COMPARATIVE
INCOME TAXATION:
A STRUCTURAL ANALYSIS

COMPARATIVE INCOME TAXATION: A STRUCTURAL ANALYSIS

Principal Author

Hugh J. Ault, Boston College Law School

Contributing Authors

Brian J. Arnold, University of Western Ontario
Guy Gest, University of Paris I
Peter Melz, Stockholm University
Minoru Nakazato, University of Tokyo
Albert J. Rädler, University of Hamburg
J. Mark Ramseyer, University of Chicago Law School
John Tiley, University of Cambridge
Richard J. Vann, University of Sydney
Kees van Raad, University of Leyden

KLUWER LAW INTERNATIONAL
The Hague • London • Boston

Published by Kluwer Law International
POBox 85889
2508 CN Den Haag
The Netherlands

Tel. +31 70 308 1560
Fax. +31 70 308 1515

Distribution in the USA and Canada
Kluwer Law International
675 Massachusetts Avenue
Cambridge, MA 02139
USA

Tel. 617 354 0140
Fax. 617 354 8595

Library of Congress Cataloging-in-Publication Data
is available for this title

ISBN 90-411-0605-7

© 1997.
Kluwer Law International
Den Haag, The Netherlands

Kluwer Law International incorporates the publishing programs of Graham and Trotman Ltd.,
Kluwer Law and Taxation Publishers, and Martinus Nijhoff Publishers.

Acknowledgments

A number of people were involved in this project and the authors gratefully acknowledge their contributions. We would like to thank Dr. Georg Thurmayr, Dr. Jens Blumenberg and Martin Lausterer for research assistance and Daniela Walter and Tanya Hoff for secretarial help in connection with the German materials; Martijn Juddu, Rijkele Betten and Ruud Sommerhalder for assistance in the preparation of the bibliography and with the Dutch materials; Dr. Peter Harris for a review of the United Kingdom materials; François Hellio for research assistance in connection with France; and Celeste M. Black for research assistance funded by the Australian Research Council.

Professor Hiroshi Kaneko gave help and advice on the Japanese materials. Professor James R. Repetti, in addition to authoring the United States Country Description, made valuable suggestions with respect to a number of aspects of the project. The comments of the participants at the Harvard Seminar on Comparative Income Taxation were also extremely helpful. Elizabeth Sponheim provided valuable logistical assistance in the organization of the seminar. Finally, thanks go to Alice Drew who was principally responsible for the preparation of the manuscript. Her unfailing good spirits and patience made a difficult task manageable.

Preface

The purpose of this book is to compare different solutions adopted by nine industrialized countries to common problems of income tax design. As in other legal domains, comparative study of income taxation can provide fresh perspectives from which to examine a particular national system. Increasing economic globalization also makes understanding foreign tax systems relevant to a growing set of transnational business transactions.

Comparative study is, however, notoriously difficult. Full understanding of a foreign tax system may require mastery not only of a foreign language, but also of foreign business and legal cultures. It would be the work of a lifetime for a single individual to achieve that level of understanding of the nine income taxes compared in this volume.

Suppose, however, that an international group of tax law professors, each expert in his own national system, were asked to describe how that system resolved specific problems of income tax design with respect to individuals, business organizations, and international transactions. Suppose further that the leader of the group wove the resulting answers into a single continuous exposition, which was then reviewed and critiqued by a wider group of tax teachers. The resulting text would provide a convenient and comprehensive introduction to foreign approaches to income taxation for teachers, students, policy-makers and practitioners.

That is the path followed by Hugh Ault and his collaborators in the development of this fascinating book. Henceforth, a reader interested in how other developed countries resolve such structural issues as the taxation of fringe benefits, the effect of unrealized appreciation at death, the classification of business entities, expatriation to avoid taxes, and so on, can turn to this volume for an initial answer. I am delighted that the Harvard Law School Fund for Tax and Fiscal Research was able to provide financial support for this important project. The resulting book should greatly facilitate comparative analysis in teaching and writing about taxation in the U.S. and elsewhere.

Professor Alvin C. Warren, Jr.
Director, Harvard Law School Fund for Tax and Fiscal Research

Table of Contents

Introduction

This work presents a comparative analysis of some of the structural and design issues which are involved in mature income tax systems. It is aimed primarily at professors and students of tax law, both in the United States and abroad, whose central concern lies naturally in working with the concepts and principles of their own domestic systems. For them, the material is intended both to provide information on what other systems actually do, which is interesting in itself, and to suggest other approaches which might represent alternative ways of dealing with corresponding issues in a domestic setting. By introducing a comparative dimension, the materials can be used both to enrich the classroom discussion of domestic problems and to give a starting point for further research and study. For example, who has not wondered, when discussing an interesting question like the child care deduction or the taxation of imputed income, what other countries do in their systems? While the answers are there, they are hard to find and harder to evaluate. This work is at least a beginning in making the approaches of other systems more accessible.

The countries selected for the study, Australia, Canada, France, Germany, Japan, The Netherlands, Sweden, the United Kingdom and the United States, all have relatively mature and sophisticated tax systems. One would expect a priori that many similar issues and questions would emerge and this intuition is confirmed by the materials. The responses to the issues, however, vary substantially in many cases though also showing some areas of congruence.

Several of the systems belong to the same broad legal "family." The approaches of the United Kingdom, Canada and Australia all display some of the expected degree of similarity, given their common historical roots. The Continental systems likewise, though to a lesser extent, have similarities in structure and result. The United States system has developed without much influence from other systems and the Japanese system has both Continental, especially German, features as well as displaying a strong influence from American ideas in the postwar developments.

Thus while the details differ, there are some recognizable "family resemblances." The Commonwealth systems all have, in varying degrees, schedular features. Different classes or categories of income may be taxed in different ways and at different rates, with varying rules for inclusion and deduction. Trust notions of "income" and "corpus" have also played an important role in developing tax concepts. Partly as a result of this latter phenomenon, the taxation of capital gains has been the subject of special legislation, often structured as a separate tax regime.

Continental systems, as well, have significant points of resemblance. Financial accounting rules have often been important in the development of tax principles, especially in the computation of business income. In addition, and unlike the Commonwealth tradition, capital gains realized in a business setting have usually been subject to the normal tax rules dealing with business profits. Capital gains of individual investors, however, have at least initially escaped tax, though the traditional approaches have often been modified, extending taxation to certain limited classes of gains.

Beyond these broad features, each of the systems has evolved its own particular set of approaches and principles. These are outlined in some detail in the individual Country Descriptions contained in Part One. These individually-authored pieces present the overall structure of the systems and try to provide some feel for the "tax culture" or climate and the institutional framework in which the substantive rules operate. They can be read as "stand alone" descriptions of the systems or referred to subsequently for a better understanding of the later discussion of a particular rule. It is essential to keep in mind some of the basic features outlined in the Country Descriptions when dealing with the later substantive material. For example, in thinking about the structure of the rules on corporate liquidations, it is crucial to remember that in some countries private capital gains of an individual will not be taxed while business gains will be subject to full taxation. Similarly, in considering items included in the tax base, taxation may depend on into which, if any, of the various taxable categories the item can be fitted. To facilitate the necessary cross-references, some of the more important features of each system are summarized in tabular form at the end of the Part One.

The following three Parts deal with Basic Income Taxation, Taxation of Business Organizations and International Taxation respectively. As will be apparent, the organization is based on an American format and follows in broad outline the issues and questions typically covered in an American law school course on each particular topic.

Within each Part, the various substantive Subparts and Sections begin by outlining some of the structural issues or problems which have arisen in the area under consideration. The responses of the countries to the problems are described together with an attempt to identify common patterns or approaches and to highlight unique or interesting solutions. The descriptions of the substantive rules vary in completeness and not every issue is discussed in connection with every country. The focus is on structural and design issues, though there is some consideration of extra-fiscal measures.

The analysis reflects state of the law in the Spring of 1996 and no attempt has been made to include developments since that time, though reference is occasionally made to anticipated future trends. Given the nature of the materials, they clearly should not be used to give legal advice; they are intended to be solely of "academic" interest.

The materials conclude with a Bibliography in Part Five which will enable the interested student or teacher to pursue a particular topic in more detail. In some of the jurisdictions there is little material in English and foreign language references have been supplied.

There is of course always a danger in attempting to relate legal rules or concepts in one system to a seemingly similar situation in another system. The institutional and cultural backgrounds may be different and the actual operation of each individual rule depends on the overall structure of both the tax system and the legal system generally. Doing meaningful comparative analysis is especially difficult in the tax area, where political pressure, chance and historical accident have all had an important influence on the development of the systems. However, with appropriate caveats and cautions, there is much to learn in the tax field from a comparative analysis of common problems. One need not believe in the existence of a Platonic Tax Form to find useful insights in the experience of others.

Part One

General Description: Australia

Professor Richard Vann

1. History of the income tax

The federal income tax was introduced in 1915 as a measure to finance the war effort. The first income tax in Australia had been introduced in South Australia in 1884, prior to federation in 1901, and by 1907 all states had an income tax. Interestingly, both at the state and federal level, the income tax was usually introduced in conjunction with a land tax, reflecting the significant influence in Australia of Henry George's work *Progress and Poverty*. Concerns about the equity, efficiency, and simplicity of the income tax systems led to a Royal Commission in the early 1920s and a new federal income tax statute in 1922. Harmonization of state and federal income taxes was not achieved in this exercise and a further Royal Commission in the early 1930s produced a new federal tax statute, the Income Tax Assessment Act 1936, which is the current legislation and was the model for all state income taxes, that is, harmonization was achieved on this occasion.

The harmonization was short-lived since with the advent of World War II the federal government decided to take over the state income taxes and levy a single federal income tax. The drastic legislative measures adopted for this purpose, including a forcible seizure of state income tax offices, were upheld in the High Court of Australia relying in part on the defense power in a major constitutional challenge by the states. Since that time no state income tax has been levied in Australia and the federal tax is the sole tax. The federal government was able to maintain this dominance in peacetime mainly through the grants power in the Constitution, which the High Court held permitted the federal government to make grants to the states conditional on the states not levying an income tax.

A new emphasis on federalism in the 1970s saw the federal legislation amended in a way which permitted states to levy income taxes if they wished, but the necessary precondition for making this a reality —

namely a cut in federal income tax rates to create room for state taxes — did not occur. The more centralist Labor Government of the 1980s and 1990s repealed the legislation permitting states to levy incomes taxes. As the federal Constitution confers an exclusive power on the federal government to levy customs and excise duties (which has been interpreted to include sales taxes on goods), it follows that the states in Australia are denied access to the major tax bases in modern societies. Australia does not have a history of levying social security taxes which in any event would almost certainly be at the federal level under constitutional powers conferred on the federal government by referendum in 1946 in the social security area. The states nowadays rely on a miscellany of taxes (mainly payroll tax, stamp duties on a variety of transactions, land tax, and taxes on credits and debits with financial institutions) for half their revenues, the remaining half coming in the form of grants from the federal government.

Although several other commissions of inquiry were instituted in the 1950s to the 1970s, they had little effect other than giving rise to legislative measures to counter various forms of tax avoidance. No major overhaul of the income tax system occurred until the mid-1980s when a federal Labor Government introduced a capital gains tax, a fringe benefits tax, imputation, and a complete overhaul of the taxation of foreign source income of residents, following the general 1980s tax reform strategy of base broadening, and rate cutting (with maximum individual tax rates falling from 60 % to less than 49 %).

2. Composition of fiscal system

The following statistics are based on the OECD Revenue Statistics for 1993, the latest available. The federal income tax is far and away the most important tax in Australia, raising 53.7 % of total revenues. Next comes taxes on goods and services at 29.8 %. Unlike most other countries where the percentage of goods and services is about the same, Australia's revenue in this area does not come primarily from value-added tax. About one-third of the figure comes from excises, just under one-third from the federal wholesale sales tax that is the general sales tax in Australia, and the remainder from a variety of sources, the most important being customs and import duties, and state taxes on gambling, motor vehicles, and business franchises. Taxes on property account for 10.4 % of total tax revenues divided about equally between land tax and stamp duties on land and financial transactions. The state payroll tax accounts for 6.1 % of revenues.

Among OECD countries, Australia now ranks second lowest in terms of taxes as a percentage of GDP at 28.7 % (just below Japan and the United States and only above Turkey). Although politicians are fond of quoting this figure, it is particularly misleading as Australia does not levy social security taxes but instead has a form of compulsory private pension plans that are functionally equivalent in most respects with the social security schemes of other OECD countries. If social security taxes are excluded, there are ten OECD countries with lower taxes than Australia and most of the others are only slightly above Australia with the exception of Denmark. The OECD Revenue Statistics also do not take account of tax expenditures and these vary quite significantly among OECD countries.

The predominance of the income tax in Australia has existed for many years. Since the OECD first began to collect statistics in 1965 it has been in excess of 50 % of total taxation. When the federal income tax became the only income tax in Australia in World War II, even then the income tax represented 42 % of total revenues. In 1993 income tax revenue was $66 billion out of a total Australia-wide revenue of $123 billion. The Treasury estimate for income tax revenues in the 1995-1996 financial year is $86.5 billion.

3. Tax rates

The 1995-1996 federal income tax rates for resident individuals are as follows:

$0-5,400	0%
$5,401-20,700	20%
$20,701-38,000	34%
$38,001-50,000	43%
$50,001 and above:	47%

In addition, all taxable income of individuals is subject to the 1.5% Medicare levy which is used to provide part of the funding for Australia's universal health care system. This levy cannot be separately identified in revenue statistics other than by estimate, as it is collected as part of the income tax and it is not treated as a social security tax in the OECD classification. There is a shading in of the levy at lower levels of income so that it is not collected from the very poor but the shading in is recaptured by a surcharge so that above moderate levels of income it operates as a flat rate charge. As a result the maximum individual rate is usually treated as 48.5 % which rate is used in fact in the legislation which is designed to levy tax at top rates, for example, the undistributed income of trusts. The fringe benefits tax rate is also 48.5 %.

The basic corporate tax rate for 1995-1996 is 36 %. There are some limited cases where higher or lower rates are charged, for example, life insurance companies income with respect to life policies is charged at a rate of 39 % (as a proxy rate for the income attributable to policy holders) while pooled development funds generally pay tax at 25% (these funds provide venture capital to small and medium-sized enterprises).

4. The basic structure of income tax system

Nominally Australia has a global income tax system, as the basic inclusion provision covers the "gross income" derived by the taxpayer without reference to categories of income. There are many specific inclusion provisions dealing with particular kinds of income, though it is still the case that the vast majority of assessable income in Australia enters through the basic concept contained in the general provisions. Despite its apparently global nature, the Australian courts in fleshing out the concept have adopted a fairly narrow approach to what is income. This outcome can be attributed to a number of influences.

First, although Australian judges have always recognized that the Australian system is structured quite differently from the explicit schedular nature of the U.K. system, nonetheless U.K. concepts in cases have often been applied in determining whether specific items are income, and in this way the U.K. schedules and concept of sources of income have influenced developments in Australia. This explains why, for example, gambling and lottery winnings are not included in the general concept of income.

Secondly, as in the U.K. which has always had a category of

"other income" in its schedular structure, there are deeper and more ancient sources at work. The most influential concept of income existing in the law when the income tax was introduced in the U.K. and Australia was the trust law concept of income. Trust law distinguishes between the capital beneficiary of the trust and the income beneficiary of the trust with the former being entitled to any increments in value of the property of the trust which generates its income. The influence of the trust law has been most apparent in the exclusion of capital gains from the basic concept of income in the U.K. and Australia.

Thirdly, accounting concepts of profit have had an influence, but as Australia does not use the concept of profit explicitly in the tax legislation in dealing with business income (in contrast to the U.K.), the influence has been muted in Australia.

The general valuation rule adopted in the income tax in Australia has also followed the U.K., being the amount of money into which a nonmonetary item can be converted. This has been a significant limiting factor in the taxation of benefits in kind, especially employment fringe benefits prior to 1986, though the lack of detailed valuation rules and administrative unwillingness to issue them were also important. Two doctrines which seem to be more peculiarly Australian have been the cause of limitations on the income concept. First, it is clearly established that there is no doctrine that the reimbursement of an expense that is deductible to a taxpayer will amount to income (though it will be income in certain cases such as general business receipts). Secondly, the Australian courts have held that where an amount is received in a lump sum which has income and non-income elements, then it is not possible to apportion out the income elements unless there is clear agreement between the parties to the payment on the breakdown of the amount and the whole is treated as not being income.

In the tax reform of the 1980s, the introduction of a capital gains tax and a fringe benefits tax added significantly to the tax base and overcame most of these problems, though curiously there still has been no direct and general abolition of the basic valuation and apportionment rules that limit the amount brought into income.

Although the Australian system has thus adopted many of the limiting features of the U.K. schedular system, the nominal global nature of the system means that many of the features of the U.K. system are not applied. In particular, generally speaking, special rules are not enacted for the detailed treatment of different categories of income with the result that all items of income are included on a current year basis (rather than some being on a current year and some on a prior year basis as in the U.K.) and losses on one kind of income category generally can be offset against income in other categories (the major exception here being capital losses but this is partly explained by the fact that the capital gains regime was enacted as a completely separate income inclusion even though it is included in the basic income tax law). Australia has also not been as much influenced by the U.K. source concept as has, say, Canada although from time to time there are hints of such a concept. For example, it is still unclear whether losses arising after a particular income earning activity has come to an end can be deducted.

5. Statutory style

Although the basic income inclusion and deduction provisions of the 1936 legislation retain their original form of a few lines each, they still account for the vast majority of income and deductions. Since the 1960s, the legislative drafting of Australian income tax has adopted a peculiarly turgid and convoluted style so that it may now lay claim to the dubious twin titles of being the longest income tax statute in the world and the most unreadable. The basic income tax statute, the Income Tax Assessment Act 1936, is now approaching 6,000 pages in length and together with an ancillary legislation such as the Fringe Benefits Tax and the International Tax Agreements Act, occupies four volumes more than 20 cms. thick printed on wafer-thin pages in closely crowded type. To the original 126 pages of 1936, 500 pages were added in the four decades to 1976, 1,000 pages in the next decade to 1986, and over 3,000 pages since (the last being attributable to the extensive tax reform starting in the mid-1980s). The problem is compounded by including virtually all the rules in legislation and leaving little or nothing to regulations (unlike the U.S. which with Code and Regulations combined can still claim to be the world champion in terms of verbiage).

Part of the peculiar style and mind-numbing detail can be blamed on the literal, nit-picking approach to interpretation of tax legislation by the judges until recently, which meant that the legislative drafter felt compelled to hedge every rule with a host of anti-avoidance provisions and to seek to cover every possible factual permutation that might arise under the rules. However, part at least of the responsibility or blame seems to rest with the unsatisfactory drafting arrangements which exist in Australia, where the Office of Parliamentary Counsel has a monopoly on drafting and coordination among this Office, the policy makers in Treasury, and the technical and administrative people in the Australian Taxation Office does not seem to work as well as in other countries.

Currently, the government has invested substantial resources in the Tax Law Improvement Project whose brief is to redraft the legislation in plain English, user-friendly form without, however, effecting any significant changes in policy or meaning. The first major product of this project, the Income Tax Assessment Bill 1995, which is intended to be the first in a series of bills that will entirely replace the existing legislation, was introduced into Parliament at the end of 1995. With the use of diagrams, flow charts, signposts, lists, etc., this redraft is considerably easier to read and eliminates redundant and duplicated provisions, but at the end of the day there is still likely to be more than 3,000 pages in the basic taxing statute. The redraft adopts the unusual approach of addressing the taxpayer as "you" so that the basic charging provision now reads "You must pay income tax for each year ending on 30 June."

One highly undesirable feature of the statutory style that is an outgrowth of the tax avoidance problems discussed below is that tax legislation is routinely made retrospective to announcement date even where major changes in the announcement occur and the legislation concerns systemic issues rather than tax avoidance. In some cases there have been delays of years rather than months in introducing the announced legislation. The Senate has now adopted procedural rules to curb the worst features of this practice - unless the legislation is introduced into Parliament within six months after announcement, the Senate will only pass the legislation on a prospective basis. Still, the legislation can take up to a year to go through the Parliament and considerable uncertainty among taxpayers results.

6. Statutory interpretation

Until the early 1980s, the Courts adopted a very strict and literal approach to the interpretation of tax legislation excluding any reference to extrinsic materials or the purpose of the legislature except insofar as that purpose was ascertainable from the words used. The approach is typified in the following quote:

> It is for the Parliament to specify, and to do so, in my opinion as far as language will permit, with unambiguous clarity, the circumstances which will attract an obligation on the part of the citizen to pay tax. The function of the court is to interpret and apply the language in which the Parliament has specified those circumstances.
>
> The court is to do so by determining the meaning of the words employed by the Parliament which is discoverable from the language used by the Parliament. It is not for the court to mould or to attempt to mould the language of the statute so as to produce some result which it might be thought the Parliament may have intended to achieve, though not expressed in the actual language employed. . .
>
> Parliament having prescribed the circumstances which will attract tax, or provide occasion for its reduction or elimination, the citizen has every right to mould the transaction into which he is about to enter into a form which satisfies the requirements of the statute. It is nothing to the point that he might have attained the same or similar result as that achieved by the transaction into which he in fact entered by some other transaction, which, if he had entered into it, would or might have involved him in a liability to tax, or to more tax than that attracted by the transaction into which he in fact entered. Nor can it matter that his choice of transaction was influenced wholly or in part by its effect upon his obligation to pay tax. The freedom to choose the form of transaction into

which he shall enter is basic to the maintenance of
a free society.[1]

From this time, three related developments have substantially
improved the interpretation process though it still can hardly be
described as ideal. First, the judges began to take a more purposive
approach to their interpretation of tax legislation and permit themselves to look at extrinsic material on their own motion, though it is
true to say that the Courts have yet to settle on an agreed and generally
applied approach to interpretation. Secondly, the Acts Interpretation
Act 1901 which contains many rules as to the interpretation of
statutes, was amended to require a purposive approach in interpretation
and access to extrinsic material where the statute was ambiguous. This
both confirmed and encouraged the change in judicial attitude which
was already underway. Thirdly, the approach to drafting the legislation
began to change. The style was simplified, purpose statements, examples and other reading guides began to be included, and more detailed
and helpful explanatory memoranda began to be produced (the
explanatory memorandum is the official government explanation that
is introduced into Parliament at the same time as the legislation). The
current Tax Law Improvement Project mentioned above is the culmi-
nation of this process, though it has been substantially criticized for the
narrowness of its brief — rewriting without changing policy — as a significant amount of current complexity stems from overly elaborate policy in response to the former attitude of the courts.
    This transition phase is still underway and it remains to be seen
whether a coherent and sustainable system of interpretation involving
the cooperation of the legislature, the courts and the administration will
emerge. The signs so far are not encouraging, however, as appears below.

---

1. Barwick, CJ in *Westraders Pty Ltd*, (1980) 144 CLR 55, 60-61. The Barwick court (1965-
1981) is generally regarded as having taken literal, indeed taxpayer biased, interpretations to
extremes.

7. Administrative, taxpayer, and judicial style

A visitor from another planet might be forgiven for thinking that the advanced Anglo-Saxon countries suffer from a disease that may be called tax rule madness, with Australia having a particularly virulent form. The common-law method and a perverted version of the rule of law seem to be the basic cause. The common-law method focuses on specific cases rather than general principles and the rule of law requires that citizens know their rights and obligations (which is perversely interpreted in the tax area as meaning each and every one of the myriad rules and interpretations which can go into the calculation of taxable income). Put together with a judiciary which in the past did not admit the impossibility of stating a rule in legislation for every conceivable circumstance, it is no wonder that Australia has ended up with such a mountain of legislation.

Further, in Australia, self-assessment is interpreted by the Australian Taxation Office in the sense that taxpayers must have or be able to obtain a rule (ruling) for every situation in preparing their tax returns and correspondingly tax audits are to be conducted on an issue-by-issue basis with no trade-offs between issues in settlements. Taken to its extreme, this approach means that there should be no discretions in the tax legislation and even taxpayer elections are felt to create problems in the self-assessment realm. Taxpayers have contributed and responded to these developments by on the one hand pushing the system to its limits in terms of aggressive tax avoidance, and on the other hand complaining about the enormous compliance costs resulting from the system put in place to deal with the tax avoidance. In passing, it is worthwhile to note that Australia seems to have the highest compliance costs in the world on the basis of a number of studies undertaken in the late 1980's. This is reflected, for example, in the fact that about three quarters of Australian individual taxpayers (Australia uses the universal filing system) require professional help in the preparation of their tax returns. On the other hand, this latter phenomena has led extensive use of electronic filing which has a positive impact on costs.

7.1 Administrative style

Because of the aftermath of the tax avoidance industry of the

1970s referred to below, the attitude of the Australian Taxation Office (ATO) toward taxpayers in the 1980s was seen as particularly aggressive. Some of this apparent aggression was the result of a major system change in the mid-1980s. The changes started with the appointment of Commissioner Trevor Boucher in 1984 and have been continued by his successor. Another catalyst for change was the Australian Audit Office which produced a number of highly critical efficiency audits of the ATO in the mid-1980s (and was followed by major reviews by the House of Representatives Standing Committee on Finance and Public Administration in the late 1980s and by the Parliamentary Joint Committee on Public Accounts in the early 1990s).

Until the mid-1980s all tax returns had been manually processed by officers who issued assessments on the basis of the returns and with virtually no follow-up audit activity. Where the officer did not agree with the return as filed, an assessment was issued with an adjustment sheet (handwritten with special purple pens) and the taxpayer could then object to the assessment which initiated the appeal process. While many cases were settled at this stage there was very little direct contact between tax officials and taxpayers, matters being dealt with by correspondence. Most of the non-assessment resources of the ATO were devoted to withholding, collection, and appeals (with the cleanup of the 1970s avoidance industry absorbing many of these resources).

In the mid-1980s the ATO took the first tentative steps toward self-assessment for companies (which was finally completed in the early 1990s). The most obvious initial effect of this change was to move resources out of assessing into audit, and for the first time many taxpayers actually came face-to-face with tax officers. The large corporate audits in particular generated a lot of heat, and were not assisted from a public relations point of view by well-publicized dawn raids on banks and professionals seeking copies of documents about suspected tax schemes.

In the early 1990s client service became the focus of activities of the ATO, with audit activity being reduced from late 1980s levels (when coverage was still not great) and resources moved into service areas. For the average taxpayer the main manifestation of this has been TaxPack, a magazine-style explanation kit for completing and filing tax returns that is mailed to millions of people. The kit has been developed in consultation with communication and language professionals and is backed up by toll-free help lines, etc. For tax professionals the main change has been the introduction of an extensive public and private ruling system that is binding on the ATO. An informal private ruling system had been in operation for many years and nonbinding public rulings began to be issued in 1982. In 1992 legislation was passed formalizing this process (as part of the final stages of self-assessment), which has lead to significant growth in the numbers of public and private rulings.

The collection and information matching capabilities of the ATO have also been greatly improved over the last decade. A large computer reequipment process is in its final stages. The tax file number used for many years has been given a formal statutory basis and is now used for reporting and backup withholding purposes (rather than just for internal tracking of files), with some significant improvements in detection and compliance. The annual federal budget now often contains a quite significant revenue increase arising from administration improvements based around technology.

During the last decade the ATO has also gone through a revolution in management practice, adopting most of the corporatization efficiency rhetoric that has seized the government sector in Australia and New Zealand. In terms of administrative and operational structure, these changes are most evident to taxpayers from the opening of many regional and suburban offices of the ATO (in the former manual assessment days there was one tax office in each state or territory), specialization among these offices, and reorganization of work along business lines (permitting one-stop tax shopping) rather than functional or tax lines.

7.2 Taxpayer style

The former manual assessment system and the apparent taxpayer bias of the judiciary from the mid-1960s encouraged very aggressive tax avoidance activities by taxpayers and their advisers, which still lingers today. There was little chance of getting caught and if you did, then as likely as not the courts would uphold the scheme. A large scale publicly marketed tax-avoidance industry flourished as a result from about the mid-1970s which to some extent made the payment of tax optional. The government was initially slow to react to these developments and the early amendments were themselves full of loopholes, which suggested to some observers tacit acceptance of the industry by the government.

By the late 1970s, when lengthy unreadable anti-avoidance legislation seemed to have closed off most of the abuses, advertisements still appeared in the financial press offering to purchase companies for the value of their pretax income (less a percentage being the purchaser's fee or commission). There was no shortage of sellers who did not stay to ask what was being done with the companies (the assumption being that they would be put into a tax scheme which wiped out their tax liability). It came to the surface in a royal commission investigating a notorious labor union heavily involved in criminal activities that the companies were simply being stripped of their assets by the purchasers, dummy directors with criminal backgrounds appointed and the records of the companies destroyed (metaphorically consigned to the "bottom of the harbor" as the scandal came to be called — that is, Sydney Harbor —though the activities were by no means confined to Sydney).

The legislative reaction was very severe. It was made a specific criminal offense to render a company unable to pay its tax (though arguably the general criminal law already had this result), and more importantly retrospective legislation was passed making the vendors of the shares in the companies liable for the company tax which was not paid (even where small listed companies were involved). A new anti-avoidance rule was enacted that overcame, it was thought, the defects of the existing rule. As already noted, a significant share of some of the best people resources in the ATO were involved in the washup well into the 1980s. This included attacking not only the "bottom of the harbor" cases but many of the real avoidance schemes. There was considerable success in the courts as the judicial tide turned (one notorious 1974 High Court of Australia case often considered to be the start of the real rot was ultimately reversed as a precedent in 1989).

One of the root causes of the problem in a policy sense was the combination of a classical corporate tax system with no capital gains tax, so that most share sales were tax free. The policy remedy came with the tax reform of 1985. At the same time, the tax administration was undergoing its own reform as noted above, partly to ensure that the same debacle could never occur in the future. This development, combined with the not surprising suspicion of the tax profession among tax administrators arising from the tax avoidance era, has meant that relations between profession and administration remain strained despite expressions and intentions of goodwill and cooperation on both sides.

Tax planning went into a less aggressive mode in the 1980s —

rather than seeking to wipe out all tax liability through paper shuffling circular transactions, tax reduction through exploiting the debt-equity borderline, tax shelters, and timing differences became the main focus of attention, though more aggressive planning on the international scene was also evident. At the moment there are signs that the judicial pendulum is starting to swing back in favor of taxpayers and it seems likely that the tax profession will be quick to exploit any opportunities that arise. For although the law and administration have undergone extensive reform, little has happened on the professional standards and ethical front. A review of the tax agents system has been underway for some time to raise educational standards (tax agents are licensed under the tax legislation to prepare tax returns and represent taxpayers), but this mainly affects the bottom end of the market (return preparers for normal individuals). Specialist tax accountants and lawyers acting for the wealthy and the corporate sector are not engaged because registration is either automatic (specialist tax accountants) or not required (lawyers).

7.3 Judicial style

In many ways judges remain bemused bystanders in the tax game in Australia. It seems likely that they did not understand the implications of their decisions that led to the tax avoidance industry in the 1970s and similarly nowadays they do not know a deduction for principal dressed up as interest when confronted with it. There is only one judge in the system who could be regarded as a tax expert. Again, history is the reason for this peculiar outcome.

Tax was probably the first area in Australia to have specialist administrative tribunals (originally called Boards of Review, now a division in the Administrative Appeals Tribunal) and by a quirk of the federal constitution, tax cases went from this tribunal directly to the High Court of Australia, the highest court in the land. For a time the system worked well, as the best judges in Australia had a certain expertise in taxation and usually produced sensible decisions. With the advent of the Barwick court there seemed to be a decline in expertise (perhaps a reflection of the very heavy load of the court which exceeded the House of Lords in the U.K. and the Supreme Court in the U.S. by a factor of three in the 1970s) and Barwick, CJ was generally regarded as strongly pro-taxpayer and influential with the other judges. While the judges seem to have moved during the 1980s to a position that favors the tax administration against the taxpayer, the approach to tax cases is still not founded on any consistent or coherent theory of interpretation of tax law, though at least attention is now given to purpose and extrinsic materials. Some recent cases on the general anti-avoidance provision in the tax law might be regarded as a pro-taxpayer shift in the courts.

The High Court managed to dispense with its constitutional jurisdiction in tax matters to state courts and then the newly created federal court from the latter part of the 1970s. There is no special tax court with the result that there are virtually no specialist tax judges. The Boards of Review were constituted by three members — one from the tax office, one an accountant, and one a lawyer. Because of the influence of the tax office in the appointments, the tribunal was often regarded as pro-tax administration and not highly respected. The advent of the Administrative Appeals Tribunal does not seem to have greatly improved matters at this level. Appeals to the High Court are now by special leave and fairly rare; whether for this reason or not, the technical quality of recent tax judgments at this level seems clearly to have gone down even though the heart may now be in or about the right place.

8. General principles

8.1 Relation of tax and financial accounting

The Australian courts generally give the tax legislation primacy over accounting principle. The legislation uses the global system nominally and does not adopt "profits" as the measure of business income. It is thus easy to interpret the legislation as setting out its own criteria of taxability completely independent of accounting rules. Equally, at many crucial points the legislation does not provide guidance on accounting rules and the courts could have easily adopted accounting principles as the guide in such cases. In the result, the attitude is very similar to that adopted toward U.K. cases — take it or leave it, as suits the particular judge.

So far as any trend can be discerned, the courts seem over time to be moving toward greater consistency with accounting principle. On the other hand, the legislation increasingly specifies tax accounting rules for many areas, partly arising out of bad judicial decisions. Even where these follow generally accepted accounting concepts they do so through detailed statutory language and so do not have the capacity to change when accounting practice changes (not to mention that the accounting concepts are sometimes mistranslated — for example, in the limited area where the concept of the financial lease governs, a finance lease is defined in one respect as existing where the total payments under the lease exceed 90 % of the market value of the property at the time of the lease, rather than the present value of those payments).

There does not seem to be any general movement in Australia to leave the determination of business income to accounting concepts, despite the potential simplification of the legislation that could be achieved. In part this results from the global nature of the system and a misunderstanding of the systems in Europe which operate in this way.

8.2 Respect for civil law form

Unless a transaction can be characterized as a sham in the sense of not having under general law the legal effect that it purports to, then the courts generally respect the form of the transaction adopted for income tax purposes. Thus, the transfer of a right to income which is effective under property law is generally regarded as carrying the income with it for tax purposes (although there is specific legislation directed at this result for shorter term assignments). Recently it has been held that an embezzler was not assessable on interest earned on embezzled funds because the interest was subject to a constructive trust in favor of the company embezzled. There is, however, no uniform practice on this matter. Courts have been prepared to look at substance in the area of services income (whether payments under restrictive covenants are for genuine restrictions or not), but in the area of deductions some of the most destructive court decisions in the tax avoidance era elevated form over substance (e.g., what was really purchase price became deductible if given the form of rent for the use of the property).

Relatedly, there has been much debate in cases recently whether tax motivations for transactions can affect the tax outcome—the traditional answer as found in the quote from Barwick, CJ in *Westraders* above has been no. After acceptance in the lower courts, the High Court of Australia has rejected the U.K. fiscal nullity judicial doctrine on the basis that there is a statutory anti-avoidance regime so that judicial activism is unnecessary in the area. Nonetheless, in some recent cases including in the High Court, deductions have been denied on the basis that the expenses were tax motivated. For example, in a complex annuity scheme that featured large interest deductions early in the period of the annuity and most of the income toward the end with a power to unwind the transaction before the income arose, the High Court said that where income exceeded deductions then generally there was no need to look at motivation. However, if deductions exceeded income then motivation was relevant and if in this case the parties intended to unwind the scheme before the income arose (as was ultimately found to be the case) then the interest deduction was reduced to the amount of income derived in each year. Similarly a collapsing prepaid interest scheme was found in a lower court not to work, because the purpose of paying the interest was to obtain a tax deduction and not to earn income, so that it failed the income-earning test of the statute. Once again, however, it is difficult to find consistency of approach in the courts.

9. Anti-avoidance legislation

As already noted, there is no clear doctrine in case law on tax avoidance and one of the reasons for this is the long-standing existence of a legislative provision. Originally the provision was s. 260 which reads as follows:

"Every contract, agreement, or arrangement made or entered into, orally or in writing, . . . shall so far as it purports to have the purpose or effect of in any way, directly or indirectly—

(a) altering the incidence of any income tax;
(b) relieving any person from liability to pay any income tax or make any return;
(c) defeating, evading, or avoiding any duty or liability imposed on any person by this Act; or
(d) preventing the operation of this Act in any respect, be absolutely void, as against the Commissioner, or in regard to any proceeding under this Act, but without prejudice to such validity as it may have in any other respect or for any other purpose."

Although there were ups and downs in the history, over a series of decisions prior to 1980 the courts deprived the provision of virtually any meaning. The major problems were as follows:

1. With regard to the general inclusion and deduction provisions of the Act, the courts held that they had their own built-in protection if they were interpreted properly (which the courts demonstrably failed to do) and so did not need the assistance of the anti-avoidance provision.

2. With regard to the specific provisions of the Act the courts held that where the legislation offered the taxpayer a choice, then the anti-avoidance provision did not apply if the taxpayer exercised such a choice. This was taken to extremes. For example, the Act has different rules for private and public companies and much elaborate tax planning was directed to avoiding characterization as a private company which the courts held was the exercise of a choice.

3. To supply the counterfactual for the application of the provision (what would have happened in the absence of the contract etc.), the courts tended to look only to what the taxpayer did so that it seemed necessary for the taxpayer to start down one direction with a transaction and then to change course midway for tax reasons. A well-executed tax plan carried out from the very beginning was thus immune (the false start principle).

4. If the section applied, its effect was simply destructive of the contract, etc. It did not allow the Commissioner to construct an alternative that would give rise to tax; the tax liability had to be found in the ruins of the contract, etc.

The legislature had had enough by 1981 and enacted the more elaborate Part IVA to take the place of s. 260. Under this Part, three elements have to be found: a scheme, a tax benefit, and an objective conclusion (not having regard to the parties' actual intentions) that the primary purpose of the scheme was to obtain the tax benefit. A scheme is defined so broadly as to cover virtually any transaction, though the courts have held that it must be something that can stand and make sense on its own. A tax benefit is obtained when an amount is not included in assessable income of a taxpayer in a year of income where it would have been included or might reasonably be expected to have been included if the scheme had not been entered into; there is a specific exclusion for elections under the Act such as valuing inventory on the basis of cost or market value. A similar tax benefit rule applies in the case of deductions. In determining whether the purpose of the scheme was to obtain the tax benefit, eight listed criteria such as the form and substance of the scheme, the timing of the scheme, the change in financial positions that result from the scheme, and the connection between the parties were used. The Commissioner is given power when these criteria are satisfied to determine that the Part applies and then reconstruct the transaction so as to produce the tax outcome that would prevail in the absence of the scheme.

At the time the new rules were introduced, it was stated that they applied to transactions that were "blatant, artificial or contrived arrangements" as compared to "normal commercial transactions by which taxpayers legitimately take advantage of opportunities available for the arrangement of their affairs." They have been successful in closing down the round-robin collapsible paper schemes and for many years acted in terrorem against aggressive tax planning in genuine transactions. Very recently, however, the first important court decisions on the Part have appeared and they seem to confine it to the first kind of case. In particular, in all the cases it has been said in one way or another that the Part is unlikely to apply to bona fide investment or business transactions even where aspects of the transactions are structured to reduce tax that would otherwise be payable. One decision holds that the choice principle still applies and the ATO has had trouble in establishing the counterfactual that gives rise to a tax benefit. Thus the courts have held redeemable preference schemes that convert debt to equity, shifting interest income offshore to take advantage of the exemption system that applied before 1987 and the use of captive offshore insurers are not struck down by the Part. One particular weakness is that the Part does not apply to schemes which seek to obtain tax credits that otherwise would not be available.

Ironically, in the meantime, the courts have revived s. 260 in the many schemes taken to the courts in the cleanup of the tax avoidance era so that it now appears to be more effective than Part IVA (s. 260 applies to transactions prior to 1981). It has been used to strike down arrangements when personal services income is moved into entities where lower tax rates apply, and to the various stripping schemes that were featured in the tax avoidance era. It may be that Australia would have been better off without these anti-avoidance measures so that greater responsibility would have fallen on the courts to produce a workable approach to interpretation of tax legislation.

The courts are not entirely to blame for this sorry story. The government and legislature have never solved satisfactorily the inherent conflict with anti-avoidance rules that arises from tax concessions which encourage certain forms of activity and transactions. These arms of government were also slow to act in the early part of the tax avoidance era and now have swung to the other extreme where virtually all tax legislation has elements of retrospectivity, including not just measures directed against tax avoidance schemes but major changes like the capital gains tax and the CFC and FIF regimes. And such draconian measures encourage the tax profession in adopting a confrontational approach to the tax system.

General Description: Canada

Professor Brian J. Arnold

1. History of the income tax act

Canadian federal income tax was first imposed in 1917 as a temporary measure to help finance World War I. Until then, the major sources of federal revenue were customs and excise taxes. Over the period from 1917 to the early 1960s the income tax became an increasingly important source of government revenue. Rates increased and the tax base expanded on a rather ad hoc basis. Dissatisfaction with the resulting "system" led to the establishment of a Royal Commission (the Carter Commission) in 1962 to make a comprehensive study of the Canadian tax system. In 1966 the Carter Commission issued its famous report proposing the adoption of a comprehensive tax base. The report led to a major overhaul of the income tax in 1972. The revised system was much more sophisticated and the legislation much more complex. Another less significant tax reform occurred in 1986-87 in conjunction with and partly in response to the worldwide tax reform phenomenon.

2. Constitiutional issues

Under the Canadian constitution, the federal government has unlimited powers of taxation. The provinces have the power to levy "direct taxation" within the province on income earned in the province and on the worldwide income of persons who are resident in the province. All of the provinces levy income tax on individuals and corporations. The federal individual tax rates are set in light of the fact that the provinces also levy income tax at rates of approximately 50 % of the federal tax. The federal corporate income tax contains a 10 % abatement to make room for the provincial corporate tax. Pursuant to a long-standing tax collection agreement between the federal and provincial governments, the federal government collects both individual and corporate tax on behalf of most of the provinces. In consideration, the provinces agree to adopt the federal income tax base. Only Quebec collects its own individual income tax; Alberta, Ontario, and Quebec collect their own corporate taxes.

3. Composition of fiscal system

Income taxes are estimated to comprise about 57 % of total federal government revenues. Of this amount, corporate income taxes account for about 11.6 %, while personal income taxes make up the remaining 45.3 %. Other sources of federal revenue include unemployment insurance contributions (14.8 %), the goods and services tax (a form of value added tax) (13.1 %), customs and import duties (.025 %), excise taxes (0.56 %), and other (0.14 %). For the year ended March 31, 1994, personal and corporate income taxes generated $96.5 billion and $14.6 billion respectively out of total revenues of $286.9 billion. For calendar year 1994, tax revenues constituted 35.9 % of GDP.

4. Tax rates

For 1996, federal income tax rates for individuals are as follows:

Taxable income	Tax rate
$29,590 or less	17%
$29,591 - $59,180	26%
$59,181 and over	29%

The brackets are indexed for inflation in excess of 3 % annually. In addition, various personal credits are similarly indexed for inflation. There is, however, no comprehensive relief for inflation with respect to amounts included in computing income.

Except for Quebec, provincial tax rates are expressed as a percentage of the basic federal rate, ranging from 45.5 % in Alberta to 69 % in Newfoundland. Hence, the maximum combined federal and provincial tax rates, excluding surtaxes, range from approximately 42.2 % in Alberta to 49 % in Newfoundland.

The basic federal tax rate for corporations is currently 38 %. However, this rate is reduced by the 10 % abatement for income earned in a province. The provincial corporate tax rates vary considerably from 5 % to 17 %. Thus, combined federal/provincial rates vary from 33 % to 45 %.

5. Basic structure of the system

In Canada, income is calculated on a source basis. Income in the broad economic sense that does not have a source is not income in the legal sense. Amounts that lack a source cannot be characterized as income and are not taxable unless they are expressly included in income by statute. Windfall gains, such as lottery prizes, are perhaps the best example of this fundamental principle. Capital gains are another example, although since 1972 a portion of such gains has been expressly required to be included in income. Capital gains are considered to be derived from the disposition of a source of income rather than income from a source; or, to use the well-worn metaphor, capital gains represent the tree (capital) rather than the fruit (income) from the tree.

The source concept of income finds statutory expression in section 3 of the Act, which defines a taxpayer's income as: "income for the year from a source inside or outside Canada, including . . . the taxpayer's income for the year from each office, employment, business, and property." Section 4 goes on to provide that a taxpayer's income or loss from any source must be calculated on the assumption that the taxpayer had no income or loss from any other source during the taxation year, and that only amounts reasonably applicable to that source of income are deductible.

It is clear from paragraph 4(1)(a) of the Act that amounts are deductible in computing income from a generic source only if they can reasonably be regarded as applicable to that source. Although it does not necessarily follow that a source of income must exist at the time an expense is incurred in order for the expense to be deductible, the courts have so held. Expenses incurred either before a source of income exists or after it ceases to exist are not deductible because they are not applicable to a source of income.

The source concept of income has its roots in the "schedular" basis used in early U.K. income tax statutes. Under this approach, income tax is levied only in respect of amounts included in various schedules. If an amount is not specifically included in one of these schedules, it is not subject to tax. The schedules specify the types of income subject to tax, and also the persons subject to tax on such amounts. Generally, income and losses from different schedules cannot be aggregated as each schedule has its own computation rules.

The Canadian income tax system has never followed the U.K. schedular approach. Since 1917, the Canadian Income Tax Act has required the inclusion of income from all sources —a clear attempt to escape the narrow confines of a schedular approach. Generally, however, the courts have limited section 3 to income from the specifically enumerated sources. In addition, the Canadian system has permitted the aggregation of income and losses from various sources for over thirty years.

In Canada, as in the United Kingdom, the courts' exclusion of amounts from income on the basis of the source concept has been largely reversed by statute. For example, as mentioned earlier, since 1972 a portion of capital gains has been included in income. Also, subsection 6(3) of the Act ensures that amounts received before employment commences or after it ceases must be included in income if they constitute compensation for services rendered. The increased use of accrual accounting for income tax purposes in recent times has effectively eliminated the problem of including in income amounts received after the cessation of a source of income. Consequently, the Canadian tax base includes most significant items of income whether or not they have a source under the case law. Windfall gains are the only significant items of income that are currently excluded from the tax base because they lack a source.

Although the source concept has been overridden by specific statutory provisions with respect to income items, it has not often been overridden with respect to deductions. When the Act provides for the inclusion in income of amounts that lack a source, the inclusion is generally net of any expenses incurred in connection with the amounts. For example, the amount of a capital gain is the proceeds of disposition less the cost of the property and any selling expenses. Generally, however, expenses are not deductible under the Act unless they relate to income from an existing source. Moreover, there are many instances (those involving interest probably being the most important) in which expenses are incurred after a source of income has ceased to exist and there is no ongoing income against which these expenses can be offset.

In summary, there are five sources of income: office or employment, business, property, capital gains, and miscellaneous. The taxpayer must calculate income and loss from each source separately and allocate reasonable deductions to each respective source. The rules for calculating income from the various sources differ, although for income from business and property the differences are minor. The major difference between income from employment and income from business or property is that the deductions permitted in computing employment income are severely limited. Once income and losses from the various sources have been computed they are aggregated to obtain the taxpayer's "income."

6. Statutory style

Prior to tax reform in 1972, the general style of the Canadian Income Tax Act tended to be broad, generally worded provisions. For example, an income tax was levied on the income of residents of Canada, but there was no definition of a resident of Canada for this purpose. Similarly, the Canadian transfer pricing rules consisted of two simple subsections providing that the amount charged in any transactions between a resident and a related nonresident person must be reasonable in the circumstances.

With tax reform in 1972, there was a clear change in the style of statutory drafting. The Act expanded dramatically. The 1972 Act and virtually all amendments since that time have reflected a high degree of technical complexity. Increasingly, the government places reliance on excessively detailed technical rules. Often it seems that these rules are intended to preclude the courts from playing any role in the development of tax law. Tax professionals complain bitterly about the pace of legislative change and the length and technical complexity of the provisions. Another recent development in the style of statutory drafting is the frequent use of algebraic formulae. Despite these modern developments, there are still several aspects of the Canadian income tax system that are holdovers from the pre-1972 Act, such as the transfer pricing provisions mentioned earlier.

7. Statutory interpretation

Until 1984, Canadian courts used the strict or literal approach to the interpretation of taxing statutes. This approach was originally adopted from the U.K. judicial traditions and was deeply ingrained, despite being so obviously inappropriate. Strict interpretation resulted in some shocking judicial decisions.

In 1984 the Supreme Court of Canada, in the *Stubart Investments* case, abandoned strict interpretation in favor of a so-called modern approach:

> Today there is only one principle or approach, namely, the words of an Act are to be read in their entire context in their grammatical and ordinary sense harmoniously with the scheme of the Act, the object of the Act and the intention of Parliament.

Even after the Supreme Court's endorsement of the modern approach, some judges continued to apply strict interpretation. In effect, they argued that the ordinary meaning of the words was an important ingredient of the modern approach, and if the ordinary meaning of the words was clear it was unnecessary to consider anything else. This narrow view of the modern approach was apparently laid to rest by the Supreme Court in a 1994 case in which a teleological approach was endorsed:

> Whether strict or liberal interpretation is given should depend on the purpose underlying it, and the purpose must be identified in light of the context of the statute, its objective, and the legislative intent. This is the teleological approach.

However, in a 1995 case, the Supreme Court reverted to a plain meaning approach under which it is permissible to consider legislative purpose only if the meaning of the statutory language is ambiguous.

It may seem strange in light of the purposive approach to statutory interpretation, but Canadian courts will not admit into evidence the legislative history of a provision for the purpose of interpreting it. There is an exception to this "*Hansard*" rule if the extrinsic material is used only for the purpose of showing the mischief or problem which the legislation was intended to correct. The *Hansard* rule was adopted from the United Kingdom, although it has recently been abandoned by the House of Lords in certain limited circumstances. It seems likely that Canadian courts will follow the U.K. courts in expanding access to legislative history. Indeed, in practice, many Canadian judges have been considering legislative history in one way or another for many years.

8. The role of the courts

Taxpayers who choose to dispute the tax, interest, or penalties levied by the Minister of National Revenue must file a notice of objection to their assessment. This notice triggers an internal appeal process. If, however, the assessment is confirmed, the taxpayer may appeal to the courts. The amount of tax in dispute does not have to be paid until the dispute is finally resolved.

All tax appeals are heard in the first instance by the Tax Court of Canada, which has a general procedure and an informal procedure which is available for appeals involving less than $12,000 of federal tax and penalties. Under the informal procedure there are no formal rules of evidence and taxpayers need not be represented by counsel. An adverse judgment of the Tax Court may be appealed to the Federal Court of Appeal. The final appeal lies to the Supreme Court of Canada whose jurisdiction is largely discretionary.

The number of tax cases decided annually by the three levels of courts is shown in the following table.

Year	Tax Court of Canada	Federal Court of Appeal	Supreme Court of Canada
1990	218	33	3
1991	257	36	1
1992	201	45	1
1993	330	31	5
1994	252	50	2

Case law is an important aspect of Canadian income tax law. As explained earlier, many provisions of the Income Tax Act are still generally worded, and the cases are important in giving more precise meaning to these general provisions. A considerable amount of case law each year involves the distinction between capital gains and ordinary income.

Judicial decisions are binding unless reversed on appeal. The government will often reverse by statute a judicial precedent with which it disagrees. The necessity for corrective legislation arises more often than it should because, in my opinion, Canadian courts are not very good with respect to tax issues.

9. The Canadian self-assessment system

The Canadian administration of tax collection is based on a system of "voluntary compliance" or self-assessment. All taxpayers are legally obligated to file an annual tax return reporting their income and expenses accurately, along with a calculation of the amount of tax owing or the refund due. The tax returns are then checked by Revenue Canada to ensure that the required information is correct, the necessary receipts are attached, and the computations are mathematically correct. A notice of assessment showing the amount of tax owing is then sent to the taxpayer. Since less than 1 % of all individual tax returns are actually audited by Revenue Canada, the income tax system depends largely on voluntary compliance by taxpayers.

However, the system is not exclusively voluntary. Payments of salary and wages and other amounts are subject to withholding at source. In addition, the self-assessment system is supported by broad information reporting requirements.

The rationale for the self-assessment system is cost-effectiveness. Costs to the government include the cost of printing returns, providing information and assistance to taxpayers, processing returns, and auditing a minimal number of returns filed. No other system is nearly as economical.

10. Revenue Canada's administrative style

The administrative style of Revenue Canada has varied considerably over the past fifteen years. In the late 1970s and early 1980s Revenue Canada was accused of using "Gestapo" tactics and being insensitive to taxpayers' legitimate concerns. Indeed, Revenue Canada's performance was an important issue in the 1984 federal election. When the Conservative Party was elected in that year, it set out to make significant reforms to Revenue Canada. The central thrust of these reforms was to convert Revenue Canada from an enforcement agency to a service agency. This shift in attitude had many consequences, from the silly (taxpayers became referred to as "clients") to the serious (Revenue Canada started to take a rather benign attitude to tax avoidance transactions that complied literally with the words of the Act). There are some signs that the Department's overemphasis on service compared to enforcement is beginning to change.

As a public relations exercise, Revenue Canada issued a "Declaration of Taxpayer Rights" on February 28, 1985. This Declaration is administrative rather than legislative. It proclaims that taxpayers are entitled to complete, accurate, and timely information about the Income Tax Act, impartiality, courtesy, and consideration, and the presumption of honesty. It also notes that personal and financial information will be kept confidential. In addition, the Declaration informs taxpayers of the availability of independent review of assessments, along with the freedom to withhold amounts disputed in formal objections until the review is completed.

Revenue Canada's administrative practices are extremely important in many areas of the tax system. In some areas, the law consists of little more than a generally worded statutory provision and a series of well-known administrative practices. In general, Revenue Canada makes its administrative practices widely known to the public. The Department publishes its administrative positions and they are available through the Department's on-line services. The open access to Revenue Canada's administrative positions was effectively forced upon the Department after the introduction of access-to-information legislation. Commercial publishers used the access-to-information legislation to publish information about administrative positions that were important to tax practitioners.

There is very little administrative discretion expressly permitted by the provisions of the Income Tax Act. Such administrative discretion is viewed with disfavor by both the government and tax practitioners. As a general matter, of course, Revenue Canada officials have significant amounts of administrative discretion in administering the Income Tax Act. However, any exercise of such discretion is subject to judicial review through the normal objection and appeal process.

Revenue Canada is currently a government department under the control of a cabinet minister. Occasionally, this administrative structure has given rise to concerns about political influence on the resolution of tax disputes. Early in 1996 the government announced its intention to convert Revenue Canada from a government department to a commission responsible to Parliament.

11. Taxpayers' style

The behavior of Canadian taxpayers is probably broadly similar to that of American taxpayers. The general public meets its tax obligations grudgingly and there is probably a good deal of small-scale cheating. Large corporations are sensitive to tax issues, and most do not hesitate to engage in reasonably aggressive tax planning. Tax professionals have become increasingly aggressive over the last twenty-five years.

12. Relation of tax and financial accounting

Section 9 of the Income Tax Act provides that a taxpayer's income from a business or property for a year is the "profit" from the business or property for the year. The term "profit" is not defined in the Act. The courts have held that profit is a net amount of gross revenue in excess of expenses computed in accordance with the ordinary principles of commercial accounting and business practice. Although accounting principles and practices are extremely important in the computation of profit, the Supreme Court has recently reiterated that the computation of profit for tax purposes is a question of law, and accounting practice is not controlling. In many instances the use of accounting principles of practices is expressly overridden by the provisions of the Act. For example, accounting depreciation is not allowed for tax purposes; instead, a separate system of capital cost allowance has been established for income tax purposes. In addition, accounting practice may be displaced by overriding principles of income tax law such as the realization principle. The courts have indicated that there is no requirement of conformity between the treatment of an item for financial accounting purposes and income tax purposes.

13. Respect of civil or private law form

It is clearly recognized in Canada that the income tax law is generally applied to legal rights and obligations determined under the general law. The Income Tax Act is replete with terms such as "employment," "corporation," "person," and "paid-up capital" that derive their meaning from the general law.

There are two difficult aspects of this issue. First, because Canada is a federal state, occasionally the legal meaning is different in different provinces. This is particularly the case with respect to the province of Quebec, which follows a civil code system. Ordinarily, the drafters and the courts strive to achieve consistency in the application of the income tax law to taxpayers in various parts of the country. Special provisions are sometimes required with respect to legal concepts in the province of Quebec. The courts and Revenue Canada generally adhere to the relevant provincial law, although they have sometimes been known to take very flexible positions in order to achieve consistency. Second, the application of the provisions of the Income Tax Act to the offshore activities of Canadian taxpayers involves applying the Act to foreign legal rights and obligations. In general, the legal rights and obligations are determined under the foreign law; the Canadian tax law is then applied to those findings, which are in effect treated as findings of fact rather than law.

14. Substance over form

There is considerable confusion in Canada concerning the doctrine of substance over form. Canadian law derives from the House of Lords decision in the *Duke of Westminster* case in 1936. In that case, the House of Lords clearly rejected any doctrine under which the legal form of a transaction could be disregarded in favor of its economic substance. However, the House of Lords did recognize that the legal substance of a transaction prevails over the nomenclature used by the taxpayer to describe the transaction.

The Supreme Court of Canada has reaffirmed on several occasions that the *Duke of Westminster* case is deeply entrenched in Canadian tax law. Nevertheless, on several occasions the Canadian courts, including the Supreme Court, have made references to the doctrine of substance over form, which seems to suggest that economic substance will prevail over legal form in certain circumstances. For example, in the *Bronfman Trust* case in 1987, the Supreme Court of Canada stated:

> . . . The recent trend in tax cases [has] been towards attempting to ascertain the true commercial and practical nature of the taxpayer's transactions. . . Assessment of taxpayers' transactions with an eye to commercial and economic realities, rather than juristic classification of form, may help to avoid the inequity of tax liability being dependent upon the taxpayer's sophistication at manipulating a sequence of events to achieve a patina of compliance with the apparent prerequisites for a tax deduction.

Unfortunately, the Supreme Court did not analyze the connection between this statement and the *Duke of Westminster* case. In a more recent case, the Supreme Court stated rather vaguely that substance would apply over form where it was consistent with the wording and purpose of the particular provision. Once again, the Court did not bother to analyze the relationship between its statement and deeply-entrenched principles from the *Duke of Westminster* case.

15. Anti-avoidance doctrines and legislation

The main anti-avoidance doctrines used by Canadian courts to control tax avoidance are:

- the sham transaction doctrine. Under this doctrine, a transaction which attempts to give the appearance of legal rights and obligations different from the actual legal rights and obligations created between the parties can be disregarded for tax purposes.

- substance over form. This doctrine is discussed above.

- step transaction doctrine. This doctrine is not well developed in Canadian law, although it has been applied occasionally.

- the business purpose test. This doctrine was rejected by the Supreme Court of Canada in the *Stubart* case in 1984. The Supreme Court's rejection of the doctrine, under which transactions which lack a nontax purpose may be disregarded, ultimately led to the enactment of a general anti-avoidance rule in 1987.

Although these judicial doctrines are quite limited in scope, Canadian courts have not had difficulty in striking down avoidance schemes simply by means of the ordinary rules of statutory interpretation. However, their application of these rules has been very inconsistent.

In 1987 the government enacted section 245 of the Income Tax Act as a general anti-avoidance rule. Under this rule, if a transaction is an "avoidance transaction" then the tax consequences of the transaction may be determined so as to disallow any tax benefit arising from the transaction. An avoidance transaction is defined to be any transaction that results in a tax benefit, which is broadly defined, unless the primary purpose of the transaction is something other than tax avoidance. Even if a transaction is an avoidance transaction, however, there is an exception for transactions that do not involve a misuse of the provisions of the Act or an abuse of the provisions of the Act read as a whole.

The courts have not yet had an opportunity to deal with the application of the general anti-avoidance rule. In general, the rule has not had any significant impact on aggressive tax planning.

General Description: France

Professor Guy Gest

1. History and basic structure of the income tax system

1.1 General outline

The first French income tax system was instituted by three statutes in 1914 and 1917. It was a mixture of the then English and Prussian systems in that it was characterized by the superposition of seven flat rate taxes on seven different *schedular* categories of income (almost the same as today) at the first level and a progressive tax on the total of incomes from all schedular categories accrued to or received by the taxpayer at the second level.

The system remained fundamentally unchanged until 1960, except that a distinct *corporate income tax* — of a global type — was created in 1948 (*impôt sur les sociétés*, IS), the base of which was and is still fundamentally determined according to the rules applicable to the industrial and commercial schedular category of income. Previously, the profits of corporations were subjected to one of the seven then existing flat rate schedular taxes according to the type of activity carried out (industrial and commercial, agricultural, noncommercial, etc.).

In 1960, the different existing proportional and progressive income taxes levied on individuals were replaced by a then unique progressive *individual income tax* (*impôt sur le revenu*, IR).

An integration system was introduced by a 1965 statute. The resident shareholder (or even nonresident under some tax treaties) is granted a credit (*avoir fiscal*) equal to one-half of the dividend received. Since the corporate tax rate is now 33.33%, no double taxation remains on distributed profits.

1.2 The individual income taxation system

Today, the French tax system comprises no less than three different taxes on the income of individuals.

As far as the traditional individual income tax (IR) is concerned, gross taxable income necessary falls into one of the following eight *categories*:

- salary and pension income
- remuneration received by certain company managers
- industrial and commercial profits
- agricultural profits
- real estate income
- securities income
- private capital gains
- personal (noncommercial) services income and other income (catchall category).

From the beginning, the concept of income has been based on the *civil law source theory* according to which income only encompasses sums of money which are likely to flow on a periodical basis from a steady source as opposed to one-off resources or to those which can be considered as part of the source itself (especially capital gains). And this theory still fundamentally inspires the criteria that can be found in the "other income" category in order to determine whether income which does not fall within any one of the other existing categories is taxable or not. But in a number of respects, especially as far as capital gains are concerned, the source theory was reversed by statute.

Business capital gains and losses have systematically been taken into account (except for very small businesses) since the 1930's and taxed within the industrial and commercial, agricultural, and noncommercial schedular categories. In contrast, the principle of the taxation of private — i.e., non-business — capital gains was only established in 1976, and there still exist many exemptions and favorable rules governing their taxation.

Each category has its own specific set of rules (and often several different sets of rules) used to calculate the net income or loss.

Except for gains on the sale of securities, fixed securities income, and business long-term capital gains which are generally subject to a flat rate tax, the individual progressive income tax base is the *algebraic sum of net incomes and losses* (subject to certain limitations) accrued to or received by the different members of the same fiscal household, i.e., the taxable unit, composed of a married couple or a single person with their/his/her dependent persons, mainly children.

According to the family share system (*quotient familial*) created in 1945, the household net income is divided by the number of shares corresponding to the number of people in the family, before being subjected to the single progressive tax schedule. The tax so obtained is then multiplied by the relevant number of shares.

The new and additional individual income taxes, called the generalized social contribution (*contribution sociale généralisée*, CSG) and the social debt reimbursement contribution (*contribution au remboursement de la dette sociale*, CRDS), were created in 1991 and 1996 respectively in order to help finance the social security system. In spite of their names, they are not social security contributions. And they differ from the traditional individual income tax (IR) in many important ways. Their rate is not progressive and their base is wider (fewer exemptions and fewer deductions) and they do not take into account the size of the family.

2. Rate structure

2.1 Individual income tax

The 1995 individual income tax schedule contains seven rate brackets (thirteen before 1994):

Taxable income	Tax rate
ca. $45,000 or less	0%
$45,000 - $9,900	12%
$9,900 - $17,400	25%
$17,400 - $28,200	35%
$28,200 - $45,850	45%
$45,850 - $56,550	50%
$56,550 and over	56.8%

This schedule applies to one share of the global annual income of each fiscal household. Thus it typically corresponds to the taxable income of a single person (with no children).

The brackets are de facto indexed for inflation. In addition, inflation is taken into account when calculating net long-term private gains and indirectly in the case of long-term capital gains in business which are taxed at a preferential rate.

While it exceeded 70 % in the early eighties, the highest marginal rate has not changed since 1987. But, since 1991 the 2.4 % CSG and, beginning in 1996, the 0.5 % CRDS flat rates have to be added so the marginal rate of tax on income is not far from 60 %.

The combined application of this schedule and the family share system gives the gross tax. But several additional calculations (especially tax reductions for personal expenses) have then to be made before arriving at the net payable tax. So, though it was somewhat simplified in 1994, the computation of French individual income tax probably remains one of the most complicated in the world. Fortunately it is not made by the taxpayer himself.

2.2 Corporate income tax

From the beginning, the corporate income tax has been a *flat rate* tax. Initially 24 % (the rate of the former individual income tax on industrial and commercial profits), the normal rate (i.e., the rate of the tax on ordinary income as opposed to capital gains) progressively rose up to 50 % in 1958. It remained at that level until 1986, then *progressively decreased to 33.33 %* for fiscal years beginning January 1, 1993. And, for several years, from 1989 to 1992, French corporations have been subject to a split rate system. A surtax was assessed when, after having been taxed at normal rate when realized, the corporate income was distributed; it was designed to bring the standard corporate tax rate on distributed income up to 42 %.

There is no small corporations special rate. But a 24 % reduced rate applies to certain passive income (rents, interest, dividends) and agricultural income of non profit-seeking entities ("associations"). And, more importantly, net long-term capital gains (i.e., realized more than two years after the asset was acquired, except depreciation recapture which is always ordinary income) may be subjected to another reduced rate (19 % at present).

Lastly, a *temporary surtax* (equal to 10 % of the 33.33 % or 19 % corporate tax) was created in 1995.

3. Basic structure of the tax system

One of the basic features of the French tax system is that income taxes represent a small proportion of the tax revenues compared to other developed countries; they amount to less than 8 % of GDP. The individual income tax is highly progressive and its burden is concentrated on the highest income categories, while almost one out of two fiscal households is exempt.

But social security contributions, which account for more than 19 % of GDP, are also essentially levied on income, and more specially on earned income. The main trends of fiscal reform in the next few years will probably consist in financing welfare benefits in greater proportions through new-style income taxes with wide bases and flat rates, while the old wheezy individual income tax will be modernized.

Tax revenues as percentage of GDP have been rather stable for the last ten years (about 44/45 %) after having steadily and quickly grown in the ten previous years. They are expected to rise dramatically in late 1996 and 1997 (possibly up to 46 %) because of new additional taxes on individual and corporate income and VAT tax rate increase.

4. Statutory style

As in many other legal systems, the statutory style has greatly changed during the last few decades, in that statutes tend to be much more numerous, detailed, and complex than before. Statutory tax law is also nowadays characterized by a great instability. Such an evolution reflects the growing complexity of the technical, economic, and social background of the law as well as the growing number of tax incentives. It explains why the volume of the statutory part of the tax code increased by 35 % from 1975 to 1990.

However, the tax code, even considered together with its schedules (Government decrees), is by far less voluminous than the IRC. This is probably because, in spite of the abovementioned evolution, the French Parliament still generally does not seek to contemplate every particular situation and still often prefers, rather than setting out precise and specific and rigid rules or comprehensive definitions and enumerations, to formulate principles and generally-worded and concise provisions likely to adapt to various and/or new situations thanks to appropriate constructions. Many old-style provisions remain in effect, such as, for instance, the statutory rules concerning the taxation of corporations in the international field, which are condensed in several lines in the tax code. Thus much is left to judicial and administrative interpretation.

5. Statutory interpretation and judicial style

Case law is a major source of tax law. This is because many statutes (and even Government decrees) are generally worded and administrative interpretations are never binding upon courts (see infra). Many tax principles and rules have been set by the tax courts and judicial interpretations are part of the law.

The courts may set aside a statutory provision when they consider it contrary to a treaty or to a European Union directive or regulation. But they do not verify the conformity of the statutes to the 1958 Constitution and the 1789 and 1946 Bills of Rights; nothing, however, prevents them from construing them according to the principles contained in those texts.

No interpretation act has ever been enacted; the judgments never explicitly set out the construction principles and methods used; and there are very few academic studies on the subject. So it is somewhat difficult to explain how statutes (and decrees) are construed by the courts.

It can, however, be said that, as a matter of principle, the clear wording of the texts always prevails over the preparatory works and over tax equity or economic logic considerations. But it is the judge who says if the text is clear or not, and even if a provision is clear, it may be incomplete or imprecise or inappropriate to the particular situation in hand. In such cases, as well as when the texts are ambiguous, contradictory or silent, the judge may use every available method of intrinsic or extrinsic interpretation likely to reveal what the intent of the legislator may have been, though he is rather reluctant to use reasoning by analogy or *a contrario* reasoning and he rarely explicitly relies on the preparatory works. In practice he is very much at liberty to decide what the law is.

This is particularly true for the administrative judges, who are in charge of the litigation concerning the main levies (individual and corporate income taxes and VAT); civil courts, which deal with litigation arising from registration, death, gift, and wealth taxes as well as stamp or excise duties, tend to adopt a more literal and strict style of construction.

Judgments are generally short (rarely more than two or three pages long) and written in a very concise, and even sometimes over-laconic style. The opinions of the judges — either concurring or dissenting — are not published. The doctrine of binding precedent is not applied as such.

6. Administrative style

6.1 Administrative interpretations

After Parliament has enacted a statute, Government decrees (*décrets*) often outline the meaning and scope of the statutory provisions, but this is not systematic unless Parliament has specifically asked the Government to do so. The decrees are codified in different schedules to the Code. The rules they establish can be set aside by the courts if they consider them as contrary to the corresponding statute.

Published administrative circulars (*circulaires* or *instructions*) issued by the Minister of Finance or, under his authority, by the heads of the two main tax departments of the ministry of Finance (*Direction générale des impôts* and *Service de la Législation fiscale*) then explain and interpret statutes and decrees as well as outline the practical measures for the application of the same. They cannot set new rules, and they are deprived of any force of law in that they are not binding upon taxpayers and courts, except when they establish an interpretation which is illegal but favorable to taxpayers. In the latter situation, no additional assessment is possible against a taxpayer who has complied with such interpretation.

There has been a growing tendency, especially in the eighties, to reverse by statute case law running contrary to administrative interpretations and practices and with which the tax authorities disagreed. This trend has been much criticized because such statutes were very often retroactive.

The circulars tend to be more and more precise and are more and more illustrated with examples. They are of course very important and useful to taxpayers. But fields of tax law where decrees and circulars are non-existent or of a very limited help are not so rare, even when the statute is itself very generally worded, for instance in transfer pricing matters.

The French tax authorities have always been reluctant to issue advance rulings. And taxpayers themselves are rather suspicious about them.

6.2 Tax audits

In the past few decades the tax audit services have been reorganized, the skill of tax auditors has been improved, and the use of computers has made tax auditing more efficient. But at the same time the tax auditing process has been more and more precisely regulated and many detailed procedural rules which courts generally strictly enforce are now affording the taxpayer a very complete protection.

The tax files of the individual taxpayers seem to be periodically reviewed, and the necessarily limited funds devoted to tax auditing are concentrated on the control of big businesses, as the tax result of many small sole proprietorships is still determined through an agreement between the taxpayer and the tax collector (*forfait* method).

7. Taxpayers' style

French taxpayers do not like taxes, and they say they don't. In the past fifty years there have been some revolts against taxation, especially by small individual businesses. But, even if many taxpayers still consider tax evasion as legitimate and the amount involved in tax evasion is indeed not inconsiderable, the relationships between taxpayers and the revenue services seem to have reached a relatively peaceful *modus vivendi* in spite of the dramatic increase of tax burdens and of the improved efficiency of tax auditing. This is probably because of the new and numerous statutory rights granted to taxpayers, a growing understanding of the link between taxes and State benefits and the growing number of employees compared to small businesses. At the same time, more and more taxpayers do not hesitate to go to court.

In the past, French taxpayers and tax professionals have apparently not shown an outstanding skill in tax planning, or at least they have not been engaged in aggressive tax planning. But under the influence of Anglo-American practice, things may be changing, especially in the international tax field. In response, many loopholes have been closed and the tax services have now been granted many anti-avoidance tools which they now use with an ever-increasing efficiency.

8. Relation of tax and financial accounting

The link between the two is very close. The taxable income of corporations and, in principle, of sole proprietorships carrying on an industrial, commercial, or agricultural activity is fundamentally their book income, to which adjustments are made whenever tax law departs from accounting law. In case of uncertainty, the courts have shown in the last few years a growing tendency to apply the accounting concepts and principles unless there are strong reasons to the contrary derived from the purpose of the tax provision in hand.

Symmetrically, it is often regretted that tax considerations sometimes "pollute" the development of accounting rules.

9. Respect for civil law

The doctrine of the autonomy of tax law is nowadays out of favor. Civil, commercial, or corporate law concepts used in tax law normally have the same meaning as under the branch of law to which they belong. This is a major principle of interpretation in civil courts when they deal with tax cases. On the other hand, administrative courts, when judging income tax or VAT cases, may still be more sensitive to the purpose of the particular tax provision involved and consider that it can justify giving a particular term a meaning different from the one it has in civil law.

If the parties to a transaction have erroneously characterized this transaction for tax purposes, the tax service is entitled to recharacterize it. In the case when it has been deliberately mischaracterized in order to avoid or unduly decrease taxation, it must invoke the "abuse of law" doctrine which constitutes one of the major anti-avoidance weapons.

10. Anti-avoidance doctrines and rules

Two main doctrines have been traditionally used in French tax law to combat tax avoidance.

The abuse of law (*abus de droit*) doctrine, which has been specifically embodied in a particular section of the tax code, authorizes the revenue service to recharacterize a specific transaction (e.g., a sale) that in fact disguises another transaction (e.g., a donation), the tax cost of which is higher (simulation) and more generally, according to case law, to set aside any scheme which is devoid of any business purpose and has been set up by the taxpayer exclusively for tax purposes (*fraus legis*).

The second anti-avoidance doctrine, which is much more widely used by tax auditors, is the abnormal management decision (*acte anormal de gestion*) doctrine, according to which the consequences of any management decision can be set aside when it unduly deprives a business from receiving income or makes it incur useless expenses or loss or more generally is not in the interest of the business; such income is taxed as if it had been received and such loss or expense is not deductible for tax purposes.

Those two doctrines are applicable in domestic and international tax matters as well. But they have inspired several specific anti-avoidance statutory provisions in the international tax field, such as those against transfer pricing, payments to low-tax jurisdictions, "rent-a-star" companies, or controlled foreign corporations. These are discussed in Part Four.

11. Tax assessment

Corporate and individual taxpayers have to file annual tax returns. All the incomes from all schedular categories realized by the different members of each fiscal household have to be indicated in the individual income tax general return. Special tax returns concerning the various categories of business profits (industrial or commercial, agricultural, and non-commercial profits) have also to be filed, where the taxpayer declares its taxable income after having calculated it, but the taxable income of many small sole proprietorships results from an agreement between the taxpayer and the tax collector; such schedular net income is then transferred to the general household tax return.

The amount of individual tax payable is no longer assessed by the taxpayer himself, which is a good thing given the great complexity of the method of calculation. And the tax is withheld at source only on some fixed securities incomes and in an international context.

General Description: Germany

Prof. Dr. Albert J. Rädler

1. Power to enact tax laws

Until the end of World War I, the German federal states but not the German Reich had the power to impose income taxes. In 1919/20 this power was shifted to the German Reich by the Weimar Constitution. In the subsequent tax reform, the first Corporate Income Tax Act became law.

The German Federal Constitution (*Grundgesetz*) of 1949 gives the Federation (*Bund*) the right to enact tax laws if the Bund is at least partly entitled to the tax revenues or if federal legislation is necessary to ensure equal living conditions or to maintain legal or economic unity in Germany (art. 105 (2); art. 72 (2) *Grundgesetz*). If the Bund makes use of this right, the individual states (*Länder*) are no longer authorized to legislate in this area.

Under the federal constitution, the federal states take part in federal legislation through the instrument of the Council of States (*Bundesrat*). Tax laws adopted by the Federal Parliament (*Bundestag*) can be blocked by the states; currently, this occurs quite often.

2. Sharing of tax revenue

While tax legislation is mainly a federal matter and tax administration mainly a state matter, the revenue from most of the more important taxes is shared between the Bund, the Länder and sometimes also the municipalities. The revenue of some taxes is only for the benefit of one level of government.

The constitutional revenue sharing is one of the major inroads on the constitutional separation of federal and state budgets.

In addition, there are horizontal payments between rich and poor states; there are also vertical payments from the Federation to individual states (*horizontaler und vertikaler Finanzausgleich*).

3. Administrating taxes

When the Grundgesetz came into existence in 1949, the Western powers insisted that there be no centralized collection of taxes but that taxes should be collected by the Länder. Today, collection of taxes is decentralized, but uniform.

Conceptually, Federal and State tax administration is exercised by a separated hierarchy of Federal and State authorities.

The Federal authorities are, in particular, the Federal Ministry of Finance (*Bundesfinanzministerium*) and the main customs offices (*Hauptzollämter*) which are in the field of customs the counterpart to the tax offices. The regional finance offices (*Oberfinanzdirektionen/ OFD*) are mixed entities, consisting of federal authorities in the customs field and state authorities in the tax field. The head of each regional finance office is simultaneously a federal and a state government official.

While the constitutional provisions on tax administration may indicate strong differences between the federal states, the reality shows strong uniformity. The general laws on tax procedure and on administrative procedural rules are identical as are career and salary provisions for tax officials. The heads of the special tax divisions of the federal states meet regularly, together with their federal counterpart. Identical application of tax law is also safeguarded by the Bundesamt für Finanzen which sends its tax auditors all over Germany to take part in tax audits of larger companies.

Other than for customs and excise taxes, the Bund has expanded its own tax service in certain areas over the years, particularly in international taxation. The administrative arm of the Bund is the Bundesamt für Finanzen, which administers refunds of withholding taxes, refunds of VAT, attribution of ID-numbers for EU purposes, etc.

4. Significance of taxes

4.1 Importance of individual taxes

Germany is a high-tax country levying a variety of different taxes. Many of these taxes are transaction taxes generating only a small volume of revenue. In 1994, the total tax revenue of the Bund, the Länder and the municipalities amounted to DM 786.3 billion (approx. US-$ 524.2

billion; 1 US-$ = 1.50 DM)[1]. In relation to the estimated 1994 Gross Domestic Product (GDP) of DM 3,321.1 billion (approx. US-$ 2,214 billion),[2] the total tax revenue is 23.67 %. In relation to the GDP the share of the taxes (not including social security contributions) varied only between 23 % and 25 % during the last 25 years. In terms of 1994 tax revenue, the most important taxes are listed in the following chart:

---

1. Source: Bundestags-Drucksache 13/2009 of 18 July 1995, Entwicklung des Steueraufkommens und der Steuerstruktur. Under the German Federal structure there exists a distinct system of revenue sharing among the different government levels. (An exchange rate of $1 = DM 1.5 is used throughout.)

2. Source: Statistisches Jahrbuch 1995 für die Bundesrepublik Deutschland, p. 655 et seq.

Total German Tax Collection 1994 (excluding social security contributions)	bn. DM	% of Tax Revenue	% of GDP
Personal income tax (*Einkommensteuer*), including Wage withholding tax (*Lohnsteuer*)	266.5.	33.9%	8.02%
Assessed income tax (*veranlagte Einkommenst.*)*	25.5	3.2%	0.77%
Interest withholding tax (*Zinsabschlagsteuer*)	13.7	1.7%	0.42%
Other withholding taxes (incl. corporations)	<u>17.7</u>	<u>2.3%</u>	<u>0.53%</u>
Subtotal	323.4	41.1%	9.74%
Value added tax (*Umsatzsteuer*)	235.7	30.0%	7.10%
Mineral oil tax (*Mineralölsteuer*)	63.8	8.1%	1.92%
Trade tax on income and on capital (*Gewerbesteuer*)	44.1	5.6%	1.33%
Tobacco tax (*Tabaksteuer*)	20.3	2.6%	0.61%
Corporate income tax (*Körperschaftsteuer*)	19.6	2.5%	0.59%
Car tax (*Kraftfahrzeugsteuer*)	14.2	1.81%	0.43%
Real property tax (*Grundsteuer*)	12.7	1.62%	0.38%
Insurance tax (*Versicherungssteuer*)	11.4	1.45%	0.34%
Customs (*Zölle*)	7.2	0.92%	0.22%
Real estate transfer tax (*Grunderwerbsteuer*)	7.0	0.89%	0.21%
Networth tax (*Vermögensteuer*)	6.6	0.84%	0.20%
Liquor excise tax (*Branntweinsteuer*)	4.9	0.62%	0.15%
Inheritance tax (*Erbschaftsteuer*)	3.5	0.45%	0.10%
Total of approx. 20 other taxes	11.8	1.50%	0.35%
Total tax revenue	786.2	100%	23.67%

* Refunds on withholding taxes, in particularly wage withholding tax, may be given through the assessed income tax

The revenue from assessed income tax, corporation tax, networth tax, inheritance tax appears rather low in an international comparison.

Over the last years, assessed income tax has been reduced by several factors. These include the following:

(1) substantial refunds from wage withholding tax are effected through the assessed income tax;

(2) substantial tax-effective writeoffs have been made on investments made in Eastern Germany, in part by high income individuals; and

(3) in 1994 particularly, substantial dividend payments were made to benefit from a change in the corporate income tax rates on retained earnings and on distributed profits resulting in substantial tax credits for domestic shareholders.

The low revenue from the corporation tax is explained in part by tax-effective writeoffs from Eastern Germany, and also since many important businesses are still organized as partnerships. In addition, many big companies are going more and more global which results in less corporation tax under the exemption system.

Members of Catholic or Protestant churches as well as some other churches pay an 8 % or 9 % surcharge on their income tax (church tax, *Kirchensteuer*) which qualifies as an itemized deduction. The total revenue for the Catholic and Protestant churches amounts to 17.6 billion DM (approx. 11.7 billion US-$) which is not included in the chart above.

4.2 Shift from direct taxes to indirect taxes

Since the German unification in 1990, a variety of special tax provisions and subsidies have been introduced to promote investment in East Germany and to restructure the East German economy. Because of the unexpectedly high costs of unification (and a shortfall of tax revenues as of 1993), the German government felt compelled to increase taxes, in particular VAT, mineral oil tax and other indirect taxes, thereby effecting a shift from direct to indirect taxes. In addition, a "solidarity" surcharge (*Solidaritätszuschlag*) on income tax (on both personal and corporate income tax) was put into effect from mid-1991 until mid-1992 and was reintroduced without time limitation as of 1995 at a rate of 7.5 % of the personal and corporate income tax liability.

In relation to the total tax revenue, direct taxes (personal and corporate income tax, trade tax, interest withholding tax, networth tax and similar taxes) developed as follows:[3]

1970	48.2%	1990	52.3%
1975	54.7%	1995	48.6% (estimated)
1980	55.3%	1999	52.4% (estimated)
1985	56.0%		

4.3 Social security contributions

German social security contributions currently amount to 41.2%[4] of the wages, salaries and other compensations paid to employees up to the following maximum limits: In 1996, the maximum annual tax base for pension insurance contributions amounted to DM 96,000 (approx. US-$ 64,000) in the old German Länder and the one for the obligatory health insurance to DM 72.000 (approx US-$ 48,000). In the new German Länder the maximum tax base is 85 % of the one in the old German Länder. The social security contributions are equally shared between employer and employee.

In contrast to taxes, the share of social security contributions as a percentage of GDP has dramatically increased over the last 20 years; such increase was caused by a longer-living population, better and more expensive medical services including dentistry and eye-glasses, longer periods for study and earlier retirement.

5. Personal income tax

5.1 Tax Base

In Germany, the existence of several categories of income indicates a certain schedular aspect, although the general approach is, to some extent, global in nature. Recent developments during the last ten years, however, seem to go more into the direction of the schedular

---

3. Source: Bundestags-Drucksache 13/2009 of 18 July 1995, Entwicklung des Steueraufkommens und der Steuerstruktur.

4. As of mid-1996, the social security tax rates amount to 19.2 % for pension insurance contributions, 13.8 % for health insurance contributions (on average), 6.5 % for unemployment insurance and 1.7 % for care insurance contributions.

system. Thus, the number of categories of income where losses are not currently deductible from other categories of income increased; in 1994 a reduced maximum income tax rate on business income for individuals (47 %) instead of the general maximum tax rate (53 %) was introduced; and for capital investments every individual taxpayer gets a tax-free allowance of DM 6,000 (ca. $4,000)

The German Income Tax Act (ITA) lists the following seven categories of income (sec. 2 (1) ITA):

(1)   income from agriculture and forestry (secs. 13 - 14a ITA);
(2)   income from trade or business enterprises (secs. 15 - 17 ITA);
(3)   income from professional and certain other independent personal services (sec. 18 ITA);
(4)   income from dependent personal services (wages and salaries, sec. 19, 19a ITA);
(5)   income from capital investments (in particular interest and dividends, sec. 20 ITA);
(6)   rental and royalty income (secs. 21, 21a ITA);
(7)   income from certain other sources specifically defined in the ITA, such as from so-called speculative transactions (secs. 22, 23 ITA).

Non-resident individuals are taxed on their German source income only (sec. 49 ITA).

For purposes of the first three categories of income, "income" is defined as "profit" (*Gewinn*), i.e. as the difference between the business assets at the end of the tax year and at the end of the preceding tax year, plus withdrawals and less contributions (sec. 2 (2), 4 (1) ITA). For the last four categories of income, "income" is defined as the excess of receipts over expenditures to acquire, secure, and/or maintain revenue (secs. 2(2), 8-9a ITA), i.e. the cash method applies, supplemented by a deduction for straight-line depreciation.

Capital gains or losses from the disposition of assets related to a trade or business (including farming and professional services) are generally fully included in the tax base and taxed at ordinary tax rates upon realization. However, under certain conditions, business capital gains may be carried-over if they are earmarked to cover the acquisition or production costs of certain assets to be acquired (upon acquisition/production of such assets the acquisition or production costs are reduced by the deferred capital gain). Capital gains derived from the sale of a whole business or division or sale of a partnership interest are subject to German taxation at half the ordinary tax rate after specific tax-free amounts; this privileged tax rate treatment is limited to gains of up to DM 30 million (approx. US-$ 20 million).

Capital gains or losses from the disposition of private assets are taxable only if they derive from the sale of a substantial participation (more than 25 %) in the shares of a company (sec. 17 ITA) or from so-called speculative transactions specifically defined in the ITA. A speculative transaction is assumed if the private asset is sold within two years after the acquisition in case of real property or within six months in the case of securities and other assets (secs. 22, 23 ITA). Speculative losses, in principle, can only be offset with speculative gains of the same character.

Taxable income is defined as income from all (seven) categories reduced by special costs (*Sonderausgaben*) and extraordinary costs (*aussergewöhnliche Belastungen*) as well as certain personal allowances. The latter are intended to exempt a certain minimum level of subsistence from tax.

According to the statutory definition, special costs are expenses which are expressly deductible but which are neither business expenses nor income-related expenses (sec. 10(1)ITA). As private expenses they would normally not be tax-deductible (sec. 12 ITA). There is no clear concept of what sorts of personal expenses should be deductible. There is a wide range of expenses which are treated as special costs, such as certain alimony payments, certain annuities, church tax, tax consulting fees, certain educational expenses, social security contributions, specific insurance premiums, employment of a maid under certain conditions, donations for scientific, charitable, and specific cultural purposes.

Extraordinary costs are, like special costs, basically private expenses. In order to be considered extraordinary, the costs incurred must be unavoidable, based on legal, factual or moral reasons and must be higher in comparison to similar expenses of most other taxpayers. A threshold of between one and seven percent is nondeductible, depending on total income, marital status and number of children.

Social considerations and the ability-to-pay concept are seen as reasons for the introduction of the deduction for extraordinary expenses. Since the distinction between special costs and extraordinary costs in somewhat arbitrary and vague, it has been proposed to combine both into one allowance.

Nondeductible expenses include the expenses the taxpayer incurs for family expenses, voluntary contributions to persons entitled to support, taxes on income and other personal taxes such as networth tax, and penalties.

5.2 Tax rates

The German personal income tax rate schedule is based on a formula approach (contained in sec. 32a ITA). Individuals pay taxes according to a progressive rate at between 25.9 % (effective 1996, 19 % before) and 53 %. The top marginal income tax rate on business income was reduced from 53 % to 47 %, effective 1994 (plus local trade tax).

Since German income tax law is strictly based on the nominal-value principle, it does not provide for indexation with the effect that the average tax rate on real income increases constantly with inflation. The last adjustment of personal income tax rate before 1996 was in 1990 when the marginal tax rates in the progressive tax rate scheme were slightly reduced .

In 1996, the basic personal exemption for a single person was DM 12,095 (ca. $8,100) and DM 24,190 (ca. $16,200) for a married couple.[5] Before 1996, the basic personal exemption amounted to DM 5,616 (ca. $3,750) which was held unconstitutional according to a decision by the Federal Constitutional Court in 1992.[6] The 1996 federal income tax rates for individuals are as follows (marginal tax rates for individuals; for married couples the total amounts must be doubled):

DM 12,095	or less		0 %
DM 12,095	up to	55,727	25.9 % up to 33.3 %
DM 55,728	up to	120,041	33.4 % up to 52.7 %
DM 120,041	and more		53 %

Effective 1995, a solidarity surcharge of 7.5 % of the income and corporate income tax liability (*Solidaritätszuschlag*) was reintroduced to raise additional revenue to cope with the financial needs caused by German unification.

---

5. For 1997 and 1998, the basic personal exemption is increased to DM 12,365 (DM 24,730 for married couples) and for 1999 to DM 13,067 (DM 26,134 for married couples).

6. Federal Constitutional Court of 25 September 1992, BStBl. I 1993, p. 413.

6. Corporate income tax

The most important entities subject to corporate income tax are corporations (stock companies, limited partnerships with shares and limited liability companies). Other entities, such as commercial cooperatives, mutual insurance associations and other juridical persons under private law are from an overall point of view less important.

All income earned by corporations is deemed to be income from trade or business (sec. 8 (2) CTA). Other entities subject to corporate income tax, particularly associations without legal existence, institutions, certain foundations and other asset-conglomerations under civil law may earn most types of income like individuals.

Partnerships, including a limited partnership with a corporate general partner (*GmbH & Co. KG*) (of which approx. 80,000 exist in Germany) are not subject to corporate income tax. Their income is assessed jointly and separately and allocated to the single partners.

For retained earnings, the tax rate for corporations is 45 %, for distributed profits 30 %. For certain entities (including German branches of foreign corporations), the tax rate is 42 %.

One of the most important factors in German tax policy is the relationship between the top rate of personal income tax and corporate income tax on retained income. Particularly in today's situation with strong tax competition between the member states of the European Community, it is difficult to further reduce the rate on retained earnings (currently 45 %, not including trade tax) because this rate should be comparable to the top rate of personal income tax rate, which is currently 47 % for business income and 53 % for other categories of income. The proposal made in the Ruding Report to give partnerships an option to be taxed as a corporation has been rejected.

In case of dividend payments, a withholding tax of 25 % is retained on the payments.

The current corporate tax structure combines a reduced rate for distributions and an imputation credit to eliminate all economic double taxation on distributions to domestic taxable shareholders.

The current system has brought substantial advantages in the purely domestic context since through the corporation tax and dividend withholding tax, the possibilities for tax evasion are very small. In most cases, it does not make a difference whether the domestic individual shareholder declares his dividend income. However, the great expectations for a rapid expansion of the domestic stock market when the system was introduced in 1977 did not materialize.

There is growing criticism of the current corporation tax system concerning its cross-border aspects. The main reason for criticism is that the imputation system no longer complies with the needs of the internal market and may even violate Community law.

For example, domestic permanent establishments of companies from other member states are effectively taxed higher than subsidiaries from the same state; they are subject to a straight 42 % rate, whereas foreign subsidiaries usually follow a tax-induced policy in which they distribute most of their current income to take advantage of the reduced rate of corporation tax of 30 %. Needless to say, that subsequently capital may be brought back either as equity or as loans, as long as it stays within the limits set by thin capitalization rules.

On the other hand, German-controlled corporations have a competitive disadvantage compared to domestic subsidiaries of foreign groups because they can not make full use of the reduced rate on distributions of 30 % for business reasons, but have to subject a substantial part of their income to the higher rate of 45 % on retained earnings.

German groups complain that dividends received from foreign subsidiaries cannot be passed on to their German shareholders without them paying a tax penalty.

A similar point concerns domestic private investors. Whereas on dividends from German corporations they generally receive the domestic imputation tax credit which now amounts to over 42 % of the nominal dividend, they do not get any such imputation tax credit on dividends from other member states, with the exception of France. Thus the individual investment decision is clearly directed towards domestic shares.

7. Trade tax on income and capital

The second major tax to which a German business (whether incorporated or not) is subject is the trade tax on income and on capital (*Gewerbeertragsteuer* and *Gewerbekapitalsteuer*, respectively) which is levied by the German municipalities. A foreign business is subject to trade tax if it has a permanent establishment in Germany (sec. 2 GewStG). According to trade tax statistics, about 60 % of the revenue from that tax is generated by unincorporated businesses and only 40 % by corporations.

The tax base for the trade tax on income is the profit determined under the income tax rules subject to various adjustments.

The tax rate for trade tax on income is 5 % (base tax rate) multiplied by a municipal factor (*Hebesatz*) which is determined by the respective municipality. At present, the average factor is close to 400 % which results in an effective tax rate of 16.7 % for trade tax on income.

The tax base for the trade tax on capital, which is effectively a separate tax, is the total of net assets subject to adjustments similar to those applicable to the trade tax on income. The tax rate for trade tax on capital is 0.2 % (base tax rate) multiplied by the respective municipal factor as for trade tax on income. No trade tax on capital is levied in the new German Länder until 1 January 1997.

The trade tax is criticized because it constitutes a special burden for taxpayers receiving income from business activities, compared with income from self-employment, agriculture and forestry which is not subject to trade tax (this disadvantage was only partly eliminated by the introduction of the 47 % maximum personal income tax rate for business income). Furthermore, the trade tax on capital (like the net-worth tax) must be paid even in case of losses.

8. Statutory style

As in many other countries, German tax legislation is earmarked by:

(1) frequent changes of the tax laws (the income tax act is modified at least once a year, sometimes even three times a year);

(2) the attempt to encourage or discourage certain activities (e.g. environmental protection);

(3) the attempt to prevent abuses;

(4) the intention to achieve fairness in each single case (*Einzelfallgerechtigkeit*).

At present, the tax laws are highly complex and sometimes may be even contradictory. Even tax professionals can sometimes be confused by the specific provisions.

Together with the high tax rates, the complexity of German tax laws may encourage tax avoidance or even tax evasion.

9. Impact of the Constitution and the Federal Constitutional Court

In addition to the provisions which concern the powers of different levels of government in taxation, the Constitution has played an important direct role in developing German tax law after World War II. This has happened by interpreting fundamental constitutional rights in the tax area.

9.1 Basic rights

Among the "Bill of Rights" contained in articles 1 to 19 of the Federal Constitution, the following have had a special impact on tax matters:

- Art. 2 para. 1 in connection with Art. 20 para. 3 (free development of the individual and due process of law which, for example, prohibit retroactive tax legislation),
- Art. 3 (equality),
- Art. 6 para. 1 (marriage and family are under the special protection of the state),
- Art. 14 (protection of property),
- Art. 19 para. 4 (the right to bring any violation of rights by the administration before an independent court of justice).

These constitutional rights may be directly invoked by the taxpayers.

9.2 Important decisions

The following decisions of the Federal Constitutional Court had a special impact on taxation:

- The simple fact of marriage may not increase the total tax burden of the spouses; therefore, the joint assessment of husband and wife was declared null and void; subsequent legislation provided for income splitting (1957);
- The income of minor children must be assessed separately (1964);
- The old system of multi-stage sales tax was found unconstitutional, because it gave unfair advantages to integrated multi-stage businesses (1966);

- The principle of separation of powers disallows the tax authorities to levy administrative penalties (other than those for late payment) (1967);

- The former system of taxation of interest was unconstitutional because it did not provide for proper enforcement (1991);

- The basic exemption for personal income tax may not be lower than the minimum amount necessary for existence which corresponds to the amount which is paid to the poor by the state welfare authorities. Currently this is fixed at DM 12,095 per person annually (1992).

- The networth tax and inheritance tax have to be changed because the value of real estate was unreasonably lower than the fair market value, which was the value of most other assets (1995).

10. Statutory interpretation

Both the Federal Constitutional Court and the Federal Tax Court use in principle the objective approach.[7] The principal aim of interpreting the law is to apply the objective intention of the legislator.

Although there is no mechanism and hierarchy in applying various criteria of interpretation, the most important criteria is the wording of the statute (literal interpretation). Furthermore, the context of the statute, its purpose, the legislative intent and finally the legislative history are important.

Teleological, systematic or historical arguments are applied, particularly if the wording of a statutory provision is ambiguous. In addition, it is very often common to use these arguments to justify the result of a literal interpretation.

The role of economic arguments (*wirtschaftliche Betrachtungsweise*) is unclear. On the one hand, the Federal Tax Court decides very often that the literal interpretation is limited by the possible meaning of the statutory wording. Thus, economic arguments do not justify the filling in of missing definitional elements or changing the meaning of the law. On the other hand, in several cases the Federal Tax Court interpreted the statute in such a way that the interpretation differed from the statute's

---

7. For details see Ruppe in Herrmann/Heuer/Raupach, Einf. ESt, note 652.

wording. However, such interpretation is only possible in very limited cases, i.e., in cases in which the literal approach would lead to an outcome which does not make sense and in cases in which there are clear signs that the wording of the statute does not properly reflect the legislative intention.

11. Role of the courts

The Federal Constitutional Court has the power to review the compatibility of federal legislation with the German Constitution. In other cases, its decisions are binding for the other governmental bodies of the Bund and the Länder.

The decisions of the Federal Tax Court (*Bundesfinanzhof*) are only binding for the parties of the specific case. Nevertheless, the decisions of the Federal Tax Court are of great importance because only cases of fundamental importance may be brought before the Federal Tax Court

The publication of a particular decision in the Federal Tax Gazette (*Bundessteuerblatt*) or in the tax regulations indicates that the tax authorities in general apply the specific decision of the Federal Tax Court. Sometimes tax authorities release a decree of non-application regarding a particular decision, which may be both to the advantage or the disadvantage of taxpayers; this degree may be simultaneously published in the Federal Tax Gazette with the decision of the Federal Tax Court concerned.

If the tax authorities believe that the Federal Tax Court will confirm a decision in subsequent cases, they may propose a legislative change.

12. The German assessment system

German tax administration works in a quite bureaucratic and formalistic way, governed by strict adherence to the rule of law.

Roughly 200 million tax assessments are made every year. This estimate includes also separate assessments, for example for real estate valuation, partnerships, church tax etc. Some taxpayers may even get more than a dozen assessments for the income tax for a particular year, taking into account subsequent adjustments and corrections, some of them based on separate assessments for partnerships in which the taxpayer is a member.

12.1 Tax filing and audit enforcement

In Germany, all taxpayers are obligated to file an annual income tax return and report their income and expenses accurately. An exception exists only for taxpayers with relatively low income from employment and no significant further taxable income from other sources. However, such taxpayers may be assessed upon request.

The tax returns are checked by a medium level tax inspector who examines the relevant facts and ensures that the information is sufficient and correct. If there are any doubts, more detailed information may be requested. If the taxpayer does not fulfill his obligations, all uncertainties may be interpreted to his disadvantage.

This desk audit is mainly concerned with plausibility, i.e. reviewing how the different categories of income of the taxpayer have developed compared with earlier years as well as with taxpayers of the same trade or professions etc.

Tax payments must be made within one month after the notification of the tax assessments. Tax refunds are paid out upon notification.

Very often desk audits do not lead to final tax assessments, but to tax assessments subject to review. In such cases, desk audits are very often followed by field audits. Field audits are highly developed in Germany and most businesses or professional firms of any significant size will typically be subject to a field audit. Smaller businesses are audited less frequently; their selection may depend on the existence of certain indications. The system of field audits is criticized because the audit periods are too long. Quite often transactions reviewed had happened six or more years before.

Altogether, the German tax administration employs more than 10,000 field auditors.

12.2 Differences in tax compliance

The ability of the tax authorities to check whether the declaration of income by a taxpayer is accurate varies significantly between the different types of income.

Due to the field audits in the area of business and professional income tax, compliance appears to be very high in an international comparison. The same is true for an income from employment. Wage withholding is audited in the offices of the employer at shorter intervals (usually one or two years). Smaller enterprises are audited for wage withholding tax on a regular basis. Separately, the payment of social security contributions is field-audited by agents of the social security organizations.

In case of income from capital investment, in contrast, tax compliance seems to be very low. For many years there was no serious effort to enforce the declaration of interest from bank accounts and bonds. There was no withholding tax on interest, and banks were not required to provide information reporting on interest payments automatically. The tax auditors of banks have not been authorized to copy lists of bank customers who receive interest. Consequently, according to estimates accepted by the Federal Constitutional Court, about 60 % to 70 % of domestic interest received by private investors was not reported. Finally, the Constitutional Court declared the system of interest taxation as unconstitutional because it violated the principle of equal treatment.

As a consequence, in 1993 a withholding tax of 30 % was introduced on interest received by residents but not by nonresidents. At the same time a basic exemption for capital income of DM 6.000 (approx. US-$ 4.000) per taxpayer was introduced. Because the withholding tax applies to banks resident in Germany, there was a substantial outflow of capital particularly to the subsidiaries of German banks in Luxembourg and in Switzerland, in total estimated to be more than DM 500 billion. (ca. $333.3 billion). Today, it is again asserted that the new system is unconstitutional because it does not safeguard that the tax on interest is fully paid because most taxpayers will have a higher marginal tax rate than 30 %.

Compared to other countries, Germany has an extremely high number of criminal tax investigations. It seems that it is the fear of a criminal investigation which keeps the rather complicated tax system running. During the last years, prominent taxpayers, including executives of major companies have been under investigation. When a normal tax official, particularly a field agent, is seriously convinced that the taxpayer has acted in a fraudulent way, he has to stop further investigations and transfer the case to the criminal investigation division.

One of the reasons for this situation is the absence of administrative penalties. The interdiction of administrative penalties by the Federal Constitutional Court was first regarded as a great victory by taxpayers; in hindsight it may be seen differently.

Every year about 30,000 cases of criminal tax investigations are initiated, of which over 10,000 are terminated by a conviction of tax fraud by a criminal court. The conviction is registered in the criminal records of the taxpayers.

The penalties pronounced by the criminal court are usually monetary; effective imprisonment is rare as far as direct taxes are the cause: prison terms are usually suspended. It is not unusual, however, that a suspect is put into preliminary detention in order to prevent him from disrupting the investigation or disappearing to a foreign country.

13. Appeals against tax assessments

A notice of assessment or other formal act of the tax administration may be appealed. This administrative appeal is directed to the same tax office which has made the assessment on the administrative level. After the administrative appeal has failed, the appeal can be brought before the courts. Only in rare cases, the taxpayer can go directly to the tax court.

Whether or not an appeal is filed, the amount of tax fixed by the assessment has to be paid within the time given (usually one month) unless the execution of the assessment is suspended. This suspension usually requires a request of the taxpayer. Therefore, it is common that the taxpayer files an application for suspension of execution together with the appeal. This application is usually filed with the tax office.

14. Appeal to court

In Germany there are two levels of tax courts, the (Lower) Tax Courts (established by the Länder) and the Federal Tax Court.

Within one month after the receipt of the negative decision on the administrative appeal, the taxpayer may file a suit to the tax court. The tax courts are responsible both for the investigation of the relevant facts of the underlying case and the proper application and interpretation of the law.

56,113 new cases came before the tax courts in 1994. Over the last years, the number of new cases stayed rather stable but it was about 10 % higher in 1988. The number of the cases which were terminated in 1994 was 63,413. It is interesting to note that only about one quarter of the cases which were terminated were decided by the court. Obviously the time while the case is pending before the tax court is used for negotiations between the taxpayer and the tax administration. The tax courts themselves estimate that in total about one third of the cases terminated end in favor of the taxpayer.

14.1 Federal Tax Court (*Bundesfinanzhof*)

The Federal Tax Court in Munich sits with 11 chambers (Senate), each with 5 judges. It is only responsible for the proper application of tax law. Therefore, it is not possible for the taxpayer and/or the tax authorities to introduce new facts once the case is brought before the Federal Tax Court unless the tax court has infringed its obligation to ascertain the facts properly.

A case may only be brought before the Federal Tax Court if it is of fundamental importance.

In total, about 20 % of the cases are decided in favor of the taxpayer; this percentage would be higher if one takes into account the high number of cases which are rejected for formal reasons.

15. Administrative style

German tax officials are usually well-trained and expected to strictly follow the rule of law. Consequently, the power of discretion of the individual tax official is relatively small within the frame-work of numerous regulations, decrees, circular letters, etc. Most of the internal circular letters are also published. Cases of corruption are almost unheard of. An important factor in this context is that salaries of tax officials are thought to be competitive with the private sector if the more generous retirement plan is included. Promotions are based on merit and seniority.

The Federal Ministry of Finance publishes every two or three years new regulations concerning the most important taxes (income tax, corporate income tax, turnover tax, trade tax). These regulations are intended to facilitate dealing with these taxes and ensure a uniform application of the laws throughout Germany.

It cannot be said that the tax administration has become stricter in recent years. However, some people fear that the huge budget deficits resulting from the German unification may lead to more detailed examinations and tax audits. Tax officials like taxpayers and their representatives deplore the fast change in tax laws, when it even happens that a new law is amended again before it becomes effective.

Sometimes the tax administration develops its own policy with respect to certain ongoing transactions, either through administration interpretation of existing provisions or by applying the general anti-abuse-provision (sec. 42 BTA). A recent example of the latter is the treatment of the setting-up of Ireland-based subsidiaries to make use of Irish fiscal incentives in the period from 1989 until 1991.[8] Finally, the tax authorities may propose a change in the tax law.

Contracts concerning the amount of the tax and the applicable tax law are not permitted. This results from the principle of the rule of the law. However, if the underlying facts of a particular case are difficult to investigate, a mutual agreement on the facts is possible. Mutual agreements on the facts must not lead to an obviously wrong taxation.[9]

Rulings can be obtained on legal matters and must be given in certain situations. However, the tax office can refrain from giving a ruling when the object of the application would be the achievement of a specific tax advantage such as tax-shelter operations or a borderline of tax abuse.

16. Taxpayer style

It is rather obvious that due to the high German tax rates and the complexity of the German tax base, most taxpayers try to reduce their tax liability. However, the possibilities for the taxpayers differ significantly.

On the one hand, taxpayers earning income exclusively from employment have very limited possibilities to reduce their tax burden because most deductions available are standardized and income is subject to withholding.

On the other hand, most multinational corporations are sensitive to tax issues and most do not hesitate to engage in reasonably aggressive tax planning. Based on decisions of the Federal Tax Court the right of the taxpayer to test the limits of tax abuse is recognized, as long as the facts are fully and correctly disclosed to the tax authorities.[10]

---

8. For more details see Rädler/Lausterer/Blumenberg, DB 1996, Supplementary 3/1996.

9. Federal Tax Court 11 December 1984 VIII R 131/76, BStBl. II 1985, p. 354, 358.

10. For more details see Rädler/Lausterer/Blumenberg, DB 1996, Supplementary 3/1996.

Also, medium-size corporations are getting more and more sophisticated in international tax-planning.

17. Relation of tax and financial accounting

German taxation of business income earned by both individual entrepreneurs and corporations is marked by a strong connection between taxable income and accounting income. This "linkage" (*Maßgeblichkeit*) is based on the principle that the financial accounting treatment controls for tax accounting provided there are no divergent tax provisions. An interpretation by the Federal Tax Court deals with the treatment of accounting elections; whenever there is such an election, the taxpayer has to use in his tax return the election which results in a higher taxable income.

This linkage rule, in combination with the absence of express tax limitations, has the result that reserves and provisions are accepted as tax deductions in Germany more than in other countries. In spite of high nominal tax rates, this timing rule gives fast-growing enterprises a temporary tax advantage compared to other countries. On the other hand, mature enterprises suffer under the high tax rates, particularly in periods of high inflation rates.

18. Respect of civil or private law

In Germany, it is clearly recognized that income tax law is generally applied to rights and liabilities determined under general civil law. Tax law is not autonomous. It must respect principles of other fields of German (and EU) law (so-called *Einheit der Rechtsordnung*). For example, tax law must not encourage any activity which is penalized by civil or penal law (no deductibility of penalties).[11]

19. Substance over form

German tax administration and, to a lesser extent, tax courts have always followed the principle of "substance over form", with different intensity in different periods. This principle is based on the general anti-

---

11. See Tipke/Lang, Steuerrecht, 13 ed. 1991, p. 9.

avoidance clause of sec. 42 BTA which is aimed at abusive structures.

According to the Federal Tax Court, a legal structure is to be considered abusive if:

(1) the structure is inadequate (in the meaning of unusual) to achieve the (economic) goal strived for,

(2) the realization of this structure shall reduce the tax burden, and

(3) the legal structure lacks good business reasons.[12]

Furthermore, the taxpayer must have the intention to carry out the abusive structure.[13] Thus, if a taxpayer can prove that a lack of experience or of legal knowledge was the cause for the structure, no abuse will be assumed.[14] On the other hand, the taxpayer's intention itself to save taxes is not abusive[15] if the chosen structure is adequate.

---

12. Federal Tax Court, 16 January 1992 V R 1/91, BStBl. II 1992, p. 541, 542; Federal Tax Court, 14 January 1992 IX R 33/89, BStBl. II 1992, p. 549, 550 with further references.

13. Federal Tax Court, 5 February 1992 I R 127/90, BStBl. II 1992, p. 532, 536.

14. See Tipke/Kruse, sec. 42 Basic Tax Code, note 18; critical: Fischer in Hübschmann/Hepp/ Spitaler, sec. 42 Basic Tax Code, note 107.

15. Federal Tax Court, 20 October 1965 II 119/62, BStBl. III 1965, p. 697.

General Description: Japan

Professor Minoru Nakazato

Professor Mark Ramseyer

1. History

The Japanese Imperial Constitution was promulgated in February of 1889. Yet the income tax had already been enacted in 1887. Prior to that time, Japanese national revenues had been heavily dependent on the land tax and the liquor tax. As a result, the notion behind the income tax was that the tax burden should be made more fair by assessing tax on those engaged in commerce and industry as well. The new income tax was a progressive tax with five brackets ranging from 1 % to 5 %. Corporations were not taxed. Since that time, there have been several major revisions to the income tax. The more prominent are:

    a. In 1899, income was divided into three categories: Type I (corporate income), Type II (interest on bonds), and Type III (individual income). Of these, the first two were taxed at a low rate, and the last was taxed at progressive rates. The corporate bond interest was taxed independently through withholding provisions — it was not taxed further. Because dividends were not taxed, there was no double tax on corporate income.

    b. In 1920, interest on bank time deposits was added to Type II income. Dividends received were now added to Type III income, but only after a 40 % deduction of the amount received.

    c. In 1940, taxes were raised to cover the high war costs. The income tax was now assessed on a wider swath of the population, and became central to the national tax structure.

    d. In 1947, a self-assessment system was introduced on a broad scale. What had been a distinctively

Japanese amalgam of a schedular and global system was replaced with a single global system. The scope of taxable income was broadened, and capital gains were made taxable. The unit of taxation was changed from the household to the individual.

e. In 1950, the system was changed yet again to incorporate most of the provisions of a study commission headed by Columbia economist Carl Shoup. The new system incorporated the latest in tax theory from the U.S., and used a global progressive tax that took a comprehensive tax base as its ideal. Inter alia, capital gains were taxed on their full amount; capital losses were deductible in full; provisions were adopted to integrate the corporate and the individual tax; many special tax measures were abolished; and tax administration was improved.

f. In 1987, the tax rate structure was flattened; the exemption for deposit interest income was abolished; the tax-exemption for capital gains from the sale or exchange of securities was abolished; and the consumption tax was introduced.

g. The future: One can predict a gradual aging of Japanese society toward 2025. This necessarily has implications for Japanese tax reform. First, it is thought that the consumption tax rate will need to be increased. Second, the corporate tax rates will have to be lowered to slow the flow of Japanese investment overseas.

The single event with the most influence on postwar tax policy was the 1949 Shoup Report (*Report on Japanese Taxation by the Shoup Mission*, 4 vols.). Regarding this report, Professor Kaneko writes:

In 1949, in order to realize the nine principles of economic stabilization, a long-term balanced budget under the Dodge Line was established, and inflation rapidly came under control. Furthermore, in order to accomplish the (long-envisioned) comprehensive reconsideration of the national tax system, SCAP invited from the U.S. [a group of experts organized around] Columbia Professor Carl Shoup (the "Shoup mission"). This mission included Shoup and six other specialists in tax theory or tax law. They arrived on May 10, 1949, and investigated and considered the national tax system for about 3-1/2 months. On September 15, they published their large-scale report, the so-called Shoup Report. The mission returned to Japan again in July 1950, and on September 21 published a second report (the *Second Report on Japanese Taxation by the Shoup Mission*). This was a form of "after care" for the 1949 report. These studies are often referred to together as the "Shoup Report."

The Shoup Report recommended, on a long-term basis, the way our tax system (both the national and the local systems) ought to be. Its main principles can be summarized by three goals: (a) the establishment of a fair tax system, (b) the reform of tax administration, and (c) the strengthening of local fiscal capacity. In suggesting measures like the revaluation of assets, however, it also considered the need for capital accumulation and economic recovery. As a whole, the Shoup Report urged the establishment of a theoretically coherent fair tax system. . .

The Shoup Report designed a single country's tax system around a coherent theoretical structure. As a result, it was a grand experiment. In content, it systematized the latest in tax theory in the U.S. (from the perspective of tax-system theory, that was the most advanced in the world). As scholarship too, it was a magnificent achievement. Moreover, as one could tell from looking at the members of the mission, it was a heavily reformist group. They understood the vicissitudes of the American tax system, and had high hopes about how that system should be reformed. Precisely because of that, they strove hard to establish a modern idealist tax system that was extremely fair.

In other words, the Shoup Report pointed toward reformist legislation. It contributed greatly toward the modernization of our country's tax system. Moreover, as one can see from the proposals to revalue capital assets, it contained many realistic elements, and contributed to economic stabilization and growth. In part stimulated by the Shoup Report, the study of tax theory and tax law in our country also grew steadily and has now reached a vigorous state. At least indirectly, these scholarly achievements too are a legacy of the Shoup Report.[1]

2. Basic structure of the system

Japan currently maintains a formally schedular system — in the way that income is divided into categories, and computed according to distinctive rules of calculation. The theory behind this is sometimes said to be that the "ability to pay" varies by category of income. Other evidence of the schedular character of the Japanese system includes the limits on the deductibility of losses in one category against income in other categories. As discussed above, the system is in substance closer to a global regime.

3. Rate structure

The personal income tax rates, for 1995, are:

Income (x ¥1000)	Marginal rates
under 3,300	10 %
to 9,000	20
to 18,000	30
to 30,000	40
above 30,000	50

---

1. Hiroshi Kaneko, Sozei ho [Tax Law] (Tokyo: Yuhikaku, 5th ed., 1996) pp. 61-62, 67.

There are no formal rate bracket adjustments for inflation but in the 1960's and 1970's the government reduced frequently made ad hoc bracket adjustments, which had somewhat similar effects.

The corporate income tax rate, for 1995, is 37.5 %. This rate is widely seen as too high, and as having a detrimental effect on the economy. Nonetheless, if corporate tax reform is to remain revenue-neutral, then any lowering of the rates will have to be paired with an expansion of the tax base.

4. Composition of fiscal system

The percentage of the different taxes in national revenues are:

Income tax (37.8 %), Corporate tax (23.0 %), Inheritance tax (5.1 %), Land tax (0.9 %), Consumption tax (13.2 %), Liquor tax (3.9 %), Tobacco tax (1.9 %), and other taxes (4.4 %).

Compared to other countries, Japan obtains a relatively large percentage of its revenues from the corporate tax. The ratio of national to local tax revenues is about 7:3. Total local and national taxes are 23.2 % of national income.

5. Statutory style

Compared to statutes in other fields, Japanese tax statutes are detailed affairs. Note, however, that the statutes — detailed as they may be — still contain flexible terms like "extremely low price" or "appropriate amount."

Legal provisions related to the tax system include: the constitution, treaties, statutes, regulations (*seirei*, issued by the cabinet), orders (*shorei*, issued by the Ministry of Finance), circulars (*tsutatsu*, issued by the head of the National Tax Office [NTO] or the heads of the regional offices and directed at subordinates), and provisions (*jorei*, issued by local organizations). In theory, the circulars are simply internal instructions from bureaucratic superiors to inferiors, and thus do not bind citizens. In fact, as discussed below, courts often defer to these circulars. These circulars should be understood as playing an important role in making tax administration predictable to taxpayers.

Using ambiguous terms (those not readily understood through standard interpretive principles) in statutes formally violates Article 84 of the Constitution: "No new taxes shall be imposed or existing ones modified except by law or under such conditions as law may prescribe." (official translation; the term "law" here is the Japanese *horitsu*, which might better be translated "statute"). Often, however, concepts one might otherwise think unclear are held to be clear upon interpretation.

As a structural matter, there are separate statutes for the income and corporate tax, and there is an additional statute for "special tax measures" which contains provisions that could broadly be considered tax expenditures.

6. Statutory interpretation

Courts are sometimes said to pay more attention to the actual text of the statute in tax law than in other fields (though this is obviously a hard claim to measure). This is because of Article 84 of the Constitution (quoted immediately above).

Within legislative history, emphasis is placed on (a) answers given by the tax investigative committee in response to questions at the time of the revision of the statute, and (b) interpretations (not official) given by the staff of the tax office within the Ministry of Finance.

The actual legislative drafting is done by young bureaucrats in the Ministry of Finance tax bureau. As a result, it sometimes happens that the most valuable tax legislative materials exist only as internal documents within the Ministry of Finance or the bureau. Sometimes this internal information becomes public when a bureaucrat at the Ministry of Finance or the bureau publishes a book or article in his "private" capacity.

Not infrequently, judges seldom have deep specialist knowledge of the tax law. As a result, perhaps it is not surprising that they often defer to the opinions of the tax office in tax litigation.

7. Administrative style

The principle of administration only according to law is a basic constitutional principle in Japan, and the notion is particularly important in tax because of Article 84 of the Constitution. Administrative interpretation is provided mostly in the form of circulars issued by the NTO. Although circulars are not binding interpretations of law, necessarily they are the result of careful consideration by a group of very knowledgeable and sophisticated specialists. This, together with the fact that courts rarely have expertise in tax, results in considerable judicial deference to these circulars.

The whole question of Japanese administrative style is a matter of some controversy. The conventional interpretation is that the system is characterized by a strong bureaucracy using informal "administrative guidance" which is typically followed by the private sector. As applied in the tax area, this would mean that informal interpretations would perform the same role as formally issued regulations in a more rule-oriented system. On the other hand, some commentators (including one of the authors of this description) have taken the position that the Japanese system is not unique in its use of informal regulation. Informal regulations are only followed if and to the extent that the parties believe that the positions taken could be transferred into formal rules. By governing informally, both the government and the private parties save the costs of formality.

8. Taxpayer style

At least according to conventional wisdom, Japanese taxpayers do not approach tax planning as aggressively as American taxpayers do. Recently, however, aggressive tax shelters have begun to be marketed. For example, an American bank is pushing the following tax-planning scheme as a way of minimizing inheritance-gift tax liability: (a) child becomes an American resident; (b) parent, in Japan, buys American treasury bonds; (c) parent gives bonds to child. The Japanese gift tax applies to the recipient of the gift. If the recipient is a nonresident, the tax applies only to domestic assets, and U.S. treasury bonds (even if physically located in Japan) are considered foreign assets. Accordingly, the Japanese gift tax does not apply. On the other hand, the U.S. gift tax applies in principle to the donor but does not cover intangible property. As a result, the gift by a nonresident of treasury bonds is not subject to tax in either jurisdiction.

Among taxpayer organizations, there are those that are cooperative to the National Tax Office (e.g., the Blue Return Organization), and those that are uncooperative (e.g., the Democratic Chamber of Commerce). The Democratic Chamber of Commerce has launched many legal challenges against the NTO. Among the leftist tax adviser (*zeirishi*) groups, there is the Young Tax Advisers Association.

9. Judicial role and style

Following the continental influence on the Japanese legal system, judicial opinions are not formally the source of law, at least among equal levels in the judicial hierarchy. This does not mean, however, that judicial opinions have no authority. Quite to the contrary— they have enormous authority. For example, should the tax office lose a case, even if the court is an obscure district court, the tax office often changes its policies to comport with the court decision. In general, if a court rejects an NTO circular, the circular is amended.

Japanese courts tend to be conservative in the exercise of their powers, and to defer broadly to the legislative branch. This is particularly noticeable in fields like tax where technical sophistication is at a premium. As the Supreme Court put it:

> Tax today involves more than its basic function of providing for the national fiscal needs. It also redistributes income, appropriately allocates resources, and adjusts economic performance. In deciding each citizen's tax burden, the determination of national fiscal, economic and social policy on a comprehensive national scale becomes necessary. Because the prerequisites of tax liability must also be decided, however, the process requires specialized technical judgment as well. Accordingly, in the determination of tax law, it is necessary to defer to the policy and technical judgment (based on accurate data regarding such issues as the national fiscal situation, the social economy, the national income, and the national living situation) of the legislative branch. At root, the courts have no choice but to respect the discretionary judgment of that branch.[2]

---

2. Oshima v. Sakyo zeimu shocho, 39 Saihan minshu 247 (S.Ct. Mar. 27, 1985) (*en banc*).

10. General principles

10.1 Relation of tax to financial accounting

The taxable income of a firm is calculated by taking the profit-and-loss statement dictated by the Commercial Code and making the adjustments required by the Corporate Tax Act. The accounting provisions dictated by the Commercial Code, in turn, are based on generally accepted accounting principles.

All this is generally explained as based on the need to simplify tax law, but it remains problematic. For example, suppose that the rules for annual accounting change. By this logic, the tax rules would automatically change as well. Yet that seems to violate the general constitutional requirement of taxation according to law. One current issue, for instance, is whether mark-to-market principles generally used for financial derivatives will be adopted into the tax system — wholly without a statutory change.

10.2 Extent of respect for civil law form

In general, the Supreme Court's position has been that, where the tax code uses concepts common to the Civil and Commercial Codes, the concepts are interpreted in the same manner as in the Civil and Commercial Codes.

At least according to most observers, courts do not ignore contractual form and impose a tax based on the underlying economic substance. Because the approach generally taken has the potential for tax evasion, the tax office sometimes asserts substance-over-form arguments.

10.3 Anti-avoidance doctrines or legislation

There are in Japan no general provisions that require courts to recharacterize tax avoidance schemes. There are, however, some more narrow provisions to that effect. Perhaps the most important is the rule that authorizes courts to recharacterize the transactions of family corporations. According to this rule (stripped of a variety of details), should transactions among such corporations unreasonably reduce their tax liability, the courts can recharacterize the transactions and recompute the tax liability.

11. Procedure

In principle, Japan adopts the self-assessment system. In fact, however, withholding rules play a large role. Indeed, 80 % of the income tax is collected through withholding. For a couple of reasons, this withholding largely obviates the need for self-assessment.

First, wage earners generally make appropriate adjustments to their withholding at the end of the year and thereby eliminate the need to file a return.

Second, much of the nonwage income is also subject to withholding.

General Description:
The Netherlands

Professor Kees van Raad

1. Tax system

The authority to levy taxes is vested primarily in the central government. Provinces and municipalities are generally restricted to levy various user fees. Municipalities, however, may also impose an (annual) tax on the value of real property. The budgetary needs of provinces and municipalities are met mostly through revenue sharing with the central government. The various taxes imposed by the central government are listed below, along with the percentage each of them contributed to the total amount of taxes raised in 1995:

<u>Direct taxes</u>

Income tax (individual)	5.8
Wages (withholding) tax	28.8
Dividend tax	1.3
Company tax	12.3
Wealth tax	0.9
Gift and succession duties	1.0

<u>Indirect taxes</u>

Import duties	2.1
VAT	28.2
Excise duties	9.2
Tax on legal transactions	2.7
Car taxes	5.5
Environmental taxes	1.3

In addition to these taxes, which along with taxes imposed by local governments amount to about 26 % of the Netherlands GNP, social security contributions (both general and employment-related) amount to an additional 20 % of the GNP. The "general" social security contributions are levied together with the wages and income taxes by adding the social security contribution rates to the tax rates (see further paragraph 4.3, below).

2. History of the Netherlands tax system, tax morale and tax simplification

An 1821 Act provided the first conceptual framework for taxes that were levied at that time. Most of these taxes were excise taxes, except for the tax levied under the Patent Right Act of 1819, which was imposed on trades and businesses (operated under a license or "patent") according to their deemed income as apparent from external characteristics, such as number of employees. The first true income taxes were introduced in 1892-1893. Income from capital was taxed under the Wealth Tax Act of 1892 under which income from capital was deemed to amount to 4 percent of the value of the capital. In addition, the Business Tax Act of 1893 subjected to tax business and employment income.

The reason for taxing income under two separate acts was the desire to tax passive income more heavily than active income. This difference in income taxation disappeared when the two acts were replaced by the Income Tax Act of 1914. In order to still subject wealthy individuals to a higher tax burden, however, a true wealth tax was introduced in the same year. The 1914 income tax was levied not on the income earned during the preceding year but on the income the taxpayer concerned could be expected to earn during the current year from income sources available to him at the beginning of the taxable year (May 1), and on the basis of the actual amount of income derived from such sources in the preceding year. Disposition of sources of income just before May 1 was therefore a widely-spread tactic to avoid taxation on income from such sources. Whereas the 1914 Income Tax Act originally covered the income of companies as well, in 1918 a special tax on the corporate distributions was introduced (while nondistributed income remained tax-free).

After Germany occupied The Netherlands in 1940, it introduced in The Netherlands in 1941 an individual income tax and in 1942 a company income tax, both based to a large extent on the then existing German tax and both taxing real income rather than deemed income as under previous acts. Although after the war both acts were substantially amended, it was not until the 1960s that they were replaced (the current Income Tax Act of 1964 and the Company Tax Act of 1969). At the time they were enacted, these two statutes, which still reflected many of the notions of the old tax codes introduced by Germany, were models of clear and concise tax legislation. As a result, however, of a considerable decrease of tax morale in The Netherlands starting in the 1970s and the subsequent (international) avoidance tactics resorted to by taxpayers (cf. paragraph 5.3, below), the Government was forced to add detailed, complex counteracting measures, which often contained elements of overkill, which in their turn led to further taxpayer reactions and, on the Government side, to increases in both size and detail of the statute and a corresponding reduction of the clarity and conciseness of the tax acts.

In the 1980s The Netherlands joined the worldwide move toward rate reduction and base widening of the income tax. In addition, it paid some lip service to tax simplification. The simplification, however, remained restricted mostly to a replacement of a detailed rate structure of the individual income tax by three tax brackets and an integration of individual income tax rates and general social security contributions. The proposals of a Government Commission appointed in the early 1990s to come up with suggestions for a true simplification of the individual income tax law received only lukewarm support from the Government. Various elements, however, were in later years strongly backed by prominent commentators. In 1995 the current Under Minister of Finance appointed distinguished members of the business and academic tax communities to various working parties to produce solutions to a range of pressing issues, such as the taxation of "substantial interests" (see paragraph 4.2).

3. Statutory and judicial style and role

3.1 Statutory style

Most of the important tax acts were drafted in the 1960s. Their overall design at that time was to provide a clear and lean framework of fundamental rules. The entire individual income tax act, comprising provisions on taxable persons, categories of taxable income, personal deductions, loss compensation, tax rates, and special rules, was covered at that time in most text editions in less than 20 pages of print. The other acts were even briefer. Practical details and other specific matters (*inter alia*, amounts that may change frequently, lists, etc.) were typically relegated to implementing decrees.

By 1996, the size of individual income tax act has grown to more than four times its original size. Three decades of additions have obfuscated the act's original well-balanced structure. Mostly as a result of the legislator's recurring attempts to counter particular tax avoidance practices of taxpayers, highly detailed rules have been inserted, greatly adding to the size and affecting the accessibility of the statute. The individual and company income tax acts, and the wages, dividend and wealth tax acts and implementing decrees jointly typically comprise now some 350 pages of print.

In respect of many income tax provisions the Minister of Finance has issued "resolutions" and other communications in which he may take a particular interpretative position. When such a position is more favorable to the taxpayer than under a strict application of the statute, the taxpayer is entitled to use that interpretation in his tax return. To the extent a position taken by the tax administration in a resolution appears stricter than the law, the taxpayer may challenge the resolution as nonbinding.

Newly enacted tax legislation, like all law, is generally not retroactively effective. However, in a 1996 memorandum the Government takes the position that in three situations there may be a justification for retroactive effect of newly enacted tax rules: the measure concerns anti-abuse, the measure corrects an obvious legislative error, and cases where the announcement of the new rule would result in taxpayer actions to effectuate plans quickly before the new law will render that impossible.

3.2 Judicial role and style

Strictly, court decisions are only binding for the case decided. In practice, they are given much greater weight, particularly when the court's phrasing of the decision is more general than the case warrants. Nevertheless in cases where the Government strongly disagrees with a position taken by the Supreme Court (*Hoge Raad*), it occasionally submits to the Court a second case on the same issue. If the Court maintains its position, the Government will typically consider to submit a legislative proposal to amend the law.

Netherlands courts do not issue dissenting opinions. Partly as a consequence thereof, the opinions are often quite brief. Occasionally, the grounds for a decision are phrased so tersely that the decision reads like a pronouncement by the Delphi oracle, giving ample room for widely divergent interpretations as to its scope.

As tax proceedings in court are not public, the decisions are anonymous when made public by the court. Curiously, the courts themselves select which cases to publish and which not. While it appears that most cases that are not made public are of no interest beyond that of the litigating parties, in some cases, decisions of wider significance may not be made public. There is a growing sentiment to give to an outside authority the power to select for publication the court decisions in tax matters.

4. Basic structure of the income tax system

4.1 Types of income taxes

The income of individuals is subject to income tax as provided for in the Income Tax Act of 1964 (ITA, *Wet op de inkomstenbelasting 1964*). Companies are taxed on the basis of the Companies Tax Act of 1969 (CTA *Wet op de vennootschapsbelasting 1969*). For the general rules on the determination of business income and for the taxation of nonresident companies, the CTA refers to the ITA.

Individuals who earn income from (current or past) employment or receive public benefits are, in addition to income tax provisions, subject to the rules of the Wages Tax Act of 1965 (WTA, *Wet op de loonbelasting 1965*) with the result that the wages tax withheld generally satisfies the income tax liability. The rates of the wages tax are identical to those of the income tax. If the annual amount of income subject to the wages tax does not exceed about Dfl 80,000 (US$ 50,000) no income tax return needs to be filed, unless the taxpayer derives more than nominal amounts of income from other sources or unless he chooses to file a return (e.g., because of deductions he did not or could not claim under the wages tax). As appears from the percentages presented in paragraph 1, above, the wages tax is from a budgetary point of view far more important than the income tax.

Dividends distributed by a Netherlands resident company are subject to a 25 % tax, to be withheld by the distributing company. There is no withholding on interest and royalty payments. In respect of interest, however, banks are required to report to the tax administration the amounts of interest they pay on savings accounts and the names of the (resident) individuals holding such accounts.

4.2 Source of income

Particularly with regard to income taxation of individuals, Netherlands tax law employs a "source of income" concept. Only income derived from a "source" is taxable. This term does not refer to the territorial source of the income, i.e., the concept used by most countries to distinguish between domestic source and foreign source income. "Source of income" refers to sources that produce a flow of income. Generally, only income that is derived from a "flowing" source is taxable. Consequently, incidental income, i.e., income from an isolated activity or incident, is not subject to tax. In addition, activities that are not expected to produce any positive amount of income (hobby farms, "inventing," etc.), are not considered to constitute a source of income.

As a result of the application of the "source of income" concept, capital gains are generally not subject to taxation. Exceptions apply to business capital gains and gains on the disposition of a so-called substantial interest or participation (shares belonging to a 33.3 %-plus interest in a company). With respect to other capital gains, the absence of capital gains taxation and the high tax rates applicable to ordinary income (37.5 %, 50 % and 60 %) constitute a strong incentive for taxpayers to try to convert ordinary income into a tax-free capital gain or into a substantial interest gain that is taxed at only 20 %. Some of these attempts have met with success, while others have been struck down by the courts through application of the *fraus legis* doctrine (see paragraph 5.3, below). Taxpayers, however, by effecting the conversion of ordinary income into substantial interest gains in an international rather than a domestic setting, have attempted to escape from the reach of *fraus legis*, as courts have so far been quite reluctant to apply this doctrine to tax treaty rules. The resulting complicated and unsatisfactory situation is the subject of one of the tax reform projects that are currently underway.

The categories of income from sources in respect of which individuals are subject to income taxation are enumerated exhaustively in the ITA: (1) income from business and professions; (2) income from (present and past) employment; (3) income from capital (e.g., dividends, interest, insurance payments); (4) income from rights to periodical payments and, (5) gains and losses on a substantial interest.

With the exception of gains and losses on substantial interests, in respect of which the special 20 % rate applies, the (positive and negative) amounts of income from the various categories are added up and certain personal and standard deductions are applied. To the resulting amount, if positive, the normal tax rate (see paragraph 4.3, below) is applied. If the resulting amount is negative, it constitutes a net operating loss that may be carried back three years and carried forward indefinitely.

4.3 Tax rates

Effective 1989 the (individual) income tax brackets were reduced to three. For 1996, a lower bracket of about 37.5 % applies to income of amounts up to Dfl 45,500, (US$ 27,500), a middle bracket of 50 % to the next Dfl 47,500 (US$ 28,500) of income, and a 60 % rate is applicable to the income segment over Dfl 93,000 (US$ 56,000). The lower rate of about 37.5 % is in fact a combined income tax rate (of about 6.5 %) and a general social security contribution rate (of 31 %). Contributions for general social security benefits (for old-age, disability, etc.) are widely felt to constitute taxes rather than insurance premiums because every resident of The Netherlands is obliged to contribute and the amount of the contribution is based on the individual's capacity to pay (i.e., income) rather than on the right to benefits (which is generally equal for everyone). It was therefore decided in 1989 to combine the two levies into one by having the first bracket of the income tax coincide with the maximum amount in respect of which general social security contributions must be paid (about Dfl 45,500 or US$ 27,500). No general social security contribution is due in respect of income in excess of the first income bracket; the 50 % and 60 % brackets are exclusively income tax.

Because nonresident taxpayers are generally not subject to Netherlands social security levies (exception: residents of other EU Member States who earn active income from Netherlands sources), nonresidents should be subject only to the 6.5 % income tax component of the 37.5 % rate. As the 6.5 % rate was considered by the Government too low an income tax rate for nonresident taxpayers, the lower rate for nonresident individual taxpayers who are not subject to general social security levies was set at 25 %. In respect of business income that residents of treaty countries derive through a Netherlands permanent establishment, the taxation of which is covered by a treaty permanent establishment-nondiscrimination clause, however, the rate has been reduced to the 6.5 % rate as is applied to resident taxpayers. Furthermore, in a 1996 decision of the EC Court of Justice, the

Netherlands 25 % rate was found to be in violation of the EC Treaty's nondiscrimination provision in respect of business income.

The corporation tax rate is 35 %, with a slightly higher rate - that is being phased out - for income up to Dfl 100,000 (about US$ 60,000). As The Netherlands employs a classical system of corporation and individual income taxation (see paragraph 8.3 below), the tax burden on income distributed by a corporation may reach 35 % + (60 % of 65 =) 74 %. As minor relief resident taxpayers are entitled to exclude from taxable income the first Dfl 1,000 (about US$ 600) of dividends received from Dutch companies.

4.4 Indexation to inflation

The individual income tax brackets have been indexed for over twenty-five years. Some twenty years ago the Government commissioned a high-level independent study of full indexation of the income tax system to inflation (particularly dealing with the inflation element in claims, debts, and capital in general, and in business inventory). Although the report contained clever and practicable solutions to these thorny issues and at the time the report was presented inflation was fairly low permitting a smooth phase-in of the proposed rules, the Government moved away from implementing the proposals and restricted itself to some rather general measures relating to business taxation.

5. Statutory interpretation

5.1 In general

The Netherlands Constitution provides that taxes may be levied only on the basis of a statute. In the Constitution it is also provided, however, that courts may not test the constitutionality of statutes, including tax statutes (but they may test rules enacted by local governments and administrative positions taken by the Revenue Service). Equal treatment provisions laid down in the Netherlands Constitution only provide guiding principles when applying statutory provisions rather than strictly enforceable rules. As a result, the impact of the nondiscrimination provisions of the human rights conventions has been much greater in The Netherlands than in countries where such guarantees are provided for in national law (see also below, paragraph 7.2).

As statutory tax provisions may not always be clear and may need interpretation, a substantial body of case law has been developed over the years on the interpretation of statutory law in general and of tax statutes in particular. In general, four methods are applied, without any clear hierarchy among them. In the "grammatical" method stress is put on the literal meaning of statutory terms. The "historical" method puts the emphasis on explanatory memoranda published on the draft legislation and on the parliamentary memoranda and debates on the provision concerned. In addition, there is the "systematic" method in which particular attention is paid to the structure and cohesion of the statute involved, and finally the "teleological" method in which purpose and intent of the statute are decisive factors for its interpretation. However, as courts are free in tax matters to choose the means of interpretation, there is no prevailing order in the use of these four methods.

5.2 Respect under tax law for the civil (private) law form of contracts

Netherlands tax law employs many terms and concepts that are based on civil (private) law. The question may arise whether for tax law purposes these terms and concepts necessarily have the same meaning as they have under civil law. Under current doctrine, civil law terms and concepts used in tax law are generally to be understood in their civil law meaning. However, aim and purpose of a given tax law provision may justify giving to a particular term or expression a meaning that differs from its general civil law meaning.

5.3 Substance over form

Application of tax law rules generally involves three steps. First, it must be ascertained whether what is presented as a fact is indeed a fact. Next, it has to be determined whether the (truly existing) facts are to be recognized for tax purposes. Finally, the law must be applied to these ascertained and recognized facts. At either of the last two levels the issue of substance over form may arise.

For tax law purposes, facts need not be accepted by the tax authorities as they are presented by the taxpayer. Something presented as a fact may not be a fact. E.g., if a hobby artist donates a worthless painting to a local museum in order to obtain a charitable deduction, the "gift" may be found to be nonexistent because what was given had no value (this is called "simulation": nonexistent facts are suggested to be true facts). To the extent facts — or legal situations — truly exist, the next step is to examine whether they should be recognized for tax purposes or whether on the basis of their substance they should be recharacterized. E.g., illegal income (for instance, income obtained through embezzlement) is subject to tax despite the fact that it does not constitute true income as the recipient may be under the legal obligation to return to the owner the funds obtained (when the funds are returned, a deduction ("negative income") will be allowed at the time of the payment). Other examples include rental income in cases in which the lessee is related to the lessor and pays an unrealistically low rent, and income from a void contract that nevertheless has been implemented.

After the facts have been accepted for tax purposes, the courts may apply the (nonstatutory) *fraus legis* doctrine to attach to facts tax consequences different from the consequences these facts normally have. While a taxpayer is generally free to organize his affairs in a manner that is most advantageous to him from a tax point of view, there are limits to this freedom. One such limit is reached when the taxpayer (alone, or in collaboration with other taxpayers) is able to lower the amount of his tax liability entirely at his own discretion (e.g., if a parent company pays tax deductible interest to its subsidiary company on a loan obtained from the subsidiary and the subsidiary subsequently returns to the parent as a tax free intercorporate dividend the amount it received from the parent as interest).

To apply the *fraus legis* doctrine the following requirements must be met: (1) the extraordinary — nontaxable — situation created by the taxpayer is in its nontax effects identical or similar to the more ordinary — taxable — situation; (2) tax avoidance is the controlling ("primary") motive of the taxpayer, and (3) the tax effects of the situation created by the taxpayer conflict with the purpose and intent of the tax law.

While twenty-five years ago *fraus legis* (and a related statutory substance-over-form rule) were rarely applied, during the last ten years cases involving the application of this doctrine make up a substantial part of the case load of the tax chambers of the Courts of Appeal and the Supreme Court. Many of these cases involve the erosion of the corporate tax basis through interest payments and, with respect to individuals, the taxation of income derived from closely-held companies (see paragraph 4.2, above). So far the courts have restricted the application of this doctrine to national law and have refused to extend it to the application of tax treaties. Consequently, nonresident taxpayers (where individuals, often former Netherlands residents) in particular have been able to shield their transactions from the application of *fraus legis*.

6. Tax administration

6.1 Organization of the Revenue Service

Traditionally the Netherlands Revenue Service has been organized in a manner that reflects the categorization of taxes. There were separate departments for direct taxes and indirect taxes. Both departments consisted of divisions, each of which dealt with a distinct tax. As a result, in its contacts with the tax administration a company typically would have to deal with different officials for each of the taxes it is subject to (company tax, wages tax, turnover tax and, occasionally, dividend tax and tax on legal transactions).

In the 1980s the tax administration underwent a complete overhaul to change it from a government-oriented into a taxpayer-oriented organization. Departments and their divisions merged and to the extent they did not merge each (corporate) taxpayer was assigned a coordinating official who generally acts as the single contact for the company. To the extent questions arise that are outside the area of expertise of this official, he would discuss them with the officials in charge of the tax concerned.

While this reorganization has not changed the fact that taxpayers and Revenue Service have opposite interests, it has certainly improved the efficiency of the taxpayers' dealings with the tax Revenue Service. In addition, it has improved the efficiency of the tax administration's operations, e.g., by conducting combined rather than separate audits for company income tax, wages tax, and turnover tax.

6.2 Taxpayer bill of rights; ombudsman

Along with the reorganization of the tax administration, attempts were made to further improve the position of the taxpayer vis-a-vis the Revenue Service. In 1991 the Ministry of Finance promulgated a "Taxpayers' Bill of Rights," after the example of the United States. In The Netherlands, however, the importance of this Bill is more of a psychological nature than real because the Bill is mainly restricted to restating the taxpayers' statutory rights.

Of more substantive importance to taxpayers, however, has been the extension of the scope of Government's actions in respect of which the "Ombudsman" (an independent authority with whom complaints against Government may be lodged) is entitled to receive complaints from citizens (and companies) or to undertake investigations on his own initiative. The Ombudsman is not permitted to investigate general government policy and individual cases where the taxpayer had access to regular administrative or judicial remedies. Despite these restrictions, he is called upon by taxpayers in a large number of cases and in a substantial number of these cases he usually finds that the Government has been acting wholly or partly in an inappropriate manner. While the Ombudsman has no legal means to enforce his findings, by publishing his reports in which he may suggest to the Revenue Service to take specific remedial action, he is usually successful in having the Government comply with his recommendations.

6.3 Release of Government information to taxpayers

The 1991 Act on Public Access to Government Information has proved to provide to taxpayers and their advisers an important instrument to obtain knowledge and insight in tax administration policy in general and in individual cases. Over the past decade a body of case law has emerged on the basis of decisions by the Council of State (*Raad van State*). This Council is the highest administrative court that rules upon appeals by individuals and companies against refusals of the Government to divulge information. The information may range from an audit report on individual taxpayers (under current case law the entire report must be made available to the taxpayer except for those parts that contain information on sensitive issues like audit strategies, etc.) to internal government studies, private rulings, etc.

6.4 Advance rulings

These rulings are typically issued on a request submitted by Netherlands- and foreign-controlled internationally operating companies. Currently, there are three categories of rulings, issued by different tax offices. Rulings on the determination of an arm's length price in individual transactions are issued by the taxpayer's local tax office. If a request for a ruling concerns the taxation of large direct investment projects of (prospective) foreign investors, the Rotterdam Tax Office for New Foreign Investment in The Netherlands is authorized to issue an advance ruling. Finally, when the ruling request concerns the determination of the income of a Netherlands member of an internationally operating company, a Rotterdam-based team of tax inspectors (the "Ruling Team") is in charge of these rulings. Most of the rulings issued by this team are of one of eight standard types, "cost plus"-rulings and rulings for holding companies, finance companies, and royalty companies being the most common types.

7. Tax procedure

7.1 Assessment, administrative appeal and appeal to courts

In respect of income tax and wealth tax (individuals), and company tax (companies), the tax inspector issues a tax assessment after having reviewed the tax return filed by the taxpayer and received that taxpayer's answers to questions that the inspector asked on the basis of his review. With respect to corporate taxpayers the questions may pertain to foreign subsidiaries of the taxpayer and to its foreign parent company. Failure to provide adequate answers to such questions may result in the burden of proof shifting from the tax inspector, where it usually rests, to the taxpayer.

In respect of business taxpayers, the inspector will order a field audit every few years before issuing the assessment The 200 largest companies are subject to a field audit every year. To arrive at an agreement on the facts of the case the tax inspector may conclude with the taxpayer a contract ("*compromis*") in which these facts are determined. If the tax inspector, after he has issued an assessment, learns facts which he did not know (and could not reasonably have known) at the time of issuing the assessment and which increase the taxpayer's tax liability, the tax inspector will issue a supplemental assessment (increased with a penalty if the taxpayer was at fault). Both the original assessment and the supplemental assessment may be appealed by the taxpayer administratively. This appeal is usually decided upon by the same tax inspector who issued the assessment.

The wages tax and value-added tax (companies and individuals) and the dividend tax (companies) are self-assessment taxes. If the tax inspector disagrees with the self-assessed amount, he may issue a supplemental assessment (with or without a penalty). This assessment is also subject to administrative appeal by the taxpayer.

The decision made by the tax inspector upon the appeal lodged against an assessment may be appealed to the Tax Chamber of one of the five Courts of Appeal (*Gerechtshof*). The taxpayer does not need legal representation for making such an appeal. Cases are heard in this Court by one- or three-member panels of judges. These judges are typically recruited from the circles of senior government tax officials, senior tax advisers and tax academics. In addition, prominent tax advisers and tax professors may serve as part-time deputy judges. A decision by the Tax Chamber of a Court of Appeal may be appealed to one of the Tax Chambers of the Supreme Court (*Hoge Raad*). In addition to a Civil Chamber and a Criminal Chamber, the Supreme Court has two Tax Chambers (reflecting the prominent role of tax law in The Netherlands judicial process), each consisting of five justices, two or three of whom will typically have a tax background. The Supreme Court has no right to refuse to hear a case, but will only consider questions of law. For appeal to the Supreme Court in tax matters, the taxpayer again does not need legal representation. On complex issues presented to the Supreme Court one of the three independent Advocates General of the Court may issue in advance an Opinion to the Court. These Opinions usually provide excellent analyses of the law at issue. The number of tax appeals, which has kept rising over the last two decades, seems to have stabilized now at an annual number of about 13,000 per year for appeals to any of the five Courts of Appeal, and at about 750 per year for further appeals to the Supreme Court.

7.2 Impact of human rights conventions and EC Treaty fundamental freedom provisions

As Netherlands statutory law cannot be challenged on the basis of violation of any Netherlands constitutional provision, individuals and companies cannot base their viewpoint on such provision. Consequently, the nondiscrimination clause laid down in Article 1 of the Constitution is mostly of symbolic rather than effective importance to taxpayers (see paragraph 5.1, above). For that reason, the nondiscrimination provisions in the human rights conventions that The Netherlands has acceded to are in The Netherlands of greater importance to litigants than in other countries. So far, some of the statutory tax provisions and several administrative positions taken by the Revenue Service have been found by the courts to violate these treaty nondiscrimination provisions.

In addition, the fundamental freedom provisions of the European Community Treaty, notably those on the freedom of workers (Article 48) and the freedom of establishment (Article 52), have been decided by the EC Court of Justice to forbid differential tax treatment of non-resident taxpayers. For example, in a 1995 decision the EC Court found the restriction to resident taxpayers of the right for individuals engaged in business to set up a tax-free old-age reserve violated Article 52 of the EC Treaty. And a June 1996 decision of the EC Court found the Netherlands 25 % income tax bracket for nonresidents (see paragraph 4.3, above) to be in violation of one of the Treaty's nondiscrimination provisions.

8. International

8.1 Historically-based foreign orientation

In trade and investment matters, The Netherlands has historically been oriented toward foreign countries. Although it has given up most of the vast foreign territories it once controlled (among them the present Indonesia), it has remained an important international trading country, deriving an unusually large share of its GNP from import and export activities. In addition, both foreign direct investment by Netherlands companies and investment in The Netherlands by foreign companies are large both in comparative and in absolute terms.

This foreign orientation is apparent from the Netherlands tax system. Apart from a dividend tax, The Netherlands has no withholding tax on outgoing income from capital. The dividend tax rate which amounted originally to 15 % only, was increased in 1965 to 25 % primarily to improve the Netherlands tax treaty negotiating position.

8.2 Double taxation relief

The Netherlands has traditionally preferred the exemption rather than the credit method with regard to both juridical and economic double taxation. From the first act on company taxation, dividends received from foreign (as well as domestic) subsidiaries have been exempt from (economic) double taxation through the so-called participation exemption. In addition, both under tax treaties and unilaterally, active income (i.e., income from business and professional activities and from employment) and real property income are exempt from taxation (while foreign losses are still taken into account, with a later recapture). An exception applies to foreign dividends, interest and royalties in respect of which double taxation is relieved through a foreign tax credit (with tax sparing provided in many treaties with developing countries).

8.3 Classical system

Some very large multinational companies reside in The Netherlands. A significant amount of the shares of these companies are in the hands of shareholders that reside in countries with which The Netherlands does not have a tax treaty (countries in the Middle East, tax haven countries). This situation has greatly contributed to Netherlands resistance to moving away from its currently applied classical system and adopting an imputation system as applied in most other countries of the European Union. In an imputation system, qualifying shareholders are entitled to an imputation credit that is either funded by the company tax paid by the corporation (to the extent dividends are paid from income that has been subject to domestic taxation) or by a specially imposed equalization tax (to the extent domestic income is tax-free or, if foreign, qualifies for double taxation relief). Since the profits distributed by those large Netherlands multinational companies have to a large extent been derived from abroad and, as a result of the exemption system, are not subject to Netherlands taxation, large amounts of equalization tax would be due upon their distribution. However, as shareholders resident in nontreaty countries would typically not qualify for the imputation credit, in respect of these shareholders the equalization tax would amount to an increase of pre-distribution tax though they would not be entitled to the corresponding shareholder-level credit. Consequently, the effective amount of dividend paid to these shareholders would be lower, with the result that they would move away from Netherlands shares. To avoid this consequence, The Netherlands has so far resisted attempts to create a harmonized EC system of corporate-individual imputation taxation.

General Description: Sweden

Professor Peter Melz

1. Historic development

The income tax originated as a schedular income tax system. The first income tax law was enacted in 1810, influenced by English liberal thought. However, it was repealed in 1812 and instead a schedular system with eight income sources was introduced. During the 19th and beginning of the 20th century the development towards a modern income tax went on with important reforms 1860, 1902, 1910 and 1928.

As a result of successive reforms, schedular differences have decreased. The income concept was broadened by successive inclusions of capital gains. In 1991 a major reform was enacted. The sources were reduced to three for individuals: income from employment, business income, and income from capital. In principle, however, the Swedish system is still a schedular system, which means that there is no general income definition. The definitions of income in the different sources, however, are quite broad.

The source principle nonetheless still has some importance since if a specific potential income item cannot be fit in as income in any of the three sources, it will be excluded from the income tax base. In general it can be said that the taxable income consists of all remunerations for a performance of services, yield and gains on capital, and income from the combination of those two factors in a business.

2. Basic structure

In Sweden income taxes are paid by individuals to the national government and to different municipalities. Corporations only pay income tax to the national government. The taxable income for national and municipal purposes is calculated according to the Municipal Tax Law (*Kommunalskattelagen*, KL) and the calculation for corporations is modified in some aspects by rules in the National Income Tax Law (*Lagen om statlig inkomstskatt*, SIL).

For individuals, income is calculated in three sources: income from employment, business income and income from capital. The first two sources consist principally of income derived from work, as an employee or as self-employed. The income from business source contains all forms of an independent business including e.g., agriculture and commercial real estate.

Income from employment and business are added together and the combined income is subject to municipal income tax. Municipal tax rates vary according to locality and average around 31 %. Above a limit (ca. $35,000) national income tax (currently 25 %) is levied on the income. The combined maximum rate averages 56 %. Rate brackets are adjusted for inflation.

On income from capital, a national income tax is levied with a flat rate of 30 % and no municipal tax is imposed. This means that there is often a major difference between the tax rate on capital income on the one hand and the tax rate on employment and business income on the other hand which makes characterization an important issue. In addition, measures are necessary to prevent taxpayers from converting income from business or employment to capital.

The lower tax rate on capital income is intended to be a standardized compensation for the inflationary losses incurred in connection with capital income. In the preparatory works for the tax reform, the derivation of the tax rate is shown to be based on a rather simple calculation: A real interest rate of 3 % and an inflation rate of 4 % was anticipated. Thirty percent tax on a nominal interest rate of 7 % means a tax of 2.1 % which is 70 % of the real interest rate. Seventy percent is a tax rate that is roughly the same as — actually some percentage points above — the rate for a high income earner on earned income, if social security contribution fees are included.

Presently the inflation is lower than expected (2 %) and the real interest rate is higher (5 %). That results in a tax rate on the real interest of 42 %. In a recent Government Report this is taken as a justification for retaining a Net Wealth Tax of 1.5 % of the net wealth. The Report argues that the two taxes combined would result in the same real tax rate on capital income as on earned income.

Another reason for the choice of the tax rate on capital income was that the tax rate on income from capital, corporations' income and the municipal tax rate should be roughly the same, which would counter tax planning. A flat rate was also chosen to counter tax planning. Since the capital income rate was calculated to equal the rate a high income earner pays on his marginal earned income, the capital income rate represents a heavier taxation on capital income than on earned income for a low income earner. However, there has been little opposition to this. One reason for this may be that the tax rate in any event meant a decrease or at least not an increase compared with the tax rate on interest — which probably is the most common form of capital income for low income owners — before the reform.

Corporations calculate all income in one source, income from business. A national income tax with a flat rate of 28 % is levied on the income. The effective tax rate is lower because 25 % of the income can be set aside in a reserve (*periodiseringsfond*) for five years. Apart from that reserve, the intention is that there should be no more possibilities for special tax reserves as had existed under prior law so that the tax is on the effective income of the corporation.

Income distributed from a company as dividends are taxed by individuals as income from capital with a tax rate of 30 %. This means a combined tax rate of ca. 28 % + 0.7 x 30 % = 49 % on the income earned in a corporation. Income from business carried on directly by an individual is subject to social security contributions, municipal income tax, and (if the combined income for the individual is high enough) state income tax. The combined effect could result in a ca. 66 % marginal rate. The tax burden of an individual partner's share in a partnership's income is the same.

This difference could in most cases encourage the incorporation of individual businesses. Special rules have therefore been enacted in order to level the playing field. For individuals who participate actively in a closely held company in which they or relatives are shareholders, dividends and capital gains above a certain level are taxed as employment income. Furthermore, for individual businesses the income will only be subject to the special state income tax of 28 % as long as the income is reinvested in the business. The tax burden will therefore be the same on reinvested income in individual and corporate businesses.

3. Composition of fiscal system

The vast majority of revenues for the national Government are taxes (85 %). For the municipalities, the municipal income tax is 57 % of the revenues. Another 20 % are contributions from the government, which principally is financed by national taxes. Taxes are therefore a very important basis for the public sector in Sweden.

In the beginning of the twentieth century, indirect taxes on trade, consumption etc. were the most important type of taxes. The trend since then has been an increasing importance for the income taxation. However, in the last decades, impelled by the need to increase the tax revenues, the importance of income taxes has declined. Social security contributions (which principally is a concealed tax in Sweden) have increased substantially in the last decades. In the tax reform of 1991, the income tax was further decreased and instead the VAT was increased by broadening the tax base.

The present situation is that the revenue in the national Government budget is composed as follows: 10 % income taxes, 20 % social security contributions, 10 % taxes on property, and 60 % taxes on goods and services. Almost every type of tax is used in Sweden: municipal and national income tax on individuals, national income tax on corporations, net wealth tax, inheritance and gift tax, value added tax, taxes on alcohol and tobacco, petrol, and energy in general, etc., sales (stamp) tax on real estate, and real estate tax. Although the national income tax forms a small part of the total revenues, the combined income tax for the municipalities and the national Government is still a major source of revenue, constituting some 20 % of GDP. Furthermore, the social security contributions function as an income tax as they are levied on the same bases as the income tax and normally ensure no individually earmarked future benefits. The income tax is still the most important tax form for lawyers and accountants in tax planning and tax litigation, because of its economic importance and its still rather complicated rules. Some taxes such as the net wealth tax (1.5 % of the net wealth above ca. $125,000) and the inheritance and gift tax have little fiscal importance and are maintained primarily for ideological reasons (leveling of wealth).

Most taxes are levied and constructed only to pursue fiscal goals. However, at least officially it is considered that the income tax to a certain extent will equalize the income distribution. Certain sales taxes such as the tobacco and the alcohol taxes, as well as taxes on energy consumption, obviously influence consumption behavior.

4. Statutory style

The major changes in the Swedish tax law have been enacted through statutory rules. The statutes have been written in a rather broad way and therefore case law has had the possibility to create law in some important cases. As an example, it is not stated in the statutory law whether a bankruptcy estate should be a taxable person or not. Case law, however, has determined that it is not a person for income tax purposes, but that it is so treated for VAT purposes. In later years, especially in the tax reform of 1991, the tendency is to codify case law into statutory rules.

The Swedish tax codes in the 1930s and the following decades were written in a special way. There was first a rather short and principal statutory rule (paragraph), and then this rule was explained more in detail in a regulation (which also was a statutory rule). In the beginning, the regulations were not intended to add any new content but only to explain. Sometimes there were even arithmetic examples in the regulations. In later decades, there is no longer any difference in principle between paragraphs and statutory regulations. At present some paragraphs are almost only a sort of heading telling what will be said in the regulations. The statutory rules are rather detailed. However, the aim in the last decade has been to avoid complicated rules, and thereby complicated statutes. This is, however, more a question of the structure of the system (avoiding different treatment of different kinds of income etc.) than a question of statutory style.

A more general tendency in statutory style in the last decade is to avoid enumerations and instead to give a more abstract definition. This is intended to give the courts possibility of dealing with new phenomena (e.g., financial instruments) and placing them in the proper categories. On the other hand, a lot of new mechanical rules have been introduced recently and because of their mechanical character the statutory rules regulating them are rather comprehensive. As mentioned below, in Sweden the Constitution states that taxes should be levied under the law. The need for a more clear ground in the statutes for a tax imposition has been stressed more in the last decade.

This has of course influenced the statutory style and one can see a tendency of writing statutes more comprehensively, and not expecting the courts to remedy shortcomings.

Sweden has a tradition of extensive preparation of legislation by work in Government Commissions. A Commission could either be Parliamentary (members on the commission are M.P.'s) or an expert commission. Commission Reports (*Statens Offentliga Utredningar*, SOU) are circulated for comments to organizations, courts, universities etc. Based on these comments, the Government presents a bill (*proposition*) to the Parliament (*Riksdagen*). For important proposals, the bill is preceded by a draft which is examined by three Supreme Court judges in the Law Council (*lagrådet*). Amendments in the Parliament are rare, probably principally because the Government usually has a controlling majority in the Parliament.

5. Statutory interpretation

There is no uniform system of statutory interpretation in Sweden. In the Supreme Administrative Court (which handles tax cases and other administrative law matters) one method has been in general use, with few exceptions, and that is to give great value to opinions expressed in preparatory works to the legislation, primarily the Government's proposition to Parliament. In some recent cases, however, a new tendency by some judges can be seen. There is more willingness to ignore the preparatory opinions when they are not clearly reflected in the statutes. Among academics there are various opinions of the degree of authority that should be given the preparatory works. Among those judges not giving great weight to preparatory works, there is also a tendency to literal interpretation, or at least great respect for the literal meaning of the statutes.

In a case where the preparatory works and the statutory rule clearly are contradictory there is a consensus that the statute could not be set aside. Among those judges giving more authority to preparatory works there are variations in interpretational style. The old school tends to follow a statement in the preparatory works as long as it is not contrary to the literal meaning of the statute. The more modern school pays more respect to general intent expressed in preparatory works and what it, combined with the context of the statute, means.

As a summary all variations prevail, but the most common trait for Sweden is the respect for opinions in preparatory works.

6. Administrative style

In Sweden the rule of law prevails. In the Swedish Constitution it is stated that rules about taxation should be made in the form of parliamentary statutes. As a consequence, there are very limited possibilities to delegate the right to create binding tax rules to the Government or tax authorities. Delegated rules may only prescribe how to comply with the statutory rules and no new rules may be implemented through them. In reality regulations have great impact in some areas, especially in the procedure to establish assessed values on real estate. This is such a technical field that the complete procedure could not be prescribed in the statutory rules and a number of things must therefore be prescribed in regulations.

The National Tax Authority issues Tax Advices (*RSV's rekommendationer*) in a lot of fields. In these advices, the state of law is described based on statutory rules, case law, and preparatory works. In questions where the state of law is not clear NTA issues official advices. These advices are not binding for the courts and, more surprisingly but in line with the Swedish Constitution, not even for the local tax authorities. In reality these advices are almost always followed by the local tax authorities and have considerable impact on the tax courts' decisions.

The amount of field auditing has been fairly low in Sweden. The resources of the tax authorities have been tied up to a considerable extent by reorganizations in the 1980s and 1990s. The administrative reform now seems to be completed (for this time) and the procedure for assessment of normal taxpayers is today to a large extent computerized. The auditing resources should therefore be concentrated on businesses, especially big enterprises. In the last years a lot of large Swedish multinational companies have been audited, and tax claims of billions have been raised. The tax courts largely upheld the assessments One could be surprised that these big companies have erred in their tax accounting to this extent. In a number of cases, however, the issues involved are nonrecurring questions of timing. To the extent the government has lost, it has been in part because of too aggressive positions and in part because of fair but arguable questions.

7. Taxpayer style

The tax rates in Sweden are high and have been even higher. In the tax system before 1991 the impact of the high formal income tax rates was mitigated through "tax planning." A lot of these transactions were not primarily made for tax reasons, but were such simple things as the fact that the tax system encouraged investment with borrowed funds in real estate, stocks, etc. But there were also real tax planning structures such as creation of partnerships which nominally invested in films, bonds, etc. in order to get double deductions (a loophole). With the tax reform of 1991 most of these tax planning opportunities were reduced or mitigated. Now the tax planning opportunities are more in the field of international transactions. The attitudes between taxpayers and tax authorities are good in general. The level of service from the authorities is high, although constant changes of material and procedural rules and reorganizations create problems. In the above mentioned audits, the tax authorities have been a bit disturbed that some of the big companies have not complied fully in the way the authorities expected.

8. Judicial style

As a formal matter, it is the role of the legislature to enact measures imposing taxation. The role for the courts is therefore in principle to interpret the statutes. In reality a lot of questions are not clearly answered by the statutes, and case law therefore is an important source of law. Cases decided by the Supreme Administrative Court are deemed binding for lower courts. There is no statutory rule stating this, but precedents are with rare exceptions followed. The court seldom changes a precedent, and if it does, the change must be made in a plenary session.

9. General principles

9.1 Relation of tax and financial accounting

Income of business is required to be calculated on the basis of generally accepted accounting principles (GAAP), if tax rules do not state something else. Tax rules exist mostly for practical reasons in a variety of fields. Almost every form of depreciation is regulated in statutory tax rules. As there are a lot of questions that are not regulated in tax rules, GAAP have great impact on the calculation of taxable income. On the other hand, this means that tax considerations have great impact when developing GAAP. This has been criticized, but so far no changes have been made.

9.2 Respect of civil law

In general, words and concepts in tax law which are similar to civil law are interpreted in accordance with civil law. In many cases the situation is not regulated in detail in civil law and has not before been considered in a civil court, e.g., because the question of whether a contract should be deemed a lease or a sale has minor civil law consequences. The tax courts in these instances have to consider what is the correct decision based on civil law.

The form is respected, as long as there is enough substance behind the form. If a transaction is only stated as, e.g., a lease in the contract, but it is in substance a sale, it will be treated according to its real economic significance. However, the courts are mostly not willing to set the form aside when some substantial consequences of the contract are in accordance with the form. For instance, a sale and lease back of real estate has been ruled to be treated as a sale, although in reality it was most likely that the transaction in fact functioned as a loan with a collateral. However, there existed some risk that the "lender" might be stuck with the real estate, with no right to repayment. Special tax aspects may be taken into consideration when interpreting the meaning of complicated transactions, because some civil law concepts are vague.

9.3 Anti-avoidance

A special Tax Avoidance Act has been in force for several years. It was abolished by the former nonsocialist Government for some years but reintroduced by the present socialist Government. Transactions can be set aside according to the Tax Avoidance Act (*Lagen om skatte-flykt*), if three conditions are fulfilled: (1) the main purpose of the transaction is to avoid tax; (2) the tax reduction is substantial; and (3) an assessment based on the form of the transaction contravenes the purpose of the relevant tax rules. The law has seldom been used because it is hard to show that the conditions are fulfilled. A commission is reviewing the law in order to make it easier to apply. In the doctrine, the law has been criticized because it states that a rule in a tax law (interpreted with common methods) should be set aside, if the above-mentioned conditions are fulfilled. That would mean that the taxation would be based on a purpose expressed in preparatory works instead of the wording of the tax statute, and that would be contrary to the constitutional demand that the taxation should be based on statutory rules.

The courts have been rather strict, besides the Tax Avoidance Act, in using anti-avoidance doctrines. As mentioned above, they normally do use the form-over-substance approach, although they set aside a form that has no substance at all. In a few cases, they have applied what some call a "lifting-the-veil" concept and set the form aside in more complex cases.

10. Procedure

All individuals with taxable income during the tax year must file a tax return and submit it to the tax office of the relevant tax district. For most taxpayers, the tax return is simplified. Where statements of earnings, interest, etc. are supplied by third parties, e.g., employers or banks, this income is already filled in by the tax authority and the taxpayer simply indicates if they have other income than that in the statements.

Mandatory statements are required for income from employers and other contractors who make payments which are employment income for the receiver. Banks and other financial institutions are required to provide statements of interest income The Securities Register Center is required to provide statements of dividends paid out by the Center.

The bulk of tax revenues is collected by withholdings and prepayments. Taxes on income from business are preassessed in twelve installments. If the final tax due exceeds the mandatory prepayments, further prepayments can be made to avoid a surcharge.

A surcharge is levied if the taxpayer has provided false information on his tax return. The surcharge is normally 40 % of the tax that would have been evaded. The surcharge is decreased to 20 % in those cases where the tax officials could correct the fault by information from mandatory statements of earnings, the previous years' tax returns, etc. The surcharge may not be levied in cases where the false information is deemed to be excusable.

The administrative surcharges are the most important penalties for misconduct. Criminal sanctions can be applied for more serious wrong-doing under the Tax Crime Code. The punishment for tax fraud is imprisonment for up to two years and for serious tax fraud up to six years.

A taxpayer who is dissatisfied with the assessment may either request a review by the tax authority or appeal to a county administrative court within five years of the assessment year. Decisions of the county administrative courts may be appealed to administrative courts of appeal. Their decisions may be appealed to the Supreme Administrative Court. This right to appeal is, however, restricted to cases with a precedent value or where the decision is seriously questionable.

General Description: United Kingdom

Professor John Tiley, University of Cambridge

It has been said that when trying to understand anything about the United Kingdom and in particular England one should not ask the question "why" but "since when". History is all important in the U.K. tax system especially when dealing with income tax; so what follows is an account of the history of the U.K. direct tax system

The history can be traced not only in the legislation passed year by year together with the accompanying debates but also in the annual reports made to Parliament by the Inland Revenue. These are now accompanied by a separate volume of Inland Revenue Statistics, although at one time these formed part of the Annual Report itself. There is also useful information of a background variety in another government publication called Social Trends.

The different taxes have different yields. The OECD survey shows that in 1992 total tax revenues including Social Security taxes took 35.8 % of the UK's GDP. That figure of 35.8 % breaks down into 10.3 % from taxes on personal income, 3.2 % from taxes on corporate income, 6.4 % from social security taxes 11.8 % from taxes on goods and services and 3.3 % from taxes on property.

1. The principal direct taxes

1.1 Income Tax

Income tax was introduced in 1798 and has remained in force save for a gap between 1816 and 1842 ever since. It is, however, a temporary tax in that Parliament has to provide each year that there is to be an income tax for that year. This doctrine of the annual tax is a relic from the days when Parliament wanted to make sure that the King would summon a Parliament each year; a perpetual source of income would make a calling of the Parliament less necessary. This doctrine applies also to corporation tax but not to capital gains tax or inheritance tax.

Income was first used as a measure in the U.K. tax system as a means of giving relief from another tax. By an Act of 1797 Pitt imposed the so-called Triple Assessment, a tax based on property and expenditure: this involved a sharp increase on the tax levied on that basis in the previous year; the full increase was to be charged on those whose income was more than £50 the previous year and there were smaller increases for those with incomes below that figure; further the tax payable was not to exceed 10 % of total income. The process was not a success and the following year Pitt introduced the Property and Income Tax Act to be effective from January 1799. The tax was based on a general return by the taxpayer of his income for the year, a return which could be challenged by the Surveyors who could ask for details under nineteen different heads. The tax was charged at 10p in the £ on all income over £200 with a graduated rate between £60 and £200 and exemption below £60. Among permitted deductions were allowances for children, interest payments, and life assurance.

This tax was a partial success and was completely overhauled in 1803 by the introduction of the system of the taxation of income as opposed to total income, the abandonment of the general return of income, and the introduction of the schedular system backed up an extensive system of withholding at source. The 1803 changes were well described in the 28th Report of the Inland Revenue C.4474 (1885) p. 30:

"As the former duty was imposed on a general account of income from all sources, the present duty is imposed on each source, by itself, in the hands of the first possessor, at the same time permitting its diffusion through every natural channel in its course to the hands of the ultimate proprietor. Instead of the landlord and the various claimants upon him in succession, it looks to the occupier only. Instead of the creditor, it looks to the fund from which the debt is answered. In the place of a complicated account collected from various sources from which the income of an individual is derived, it applies to the source itself to answer for its increase. By these means its object is attained with more facility and celerity, and with less intricacy and disclosure, diminishing the occasion of evasion by means of exaction; thus the charge is gradually diffused from the first possessor to the ultimate proprietor, the private transactions of life are protected from the public eye and the Revenue is more effectually guarded."

The reference to the taxation of the landlord is a reference to the system of taxing imputed income arising from the occupation of property under the original Schedule A, a system that remained in place until 1963. The reference to the system of deduction at source is a reference to provisions currently known as TA 1988 ss. 348 and 349, the scope of which have over the years has been progressively reduced but which remain in place.

The influence of this overall system is still with us. Thus even today there is no provision in TA 1988 stating that income tax is levied on a person's income. Section 1 states simply that income tax is levied on the property, profits or gains stated in the schedules, and goes on to provide first that basic rate income tax is levied on "income" and then that if an individual's total "income" exceeds a certain figure income tax may be levied at higher rates while if it is lower then the lower rate will be taxed.

One effect of this system was to make the introduction of graduation and differentiation a much more difficult task since such a system demanded a personal return of total income and was quite inconsistent with the final character of the scheme of deduction at source. When introduced in 1907, differentiation originally took the form of a lower rate of tax on earned income but this soon became a relief from income tax; only in 1973 was the tax rate expressed in terms of earned income and a new additional rate applied to investment income; this additional rate was itself repealed in 1984.

Graduation took the form of a new tax, super tax, later remodeled and renamed surtax. Income tax was levied on income; surtax on the total income of an individual. Surtax being additional to income tax, a particular piece of an individual's income might be subject to income tax at 40 % and surtax at 20 %; it was an excess liability on those better able to pay. Only in 1973 were the two taxes merged, although this is often a matter of form rather than substance as the continued existence of excess liability shows.

Another historical effect has been the astonishing longevity (1996) of the preceding year basis of assessment even if the end is now at hand. Under this system the income arising for a source in, say, year three is used as the measure of income from that source in year four; it is taxed in year four at the rates relevant to year four, not year three. So artificial a system with its inelegances and its absurdities probably owes its origins to the system of direct assessment by the Revenue rather than self-assessment by the taxpayer. In the nineteenth century it would have been unthinkable to allow the Revenue to make an assessment when the amount due was not certain. To tax on a current year basis would mean that the tax could not be assessed until after the tax year had ended. The preceding year basis enabled the Revenue to tax quickly and certainly but artificially.

However, probably the greatest legacy of history is a view of the scope of income and the distinction between income and capital. When income tax was first introduced in 1799, not only were various existing forms of capital already subject to other taxes, but there was also a substantial area of law, that of trusts, where a very sharp distinction between income and capital receipts had been drawn. Further, insofar as business was concerned, Adam Smith had already set out the distinction between circulating and fixed capital, between income profits and capital gains. The details of trading income had to be worked out at a time well before the first Companies Act and when the business unit was relatively small and when ownership and management were not completely distinct concepts. A tax on income introduced against such a legal and intellectual background would find little room for arguments based on a comprehensive income tax base. The distinction between capital and income remains central to the tax system despite a certain amount of convergence, especially with regard to rates of tax, in 1987 (for the corporate sector) and 1988 (for the personal sector).

Although there is an Act known as the Income and Corporation Taxes Act 1988, this is not a complete code of provisions. Rather it is the latest in a series of consolidations; these occurred in 1918, 1952, 1970, and 1988. The 1988 Act may be amended each year by the annual Finance Act; however, there is no need for the annual Act to do that and it may instead add its own provisions to the overall patchwork of legislation.

1.2 Capital Gains Tax (CGT)

The refusal of the courts and of the legislature to widen the scope of income tax to cover capital gains is of great importance in the history of the U.K. tax system. Opportunities to convert income into capital were exploited by taxpayers and only occasionally were stopped, and then on a piecemeal basis, by the legislature. Reform eventually came in 1965 with the introduction of the long-term capital gains tax. A short-term gains provision had been introduced in 1962 that was designed to tax gains realized within six months of acquisition and to tax them as income. This was extended in 1965 to gains realized within twelve months and was preserved until 1971 despite the introduction of the long-term CGT in 1965 because of the difference in tax rates — CGT had a flat rate of 30 % while income tax could go over 90 %. The rates of CGT and income tax were assimilated for companies in 1987 and for individuals in 1988

CGT contains its own fundamental doctrines. It is restricted in that there must be a disposal (whether actual or deemed) for there to be a charge and the disposal must be of an asset that is relevant to the tax system. Assets relevant to the system include shares and debts on a security, although there is a very important exception for qualifying corporate bonds: other debts are not generally relevant assets although exceptions are made for debts on a security, for certain loans to traders, and for assignees of debts. A liability is not an asset so that a loss on a loan (e.g., due to the extra cost of paying off a foreign currency loan when sterling has declined against that currency since the original borrowing) cannot give rise to any relief under CGT. This gap was the source of much frustration for many taxpayers and led to the introduction of new rules for foreign exchange transactions and risk management instruments in 1995 and a comprehensive new regime for all loan instruments in 1996 — but only for companies subject to corporation tax. It also opened the doors to planning for other taxpayers who would not be subject to tax on a gain they might make on a liability, while obtaining full relief for interest payments even though the exchange risk was one of the reasons why the rate of interest charged was high.

Capital losses may only be set against capital gains of the same or any subsequent tax year, a rule which encourages a certain amount of tax planning.

CGT has two other major restrictions. The first, introduced in 1988, is that it does not usually attempt to tax gains that accrued during a period before March 31, 1982. The second, originally introduced in 1982, is that there is relief for inflation through the "indexation allowance." This relief cannot at present be used to turn a gain into a loss, although this has been so in the past.

Where the asset has a useful life of less than fifty years, it will be classified as a wasting asset and the costs will be written off over the life of the asset to avoid giving relief for the inevitable loss.

The CGT legislation was consolidated in the Capital Gains Tax Act 1979 and again in the Taxation of Chargeable Gains Act 1992. The reason for the change in title is that corporations do not pay CGT on their capital gains but corporation tax instead. The 1992 Act consolidates not only the rules for CGT but also a number of the corporation tax rules that had not been consolidated in the 1988 Act.

1.3 Corporation Tax

Corporation tax as such was introduced in 1965, at the same time as CGT. Before that time companies paid tax on their profits but did so through a combination of the income tax (as opposed to surtax or supertax) and special taxes. Dividends were not subject to income tax but were grossed up to give a figure for surtax; this was so, whether or not the company paid income tax on its profits.

This system was subject to two major modifications. First, the fact that a company was subject to income tax, but not to surtax, meant that it was advantageous for a high-rate taxpayer to leave income behind the veil of a company where it would be taxed at lower rates and so multiply more rapidly. Legislation was therefore introduced in 1922 to deal with what were then called one-man companies, in the form of a surtax direction that treated the income of the companies as if it were the income of its owners and so liable to surtax. This was the forerunner of the modern close company legislation; the reduction in tax rates over the last fifteen years has enabled Parliament to repeal almost all of these attributions of income rules.

The second modification was the special tax on profits; the National Defence Contribution, which in due course became profits tax, was introduced in 1937. This was an extra tax on the profits of the company, which, not being income tax, could not be recovered by the taxpayer through the mechanism now contained in TA 1988, ss. 348 and 349. This device could be used to levy tax at differential rates on distributed and retained profits and was so used between 1947 and 1958.

The two-tax system was subject to a number of disadvantages quite separate from the issue of whether the tax system should encourage the retention of profits. First, since the basic tax on the company was income tax, not only was it subject to all the complexities of matters such as the commencement and cessation provisions, but also the rate would alter whenever the government thought it right to alter the rate in the personal sector. Second, profits under the two taxes were computed differently. Not only was profits tax levied on a current as opposed to a preceding year, but some items were deductible in computing profits for profits tax that were not for income tax, necessitating two sets of calculations; thus until 1952 profits tax was deductible for income tax. Further, companies whose profits were less than £2,000 were exempt from profits tax.

This untidy system was replaced in 1965 by a corporation tax based on the classical system. This was in turn replaced in 1973 by the current imputation system.

The legislation on corporation tax is consolidated in the Income and Corporation Taxes Act 1988 but as seen above certain rules dealing with capital gains are to be found in the Taxation of Chargeable Gains Act 1992. Both Acts are supplemented by (many) provisions in the annual Finance Acts.

2. Indirect taxes

Though not the subject of this study, mention must be made of the value-added tax. This tax is based on a single model drawn up by the European Community and implemented in the different countries in their own legislative form. Although the structure of the tax is meant to be identical (and the courts can prefer the words of the directive to those of national legislation if the latter does not correctly implement the former) the rates of tax are not yet completely harmonized.

In the U.K. the standard rate of VAT is 17,5%; the reduced rate is 8%. There is also a zero rate which attracts considerable hostility from certain parts of the European commission.

The importance of the VAT is as a highly successful revenue raiser. In 1993 it raised almost £44bn out of a total government Revenue of £191bn; income tax raised £59bn and corporation tax £15bn while CGT raised £1.1bn and IHT £1.2bn. Social security taxes (known as National Insurance Contributions) raise £38.5bn

3. Constitutional structure.

It is axiomatic that the U.K. has no written constitution and no basic law against which legislation can be assessed for constitutional validity. However, the U.K. does have experience of finding its legislation overruled by the European Court of Justice in Luxembourg as a result of its membership of the European Community.

Within the U.K. the central government enjoys an almost unparalleled degree of power. There are local authorities in different parts of the country but they are subject to tight control from Whitehall in a number of ways. First, a substantial part of their responsibilities are funded from Whitehall rather than through local taxes. Secondly, their revenue raising powers have been made the subject of capping powers. Thirdly, their ability to raise money from businesses has been reduced by the device of the business rate. This leaves them with little power to raise much money from the local residents; the local tax is called the council tax. The level is fixed by the authority — subject to capping — and that rate is then applied to each house, the house being placed in one of a number of bands of value.

The council tax replaced the very short-lived community charge, or poll tax as it came to be known. The theory of the community charge was that it was a charge for local services paid locally by all who lived there. It was an attempt to link liability to pay with the right to enjoy benefits. The community charge had replaced the earlier (and much longer lasting) "rates" which were strongly criticized by successive governments Rates were based on the imputed income of property occupied by the owner; those who did not pay rates (e.g., because their income was too low) still had the vote at local elections, a situation which led to a divorce between liability to pay from the right to enjoy benefits. It was Mrs. Thatcher's insistence on standing by the community charge that led in part to her downfall, but then only a politician of her determination would have done something to replace the rating system.

A local income tax has rarely been considered in the U.K. and never implemented. Current suggestions for devolving powers to a Scottish Parliament include the power to raise a local income tax of up to 3p in the £.

4. Rates of tax

4.1 History and politics

Of all the aspects of the U.K. tax system the rates of income tax provide the most striking examples of the influence of history — and of politics. The English reputation for moderation is not justified by the record in this area. Rates of income tax in the last year of the Labour administration (1978-79) reached 83 %; however, if the income was classified as investment income and exceeded a certain figure, a supplementary tax of 15 % was due - making a marginal rate of 98 %. This was fairly typical of the period after 1945 and showed the great doctrinal belief in equity in the sense of shared misery. It was highlighted by the very occasional (twice) surcharge on income, which being expressed as percentage of tax normally due could (and did) mean that the marginal rate of tax could exceed 100 %. The ferocity of these rates emphasizes the gap between income and capital gain (not generally taxed until 1965) and the importance of any gaps in the tax base and of the generally neutral attitude of the courts toward straightforward tax avoidance schemes.

Since the election of the Conservative administration in 1979 the top rates have been reduced - in 1979 the general rate dropped from 83 % to 60 %; in 1984 the surcharge on investment income was abolished and in 1988 the top rate was cut to 40 %. In these ways, the doctrinal writings of the 1970s with their emphasis on neutrality rather than equity, have come to hold sway with the same fervour as their predecessors arguing for equity.

4.2 Inflation

Indexation and inflation adjustments have been part of the U.K. tax system for many years. Income tax rate brackets are liable to be adjusted for inflation or other causes each year; the same was true of the personal reliefs. In part this was attributable to the fact that the income tax was an annual tax and was therefore subject to annual review. However all depended on the needs of the Chancellor of the Exchequer of the day. In recent years adjustment of these values for inflation has been formalized in that they will be changed unless the annual Finance Bill directs otherwise - the annual Finance Bill has directed otherwise more often than not with smaller (or no) adjustments in years when the government needs money and larger adjustments when the government needs votes.

Adjustment for inflation has formed part of the Capital Gains system since 1982. The current position is that inflation adjustments are made to the base cost of the asset in determining a gain. However while the adjustment can remove a gain altogether it cannot create a loss.

There are no adjustments to the base cost used in determining the amount which may be claimed under the capital allowance system (depreciation).

4.3 Rate structure and reliefs, 1996[1]

The income tax rate structure is as follows:

0 - £3,900	20 % (lower)
£3,901 - £25,500	24 %(basic)
over £25,500	40 % (higher)

Rate brackets and reliefs are index linked but the effects of this are more often than not overridden; this overriding sometimes makes the increase smaller (or non existent) but sometimes makes the increase larger. The capital gains tax is charged as if the gain were added to the taxpayer's other income, after an annual exemption of £6,300. In addition, national insurance contributions are imposed on both employer and employer and range from 2 % to 10.2 % of earnings.

Income in the form of dividends or interest is now taxed at 20 % rather than 24 % - but both are liable to be taxed at 40 %.

The following basic personal allowances are granted:

Personal allowance (under 65)	£3,765
Married couple's allowance[2] (both spouses under 65)	£1,790*

---

1. All amounts shown are expressed in pounds sterling. The current exchange rate is ca. £1 = $1.55

2. All amounts marked with a star (*) not given at the taxpayer's actual marginal rate but at a notional 15% rate. Amounts marked with two stars (**) are phased out at higher income levels.

In addition to the basic personal allowance, a number of complex exemptions or reliefs, sometimes phased out based on income levels of the taxpayer or spouse, are give based on age, marital status and other factors. They include the following:

Age allowances:

Personal allowance (65-74)	£4,910**
Personal allowance (75 or over)	£5,090**
Married couple's allowance (elder spouse 65-74)	£3,115* **
Married couple's allowance (elder spouse 75 or over)	£3,155* **
Widow's and widower's bereavement allowance	£1,790*
Additional relief for children	£1,790*
Blind persons (each)	£1,250

For corporations, in 1996 the full rate is 33 % with a reduced rate reduced rate of 24 % which is phased out once profits pass £300,000. The rate of ACT is 1/4 of the qualifying distribution.

5. Tax setting

5.1 Administration

The direct taxes are administered by the Inland Revenue; indirect taxes, including VAT, by the Customs and Excise. Both departments work closely with the Treasury but are not subordinate departments of the Treasury, even though they share common Ministers.

The Inland Revenue divides the country up into districts and each district has an Inspector of Taxes in charge; other inspectors assist in carrying out the duties stated in the legislation. At one time all the tax affairs of a taxpayer would be dealt with in a local office, i.e., local to the place of employment or residence. The values inherent in this very personal service do not appeal to today's style of management and it is regrettably the case that a taxpayer's affairs are dealt with miles away. The Revenue try to compensate by providing help locally.

For many years the system has depended upon assessment of the taxpayer to tax by the Revenue. The system was similar to that which used to prevail in Australia and which is outlined in that Country Description. The taxpayer would make a return of income and the Revenue would calculate the tax due. There was no binding obligation on the Revenue to accept at face value what the taxpayer reported as income and the inspector of taxes has power to make an assessment to the best of his judgement "if it appears to the inspector that there are any profits in respect of which tax is chargeable and which have not been included or if the inspector is dissatisfied with any return". Equally there is power to make further assessments if the inspector "discovers" that any profits that ought to have been assessed have not been assessed to tax or that an assessment is or has become insufficient. The term "discovers" has been given a wide interpretation by the courts; an inspector was held to have made a discovery when he changed his mind about the correct legal position. The time limit is ordinarily six years but is extended to twenty in cases of fraudulent or negligent conduct.

Although an assessment once made is final (in the sense that formal acts or agreements are needed to change the obligations resulting from it), the Revenue may use their discovery powers extensively. Moreover, the burden of proof is on the taxpayer to disprove an assessment. There are extensive penalty powers as well as interest on arrears of tax. Since a favourite explanation of undeclared wealth is a gambling win, the Revenue, at least according to rumour, keep a list of all horse race results (complete with betting news).

This system of Revenue assessment worked well because of a number of other features of the tax system. One was the wide band of income taxed at the basic rate of tax and the absence of a lower rate of tax. The second was the scheme for withholding tax at source on many types of investment income, including dividends and interest. In combination with the first feature, this meant that there would be few adjustments to be made for most taxpayers if tax at basic rate were withheld at source. However, perhaps the most important feature was the introduction during the World War II of the rules known as Pay as You Earn (PAYE). This was a system of cumulative withholding at source on all income from employment. The taxpayer would be given a code that would be based on the deductions available to that person that year; the deductions would then be allocated on a week-by-week cumulative basis. The rules allowed for an accurate deduction of tax even where the person's income level or employment changed during the year. A drop in income level would bring not simply a reduced tax deduction for the rest of the year but sometimes even a repayment. The purpose of this system was to get the taxpayer's total of the income tax deducted at source right by the end of the year so as to avoid any more paperwork. This imposed a substantial extra cost on employers but the system worked well. One last factor should be mentioned when assessing the workability of the system of revenue assessment. This was the aversion of the Revenue to posturing — if a new tax rule was to be introduced it would have to be workable, even if this meant narrowing the theoretically ideal scope of the charge.

The system of assessment by the Revenue is about to pass into history. A first step towards self-assessment for corporation tax came into force in 1993; it is known as Pay and File. Self assessment comes into force for all taxpayers for the year 1996-97.

For many years relations between the Revenue and the general body of taxpayers were generally cordial. Tax was due and was generally regarded as a legitimate charge. Although there was considerable resistance to the very high rates of income tax charged during and after the Second World War this was tempered by the absence of any charge on capital gains, the existence of a number of reliefs e.g. for pension contributions, the system of allowing income to be assigned (otherwise than to one's spouse or infant children) through the system of covenants and a strict, even legalistic, attitude to tax avoidance schemes. Some might see in this a certain element of hypocrisy; others might see the last embers of a civilized society summed up in the condemnatory expression "it isn't cricket". For whatever reason, it has to be said that the Revenue were at least during the 1960s and early 1970s slow to use some of the powers at their disposal e.g. in relation to transfer pricing.

Once the Revenue had decided that the old consensus had broken down they persuaded Parliament to grant them extra powers including the right of entry on to a taxpayer's premises.

5.2 Avoidance of tax

The periodic shifts in the UK tax environment can also be seen in the willingness or unwillingness of the courts to control tax avoidance by judicial doctrine.

The earliest doctrine of the courts was one of strict construction - there is no equity about a tax as one judge famously remarked, (*Cape Brandy Syndicate v IRC* [1921] 1 KB 64 at 71, 12 TC 358 at 366). On this approach there is no presumption as to a tax; nothing is to be read in, nothing is to be implied. One can only look fairly at the language used. This strict approach however was not confined to avoidance schemes; it was applied with equal consistency to exemptions from tax.

More recently the courts have sometimes tried openly to look for the purpose behind the statute or, in a less confrontational way, to look for the structure of the Act. However, all too often the purpose of the Act does not help to determine the answer in the very precise circumstances before the court. Moreover, when the structure of the Act is looked to events may change some of the assumptions on the basis of which a judgement might be made. Thus the general definition of a distribution by a company that would be taxed as if it were a dividend clearly assumed that taxpayers would try to dress up dividend payments as interest, and the definition therefore widened the concept of a distribution to include certain types of interest. Some time later, at a time of deep recession, banks in particular found it attractive to dress up what would have been interest as dividends so attracting a tax credit that could be used to frank their own distributions; the choice was usually indifferent to the company as it had no profits against which to put its own ACT. Again the rules about companies buying their own shares clearly assumed that qualifying companies would try to take advantage of the new rules allowing the transaction to be treated as one involving only capital gains legislation; changes in the various rates of tax including corporation tax, ACT, CGT, and income tax made this assumption quite false and companies might try to make their transactions fall outside the supposedly beneficial rules.

The courts have shown a willingness to interpret anti-avoidance provisions phrased in broad language that deliberately eschews legal terms of art in a broad way. As one judge put it,

"We seem to have traveled a long way from the general and salutary rule that the subject is not to be taxed except by plain words. But I must recognize that plain words are seldom adequate to anticipate and forestall the multiplicity of ingenious schemes which are constantly being devised to evade (sic) taxation. Parliament is very properly determined to prevent this kind of tax evasion (sic) and, if the courts find it impossible to give very wide meanings to general phrases, the only alternative may be for Parliament to do as some other countries have done, and introduce legislation of a more sweeping character which will put the ordinary well-intentioned person at much greater risk than is now created by a wide interpretation of such provisions as those which we are now considering."

The House of Lords has shown itself capable on the one hand of depriving a provision of any effect and on the other of imposing double taxation.

In 1992 the House, reversing centuries of case law, held that the court could consult *Hansard*, the compilation of legislative material and history, in order to interpret the words of the legislation. As Lord Browne-Wilkinson put it in the landmark case of *Pepper v. Hart* :

". . . subject to any question of Parliamentary privilege, the exclusionary rule should be relaxed so as to permit reference to Parliamentary materials where:

(a) legislation is ambiguous or obscure, or leads to an absurdity;
(b) the material relied on consists of one or more statements by a minister or other promoter of the Bill together if necessary with such other Parliamentary material as is necessary to understand such statements and their effects; and
(c) the statements relied on are clear." ([1992] STC 898 at 922)

In assessing this apparently complacent attitude on the part of the judges it should not be forgotten that Parliament passes a Finance Bill every year and that loopholes could be filled by appropriate provisions. Moreover the traditions of party discipline and of allowing clauses drafted by good professional draftsmen meant that the government would usually get its way and do so in a workable form.

Apart from the question of the strictness or otherwise with which statutes are construed is the closely related issue of the characterization of the facts, particularly where avoidance schemes are concerned. There has been no shortage of leading cases on the judicial approach to problems of tax avoidance but one still begins with *IRC v Duke of Westminster* [1936] AC 1; 19 TC 490. This case lays down that in applying the tax legislation to the facts the courts must have respect for the legal rights which the parties have created even if for tax avoidance purposes. In this form the decision is still good law.

As a result of some occasional odd drafting and a very aggressive tax-avoidance industry, a number of schemes were peddled in the 1970s. These schemes frequently involved circular and ultimately self-canceling transactions carried though according to some timetable. A typical example was *Ramsay v IRC* [1981] STC 174; [1982] AC 300 where the House determined that it would be consistent with the *Westminster* doctrine to treat such circular and self-canceling transactions as one single transaction for tax purposes. Although the scheme in *Ramsay* failed not only at this abstract level but also on a narrow point of tax law, the decision was very important; if the scheme had succeeded, the tax (CGT) would have become voluntary — one would have paid either the Revenue or the tax adviser.

This decision was extended to a linear transaction in a preordained series having no purpose (as opposed to effect) other than the avoidance of tax in *Furniss v Dawson* [1984] STC 153; [1984] AC 474. This was the high-water mark of what became known as the New Approach or the *Ramsay* doctrine. The case itself involved the use of a share-for-share exchange to achieve a deferral of capital gains tax on a corporate reorganization. The effect of that decision, exacerbated by some very wide statements by some members of the court, was to reduce much tax advice to a valueless exercise in guessing what the courts might do next. This period of uncertainty was ended in 1988 when the court in considering what was meant by a preordained series of transactions, concluded that this was only so when it was "practically certain" at the time of the first step that the second would follow - *Craven v. White; Bayliss v. Gregory* and *IRC v. Bowater* [1988] STC 476. This case also confined the new approach to such cases so that the UK is left with a narrow step transaction doctrine that applies where there is no business purpose other than the avoidance of tax.

However, the New Approach may well have other effects, particularly in encouraging the courts to look more broadly at the facts even if there is no tax-avoidance motive around. Meanwhile, the courts have stressed the need for tax to live in the "real world," e.g., *Ensign Tankers (Leasing) Ltd v Stokes* [1992] STC 226. The case law since 1988 is generally one of Revenue failure e.g., *Pigott v Staines Investments Co Ltd* [1995] STC 114.

Before leaving this topic two other points need to be made. The first is that while the courts have taken their time to evolve the New Approach, Parliament has been willing to pass legislation to deal with specific schemes and in particular to stop such schemes retrospectively. Thus the 1978 Finance Act countered one scheme back to March 1976 and effectively ended the tax-avoidance industry which had sprung up. There is as yet no constitutional principle that can be invoked to challenge such legislation on grounds of retroactivity. The other is that while some of the schemes were of an artificiality that was a tribute to the ingenuity of their designers (but little else), some of the schemes were very elegant.

5.3 Sources of law, official practice and rulings

The sources of U.K. tax law include the customary Statutes and Cases. In addition, the Revenue for many years published extra-statutory concessions and statements of practice. The latter became more systematic in 1978. More recently the revenue began publishing Revenue Interpretations and Decisions in their own magazine called *Tax Bulletin*. They are currently experimenting with post-transaction rulings, a necessary part of a system based on self-assessment.

Other sources include the publication of the Revenue's own manuals for the guidance of inspectors; some of these are particularly useful, e.g., those dealing with specialized matters such as banking and international transactions.

Pretransaction rulings have been a feature of some parts of the tax code but not generalized. Informal advance clearances have long been available provided full disclosure was made.

The question whether one can use concessions for tax-avoidance purposes was considered in *R v IRC ex parte Fulford-Dobson* [1987] STC 344; 60 TC 168. The court held that since the official booklet published by the Inland Revenue and setting out these concessions stated that the Revenue would not allow them to be used for avoidance purposes, the taxpayer could not reverse that refusal by judicial review. This is of considerable interest since there is of course no general anti-avoidance provision in the tax legislation itself.

Where an application for judicial review is made on the basis of a ruling, the Revenue will only be bound in the case of an informal approach if the taxpayer gave full details of the specific transaction on which he sought the Revenue's ruling, indicated the ruling sought and made it plain that a fully considered ruling was sought, indicated the use he intended to make of any ruling given, and the ruling or statement made was clear, unambiguous, and devoid of qualification. A breach of a representation by the Revenue will not amount to an abuse of power if the taxpayer knows that clearance at local level is not to be treated as binding on the Revenue or if the taxpayer has not fully disclosed all relevant material to the inspectors. There is not necessarily full disclosure merely because sufficient information has been disclosed to enable inferences to be drawn.

6. Role of courts

6.1 Judicial review

One of the recent features of the U.K. tax system has been the use made of judicial review. It is one of the few ways in which an assessment may be disturbed. In recent years it has been used to challenge the Commissioners' decision at the hearing of an appeal or at some other procedural steps; for example, a hearing was unfair when the taxpayer was not given enough notice. However, judicial review may also be used to challenge decisions by the Revenue before and independent of any appeal hearing. Consequently, it has been used to question the Revenue's withdrawal of an informal clearance given by an inspector (*R v. IRC ex parte Matrix Securities Ltd)* [1994] STC 272 HL), its revocation of a company's right to pay dividends gross to a nonresident (*R v. IRC ex parte Preston* [1985] STC 282 HL), its decision to prosecute some parties to a tax fraud and not others (*R v. IRC ex parte Mead and Cook* [1992] STC 482 QB), its decision not to treat a taxpayer as falling within an extra-statutory concession, (*R v. IRC ex parte Fulford-Dobson* 1987 STC 344) or a statement of practice (*R v. IRC ex parte Kaye)* [1992] STC 581) and not to assess another taxpayer (*IRC v. National Federation of Self Employed and Small Business Ltd* [1981] STC 260).

Judicial review has to be distinguished from appeal. On an appeal the court may uphold an assessment or vary it; in judicial review the court either upholds the act complained of or quashes it and, if it quashes it, it sends the matter back to the original body to exercise its jurisdiction correctly — the court does not substitute its own decision for that of the body reviewed. If commissioners have conducted the hearing of an appeal in way which breaches the rules of natural justice they will have to hear the appeal again. If an assessment by an inspector is quashed, a new assessment must be made — although it may sometimes be too late for the Revenue to make a new one. On appeal the court goes into the merits of the decision; in judicial review the court looks at the procedures followed and ensures that the public body whose acts are being scrutinized had power to do what it has done. In judicial review the court does not interfere with the proper exercise of a power or jurisdiction.

Another difference is that an appeal lies if a statute gives a right of appeal whereas judicial review is always available unless it is expressly excluded; moreover a right of appeal will usually be as of right whereas judicial review is always a matter of discretion.

The court will not usually grant leave to apply for judicial review if the taxpayer has another route open, such as the right to appeal against the assessment or the determination by the commissioners. However, the court clearly has jurisdiction to grant judicial review in such cases —it simply declines to exercise it in most cases where appeal is still open.

Judicial review is not to be undertaken lightly. Where a taxpayer obtained leave to apply against the Revenue on an ex parte basis and the Revenue remedied the matter before the full hearing the taxpayer was not allowed his costs. (R v. IRC ex parte Opman International U.K. [1986] STC 18).

6.2 Appeal system.

A taxpayer who is dissatisfied with an assessment made by an inspector may appeal to a body known as the Commissioners. This term is confusing since the Members of the Board of Inland Revenue are known as the Commissioners of the Inland Revenue. The appellate commissioners are either General or Special and their full title is General (or Special) Commissioners for the purposes of the Income Tax; despite the mention of Income Tax their jurisdiction extends to other taxes, but not to VAT which has its own appeal tribunal.

General Commissioners reflect the English appreciation of the amateur; like the magistrates these are lay people who sit in panels and are advised on the law by their clerk. The term "amateur" should not be seen as a condemnation; the tribunal usually comprises people of a wide range of experience who bring considerable expertise to their tax role. The Special Commissioners by contrast are highly trained specialists appointed from the ranks of barristers solicitors or accountants and from the Inland Revenue itself.

The respective roles of these two bodies is changing. At one time their jurisdictions overlapped quite extensively. Today the Special Commissioners are becoming more specialized; they frequently sit on their own instead of, as previously, in pairs. They may also sit with an expert assessor. It is expected that they will shortly be merged with the

Value-Added Tax Tribunal to make a single Tax Court in a form recognizable to those from other jurisdictions. The burden of proof lies on the taxpayer to disprove the assessment. Publication of the decisions of the Special Commissioners began in 1995; previously these were regarded as confidential to the parties. The commissioners still sit in private; they have just obtained the power to award costs in appropriate cases in accordance with the normal rules of litigation in the U.K., i.e., costs follow the cause. Appeals from their decisions lie to the High Court and from there to the Court of Appeal; appeals may also go straight to the Court of Appeal, with leave; appeals lie from the Court of Appeal to the House of Lords.

The General Commissioners have had the more exotic areas of tax law removed from their jurisdiction. They still hear appeals against assessments. The burden of proof lies on the taxpayer to disprove the assessment. They sit in private; their decisions are not published; they have no power to award costs. Appeal from their decisions lies by an archaic process still used in criminal appeals from decisions of magistrates and known as the case stated.

Since appeals lie from Commissioners only on questions of law and not of fact the issue of the distinction between the two is important. Apart from errors of law in the most obvious sense, the courts have said that they will intervene in three situations which may well amount to the same thing: where there is no evidence to support the determination reached by the commissioners, where the evidence contradicts that determination, and where the true and only reasonable conclusion contradicts that determination (*Edwards v Bairstow and Harrison* 36 TC 207 at 229).

7. The current situation.

The U.K. tax system is going through a period of profound change. At the risk of repetition these changes may be grouped in the following ways:

a) Self-assessment. After a long and honourable tradition of assessment to tax by the Revenue, the system is to change to one of self-assessment as from 1996. This change is presented as a cost saving exercise and has little else to commend it. One of the casualties of the change will be the relationship between taxpayer and Revenue official; a more confrontational approach by the latter seems inevitable - and regrettable.

b) Simplification. One benefit of a) has been the simplification of the tax system, especially as concerns the income tax payer; not even the Revenue could hope that taxpayers would understand some of the concepts previously current in the tax system. This is not all attributable to a) but the list of changes is becoming impressive:

i) The rewriting of Schedule A in 1995 so as to be based on something close to business principles in the calculation of income; this meant the abandonment of much ancient and unnecessary learning.

ii) The abolition of Schedule B in 1988; in future, income under this head is simply not taxed at all but equally there are no tax effects of expenditure connected with it.

iii) The abolition of Schedule C in 1996; Schedule C was merged with D Case III.

iv) The abolition of the preceding-year system of assessment first promulgated in 1993 and to come into effect in full effect in 1997-98 with 1996-97 as a straddle year.

v) new rules for foreign exchange transaction (1993), financial instruments (1994), and interest and related matters (1996). One thing these provisions have in common is a willingness to abandon the old doctrines, such as the distinction between income and capital and the requirement that income must be realized in order that it can be taxable. In place of the old doctrines is an accrual system of taxation covering both gains and losses and allowing a choice of accounting systems.

c) More stress on accounting principles. b) v) provides some statutory examples of the use of accounting principles but no less important has been the willingness of the courts to use such practice in solving other problems in the determination of business income. These developments will bring the U.K. closer to its continental European counterparts.

d) The legislative process. This process has come under scrutiny thanks to various factors these include the work of the Deregulation Unit at the Department of Trade and Industry, the Institute for Fiscal Studies, and the Inland Revenue itself. One objective has been to make the tax legislation clearer. It is too early to assess results. In certain areas the Revenue has shown a much greater willingness to allow discussion of proposals - again the instances at b) v) are good examples of this. However it has to be said that one effect of this consultation has been a greater willingness to have very detailed legislation backed up by even more detailed statutory instruments. As the power to make these statutory instruments often includes a power to change the primary legislation, such powers are rare elsewhere in the tax system. They are needed in the areas mentioned to enable the Revenue to adapt the legislation as new instruments or arrangements come along.

e) New taxes. One of the boasts of Nigel Lawson in the 1980s was that he reduced the number of taxes. Since his departure all has changed and we are in danger of reverting to an eighteenth century picture of many little taxes. In part this is due to the government's wish to be seen as reducing income tax. New taxes include charges on insurance premiums (1994), airport passengers (1994), and landfill (1996).

f) The sacred cow of the marginal rate of income tax. When Keynes was asked why he had changed his opinion on something he is said to have replied, "When the evidence changes, I change my conclusions. What do you do?" No such honesty grips the present government, as it will do anything rather than be accused of "making a U-turn." The huge political investment in cutting the basic rate of income tax has been apparently preserved by freezing rate bands, freezing the value of reliefs, restricting the value of other reliefs, e.g., by allowing mortgage interest relief only at 15 % and by reducing value of tax repayments to charities, pensions plans and other exempt bodies. If the government had subjected these bodies to a 5 % tax there would have been severe political trouble; as it only reduced the repayment by 5 % there was very little. It all goes to show that the level of tax sophistication in the U.K. is patchy. The general price paid under this heading in terms of loss of elegance and cohesion should not be underestimated.

g) Role of Europe. Although a single Europe-wide tax base is a long way off, the law of the European Union is having a distinct effect on the U.K. tax system. What we do not yet know is whether the traditions of interpretation prevalent on the continent and which have to be applied when considering such matters will have any effect on the interpretation of U.K. legislation. The move towards monetary union if implemented may well lead to demands for fiscal union; hence some of the present U.K. anxieties about the enterprise.

General Description: United States

Professor James R. Repetti *

1. History of the federal income tax

The U.S. first briefly adopted a tax on the income of individuals during the period 1864 to 1872 to finance the Civil War. The tax affected only 1 % of potential taxpayers. Income from corporations was taxed directly to the individual taxpayer. Over thirty years after the repeal of the Civil War income tax, Congress adopted in 1895 a new act which imposed a tax on the income of both individuals and corporations. The U.S. Supreme Court declared this act unconstitutional on the grounds that Congress lacked authority under the U.S. Constitution to adopt an income tax on individuals without apportioning that tax among the states based on their relative populations. The final enactment of an income tax for individuals required the adoption of the Sixteenth Amendment to the Constitution which was ratified by the states in 1913.

The original 1913 income tax and subsequent changes through 1938 were enacted as self-contained Revenue Acts. Each new Revenue Act would supersede the prior Revenue Act and would contain all the income tax provisions. As a result, the process of referencing and amending the statutes was very complex and cumbersome. To remedy this problem, Congress codified all the revenue provisions in effect in 1939 into the Internal Revenue Code of 1939. The change to a Code allowed subsequent statutory enactments to occur as amendments to the Code, rather than as a reenactment of the entire Revenue Act.

Congress replaced the 1939 Code with the Internal Revenue Code of 1954. The 1954 Code revised the income tax treatment of partnerships, trusts and estates, annuities and corporate distributions. It also introduced several new deductions, and provided more accelerated depreciation rates. The most important changes in the 1954 Code

---

* Professor of Law, Boston College Law School

occurred in the 1980s. In 1981 Congress substantially reduced individual rates, and adopted extensive new tax incentives for savings and investments, including greatly accelerated depreciation rates. In 1986, Congress adopted additional significant changes in the income tax structure. The Tax Reform Act of 1986 broadened the tax base, substantially eliminating many tax incentive provisions, and reduced individual rates still further. The deduction for personal interest was eliminated (except for home mortgage interest), as was the preference for capital gains. To mark the significance of the changes, Congress renamed the Code as the Internal Revenue Code of 1986.

Since 1986 there have been a number of amendments to the Code. The amendments have tended to increase the maximum statutory rates for individuals. Concerns with the budget deficits have dominated recent tax legislation with little attention paid to the impact of the changes on the overall structure of the Code. Frequently, Congress has hastily adopted the amendments with the result that still more amendments are necessary to correct the earlier amendments.

2. Constitutional issues

The Sixteenth Amendment to the United States Constitution grants Congress very broad powers to assess an income tax. Earlier cases that seemed to impose some bounds under the Sixteenth Amendment on the ability of Congress to use tax statutes to accomplish objectives not related to raising revenue are now commonly disregarded. For example, it is now clear that Congress may use taxes to discourage certain activities without any consideration of whether the tax will in fact raise revenues. See e.g. Sunshine Anthracite Coal Co. v. Adkins, 310 U.S. 381 (1947). Moreover, Congress may favor some groups with tax preferences without favoring all groups so long as the distinction among groups is not based on a suspect classification such as race. For example, in Regan v. Taxation With Representation of Washington, 461 U.S. 540 (1983), the Supreme Court ruled that the fact that Congress allows veterans' organizations to use tax deductible contributions to engage in political lobbying did not mean that Congress has to extend the same tax subsidy to other organizations. The Court explained that Congress has "broad latitude in creating classifications and distinctions in tax statutes."

Consistent with this "broad latitude" is the Supreme Court's treatment of tax statutes that apply retroactively. The Court has stated that the enactment or amendment of a tax statute that applies retroactively will be held unconstitutional under the due process clause of the Fifth Amendment only where "the nature of the tax and the circumstances in which it is laid [are] so harsh and oppressive as to transgress the constitutional limitation." Welch v. Henry 305 U.S. 134, 147 (1948). Under this standard the Supreme Court has permitted tax rates to increase for the calendar year in which the legislation was adopted, although adopted late in the year. See e.g. United States v. Darusmont, 449 U.S. 292, 297 (1981); United States v. Hudson, 299 U.S. 495, 500-01 (1937). Similarly, in United States v. Carlton, 512 U.S. 26 (1994), the Court held that an amendment in 1987 that applied retroactively to 1986 was not unconstitutional where Congress had acted promptly to correct a mistake in the statute adopted in 1986.

Another area illustrating the U.S. courts' view of the expansive nature of Congressional taxing power is the courts' application of Article 1, Section 7, clause 1 of the U.S. Constitution. That provision states, "All Bills for raising Revenue shall originate in the House of Representatives; but the Senate may propose or concur with amendments as on other bills." In 1982 the House of Representatives adopted a tax bill consisting of three pages which it then sent to the Senate. The Senate removed the provisions which the House had adopted and substituted over 500 pages of new amendments to the Code. Both the House and the Senate then adopted the "revised" bill and it was signed by the President. All the U.S. Courts of Appeals which have addressed the validity of this process have held that the Senate's "revision" did not violate the above quoted Article 1, Section 7, clause 1.

3. Tax rates

The rates of the U.S. income tax have fluctuated widely depending upon revenue needs and economic objectives of Congress. Initially, the maximum statutory tax rate was 6 % for individuals and 1 % for corporations in 1913. In subsequent years the rate for individuals peaked at 91 % and for corporations at 52 % (excluding the excess profits tax which during World War II subjected corporations to an overall maximum rate of 80 %).

The Internal Revenue Code of 1986 significantly reduced both the level and progressivity of the rate structure, establishing the maximum statutory rate for individuals at 28 % and the corporate rate at 34 %. Since 1986, the rates have increased to 39.6 % for individuals and 35 % for corporations.

Different rate schedules are provided for different categories of individuals. In general, the brackets for the two lowest rates, 15 % and 28 %, are broader for married individuals filing joint returns and for heads of household as compared to the brackets for unmarried individuals. The brackets for rates that apply to all individuals are adjusted annually to reflect inflation. The rates currently projected for the 1996 taxable year are as follows:

Unmarried Taxpayer

Taxable Income Over	But Not Over	Rate
$0	24,000	15%
24,000	58,150	28%
58,150	121,300	31%
121,300	263,750	36%
263,750		39.6%

Married Taxpayers Filing Jointly

Taxable Income Over	But Not Over	Rate
$0	40,100	15%
40,100	96,900	28%
147,700	263,750	31%
263,750		39.6%

Taxpayer who Is Head of Household

Taxable Income Over	But Not Over	Rate
$0	32,150	15%
32,150	83,050	28%
83,050	134,500	31%
134,500	263,750	36%
263,750		39.6%

The tax rates for corporations are not adjusted annually to reflect inflation. The corporate tax rates are complex due to the phase out of lower bracket rates and are as follows:

Corporations

Taxable Income Over	But Not Over	Rate
$0	50,000	15 %
50,000	75,000	25 %
75,000	100,000	34 %
100,000	335,000	39 %
335,000	10,000,000	34 %
10,000,000	15,000,000	35 %
15,000,000	18,333,333	38 %
18,333,333		35 %

4. Composition of fiscal system

In addition to the income tax, the U.S. government also imposes a wealth transfer tax, social security taxes and various excise taxes. Each state is also allowed to impose taxes. The states in general impose some combination of income, property, wealth, sales and excise taxes.

Federal receipts as a percentage of gross domestic product ("GDP") have been remarkably steady since 1960. During the period 1960 through 1994, federal receipts ranged from a low of 17.41 % of GDP for the year 1965 to a high of 20.22 % of GDP for the year 1981[1] The past ten years has seen an even narrower range of variation. As shown below for the period 1984 through 1994, revenues as a percentage of GDP only ranged from 18.04 % to a high of 19.18 %.[2]

---

1. Joint Committee on Taxation, Selected Materials Relating To The Federal Tax System Under Present Law and Various Alternative Tax Systems (JCS-1-96), Table A-4 (March 14, 1996).
   2. Id.

Federal Receipts As A percentage Of Gross Domestic Product[3]

Year	Receipts as percentage of GDP
1994	18.96
1993	18.43
1992	18.42
1991	18.57
1990	18.81
1989	19.15
1988	18.90
1987	19.18
1986	18.23
1985	18.50
1984	18.04

The largest source of receipts for the U.S. government is the individual income tax. In 1994, 43.18 % of Federal receipts were from the individual income tax.[4] The next largest category of receipts by the IRS were the employment taxes. They accounted for 36.69 % of IRS receipts.[5] Taxes from corporations accounted for only 11.16 % of receipts in 1994.[6] Receipts from the estate and gift tax represented only 1.21 % of Federal receipts in 1994.[7]

It is interesting to note that the relative contributions of the corporate income tax and employment taxes have become reversed over the past 50 years. In 1945, employment taxes accounted for 7.64 % of

3. Id.
4. Id. at Table A-5.
5. Id.
6. Id.
7. Id. at Table A-6.
8. Id at Table A-5.

federal receipts, while the corporate income tax accounted for 35.40 % of receipts.[8] In 1994, corporate income taxes accounted for only 11.16 % of receipts while employment taxes accounted for 36.96 %.[9]

5. Basic structure of the income tax for individuals

The U.S. income tax is a global tax which taxes income of U.S. citizens and U.S. residents regardless of source or type. The starting point for calculating the tax is gross income. The term "gross income" is defined broadly to include all accessions to wealth with a few well-defined exclusions. Significant exclusions from income include gifts, bequests, and proceeds from life insurance policies. Scholarships paid to degree-seeking students are also excludable from income if the scholarship is for tuition or book expenses and if the student is not required to perform services. A broad range of fringe benefits is excluded from income, the most important ones being employer-provided health insurance and employer contributions to pension plans.

Income from the cancellation of debt is only excluded from income in certain narrow situations, such as when the taxpayer is insolvent or in a bankruptcy proceeding. Windfalls and gambling wins are clearly includable in income.

Although no statutory provision addresses the issue, imputed income is not taxed in the U.S. For example, taxpayers do not recognize income for the imputed rental value of their homes. Similarly, a taxpayer is not taxed with respect to the care provided by a spouse, parent or child.

Gross income is recognized upon the occurrence of a realization event. The scope of transactions that result in a realization event is fairly broad. For example, an exchange of one item of property for another qualifies as a realization event where the properties differ "materially in kind or in extent." Under this approach, the change in the yield of a debt instrument by more then 25 basis points will gener-

---

8. Id at Table A-5.
9. Id.

ally be treated as an exchange of an old debt instrument for a new instrument. In the corporate context, the distribution of appreciated property is now normally a realization event, though it took a surprisingly long time to reach this result.

The U.S. does not treat transfers by gift or at death as realization events. Indeed, in the U.S., the appreciation inherent in property held by a taxpayer at death permanently escapes income taxation because the tax basis of the property is stepped up to its fair market value at the time of death (or its fair market value at the time 6 months after death if the alternative valuation date is selected). Property owned by the taxpayer at death is subject, however, to the U.S. estate tax, which is a wealth transfer tax.

An old Supreme Court decision, Eisner v. Macomber, 252 U.S. 189 (1920), initially created some doubt about whether Congress had the authority to treat the mere appreciation of an asset as a realization event. However, the Court's statement in a subsequent decision, Helvering v. Horst, 311 U.S. 112, 115 (1940), that described the realization requirement as "founded on administrative convenience", has largely eliminated any doubt about the authority of Congress to define a realization event in any way it wishes. However, Congress has elected to take a "mark-to-market" approach only in narrow circumstances, for example, with respect to certain futures contracts and options.

After calculating gross income, individual taxpayers may deduct expenditures that the statutes expressly provide are deductible. Taxpayers are permitted to deduct expenses that they have incurred in producing income in a trade or business. Difficult judgments occur, however, where expenses that are incurred in the conduct of a trade or business also involve aspects of personal consumption. The U.S. tax system's treatment of such expenditures has been somewhat arbitrary. Some expenditures that involve mixed aspects of income production and personal consumption are always nondeductible regardless of whether the income - producing aspect dominates. For example child care expenses and the costs of commuting from a taxpayer's residence to her principal place of business are not deductible. Other expenses, such as business related meals and entertainment are partially deductible pursuant to a statute that arbitrarily allows a deduction for 50 % of such expenditures.

The trade or business expenses that may be currently deducted are limited to expenses that do not have a significant benefit extending beyond the current taxable year. In general, expenses that have a benefit extending beyond the current year must be capitalized, though there has been substantial disagreement as to exactly how the test should be formulated. These capitalized expenses may be amortized or depreciated under various Code provisions. In general, the period for depreciation or amortization is determined by statute. Currently, the periods for personal tangible property and real property correspond very roughly to their economic useful life, although in the past Congress had significantly reduced the depreciation period below economic useful lives in order to encourage investment.

The trade or business expenses are generally deductible from gross income to obtain the statutorily defined amount of "adjusted gross income." Most other deductions (the "itemized deductions") are then taken from adjusted gross income to determine taxable income. The calculation of adjusted gross income is significant because many of the itemized deductions are limited by reference to adjusted gross income. For example, the deduction for charitable contributions of appreciated property is in general limited to 30 % of adjusted gross income. Medical expenses are only deductible to the extent they exceed 7.5 % of adjusted gross income.

Most of the itemized deductions represent tax expenditures. These deductions include medical expenses, casualty losses and interest on loans secured by residences. In addition to the tax expenditure deductions, expenses incurred in a profit seeking activity that does not rise to the level of a trade or business and that are not related to rent or royalty producing property are also deductible only from adjusted gross income in calculating taxable income.

Most of the expenses deductible from adjusted gross income in calculating taxable income are decreased by up to 80 % for high income taxpayers. The decrease takes the form of a "phase out" of the deductions as income increases. Congress indicated that the purpose of the phase out was to more closely match tax burdens with ability to pay.[10] Excluded from this phasing out are medical expenses, casualty losses and interest expenses incurred in connection with the production of investment income.

---

10. H.R. Rep. No. 881, 101st Cong., 2d Sess. 361 (1990).

Moreover, some itemized deductions, (the so-called "miscella-neous" itemized deductions), such as expenses incurred in a profit-seek-ing activity and expenses of an employee that have not been reim-bursed by the employer, are only deductible to the extent they exceed in the aggregate 2 % of adjusted gross income. Congress stated that the purpose for the 2 % floor was to reduce the burden of record keeping and to account for the fact that the expenses subject to the 2 % floor often contained some element of voluntary personal expenditure.[11]

In lieu of itemized deductions, individual taxpayers may deduct a so-called "standard deduction". Usually, taxpayers will deduct the stan-dard deduction if it exceeds the total amount of their itemized deductions which may be deducted. The standard deduction is not subject to the 2 % floor rule or to the phase out that applies to many itemized deductions. The purpose of the standard deduction is to reduce the need for record keeping. The standard deduction is adjusted annually to reflect inflation. For the 1995 taxable year the standard deduction was $3,900 for unmar-ried individuals, $5,750 for heads of households, $3,275 for married indi-viduals filing separately and $6,550 for spouses filing jointly.

All individual taxpayers may also deduct a "personal exemption" amount. The personal exemption amount is adjusted annually to reflect inflation. For the 1995 taxable year, the personal exemption amount was $2,500. Taxpayers are also allowed additional exemptions for dependents. The exemptions are phased out for higher income taxpayers.

After the various deductions, a tentative tax using the progres-sive tax rate is then calculated. Allowable tax credits, such as the child care credit and earned income tax credit, are subtracted to determine tax liability. Most credits are not refundable, i.e. the taxpayer does not receive a payment from the IRS to the extent the tax credit exceeds the taxpayer's tentative tax liability. However, the earned income credit is a refundable credit which causes it to function as an income supplement system for low income workers.

In calculating the tentative tax liability and actual tax liability, the maximum tax rate applied to certain capital gains may not exceed 28 %. In general, qualifying capital gains are the gains attributable to

---

11. Staff of the Joint Committee on Taxation, General Explanation of the Tax Reform Act of 1986 p.78 (1987).

capital assets that have been held for more than one year. A capital asset is in general defined in the Code as property which the taxpayer did not hold for sale to customers in the ordinary course of business and which was not depreciable property used in a trade or business. Special rules extend this preferential tax rate to gain from depreciable property used in a trade or business that is also not held for sale to customers in the ordinary course of business, except that the portion of gain from depreciable personal property that is attributable to depreciation is recaptured as ordinary income.

In recent years, the U.S. tax system for individuals has tended towards a schedular system. Several categories of expenses are limited in their deductibility to similar categories of income. For example, losses from passive activities may only be deducted from income generated by passive activities. In general, a passive activity is a profit-seeking activity to which the taxpayer does not devote a significant amount of time. Similarly, investment interest expenses are only deductible from investment income. Expenses attributable to a personal residence (other than mortgage interest expenses) may only be deducted from rental income generated by the residence or may be deducted if the residence was the taxpayer's principal place of business. Lastly, the treatment of capital gains is also a schedular approach. Taxpayers may fully deduct capital losses from capital gains but can only deduct $3,000 of capital losses from ordinary income.

Another aspect of the individual income tax is the alternative minimum tax (the "AMT"). The AMT is, in effect, a "shadow" tax system which accompanies the regular U.S. tax system. Congress adopted the alternative minimum tax "to ensure that no taxpayer with substantial economic income can avoid significant tax liability by using exclusions, deductions and credits."[12] The AMT in effect recalculates a taxpayer's taxable income by limiting or eliminating many tax expenditure deductions and exclusions. Where the taxpayer's AMT liability exceeds his regular income tax liability, the taxpayers must pay the AMT liability. Although Congress sought to apply the AMT to a taxpayer's "economic income," the AMT frequently overestimates economic income because it denies a deduction for expenses incurred in a profit-seeking activity.

12. Staff of the Joint Committee on Taxation, General Explanation of the Tax Reform Act of 1986, p. 432 (1987).

6. Basic structure of the corporate income tax

The U.S. has a classical corporate tax system which taxes income at the corporate level and taxes distributions of such income at the stockholder level.

The income of a corporation is calculated in a manner similar to individuals, but with several important variations. There is no adjusted gross income for a corporation since expenses and losses incurred by a corporation are generally assumed to be connected to a trade or business. Instead, deductions are subtracted directly from gross income to calculate taxable income.

Capital gains are not taxed at a preferential rate, as they are for individuals. However, corporations are restricted to deducting their capital losses against capital gains. Unused capital loss may be carried back 3 years and forward 5 years.

Since the corporation is treated as a separate taxable entity, special rules are necessary to prevent the recognition of income upon the formation of the corporation. In general, stockholders will not recognize income when they transfer appreciated property to the corporation in exchange for stock if they will own 80 % of the corporation's stock after the transfer. The corporation, itself, never recognizes gain upon the transfer of its own stock to a stockholder in exchange for property.

Because corporate income is taxable to the corporation when recognized and is taxable again when distributed to stockholders, special rules are necessary to prevent the "cascading" of corporate level tax with respect to intercorporate distributions. These rules allow a deduction for a percentage of the dividend received by a corporate shareholder receives with the amount of the deduction depending on the level of shareholding. The entire dividend can be deducted if the corporate shareholder owns 80 % of the stock of the distributing corporation. Special rules apply to curtail the tax arbitrage possibilities offered by the dividends received deductions. For example, a provision prevents corporations from purchasing portfolio stock with borrowed proceeds in order to obtain the tax benefits of the interest deduction with respect to the borrowed proceeds and the dividends-received deduction with respect to amounts paid on the debt-financed portfolio stock. Similarly, Congress has sought to prevent corporations from obtaining capital loss deductions that are attributable to declines in the value of stock as the result of dividends paid to the corporations that were not taxed at all or only partially taxed.

Corporations are also allowed to acquire other corporations without triggering a corporate or stockholder level tax in certain transactions called "reorganizations". To qualify as a reorganization, several requirements must be satisfied. A business purpose for the transaction must exist and a significant portion of the stockholders in the acquired corporation must continue to own stock in the acquiring corporation. Also, the acquiring corporation must continue to conduct at least one of the target's historic businesses or to use a significant amount of the target's assets. Finally, the structure of the transaction must correspond to one of the forms set forth in the statute. There appears to be no substantive purpose for the transactional forms set forth in the statute. The rationales supporting nonrecognition, that the stockholders have not significantly changed their relationship to the target's business, appear to be better addressed by the continuity of interest and business requirements.

Dividend distributions to stockholders who are individuals are taxed as ordinary income. In contrast, an individual's gain on the sale of her stock will qualify for preferential capital gain treatment. The result is the substantial portion of the corporate tax rules are aimed at preventing stockholders from "bailing out" corporate earnings at capital gains tax rates. For example, special rules have been formulated to determine whether a sale of stock to a corporation or a related corporation will be treated as a disguised dividend or as a sale. In general, the form of the transaction as a sale will be respected where there has been a significant reduction in the stockholder's stock ownership of the company. Similarly, special rules have been adopted to prevent stockholders from recognizing capital gains with respect to preferred stock that was distributed to them by the issuing corporation to the extent the corporation had earnings and profits at the time the stock was issued.

As in the case with the individual income tax, the corporate income tax also has an AMT. The AMT rate for corporations is 20 % after allowance for a $40,000 exemption which is phased out. The corporate AMT was adopted to ensure that corporations will pay a minimal income tax. It also attempts to measure the economic income of the corporation more accurately than the regular corporate income tax. Because of the complexity of the computations and the lack of guidance for some key aspects of the corporate AMT, it is not clear that the benefits arising from the corporate AMT outweigh the significant burdens imposed on corporate taxpayers.

7. Statutory style

The Internal Revenue Code is immense. What initially started as 16 pages in Section II of the Tariff Act of 1913 has blossomed into a tome of approximately 6000 pages.

There are many reasons for the current complexity of the Code. First, the existence of tax expenditures contributes to complexity. The presence of tax expenditures usually requires additional provisions to prevent taxpayer abuse of the expenditures. For example, a preferential rate for capital gains requires many additional provisions to prevent taxpayers from converting ordinary income into capital gain. It also requires courts to engage in difficult factual inquiries about whether the taxpayer has satisfied the statutory requirements. Moreover, the ability of taxpayers to use tax expenditures to eliminate or significantly reduce their tax liabilities has caused Congress to adopt the AMT, which is supposed to insure that all taxpayers pay a minimal income tax when tax expenditures would otherwise eliminate or reduce tax liability.

Another source of complexity has been the reluctance of Congress to admit that it was enacting tax increases. In 1990, rather than merely raising the maximum statutory rate, Congress adopted provisions that decrease many of the itemized deductions for high income individuals. Moreover, Congress had earlier adopted another provision which allows deductions for "miscellaneous itemized deductions" only to the extent the total of such deductions exceeds 2 % of the taxpayer's adjusted gross income. Both of these provisions require classification of deductions which are subject to the limitations. Based on no overriding principles, they reduce or eliminate the "transparency" of the system for the ordinary taxpayer to whom they apply.

Complexity is also produced by the tendency of the Code to assign different meanings to the same word in different parts of the Code. For example, the term "property" often has a different definition for different Code sections.

Lastly, in recent years, Congress has tried to anticipate many of the ways that taxpayers will attempt to abuse tax provisions and address them in the statute. This practice is in contrast to earlier years when Congress would rely on the courts to police the boundaries of compliance. It is not clear that this approach is productive. The failure of Congress to address all abuse situations may create an inference that Congress intended to permit the abuses not addressed in the statute.

8. Statutory interpretation

In the U.S., as in all systems, there is a tension between a strict and literal approach to statutory interpretation and an approach which attempts to achieve the intent of the legislature. The Supreme Court has stated:

> There is, of course, no more persuasive evidence of a statute than the words by which the legislature under-took to give expression to its wishes. Often these words are sufficient in and of themselves to determine the purpose of the legislation. In such cases we have followed their plain meaning. When that meaning has led to absurd or futile results, however, this court has looked beyond the words to the purpose of the act. Frequently, however, even when the plain meaning did not produce absurd results but merely an unreasonable one "plainly at variance with the policy of the legislation as a whole" this Court has followed the purpose, rather than the literal words.[13]

As the foregoing statement clearly illustrates, the U.S. courts will normally seek to determine the legislative intent for a specific statute in order to determine whether the statute's plain meaning is unreasonable. In seeking to identify the legislative intent for a particular Code section, the courts will normally examine reports from the House Ways and Means Committee, the Senate Finance Committee and the Conference Committee. They may also examine an explanation of the statute drafted by the staff of Joint Committee on Taxation, records of hearings and analyses by commentators, although they will normally accord less weight to these sources.

Although the inclusion of the word "Code" in the name "Internal Revenue Code" implies a self-contained, systematic statutory treatment of the tax laws, the courts have developed many common law principles that aid their efforts to apply tax provisions. In general, the courts will narrowly interpret exclusions from gross income. That

---

13. United States v. American Trucking Ass'n, 310 U.S. 534, 543 (1945).

is, an item (other than imputed income) is generally excluded from gross income only where an express statute authorizes such exclusion. Similarly, the courts view deductions as a matter of legislative grace and, therefore, do not allow deductions unless permitted by statute and interpret the statute allowing such deductions narrowly.

The courts have also created several requirements that are not in the statute. In order for a transaction to be given effect for tax purposes, the courts may require that transaction have been entered into for nontax purposes. For example, the courts will ignore an entity's existence when it was not formed for a business purpose and has no business activity. See e.g., Moline Properties Inc., v. Commissioner, 319 U.S. 436, 438-439 (1943).

Similarly, the courts will seek to identify the substance of a transaction in order to apply the tax laws. They will not blindly follow the form cast by the taxpayer. For example, even though the taxpayer may have drafted a financial instrument in the legal form of debt, the courts will treat it as equity if the taxpayer fails to respect the formalities of debt such as prompt payment of interest and principal. Moreover, rather then accepting a transaction as a sale or lease because it has such formal legal structure, the courts will analyze whether the burdens and benefits of ownership have shifted. Lastly, the courts may combine several steps into a single transaction where it appears that the taxpayer intended a single transaction. Under the "step transaction" approach, for example, if a taxpayer sells stock shortly after having acquired it in a tax-free corporate acquisition, the court will treat the taxpayer as though he received cash in the transaction rather than stock if the court determines that the taxpayer, at the time of the reorganization, already possessed an intent to sell the stock.

The approach of the courts to statutory interpretation in the tax area, which is marked by some special features, is of course also affected by general judicial trends. Currently, a vocal minority on the Supreme Court has been urging more limitations on the use of extra-statutory material in statutory interpretation. Such an approach, if adopted by the majority, would have a significant effect in the tax field where the courts routinely consult legislative history.

9. Administrative, taxpayer and judicial style

9.1 Administrative style

The U.S. tax system is a self assessing system that is backed up with extensive informational reporting and withholding. For example, most employers who pay wages must file with the IRS the amounts paid to each of their employees and are also required to withhold income taxes. The bulk of individual income taxes collected by the U.S. are through employer withholding. In 1995, for example, approximately 79 % of individual income taxes were collected from withholding.[14] There are also reporting requirements for persons who employ independent contractors in the course of their business and for persons receiving more than $10,000 of cash and for most forms of capital income, including gains on sale of investment assets.

In comparison to other countries, the audit level in the United States is extremely low. In 1995, the U.S. audited 1.67 % of individual income tax returns.[15] For individuals with income over $100,000, the audit rate was 2.79 %.[16] For individuals with business income over $100,000, the audit rate was 3.47 %.[17]

In 1995, the U.S. audited 2.05 % of all corporate tax returns.[18] The audit rate for large corporations, however, was significantly higher. The audit rate for corporations in 1995 with assets between 10 million dollars and 50 million dollars was 19.79 %.[19] For corporations with assets of 250 million dollars or more, the audit rate was 51.77 %.

To discourage taxpayers from playing the "audit lottery" resulting from low audit rules, Congress has increased substantially the interest rates on tax deficiencies and introduced a set of "accuracy related" penalties. These latter rules apply, for example, if the taxpayer fails to

---

14. See Internal Revenue Service, 1995 Data Book Table 1 (1996) (noting 49.1 percent of all receipts by the U.S. in 1995 was from the individual income tax and that 38.8 percent of all receipts was from the individual income tax that had been withheld by employers).

15. GAO, Tax Administration Audit Trends And Results For Individual Taxpayers, Table I.1 (April 26, 1996).

16. Id. at Table I.4.

17. Id.

18. I.R.S., 1995 Data Book, Table 11 (1996).

19. Id.

include on his return an item which has been reported to him on an information return. In addition, increasingly sophisticated use of computer checking of information returns reduce the audit lottery odds.

Perhaps because of the self-assessing nature of the U.S. income tax, the Internal Revenue Service has tended in recent years to provide very detailed regulations. In addition, the Service publishes "revenue rulings" that are similar to memoranda of law addressing various issues not resolved in the regulations and setting forth the government position. Taxpayers seeking additional advice may request the Service to issue a private ruling to the taxpayer stating how the law will be applied in a situation which the taxpayer has presented to the Service.

9.2 Taxpayer style

Taxpayers in the U.S., both corporate and individual, tend to be aggressive in interpreting the law to their advantage. The high water mark in aggressive tax planning was probably reached in the late 1970s and 1980s with an explosion of "tax shelter" investments. The shelters were typically based on financing for which the taxpayer had no personal liability and took advantage of accelerated deduction provisions. With overly-optimistic valuations of the assets involved, the worst of the shelters were often essentially paper transactions which generated tax deductions and nothing else. The Congressional response was to raise the standard for avoiding penalties and the interest rate assessed on tax deficiencies. Congress retained the threshold standard which requires the taxpayer to establish that there is "reasonable basis" for the taxpayer's position to avoid penalties. However, for substantial underpayments of tax, Congress added the requirement that the taxpayer can only avoid penalties if he shows that "substantial authority" existed for the position. The regulations state that the "substantial authority" standard is less stringent then a 50 % probability of success standard but more stringent than the "reasonable basis" standard.

These relatively low thresholds, coupled with the low audit rate, may still encourage, or at least not adequately discourage, many taxpayers to adopt a "frontier" attitude in seeking to minimize tax liability. It is estimated that in 1992 individuals paid approximately 83.1 to 83.6 % of taxes actually owed, while corporations paid approximately 81.1 to 88.1 % of their actual tax liabilities.[20]

---

20. Joint Committee on Taxation, supra note 1, at Table E-2.

9.3. Judicial structure and style

The United States has no specialized system of courts which hears only tax cases. One court of first instance, the Tax Court, is specialized in tax matters and has jurisdiction if the taxpayer resists the payment of a tax asserted by the Internal Revenue Service. Alternatively, the taxpayer can pay the tax asserted and sue for a refund, either in the Federal District Court or in the Claims Court, a special court which handles other claims against the government. The taxpayer may request that a jury be the finder of facts in the Federal District Court but is limited to a judge as the fact finder in the Tax Court or Claims Court. Decisions from the Federal District Court and Tax Courts may be appealed to the Court of Appeals for the circuit in which the taxpayer resides. Decisions from the Claims Court may be appealed to the Court of Appeals for the Federal Circuit. Thus, the taxpayer has a number of judicial options in contesting his tax liability and this structure creates a certain amount of "forum shopping."

All decisions may then be reviewed by the Supreme Court, though there is generally no right to review. In the event that the Courts of Appeals reach differing results on the same issue, the Supreme Court will usually agree to hear a case which will resolve the issue.

Judicial decisions are issued in the form of full opinions which set forth the relevant facts and apply the law to those facts. Because cases are relied on by courts as precedent in deciding future cases, the judges are usually careful to set forth their reasoning in full.

Despite the extensive statutory material in the United States system, the courts have been responsible for a significant part of the doctrinal development in the tax area. In some cases, case law based principles have subsequently been taken over in the statute. In others, the case law remains the primary source of law. For example, the determination of the taxpayer to whom income should be attributed is almost entirely based on case law. In addition, the case law principles of statutory interpretation discussed above have had an important influence on the development of the law.

10. Relationship of tax and financial accounting

In general, tax accounting is totally distinct from financial accounting. While financial accounting in general seeks to recognize expenses as soon as possible and postpone the recognition of income as long as possible, tax accounting seeks, broadly speaking, exactly the opposite. That is, tax accounting seeks generally to recognize income as soon as it is reasonable to expect the taxpayer to pay tax but to only recognize expenses to the extent they can be matched to the recognized income.

For example, taxpayers who receive a cash payment before they have earned it by performing services or delivering property are generally required to include the payment income regardless of whether they use the cash or accrual method of accounting. Moreover, even though an accrual method taxpayer has a fixed liability which would normally justify a current deduction, the taxpayer may frequently not recognize the expense until it is actually paid. Similarly, while financial accounting principles require the establishment of reserves for estimated expenses that relate to current income, tax accounting does not generally permit such reserves.

Like financial accounting, tax accounting employs an annual accounting period which has been interpreted fairly strictly by the courts. Events which occur after the close of the year will not in general affect the tax treatment in the earlier year. Nonetheless, taxpayers are allowed a deduction for items that they have included in income and are subsequently required to return. Moreover, in certain situations, the taxpayer may, in lieu of a deduction, be able to reduce current tax liability by the amount of taxes paid in the prior year attributable to the inclusion of the item in income. In the converse situation, taxpayers who have deducted as an expense an expenditure that is subsequently refunded must recognize income to the extent the earlier deduction resulted in a tax saving. Expenses incurred in a trade or business that exceed business income may be carried back 3 years and forward 15 years.

11. Anti-avoidance legislation

As discussed earlier in the section on statutory interpretation, the courts have created several common law doctrines to curtail taxpayer avoidance activities. As a result, Congress has not adopted broad anti-avoidance statutes.

In narrow contexts, Congress has either adopted anti-avoidance legislation or expressly authorized the IRS to adopt anti-avoidance regulations. In Section 269, Congress sought to prevent a corporation that has acquired another corporation from deducting expenses or claiming credits with respect to the acquired corporation where "the principal purpose for which such acquisition is made is evasion or avoidance of Federal income tax by securing the benefit of a deduction, credit or other allowance...." In 1993, Congress also adopted § 7701(l) which authorizes the Secretary to "prescribe regulations recharacterizing any multiple-party financing transaction as a transaction directly among any two or more of such parties when the Secretary determines that such recharacterization is appropriate to present avoidance of any tax by this title." Pursuant to this statute, the IRS has promulgated regulations which allow it to treat an entity as a conduit if a principal purpose for using the entity in the transaction was to avoid the U.S. income tax on income of foreign corporations which is not effectively connected with a U.S. trade or business. See Treas. Reg. § 1.881-3(b)(1).

As discussed earlier, the courts will recharacterize a business transaction if it lacks a business purpose. Recently, the IRS has sought through regulations to change the business purpose test as applied to partnership transactions. Treas. Reg. § 1.704-2 seeks to raise the standard from merely requiring the presence of a business purpose to requiring the presence of a substantial business purpose. It is not clear that the IRS has the regulatory authority to elevate the standard in this context without a directive from Congress.

12. Future developments

Over the past twenty years there have been various proposals to change significantly both the corporate and individual income taxes. The most significant proposals for the corporate tax have been to eliminate the double tax on corporate income through some form of integration. To date, Congress has not adopted these proposals in part because of concerns about the revenue loss from integration. In addition, given the uncertainty as to the economic incidence of the corporate tax, it is unclear which groups of taxpayers would in fact benefit from integration.

There have been a number of proposals for change in the income tax. They range from some adjustments in the tax rate and tax base to the complete replacement of the income tax with some sort of consumption tax. In the recent Presidential campaign, substantial attention was given to "flat tax" proposals which established a single flat tax rate and denied most deductions. Though not described as such, the proposals were variations on a subtraction-method value added tax. They effectively exempted income from capital while providing some degree of progressivity in the remaining wage income base by allowing a substantial exemption amount.

Others have argued more explicitly for the replacement of the current income tax with a consumption tax, usually in the form of a "cash flow" tax. However, to date concern about the potentially regressive nature of such a tax and the complexity of making the transition from an income tax to a tax focused on consumption have prevented the proposals from generating much political support. Nonetheless, the question of fundamental changes in the tax system has attracted increasing attention in the last several years and will undoubtedly remain on the policy agenda.

The following **Table I** summarizes some of the important features of the various country systems described in Part One. It is necessarily general and involves a certain amount of arbitrariness in the various classifications or descriptions.. For example, while the United States system is classified as a "global" system, it has many important schedular features and, indeed, one important recent development is the increasing use of a schedular approach. Nonetheless, in comparison with the other systems considered here, it seems appropriate to treat the U.S. system as fundamentally global. Similar qualifications can be made about many of the other classifications.

Overview of some basic structural features

	Individual rate structure	Global/ Schedular	Private capital gains	Business capital gains	Impact of financial accounting on tax rules	Taxable unit	Corporate tax structure	Realization events[1]
Australia	20-47% (max. rate at ca. $38,000)	global	full tax (with indexation)	full tax (with indexation)	limited	individual	full imputation	S, G, E
Canada	(17-49% incl. provincial) (max. rate at ca. $45,000)	global with minor schedular features	pref. rate	pref. rate	limited	individual	partial imputation	S, G, D, E, W
France	12-56.8% (max. rate at ca. $56,000 = one family share)	modified schedular	pref. rate (with many exemptions)	pref. rate	strong	fiscal house-hold	full imputation	S, W
Germany	25.9-53% (max. rate at ca. $85,000)	modified schedular	generally exempt (substantial participation taxed at pref. rates)	full tax (pref. rate on sale of business)	very strong	joint (full income splitting)	imputa-tion/split rate (full relief)	S,W
Japan	10-50% (max. rate at ca. $280,000) (some schedular aspects)	schedular	pref. rate	full tax for corp; pref. rate for indiv.	strong	individual	very limited integration	S

1. S=Sale; W=withdrawal from business; E=Emigration; G=gift; D=death

Overview of some basic structural features

	Individual rate structure	Global/ Schedular	Private capital gains	Business capital gains	Impact of financial accounting on tax rules	Taxable unit	Corporate tax structure	Realization events[1]
The Netherlands	37.5-60% (max. rate at ca. $56,000)	schedular	generally exempt (substantial. interest taxed at pref. rates)	full tax (substantial. participation exempt for corps.)	limited	individual (some exceptions)	classical	S,W,G,D (some exceptions)
Sweden	schedular: capital inc. 30%; bus/ employ. 31-56% (max. rate at ca. $32,000)	schedular	full tax (cap. inc. rate)	full tax	moderate	individual	classical	S,W
United Kingdom	20-40% (max. rate at ca. $38,000)	schedular	full tax (with indexation)	full tax (with indexation)	limited	individual	partial imputation	S,G
United States	15-39.6% (max. rate at ca. $270,000)	global	pref. rate for high bracket indiv.	pref. rate for high bracket indiv.; full tax for corp.	limited	joint (elective)	classical	S

1. S=Sale; W=withdrawal from business; E=Emigration; G=gift; D=death

Part Two: Basic Income Taxation

Subpart A: Inclusions in the tax base

The determination of the items to be included in the tax base is a central question in all income tax systems. A global system typically has a single, comprehensive concept of income, often based on an economic notion of income,[1] and a single rate structure. In contrast, a schedular system focuses on particular classes or categories of receipts and often has different rates and different substantive and procedural rules for each class.

In practice, the distinction between the two approaches is invariably blurred. Nominally global systems may have schedular elements, particularly with respect to limitations on the ability to use deductions incurred in one type of activity against income from another type of activity. In addition, even with the most extensive statutory definition of income, the system must deal with the classification of "borderline" items in terms of the basic income definition. Similarly, nominally schedular systems may have a global character in practice. Often income or losses from particular categories are combined in the final income calculations. There is frequently a catchall "other" category of income which captures any additional items that the system wishes to tax. In other cases, the elastic interpretation of the various categories approaches that of a global system. Still, at the margin, the inclusion of particular items in the tax base is influenced to some extent by the basic underlying approach to tax base definition. As the materials in Part One have shown, the countries here under consideration vary substantially in their formal definitions of income.

The *United States* has the most extensive statutory definition of income, essentially a tautological statement that income is income "from whatever source" and then a nonexclusive list containing the

---

1. The most frequently used economic reference point in global tax systems is the tax base composed of consumption and net accretion in wealth over a period, a concept associated in the Anglo-Saxon literature with Haig and Simons and in the Continental context with Schanz and Davidson.

most commonly occurring items. Specific items which would otherwise fall within the broad definition are expressly excluded. The *Australian* system, as well, has a global income approach but, influenced by trust concepts, the judicially developed concept was not extended to capital gains, which required separate legislation.

In contrast, the *United Kingdom* definition is based on a number of categories or Schedules (sometimes subdivided into Cases) and to be taxable, a particular item must fall within one of the Schedules. The Schedules have evolved historically and are in no sense "scientific," either in content or in organization. Some Schedules have broad coverage, for example, profits of a trade, and others are very narrow, income from foreign securities. Where income falls into a particular Schedule, the rules of that category must be applied, which affects both the method of computation and the ability to offset losses in one category against income in another category.

The existence of the Schedules has also influenced other aspects of the system. Conceptually, each Schedule is viewed as a separate "source." Correspondingly, if a receipt has no taxable source, it cannot be included in income. In addition, the disposition of a "source" is not itself treated as an item of income, thus leading to the necessity of special rules to capture such receipts as capital gains.

The *Canadian* system, influenced historically by the United Kingdom and the United States, has a global definition of income based on the source concept. Only amounts that have a source constitute income subject to tax. The principal sources of income - business, property, and employment - are specifically mentioned in the statutory definition of income. Like the United Kingdom and Australia, special legislation was required to extend taxation to capital gains, but unlike the United Kingdom, losses from various sources can, in general, offset income from other sources. In addition, the statute has been amended to include in income most amounts lacking a source. Consequently, the source basis of taxation is of relatively minor significance.

The *Swedish* system, though growing out of a different tradition, also distinguishes between income from employment, business, and capital. The *Dutch* system likewise separates employment, business, and investment categories, with an additional category for periodic income. The *German* system provides in the statutory structure for seven income categories, with two basic methods of income calculation applicable to the various categories. Capital gains realized outside of business generally do not fall into any taxable category and thus are not taxed, though there are exceptions. The French system has similar statutorily delimited categories, though the extent of capital gains taxation is broader.

In *Japan*, the approach to income definition is an intermediate one and reflects both the prewar European schedular tradition and the postwar American global view. While income is divided into several categories in accordance with a schedular approach, capital gains on nonbusiness assets are subject to tax and a broad category of "Miscellaneous" income gives the system a global character.

Despite these differences in starting point, however, there is more similarity in results than the formal definitions would suggest. The following material analyzes the treatment of a number of specific items in the determination of the tax base in each country. Subpart B will consider deduction issues.

1. Employee fringe benefits

1.1 General

The issue of the appropriate treatment of employee fringe benefits arises in a similar fashion in both schedular and global systems. The inclusion of fringe benefits in the tax base is necessary both in terms of horizontal equity and in order to prevent the erosion of the cash compensation base. A number of structural issues, however, are involved in the taxation of fringe benefits. In the first place, there is the question of whether the employee can be said to have obtained a personal or consumption benefit from the item in question or whether it is simply part of the "working conditions" of his employment. Even where some nonwork-related personal benefit is clearly present, there is an important issue of valuation. Often the employee does not have a choice as to whether or not to accept the benefit and including the full market value in income may be an inappropriate measure. From an administrative point of view, ensuring that the item is in fact included in the employee's tax base can be difficult, particularly in the case of small amounts or benefits which are shared among many employees. Similarly, where wage income is subject to withholding at source, the inclusion of fringe benefits provided in kind can be a problem. Finally, some categories of fringe benefit may be expressly excluded from the tax base for extra-fiscal reasons.

The systems here under consideration show a wide range of responses to the taxation of fringe benefits. They include the outright exclusion of some significant benefits, some arbitrary "standard" values used for employee inclusion of specific benefits, valuations which clearly undervalue the benefits, denial or limitation of the employer's deduction for benefits which are not included by the employee, and finally, a separate employer-level fringe benefits tax which in effect includes the value of the benefit in the employer's tax base in lieu of taxing the employee. To some extent, exclusions apparently reflect differing societal views on what is appropriately viewed as a nontaxable working condition, for example, a free glass of beer in Germany and Australia (provided it is consumed on the employer's premises) and free coffee in Sweden. More generally, they differ in the extent to which a real attempt is made to tax the economic benefit accruing to employees.

In the *United States* system, detailed statutory provisions deal with fringe benefits. The principal rules, enacted in 1984, supplanted administrative practice which was increasingly unable to deal with the proliferation of fringe benefit programs. The statutory pattern establishes a general rule that fringe benefits are taxable but then creates a number of exceptions. Under the "working condition fringe" exception, an employer-provided benefit is not taxable if the expense would have been deductible if incurred directly by the employee. In addition, de minimis amounts of fringe benefits are excluded. In a concession to the transportation industry, "no additional cost" services are not taxed, thus allowing that form of compensation to be given to transportation employees on a tax-free basis. Employer discounts are also excluded, subject to some limitations. Exclusion is also available, usually subject to dollar limitations, for certain employer-provided transportation, reimbursed moving expenses, daycare programs, educational assistance, group life insurance, and meals and lodging in certain situations. One of the most important nontaxable fringe benefits from an economic point of view is employer-funded medical care. Medical benefits provided directly or under insurance financed plans are not taxable. The ability to obtain medical care on a before-tax basis has been identified as one of the factors affecting the escalation of medical care costs.

Where fringe benefits are taxable, they are in principle taxed at fair market value. The employee's "subjective perception" of the value of the benefit is not relevant. Detailed regulations establish the values of employer-provided automobiles and aircraft. A statutory provision requires the taxation of employer-provided parking to the extent that the value of the parking exceeds $155 per month.

In *Germany*, the employment income category in principle includes all "benefits" which are received by the employee to the extent they can be determined to have a cash value. The theoretical justification for the inclusion is based on both the notion that the benefit results in an increased "ability to pay" and that the employee has been saved an expense which he would have otherwise incurred. The fact that the benefit cannot be converted to cash is not relevant. There is a de minimis rule which excludes from income up to ca. $35 per month of otherwise taxable benefits other than company cars or special employer discounts. If the $35 amount is exceeded the entire amount is taxable.

There is a long statutory catalogue of items that are not taxed for what are perceived to be social policy reasons including cash payments within certain limits on the occasion of the employee's wedding, birth of a child, anniversary of commencing work, anniversary of the founding of the firm, and extra pay for overtime work on Sundays, holidays, or at night. In addition, exemption is granted for employer discounts up to certain amounts, employer-provided daycare and employer-provided passes for public transportation between home and workplace.

There are also a number of case law-based exceptions which focus on the benefit to the employer of a happy work-force (firm outings, "occasional" gifts, free beer) but seem to ignore the parallel benefit to the employee. Recent cases have tended to reduce the scope of the case law exceptions and find the statutory exemptions as exclusive.

Benefits are, in principle, valued at retail market value. There are, however, standard value tables for meals and lodging, and other benefits which apply unless there are unusual circumstances, e.g., a luxury apartment provided to an executive. They generally undervalue the benefits. In the case of employer-provided cars, the employee may choose between a standard value method or an "exact" method. The standard value method is based on the list price of the car and requires a percentage of that value to be included in income. Alternatively, the employee can use the "exact" method based on actual costs and a driving record establishing private and business-related driving. Employer-provided parking is not taxable unless the employee would otherwise have had to pay a parking fee at the lot.

Special "lump sum" rules apply at the employer level with respect to certain fringe benefits. In effect, these rules make the employer-level tax the final tax on the benefit; it is not included in the employee's assessable income. The rules also provide a lower rate of tax on certain benefits for policy reasons. Thus employer payments to provide certain retirement annuities and insurance for an employee are taxed at a flat 20 % rate at the employer level.

In *Sweden*, in principle all benefits which fall into the category of income from employment are taxable. However, no attempt is made to tax employee benefits like free coffee, sport training facilities, and the like. The justification is principally one of administrability. Where benefits are taxable, valuation in principle should be done on the basis of fair market value. In special cases, where the employee's ability to choose the benefit is restricted, a lower value may be used if the benefit could not be exchanged for money and the employee presumably would not have purchased it himself.

Standard values are used for meals and cars, the two most often provided fringe benefits. For meals, average restaurant prices for "normal" meals are calculated periodically and that valuation is generally controlling. For employer-provided cars, a taxable standardized amount is calculated based on an presumed personal use of 15,000 km. per year. The excess is assumed to be business use. Only in very unusual circumstances can this presumption be overturned by showing a greater use in business in relation to the total use. The rule has been criticized from an environmental point of view in that it, in effect, establishes a zero marginal cost for additional personal driving.

Another item which is treated specially is employer-provided health care. Sweden has an extensive public health care system which involves long waits for certain kinds of services. If the employer pays the costs of private care, the amount is not deductible to the employer but is not taxed to the employee. The tax rate of the (corporate) employer is usually lower than the employee rate (and the employer does not bear the burden of social security contributions) and thus an incentive is provided for this kind of benefit. A partial justification is the advantage to the employer of getting the employee back to work sooner.

In *The Netherlands*, most fringe benefits are included in income. Valuation is based on resale value or, if it is not possible or usual to sell the benefit received, the amount which the employee is assumed to have saved because of the employer benefit. In the case of employer-provided housing, a fair market rental must be established. Special— and generally realistic— rules apply to, inter alia, meals, low-interest loans, stock options, and transportation provided by the employer. Cars provided by the employer and also used privately are taxed to the employee at 20 % or 24 % of the car's list price (depending, among other things, on the distance between home and office).

The *French* system generally includes benefits at retail value but there are several exceptions and special rules which result in undervaluation, especially in connection with meals and lodging. If the employee's income is below a certain level, the value is determined by multiplying the minimum hourly wage by certain coefficients. If the wages exceed the threshold, in principle fair market value should control but in practice a higher coefficient is used for food and, in the case of lodging, the value used for a separately imposed "housing tax" is applicable which is not in fact related to fair market value. A special valuation rule applies to employer-provided cars based on the amount of horse power and the number of kilometers driven.

Canada has a broad statutory provision which taxes "benefits of any kind" received by an employee but there are number of benefits which are excluded by statute (health benefits, group term life insurance) or by administrative decision (merchandise discounts, subsidized meals where the employee pays cost, recreational facilities). Courts have also held that reimbursement of moving expenses, of the loss on the sale of a house and even increased mortgage expenses arising in connection with a move are not required to be included in income. Free parking spaces have generally not been considered to be a taxable benefit except in metropolitan areas where parking is expensive. Complex rules attempt to value employer-provided automobiles. In general, it is difficult to find any consistent strand in either the administrative practice or the jurisprudence.

In *Japan*, while all benefits are in principle taxable, there are a number of administratively sanctioned exemptions which include gifts related to years of service or the anniversary of the company, discount sales of employer goods and services, as well as meals and housing provided at below-market rates to employees.

The *United Kingdom* initially had difficulty in taxing fringe benefits because of a court-developed principle that benefits could only be taxed to the extent that they could be reduced to cash. This led to a widespread use of fringe benefits which could not be resold or where real or nominal restrictions reduced or eliminated the resale value. In response, a special statutory regime was introduced which was applicable to employees with incomes over a certain level (ca. $13,000). The income level was originally set to cover only higher paid employees but has not been increased for inflation thus expanding the coverage of the statutory rules. The rules apply to a wide range of benefits. However, the benefits are generally valued at the marginal cost to the employer, which allows substantial value to be derived free from tax by the employee. A standard value approach is used for company cars and other commonly recurring situations. Free parking is expressly excluded from taxation. The court-developed principles remain applicable outside of the statutory regime and continue to limit inclusion of such benefits to their cash conversion value, i.e. the resale price for employer-provided goods.

While the contours of the rules differ, most of the systems described above allow substantial amounts of employment income in the form of fringe benefits to escape tax because of the administrative and valuation problems which such benefits entail. *Australia* has taken a different approach to the treatment of fringe benefits. In general terms, rather than attempting to value the benefit and collect the tax at the employee level, Australia in 1986 introduced a separate employer-level tax on fringe benefits while excluding such benefits from the employee's tax base.

Apart from the technical aspects referred to below, the decision to impose a fringe benefits tax was very much a political one. The tax was introduced by a labor (centrist-socialist) government whose constituency was to a large extent based in the trade union movement. Because of defects in the system of trying to tax fringe benefits at the employee level, untaxed or low-taxed fringe benefits had become widespread among all classes of employees and had been at least in part capitalized into wage rates. If the income tax had been imposed on employees, there would have been an immediate reduction in after-tax wages while the levy of the tax on the employer meant that the initial incidence of the tax in most cases fell on the employer. This resulted largely from the fact that wage rates in Australia are set out in officially approved awards and can only be changed by elaborate procedures. After enactment, the burden of the tax has gradually been shifted through the bargaining process.

From a technical point of view, the fringe benefits tax (FBT) was introduced primarily because of the perceived administrative difficulties of assessing and collecting the tax at the employee level. In addition, imposing the tax at the employer level allowed the tax in principle to be collected without the allocation of the value of the total benefit to individual employees, one of the major administrative difficulties in the case of shared benefits.[2] The basic issue of the valuation of the total amount of the benefit, of course, remains though the level of the inquiry is shifted to the employer. There the legislation sets up a variety of valuation rules which roughly parallel the types of rules used in the income tax system in other countries. However, since the tax was completely new, more attention was given to details and to the logical structure of the rules than is usually the case for the gradually evolving rules trying to tax employees. On the other hand, commonly recurring items like employer-provided parking have continued to be a problem in the fringe benefit tax and complicated and arbitrary valuation rules have been required.

The use of a separate tax to deal with fringe benefits, while it has administrative advantages, raises its own set of problems. There are a number of issues involved in the interaction between the FBT and the income tax. In the first place, while the income tax is imposed on a "tax inclusive" basis, the fringe benefits tax is in effect "tax exclusive" since the tax itself is not generally included as part of the fringe benefit tax base. That is, if the tax inclusive income tax rate is 25 %, the fringe benefit tax must be set at 33 % to impose a corresponding tax burden. This difference in rates detracts from the "transparency" of the tax and its relation to the income tax.

In addition, if the rate of the fringe benefit tax (as appropriately adjusted) is set at below the maximum individual rate, there will be an advantage for fringe benefits to highly compensated employees who would be taxed at a higher rate under the income tax. On the other hand, using the maximum individual rate indirectly overtaxes other employees. Australia initially imposed the FBT at the highest individual level at a time when that rate and corporate rates were the same.

---

2. In fact, the Australian system requires the allocation of benefits to employees in many situations, for example, in order to apply a fixed exemption level which is allowed for each employee. However, the possibility in principle of avoiding an allocation of benefits is present in the fringe benefit tax approach.

The amount of the fringe benefit was deductible for income tax purposes but the FBT itself was not deductible (thus in effect making the FBT "tax inclusive" when the rates were the same). As a result, for a taxable employer, the after-tax cost of providing a fringe benefit subject to the FBT but not taxed to the employee was the same as a fully deductible cash payment taxed at the employee level.[3] When tax-exempt employers are involved, however, or when, as was subsequently the case in Australia, the corporate rate is lower than the highest individual rate, this equivalence is not maintained and there is an advantage in the provision of fringe benefits in comparison to taxable compensation.[4] This was especially a concern in connection with the tax exempt sector. The response to this problem in Australia was to require the employer in most cases to "gross up" the amount of the fringe benefit by the FBT rate, while allowing a deduction for both the benefit and FBT itself for income tax purposes. This approach makes the employer tax rate (or tax exempt status) irrelevant in the comparison of the cost of compensation in the form of cash or fringe benefits.[5]

Another problem involves the treatment of fringe benefits which would be deductible by the employee if paid directly. Since the FBT taxation takes place at the employer level, there is no way to "wash" the employee inclusion and deduction as would normally be the case with employee-level taxation. Here an exception to the fringe benefits tax, the "otherwise deductible" rule, was created which exempted from the FBT the value of fringe benefits which would have been deductible if paid for directly by the employee. Thus in the case of, for example, a company car which is used for both business and personal travel, the same sort of allocation must be made in the context of the fringe benefits tax as is required in the case of benefits taxable at the employee

---

3. Assume a corporate, individual, and FBT rate of 40 %. A deductible cash payment of 100 of salary will have a before-tax cost of 100 and an after-tax cost of 60 to the employer and an after-tax benefit of 60 to the employee. If 60 of fringe benefit is substituted, the employer-level FBT will be 24 but since that amount is nondeductible, it requires 40 of pretax income $(24/1\text{-}0.4)$ to fund the payment, on which 16 of income tax will be due for a total before-tax cost of 100 and after-tax cost of 60 providing the employee with 60 of after-tax benefit.

4. If in the prior example, the corporate rate was 30%, the total cost of providing 60 of fringe benefit to the employee would be 60 + 24 + 10.3 or 94.3. The cost of providing 60 of after-tax cash compensation would remain 100, thus favoring the use of fringe benefits.

5. The cost of providing 60 of fringe benefit would be 60 of benefit and 40 of fringe benefit tax $(60/1\text{-}.4) \times 40\ \%)$ or 100, the same as the cost of 60 of after-tax cash compensation. In New Zealand, the same result was achieved by grossing up the FBT rate itself (in relation to the top individual marginal rate) rather than the FBT tax base.

level. Under the fringe benefits tax, the business use can be established by a travel log or through a statutory formula which applies a percentage to the cost of the car depending on the number of miles driven. While the "otherwise deductible" approach solved the "wash" problem, it reintroduced the question of allocation of benefits since, to determine if the amount would be "otherwise deductible," it must be allocated to a particular employee (or class of employees) to know if an employee-level deduction would have been available.

There are other difficulties with having two parallel systems for dealing with normal compensation in the income tax and fringe benefits in a separate tax. There are borderline classification issues between normal compensation taxable to the employee and fringe benefits taxed at the employer level which have complicated the administration of the system. Eliminating the fringe benefit from employee taxation creates problems with means-tested benefits and other programs which are based on taxable income. It is not simple to adapt fringe benefit taxation to international tax and treaties relationships. On the whole, the introduction of the fringe benefits tax in Australia has improved the tax treatment of such benefits. Nonetheless, some feel that if as much legislative and administrative effort had been put into improving the income tax treatment of fringe benefits as went into the construction of the new tax, the overall results would have been even better.

1.2 Employer-provided pension benefits

Employer-sponsored pension or retirement plans are fringe benefits which frequently receive special tax treatment. The importance of the privately-based pension plans is directly related to the extent to which public or quasi-public retirement arrangements exist. While the details of the provisions vary, they typically allow a current deduction to the employer for amounts set aside for employee retirement payments to be made in the future with no current tax to the employee. In some cases, the amounts must be transferred to a separate fund or trust while in others they simply represent a liability of the employer. Where the contributions are set aside in a special trust, the earnings accumulated prior to distribution are often not taxed.

In the *United States*, there is an extensive system of employer-provided pensions plans which cover nearly one half of the full time workers and supplement the somewhat limited public social security benefits. There are extensive and complex rules governing the "qualification" of the plan, including requirements dealing with funding, nondiscriminatory coverage, limitations on contributions and benefits, and the "vesting" of employee rights. From a structural point of view, the plan utilizes a trust to which both employer and employee contributions are made. The plans take basically two forms, a "defined benefit" plan and a "defined contribution" plan. Under a defined benefit plan, the employee is entitled to specific benefits on retirement, typically tied to the period of service and level of compensation. The employer makes whatever contributions are actuarially required to fund the anticipated payments. In a defined contribution plan, a specified percentage of the employee's salary is contributed to the plan and the benefit is whatever the accumulated fund will generate.

From a tax point of view, employer contributions are currently deductible but are not currently included in the employee's income. Similarly, employee contributions, when present, are currently deductible. Both employer and employee contributions are subject to absolute and percentage limitations. Employees can also make nondeductible after-tax contributions to the plan. The earnings of the qualified plan are not subject to tax in the hands of the trust and the distributions when made are fully taxable to the employee. A special rule imposes an additional 10% tax if withdrawals are made before reaching the age of 59 1/2 thus trying to ensure that the tax-preferred savings are really being used for retirement. Similarly, benefits have to begin at age 70 1/2. Rollover provisions are broadly available on change of employment.

There are a number of other tax-favored mechanisms related to employees' retirement income. So-called "cash or deferred" plans allow employees to make their own contributions in lieu of current cash salary to plans subject to generally the same rules and restrictions as qualified plans. In addition, certain specially-favored qualified plans ("Employee Stock Ownership Plans") are allowed to make investments in the stock of the employer corporation and give the employees the right to receive the stock on retirement.

The overall economic impact of qualified plans in the U.S. is substantial, accounting for over $62 billion in lost revenues in 1996.

Employee pension plans are the most important source of retirement income in *Canada*. The government-provided pensions - Canada (or Quebec) Pension Plan, to which all employees must contribute, and Old Age Security - are relatively modest. Payroll taxes, which consist primarily of Canada and Quebec Pension Plan contributions, unemployment insurance premiums, and workers' compensation, represented about 5 % of GDP in 1995.

To qualify for tax benefits, employee pension plans must be registered with the tax authorities and registration is permitted only if various conditions are met. In addition, pension plans must meet several conditions imposed by provincial law. Legally, the plans are trusts. Registered plans must be either money purchase plans or defined benefit plans. There are limits on the contributions by both employers and employees which are related to the maximum pension benefit that can be received by an individual. In addition, the limits are integrated with the limits on contributions to private retirement savings plans.

Both employer and employee contributions to registered pension plans are tax deductible within limits. In addition, income earned by the plan is not taxable. There are restrictions on the investments that can be made by registered pension plans. For example, no more than 20 percent of a plan's assets can be invested in foreign property. Amounts are taxable when withdrawn from the plan.

The situation in *Japan* is somewhat different. Although initially employer pensions were uncommon, beginning in the late 1950's it became more usual for employers to provide for employees' pensions, typically by paying premiums to a bank or insurance company which undertakes to pay the retirement income. The premiums are currently deductible by the employer, and, if the plan is qualified, are not currently taxed to the employee who is only taxed on the pension when paid. However, the pension reserves are subject to a special corporate tax in the hands of the company providing the benefit to compensate for the fact that the premium is currently deductible by the employer and not included currently by the employee.

In *Sweden*, employer deduction is available for future pension costs either through a deductible reserve against profits, a transfer to qualified pension fund or the purchase of pension insurance. The deduction is limited to those amounts required by a general pension plan negotiated with a union or similar association (Sweden has a highly organized and centralized union structure) or amounts of similar magnitude if there is no actual union plan. In addition, there are limits on the absolute amounts which can be deducted currently. The amounts are not taxed currently to the employees.

In *The Netherlands* an employer may deduct as a business expense pension premiums paid to an insurance company or to a pension fund that operates for an entire industry or branch of business activities. Alternatively, the employer may create, but not control, a special pension fund for the business which meets certain statutory requirements and can deduct contributions to the fund. The employer may also deduct an addition to a pension reserve in certain circumstances where the legal right to the pension has not yet vested in the employee though the employer has expressed an intention of granting a pension on retirement.

The employee's right to future benefits is treated as postponed wage income and is not taxed until actually received. Most pension funds are exempt from tax with the result that the accumulated earnings of these funds typically go untaxed. There have been proposals to tax the capital surplus of such funds but no legislation was forthcoming.

Dutch pension benefits are typically quite generous. Many employees are entitled to a pension which, when combined with the relatively substantial governmental social security payment, is equal to 70 % of their last year's earnings. The amount is sometimes indexed for inflation or even changes in general wage levels. In light of the demographic situation and the potentially increasing number of retired persons, there is discussion to move the 70 % benchmark to a weighted average lifetime salary.

In *Germany*, the use of employer-provided pension plans is fairly widespread, with nearly one third of all companies providing a plan. Close to one-half of the working population is covered by an employer plan. On the other hand, the benefits provided by the plans are relatively low, with the most of the retirement benefits coming from the social security system.

Plans can be structured by a direct commitment by the employer to pay the pension, through third party pension insurance, as a pension fund or as a "benevolent" fund. Large and medium-sized companies typically use the direct method while smaller enterprises fund the pension obligation by purchasing insurance. Direct pension commitments are funded through the creation of deductible pension reserves. For tax purposes, the reserve can be first established when the employee reaches the age of 30 and is based on the actuarial calculations of the future pension obligation, using a 6 % discount rate. Subsequent adjustments to the reserve can be made. There is no restriction on the employer's use of the funds reflected in the reserve. However, employers are legally required to participate in a special guarantee fund. Though the employee has a legal right to the future pension at the time the reserve is formed, there is no taxation at the employee level until payments are made.

In contrast, if the employer finances the retirement benefits through insurance, the payment of the premium is currently deductible by the employer and currently taxable to the employee, though the amounts included can be deducted as an "extraordinary expense" up to certain limits and under certain circumstances may qualify for a special 20% flat rate. When the retirement payments are made by the insurer, an annuity approach is taken which taxes the interest portion of the deferred payment. If pension benefits are funded through qualified pension plans set up by the employer, the pattern of taxation is the same as third party insurance; the employer has a current deduction for additions to the fund and the employee has current income. The fund itself is generally tax-exempt and is subject to substantial governmental oversight and regulation. A final method for funding involves so-called benevolent or relief funds, in which the employee does not have a legal right to the future pension. Benevolent funds are subject to less governmental supervision than formal pension funds, and correspondingly, there are substantial restrictions on the employer's deduction.

In the *United Kingdom*, legislation dealing with employer-provided pensions requires that a fund be established under a trust complete with an administrator who is responsible for dealing with the Inland Revenue. However, The Revenue have power to approve other arrangements; in practice they only grant approval for the purchase of an immediate annuity for a person about to retire or where the contract is to be underwritten by a special type of investment company known as a friendly society. Employer contributions are deductible and the funds held by the pension scheme are exempt from tax on both income and capital gains.

The United Kingdom permits various types of entitlements including terminal salary schemes (defined benefit plans). These are subject to a maximum by which the total retirement benefit may not exceed 2/3 of the final salary as defined. Many taxpayers commute a part of their pension in return for a fixed sum; the effect of this sum is to reduce the remaining pension to 1/2 of the final salary; the fixed sum is equal to 1.5 times the final salary and is tax free (which accounts for its popularity). There are also defined contribution schemes known as contracted out money purchase schemes; these may not be tied to terminal salaries.

There is a further limit in that the schemes do not permit deductions in respect of earnings over a set figure; this amount is index linked and for 1996-97 the limit is set at ca. $123,000.

When there is a refund of contributions there is a special charge of 20 % of the amount returned; the charge falls on the administrator of the fund and not on the member of the scheme. Where the administrator is obliged to return the fund to the employees there is a charge of 35 % on the administrator; here the employee is treated as having been charged tax not at 35 % but at the basic rate (now 24 %). If The Revenue withdraw approval of the scheme there is a charge of 40 % on the value of the assets immediately before withdrawal of the approval.

Australia's arrangements for private retirement income, which is generally referred to as superannuation, have been undergoing rapid development for over a decade and are worth examining in some detail. In contrast to some other countries here considered, there is no public social security scheme funded by a special tax in Australia and the universal old age pension funded out of government general revenues is basically a flat rate payment which is equal to 25 % of average weekly earnings and is very strictly means tested. Thus employer-provided benefits are extremely important.

Prior to 1983, employer contributions to superannuation funds (in the legal form of trusts) were deductible within generous limits, superannuation funds were tax exempt and lump sum payments on retirement were effectively tax free while pensions were taxable. Less than half the labor force was covered by private superannuation and coverage was heavily skewed in favor of upper income groups. In 1983 taxation on lump sum payouts was introduced, and in 1988 (mainly to fund a reduction in the company tax rate and to overcome arbitrage activities involving superannuation funds) a 15 % tax on employer contributions and on fund income was introduced along with a 15 % tax rebate for pensions. That is, the intention was to accelerate revenue, rather than significantly affect the tax expenditure involved in the superannuation area. (In 1994 the tax expenditure in respect of the superannuation system was $5.5 billion, far and away the largest item in total tax expenditures of $13 billion).

In 1992 a superannuation guarantee charge was introduced to make superannuation contributions compulsory in respect of all employees, with the required rate of employer contribution being phased in over a number of years to reach a maximum of 9% of salary in 2002.

The proceeds of this charge, which only applies when employers do not provide "voluntarily" the required level of private superannuation coverage, are paid into a special fund for the benefit of the relevant employee who may direct payment into a superannuation fund. To prevent the system from being burdened by small amounts which are eaten up by administration charges, employers can opt out of the compulsory part of the system for employees with incomes below a certain level.

Employee contributions to a superannuation fund are out of after tax income and not subject to the contribution tax or to tax on payout from the fund. There is thus a bias against employee contributions in the system, but many of the larger and longer established schemes provide for matching employer and employee contributions which effectively removes any choice from the employee in respect of employee contributions. Employer contributions are deductible within limits indexed for inflation and based on an age-related scale. Deductible employer contributions are not included in the income of the employee but, as mentioned, are subject to the 15 % contributions tax in the hands of the superannuation fund.

The income of a complying superannuation fund (one which has been approved by the Insurance and Superannuation Commission as meeting the necessary criteria for vesting, preservation to certain age limits, portability, general protection of fund members etc.) is taxed at a rate of 15 %, in contrast to the 47 % top individual rate. Superannuation funds are entitled to the benefit of corporate imputation credits to reduce the contributions tax and the tax on investment income. A fund may not invest more than 10 % of its assets in the sponsoring employer or its associates but otherwise is unrestricted in investment policy though the trustee must formulate and implement an investment strategy.

In general, superannuation pensions are taxable in the ordinary way as other income (apart from the employee's non-deductible contributions) but subject to a flat tax rebate of 15 % in recognition of the tax paid on deducted contributions and fund income. In addition, pension payouts are subject to a complex scheme of so-called "reasonable benefit" limits which apply to both preferentially treated pensions and other items such as "golden handshake" payments. In general terms, there is a flat dollar limit on the amount of benefits which may be received and when that limit is exceeded, additional benefits are taxed at the top individual rate. The limit is much higher for payments in the form of a pension than for lump sum payments as a way of encouraging the provision of ongoing retirement income.

There is an elaborate system for rolling over amounts paid from superannuation funds on change of employment, etc., to ensure that they remain within the special tax regime until retirement (generally not earlier than age 55). Contributions and income can be made and accumulated within the system until age 70 (up from age 65 in the 1996 budget). Schemes can take defined contribution and defined benefit forms and there are many special rules in relation to unfunded schemes for public sector employees.

As noted above, although the superannuation system is private rather than public, it is compulsory for all employees as from 1992 with gradually increasing contributions required of employers and enforced by the superannuation guarantee charge. The government has made the superannuation system the centerpiece of achieving the twin objectives of increasing the private savings rate in Australia and insuring against effective bankruptcy of the public sector as the population ages.

2. Imputed income from owner-occupied housing

The in-kind return from the ownership of consumer assets and self-provided services has long been recognized as an economic benefit but only in the case of owner-occupied housing has there been a serious effort to include the benefit in the income tax base. The treatment of imputed income from owner-occupied housing is an important part of the overall treatment of housing for tax purposes. Failure to tax imputed income, when coupled, as it often is, with a deduction for interest costs incurred in purchasing a personal residence, and preferential treatment of gain on sale, may lead to a serious undertaxation of housing expenditures and a corresponding overinvestment in this sector. This has clearly been the case in the United States. Failure to tax also creates equity problems in the relative treatment of renters and homeowners. On the other hand, real property taxes may to some extent operate as a surrogate for the taxation of imputed rental income. Thus, in France, for example, the taxation of owner-occupied housing was abandoned in 1966 but local taxes apply both to the owner of the property and to the occupant.

In the systems considered here, the results with respect to the taxation of owner-occupied housing are varied. In the *United States,* though the matter has been discussed from time to time, no legislative proposals to tax income from owner-occupied housing have been seriously considered. In other countries, the taxation of imputed housing income was attempted but then dropped because of difficulties in applying the tax on a realistic basis. For example, prior to 1987, *Germany* included in the category of rental income the income from owner-occupied housing. The rental value was based on either the assessed value of the real estate, which was seldom an accurate measure of the market value, or on comparable rentals which also presented some valuation problems. Since interest costs (as well as maintenance costs in the case of a comparable rental approach) were deductible, the result was very often a loss which could be used against other income. After a transition period beginning in 1987, taxation of imputed income was eliminated.

Similar results occurred earlier in *Australia* and *France*. France, however, continues to tax the imputed value of forests and bodies of water used for private hunting or fishing, as well as nonresident ownership of real estate in some cases. In the *United Kingdom*, the tax was abandoned because of the perceived difficulty of obtaining accurate valuation of property for purposes of the tax.

Other countries have been more successful in taxing imputed rental income. In *The Netherlands*, imputed housing income is, in principle, subject to tax. From a policy point of view, the taxation of imputed income from home ownership is intended to help equalize the after-tax living costs of owners and renters. The imputed income is calculated through a procedure intended to reach results approximating the market rental value of similar occupied properties. The procedure is revised periodically to take into account changes in actual rentals and in recent years the required inclusion has been about 2.8 % of the fair market value of the property. The rental value is assumed to be a net value, i.e., all expenses which are normally deductible from rental income are deemed to have been deducted, with the exception of interest on loans taken up to purchase or improve the house. Because of this interest deduction, most home owners actually show a loss for income tax purposes. However, since personal interest is deductible in any event, the taxation of the net imputed income does produce some revenue. Gain on the sale of the residence is not taxed, consistent with the general pattern of nontaxation of capital gains.

Similarly, imputed income from owner-occupied housing has historically been subject to income tax in *Sweden*. Originally, the fair market rental value was included in the tax base. The same rule was applied (and still is applied) to the use by the owner of property held in a business, for example, personal use of an apartment in an apartment building. Valuation problems made the application of the system difficult in the case of owner-occupied private housing and was replaced with a system of standardized income calculation. The imputed return was taken to be the interest rate on long-term government bonds with no deductions for any expenses except interest expense. Thus, in effect, the return on the taxpayer's equity invested in the house was taxed.

In the most recent tax reform in 1991, the basic principle of taxing imputed income was retained for equity reasons but the structure of the tax was changed. A separate real estate tax was imposed at a rate of 1.5 % (subsequently 1.7 %) of the assessed value of the property which should, in principle, be equal to 75 % of the market value. Indexation of the assessed value is provided for in the periods between assessment. A deduction is allowed for interest. The rate was set with reference to the historical real yield on government securities. The combination of the tax rate and the calculation of the base is intended to tax the return at a rate equivalent to the rate for income from capital, after inflation adjustments are taken into account, though there is some necessary standardization in the yield and rate calculations. (It should be noted that real estate is also included in the net wealth tax).

Special rules are necessary to deal with cooperative apartment houses, a common legal construction in Sweden. The general impression is that the system works fairly well for single family residences though cooperatives still are a problem. No other types of imputed income from private assets are taxed in Sweden.

Japan does not, in principle, tax the imputed value of privately held assets. However, there is a mechanism which in effect may allow for the taxation of some imputed income if a personal asset is later sold. In general, a deduction for depreciation is not allowed with respect to personal assets. Nonetheless, the taxpayer must adjust the basis of the personal asset as if depreciation had been taken. If the personal asset is later sold at a gain, the gain must be calculated from the adjusted basis. In effect, a portion of the imputed income in the amount of the depreciation is included in the tax base when it occurs but is offset by the corresponding depreciation deduction with the attendant basis adjustment. If the asset is later sold for a gain, the economic equivalent of that portion of the imputed income is included in the tax base at that time.

3. Gifts

The proper taxation of gifts in a family context has been a matter of some discussion from a theoretical point of view in systems with a global approach to income definition. Since the donee who receives the gift has the power to consume or save the proceeds, there would be some logic in including the gift in his income. On the other hand, since the donor has typically paid tax on the funds representing the source of the gift initially, taxing the donee would represent a second tax on what is the same economic income. A response to this problem would be to give a deduction to the donor for the gift, but in systems with a progressive rate structure that approach would encourage income shifting to reduce taxes. The final possibility, which is the rule generally adopted, is to not tax the donee but also to give no deduction to the donor, thus ensuring that the initial income stream from which the gift is made is only taxed once (though, from one point of view, to the wrong person).

In schedular systems, the issues arise somewhat differently. In the case of private gifts, the issue of income inclusion generally does not come up since typically the receipt does not fall within any taxable schedule. In some systems, the "other" category of income includes receipts from whatever source when they arise on a periodic basis, e.g., a series of gifts over a period of time, reflecting an underlying notion of periodicity as an important characteristic of income. In all of these situations, the existence of transfer taxes also may have an impact on the view taken of gifts from an income tax perspective.

A related problem involves gifts or bequests of appreciated or depreciated property. Some systems treat the gift or bequest as a realization event. Others postpone current taxation and preserve the potential taxation of the appreciation at the time of the gift by providing a carryover tax cost[6] in the property to the donee. Still others, in

---

6. The various systems use different terminology to express the notion of the taxpayer's capital investment in an asset for tax purposes. The United States term is "basis" or "tax basis." Other systems refer to "cost", "tax cost," "acquisition cost," " tax book cost," or some equivalent term. These materials will generally use the term "tax cost" to refer to this basic concept.

particular the United States and the United Kingdom, allow a fair market value tax cost in the hands of the transferee on transfers at death without treating the transfer as a realization event. These aspects are dealt with briefly here and discussed in more detail in the subsequent section dealing with realization generally.

Additional issues are raised by gifts in a business context, when the donor is typically deducting the payment, and are considered after the treatment of nonbusiness gifts.

3.1 Gifts outside of a business context ("personal" gifts)

The *United States* is an example of the treatment of personal gifts in a global income setting. Gifts in a private context are not taxable to the donee and are not deductible for the donor. In the case of appreciated property, the gift is not treated as a realization event and the donee takes as his tax cost the tax cost of the donor, thus preserving the possibility of tax on the appreciation in the hands of the donee. A special rule prevents the shifting of loss in the case of depreciated property. Bequests are treated similarly as regards deduction and inclusion but the property receives a tax cost equal to fair market value in the hands of the transferee, thus allowing predeath appreciation to escape tax altogether.

In *Germany*, gifts of private assets between private persons are neither taxable to the donee nor deductible by the donor. The tax cost of appreciated assets carries over. In *France*, the same pattern of taxation applies but the transferee takes a fair market value tax cost for both gifts and transfers at death.

Similar principles are applied in the *U.K.*, *Canadian*, and *Australian* systems as regards deduction and inclusion. Personal gifts are nontaxable, since they are not derived from a taxable "source" and similarly not deductible. The Commonwealth systems differ, however, in their treatment of gifts and bequests of appreciated property. In Canada, both inter vivos transfers and transfers at death are treated as realization events for the transferor, with the transferee taking a fair market value tax cost. In Australia, inter vivos transfers are similarly realization events while transfers at death result in a carryover of tax cost, thus preserving the possible taxation of predeath appreciation. The United Kingdom treats an inter vivos gift as a realization event. As in the United States, however, in the case of a transfer at death, there is no realization and the transferee takes a fair market value tax cost.

Japan, *Sweden*, and *The Netherlands* reach the same results as to deduction and income inclusion and generally provide for a carryover of tax cost if the asset would be taxable on resale.

3.2 Gifts in a business or employment context

Gifts in a business or employment context raise somewhat different issues. The donor who has made the gift for business reasons will typically have deducted the gift as a cost of doing business so if, as in the case of personal gifts, the gift continues to be exempt in the hands of the donee, the entire amount will have escaped tax. The response to this problem would either deny the deduction to the donor or require the deducted gift to be taxed to the donee. Both approaches have been taken in the systems under consideration.

In the *United States*, most gifts over a de minimis amount from an employer to an employee are taxable to the employee and deductible as a business expense by the employer. Special rules apply to exclude tangible property awarded for length of service and other similar achievements (the "golden watch" exception). In the case of gifts in the business context to nonemployees, the donee may be able in principle to exclude the gift as an expression of disinterested generosity by the donor, but in that case, the deduction is denied to the donor, thus ensuring that the gift is not excluded from the tax base entirely.

In the *Commonwealth* countries, business gifts are typically taxable to the recipient (or subject to the fringe benefits tax) as arising from an employment relation or other business relation. The gift can be excluded if the taxpayer shows that it arose out of personal regard, but the fact that the payor has deducted the payment raises a presumption that it is taxable.

In *Germany*, in general, gifts over a de minimis amount (ca. $50) are not deductible by the donor as a business or income-related expense but may be excluded by the donee if a true gift is present. If the purported "gift" is sufficiently related to a clearly identifiable service, then the cost of the transfer is deductible and includable by the recipient.

Gifts of property in a business context in Germany are subject to a complex set of rules growing out of the general principles dealing with the withdrawal and contribution of business assets. In general terms, the donation of an asset for nonbusiness reasons is treated as the withdrawal of an asset from the business sphere and is a realization event. There is no deduction for the transfer under the general rule denying deduction for gifts. The recipient takes the gift with a fair market value tax cost at the time of transfer but does not include the gift in income as it falls within no taxable category. If the transfer is for business reasons, it is no longer treated as a withdrawal. It is not clear if the deduction and corresponding inclusion are based on tax cost or on fair market value.

The *Swedish* rules are similar, except that the transfer for business reasons results in realization and a corresponding fair market value deduction for the transferor.

Gifts made by corporations or commercial law partnerships in *Japan* are, in principle, subject to income tax in the hands of the recipient and deductible by the payor. If the gift is not related to any particular category of income of the recipient, it is taxed as Occasional Income which is subject to a preferential rate and special deductions. Otherwise, the gift falls into the appropriate income category, sometimes subject to a special rate.

In *The Netherlands*, gifts which occur in a business or employment relation are treated as deductible by the payor and taxable to the recipient. In the case of appreciated property, the transfer is a realization event.

In *France*, business gifts to clients, employees, etc. are generally not taxable if they are not directly related to services performed. They are, however, deductible if they are made in the interests of the business and the amounts are not too large. The gift of a capital asset would be considered a realization event for capital gains taxation purposes.

4. Prizes and awards

As in the case of gifts, the income definitional issues for prizes and awards arise somewhat differently in global and schedular systems. In a global system, the logic of the system would clearly point toward taxation of the recipient unless extra-fiscal considerations are thought to justify exclusion. In schedular systems, the question is whether the prize "fits" in a taxable category. Special rules sometimes apply to prizes or awards in the employment context.

In the *United States*, after recent statutory changes, prizes and awards are in general fully taxable, regardless of the nature of the activity or accomplishment which is being recognized. Thus, for example, the Nobel prize is taxable, as are athletic awards. Special rules exempt certain prizes and awards in the form of tangible property for employee service or achievement and since the amounts remain deductible by the employer, the entire amount escapes the tax.

In *Germany*, prizes and awards are taxable if they can be related in a loose way to one of the income categories. In addition, they may be taxed as "other" income if they are awarded for a specific accomplishment. Awards to employees for suggestions, improvements, etc. are taxable. On the other hand, prizes in recognition of a life's work, the Nobel prize, Goethe prize, etc. are not taxable. Prize drawings are exempt even if the drawing takes place in a business setting as long as the chances of winning are low and all employees are entitled to participate.

Similarly, in *The Netherlands*, prizes and awards are taxable if they relate to the recipient's professional or business activities, e.g., a prize to a professional author if the recipient could reasonably have expected to have received the award. Prizes for "hobby" activities, e.g., an amateur dog show, would not be taxable since there is no taxable source. However, if too much effort is involved, a business or profession may be present.

In *Japan*, prizes and awards received from corporations or commercial partnerships as part of advertising and publicity campaigns are taxable as Occasional Income. Scholarly and scientific prizes are not taxable.

Under the *Swedish* schedular system, prizes and awards which cannot be characterized as being "remuneration" for a "performance" are not taxable. Thus lottery prizes where the winner is chosen by chance are not taxable. On the other hand, a case held that a prize for entering an advertising slogan in a contest was taxable. The court rejected the taxpayer's argument that there were so many entries that the jury could not have read all of them and thus the prize was in fact based on chance. It was not relevant that the amount of the prize had no relation to the value of the performance. Prizes won on TV shows are taxable even if based on chance; the element of performance is supplied by the act of appearing on the program. In addition, lottery prizes won in a drawing which is limited to employees of the firm are taxable as fringe benefits arising out of the employment relation. In Sweden, the Nobel prize has been held (not surprisingly) to be nontaxable, in part on the theory that the accomplishments on which the prize was based were not undertaken in order to obtain the prize. (The case was decided before *The Double Helix* was written.)

The *Australian, U.K.*, and *Canadian* rules reveal similar principles, with prizes arising in a field of endeavor regularly carried on by the taxpayer or paid on a periodic basis being taxable, as income resulting from a taxable "source." There is an exemption for general public prizes like the Nobel prize.

In *France* as well, prizes and awards are taxed only if they are related to the recipient's profession or business. Literary and academic prizes awarded by an independent jury are likewise excluded, as is the Nobel prize.

5. Scholarships and grants

The tax treatment of scholarships is related both to the global or schedular structure of the tax system and to the overall system for the provision of educational services in the country. In countries which provide extensive no-fee or low-fee public education, scholarships involving tuition are generally not an issue and scholarship payments are usually in the form of support for living expenses. Since one of the typical schedules of taxable income is periodic payments for living expenses, scholarships would easily fit into this taxable category. Similarly, in a global system which focuses on consumption as an important component of the tax base, payments for living expenses would be a clear candidate for taxation.

In addition, where tuition is generally privately financed, the issue of scholarships covering tuition must be faced, as well, with potentially different outcomes in global and schedular systems. General, nonfiscal arguments concerning the importance of supporting education also play a role. Finally, even if, in principle, some scholarships are exempt, if the payment in the form of scholarship is sufficiently related to employment or some other taxable category of income, taxability might result. The systems under consideration here combine these principles in various forms.

In the *United States*, scholarships which cover tuition and related educational expenses are excluded from income. Payment for other expenses such as lodging or meals do not qualify. The recipient must be a candidate for a degree at a recognized educational institution. The exclusion is not available to the extent that the student is required to perform teaching, research, or other services as a condition of the grant. In that situation, the amount equal to the fair market value of the services performed is taxable and the remainder, if any, can be excluded as a scholarship. A special rule treats as a qualified scholarship the tuition reduction or remission for the children of employees of an educational institution, as long as such reduction is available on a nondiscriminatory basis, i.e., not limited to professors.

In *Sweden*, despite the extensive low-cost public education system, a special statutory provision exempts scholarships. There have been discussions in the context of the 1991 tax reform to repeal the exemption but it survived based on arguments about the necessity of supporting research. Payments in support of education which can be characterized as remuneration for services are taxable. For example, a "scholarship" paid by a publishing house to an author whose works were published by the publisher was taxable. In some cases, a series of payments in support of research may be taxable based on the historical notion that periodicity is an essential characteristic of income. Periodic payments by domestic tax-exempt organizations have been made exempt by statute; a series of payments over three years from a foreign foundation was held taxable.

In *Germany*, scholarships are explicitly exempted from tax by statute. To qualify, the payments must be made by governmental or charitable organizations and must not require any specific performance of services on the part of the recipient. The payments must be to further research or education.

In contrast, in *The Netherlands*, while public "study grants" are exempt from tax, private scholarships and grants are taxable if they take the form of periodic payments. This reflects the early role of periodicity in income definition. On the other hand, lump-sum payments are not taxed.

In *Canada*, which also has extensive public education, scholarships in excess of $375 are explicitly recognized as a taxable "source" of income. The same principle applies to research grants. In contrast, in *Australia*, while scholarships would normally be taxable as periodic payments covering living expenses, there is a specific statutory exclusion which applies unless the purported scholarship is conditioned on providing services currently or in the future. The *United Kingdom* similarly exempts scholarships, though amounts in support of study provided to children of employees by an employer are taxable to the employee under the fringe benefits legislation. The latter rule does not apply if the scholarships are provided under a trust scheme in which at least 75 % of the beneficiaries are not relatives of employees.

In *France*, state-provided educational assistance, which is awarded on the basis of social criteria, is not subject to tax but is treated as social assistance.

6. Cancellation of indebtedness

Where funds are borrowed, income is typically not realized under any of the systems here under consideration. The traditional explanation is that the increase in assets caused by the loan is offset by the corresponding liability so, in balance sheet terms, there is no increase on net worth at the time the loan is taken out. Taking this approach, all systems must deal with the situation where, contrary to expectations, the loan is not fully repaid. In principle, the failure to repay the loan in full would result in additional taxable income to the borrower, reflecting the fact that the loan proceeds were originally received on a tax-free basis on the expectation that they would be repaid in full. In many cases, however, where the debt is being forgiven or reduced, it is because the taxpayer is in financial difficulty, raising the practical issues of the desirability and feasibility of assessing and collecting a tax at this time.

The systems under consideration here have taken a wide variety of approaches to the problem. Most recognize the taxability in principle of forgiveness of indebtedness, though in the context of a schedular system, the debt must be related to a taxable category of income. However, all make some concession to the financially troubled taxpayer in terms of income inclusion. In some cases, no income is required to be recognized unless the taxpayer is made financially solvent after the forgiveness. Even here, some systems require the reduction of other tax attributes, for example, the tax cost of property or the availability of accrued operating losses in effect financed out of the loan proceeds.

The evolution of the rules in the *United States* shows some of the interplay among these principles. Income from cancellation of indebtedness is in principle subject to tax, though there are a number of exceptions. In the private context, the cancellation may qualify for exclusion as a gift. In a business setting, specific statutory rules exclude cancellation of indebtedness from income if the taxpayer is in a bankruptcy proceeding or is insolvent both before and after the forgiveness. Otherwise, cancellation in a business setting results in taxable income. Where exclusion is available, the taxpayer is generally required to reduce certain tax attributes as a condition for the exclusion. The reduction is made first in any net operating losses, which are in effect treated as if funded by the forgiven loan. If those losses are not sufficient to absorb the forgiveness, the taxpayer must reduce the tax cost of other assets, thus increasing potential income in the future by reducing deductions or losses or increasing the amount of gain on the disposition of the assets.

Under an earlier statutory regime, all business taxpayers could elect to exclude cancellation income if tax attributes were correspondingly reduced. This rule was found to be too generous and was eliminated, thus limiting the exclusion to insolvency and bankruptcy situations.

A special rule treats a discharge that arises out of the sale of property as a retroactive reduction in the original purchase price which does not result in income to the buyer. The exclusion only applies to an obligation running from the buyer to the seller; forgiveness of third-party financing could result in income.

In *Germany*, in principle, cancellation of indebtedness is taxable if the debt arises in connection with a source of taxable income. If the debt is in the private sphere, no income results from forgiveness. The conceptual basis for the inclusion is the increase in net worth that the forgiveness causes that is reflected in the changes in the right-hand side of the balance sheet. A complex administrative and judicial exception exists for cancellation in connection with the changes of financial structure of a business in financial difficulty. In general terms, the forgiveness must be part of a plan based on the need for the company to reorganize to be able to continue its business. It is often typical in such circumstances for the creditors to receive contingent rights entitling them to payment if the situation of the debtor improves. Payment of these amounts are not deductible if the cancellation income was exempt under the reorganization exception. Otherwise, there is no reduction of tax attributes as a result of the forgiveness.

In *Sweden*, cancellation of indebtedness is taxable if it takes place in a business context, unless the debtor is insolvent. Where the cancellation does not result in income, the right to deduct a loss is limited by the same amount. In effect, the cancellation income must be offset by the otherwise available loss which could reduce income in later years. It has been suggested that if there is no accrued loss, the basis of assets acquired with the loan should be reduced. Outside of the business context, cancellation of indebtedness will not result in income.

Similarly, in *The Netherlands*, cancellation occurring in a business context is not taxable if it can be established that the debt could not have been repaid. Insolvency or bankruptcy is a factor in that determination but is not controlling. While the cancellation of such a debt is not taxable, the resulting gain must be used to offset any current losses or available loss carryforwards. In *Japan*, in principle, cancellation of indebtedness results in income to the debtor. However, in administrative practice if the debt is canceled in circumstances in which it is extremely unlikely that the debt will be repaid, no income results.

The treatment of forgiveness of indebtedness income in *Canada*, *Australia*, and the *United Kingdom* has been influenced by the capital gain-ordinary income distinction. Cancellation of debts arising in the business and related to revenue items like trade payables have always been included as business income in Canada. When the taxation of capital gains was introduced, the possibility of treating the forgiveness of other types of liabilities as a taxable capital gain was considered but rejected. Instead, loss carryovers and the basis of depreciable property were required to be reduced to the extent possible by the amount of the forgiveness. If the amount forgiven exceeded the available tax attributes, there were no tax consequences to the excess of the debt forgiven. A recent proposal would extend taxation to the excess.

Similarly, in Australia, there is no general legislative rule that cancellation of indebtedness results in income. If a company involved in a finance business buys back its debt obligations at below face value, the corresponding profit will be taxed as part of business income. However, if a commercial company does the same transaction, no income results since the capital gains tax, which would seemingly be applicable to gains in this type of situation, deals explicitly with assets and not liabilities. Rules requiring the reduction of losses or tax cost similar to those in Canada have recently been introduced into Parliament but have not yet been enacted.

The *United Kingdom* continues to have very restrictive rules on cancellation of indebtedness income. In general, income arises only if the loan was employment related, made to a shareholder of a closely held corporation, or involved a liability which had previously been deducted.

In *France*, the cancellation of a debt in a private context has no tax effects. In a business setting, the cancellation results in income even if the debtor is in bankruptcy. In some circumstances, the cancellation by a parent corporation of an advance to a subsidiary may be excluded from income and treated as an increase in stated capital.

7. Gambling

The inclusion of gambling income is strongly influenced by the schedular or global nature of the system. In the global system in the *United States*, gambling winnings are in principle subject to tax whether they arise from occasional transactions or are received by a professional gambler. However, even in the case of a professional gambler, gambling losses for the year can only be deducted to the extent of gambling income. This essentially schedular approach to gambling income may be influenced to some extent by the concern with artificial gambling "losses." As well, the gambling losses may be viewed as consumption. The restrictions in *Japan* are even more strict. Gambling income is taxable as Occasional Income but losses incurred in gambling are not deductible against other types of income and gambling losses arising on other occasions cannot be deducted against gambling winnings. Each gambling occasion is a separate event. These restrictions presumably reflect both the administrative difficulties of verifying losses and possible characterization of the gambling losses as consumption.

In many schedular systems, gambling income is taxable only if the gambler can be found to be in the business of gambling. For example, in *Germany*, case law holds that gambling income of a professional card player is taxable as business income. In contrast, income from private trading in futures contracts is treated as gambling income, not as (taxable) income from speculation in property. However, in the unusual case that the futures contract is closed through an actual delivery of the product, a taxable speculative gain may be present. Similarly, in *The Netherlands* where a cafe owner bought a case of whiskey that automatically entered him in a lottery in which he won a motorcycle, he was able to exclude the prize by showing that he had not deducted the costs of the whiskey. Since the whiskey was a private asset, the attendant lottery prize was not taxable. As discussed above, Sweden taxes gambling if the income can be said to come from the performance of a service but not if purely by chance. Winnings in the Swedish lottery are expressly exempt.

In *Australia, Canada*, and the *United Kingdom*, income derived from gambling or lottery-type prizes is not taxable unless the activity amounts to a business. Otherwise, there is no taxable "source" and accordingly gains are not taxable and losses not deductible. *France* reaches the same results.

8. Illegal income

In all of the systems here considered, in general the fact that income is derived from illegal activities does not prevent its taxation (pecunia non olet). The common principle is that the taxpayer cannot use the illegal nature of his activities as a defense against taxation. In a schedular system, however, the income must of course fall into a taxable category. Thus, for example, in Germany, illegal income will often fall into the category of Miscellaneous Income from the occasional performance of services, e.g., espionage. However, income from theft or embezzlement is not taxed since it does not fit within the criteria of the Miscellaneous category.

Since illegal income typically involves a civil law obligation to repay the amounts taken, the taxpayer has no legally recognized right to keep the income and this has influenced the income inclusion issue in some situations. For example, an *Australian* case has held the earnings on embezzled funds not taxable where the embezzler was caught and had to return the funds and the interest. Some early United States cases reached similar results on the ground that the taxpayer (an embezzler) had no "claim of right" to the income, though the result was later reversed.   Sometimes a line must be drawn between embezzlement (typically with an intention to repay) and an informal loan. The latter characterization requires the real or assumed acquiescence of the "lender." A related issue involves the deduction for possible repayment of the illegally obtained funds.

In *Sweden*, there is in principle full taxation of illegal income which arises in a business. However, in most cases, illegal income will be forfeitable and as such, deductible, so there will be no net income. Illegal income which does not arise in a business is not taxable.

In *France*, according the principle known as "tax law realism," income from illegal activities is taxed like lawful income and in whatever the normal category would be. For example, income from procuring is commercial profit while the income of a prostitute is either wages or non commercial profit, depending on the circumstances.

The treatment of expenses such as bribes, fines, etc. which often arise in connection with illegal income is discussed below in Subpart B.

9. Windfalls

The logic of a global system extends to the taxation of windfall gains such as found property and this approach is followed in the *United States*. *Japan* treats windfalls as taxable Occasional Income. In *Germany*, the treatment of windfalls depends on the situation. Normally, found property is not taxable. However, if it arises in a business setting, it is included as part of the business profits. Thus, money found by the owner in a cinema is taxable. Likewise, in *The Netherlands*, windfalls are in general not taxable unless they fall within a taxable category and in *Sweden*, windfalls have historically not been taxable since they are not the result of efforts to earn income and are not periodic. In the *Commonwealth* countries, windfall is not a taxable "source" of income and is not included in the income tax base. The subsequent extension of taxation to capital gains typically did not affect this result. In *France*, windfalls are not taxed unless they arise in a business context.

Damages are a special category of windfalls. In general, in schedular systems damages are taxable to the extent they relate to assets or activities which are taxable. Damage awards for injury are typically treated as reducing the tax cost of the asset with gain resulting if the total amount recovered exceeds the cost. In some cases, the gain can be deferred through the use of a reserve if the property is going to be repaired or replaced. Damages for personal injuries are typically not taxable even if calculated with reference to lost earnings or earning capacity. In the *Commonwealth* systems, the introduction of a capital gains tax expanded the taxation of damage awards, which had previously escaped tax, though the exclusion for damages to person or profession (e.g., defamation) was typically retained.

In *France*, personal injury damages are taxed if they are paid in the form of an annuity, thus reflecting a periodic concept of income.

The proper treatment of personal injury damages has been the subject of a substantial amount of litigation in the United States. The disagreement has centered around the scope of a special statutory rule which excludes damages for "personal injuries." The Supreme Court recently ruled that recoveries based on a statutory prohibition against age discrimination did not result from a personal injury and were not excludable.

10. Subsidies

The treatment of governmental subsidies raises a number of structural issues. In the simplest case, when the payment is a form of payment for services, e.g., payments to private carriers for mail transport, it is typically taxable as business income. At the other extreme, some subsidies are so indirect or diffuse that even with a global income definition they would not be included in the tax base. In still other cases, the payment is not includable directly in income but the tax cost of assets acquired or other tax attributes must be reduced accordingly so that the payment is indirectly included over the life of the asset. Public welfare payments are typically not taxed unless they are in the form of wage supplements like unemployment compensation. The *United States'* rules follow this pattern in general.

Similarly, in *Germany*, for business-related subsidies, capital contributions may either be treated as current income or reduce the basis of property produced or acquired with the funds, at the taxpayer's election. If the payments do not involve a capital investment, they are in general currently taxable. However, if they relate to conduct to be performed over a period of years, e.g., not producing milk for five years, the payments may in effect be included over the period of the performance of the service as an accounting matter. Public welfare subsidies are not taxable, but in some cases must be taken into account in determining the applicable tax rate on other income ("exemption with progression").

In the same way, in *Sweden*, governmental subsidies are currently taxable if they are intended to subsidize current costs. If they are in the nature of capital contributions, the basis of the appropriate assets is reduced correspondingly. Subsidies provided by private organizations, for example, research foundations, are not taxable but the tax authorities in practice will attempt to deny the deductions for expenses financed with the tax-exempt payment, thus in effect making them taxable.

In *The Netherlands*, subsidies granted in respect to the acquisition of assets are not currently taxable but result in a basis reduction.

The *United Kingdom*, based on case law principles, has generally taxed current payments but exempted as a nontaxable capital receipt payments which were intended to recoup a capital investment, though the line is not easy to draw. *Australia* still follows this principle to some extent, though the introduction of the capital gains tax may have narrowed the scope of the exclusion. The rule has been supplanted in *Canada* by statute. There, subsidies for current operations are fully taxable as income from business or property. Where the subsidy relates to a depreciable asset, it reduces the tax cost of the asset. For nondepreciable property, the taxpayer has an election to include the amount currently in income or reduce the tax cost.

In *France*, public subsidies are generally exempt from tax unless they are a substitute for taxable income, as in the case of unemployment compensation. In a business context, subsidies for current costs are fully taxable. Payments for capital costs may be spread over ten years (non-depreciable assets) or taken into account at the same time and rate as depreciation. In some situations, the basis of the asset purchased may be increased by a portion of the subsidy for depreciation purposes.

11. Realization and recognition of gain

All of the systems here under consideration are in general based on the realization principle. Gain or loss is not taken into account for tax purposes until some event has caused its realization. Thus the definition of an event of realization is central in all the systems. Here, though the core of the rules is similar, there are many variations. In some jurisdictions, any disposition of an asset is treated as a realization, even if the transfer is not for consideration. Thus, as has been noted, gifts and transfers at death can result in realization of gain or loss. In other cases, a change in tax status, for example, ceasing to be a resident, is treated as a "deemed" realization with respect to certain assets held by the taxpayer.

While the concept of realization is firmly anchored in all of the systems, there are some areas in which the realization requirement has increasingly been abandoned. The first involves the treatment of financial instruments, where some sort of accrual or "mark-to-market" taxation has commonly been applied. The development began with the treatment of the implicit interest element in bonds issued at original discount and has been extended to other types of instruments. These matters are discussed in more detail in Subpart C, as the approach has historically been tied to accounting rules. In addition, the realization principle has frequently been abandoned in the taxation of foreign investment companies. There a mark-to-market approach has often been used, as well as the technique of imputing a specified rate of return on such investments for tax purposes where mark-to-market proved to be difficult to apply. These matters are discussed in Part Four.

All systems also contain rules which allow for the deferral ("rollover") of realized gain in some circumstances. These provisions typically involve property-for-property exchanges, reinvested realization proceeds, especially if the realization event was involuntary, and other similar situations. The rules vary substantially both in their requirements and in the techniques used to establish deferral. Various corporate exchanges which involve rollover treatment, usually in the context of corporate reorganizations, are discussed in Part Three.

In the *United States* system, there is substantial case law on the doctrine of realization. Originally thought to be constitutionally required, the issue of realization is now recognized as essentially a question of administrative convenience. Any exchange of properties in which there is a "material difference" between the properties exchanged will result in realization. The gratuitous transfer of property by gift or at death, however, is not treated as a realization event. In the case of gifts, a carryover of tax cost preserves the possibility of taxing accrued gains in the hands of the donee, but for transfers at death, the heir or legatee receives a fair market value tax cost and appreciation at death escapes tax altogether.

The placing of a mortgage on property, even if the mortgage is nonrecourse and involves no personal liability for the repayment of the funds, is not treated as a realization. As a corollary of this rule, the transfer (or abandonment) of property subject to a mortgage is treated as involving an amount realized equal to the face amount of the mortgage.

A special statutory rule requires securities dealers to report gains and losses on securities on a "mark-to-market" basis as if the property had been sold on the last day of the taxable year.

Recently proposed legislation would extend the notion of realization to cover situations in which the nominal owner of an asset has in effect secured protection against the risk of a decline in value of an asset and similarly given up the possibility of benefiting from its increase in value. Where the risk of loss and the opportunity for gain have been substantially eliminated, realization for tax purposes is deemed to take place. Typical transactions covered would include the "short" sale of a stock which the taxpayer already owned or an "equity swap" in which there is a contractual agreement to pay over the total return on stock held by the taxpayer in return for a corresponding right to receive the return on a different security. In addition, the rules would cover certain so-called "collars" involving simultaneous puts and calls on the same asset.

Where gain is realized there are a number of "rollover" provisions which allow realized gain to be deferred in certain situations. These include the exchange of like-kind depreciable property and real estate, the reinvestment of proceeds from damage or condemnation of property involved in an "involuntary conversion," and the reinvestment of the proceeds of sale of a principal residence. In the latter situation, there is a one-time exclusion of $125,000 of gain on the sale of a principal residence by a taxpayer who has reached the age of 55.

In *Germany*, gains on property dispositions are taxable and losses correspondingly are deductible if they occur in the context of a business or similar income category. The taxation of the gain flows from the balance sheet comparison method of income determination; the total profit of the business includes both the operating profit and the realized increase in assets caused by the disposition for consideration of assets which have appreciated. In addition, the withdrawal of assets either from a corporation or from a sole proprietorship is a realization event for the business. The transfer of assets to a foreign permanent establishment in circumstances where the gain would not be taxed in Germany was at one point treated as an immediate realization event, but the taxpayer is now allowed to take the gain into account over the assumed remaining life of the asset or at the time of actual disposition in the foreign branch.

There are a number of provisions in the German system that allow the deferral or rollover of realized gain. In the case of real estate and long-lived business assets, current recognition can be avoided if the sales proceeds are reinvested. The reinvestment rules are complex and do not require the investment in similar property. For example, gain on the disposition of certain shares can be deferred if the proceeds are invested in depreciable property. On the other hand, gain on depreciable property cannot be deferred if the proceeds are reinvested in stock. The basic purpose of the restrictions is to prevent the indefinite deferral of gain by the reinvestment in longer-lived assets but the policy is not fully carried out. The basis of the acquired asset is adjusted to reflect the deferred gain.

If current reinvestment is not possible, the taxpayer can avoid current recognition of gain by establishing a tax-deductible investment reserve which reduces current income. The reserve may be maintained for four to six years depending on the type of the asset. If the reserve must be dissolved because no reinvestment was undertaken in the prescribed period, an annual interest charge of 6 % is imposed on the amount of the reserve.

The Netherlands has the same basic pattern of rules for domestic transactions, though the technical details differ somewhat. For example, reinvestment must be in similar property and the reserve may not be maintained for more than four years.

In *Sweden*, in general, all property gains are taxed only on realization. One significant exception is gains on short-term claims denominated in foreign currency arising in a business which are taxed on a mark-to-market basis, following accounting principles. Foreign exchange gains on long-term claims are only taxed when realized but an interest charge is imposed on the deferred taxes. Gain realized on involuntary conversion can be deferred if the proceeds from insurance, damage, etc. are reinvested. Gain on the sale of a personal residence can likewise be deferred if the sales proceeds are reinvested.

In *Japan*, as well, a sale or exchange of an asset is necessary for gain realization. This includes the contribution to capital by a shareholder which is a realization event. Gain on business assets may be deferred in a like-kind exchange. Under prior law (influenced by the Shoup Commission and Stanley Surrey), a gift of appreciated property was treated as a realization event but the system was very unpopular and was replaced with a carryover basis mechanism (which extends to transfers at death).

France requires realization, though in the business context, foreign currency gains on claims are taxed on a mark-to-market basis and unrealized losses on nondepreciable capital assets can be taken into account through the use of reserves. Transfer of business property by gift or death is a realization event, as is the withdrawal of assets from a proprietorship or the cessation of the taxpayer's business. There are relatively few rollover provisions.

All of the *Commonwealth* systems are based on the realization principle. The realization requirement was originally developed by the courts in the context of trading profits. With the subsequent introduction of capital gains taxation, broad statutory realization rules were enacted which in general treat any disposal or disposition (rather than sale or exchange) of an asset as a realization event. Thus in Canada, for example, realization will be found if the taxpayer has disposed of most of the important incidents of ownership in the asset. In some cases, changes in the terms of debt or stock can, in the view of the fiscal authorities, be treated as involving a realization. In addition, as previously discussed, disposition of property by gift or a death is generally treated as a realization event (though interspousal transfers are excepted). In general, rollover relief is limited to capital gains and losses. However, recapture of capital cost allowance (depreciation) in respect of depreciable property may be deferred where the property is disposed of involuntarily and a replacement property is acquired. Similarly, a deferral is permitted with respect to dispositions of eligible capital property, including goodwill, and real property used in a business where the taxpayer acquires a replacement property. Special rules in Canada require financial institutions to account for gains and losses on certain debt and equity securities on a mark-to-market basis.

The *Australian* approach is similar, with statutory rules (principally in the capital gains tax) dealing with actual and "deemed" disposals as realization events including inter vivos (but not testamentary) gifts. The Australian system contains special provisions dealing with the taxation of assets which could be viewed as "created" at the same time they are disposed of, for example, the entering into of a covenant not to compete. A very broad rule treats as a deemed disposition any payment received with respect to an asset. Australia is considering the adoption of a comprehensive accrual system for the treatment of financial assets. Modeled on the New Zealand system, it would use a mixture of internal rate of return and mark-to-market principles for calculating income and expense on a broad range of financial instruments and is discussed in more detail in Subpart C.

Australia has a number of rollover provisions covering a wide range of circumstances including involuntary dispositions and certain property exchanges. For historical reasons, the technical details differ depending on whether the property involved is inventory, depreciable business property, or capital property.

The *United Kingdom* system similarly focuses on "disposal" as the principal test of realization, though several of the various income schedules have their own concept of realization. The term "disposal" is not defined but has been held to cover any transfer of beneficial ownership. If the disposal is other than at arm's length, it is deemed to be at fair market value. There are a number of "deemed" realization situations, including, for example, value shifting by changing rights attached to shares in a company. A case law principle treats the withdrawal of an asset from business to personal use as, in effect, a deemed sale at fair market value, resulting in realization of income. Special legislative rules govern the interaction of this case law principle with the capital gains tax regime. Rollover of realized gain is permitted in a variety of situations, including the replacement of business assets within three years of disposal.

12. Capital gains and losses

Though the term "capital gain" or its linguistic equivalent is frequently used in the tax systems here under consideration, the precise contours of the concept vary considerably from country to country. In addition, the concept plays a different role in different systems. In very general terms, the notion is of a nonrecurring gain which is not part of the normal stream of income involved in a business or investment. The distinction may rest on agricultural notions distinguishing between land and the yield from land, or the tree and its fruit. In Anglo-Saxon systems, it has its origin to some extent in trust concepts which distinguish between current income and gains which are allocated to corpus for trust accounting purposes. Gains which are attributed to corpus are generally not available for distribution to income beneficiaries.

However defined, several basic patterns of capital gain taxation emerge. In some countries, typically *Continental*, all income which aris-

es in a business is taxed in the same fashion. There is no special treatment of, for example, gain on the disposition of an asset used in the
business as opposed to gain on inventory. On the other hand, gain on
an asset not connected with a business or other taxable category of
income often will not be taxed, though sometimes with an exception
for short term gains. Thus, gains realized by individuals on investment
assets often are not taxed or taxed only in special circumstances.

In systems influenced by the *United Kingdom*, the distinction
between ordinary income and capital gain is applied both to business
enterprises and to private persons. Initially, both categories of capital
gain were not subject to tax. Subsequent legislation, typically in the
form of a separate capital gains taxing regime, ultimately brought capital gains into the tax base, often employing a preferential rate of tax.

Finally, in countries with a global approach, capital gains were
always included in the tax base, though here too preferential rate treatment was common. In most systems, capital losses are subject to limitations, reflecting either the special treatment of the gain or the fact
that timing of the realization of the gains and losses is particularly within the control of the taxpayer, especially in case of investment assets.

These differing approaches can generate different structural issues
in the various systems. In many Continental systems, since all income
arising in corporations is business income, there is no need to classify
assets as capital or ordinary in that context. On the other hand, for
assets held by individuals, the issue is whether the assets are held as
business assets or privately, leading either to full taxation or to exemption. In a global system like the United States, the corresponding issue
at the individual level will be whether the assets qualify for preferential
treatment or are subject to normal taxation. In systems which give a
preferential rate for business-related capital gains on depreciable assets,
some mechanism will be necessary to "recapture" excess depreciation
on the sale of an asset; in systems which tax all business income in the
same fashion the issue does not arise.

In all systems, the existence of a differentiated treatment for a
certain class of gains has led to statutory and jurisprudential complexity
in attempting to delimit the classification. This problem is heightened
by the lack of any consensus as to why gains from the disposition of certain types of assets should be treated specially.

The taxation of capital gains in the *United States* has had a long
and complicated history. Gain on the disposition of assets has tradition-

ally been included in the tax base whether or not arising in a business context. However, for both individuals (since 1922) and for corporations (since 1942) certain gains have usually qualified for preferential treatment. Deduction for capital losses has in general been available only to the extent of capital gains, though individual taxpayers may claim a limited amount of capital losses against ordinary income if no capital gains are present. Unused capital losses can be carried forward.

At the present time, capital gains are taxed at a lower rate for some individual taxpayers who would otherwise be taxed at higher progressive rates while corporate gains are taxed in full. Both the treatment of capital gains and the definition of the class of gains entitled to such treatment have varied substantially over time. The result has been a hodgepodge of technical rules that is impossible to rationalize.

In general terms, capital gain entitled to preferential treatment is gain realized on the sale or exchange of a capital asset which has been held for over one year. There is substantial statutory and case law material defining "capital asset," the central concept in preferential gain treatment. The definitional process is complicated by the fact that all gain is initially included in the capital gain category with a number of exceptions then applying to treat the gain as ordinary. Capital asset status is thus denied for inventory and other property held for sale to customers in the ordinary course of a business. The scope of this rule, especially in the context of real estate, has generated an enormous amount of litigation.

A special and complex provision taxes real estate and depreciable property used in a business as a capital gain if the disposition of all such property in the taxable period results in a net gain but allows the taxpayer to deduct net losses against ordinary income. To the extent that the gain on depreciable assets is attributable to depreciation deductions that reduced the tax cost of the property, all or a portion of the gain is treated as ordinary.

Copyrights and other literary or artistic property cannot qualify as capital assets in the hands of the person who created the property. Patents, on the other hand, can qualify, even in some circumstances where they would ordinarily be treated as inventory.

Gain from the disposition of personal assets is taxed but a deduction for losses is not allowed. There is a onetime exemption of a fixed dollar amount of gain on the disposition of a personal residence for persons fifty-five or over.

Germany is typical of the schedular approach to capital gains taxation on the Continent. Private capital gains are in general not taxed and all gains realized in business or certain other taxable categories are subject to ordinary taxation. A special rate of 50 % of the normal rate applies to sale of a sole proprietorship, all of the shares of a wholly owned company or a partnership interest. (The special rate is limited to gains of ca. $20 million) Correspondingly, private losses are not deductible and losses realized in business are deductible in full.

A special rule extends taxation to certain stock sales. Gain on the sale by private persons of stock in corporations in which the taxpayer owns (or has owned) a greater than 25 % stock interest ("substantial participation") is taxed at 50 % of the normal rate, as long as the gains do not exceed ca. $20 million. Gain in excess of that amount is fully taxable. The taxation of privately-held substantial participations is justified by the similarity between that type of investment and an investment in a partnership, the gain on the disposition of which would be taxed.

"Speculative" gains, i.e., gains on real property held for less than two years and other property held less than six months, are taxable at normal rates; losses can only be used to offset speculative gains in the same taxable year; they cannot be used against other types of income or carried to other years.

Basically the same pattern of rules applies in The Netherlands except the level of shareholding for a taxable "substantial interest" is different. In addition, where gains on a substantial interest are taxable, they are taxed at a favorable 20 % rate; losses on a substantial interest generate a tax credit of 20 % which can be used against the tax liability arising from other income (regardless of category) in the year in which the loss was incurred and can be carried forward if there is no current tax liability. Also, there is no special tax on short-term gains but gains are taxed if they are the result of more than normal investment activities (e.g., restoring a building) or are based on special insider knowledge so that a sale at a gain could be reasonably foreseen.

In Sweden, capital gains realized by individuals outside of a business context were initially taxed only if they were speculative and short term. However, through successive reforms, taxation was extended until now all such gains are taxable as income from capital. The tax rate is lower than the rate for business or employment income to partly reflect the impact of inflation. A special rule exempts one-half of the gain on owner-occupied housing. The justification for the rule is in part based on a desire to reduce the lock-in effect (though a rollover is available for reinvested gains).

As for losses, capital losses are deductible but the loss is limited to 70 % of the total loss. This limitation is intended to counter to some extent the taxpayer's ability to realize losses currently while deferring gains. No deduction is allowed for losses on personal assets like cars, boats, etc. Loss on personal residence is limited to 50 % of the loss, paralleling the preferential treatment of the gain. Losses on publicly traded stock can be deducted in full against corresponding gains realized in the same year.

If there is an overall loss in the capital income category, it can be used against other income in other categories after appropriate adjustment is made to reflect the fact that capital income is taxed at a favorable 30 % rate. The allowable loss is converted into a 21 % credit (70 % loss x 30 %) which reduces the tax on income in other categories.

Like some Continental systems, *Japan*, in general, has no special rules dealing with capital gains realized by a corporation. A complex set of rules deals with capital gains of individuals. In general, gains on assets held for less than five years are fully taxable. Only one-half the gain is included for assets held for more than five years. Prior to 1989, gains on securities were not taxed. Presently, the net securities gain is taxed at a special 20 % rate. Where the sale is made through a bank or brokerage house, the gain is deemed to be 5 % of the sales price, thus resulting in an effective tax of 1 % of the gross sales proceeds. A separate set of rules applies to income from real estate. In very general terms, these rules in some circumstances apply higher than normal rates to real estate gains, e.g., in the case of short-term gains. They also provide for the classification of real estate gain as business income, capital gain or Occasional Income, with differing consequences both as to the calculation of the gain and the rate of tax. They reflect the special role that real estate gains have played in the Japanese domestic economy.

In *France*, gains on fixed assets in a business are taxed at a preferential rate (19 % for corporations instead of 331/3 %) if the assets have been held for more than two years. (though gain is always treated as ordinary income to the extent of depreciation taken). Private capital gains historically were not subject to tax but since 1976 have been covered by a special tax regime. There are many exceptions, including most personal assets and personal residences. Gains on financial assets are exempted from the normally applicable progressive rates and subject to a flat 19.9 % tax. There is a limited adjustment for inflation for real estate held for more than two years.

The development of capital gains taxation in the *United Kingdom*, *Canada*, and *Australia* has, in general, taken a somewhat different course. As indicated above, initially, gains on the disposition of an asset outside of the business context generally were not taxed. Within the business context, a distinction was drawn between inventory and current assets as compared to fixed and long-term assets. Only gains on assets in the former category were subject to the income tax. In both the private and business settings, gains from the disposition of "capital assets" were not included in the tax basis because of the "source" concept of income. A capital gain was considered to be derived from the disposition of the "source" itself rather than income from a source. Subsequently, all three systems (United Kingdom [1965], Canada [1972] and Australia [1985]) adopted separate systems for the taxation of capital gains which covered both private gains and gains on the disposition of noninventory assets used in business. In addition, in the case of the United Kingdom and Australia, and to a lesser degree, Canada, the capital gains tax legislation was used to cure certain defects and problems which had emerged in the operation of the traditional income tax system. Thus, the capital gains tax system is, to some degree, a parallel taxing system which does substantially more than simply include the gain from a certain class of assets in the tax base. With their somewhat parallel histories, the Commonwealth systems have a number of features in common.

The *United Kingdom* enacted a separate tax on capital gains in 1965 and the system has been modified several times since then. In formal structure, the capital gains tax is a separate tax for individuals with rules taxing capital gains realized by corporations included in the corporate income tax, though the outcomes are generally the same. The basic structure of the tax is to impose a charge on the proceeds of all dispositions of assets and then to exempt a number of types of gains from the tax. These include gains that are otherwise subject to the income tax, e.g., profit on the sale of inventory, gain from certain private assets (cars and personal residences), gain on certain governmental securities, and a number of other miscellaneous exceptions including gain on the disposal of a decoration for valor acquired otherwise than for money or money's worth(!). A de mimimis rule excludes gains and losses on personal assets which are disposed of for less than ca. $9,300.

Capital gains have been indexed for inflation since 1982 through an adjustment to the tax cost of the asset. In its present form, the indexation system does not apply to create a loss on the disposition of a capital asset, though such treatment was previously possible.

The rate of tax on capital gains has varied, with a preferential rate applicable for certain periods. There is no preference for either corporations or individuals at the present time, though individuals have an annual exemption of ca. $9,300. Capital losses are, in general, deductible only against capital gains, though losses on securities in unlisted trading companies can be deducted in full.

In *Canada*, initially one-half of net capital gains was included in income; the includable portion was later increased to three-quarters. A substantial lifetime exemption for individuals was provided in 1988, but was controversial and has been eliminated except for family farms and shares of small business corporations. Capital losses are in general only deductible against capital gains though full deduction is allowed for certain losses incurred in investments in small business corporations. Losses can be carried back three years and forward indefinitely.

Special rules apply to "personal use" property. If the proceeds of disposition or adjusted cost base of the property are less than $1,000, the proceeds or cost are deemed to be $1,000. This provision is a type of de minimis rule that is intended to eliminate the need to keep records with respect to relatively small properties. In addition, losses are only deductible with respect to assets which have a potential investment character, e.g., coins, rare books, art works, etc. and can only be used against gains on the same type of property. Thus, deduction for losses due to the decline in value of consumer durables is not allowed. In addition, gain on the disposition of a principal residence is exempt.

In an attempt to reduce the amount of litigation concerning the distinction between ordinary income and capital gains, certain taxpayers are permitted to make a onetime irrevocable election to treat all gains in respect of all subsequent dispositions of "Canadian securities" to be on capital account. This election prevents taxpayers from claiming capital gains treatment in respect of gains and ordinary loss treatment in respect of losses from dispositions of Canadian securities. This election is not available to traders in securities, financial institutions, or nonresidents.

The *Australian* system taxes capital gains at ordinary rates with an indexation of gains but not losses. Indexation applies only if the asset is held for more than twelve months. It is based on a broad consumer price index and compares the index in the calendar quarter of acquisition and the calendar quarter of disposal. Thus, for example, for an asset acquired in the third quarter of 1985 and disposed of in the fourth quarter of 1995, the cost indexation factor would be 1.582 reflecting a 58% inflation over that period. Indexation relates only to the asset and not to associated liabilities so that the interest on a loan used to purchase an income-producing asset remains deductible on a nominal basis. To limit the tax shelter possibilities which this system offers, interest deductions related to real estate investments were at one time limited to the income the property produced. These restrictions were later repealed.

Capital losses are deductible against capital gains but not other income. Excess capital losses may be carried forward indefinitely to offset capital gains. Rules similar to those in Canada apply to gains and losses on personal assets and also exempt gain on the disposition of the principal residence.

When Canada and the United Kingdom introduced the taxation of capital gains, assets were valued at the time of enactment for purposes of calculating gain or loss, with the United Kingdom rule subsequently changed to a later valuation date in connection with the introduction of indexation. Australia applied its capital gains tax only to assets acquired after a certain date, thus necessitating complex rules preserving the "pre" and "post" character of gains, for example, in the case of rollovers.

The following **Table II-1** summarizes some of the inclusion rules discussed in Subpart A. To deal with the issues which arise in connection with schedular systems, the headings indicate the type of situation being considered. For example, for Windfalls, the assumption is that the windfall does not occur in a business setting or in connection with profit-seeking activities. Similarly, with respect to Illegal Income, the assumption is that the income would otherwise fall into a taxable category if the factor of illegality was not involved.

Some aspects of the tax base: Inclusions

	Imputed rental income from residence	Personal gifts	Business gifts	Windfalls (non-business /profit-seeking)	Illegal income (otherwise taxable)	Public subsidies (business context)	Debt cancellation (business context)
Australia	excluded	excluded	included	excluded	included	generally included	excluded but reduce tax cost or losses if capital (proposed); taxable if ordinary
Canada	excluded	excluded	included	excluded	included	reduction of tax cost	excluded but reduce tax cost or losses if capital; taxable if ordinary
France	excluded	excluded	generally excluded	excluded	included	generally included	included
Germany	excluded	excluded	included under certain conditions	excluded	included	included or tax cost reduction	generally included but some exceptions
Japan	excluded	excluded	included	included	included	included or tax cost reduction	included

	Imputed rental income from residence	Personal gifts	Business gifts	Windfalls (non-business /profit-seeking)	Illegal income (otherwise taxable)	Public subsidies (business context)	Debt cancellation (business context)
The Netherlands	included	excluded	included generally	excluded	included	generally not included	generally excluded (exception regarding prior losses)
Sweden	included	excluded	generally included	excluded	included	included or tax cost reduction	included if solvent; if not, excluded but loss reduction
United Kingdom	excluded	excluded	excluded (if not for services)	excluded	included	included (unless specific exclusion)	generally excluded (unless business tax benefit from funds)
United States	excluded	excluded	generally excluded (employee includes)	included	included	included or tax cost reduction	included or tax cost/loss reduction

Subpart B: Deductions

The basic notion that an income tax is in general imposed on gross income reduced by deductions and not some broader category of receipts is a premise of all of the systems here under consideration. Though the implementation of that principle takes numerous forms, there are some common features. All systems recognize that in general deductible expenditures involved in income definition must have some connection to taxable activities and that personal consumption should, at least in most cases, be included in the tax base. The systems also distinguish between current expenses that reduce income of the period and capital expenditures that are taken into account through some sort of capital cost recovery system. In some systems, all income-related expenses are in principle deductible unless otherwise limited. In others, deduction is restricted to a more specific catalogue of expenditures. In addition to a deduction for expenses necessary to properly determine net income, a number of systems allow a deductions for certain personal expenses.

Beyond the definition of deductible expenses, all of the systems have important schedular aspects in connection with deductions. Even where income is defined in a global fashion, various classes of deductions are often limited to certain categories of income.

Many systems have special rules dealing with deductions by employees. Some systems allow a fixed deduction from employment income but disallow specific employee deductions. In other situations, only a very limited class of employee deductions is allowed and then often only to the extent that the expenses exceed a certain floor. Limitations of this sort are based on the administrative difficulty of policing such deductions and the concern that, without limitations, substantial amounts of personal, living, and consumption costs would be deducted. The rules are usually not extended to an individual's business or professional income, though arguably the same problems exist there. Where employee deductions are restricted and not offset by some sort of lump sum or standard deduction, while professional and business deductions are allowed without limitation, the general effect is to favor high bracket taxpayers.

Other limitations typically restrict losses arising from interest and capital recovery deductions. These limitations frequently arose in response to perceived problems with "tax shelter" investments. The various limitations on deductions are discussed after consideration of the substantive deduction rules.

1. Mixed business and personal expenses

All of the systems must deal with the basic problem of expenditures which have both an income-producing and a consumption dimension, though the overall responses to the problem are somewhat different, as are the more specific rules. At one extreme, *Germany* has a general statutory provision which disallows the deduction of any expense of "mixed" character unless there is a specific statutory rule allowing a deduction, e.g., business meals. The "prohibition of division and deduction" appears based on the idea that, for reasons of tax equity, consumption should be included in the tax base, even if the consumption necessarily takes place in a business context. Only in very limited circumstances where the personal element is de minimis or the business and personal elements can be clearly separated will any deduction be allowed.

The *United Kingdom* reaches the same result using a somewhat different analysis. Deductions are allowed if they are incurred "wholly and exclusively" in connection with trade or professional activities. For business income the test is based on the purpose behind the expenditure. However, the apparent breadth of this rule is offset by an absolute prohibition on the deduction of a "dual purpose" expenditure and by the refusal of the courts to apply the purpose test simply on the basis of what the taxpayers say their purpose was. By contrast, where the deduction relates to employment income, the general test requires that the expense be incurred wholly, exclusively and necessarily in the performance of the duties of the office or employment. This language has been interpreted to mean that expenses of getting into a position to earn income, as opposed to the actual performance of the activities which generate the income, are not deductible and has influenced the treatment of expenses involving commuting, moving, child care, and the like. The divergence between business and employment income deduction rules should not be exaggerated, however. In many of these instances, the expenditure will not be deductible for business income either, usually on the grounds of mixed personal and business purposes.

In *Canada*, the treatment of mixed business/personal expenses is a hodgepodge of statutory rules and administrative practice. In general, expenses must be categorized as either personal or business. They are either deductible in full or not at all. Where, however, an expense can be apportioned on some objective, verifiable basis, such as automobile expenses, Revenue Canada will allow the appropriate portion of the cost to be deductible. There is nothing in the statute to prohibit the apportionment of mixed business and personal expenses.

Even in countries like *Australia*, where apportionment of expenses as deductions is explicitly recognized, the occasion and nature of the apportionment is still debated. For example, if a person flies to a foreign country for one week of business activities and one week of holiday, it is necessary to apportion the costs of accommodation but it is not clear if the airfare would be subject to apportionment or subject to an all-or-nothing test.

In *Sweden*, the general approach is to attempt to identify the extra cost related to the business aspect of the expense. For example, costs for books and other reading material cannot be deducted even if used in business if the material is such that it could reasonably be assumed that it would have been purchased for nonbusiness reasons. On the other hand, an instrumentalist in an orchestra was allowed to deduct dental costs necessary to continue to perform and which he would not have otherwise incurred.

The *French* approach is somewhat similar. No general principle prohibits the deduction of mixed expenses and apportionment is made on a case-by-case basis.

In *The Netherlands*, case law (subsequently modified by statute) developed a somewhat different test. Expenses were not deductible if they would normally be incurred by someone who was not in the taxpayer's occupation. In addition, if they were typical for the profession, no deduction was allowed for those expenses in excess of what would normally be incurred by others in the profession.

Whatever the general, typically case law-developed rules, commonly recurring costs like commuting, business entertainment, moving, etc. often are dealt with in special provisions setting forth the conditions for and limits on deduction. The rules are not always consistent with any general theory. One common approach is the allowance of a specified percentage of costs that typically have a high consumption content, e.g., meals and entertainment. High substantiation requirements are also usually associated with such expenses.

Another recurring feature in the treatment of employees is an inconsistency between those costs that can be deducted if incurred directly and those that are excluded if reimbursed by an employer. The exclusion rules are usually more generous than the deduction rules. This may be explained in part by the assumption that the business connection is more likely predominant if the employer is willing to bear the cost, at least in those cases where it is clear that the expense does not simply represent additional compensation. The exclusion thus serves as a netting of income and deduction for costs which are assumed to be business connected because they are reimbursed. The following material examines some selected deductions which involve business and personal aspects.

1.1 Commuting

Commuting expenses have a clear business connection in that they are necessary to place the taxpayer in a position to begin his income producing activity. On the other hand, the level of commuting expense is tied up with the personal decision as to where to live in relation to the workplace and the means of transportation used. While several systems deny commuting deductions altogether, a number give a limited deduction.

Thus, in the *United States*, commuting expenses, defined as traveling from the taxpayer's personal residence to his principal place of work, are in general nondeductible. Once the taxpayer is in "work status," traveling expenses between work sites are deductible. A complex set of case law and administrative rules deal with the myriad of issues which arise in applying this general principle. For example, the costs of occasional travel directly from the personal residence to a secondary work site are deductible; the taxpayer is not required to go first to his principal work site.

For employees, commuting expenses, like other employee expenses, are deductible only to the extent that, together with other miscellaneous deductions, they exceed 2 % of income.

Similarly, commuting expenses are not deductible in *Canada*, following earlier United Kingdom cases which had reached the same result. Costs incurred to put the taxpayer in the position to earn income are not incurred in the course of work and are viewed as essentially personal. The costs are also related to the personal choice of where to live. In some Canadian cases, taxpayers attempted to circumvent the rule by establishing home offices and claiming the home/business trip was in the course of business. Substantial restrictions on the deductibility of home office expenses eliminated this tactic.

In the *United Kingdom*, the same result was reached in the case of a barrister who worked at home by finding that his chambers was his principal place of work and the cost of travel home in the evening was personal even though he worked there. The cost of travel was not "wholly and exclusively" business related. On the other hand, travel between two (exclusive) work sites is allowed as a deduction.

Australian case law has followed the same pattern, also basing its analysis on United Kingdom cases.

In *Germany*, a complex "lex specialis" deals expressly with the deductibility of commuting expenses. In general, the deductibility depends on the method of transportation. Actual expenses of public transportation are fully deductible as long as they can be fully documented. (There is no attempt to allocate between commuting and other use for monthly transit passes.) In case of private transportation, there is a statutory per kilometer rate for cars, motorbikes, and bicycles intended to cover all costs associated with commuting. Disabled individuals can deduct the costs in full. Distances must be measured with reference to the shortest available route; however, a longer route can be taken if it is "substantially" better in terms of traffic conditions. If the taxpayer drives to a "park and ride" station and continues the commute by public transportation, the per kilometer allowance can be deducted from the home to the parking location and the full cost of the public transportation from there to the workplace. The constitutionality of the limitation of commuting expenses to the per kilometer amount has been upheld by the Federal Constitutional Court.

In *Sweden*, though commuting expenses are viewed in principle as personal, a special statutory provision allows the deduction of commuting expenses to the extent they exceed ca. $600 per year. Only "reasonable" expenses are allowed which in practice means the cost of public transportation. The taxpayer can deduct the costs of traveling by car only when he can establish that use of the car saves at least two hours per day in commuting time. The deduction is limited to a per kilometer amount intended to cover the marginal costs of the car. The trip must be between the taxpayer's "residence" and workplace which has excluded costs of traveling from a summer house to work (a common occurrence in Sweden).

In *The Netherlands*, commuting costs were originally considered personal and nondeductible. Later, as housing shortages caused more people to live at a distance from their work, case law began allowing deduction in some situations. Beginning in 1964, legislation has allowed a limited deduction for commuting expenses though the last tax reform study in 1991 again proposed the abolition of the deduction on the grounds that the expenses were essentially private.

Under the existing rules, for commuting by private car, no deduction is allowed for the first ten kilometers of travel which is considered a private cost. (Similarly, any employer reimbursement is fully taxed). For distances of over ten kilometers, a variable annual amount is deductible depending on the distance traveled with a maximum deductible amount reached at twenty kilometers, (a slightly higher amount may be reimbursed tax-free). If public transportation is used, annual deductions (and tax-free reimbursement thresholds) are higher with a maximum based on eighty kilometers of travel. These rules are intended to reflect both environmental and traffic considerations as well as the mixed nature of the expenses.

The treatment of commuting expenses in *Japan* has been revised several times. Commuting costs are usually paid by the employer and these payments are tax-free up to a certain level. Initially, deductions were not permitted for specific costs, including commuting expenses in excess of the tax-free amounts, if incurred by employees in connection with income which fell into the employment category. Instead, income in that category was subject to a large "standard" deduction, whose relative size varied with income but which amounted to 30 % to 40 % of compensation. While the deduction performed several functions, its main role was to avoid the administrative burden of dealing with itemized deductions for employee expenses.[7] This technique proved controversial and constitutional objections were raised that it discriminated against wage-earners in relation to other taxpayers, in particular the self-employed who enjoyed such deductions. Though the constitutionality of the approach was ultimately upheld, the statutory rules were changed to allow a limited number of employee deductions, including

---

7 In addition to the administrative role discussed in the text, it has been suggested that the large standard deduction was related to the fact that more wage income was likely to be reported than income in other categories, taxes were paid more promptly due to withholding and, more broadly, that it functioned as a surrogate for a deduction for "human capital."

commuting expenses, to be taken if the total of such deductions exceeded the standard deduction. Thus "ordinary and necessary" commuting expenses can be deducted individually in some circumstances. While important as a matter of principle, in practice, a very small number of taxpayers actually itemize employee deductions.

In *France*, the general principle is that commuting expenses can be deducted, either in their actual amount or based on a per kilometer rate, provided that distance between home and work is not "abnormal." In administrative practice, this has meant a maximum of forty kilometers unless the taxpayer can justify the extra distance on social or business grounds. Most employees (95 %) do not take itemized deductions for expenses like commuting but elect a standard deduction of 10 % of their compensation.

1.2 Moving expenses

Like commuting, moving expenses have both business and a personal connection. Some moves may be entirely personally motivated and others required by the employer. Again, the approaches vary. However, in many cases employer-reimbursed expenses are not included in income where directly incurred expenses in the same situation would not be deductible. This approach, in effect, uses the fact of employer reimbursement as a proxy for the establishment of a necessary business connection for the move.

In the *United States*, case law originally held moving expenses to be nondeductible in the same manner as commuting expenses. However, administrative practice allowed the exclusion of certain employer-reimbursed expenses, creating a disparity both between directly incurred expenses and those reimbursed and between different categories of reimbursed expenses. The final statutory resolution was to require all reimbursements to be included in income and then to allow a deduction for a limited category of moving expenses. To be deductible, the move must be in connection with the commencement of work at a new place of business and meet certain distance requirements. Unlike commuting expenses, moving expenses are not subject to a percentage-of-income limitation.

In *Germany*, there are no special statutory rules dealing with moving costs. They are deductible in some circumstances under case law principles interpreting the general deduction for income-producing expenses. The move must have been exclusively or nearly exclusively for a business reason. The most frequent is the change of job location (which is itself assumed to be business related). Without a change of job, a move can be business related if it results in a saving of travel time to the job of at least one hour per day. If the move is found to be business-related, a deduction will be allowed up to the amount which would have been paid as reimbursed expenses to a civil servant for a similar move without proof of actual cost. Higher costs can be deducted but the taxpayer must establish the business connection of all of the costs.

In the *Commonwealth* systems, as a matter of general principle, moving costs are considered personal in the same way as commuting expenses. However, a special statutory rule now allows moving expenses in limited circumstances in *Canada*. Moving expenses are deductible if they arise in connection with the commencement of employment or business in a new location. The move must result in the new residence being at least 40 kilometers closer to the new workplace than the old residence.

Originally, this latter limitation was interpreted by the courts as measured in a straight line. As a result, a taxpayer was denied a deduction when he moved from the Quebec side of the Ottawa River to the Ottawa side, even though the distance limitation was satisfied if measured in terms of normal driving distance. This strict interpretation has recently been reversed by the Court of Appeal in favor of a more flexible interpretation that takes into account the normal means of transportation available.

The statutory deduction was added in part to remove discrimination between employees who received moving reimbursement from their employers and those who did not. The court cases had consistently held that such reimbursements were not includable income.

In the *United Kingdom*, there are no special statutory rules on deduction and the expenses remain nondeductible, though a special statutory provision exempts employer reimbursements of certain costs up to ca. $12,000 per move. *Australia* reaches a similar result by not allowing an employee deduction for directly incurred expenses but exempting employer reimbursements from the otherwise applicable fringe benefits tax at the employer level.

In *Sweden*, in principle, moving expenses are not deductible, partly on the basis that they are personal costs and partly on the ground that they may in some circumstances be part of the costs of acquiring a new source of income and hence are capital costs. A case law exception allows a deduction where the move was the result of an order by the employer to move.

Sweden has a statutory exclusion for employer-reimbursed moving expenses of certain kinds, even when those expenses would not be deductible if incurred directly. The somewhat unsatisfactory justification of the exclusion of employer-borne costs is to encourage labor mobility in a geographically large country. Size, however, does not seem to be a consistent factor in the treatment of moving expenses given the restrictive rules in Australia and the United Kingdom and the more liberal provisions in Canada.

In *Japan*, moving expenses incurred because of a move at the request of the employer may be deducted in the same way as commuting expenses if the total of all itemized expenses exceeds the standard deduction. *The Netherlands* rules also allow a deduction for the expenses of a business-related move but limit the amount to a percentage of income and an absolute limit of ca. $7,500.

In *France*, while moving expenses are in principle deductible if the move was based on a change in job, most employees choose the 10 % standard deduction.

1.3 Clothing

Clothing is a classic example of a mixed business and personal expense and the results in all of the systems are very similar, involving an objective test as to the suitability of clothing for wear outside of work, regardless of the life-style of the particular individual.

The approach in the *United States* is to allow a deduction for clothing which is not adaptable to usual wear, is not so worn, and is required as a condition of the employment. Thus, cost of military uniforms which can be worn when off duty are not deductible while the cost of required clothing like fatigues whose off-duty use is restricted qualify for deduction.

In *Germany*, under the basic principle of no division of mixed costs, clothing expenses are either fully deductible or nondeductible. "Typical" professional clothing like uniforms for police, fire, military, airline employees, etc. which are necessary because of the nature of the business are deductible even if they can be worn privately. Special protective clothing, shoes, and the like are also deductible. Cost of "civil" clothes not associated with a particular profession and which can be worn in normal public settings are not normally deductible even if as a practical matter they are necessary for the profession, e.g., dark blue suit for lawyers. However, cases have allowed the deduction for the formal attire of a mortician, waiter's tuxedo, waiter's black trousers (criticized in the literature), and black suit of (Protestant) clergy.

The *French* rules are broadly similar but most employees take the standard deduction.

In *Canada*, clothing represents in general a personal expense and is not deductible. Special employment-related clothing expenses are not deductible by employees in Canada since that is not one of the enumerated employee deductions. However, employer-provided special clothing is not includable. Self-employed persons can deduct special clothing costs.

In the *United Kingdom*, Revenue practice provides special fixed allowances for tools and special clothing purchased by an employee which vary from job to job and depend on concession. For self-employed persons, in a leading United Kingdom case, a female barrister was not entitled to deduct the cost of cleaning ordinary clothing worn underneath court robes but which she had purchased specifically to wear in court. The cost of cleaning the wig and gown and other court robes, however, were deductible. The *Australian* rules are similar though they have one special feature. In order to prevent employers from providing on a tax-free basis "uniforms" which are not noticeably different from ordinary clothing, such clothing has to be registered in a Register of Approved Occupational Clothing which sets the standards for "borderline" clothing, specifying requirements (e.g., logos of a certain size) which must be met.

In *The Netherlands*, costs of "work clothing" can be deducted. "Work clothing" is defined as clothing that must be worn during work activity and that is exclusively or almost exclusively suited only for such use. Uniforms, overalls and professorial gowns are examples of deductible clothing.

Sweden is more restrictive and approaches the issue from a somewhat different angle. No deduction is allowed for clothing costs even if the clothes are special, like uniforms, etc. The theoretical justification is that the expenses for the business clothing are not in excess of the alternative "avoided" expenses for private clothing which would have been incurred in any event. Thus, there is no incremental cost attributable to the business connection. This reasoning is not applicable to outer clothing like overalls, etc. which are required in addition to normal clothing and the cost of such items can be deducted. Free clothing provided by the employer which is not suitable for private wear is excluded (though self-incurred costs for the same clothes would not be deductible).

1.4 Business travel

Deductions for costs incurred in business travel involve two separate issues. One is distinguishing the cost of business travel from commuting expenses in those systems in which commuting expenses are either not deductible or only entitled to limited deductions. The other is the treatment of meals and lodging which are typically involved in business travel. The systems differ in the extent to which they attempt to capture the potential consumption element in the latter expenses.

In the *United States*, travel expenses, including meals and lodging, incurred while "away from home" on business are in principle deductible. In order to prevent the deduction of commuting expenses, "home" in this context has been interpreted administratively (though not by all courts) to mean the taxpayer's principal place of business. Similarly, to prevent the deduction of "normal" expenses for meals during the business day, "away" has been interpreted to mean a situation in which a stop for sleep or rest is necessary. Thus, generally speaking, the costs of overnight business travel are deductible. However, the principles have been applied to a myriad of factual situations with results that are not easily reconcilable. If the taxpayer is away from home for more than one year, his "home" in the sense of principal place of business is, in effect, deemed to have been established in the new work location and lodging and meal expenses are no longer deductible as he is no longer "away" from home.

For domestic travel, the transportation costs are fully deductible if the "primary" purpose of the travel is business related. Meal and lodging expenses must be allocated between business and personal activities. More restrictive rules apply to foreign travel. The taxpayer may choose between substantiating actual expenses or claiming a geographically-based per diem amount. Meal expenses which would otherwise be deductible under these tests are limited to 50 % of the costs incurred, as is discussed in more detail below in connection with entertainment expenses.

In *Sweden*, travel expenses are, in principle, deductible to the extent they exceed the personal costs which would have been incurred in any event. This means that travel and lodging are fully deductible. Meals are deductible only if the trip involves a stay overnight. In that case, a standard amount is allowed as a deduction which is intended to equal the increase in expense over the meals at home. (A larger standardized amount can be excluded if the employer reimburses the meal expenses). The employee can get a larger deduction by showing that the increase in costs is, in fact, higher. For travel abroad there are special amounts for each country.

In *Canada*, travel expenses incurred while "away from home" are, in general, deductible. The deduction extends to employees as well, though subject to some restrictions. Only 50 % of the costs of business meals is deductible. If a conference fee includes meals and beverages, $50 of the fee is considered allocated to meals and subject to the limitation though no allocation is required for meals on airlines or trains.

Australia reaches roughly the same results through a combination of employee deduction and fringe benefits taxation in the case of reimbursed costs. In the former situation, there are detailed record-keeping requirements if the amounts claimed exceed the travel allowances given to public officials. If the expense is incurred by the employer, the same rules effectively apply through the operation of the fringe benefits tax.

The rules in the *United Kingdom* are more restrictive. Travel expenses must be incurred "wholly and exclusively" for the purposes of the business. In a leading case, a lawyer was denied the deduction of attending conferences where he admitted that there were social and holiday purposes associated with the trip. In another case, however, an accountant successfully argued that the social aspects of a similar trip were simply incidental to his business purpose and so was allowed a deduction. In practice, apparently some portion of the costs of "mixed" travel is allowed.

In *Germany*, transportation expenses can be established through receipts or a per kilometer allowance can be used. Lodging expenses are deductible in full based on actual costs (though the portion of the amount attributable to breakfast must be treated as a meal expense). For foreign travel, the taxpayer can use either actual costs or a per diem amount. For food costs, deduction is limited to a fixed per diem amount depending on how long the taxpayer is away from his work site. For periods of twenty-four hours or more, a deduction of ca. $31 is allowed. Corresponding tables will be published for foreign travel. If the taxpayer stays for more than three months in one place, he is no longer in travel status and the meals and lodging costs are no longer deductible and transportation costs are limited to commuting expenses.

The *French* rules on business travel are fairly relaxed, requiring only that the expenses be normal and incurred in the course of the business. Deductions for meal expenses of employees have to be reduced by the deemed cost of a meal at home, determined under the same principles as used for employer-provided meals in the context of fringe benefits.

Some jurisdictions have limitations on the cost of congresses or seminars. For example, in *The Netherlands,* only ca. $650 of expenses are fully deductible. Seventy-five percent of additional cost up to ca. $2,500 are deductible with no deduction for the expenses in excess of that amount. Employer reimbursements are not taxable but the employer deduction is limited to 75 % of the costs.

1.5 Business entertainment

While the business connection may influence the value of the entertainment somewhat compared to freely chosen personal expenditures, the consumption element is clear. Entertainment provided in a business context is particularly susceptible to abuse and, not unexpectedly, subject to special limitations. These limitations typically take the form of an overlay of additional requirements, especially substantiation, for any deduction at all and a percentage limit on qualifying expenses. In view of the administrative difficulties, none of the systems attempt to tax the recipient of the entertainment directly. The denial or limitation on the deduction ensures that some amount is included in the tax base, though not taxed to the person enjoying the consumption.

In the *United States*, entertainment expenses must meet the normal tests of deductibility and, in addition, be either "directly related" or "associated with" the taxpayer's trade or business. The rules are relaxed for meals and other recreational facilities provided on the business premises or to employees, restaurants serving the general public, etc. Deductions for club dues are disallowed entirely. Special substantiation requirements apply. Only 50 % of otherwise qualified expenditures may be deducted.

In *Germany*, entertainment expenses are limited in the first instance to "reasonable" amounts under the circumstances. Then 80 % of the amounts paid for food and beverages and 100 % of remaining amounts is deductible. Factors considered by the case law in determining reasonableness include the analysis of the situation from the point of view of a "conscientious business manager" (a construct often used in German tax law), the relation of the expenditure to particular business transactions, the size and profitability of the business, and the amounts spent by comparable businesses in this field. Proof must be provided for the amount and the business connection of the costs. With respect to meals, written documentation must be provided concerning the place, date, amount, business connection, and participants. Restaurant receipts are acceptable for the first three elements. A special statutory provision denies a deduction for all costs incurred in connection with hunting, fishing, yachting, and other similar activities which are used in business entertainment.

The pattern in *Sweden* is similar, though without an explicit percentage limitation. In addition to meeting the normal deduction tests involving the relation of the expense to a business activity, entertainment expenses must, under special statutory provisions, have a "direct connection" with the business. The expense must be incurred "solely" to establish or maintain a business relationship. This restriction would prevent, for example, the deduction of expenses of a yacht that was used to entertain customers, but also used personally.

Assuming the "direct connection" is present, the deduction is limited to a "reasonable" amount. In the case of business meals, there is a standard amount based on restaurant prices for lunches which is revised periodically. The amount may be higher if non-Nordic foreign visitors are being entertained. Until recently, no deduction was allowed for the cost of alcoholic beverages, but when the standard deductible amount was reduced to ca. $27 the special restriction on alcohol was eliminated.

When the entertainment provider is limited in the amount which can be deducted, the recipient is not required to include the value of the meal in income. Thus, if an employee participates in a business lunch with a client which is paid for by the employer, neither is required to include the meal in income. Though the employer's deduction may be less than the actual cost of the meal, the denial of the deduction for the excess still results in a lower total tax than if the meal had been fully deductible and includable in the income of the employee, e.g., as a taxable fringe benefit, given the difference in corporate and individual rates.

In general, no deduction is allowed in the *United Kingdom* for entertainment expenses incurred by employees. If amounts are reimbursed, there is no employee inclusion but the employer is denied the deduction. Otherwise, expenses must meet the "wholly and exclusively" test and then are still subject to substantial additional statutory limitations. *Australia* also has a special statutory rule which in general denies a deduction for entertainment expenses, subject to a number of exceptions such as for restaurants providing meals to customers, business trips, and the like. In addition, there is an exception for in-house dining facilities for employees. The latter exception has made it common practice for large legal and accounting firms to have quite lavish private dining facilities.

The overlay of the fringe benefit tax in Australia makes the situation quite complex as entertainment of employees and their associates is subject to the FBT while entertainment of non-employees is subject to the denial of deduction rule. To alleviate the potentially onerous record keeping burden, two alternative elective methods for dealing with entertainment expenses were introduced, a straight 50-50 split and a split based on a typical twelve week period.

In *Canada*, 50 % of directly connected entertainment expenses involved in business activities are deductible. No deduction is allowed for entertainment expenses incurred by employees. The Canadian rules expressly disallow any deduction for club dues, and the expenses of yachts, camps, lodges, and golf. *The Netherlands* similarly allows businesses to deduct only 75 % of entertainment expenses. For employees, no deduction for expenses is allowed. If the expenses are reimbursed by the employer, the reimbursement is tax-free and the employer's deduction is limited to 75 % of the amount.

The *French* rules are much more liberal. There is no particular standard of reasonableness and no percentage limitations apply. There is a special statutory provision, however, which disallows deduction for costs in connection with hunting, fishing, yachting, and similar activities.

In *Japan*, employees are not allowed any deduction for entertainment expenses. For self-employed persons, the expenses may only be deducted if the greater part of the expenses are business related and the business portion of the expense can clearly be identified. Special rules substantially restrict the deduction of entertainment expense by corporations.

The common technique of the limitation of the deduction for entertainment expenses as a substitute or surrogate for attempting to tax the beneficiary of the expenditures itself raises some problems. For example, it has no impact on tax-exempt organizations. This aspect led Australia to include under its fringe benefits tax a special rule to impose the tax on entertainment expenses of tax exempts. As a more general matter, as the Swedish situation shows, where there is a difference in tax bracket between the payor and the recipient, denial of the deduction can have quite different effects from the inclusion of the payment, though at least it ensures that some amount is included in the tax base at some point.

1.6 Child care

The treatment of child care expenses has been controversial in many systems. Historically, the courts have treated the expenses as personal and nondeductible. However, as single parent and two outside-worker families became more frequent, pressure to allow some tax relief for child care expenses increased. The impact which nondeductible child care expenses had on labor supply generally and especially with regard to secondary workers was an important factor in the policy debate. The response was typically to continue to treat the expenses as personal from an income definition point of view but provide some limited personal deduction or credit. No country allows full deduction of child care expenses as a business expense. However, a number of systems, while disallowing a deduction for directly-incurred child care expenses, allow an exclusion for employer-provided care.

The approach to child care costs in the *United States* has varied considerably over the years. Initially treated by the courts as personal expenses, early statutory provisions allowed a limited deduction for single parents and couples with low incomes. Subsequent legislation expanded the scope of the deduction but continued dollar limitations. Currently, the expenses are not deductible but a limited credit is provided for employment-related child care expenses. In addition, some forms of employer-paid child care can be provided as a nontaxable fringe benefit.

Canadian and United Kingdom courts have consistently held child care expenses personal and nondeductible. The *United Kingdom* continues to follow this approach, though there is a limited exclusion for employer-provided child care. There is no publicly provided child care assistance. In *Canada*, there is now a special statutory provision which allows a limited deduction for expenses incurred for a variety of child care services including day nursery and boarding schools or camps. The payments must be made to unrelated parties and the tax-payer must provide the social security number of the recipient. The effect of the deduction has had some positive effect on secondary work-ers entering the work force but the effect is limited by the fact that the deductible amount does not approximate actual child care costs. There is a limited amount of governmental subsidies to child care facilities. A proposal for universal child care was considered at one time but dropped for fiscal reasons.

In 1994, the Canadian Supreme Court considered an important case involving child care expenses. The taxpayer, a partner in a large law firm, whose spouse also worked, tried to deduct the full amount of child care expenses as ordinary business expenses, quite apart from the limited statutory deduction. She claimed that the limited deduction violated the Canadian Charter (Constitution) because it discriminated against women. In a 7 to 2 decision, a majority of the court (all males) disallowed the deduction, holding that the statutory deduction was exclusive. The provision was not discriminatory since there was no showing that the expenses were paid disproportionately by women. Two dissenters (both women) would have allowed the deduction. They argued that it could be inferred from the disadvantaged social and economic position of women that women bore a disproportionate amount of the costs of child care. The majority opinion intimated that, in the absence of the special statutory provision, "the changing composition of the business class and changing social structure" might require the reclassification of child care expenses as business expenses.

Case law in *Australia*, influenced by the United Kingdom, has also denied the deduction for child care expenses as business expenses, view-ing them as not being incurred "in the course of" employment. There are some limited exceptions from the fringe benefits tax for employer-provid-ed child care. There is no generally provided governmental child care, though there are some directly provided benefits and subsidies to private sector facilities. There are some studies showing a negative effect of the lack of a child care deduction on secondary workers.

In *Sweden*, child care costs are not currently deductible, though for a period there was a limited standard deduction for parents (couples or single) with children under sixteen at home which in part was to compensate for child care costs. The rule against deductibility should be viewed against the background of a heavily subsidized public child care system in Sweden. The personal choice to incur private expenses instead of using the available public facilities heightens the consumption element of the expenditure in light of the extensive government-provided child care facilities (costing some ca. $1.8 billion per year).

Germany has a number of special rules giving relief for taxpayers with children but most of them are based on the underlying notion that the expenses of children, at least up to certain levels, reduce the tax-paying capacity of the taxpayer and should not be included in the tax base. One provision which is to some degree conceptually related to those under discussion here allows a limited deduction for child care expenses if a single parent becomes employed, or is sick or disabled. In a provision added in 1986, in the case of married couples, the same deduction is allowed if both parties are sick or disabled or if one is sick or disabled and the other is employed. It is not allowed, however, if both are healthy and employed.

In *Japan*, child care expenses are considered purely personal and are not deductible. However, employer-provided child care is not taxed to the employee as a fringe benefit.

In *The Netherlands*, after a Supreme Court case in 1991 held that child care expenses were deductible, statutory limits were introduced. There are both thresholds and a fixed maximum deduction (ca. $6,000 per child). If the employer pays for child care, the amount below the threshold and above the maximum are taxable to the employee; employer-provided child care results in the threshold amount being taxable. The deduction is viewed as encouraging women with children to join the work force.

France considers child care as a nondeductible personal cost but provides a credit of 25 % of child care costs with a maximum of ca. $750 per year. There is also a credit for 50 % of the salary paid for au pair services and housecleaning (maximum credit ca. $9,000). This latter provision was intended to stimulate employment and does not require that both parents work for the credit to be available.

2. "Hobby losses" and the criteria for determining business versus personal activities

Activities which are ostensibly aimed at making a profit but which involve the potential for substantial personal consumption raise some of the same issues as mixed business and personal expenses and are frequently dealt with by special rules. The questions come up somewhat differently in schedular systems and in systems which operate with a more global income concept. In a schedular system, for either the profit to be taxable or losses deductible, the activity in question must fit within one of the taxable categories. Thus, in an occasional activity, e.g., stamp collecting, which does not fall in any taxable category, neither income nor expenses typically would be taken into account for tax purposes. In a global system, the profit will in any event be taxable; the issue involves the deduction of the costs which arise in the activity (and which will usually be larger than the income).

The *United States* has had a series of statutory provisions dealing with the "hobby loss" problem. Under the current version, if an activity carried on by an individual is found to be "not engaged in for profit," the deductions generated by the activity may only be used against the income from the activity. However, deductions which would be available even in the absence of profit-seeking activity have to be "stacked" first against the income. The effect of the provision is thus typically to deny a portion of the deduction for maintenance and depreciation expenses of the hobby activity against other income. The factors considered by the courts in determining if a profit-seeking activity is present include the nature of the activity as potentially recreation, e.g., horse raising, car racing, etc., whether the activities are carried on in a "businesslike" manner, the use of expert advisers, and the history of profits and losses of the activity and its potential for profit. The provision may be overgenerous to the taxpayer since, to some extent, it allows what are consumption expenses to be offset against the otherwise taxable income the activity generates.

While originally aimed at limiting the deduction for the consumption element in what were essentially personal activities, the provision has been applied to tax-motivated transactions which were not likely to generate a profit apart from the tax benefits.

In *Canada*, for tax purposes, a business is an enterprise that is carried on for profit or with a reasonable expectation of profit. In the absence of any reasonable expectation of profit, no deductions will be allowed. Nonetheless, the income, if any, may be taxable. The undertaking generating the income can be viewed as a taxable "source" despite the absence of a profit-seeking expectation. The reasonable expectation of profit question is an issue of fact and the results are varied.

A special rule applies to hobby farmers, a common phenomenon in Canada. Even if the reasonable expectation of profit test is met, where the hobby farmer's chief source of income is not farming or farming and some other source, there is a dollar limit on the amount of the loss which can be deducted against other income. Non-deductible farm losses can be carried forward and deducted against farm income in later years.

The *United Kingdom* approach has evolved somewhat differently. Under the basic common-law tests, it is fairly easy to establish a "trading" activity which would in principle allow the deduction of costs. However, this rule is supplemented by a special provision which requires that the trade must be carried on on a commercial basis and with a view to a realization of profit. A further special rule applies to farming which disallows losses after five consecutive years of loss unless it can be established that there was a reasonable expectation of profit if the business had been carried on by a competent person.

In *Germany*, there is extensive case law dealing with the issue of whether the taxpayer's activities constitute a "business," self-employment, rental, etc., or are private and hence not taxable. The basic test is in terms of an intention to make a profit. While formally a subjective test, the cases have consistently based their decisions on the objective facts which would indicate such an intent. The cases deal both with "classical" hobby loss situations and also with tax shelters. The statutory provision expressly states that a reduction in taxes is not considered a profit.

For the income to be taxable and the losses deductible, there must be objective evidence of the probability of a "total" profit, that is, that the activity will generate a net profit at some point in a "reasonable" time after the activities have been started. It is not sufficient that profits be made in later years after early years of losses; the income must be sufficient to cover all costs in the operation and still result in a profit. In determining if a profit is probable, it is appropriate to take into account possible increases in value of the assets involved as well as the operating income, as long as the gains on those assets would be taxable.

Thus, in the case of rental activities which do not constitute a business, the gain on sale of the property would not be taxed and thus cannot be taken into account in determining if a total profit will result. A special provision deals with losses from a business of breeding or keeping animals. Losses can only be deducted against other income of this type.

Prior to the tax reform of 1991, the *Swedish* system made a distinction between hobby activities and business which was based on the intention to make a profit. If the profit motive was not present, neither the income nor the expenses were taken into account for tax purposes. In the tax reform of 1991, changes were made in the definitions of taxable sources of income. Income from the performance of services is now taxable without regard to the existence of a profit motive. As a result, income from a hobby will be taxed in the "services" category. Deductions in principle should not be allowed but are permitted up to the amount of the income. Any excess loss cannot be deducted against other income on the theory that the costs are personal.

In *The Netherlands*, there is substantial case law dealing with the definition of a "business" (enterprise) which draws the line between taxable business and nontaxable personal activities. For a business to be present, there must be (1) a permanent organization of labor and capital; (2) participation in an economic interchange; and (3) a profit-making goal and reasonable expectation of success. These requirements, in effect, place most hobby activities on the personal side of the line with the result that no receipts are taxed and no expenses are deductible. In some cases, a hobby activity may be viewed as involving "income from other employment," but in practice, if there is a history of losses, it is unlikely that the deductions would be allowed.

Australia has no objective criterion of the likelihood of profit as the test for determining if the taxpayer is engaged in a business, and as a result there has been considerable litigation over the business/hobby borderline. There have been some unsuccessful attempts to limit the deductibility of farming losses against other income.

Hobby loss issues have not been extensively litigated or debated in *Japan*. There is, however, some administrative guidance with regard to owners of racing horses. If certain requirements as to number of horses, number of races, manner in which the operations are conducted, etc. are met, then the income will constitute business income and any net loss can be used against other income in other taxable categories. If the tests are not met, the income would be in the

Miscellaneous Income category and, while the expenses could be used to offset the racing income, any excess loss cannot be used against other income.

3. Capital costs and recovery methods

3.1 Determining capital costs

All of the systems recognize the distinction between currently deductible costs and capital costs. The latter create an amount to be recovered under some sort of capital cost recovery system or when the asset is disposed of or a loss is deemed to be realized. While the details of the rules and the formulation of the distinction differ, in general, costs that create a benefit in future years must be capitalized if they represent a relatively large and nonrecurring expenditure. In some systems, the treatment for accounting purposes is important for the tax characterization. There is an unavoidable arbitrariness in the classifications in all of the systems, though a surprising amount of similarity occurs in the results.

Taking the *United States* as an example, the formulation of the current capital distinction in the case law has varied over time. At one point the stress was on whether the expenditure could be said to have created a separate and distinct asset. More recently, however, the focus has returned to the issue of the existence of a significant benefit from the expenditure which extends beyond the taxable year. Even here, however, the test is not applied consistently. For example, advertising expenses can generally be deducted currently despite the clear benefit in later periods.

In the *German* system, there is a specific statutory provision which requires capitalization of any expenditure whose benefits will not be exhausted during the year. However, in practice, the courts and the fiscal authorities have allowed a current deduction for major outlays that have a recurring nature in the particular business involved. Similarly, current maintenance expenses are deductible but modifications that substantially alter the condition or character of the asset must be treated as capital costs. Expenses like painting which would normally be maintenance must be capitalized if incurred in connection with a major renovation of the asset. As discussed in more detail below, under the basic German approach to the relation between tax and financial accounting rules, the same treatment must be used for financial accounting purposes.

In the *Commonwealth* systems, the basic distinction has historically been between currently deductible expenditures incurred in connection with the income-earning process and capital outlays. The latter are not deductible except as specially provided for by statute. Various court developed tests have been applied in the *United Kingdom*, *Canada*, and *Australia* and parallel, to a large extent, the pattern in the United States. The formulations have included whether the expenditure brings with it an enduring benefit for the business and whether it relates to a specific and identifiable asset of a capital nature.

In Sweden, deduction is allowed currently for cost of assets whose useful life does not exceed three years and for de minimis cost in the range of ca. $700. Otherwise costs must be capitalized.

In the *French* system, the focus historically for capitalization has been on the creation or acquisition of a distinct and legally identifiable asset or a substantial modification in the condition, character or useful life of an existing asset. More recent cases, however, seem to take the position that all costs which create a steady and durable source of income have to be capitalized, e.g., the payment for a license to exploit a patent.

3.2 Capital cost recovery systems

While there is a great deal of variation in the systems of capital cost recovery, all systems seem to have three types of rules. The first are attempts, however rough, to allow a deduction for the capital costs over something like the actual useful life of wasting assets in order to properly reflect the taxpayer's income. In addition, completely arbitrary rules are sometimes used in some situations as a matter of administrative convenience. Finally, certain types of capital costs are allowed to be written off immediately or over a short period in order to encourage investments in particular types of assets or to achieve other non-fiscal goals.

The *United States* system fits this pattern. Depreciation rules have been modified a number of times and the development of the rules reflects both changes intended to simplify the administration of the system and changes in the attitude toward using accelerated depreciation allowances as an incentive for particular forms of investment. Historically, depreciation was mandatory and was based on useful lives intended to reflect actual experience with particular types of assets.

The system was initially based on the experience of the particular tax-payer but then relaxed to provide for generally applicable classes of assets which allowed the taxpayer to vary the applicable lives some-what. Straight line methods were generally used, though increasingly, accelerated methods were permitted to reflect the fact that certain assets declined more in value in early years and to provide investment incentives.

The system was changed substantially in 1981. Under the "Accelerated Cost Recovery System" (ACRS), class lives were estab-lished for all assets which generally had no relation to either the actual useful life of the asset in general, or in the hands of the particular tax-payer. For example, real estate was assigned a class life of fifteen years. Accelerated depreciation methods were applied to the class lives which substantially increased the availability of early deductions. 1981 marked the high-water mark of noneconomic depreciation policies. Since that time, while the class-life system has been retained, most class lives are now more realistic (though not entirely so) and the rates of depreciation have been reduced. For example, straight line deprecia-tion must be used on all real estate and in the case of commercial real estate the useful life has been extended to thirty-nine years. A separate set of depreciation rules based on longer useful lives and straight line depreciation must be used for some purposes and also may be elected by the taxpayer.

With respect to intangibles, traditionally all assets which had a determinable useful life could be amortized over that life. Other assets, such as goodwill, were not amortizable. These rules put substantial pres-sure on the allocation of costs between arguably short-lived intangibles such as customer lists, favorable contracts, covenants-not-to-compete, and the like and nondepreciable goodwill. In response to a large amount of litigation over these issues, a statutory amendment in 1993 allowed all nonfinancial intangibles, including goodwill, obtained in the acquisition of all or part of a business, to be amortized over a fifteen year period on a straight line basis. This simplifying rule allows a deduction for goodwill amortization but also requires that assets with actual shorter useful lives be amortized over the uniform fifteen year period.

A number of special rules continue to apply for certain types of assets and expenditures. Research and experimentation costs can be deducted currently or amortized over a five-year period at the election of the taxpayer. Pollution control facilities are subject to special rules as are some costs in natural resource exploitation. Subject to some limitations, up to $17,500 of costs for tangible property used in a trade or business can be deducted currently. Special rules limit the deductions with respect to cars, computers, and other assets which would typically be used for both business and personal reasons.

Canada has a comprehensive system of capital cost recovery for all tangible and intangible capital assets. Tangible assets and certain intangibles which have a limited useful life are classified into forty-four different "classes" and rates of depreciation are prescribed for each class based on rough estimates of their useful lives. Cost-recovery deductions are determined on a declining balance basis for all of the assets in a class or pool. The cost of purchases of property of a particular class is added to the pool. In the case of a disposition, the lesser of the cost of the asset or the proceeds of disposition are subtracted from the pool. If the result in the pool at the end of a year is negative, that amount is included in income as recaptured depreciation. In contrast, if there is a positive balance in the pool at the end of the year and there are no assets left in the class, the unrecovered balance is currently deductible. Although the maximum amount of depreciation is determined for each pool or class on the basis of the prescribed rate of depreciation, the taxpayer can choose on a year-to-year basis to deduct a smaller amount. Thus, a taxpayer without sufficient income to absorb the depreciation deduction may postpone the depreciation deduction until later years rather than taking the deduction and creating an operating loss.

Land does not qualify for depreciation. Similarly, any asset that is not acquired for the purpose of earning income cannot qualify for depreciation. Certain types of property, such as pollution control equipment and certain manufacturing and processing assets, qualify for accelerated depreciation.

Prior to 1972, the cost of goodwill and other intangibles with no limited useful life could not be deducted and was not covered by the capital cost recovery system. Legislation, later amended, now provides for the deduction of 75 % of the costs of goodwill on a declining basis at 7.5 %. On the sale of goodwill, 75 % of the proceeds are included in income. The expenses and proceeds are accounted for on a pooled basis using the same techniques as the capital cost recovery system.

The *Australian* system, like the Canadian, begins with a general prohibition on the current deductibility of capital costs. Various depreciation regimes are then provided for plants and equipment, buildings, mining, a host of specific expenditures on tangible assets, and a limited class of intangibles like patents. In general, there is no amortization for goodwill or other similar intangibles, though one-half of the capital gain on the disposal of goodwill is exempt from tax on the sale of a business with a net worth of less than ca. $1,500,000. In addition, in some situations capital costs which do not fit within the statutory or case law pattern are not taken into account for tax purposes at all. This phenomenon of so-called "nothings" underlines the lack of a comprehensive system for depreciation.

Where depreciation is available, it is based on estimated effective lives and a declining balance method. Thus, for example, plant and equipment with a life in the ten to thirteen year range is depreciated at a 25 % declining rate. Building depreciation is straight line at 2.5 % or 4 % depending on the nature of the asset. The fiscal authorities publish tables of effective lives which taxpayers may use but are not binding on taxpayers. Slower depreciation rates, including straight line, can be elected when the asset is placed in service but thereafter depreciation is mandatory. Expensing is allowed for assets with a life of less than three years and for de minimis amounts. A limited number of provisions allows expensing for incentive purposes with regard to certain activities, e.g., research and development. If on disposal of the assets the proceeds exceed the depreciated basis, the taxpayer may elect to avoid taxation by writing down the basis of other assets. A pooling system is available in some circumstances but is not widely used.

In the *United Kingdom*, the class of assets subject to depreciation is more limited than in other systems. No depreciation is allowed, for example, for office buildings or retail stores. Machinery and equipment and industrial buildings, on the other hand, are depreciable. The rate of depreciation has varied greatly and neither the period of depreciation nor the rate have had any connection to actual useful life. In the 1970s, an immediate write-off was allowed for machinery and equipment and 50 % of the cost of industrial buildings could be deducted immediately with the remainder recoverable over twenty-five years on a straight-line basis. Later changes reduced the rates of recovery to straight line over twenty-five years for buildings and a pooled basis for machinery with a 25 % rate. Taxpayers can elect to disclaim the deduction in whole or in part in a particular year thus deferring the deduction to a later period.

In *Germany*, depreciation for wasting assets is based on useful lives as determined in depreciation tables published by the Ministry.

The tables are not binding on either tax authorities or taxpayers but are followed in the vast majority of cases and deviations must be specially justified. Depreciation is mandatory, though the taxpayer can in some cases choose among methods. Rates range from 2 - 2.5 % straight-line for buildings to 30 % declining balance for tangible property. The taxpayer may switch to straight line when that is more advantageous. The justification for the declining balance method is that the decline in market value in the early years of use is high and maintenance expenses low, while in later years the reverse is true. Since 1986, business goodwill can be depreciated on a fifteen-year straight-line basis. (Different case law-based principles apply to professional goodwill). Depreciation can also be based on the production of the asset, comparing the performance in the year with the total anticipated production. Assets whose value does not exceed ca. $530 may be deducted currently.

There are a number of provisions allowing an accelerated depreciation to encourage investment in particular assets, e.g., environmental protection, hospitals, ships, small businesses, etc. With respect to investments in former East Germany, an immediate deduction of 50 % of certain acquisition and construction costs was initially allowed but is now being phased out. Special provisions also exist for investments in Berlin.

While extraordinary depreciation can be taken for technical or economic obsolescence or heavy use, in general, there is no deduction for declines in value due to market or other conditions. However, for businesses, a special statutory rule allows all assets (including land and stock interests) to be written down to "going concern value." The basic notion is that the business assets should be valued as if the entire business had to be disposed of to one potential buyer and the appropriate part of the purchase price had been allocated to the asset in question. The going concern value cannot be less than the price the asset would have obtained if sold separately or more than the replacement cost. The taxpayer has the burden of proof as to going concern value and the assets must also be written down in the books of commercial account. Though the going concern principle introduces substantial uncertainty in the calculation of income, it is an accepted part of German rules on income determination.

In *Japan*, the taxpayer can elect between either straight-line or declining balance methods based on useful life tables that are determined by the tax authorities. The tables are extremely detailed and though it is hard to generalize, seem to reflect realistic estimates of actual lives. However, there are some attempts to use artificial useful lives to encourage particular investments and there are some incentive provisions granting accelerated depreciation for certain investments.

In *France*, the same rules normally apply for accounting and tax purposes. In principle, depreciation or amortization is allowed for all assets, the benefits of which are likely to be exhausted over a determinable period. Recently, there is a tendency to allow amortization with respect to acquired goodwill, despite the difficulty of establishing a useful life.

Useful lives are determined by reference to generally accepted business practices (with a 20 % leeway) and different lives can be used under special circumstances, e.g., in the case of heavy use. Both straight-line and declining balance methods are generally used and there are a number of special incentive provisions to encourage certain investments. If the taxpayer is operating at a loss, in certain circumstances all or a portion of the otherwise available depreciation can be deferred and carried over to later years without limitation.

In *The Netherlands*, the rules regarding depreciation are extremely flexible. There are no formal rules on useful lives and all depreciation methods are allowed as long as they are used consistently and meet the standard of "good business practice." This standard requires that depreciation be based on historical cost and not replacement value. Previously, accelerated depreciation methods were used to encourage certain types of investments but were replaced with a direct grant program which was in turn allowed to expire. Currently, there are several provisions allowing arbitrary depreciation methods for certain assets, for example, property used in designated regions or involved in advanced technology, eco-technology or in research and development.

Sweden allows depreciation deductions over standardized lives which are shorter than actual useful life for machinery and equipment. Depreciation rates are 20 % straight line or 30 % declining balance, at the taxpayer's choice. For buildings, the depreciation is straight line over twenty-five years, but the rules on the deduction of maintenance costs are quite liberal and the combined deductions for real estate are generous. Research and development costs are currently deductible. Costs involved in inventory production are treated in the same manner.

4. Educational costs

Education costs can involve personal consumption, business-related current expenses, or investment in "human capital" depending on the circumstances in which they arise. All of the systems here take generally the same approach, disallowing the expenses of basic education but allowing deductions where the taxpayer is improving or maintaining existing skills. Thus in the *United States*, expenses which maintain or improve the taxpayer's skills in an existing trade or business are generally deductible. However, if the expenses in fact qualify the taxpayer for a new trade or business or are necessary to meet the minimum educational requirements of a trade or business, no deduction is allowed. The test is an objective one; even if the taxpayer never intends and never does enter the new profession, the expenses are not deductible. Thus, an accountant who attends law school cannot generally deduct the expenses even if he undertakes the expenses only to further his accountancy career, since he is in fact qualified for a new trade or business. For nondeductible expenses, there is no provision for the amortization of the investment in "human capital."

In *Sweden*, in general, the same approach is taken. Educational expenses are usually not deductible. This is especially the case where they result in qualification for a new position. On the other hand, educational expenses to maintain an existing competence are deductible. Similarly, in *Japan*, educational expenses are usually not deductible, although employees can deduct expenses of education that is required by the employer.

In *Canada*, education expenses are not deductible. The expenses are viewed as personal, capital, or a mixture of both. Continuing education expenses of a taxpayer already established in a business are deductible as business expenses. A tax credit is available for certain postsecondary school costs.

The *Australian* system is along the same lines, with only educational costs involved in an existing trade or profession being deductible, though for historical reasons they must be in excess of a fixed threshold amount. The main exception relates to student living allowances which are available from the government on a means-tested basis. These amounts are taxable and educational expenses funded out of such amounts are deductible even where there is no existing trade or business.

The *United Kingdom* followed these principles until 1991 when a deduction for qualifying vocational training payments was introduced.

In *Germany* as well, there is a distinction between "basic" and "continuing" education, with only expenses for the latter being deductible. Basic education costs are considered personal and are therefore only deductible to a limited extent under the provision for "special" personal costs.

In *The Netherlands* education expenses incurred by an employee to maintain his current skills are treated as employment expenses and as such deductible against employment income. Costs incurred in training for a higher-level job or other occupation are personal expenses which are nonetheless deductible but only to the extent they exceed certain thresholds.

The *French* system allows a deduction for educational costs to maintain or improve skills and, in the case of employees, to qualify for a new position. In addition, students may either be included in the fiscal household of the parents or taxed separately. Where separate taxation is the case, payments made by the parents to the student can be deducted within limits.

5. Deduction of personal costs

As discussed in the Country Descriptions in Part One, personal costs are in general reflected in a personal exemption or personal allowance which in effect frees from tax a certain minimum level of income. In addition, some systems allow a deduction for specific personal costs such as medical costs or personal losses.

5.1 Interest

All of the systems allow deduction in general for interest expenses incurred in connection with business or investment activities. The deduction is sometimes limited to the amount of current investment income, in order to prevent a current deduction for an expense when the income is being deferred. In addition, some systems require the capitalization of certain interest expense, typically interest incurred in connection with the production of long-lived assets such as buildings. The most striking difference in the systems here considered is in the treatment of interest expense which does not have a connection with income producing activities. From a theoretical point of view, whether personal interest, i.e., interest which is related to personal consumption, should be deductible has been the subject of considerable debate. There is general agreement that consumption should be included in the tax base. However, personal interest can be viewed, not as additional consumption, but simply the cost of a preference for current as opposed to deferred consumption. By borrowing to consume now, the cost of the consumption is increased by the amount of the interest expense but the absolute amount of the consumption, which is the appropriate measure of the tax base, has not changed. The person who borrows to finance current consumption should be treated no differently from a tax point of view than the person who finances the consumption by "dissaving" and selling income-producing assets. If this analysis is accepted, a deduction for personal interest expense would be appropriate.

On the other hand, if the starting point of the analysis is that business-related expenses are the only type that should be deducted, personal interest would be disallowed. In addition, allowing a deduction for personal interest is often thought to encourage consumption rather than savings, which may not be desirable from an economic point of view. From a structural point of view, if a distinction is made between deductible and nondeductible interest, some mechanism must be provided for distinguishing between the two classes. These varying considerations have played out differently in the systems examined here.

In the *United States*, prior to 1986, interest expense was allowed as a deduction without limitations concerning personal interest. Limits on the deduction for personal interest were imposed in 1986 that restrict the deduction for personal interest to interest on loans used to acquire a personal residence (within some dollar limitations). In addition, interest may be deducted on up to $100,000 of loans secured by a residence no matter to what use the proceeds are put. Complex tracing rules are applied to assign the interest expense to the appropriate category, based on the flow of funds with some simplifying assumptions.

In *Germany*, personal interest is in principle not deductible. Prior to 1974 such interest was fully deductible as a "special expense." Until 1994, a limited amount of interest on personal residence mortgages was deductible. There are no statutory rules for the allocation of interest expense. The case law has developed a fairly complex tracing approach. The focus is the "economic purpose" for which the loan is obtained. If the loan is used in a taxable activity, the interest is deductible even if the purchase, expense, etc. could have been funded with existing business funds. However, if there is a close connection in time and amount between a loan and the withdrawal and expenditure of invested funds, the fiscal authorities will attempt to attribute interest expense to the expended funds. The issue of the exact connection necessary between the loan and the expenditure is currently being considered by the Federal Tax Court.

A common technique to avoid the personal interest deduction limitation is to establish two accounts and use the cash flow from business or professional activities to pay off personal loans while using borrowing in the second account to pay for business expenses. As long as the amounts and timing of the payments are not too closely linked, the actual use of the funds will be respected and is not considered "abusive."

The rules in *Canada* are similar. Interest is only deductible if the borrowed funds are used for the purposes of earning income and personal interest is thus not deductible. A proposal to allow the deduction of home mortgage interest was considered but rejected as unfair and involving too much revenue loss. Nondeductible personal interest involved in the purchase of a personal asset is also not capitalized despite the fact that the gain on the sale of the asset is taxable; the expense may be viewed as relating to the untaxed imputed return on the asset. A tracing of funds method is used to establish the nature of the interest expense. It is an accepted standard practice for taxpayers to use their savings or equity to finance consumption and borrow for income-producing purposes. *Australia* follows the same basic approach, as does *Japan*.

In the *United Kingdom*, deduction for personal interest was originally allowed without restriction. However, since 1969 the deduction has been subject to substantial limitations. If the interest is not connected to a taxable source of income such as trade or rental real estate, it must be related to a "qualifying purpose" to be deductible. The statutory list of accepted purposes is quite limited and includes investment in a closely-held company or employee-controlled company, machinery and equipment used in employment (for example, a car), and certain types of life annuity. The most important qualifying purpose is the purchase of a personal residence. However, the deduction is only allowed up to ca. $45,000. In addition, recent legislation has reduced the value of this deduction by not allowing it to be set against the top rate otherwise payable but by limiting it first of all to the basic rate of 25 %, then to the lower rate of 20 % and now simply to a notional rate of 15 %.

In *France*, personal interest is not deductible and more generally, no deduction is allowed for investment-related expenses even when the acquired asset is income producing, e.g., interest on loans used to acquire investment securities. Interest incurred in connection with rental real estate, however, is deductible.

In contrast, in *Sweden*, there are no restrictions on the deductibility of interest. Interest connected with a business is deducted from the income in that category. All other interest, including personal interest, is deducted from income from capital. In general, a tracing rule is used to determine the treatment of the interest expense. Since business income is taxed at a higher rate than income from capital, there is a special rule which prevents taxpayers from allocating excessive private interest expense from capital income to business income. If the amount of debt allocated to the business results in a "negative" equity when compared to the tax bases of the business assets, interest is calculated on the "negative" equity using the Government borrowing rate. The interest amount is treated as additional income in the business category and additional expense in the capital income category, thus in effect reallocating a portion of the excess interest expense to the more lightly taxed capital income.

In *The Netherlands*, personal interest is fully deductible without limitation. The theoretical justification sometimes put forward is that this approach equalizes the treatment of consumption financed by borrowing and consumption financed by divesting. However, consideration is currently being given to possible statutory restrictions.

5.2 Personal losses

While losses incurred in connection with personal assets are generally not deductible, in some situations a deduction is allowed if the loss occurs in particular circumstances. Thus in the *United States*, a loss due to damage to personal assets can be deducted if the damage is attributable to a "casualty," which has been interpreted to mean a sudden and unexpected event. There is a substantial amount of interpretive material around the issue of what constitutes a casualty, including an administrative rule that termite damage is not sufficiently sudden to qualify for a casualty loss. When available, the amount of the loss is limited to the tax cost of the asset and then only deductible if the total of all losses exceeds a percentage of the taxpayer's income.

In *Germany*, gains and losses on the disposition of private assets are generally not taken into account and this extends to casualty losses. Even if the casualty loss has some business connection, no deduction is allowed as a business expense, e.g., loss of jewelry on a business trip or a firm outing. However, as discussed in Part One, the German tax system recognizes a general deduction for "extraordinary expenses." The expenses must be unusually high when compared with similarly situated taxpayers and must be unavoidable. This latter requirement has been interpreted by a recent case to mean that loss with respect to property damage must have been incurred in circumstances where the taxpayer was not able to obtain insurance. The deductible amount of such expenses is the excess over a certain percentage of income. In some cases, a deduction may be allowed for costs that resulted from a casualty. For example, a recent case allowed an "extraordinary expense" deduction for expenses caused by uninsured water damage. However, the deduction was limited to the value of the replaced property before the casualty damage.

In *Canada* and *Australia*, casualty losses involving personal property are in general not deductible. However, with respect to "listed personal property," i.e., stamps, coins, jewelry, art works, etc., losses are deductible but only against the gains from such property. The loss is limited to the tax basis in the property. The *United Kingdom* restricts the loss on personal-use items by excluding any gain or loss where the assets are disposed of (including worthlessness) for less than ca. $10,000. *Australia* uses a similar rule to eliminate small gains on non-listed personal assets. These results all follow from the structure of the capital gains legislation in these jurisdictions.

In *The Netherlands*, gains and losses on private assets are not taken into account regardless as to how those gains or losses come about. Thus, neither the loss on an uninsured personal residence destroyed by fire nor the gain on receiving insurance proceeds in excess of the tax cost of an insured residence are relevant for tax purposes.

Sweden similarly does not allow deduction for personal losses. Loss is allowed, however, on real estate, which may be related to the fact that imputed income from real estate is effectively subject to tax under the special real estate tax.

France allows no deduction for casualty losses incurred with respect to personal assets.

5.3 Medical expenses

Medical expenses may be deducted or give rise to a tax credit in several of the systems, though they are viewed as personal expenses. In the *United States*, where there is no comprehensive public health-care system, a deduction is available for medical expenses that exceed a percentage of income. What constitutes "medical" treatment has been interpreted quite broadly though there is a statutory prohibition against the deduction for expenses of cosmetic surgery. Premiums for private health insurance are deductible but because of the percentage-of-income threshold, persons who are insured typically do not benefit from the deduction. As discussed in the fringe benefits materials, employer-provided health care is not taxable.

Canada has a publicly-funded health-care system, though certain costs are not covered. A credit is available for 17 % (the lowest rate of Federal tax) of the medical costs over a threshold amount of the lesser of $1,500 or 3 % of income. The credit is available for a lengthy list of medical costs. The *Australian* system provides a similar credit. Health expenses in connection with work-related injuries may be deducted under the general deduction provisions where such injuries are a clear occupational hazard.

Business-related medical expenses may also be deducted in the *United Kingdom*. There is no general deduction for medical costs but a limited deduction is available to persons over 60. Where medical expenses arise outside the United Kingdom, and are thus not covered by the National Health Service system, special legislation allows an employee to avoid the income inclusion that would otherwise arise if the employer bears the cost of providing medial insurance or treatment.

In *Japan* and *The Netherlands*, medical costs are deductible to the extent they exceed an absolute and percentage-of-income limitation.

In *Germany*, there is no specific deduction for private medical expenses. A business deduction is allowed for medical costs which arise from a sickness incurred in the course of business, e.g., radiation sickness in the case of a radiologist, tuberculosis in the case of a pulmonary doctor. No deduction was allowed in the case of a heart attack by a lawyer (!).

In addition, for medical expenses with no business connection, the general deduction for "extraordinary expenses" above a certain minimum is available for some types of medical expenses. The expenses must be "direct," e.g., doctor's costs, hospital costs, medicine. "Indirect" costs are not deductible and there is considerable litigation over the "direct-indirect" distinction. An example of a nondeductible indirect expense is the cost of a move to improve breathing for bronchitis. Deduction is not allowed for preventive medicine costs.

Cost of medical insurance premiums can be deducted subject to limitations as "special" expenses.

Sweden has an extensive public health-care system which provides free or low-cost service. Personal medical costs are not deductible. Employers are not allowed a deduction for costs covering the medical expenses of employees and the benefits are not included.

In France, mandatory contributions to French public health-care systems are deductible. Nonreimbursed health costs are considered as personal, unless they are vital for carrying on an income-producing activity, e.g., dentures for someone who is in charge of public relations.

5.4 Charitable deduction

Most of the systems allow a deduction or credit for contributions to organizations, private or public, which perform charitable, religious, cultural, or educational services. There are typically limits on the deductible amounts based on a percentage of income of the taxpayer. Thus in the *United States*, gifts to qualifying organizations can, in general, be deducted up to 50 % of the taxpayer's income. More restrictive limitations apply for gifts to "private" foundations, i.e., organizations which are not supported by the general public but by one or several large donors. Excess donations can be carried over and deducted in subsequent years to the extent that current deductions do not exceed the limitations. In the case of certain gifts of property, the fair market value of the property is deductible, thus giving a deduction for the appreciation in value of the property which has not been included in the tax base. No deduction is allowed for the contribution of services, though out-of-pocket costs may be deducted. If the donor receives some benefit as a result of the contribution, the deductible amount will be reduced to that extent. There are significant substantiation requirements.

In *Canada*, individuals are entitled to a tax credit of 17 % for the first $250 of charitable contribution and 29 % for donations in excess of that amount. Seventeen percent and 29 % are the lowest and highest marginal Federal tax rates. Gifts must be evidenced by a written receipt which must be filed with the tax return. Donations are limited to 20 % of the taxpayer's income with a five year carryforward. In the case of a donation of appreciated property, the taxpayer may elect to treat any amount between the cost basis of the property and its fair market value as the contribution. The amount elected is also treated as the amount realized on the disposition of the property for purposes of realizing gain.

The *Australian* system has similar limits on gifts of appreciated property. Normally, the gift is a realization event and the deduction is then the fair market value of the property. In circumstances in which the gift is not treated as a realization event, then the deductible amount is limited to the lower of cost or fair market value. There are elaborate administrative procedures for qualifying an institution before deductions are allowed.

In the *United Kingdom*, deduction is generally allowed for payments which are subscribed for and made over a period of four years. A limited deduction is given for single annual payments. There are no special rules dealing with gifts of property.

In the *Japanese* system, charitable contributions are deductible to the extent they exceed an absolute floor of ca. $100 and do not exceed 25 % of the taxpayer's income. The contribution must be made to a government agency or a limited number of government-approved public-interest organizations. Deduction for gifts of appreciated property is limited to cost basis.

Charitable contributions are deductible in *The Netherlands* to the extent their total amount exceeds both 1 % of income and ca. $75. The deductible amount may not exceed 10 % of income.

In *Germany*, charitable contributions are deductible as "special" personal expenses. Contributions must be made to governmental agencies or government-approved organizations. Deduction is generally limited to 5 % of income with a 10 % limit for especially meritorious cultural or scientific purposes. In the case of businesses, an alternative limitation based on payroll and turnover may be used. If an individual gift which qualifies for the 10 % limitation exceeds that limit and the amount of the gift exceeds ca. $33,000, the deduction can be carried back two years and forward five, to the extent there is "excess" limitation in those years.

Normally, the deduction for contributions of property is the fair market value. Since private capital gains are not generally taxed, the problem of appreciated property contributions does not arise. If assets are withdrawn from a business and given to a charity, the withdrawal is typically a realization event. However, a special statutory provision allows the taxpayer to deduct only the tax cost of the asset and avoid recognition of gain.

The charitable contribution is denied if the donor receives consideration in return; the transfer is no longer a "contribution." The nature and amount of the contribution must be documented. There has been substantial controversy over contributions to charitable organizations formed by political parties which, in fact, channeled the funds to political activities rather than using them for charitable purposes. One of the issues was the ability of the taxpayer to rely on the documentation provided when, in fact, the funds were misappropriated.

In *France*, charitable contributions to a wide variety of organizations are entitled to a credit equal to 50 % of the total amount of the contributions, up to a limit of 1.75 % of the taxpayer's taxable income (6 % for certain public-interest organizations). Self-employed taxpayers may elect to deduction contributions to the extent of .0325 % of gross receipts and this is the only deduction allowed to corporations. Deductions for gifts of inventory are limited to cost; in the case of capital assets, the deduction is the fair market value but the donation is treated as a realization event.

Only in *Sweden* are charitable contributions not deductible to any extent and are viewed as a personal expense. Since gifts outside of a business context are not treated as realization events, however, any appreciation in gifted property will escape tax.

6. Limitations on deductions and losses

6.1 Illegal payments, fines, penalties

Where expenses are incurred which under normal principles would be deductible but are illegal, a number of the systems limit the deduction. This is sometimes the result of a specific statutory provision, for example, disallowing a deduction for bribes, and sometimes follows from a general principle of denial of deductions which offend "ordre public" or public policy. Similarly, deduction for business-related fines or penalties may also be limited.

In the *United States*, case law established the principle that illegal payments and fines were not deductible if the deduction would "frustrate sharply defined national or state policies." Using this "public policy" principle, the cases disallowed deduction where the payment itself, for example, a bribe, was illegal, or where the deductibility of a fine or penalty would reduce its effectiveness. Subsequent legislation narrowed the limitation of deductions on "public policy" grounds to several statutorily defined situations. A special provision disallows all deductions for expenses incurred in connection with the illegal sale of drugs, thus taxing drug dealers on a gross basis. Another provision deals with the circumstances in which payments to foreign governmental officials can be deducted.

In *Canada*, until 1990, illegal payments were deductible subject to the ordinary restrictions on deductibility of expenses. This rule parallels the rule with respect to the inclusion in income of illegal amounts. In 1990, a statutory amendment denied the deductibility of bribes and similar payments.

Judicial or statutory fines and penalties are not generally deductible because of public-policy considerations. Any deduction would lessen the deterrent or regulatory impact of the fine. However, case law and administrative practice permit a deduction for fines or penalties where the breach of law is relatively minor, the fine can be considered a normal risk of the business, and where the breach does not endanger public safety and is not deliberate or the result of negligence. For example, it has been held that fines for overloaded trucks are deductible.

Under a recent statutory change in the *United Kingdom*, no deduction is allowed in computing business or rental income for any payment the making of which is a criminal offense. Thus, bribes which are in violation of a corrupt practices act or other payments, such as blackmail, which would constitute the aiding or abetting of a criminal offense are not deductible.

Sweden has no statutory rules about illegal payments or bribes. The issue has not been clearly decided by the courts, though there are some cases which allow a deduction for "consultant" fees in circumstances which suggest the fees were in fact bribes. The scholarly writing in general supports the deduction. The basic reasoning is that the business connection should be sufficient to generate a deduction though some have argued that "non-normal" costs should not be deductible. In contrast, fines are not deductible.

Similarly, in *Japan*, there are no limitations on public policy grounds for illegal payments as long as the payments can be established as "necessary" for the business, though the courts may scrutinize the alleged necessity carefully. By statutory provision, fines are not deductible, though fines paid abroad can still be deducted if the other requirements for deductibility can be met.

In *France*, all expenses related to business activities are in principle deductible regardless of their nature. However, there are specific statutory rules which deny the deduction for criminal fines and penalties imposed by administrative authorities in connection with price fixing. Penalties related to the assessment of taxes are also not deductible.

In *The Netherlands*, fines and penalties imposed by a Dutch court are not deductible. Equivalent foreign fines, however, are deductible as are penalties imposed by professional bodies. Bribes paid, like any other business expense, are deductible if they are made for business purposes. The tax authorities generally assume a business purpose to exist if it is demonstrated by the taxpayer that in view of the nature of the business the amount paid does not deviate from what is commonly paid in similar circumstances. However, it may difficult in practice to prove that the bribe has actually been paid.

In *Australia*, as well, a specific statutory provision disallows deduction for fines and penalties. Illegal payments, however, seemed to be allowed in principle under the general deduction rules.

Statutory provisions in *Germany* deal with both fines and penalties and illegal payments. Fines and penalties are generally not deductible if imposed by a German, European Union or foreign court. In the latter case, however, they may be deductible if the penalty is based on considerations in the foreign jurisdiction which are inconsistent with the basic principles of the German legal system. Non-judicially imposed penalties which result from legal infractions are also not deductible, unless the purpose of the penalty is simply to make restitution.

Bribes and similar payments are not deductible if they are of such a nature as to be punishable under the German penal code. In some cases, payments to foreign recipients can be deducted if the recipient is named.

6.2 Expenses associated with tax-exempt income

The question of relating expenses to tax-exempt income in a global system arises when certain categories of income are expressly exempted from tax, for example, interest from state and local obligations in the United States context. For schedular systems, a similar problem arises in dealing with expenses that are related to items of income which are not formally exempt but simply do not fall into any taxable category.

In the *United States*, there is an express statutory rule that in general denies a deduction for expenses incurred in connection with tax-exempt income. If an expense is directly related to an item of tax-exempt income, the deduction is denied completely. If expenses are related to several categories of income, an allocation is made, based on the amounts of income, or in some cases, the value or cost of the assets generating the income. A special rule applies to interest expense incurred in connection with exempt interest income on State and municipal obligations. There, the interest deduction is denied if the purpose of the borrowing was to purchase or "carry" tax-exempt securities. Thus, interest expense can be denied if the borrowing allowed the taxpayer to continue to hold tax-exempt securities. In the case of financial institutions, interest expense must be allocated between tax-exempt interest income and other taxable income based on tax cost of the assets involved.

Deduction for expenses associated with tax-exempt income is specifically prohibited in *Canada*. However, deduction is allowed for expenses incurred in connection with effectively tax-exempt dividends received from foreign affiliates. In general, the purpose for which the expense was incurred determines its allocation under a tracing approach. Though capital gains are partially taxable, expenses incurred to generate such gains are not deductible (or capitalized). If the asset generates income apart from the potential capital gain, the expenses are fully deductible. The *Australian* system reaches similar results since the general deduction rule requires that the deduction relate to taxable income, though it does not have the foreign affiliate exception. As in Canada, there is no deduction for the costs incurred in connection with capital gains, though the costs, including carrying costs, generally can be included in the tax cost of the assets.

In *Sweden*, in general, expenses are only deductible if associated with a taxable income source. In some cases where income which would otherwise fall in a taxable source is explicitly exempt, the exemption has been interpreted to apply to the gross income and not the net income. Accordingly, the associated expenses were allowed as a deduction against other income in the source.

Japan has no explicit rule dealing with the deductions relating to tax exempt income. The limitation flows from the affirmative rule that to be deductible, expenses must be related to a taxable category of income. The same approach is taken in France. When no direct allocation can be made, expenses related to taxed and tax-exempt income in the same income category can be allocated on a gross-to-gross basis.

Germany has a specific statutory rule disallowing expenses which have "direct economic connection" with exempt income. The most important application in practice, arises in connection with foreign dividends which are typically exempt under tax treaties and is discussed in Part Four.

6.3 "Quarantining" and other limits or restrictions on certain categories of expenses

In an otherwise global system, sometimes activities or expenses are treated specially and expenses and losses in those categories cannot be used to offset other items of income. In effect, there is a schedular overlay on the global system. In explicitly schedular systems, a similar result is achieved if an overall loss in a particular category cannot be used to offset or "compensate" income in other categories. Limitations have typically been applied in response to deductions generated in tax shelter transactions or in activities in which personal consumption is likely.

The *United States* has an extensive system of limitations on deductibility, the most important of which are the so-called "passive activity loss" rules. Adopted in response to the widespread use of tax shelters in the 1970s and 1980s, the passive activity loss rules restrict the deductibility of losses which arise in any activity in which the taxpayer does not "materially participate." This requirement has been administratively interpreted to require in general that the taxpayer spend at least 500 hours per year in the activity, though there are a number of other situations in which material participation will be present. Special rules apply to real estate activities.

Losses incurred in passive activities can only be used to offset passive activity income. In this context, "portfolio" income, typically investment income, is not passive activity income and cannot be reduced by passive activity losses. Unused losses are suspended and can be used in later years against passive activity income. When the passive activity is completely disposed of in a taxable transaction, suspended losses may be used against other income. While originally aimed at the "artificial" losses arising in tax shelter activities, the rules can apply to real economic losses where the taxpayer does not meet the material participation test.

The application of the rules on an activity-by-activity basis and the special treatment of portfolio income is extremely complex. The taxpayer in effect is required to categorize each of his activities into "normal" business activity, passive activity, and portfolio investments, making an allocation of income and deductions to each category. In addition, in order to determine if an activity has been disposed of so that suspended losses may be used, the exact scope of each separate activity must be determined. The rules in effect turn the otherwise global system of income definition into a schedular system in which each activity is potentially a separate income category.

There are some other, less extensive, limitations on the deductibility of certain expenses. Investment interest expense not incurred in a trade or business is limited to investment income, including realized capital gains in some cases. Expenses incurred in connection with the business use of a residence, e.g., an office in the home or the rental of a summer house, are limited to the income which the activity generates. As discussed previously, capital losses can generally only be deducted against capital gains, though a limited deduction against ordinary income is allowed.

In the case of unreimbursed expenses of employees or expenses involved in income-producing activities which do not amount to a trade or business, the expenses can be deducted only to the extent that they exceed 2 % of income. The effect of this limitation is to reduce substantially the availability of deductions for a large number of taxpayers. Unlike other countries, there is no specific lump-sum deduction granted to employees as a substitute for the deduction of these expenses.

In *Sweden*, losses in the category of business income cannot be used to reduce income in other taxable categories. The loss can be carried forward without limitation against business income in other years. The same rule applies to income from employment. There are, however, some exceptions. Losses from business as an artist can be offset against employment income. A loss on the termination of a business can be deducted against income from capital.

A different technique is used with losses in the category of income from capital. The loss is converted into a credit at a 30 % rate (the basic rate on income from capital) for up to ca. $15,000 and at a 21 % rate for the excess. The credit can then be used to offset tax on income in the other categories. The restriction on excess losses is to limit the ability to use current losses (principally from interest deductions in highly leveraged investments) where the gain on the investment is deferred.

In *Japan*, losses are restricted as a result of the schedular system. Losses in the Dividend, Occasional, and Miscellaneous categories cannot be used against other types of income. Timber and Retirement income are calculated separately. The taxpayer can elect to have dividend income and interest income calculated separately. The system is similar in the *United Kingdom*. In some cases, for example, Schedule A dealing with income from land, losses may only be set off against other Schedule A income. In other cases, losses may only be used against income from the same source. Sometimes, for example, in the case of income from government securities, no deductions at all are allowed. On the other hand, losses arising in a business can be used against income in other categories. Capital losses can only be used against capital gains, with a carryforward, but no carryback, of excess losses.

Under the *Canadian* system, as a general rule, the net results in the various income categories are consolidated in computing total taxable income. However, there are some special rules which operate to limit certain types of losses. Capital cost recovery allowances with respect to rented depreciable property cannot be deducted in excess of the income that the particular property generates. In general, capital losses are only deductible against capital gains and capital losses on "private" assets, coins, stamps, etc. can only be deducted against gains on such assets. In addition, the lifetime exemption for capital gains in respect of farm property and shares of small business corporations is reduced by the taxpayer's cumulative net loss from investments, thus in effect, restricting the deductibility of such losses.

Australia has a similar treatment for capital losses. For a brief period, there were rules restricting interest deductions on real property investments to the income the property generated.

In *The Netherlands*, there are, in general, no restrictions on the use of losses in one income category to offset the positive income in other categories. However, in the case of losses on dispositions of a substantial participation, a credit of 20 %, the rate at which gains on such assets are taxed, is utilized in lieu of a loss deduction.

Germany, as well, allows losses in particular income categories to be used against income in other categories. The only domestic exceptions are capital losses where the corresponding gain would not be taxable, hobby losses, speculative losses, losses incurred in stock-breeding activities and the restrictions of losses of limited partnerships. Special rules in connection with foreign losses are discussed in Part Four.

In France, in principle, the positive and negative results of the various income categories are consolidated but there are a number of anti-avoidance rules which limit the offset possibilities. Typically, where those rules apply, losses can only be taken against income in the same category which arises in the same year or within the following five years.

These specially treated categories include losses from rental real estate in excess of ca. $14,000, losses from activities in which the taxpayer does not participate on a personal and permanent basis, portfolio investment losses, and losses from hobby farming. Long-term capital losses in business can only be deducted against long-term capital gains, with excess losses qualifying for a ten-year carryforward.

The following **Table II-2** summarizes some of the deduction rules discussed in Subpart B. The notation "limited deduction" indicates that either the class of costs deductible is restricted in some fashion or that there is a limit on the amount deductible, for example, a nondeductible floor or a ceiling on deductible amounts. In addition, the generality of the Table does not capture many of the refinements, for example, the distinction frequently made between domestic and foreign illegal payments.

Some aspects of the tax base: Deductions

	Commuting costs	Entertain-ment expenses	Illegal payments	Child care costs	Personal interest	Medical expenses (non-business related)	Charitable contributions
Australia	no deduction	no deduction	no general limitation	no deduction	no deduction	limited credit	deduction with generous limit
Canada	no deduction	percent-age limitation (no deduction for most employees)	no general limitation (bribes non deductible)	no deduction	no deduction	limited credit	deduction with generous limit
France	limited deduction	full deduction	no general limitation	no deduction; limited credit	no deduction	no deduction	limited credit
Germany	limited deduction	limited deduction standard values	deductible but recipient must be named	generally no deduction	no deduction (post-1974)	no specific deduction	limited deduction

Some aspects of the tax base: Deductions

	Commuting costs	Entertain- ment expenses	Illegal payments	Child care costs	Personal interest	Medical expenses (non-business related)	Charitable contributions
Japan	no deduction	full deduc. for indiv.; limited for corp.	no general limitation	no deduction	no deduction	limited deduction	limited deduction
The Netherlands	limited deduction	limited deduction	no general limitation	limited deduction	fully deductible	limited deduction	limited deduction
Sweden	limited deduction	limited deduction; standard values	uncertain	no deduction	fully deductible	no deduction	no deduction
United Kingdom	no deduction	no deduction unless own staff	no deduction	no deduction	limited deduction (e.g., personal residence)	no deduction (insur. prems. for over 59 deduc.)	limited deduction
United States	no deduction	percentage limitation	no deduction	no deduction; limited credit	limited deduction (personal residence)	limited deduction	limited deduction

Subpart C: Accounting

All systems must contain rules governing the assignment of the various items involved in the computation of taxable income to taxable periods. Since the same task must be performed for financial accounting purposes, a basic question in all systems is the extent to which the timing and other rules used in determining financial income will also be controlling for tax purposes. While all the systems considered here use commercial accounting principles and concepts to some extent, they also generally recognize the need for special tax rules in many situations. The most obvious case where tax rules are needed is where the taxpayer, typically an individual employee or investor, does not normally keep commercial books and records. Thus, all systems recognize a simplified "cash" method of accounting for some taxpayers. In addition, and more fundamentally, in some cases, the goals and purposes of financial accounting are deemed to be so different from the requirements of the tax system that the results produced by the financial accounting rules are viewed as inappropriate for tax purposes. Here, there is a wide variation among the countries concerning the degree to which financial accounting principles are followed in the tax system. The differences rest in part on the extent to which there are legally binding accounting rules that are then incorporated into the tax system, in contrast to accounting principles that are developed on the basis of professional standards. In the latter case, the flexibility allowed by the accounting principles is often not accepted for tax purposes.

The following materials examine the basic tax accounting methods used and their relation to commercial accounting principles and then consider some specific situations in which special tax rules have been developed.

1. Basic accounting methods

In the *German* system, the method of accounting is determined by the category of income which is involved. Thus, for example, a taxpayer may use one method for computing business income and another for computing income from employment. The "net income" method is used to determine income from employment, capital, rents and royalties, miscellaneous income, and the income of small proprietorships and partnerships. This is essentially a cash method of accounting.

Income is taken into account when the taxpayer has unrestricted access to the money or property involved. Checks are treated as cash and taxable on receipt as long as the check clears in the normal course. Notes are not income on receipt but income must be recognized if the note is negotiated. Deductions are taken into account at the time the payee has unrestricted access to the funds. Expenditures for depreciable assets must be capitalized and recovered through depreciation deductions; costs for other fixed assets are taken into account when the assets are disposed of. A special statutory rule applies to items of income or expense which regularly occur and are paid "shortly before or shortly after" the period to which they relate, e.g., rent for December received in January. Such amounts are taken into account for tax purposes in the period to which they economically relate.

For most taxpayers engaged in business, the use of the so-called "net worth" or balance sheet method of income computation is required. A modified version of the net worth method may also be used by those having income from independent personal services or agriculture but is not required. In general terms, income or loss for the period is determined by comparing the balance sheet at the end of the tax period with the balance sheet for the end of the preceding period. The obligation to use the net worth method is tied to the commercial and corporate law requirements to maintain certain books and records.

Correspondingly, there is a close connection between the financial balance sheet and the tax balance sheets used in the net worth comparison. Under the traditional principle of "linkage" (*Maßgeblichkeit*), the tax balance sheet must be based on the commercial balance sheet and, unless a special tax rule provides otherwise, the values of the assets and liabilities shown on the commercial balance sheet are controlling for tax purposes. This principle has far-reaching implications for income determination. For example, it incorporates in the tax system the basic principle of conservatism which is at the base of many of the German generally accepted accounting principles. Thus, in general, unrealized losses which are taken into account in valuing assets on the financial balance sheet are also effective for tax purposes. Similarly, reserves for anticipated losses or expenses, which are required for financial accounting, also reduce taxable income. On the other hand, a principle of "reverse" linkage (*umgekehrte Maßgeblichkeit*) is followed as well; if the tax law provides optional special treatment for an item and that treatment is elected for tax purposes, that treatment must be followed in the commercial statements to be effective. This can mean, for example, that the decision to accelerate deductions for tax purposes will reduce financial statement income and the ability of a corporation to pay dividends.

The net worth method of income determination operates as a kind of accrual accounting, with "accrual" taking the form of recognizing an asset or liability on the balance sheet. Thus, when performance is completed and income has been earned, an asset in the form of an account receivable is entered in the balance sheet and will be reflected as income as a result of the balance sheet comparison at year end. Similarly, a liability which is recognized for commercial accounting, and hence tax purposes, will function as the accrual of a deduction item.

The statute contains a number of special tax rules for the valuation of assets and liabilities. For example, the principle of valuation according to "going concern value" discussed above in connection with depreciation is expressly sanctioned.

The *French* system is governed by roughly the same principles as the German one. The cash method is used to account for income from employment, renting of real estate or securities, profits of small businesses (which can choose that method), and noncommercial personal services (unless the professional has opted for the accrual method). Income is then taxable when paid or available for collection, but there is no such rule as the German one concerning income or expenses paid "shortly before or shortly after" year end.

As in Germany, a balance sheet comparison method is used for computing the tax result of most taxpayers engaged in business, more precisely corporations and, in principle, sole proprietorships carrying on an industrial, commercial, or agricultural activity. The linkage between book and taxable income is particularly close. General accounting principles and concepts apply for tax purposes unless tax law explicitly or implicitly derogates from them. In particular, both for book and tax purposes, income must be recognized and an account receivable entered in the balance sheet when the property is delivered or the performance of the service is completed. The taxable net income is determined by making adjustments to book income whenever tax law departs from accounting law (e.g., expenses deductible for book but not for tax purposes, exempt dividends from subsidiaries, long-term capital gains taxable at reduced rates, etc.). Also, as in Germany, the accounting principle of prudence explains why the deduction of reserves and provisions is liberally accepted for tax purposes. On the deduction side, expenses are taken into account as liabilities as soon as they are incurred under the same principles. Conversely, accounting law has often been, in the minds of some, "tax polluted," for instance, as far as depreciation rules are concerned.

In *Sweden*, like Germany, the method of accounting is determined by the category of income. Income from capital and income from employment are accounted for on a cash basis. There is a principle of "constructive receipt" which taxes income prior to actual receipt if it was possible for the taxpayer to obtain payment earlier. Capital gains are subject to a special rule which in effect puts them on the accrual basis. The rule was introduced in 1991 to discourage deferred payment sales of property.

Business taxpayers, including all corporations, must account for tax purposes on the accrual method. Generally accepted accounting principles are controlling wherever there are no special tax rules. As a general matter, income items are usually determined under financial accounting rules, while there are some special tax rules for deductions. Under normal accounting rules, only the present value of potential future expenditures is deductible. Special tax rules limit the deduction for anticipated guarantee expenses. Because of the importance of accounting rules for tax purposes, tax considerations have often influenced the development of the financial rules. This situation has been criticized by some as resulting in a distortion of the clear presentation of income for financial purposes.

The relation between tax accounting and financial accounting is much different in the *United States* system. While the taxpayer must in general report income for tax purposes on the same method of accounting according to which he keeps his commercial books, there are special tax rules which substantially modify the accounting principles. For example, on the accrual method, the use of reserves for estimated future expenses is much more limited for tax purposes than the normally applicable rules for financial accounting. The courts have specifically recognized the "difference in objectives" between tax accounting and financial accounting in developing special tax rules. In addition, the fiscal authorities can require modifications in accounting methods to "clearly reflect income" and under this standard a number of accounting practices have been rejected for tax purposes.

The taxpayer can elect a method of accounting and the statute specifically recognizes the cash method and the accrual method as well as "other methods" which meet the above standards. For taxpayers on the cash method, typically used by individuals and small businesses, income is taxable on receipt or in situations in which the taxpayer has "constructive receipt" of the income because of his access to the income. A check is treated as cash if it clears in due course. The receipt of the promise to pay is generally not income to a cash basis taxpayer, though special rules apply in the case of the sale of property.

On the deduction side, deductions are taken into account when an expenditure has actually been incurred. Prepaid expenses are generally treated as capital expenditures. Special rules allow farmers on the cash basis to deduct prepaid expenses but those rules are in turn limited to "real" farmers to prevent the use of prepayments in tax-shelters.

The accrual method is used by most business taxpayers. If the business involves production or purchase and sale, inventories must be used and purchases and sales are required to be accounted for on the accrual method. On the income side, income must be recognized when the right to receive the income has been established and the amount can be determined. In general, any consistent method of accounting is accepted even if the right to the income has not technically accrued. The treatment of advance payments to taxpayers on the accrual basis is discussed below.

On the deduction side, deduction was historically allowed when "all events" had occurred which established the liability to make the payment. Though contingent or uncertain liabilities were not deductible, this rule allowed taxpayers to accrue fixed liabilities currently at their nominal amount even when the payment would not actually be made until some time in the future. This approach overstates the true cost of the deduction since it does not take into account the time value of money between the period the deduction is accrued and the time it is in fact paid. In extreme situations, the taxpayer could actually be better off with the current accrual of the liability than if it had not incurred the liability at all. In response to this situation, the statute was amended to require that there be "economic performance" of the obligation before the "all events" test could be met. This rule basically defers the deductions until payment is actually made or property or services are delivered or performed (for example, in mining reclamation). For "recurring" items, that is, normally occurring business expenses, deduction is allowed currently if the amount is paid within eight and one-half months after the end of the tax year, the time that a tax return would have to have been filed. This economic performance approach makes the accrual of deductions for tax purposes much more restrictive in the United States than in the other jurisdictions here under consideration.

Japan requires the use of accrual accounting as a general rule. However, small businesses have the option of using cash method principles under strict conditions (selecting the special "blue return" system) Where the accrual method is used, it usually follows financial accounting principles generally accepted to be "fair and reasonable." There are also more detailed tax accounting rules. Under the accrual system, liabilities are taken into account at face value and there are special provisions allowing reserves for mining restoration, oil spill cleanups and similar occurrences.

Under the *Canadian* system, income from business and property must be accounted for on the accrual basis. While the tax accounting rules are based on financial accounting principles, they have developed into an independent body of law. There are a number of special tax rules which specifically displace financial accounting rules. In addition, courts have sometimes rejected financial accounting rules as inconsistent with more basic tax law principles. For example, LIFO accounting for inventory costs has been held unacceptable for tax purposes despite its recognition in financial accounting. Liabilities are generally taken into account at face value in the year incurred as long as they are not contingent with respect to liability or amount. In some cases, however, present value accrual is at least acceptable and might be required. Under legislation introduced in 1994, taxpayers may make a deductible contribution to a special trust to cover mining reclamation expenses. The trust is taxable on any income earned and any amount not spent for reclamation is taxed to the taxpayer.

In the *United Kingdom*, the appropriate accounting regime is determined by the schedule in which the income falls. In some cases, the cash method is used but for trading profits, the most important income category, an "earnings" or accrual basis is generally required. There is highly developed case law concerning the relation between tax accounting and financial accounting which is still in the process of evolution. In some cases, for example, the extent to which the deduction of a fixed liability for future expenses should be allowed at face value or discounted, the tax rules follow the accounting approach. A recent case which may influence future developments places great importance on the generally accepted accounting rules and shows a willingness to follow those rules for tax purposes in most cases where there is not a specifically developed tax rule. There are a number of specific statutory rules dealing with individual issues, for example, preventing a current deduction of interest where there is no corresponding income inclusion.

The situation in *Australia* is quite different. Tax accounting rules (at least until recently) have been developed through the interpretation of the statutory terms "derived" in relation to income and "incurred" in relation to deductions. While courts have sometimes looked to accounting principles, the development of the tax rules has been to a large extent independent. For example, whether an expense has been "incurred" depends in some sense on legal liabilities rather than the commercial outcome and thus parallels the United States experience. In general, a cash method has been accepted for employees and small businesses and an accrual method for larger businesses. Under the accrual method, income is included when it is "earned" and there is case law establishing the contours of that concept. A special statutory regime is provided for inventory which in general follows financial accounting principles though it has some important deviations. For example, the use of the lower of cost or market is optional and not mandatory.

In contrast to the other Continental systems, in the *Dutch* system tax accounting rules have developed relatively independently from financial accounting. Income from employment, capital, and periodic income is accounted for on a cash basis. Amounts are included in income when received or available for collection even if not actually collected. Income from business activities is determined in accordance with "sound commercial practice" (*goed koopmansgebruik*) applied in a consistent manner. There is substantial case law developing this concept. The principles are different in many important aspects from financial accounting rules and there is no necessary connection between financial treatment and tax treatment. However, in the interests of "prudence," the rules do allow the deduction of unrealized losses if there is a good chance the loss will be incurred and it can be quantified. This tax rule is nonetheless more strict than the corresponding commercial accounting rule. The tax rules put emphasis on the "realistic" possibility of a loss.

2. Inclusion of advance payments

The treatment of advance payments is a classic example of the possible conflict between financial accounting principles and tax accounting. Where amounts are prepaid prior to delivery of goods or the performance of services, from a financial accounting point of view, income would in general not be recognized since the unconditional right to the income has not yet been established. Current recognition of the income would prevent the income from being accounted for in the period in which it was earned. On the other hand, from the perspective of the tax system, the fact that the taxpayer has received the cash and is in a position to pay the tax would suggest the appropriateness of current inclusion. In addition, the taxation of the advance payment to the seller can be seen as a surrogate for the failure to tax the implicit interest involved in the transaction to the purchaser. The systems have resolved this conflict in a variety of ways.

In the *United States*, the treatment of prepaid income has generated a substantial amount of litigation, including three cases in the United States Supreme Court. In general, the courts have upheld the fiscal authorities' assertion that the inclusion of prepayments in income currently is necessary to "clearly reflect income." The decisions rest primarily on the discretion of the tax authorities to determine what practices clearly reflect income. While establishing in litigation that prepaid income must in principle be included currently, the rule has been relaxed somewhat in administrative practice. In the case of services income, income recognition can be postponed until the taxable year after the year of receipt. For sales income, advance payments for inventory can be deferred to the next year; payments for non-inventory items can be deferred until properly accruable under the taxpayer's method of accounting. In addition, there are a number of specific statutory provisions which allow the deferral of advance payments. For example, deferral is allowed in the case of dues prepaid to an automobile club for road service, one of the situations in which the courts had required current inclusion.

Canada deals with the problem in a specific statutory provision. Prepaid income must be included in taxable income in the year in which the payment is received, even though the amount is not properly accruable. However, the taxpayer is allowed to deduct a reserve in the same amount thus neutralizing the initial inclusion. The reserve in turn must be included in income in the following year but if the amount has still not yet been earned by the end of the year, another reserve may be claimed. The period of the reserve is thus in effect unlimited, except in the case of articles of food and drink and unredeemed transportation tickets, where a special rule limits the period to one year.

Despite the general absence of financial accounting principles in the *Australian* tax system, case law doctrine has adopted the financial accounting rule for prepayments. Such amounts are only includable when earned. In the *United Kingdom*, there is also case law support for the position that prepayments may be deferred until the income has been earned where the taxpayer can establish that this is the appropriate financial accounting treatment.

Similarly, in *The Netherlands*, case law interpreting "sound commercial practices" has allowed the deferral of prepaid income until the period in which it is earned. It is essential that a consistent practice be followed. *Sweden* likewise follows general accounting principles which allow the deferral of the recognition of prepayments until the amounts are earned.

Germany, using the balance sheet comparison approach in income determination, treats advance payments as neutral from both a financial accounting and tax point of view. The transaction is treated as "pending" and its effects are thus suspended until completion. The increase in assets on the balance sheet caused by the payment is offset by the potential liability for repayment in case delivery or performance is not forthcoming and the transaction has no tax results. *France* and *Japan* reach the same results though the techniques are somewhat different.

3. Income treatment of deferred payments

Where property is sold with the financing in effect being provided by the seller in the form of some sort of purchase money security, usually applicable accounting rules would often require the immediate recognition of the gain on the transaction. This would be the normal result under accrual methods of accounting and could also be applicable under the cash method, depending on the nature of the buyer's obligation. The systems have reacted in different ways to this situation. In some cases, a special rule allows the deferral of the recognition of the gain until the payments are in fact received under the note. In other situations, the cash basis taxpayer, who would normally be able to defer the recognition of gain until receipt, is in effect put on the accrual basis and required to take gain into account when the property is delivered.

The *United States* is an example of the first approach. Under the so-called "installment sales" provisions, the taxpayer reports the gain on the disposition of non-inventory assets in the years in which the payments are received. The payment is treated partly as a tax-free return of tax cost and partly as gain, depending on the overall ratio of gain to total purchase price. The installment obligation must bear market interest. There are a number of restrictions on the use of the installment method. It does not apply if the property sold or received is publicly traded. In addition, installment treatment is not available for any gain on the property which represents previously taken depreciation deductions. Even where deferral is allowed, if the amount of the outstanding indebtedness held by the taxpayer exceeds $5,000,000 there is an interest charge on the deferred tax. The disposition of an installment obligation causes the recognition of all deferred gain, even in a transaction in which nothing is received in return.

Under the *Dutch* system, the courts have allowed the deferral of income recognition in certain cases of deferred payment as an aspect of sound commercial practice.

Sweden has taken a quite different approach to deferred payment sales. Whether the taxpayer is on the cash basis or accrual basis, gain on the disposition of capital gain property must be included in the year the sale takes place. The purpose of the rule is in part to prevent the purchaser from obtaining a tax cost in the asset equal to the purchase price while the gain on the transaction had not yet been taxed to the seller who was on the cash basis. The *Australian* system also requires profit on the sale of inventory and capital gain to be taken into account in general in the year of sale. The same result is obtained in *Japan* by the fact that almost all transactions have to be accounted for on the accrual basis. In general, the time when a taxpayer must take into account the amount realized from the sale or exchange of a capital asset is not affected by the time of the receipt of the consideration.

Similarly, in *Germany*, using the balance sheet comparison method of income determination, the existence of the claim for the payment results in an increase in assets and hence net worth. The claim is usually valued at its nominal value though it may be discounted if some sort of hidden interest is involved in the transaction.

In *France*, under the accrual method, gains from credit sales are always taxable in the year when the delivery takes place, regardless of the time of the payment and even in case of a clause permitting termination of the contract in the case of nonperformance. The taxpayer can deduct a reserve if, according to the circumstances, the debt will probably not be paid. Under the cash method, payment is generally decisive with few exceptions. For instance, gain on the sale of a building by an individual (not acting in a business context) is taxable when the sale occurs regardless of the payment date.

The *Canadian* system takes an intermediate position. When business property is sold with deferred payments, the taxpayer is entitled to set up a reserve for the portion of the profit from the sale which is not due until after the end of the taxable year. However, the maximum period for which the reserve may be claimed is three years. In the case of capital gain property, the same approach is taken. The maximum period for the reserve is five years and at least one-fifth of the amount of the capital gain must be included each year.

The *United Kingdom* also makes a distinction between capital gain property and trading property. In the former situation, gain must be recognized currently based on the value of the consideration received, with no discount for the fact that the payments will take place over time. The actual payment of the tax, however, can be deferred if the consideration is payable for a period of over eighteen months. The situation with respect to business income is more complex. A statutory rule on the deduction side allows a write-off of bad debts only when they become worthless but does not deal expressly with the issue of at what value they should be taken into income in the first place. The Inland Revenue has unsuccessfully tried to argue that this rule implicitly requires that the obligation be taken into income at face value initially, but the House of Lords has rejected the argument, while leaving uncertain exactly how the deferred payment of trade income should be treated.

4. Original issue discount obligations and other complex financial instruments

Where obligations are issued at a discount from the stated amount payable at maturity, questions of both timing and characterization of income and expense arise for the borrower and the lender.

Though from an economic point of view the difference between the issue price and the amount due on redemption clearly represents an interest cost and interest income, it has taken some time for tax systems to translate this economic reality into legal rules. In some of the systems here under consideration, there is still no satisfactory resolution of the problem of original issue discount (OID) with the legal form of the transaction controlling its tax treatment in many situations.

Similarly, the emergence of complex financial "products", typically with hybrid or derivative characteristics, has also raised difficult timing and characterization issues. In general, there is an increasing tendency to abandon traditional realization and tax accounting approaches in this area, and to tax such instruments on an internal rate of return or mark-to-market basis. The exact scope of such rules, however, is still uncertain and many of the systems are currently evolving new approaches to these issues.

In the *United States*, prior to explicit statutory provisions, the treatment of original issue discount in the case law was unclear, with some cases following the form of the transaction and treating the discount element as capital gain. Though the Supreme Court eventually determined that the discount element was properly characterized as ordinary income, Congress had, in the meantime, intervened with a specific statutory provision denying capital gain treatment to the discount realized at maturity. The next legislative response to OID was to require holders of OID bonds to include the original discount amount in income ratably over the life of the bond regardless of their normal accounting method. Subsequent provisions modified the method of inclusion to require the discount element to be treated on an "economic" or "constant interest" accrual basis, i.e., with less interest in early years and more in later years, reflecting the implicit reinvestment of the interest element.

Finally, in 1984, rules were introduced dealing with the calculation of OID when bonds are issued for property. Except in the case of traded property, where bonds are issued for property, the value of the property is uncertain and hence the issue price of the bond and the resulting discount cannot be directly ascertained. To deal with this problem, the legislation in general terms provided for the determination of the issue price by discounting the payments to be made under the bond by a stipulated discount rate and treating that amount as the current value of the property and hence the issue price of the bond. If the amounts to be received under the instrument exceed the hypothetical issue price, the excess is original issue discount and is included and deducted currently under the usually applicable OID principles.

A number of special and complex rules deal with obligations providing for contingent payments or a variable interest rate. Proposals have been made (though subsequently withdrawn) to apply original issue discount rules to "hybrid" obligations, for example, convertible bonds, under a "bifurcated" approach which would treat separately the option embedded in the convertible bond and the actual loan, applying original discount principles to the loan portion of the transaction.

A different set of rules applies to so-called "market discount", i.e., discount arising from a purchase of bonds in the market which have declined in value because of interest rate changes. No current accrual of the discount is required but the gain is not entitled to capital gain treatment on disposition. The realization rules are relaxed with respect to the disposition of market discount bonds, so that a gift of the bond would constitute a realization event. In addition, there are limitations on the deduction of interest expense incurred in connection with market discount bonds. The taxpayer may elect to accrue market discount currently, in which case the interest expense is fully deductible.

Beyond the treatment of discount bonds, the rules dealing with more complex financial instruments are still evolving. A mark-to-market approach is taken with respect to many types of commodities futures, foreign currency and options contracts. In addition, dealers in securities and derivatives are required to mark to market certain forward and option contracts and notional principal contracts which are not covered by the general rule. A broader accrual approach has been discussed in the academic literature.

The development in *Sweden* has been somewhat similar though it took place somewhat later. Prior to extensive statutory revision in 1991, it was unclear if OID was to be treated as taxable (and deductible) interest or as potentially nontaxable capital gain. Case law-developed principles taxed the income on obligations held to maturity as interest but the treatment of income on a sale during the period the bond was outstanding was never satisfactorily resolved.

Under statutory provisions enacted in 1991, OID on obligations held by private persons is treated as interest but is not taxed until actually received, either on sale or on the maturity of the bond. For corporations and individuals holding bonds as business assets, the general application of financial accounting principles for tax purposes requires the accrual of OID currently as interest income. Business issuers of OID obligations similarly can accrue the interest expense currently. A special tax rule which had previously allowed the full current deduction of OID has recently been repealed.

Japan has no general tax rules dealing with OID though if an obligation is treated on an OID basis for Commercial Code accounting purposes, it must be similarly treated for tax purposes. In addition, a special provision imposes an 18 % final withholding tax on the OID element at the time the obligation is issued.

There is a movement to adopt a mark-to-market approach with respect to derivative financial instruments but the shape of the system which will emerge is not yet clear. Since the treatment for tax purposes is closely linked to the Commercial Code accounting rules, the accounting rules must first be changed before the tax rules will be affected. In 1996, changes were made in banking and securities laws requiring mark-to-market treatment by banks and securities companies. Corresponding changes in Commercial Code accounting rules and tax rules will presumably follow.

In *France*, OID has been subject to special rules since 1985. For individuals who do not hold the obligations in a business, the difference between the issue price and the amount ultimately received (excluding annual interest actually paid) is treated as interest income in the year received. The same rule applies in a business context for small discounts but if the discount exceeds 10 % of the acquisition price, the interest must be computed on a yield-to-maturity basis and included in income annually.

With respect to futures contracts, options and derivative instruments, statutory provisions require mark-to-market treatment if the instruments are traded on an organized market or have a value determined with respect to such a market.

The *German* rules have a similar pattern. If both the issuer and the holder of an obligation are required to use the accrual method of accounting generally, that is, are business taxpayers, the original issue discount is accounted for currently as interest expense and interest income, calculated on a yield-to-maturity basis. In addition, subsequent changes in interest rates which increase the value of the liability in the hands of the issuer are also taken into account currently though the corresponding gain to the holder continues to be deferred.

In the case of a cash basis holder, the original issue discount is only taxed at redemption or on sale, but at that time is treated as interest income and not as tax-free capital gain. The cash basis taxpayer can elect between calculating the interest element on a yield-to-maturity basis, i.e., the initial yield when the bond was issued or can base the calculation on effective yield (market yield), i.e., the difference between the purchase price and the subsequent sales or redemption price. A de minimis rule exempts certain levels of implicit interest from the application of the normal rules.

The present rules for cash basis holders were introduced in 1994 in response to the increased issuance of various forms of bonds with disguised discount which arguably qualified as tax-free capital gain under the prior system.

Realized gain or loss resulting from market discount is taxable to a business taxpayer but would be treated as tax-free capital gain in the hands of a private investor.

There seems little movement in the direction of an overall mark-to-market treatment of derivative financial instruments, reflecting to some extent the impact which the basic conservative approach of accounting rules has on the German tax system generally.

In *The Netherlands*, with regard to zero-bonds, discount bonds, "cash certificates", and "saving certificates" the difference between the amount nonbusiness taxpayers receive upon maturity from the issuer (face value) and the price they originally paid to the issuer is taxed to them when received (realization) as (passive) investment income. If the form of the transaction as a capital gain were respected, there would normally be no tax under the general rules which do not reach such gains. If the bond, etc., is sold before maturity, the seller is taxed on the amount of interest that accrued during the period he has owned the bond, and the purchaser is effectively taxed for the interest accruing during his period of ownership. For business taxpayers, under tax case law (interpreting "good commercial practice") the annual amount of interest accrued on discount bonds, etc., is taken into account for tax purposes currently.

There is no case law yet on the taxation of financial derivatives. Tax inspectors generally apply the rules of "good commercial practice" (a deduction can be taken if there is a more than negligible risk that loss will be suffered; income not yet earned need not be reported) and taxpayers apparently have not been in situations where this application led to results unacceptable to them.

The *Canadian* Income Tax Act does not contain comprehensive rules dealing with original issue discount or sophisticated financial products, including derivatives. As a result, the tax consequences of these products must be determined by applying the basic provisions dealing with the character, source, and timing of income and deductions. Not surprisingly, financial products have been used by taxpayers to manipulate tax consequences. In certain cases, the government has responded with specific legislation on an ad hoc basis.

As a result of a misreading of old English cases, Canadian courts consider interest to be a non-deductible capital expense. Accordingly, there is a special statutory deduction for interest expense incurred in respect of borrowed money or the unpaid purchase price of property if the money or the property is used for the purpose of earning income. The statutory requirement for borrowed money is an important limitation on the deduction. For example, interest in respect of unpaid interest would not be deductible in the absence of a special provision since the unpaid interest is not borrowed money. This special provision permits a deduction for compound interest only when it is actually paid.

According to the express wording of the Act, interest is deductible if it is paid in the year or becomes payable in respect of the year. Nevertheless, by administrative practice, interest, other than compound interest, is deductible on an accrual basis. Interest is not defined in the Act, but the case law has established that interest is restricted to amounts that represent compensation for the use of money, that are computed in reference to a principal sum, and that accrue on a daily basis.

An OID, premium, or bonus is considered to be interest only if a loan provides for interest at less than a reasonable rate. If OID is not interest, it is deductible only when paid. In the case of a "shallow" discount (the issue price is not less than 97 % of the principal and its annual yield is not greater than 4/3 of the stipulated interest rate), the full amount of the discount is deductible. For other "deep" discounts, only 3/4 of the amount of the discount is deductible when paid. The disallowance of 25 % of the OID as a deduction reflects the fact that generally, only 75 % of the discount would be included in the income of the holder; in other words, the discount is treated as capital gain to the holder.

Taxpayers could avoid the treatment of OID as capital by issuing zero coupon bonds. Because these bonds have no stated interest, the discount is treated as interest for tax purposes. However, Revenue Canada takes the position that the interest must be bifurcated into simple interest and compound interest. The simple interest is deductible on an accrual basis, but the compound interest is deductible only when paid on the maturity of the obligation. This treatment effectively precluded Canadian corporations from using zero coupon bonds and original issue discount as an effective means of borrowing.

In 1990 the government introduced detailed provisions with respect to certain long-term prepaid debt obligations. These rules were intended to require the prepayment of interest to be treated as a reduction of the principal amount of the obligation. Inadvertently, the rules work in such a way that corporate borrowers can achieve exactly the same result as with a zero coupon bond by simply prepaying interest. In other words, under these rules the amount of the prepayment is deductible on an actuarial basis over the term of the obligation. This result was clearly unintended.

The Canadian tax system does not contain comprehensive accrual rules dealing with financial products. Accordingly, the tax consequences of various products have been established largely by administrative practice and case law. Gains and losses in respect of futures and forward contracts are considered to be on income account if the transactions are connected with the taxpayer's business. Otherwise, a taxpayer may report such gains and losses as ordinary income or loss or as capital gains or losses, but must do so consistently. Originally, Revenue Canada applied a linkage approach to the treatment of foreign exchange gains and losses and swap transactions. In other words, the treatment of the gains and losses from the foreign currency fluctuations or the swap were dependent on the treatment of the underlying transaction. This type of approach leads to a mismatching where a capital asset or liability is hedged. Accordingly, Revenue Canada recently indicated that all interest rate swaps would be treated on income account. It is unclear whether this position will be applied to all hedging products.

Financial institutions and investment dealers are required by legislation to use mark-to-market reporting for certain debt and equity securities. For other taxpayers, gains and losses are recognized only when realized. However, if the property constitutes inventory of a business, the lower of cost or market rule of inventory valuation will require the losses to be accrued.

Currently the *Australian* system is a mixture of partial regimes dealing with various aspects of the issues considered in this section. While comprehensive legislation has been proposed, with respect to existing law, doubts still persist whether original issue discount is treated as capital gain or ordinary income in a business context, though the practice is to treat it as ordinary income. Under case law both deferred interest and OID are deductible over the term of the instrument for an accrual basis taxpayer. To deal with the problem of mismatches where an accrual basis taxpayer "borrows" using OID or deferred interest from a cash basis taxpayer (the average individual investor), and problems of capital indexed securities, stripped securities etc., an accruals regime was introduced in 1984 for a wide range of debt securities issued at a discount or otherwise providing at issue for returns in forms other than periodic interest. This regime uses the internal rate of return method on both the income and deduction side, but does not apply to all debt securities. For example, market discounts where the value of a security has fallen because of a rise in interest rates are not subject to the accrual regime. However, a statutory amendment in 1989 required that such amounts be treated as ordinary income to prevent capital gains indexation being available. Similarly, foreign exchange gains and losses are subject to a special realization-based statutory regime.

The proposed comprehensive regime is a mixture of internal rate of return and mark-to-market systems. It will apply to a broad range of financial transactions, namely debt and arrangements which are in substance debt (such as redeemable preference shares), transactions where there is an amount payable or receivable in foreign currency and physical holdings of foreign currency, debt derivatives and derivatives based on an index made up of commodities or equities. The regime will not cover equity, equity and commodity derivatives not based on an index, life insurance and superannuation or financial transactions of individuals except where there is an opportunity for significant tax deferral (e.g. deep discount) or where the holdings of the individual exceed a threshold (tentatively $500,000). Further, a special regime will be developed for leasing of plant and equipment.

Hybrids will be bifurcated where possible (i.e., where cash flows can be identified and separated); otherwise the financial transactions regime will apply in full if the instrument falls within it in part. All gains and losses from financial arrangements will be treated as ordinary income and not as capital gain. The basic timing method will be daily compounding accruals, though straight line spreading will be possible if there is no undue timing distortion. Market value accounting (mark-to-market or estimated market value) will be required for a limited number of instruments such as futures contracts and forward contracts and will be optional in other cases if it is used consistently and provides a fair estimate of value. No special regime is proposed for hedging or linked transactions, that is, the financial transactions regime will apply to any part of a hedging or linked arrangement that falls within the definition, but not to any other part. Foreign exchange gains and losses will not generally be on a mark-to-market basis, as this can produce large swings in income and losses but rather will be treated in the same way as variable return instruments with assumptions made about future cash flows and progressive adjustments to reflect outcomes. Adjustments will also be made on disposals generally to align the result of the accrual with the actual outcome. Unlike the New Zealand system, there is no proposal for charging interest to capture any underaccrual when an adjustment is made on disposal.

The *United Kingdom*, like the US, began with a struggle to fit low interest and zero coupon bonds into the tax framework. The taxability of a profit arising from a discount has been part of the UK tax system since 1802 when such profits were listed as falling within Schedule D Case III. However, under Revenue practice, while the holder was taxable on the discount, a charge only arose when it was realized through redemption. This meant that the holder was not taxed on the profit made on a realization before redemption; it had the even more bizarre consequence that the holder at redemption was taxed on the whole of the profit arising from the discount, a rule which meant that anyone who held such a bond would sell it to a tax exempt body such as a charity or a pension fund so that no tax was collected at all. A court decision in 1983 made it more likely that the holder of a bond should be taxed on an intermediate profit but the introduction of the 1984 rules, discussed below, meant that this has not been explored further. Under the Revenue practice, the discount was not deductible by the issuing company until redemption, when it was deductible in full.

Statutory provisions dealing with the situation were introduced in 1984. Under the 1984 rules applicable to Deep Discount Bonds, an income element is treated as arising, strictly in line with an algebraic formula, during the life of the bond; a discount is deep if it is greater than 15% or 1/2 % per annum. The issuing company deducts the income element under the formula year-by-year. The holder, however, pays tax only on an actual (or deemed) disposal; there is no deemed disposal simply because a year has ended. When the holder disposes of the bond he is treated as receiving the income element up to that day; if the actual price difference is greater or less than that given by the formula, the balance is treated as capital gain or loss or income gain or loss under ordinary tax rules. If the discount was not deep, or for some other reason the bonds fell outside the 1984 rules, the original Revenue practice still applies.

The Deep Discount rules only apply where the gain could be calculated at the start, e.g., where the redemption price was fixed. Some other instruments fell within further rules created in 1989 for "deep gain" securities where the formulary approach was not possible but with extensive exemptions e.g., for convertible securities, qualifying indexed securities and for certain government bonds.

In 1996, the United Kingdom introduced new rules for the tax treatment of any "loan relationship" entered into by a company, thus covering discount bonds but having a much wider scope. The rules apply for both income inclusion and deduction of expense. In general terms, the legislation authorizes two accounting methods for loans, accrual and mark-to-market. If the mark-to-market method is used in the company's financial accounts, that method must be used for tax purposes; otherwise an accrual method is required. In addition, where related parties are involved, an accrual method is also required. The new rules follow the principles of legislation introduced several years earlier applying mark-to-market or accrual accounting for foreign currency and derivative instruments. It should be noted that the new rules apply only to corporate holders and issuers; for other taxpayers the 1984 and 1989 rules or, in exceptional circumstances, the original revenue practice continue to apply.

Subpart D: Attribution of Income

A final element in the structure of an income tax is the attribution of the various elements of the tax base to the taxable person. Several different questions are involved. The most fundamental is the choice of taxable unit. Who is "the taxpayer" for purposes of applying the various substantive rules of the tax system? Once that question has been answered, a second and related issue involves taxpayer attempts to shift income among taxable units in order to reduce the overall tax burden of taxpayers who are, broadly speaking, related but who constitute separate taxable persons. To what extent and under what conditions will those income transfers be respected? While the issue arises primarily in the context of progressive rate structures, where splitting the income among several taxpayers can reduce the total tax burden, it can also involve taking advantage of various special deductions or allowances.

A related problem concerns the treatment of payments arising out of divorce and separation. Where the couple is, at least for some purposes, treated as a taxable unit, a question arises as to how payments which result from the dissolution of that relationship should be dealt with. And even in systems in which the individual is the taxable unit, there may be special rules for payments between divorced spouses and payments for the support of children.

The following material first examines the basic question of the taxable unit and then explores the other related issues.

1. Definition of taxable unit

The choice of the appropriate taxable unit involves complex issues of social and economic policy and has been the subject of much discussion in many of the countries here under consideration. Any decision regarding the taxable unit involves emphasizing some policy goals and social values at the expense of others. For example, a decision to treat the individual as the taxable unit may mean that married couples with the same amount of income and otherwise similarly situated may pay a different amount of tax depending on how much income is earned by each partner. On the other hand, a decision to treat the married couple as the taxable unit may mean that such couples are treated differently from other couples whose economic and social arrangements are functionally similar. In addition, depending on the structure of the rate schedule, a decision to treat married couples as the taxable unit may result in a change in overall tax burden as a result of marriage (or divorce).

The resolution of these conflicting policy goals has taken several forms in the systems here considered. In some cases, each individual is treated as a taxable unit and there is no aggregation of income among family members. A variation on this approach is to treat the individual as the taxable unit for the purpose of taxing earned income but to have special rules dealing with unearned income. Single taxation on earned income allows the decision as to entry into the work force to be independent of the income earned by the other member of the couple. On the other hand, some type of aggregation of unearned income prevents the shifting of such income within the economic unit in order to reduce tax burdens.

Other systems either require or allow the married couple (or certain other forms of cohabitation) to be treated as a taxable unit. This approach is sometimes accompanied by a rate structure which "splits" the income between the two partners equally which means that, in the case of progressive rates, marriage will not increase the total tax burden on the couple. On the other hand, a differentiated rate for married couples raises the issue of the proper relationship in the rate schedules between the rates for married couples and single persons.

Whatever approach is taken to the taxation of adults, the treatment of the income of dependent children raises a separate issue. Should they be treated as separate taxpayers or taxed together with the adults who have the responsibility for their care?

The development of the rules on taxable unit in the *United States* illustrates the interaction of these various considerations. Prior to 1948, the individual was the only taxable unit. As a result, the tax burden on married couples varied depending on the division of taxable income between the spouses. In addition, the Supreme Court had held that, in States which had adopted the civil law community property system, each spouse was taxable on one-half of the income, regardless of who had earned the income. As a result, under the progressive rate structure, married couples in community property states could pay less tax on the same amount of combined income than couples in common law jurisdictions. In 1948, in response to this problem, couples were permitted to elect to file "joint" returns and to aggregate income and compute their tax under a rate structure which had brackets twice as wide as the corresponding brackets used by unmarried persons. The election was only available to couples who were married for civil law purposes. While the couple could still file separate returns if they desired, it was almost always advantageous to take advantage of the splitting of income which the joint return entailed.

The introduction of joint returns meant that a couple paid significantly less tax than did an individual filing separately with the same amount of income. The perception that individuals were overtaxed in relation to couples under the rate structure introduced in connection with joint returns led in 1969 to the introduction of a new system of rate schedules. The new system retained the separate schedule for married couples but changed the relation among the brackets to reduce the difference between married and single brackets. Under the new system, the bracket differences no longer represented a "splitting" of income between the spouses. The old rate schedules were retained for married couples who elected to file separately to prevent them from taking advantage of the new lower individual rates.

Moving away from a system of splitting, however, introduced a new problem. If two single persons with roughly equal income married, their tax burden would be increased since the aggregation of their income in the married rate structure would increase the impact of the progressive rates. This "marriage penalty" was partially addressed in 1981 with the introduction of a deduction for two-earner couples. The deduction was eliminated in 1986 when a substantial reduction in the progressivity of tax rates made the marriage penalty much less significant. However, as marginal tax rates have increased since that time, concern about the impact of marriage on tax burdens has reappeared.

There seems to be a growing recognition in the United States that in a system of progressive rates it is impossible to have an equal treatment of married couples, a differential between individual and married taxation which does not reflect income splitting, and no significant change in tax burdens as a result of marriage. Choices and compromises must be made and the relative importance accorded these policy objectives has varied over time. Currently, attention is focused on the "marriage penalty" present under existing law and the impact of aggregate taxation on entry into the work force by secondary workers, primary women.

Dependent children in the United States are in general treated as separate taxpayers. However, the unearned income of children under fourteen, though technically still treated as separate income and not aggregated with the parents' income, is taxed at the parents' highest marginal rate. In certain situations the income is aggregated in what could be viewed as a first step toward a wider definition of the taxable unit.

The *German* system also provides an election for joint taxation of married couples living together (though not for other couples in marriage-like relationships). For electing couples, the total income of each partner is determined, then aggregated and divided by two in determining the statutory tax rate. Prior to this "splitting" procedure, income of married couples was aggregated and subjected to the same rate schedule as single persons. The Federal Constitutional Court in 1957 held this approach unconstitutional. It was found to violate the constitutional provision which requires that marriage and the family enjoy the "special protection" of the State. Since the rate structure would increase the tax burden in any case in which both partners had income, it discouraged marriage and hence was unconstitutional. The Court indicated in its opinion that a splitting procedure would be constitutional. Subsequently, the current splitting procedure was introduced. It is not clear whether a system that allowed aggregation and a modified rate structure that took into account the fact of marriage but did not allow splitting would be found to be constitutional. Currently, the impact of splitting on the tax burden of high-income families is increasingly criticized. Children are treated as separate taxpayers for most purposes.

The *Canadian system* takes a different approach. There the individual has always been the taxable unit, though there has been periodic discussion to establish the spouses or the family as the taxable unit. However, the income of both spouses (formally married or a common-law spouse of the opposite sex) is aggregated for purposes of determining the entitlement to certain personal tax allowances. The Australian system is quite similar. The individual is treated as the taxable unit. There is a spousal tax credit which is reduced as the income of the other spouse increases, so in the case of a couple where only one partner has income, there is some limited reduction of tax for the family unit. The amount of the credit and the income level at which it cuts out are relatively low. "Spouse" for these purposes is defined as a person of the opposite sex living as husband or wife. In both systems, there are developed rules to prevent the shifting of income which are discussed below.

Historically, the *United Kingdom* in effect treated the married couple as a taxable unit by attributing all of the wife's income to the husband. Since the husband was the technical taxpayer, he was primarily responsible for the payment of the tax and for all dealings with the tax authorities. This approach was gradually liberalized, with the wife first given the authority to deal directly with the tax authorities and subsequently the couple could elect to have the wife's earned income taxed separately. Given the rate structure and other secondary consequences of the election, it was of most advantage to higher-income taxpayers. In 1990, a system of separate taxation was introduced covering both earned and unearned income. In the case of income from property, if the property is owned jointly, the income is divided evenly unless the parties can establish a different underlying ownership. Separate taxation applies for purposes of the capital gains tax as well, with a separate annual exemption for both spouses. Children are also treated as separate taxpayers for both income and capital gains tax purposes.

The *Japanese* system also adopts the individual as the taxable unit. At one time, there were rules which attempted to assess investment income of family members to the principal wage earner but they were dropped because of administrative problems. A spousal allowance is provided if the income of the one spouse is less than a certain limited amount. The allowance is phased out as the lower-earning spouse's income increases so that if both spouses earn more than the base amount, no allowance is available. The effect of this provision is criticized as discouraging women to enter the work force on a full-time basis.

The *Dutch* approach is based on individual taxation with some modifications. If the taxpayer is married or has a recognized common household with another person (partner, parent(s), siblings etc.) and has total income below the tax-free amount to which each individual is entitled, the entire tax-free amount may be transferred to another member of the household or to the spouse. A common household is recognized if the persons involved are over eighteen and have a common household for over eighteen months and are registered at the same address.

Apart from the possibility of the transfer of a tax-free amount, married couples are taxed on their business, employment and periodic income separately ("personal income"). All other income and personal deductions are attributed to the spouse with the higher personal income. This system, enacted in 1990, eliminated a complex system of special allowances which took into account various aspects of family or household circumstances. Minor children are taxed on their own earned income but investment income (other than capital gains) is taxed to the parent with the highest income.

Sweden currently also has a system of individual taxation. In the past, the system was based on a form of aggregate taxation of couples, defined for tax purposes as those formally married or living together and having (or having had) a child together or having been formerly

married. The rules were modified in 1987 to provide for individual taxation on earned income with unearned income taxed to the partner
with the highest earned income and "stacked" on top of the earned
income. A principal reason for the change was to encourage second
workers, primarily women, to enter the work force by ensuring that the
marginal tax rate on such persons was not affected by the income level
of the other partner. This system was subsequently modified again to
provide for individual taxation on unearned income. Since the rate on
capital income currently is essentially proportional, there is no significant problem with income shifting and no need for the attribution of
income to the higher-earning spouse.

The *French* system has taken a completely different approach.
There the taxable unit is the "fiscal household" *(foyer fiscal)* which is
composed of husband, wife, dependent children, and any qualified
handicapped or invalid person regardless of family relationship who
lives together with the family. The incomes of all members of the
household are first aggregated. The total income is then taxed according to the *"quotient familial"* or "family share" system. The taxpayer and
spouse are each attributed one "share"; an additional one-half share is
given for up to two additional household members. An additional full
share is given for further members. Thus a family of husband, wife, and
two children would constitute three shares; a family with three children would constitute four shares, etc.

The same system applies to single persons (unmarried, widowed.
or divorced) but, in order to decrease the tax burden of single persons,
and especially women, with dependent children, the first dependent
child is granted a full share instead of one-half share. Unmarried couples always constitute two distinct fiscal households. Married persons
may, in exceptional circumstances, file separate tax returns provided
they live separately.

The total income of the family is divided into the relevant number of shares for the purpose of applying to each share of income the
individual income tax progressive schedule (seven brackets, from 0 %
to 56.8 %). Then the total tax payable by the fiscal household (before
any tax credit) is determined by multiplying the tax on each share by
the number of shares.

The basic theory behind this system, which was instituted just
after the Second World War, is to take into account the consumption
capacity of each member of the family and to tax the family according-

ly. A family is composed of a certain number of consumption units who have to share a given amount of income; it should not globally pay an income tax different from the sum of the separate income taxes that the family members would have paid if they had been single persons among which an amount equal to the family global income would have been equally split. Initially, each dependent child or person was considered a one-half consumption unit and so was granted one-half share. But, considering a given total income, the greater the number of children, the less tax reduction from each additional child. For this reason, in the 1980s it was decided to grant a full share (instead of one-half) to each child beginning with the third one. As the reduction in income tax resulting from the combination of the family share system and the progressive rate schedule proved to be higher for high-income households than for low-income households, such reduction was at the same time limited to a set amount (ca. $3,200 in 1995) for each one-half share in addition to the full shares accorded each spouse or the single head of household, as the case may be.

The concept of a dependent child is also complex. A child who is eighteen years or older is normally taxed as a single person, but he or she may elect to be attached to his parents' fiscal household provided he or she is less than twenty-one years of age or less than twenty-five if still in school or university and whatever age if disabled or performing military service. Even married children may, up to the above limits, elect to be part of the parents' household, but this does not result in an increase in the number of shares, the only effect being the deduction of a set amount for each attached person, child, spouse, and grandchild (ca. $5,600 in 1995).

2. Alimony and child support

The treatment of payments which arise out of the dissolution of a marriage also raise attribution of income issues. Suppose, for example, that as the result of a divorce, a husband is required to pay a portion of his salary to his former wife. There are several ways such payments could be viewed. One approach would be to treat the payment as a kind of "splitting" of the income between the two former spouses. Under this view, the alimony would in effect be deductible by the husband but taxed to the wife. On the other hand, the payment could be viewed as a personal expense to the husband and nondeductible. As for the wife, the payment could be taxable, on the view that it has increased her separate net worth and power to consume or, alternatively, treated in the same manner as interfamilial gifts, which generally do not result in taxation to the recipient. The same issues arise with respect to payments of child support to the custodial parent by the non-custodial parent. The systems examined here have taken a variety of approaches to these questions.

The *United States* system makes a basic distinction between alimony and child support. Historically, both alimony and child support were treated as personal expenses, nondeductible and not includable. Successive statutory enactments beginning in 1942 allowed a deduction and corresponding inclusion for alimony payments while continuing the nondeductible-excludable treatment for child support payments. The distinction between the two types of payments, often turning on intricacies of state family law, led to substantial litigation. The law was simplified in 1984 by providing a Federal definition of alimony that gives the parties substantial leeway in determining which payments will be treated as alimony. To qualify, the payments must be in connection with a divorce decree or written agreement of separation, must be in cash, and the parties must be living apart. The payments must end after the death of the payee and cannot be linked to events which indicate that they are in the nature of child support payments, e.g., changes made when a child reaches a certain age. Special complex and largely ineffective rules also are provided to prevent "front loading" of payments in what is essentially a property settlement rather than periodic alimony.

Even when the statutory requirements for alimony treatment are present, the parties can avoid these tax results by providing in the agreement that the statutory taxing pattern is not intended to apply. This provision gives the parties maximum flexibility in allocating the tax burden of the payments.

Payments for child support and property settlements, which are essentially all payments which do not meet the statutory definition of alimony, are nondeductible and not includable. Property settlements in connection with a divorce continue to be covered by the rollover treatment usually applicable to transfers between spouses.

The *Swedish* system is essentially the same as that in the United States. Periodic payments of alimony are deductible by the payor and taxable to the recipient. Alimony is viewed as an independent source of income for the recipient and is treated as income from services. Other periodic support payments, including those to children, are not deductible and not taxable.

Canada and *Australia* offer interesting contrasts. Under the Canadian system until recently, periodic payments of both alimony and child support were deductible by the payor and taxable to the recipient. Lump sum payments and property settlements, in contrast, are neither deductible nor taxable. It is common in the determination of the level of alimony, child support, and property payments to take into account the relative tax brackets of the parties and to utilize the form of payment which maximizes the overall tax benefit. The Supreme Court of Canada has recently rejected a constitutional challenge to the inclusion of child support payments in the income of the recipient. It was argued that the rule violated the equality provision of the Charter of Rights and Freedoms since only separated custodial parents are taxed on child support. Despite its victory in court, the government has introduced sweeping changes to the treatment of child support payments, including the elimination of the deduction for such payments and the taxation of the payments to the recipient.

The Australian system, in contrast, continues to make no distinction between alimony and child support payments. Both are in effect taxed to the payor since they are not deductible and are exempt to the recipient. Administratively, child support payments are collected through the tax system. Where property has been set aside in trust to fund maintenance payments, the payments are taxable to the recipient and in effect deductible by the payer since the income is excluded from his return. As for property settlements, there is an automatic rollover on property division between divorced or separated spouses.

The *United Kingdom* similarly does not make any distinction between alimony and child support. Prior to 1988, both types of payments were deductible by the payor and taxable to the respective recipients. In 1988, a new system was introduced which eliminated the general deduction for such payments and also made them tax-free in the hands of the recipient. Initially, a very limited deduction was allowed based on the married couples allowance which had survived the switch to separate taxation. That deduction was subsequently converted to a credit. At one time the credit was expressed in terms of the lowest marginal rate but, like the home mortgage interest deduction, the credit has now been reduced to a notional 15 % rate.

The elimination of the deduction for support payments took place at a time when there was a substantial reduction in tax rates and it is unclear if the change was simply part of a general base broadening or reflected a "family values" policy intended to make it more expensive to support separated families.

In *Germany* alimony is in principle treated as a personal expense and is neither deductible nor taxable. This is based on the concept that legal obligations of support are in general personal and should not result in a reduction of income. Correspondingly, such payments are not taxable to the recipient since they do not fall in a taxable category. However, under a special statutory provision, up to ca. $18,000 of alimony payments may be deducted and correspondingly included in the income of the recipient if both parties so agree. In addition, alimony payments which do not qualify for this special treatment can be in some circumstances considered as an "extraordinary burden" and may be deducted subject to the general limitations on such expenses.

Payments for child support in the divorce setting fall under the general rule that payment of legal obligations are personal and nondeductible and correspondingly not includable, though there are a number of allowances and exemptions for payments in relation to children generally which can apply in the divorce context.

In the *Dutch* system, periodic alimony payments, whether paid to a former spouse or a spouse from whom the taxpayer lives separately, are deductible as a qualified personal expense and includable by the recipient. In addition, a lump sum payment in lieu of periodic payments is deductible when made to a former spouse. A deduction for child support payments is allowed based on a fixed statutory amount related to the age of the child. The payments are not included in income.

In *France*, amounts paid in compliance with the obligation imposed on family members by the Civil Code to support their children or parents are tax-deductible provided they are reasonable in relation to the wealth of the payor and the needs of the payee. The deduction of support to adult children is possible if the latter are not attached to his/her fiscal household but it is limited to a set amount (ca. $5,600 in 1995 or double if the child is married).

Alimony — but not capital payments — to an ex-spouse are also deductible provided they are made under a court order and the parties are separated. So is the support to minor children under the custody of the ex-spouse even if not resulting from a judicial decision, but provided that it qualifies under the Civil Code conditions including the limitation to a reasonable amount. Alimony and child support are taxable to the payees when deductible by the payor.

In *Japan*, payment of periodic alimony is not common and there are no special tax rules. Divorce settlements are typically a lump-sum payment which is neither deductible nor taxable. It is treated by analogy to tort damages for personal injury. Periodic child support payments are also nondeductible and nontaxable.

3. Limitations on assignment of income

In a system with progressive rates, taxpayers will have an incentive to attempt to shift income to related taxpayers who are not treated as part of the same taxable unit. The pressure for income shifting is a function of the definition of taxable unit and is greatest where husband and wife are treated as separate taxpayers. Techniques to shift earned income typically involve contractual arrangements which create rights to income in related parties. With respect to income from property, the transaction will often involve a transfer of the right to the income while the transferor retains the underlying property. In both situations, a basic question is the extent to which the tax system will respect the underlying civil or commercial aspects of the transaction. The systems have reached a variety of results in these situations.

In the *United States*, case law early on established the proposition that earned income was taxable to the earner and the tax burden could not be shifted by contractual arrangements, even if those arrangements were not tax motivated and were effective for civil-law purposes. With respect to income from property, the principles are more complex. Where the entire property is given away, the tax on both the gain on the disposition of the property and the current income will be shifted to the donee. Where the right to the income is given away, but the underlying property is retained, the transfer generally will not be respected for tax purposes. Where the only right the transferor has is the right to an income stream, for example, a series of royalty payments, and the entire right is transferred, the transfer may be effective if the income stream is of long enough duration. On the other hand, the transfer of the right to one year's income while retaining the remaining stream would not be effective. Special rules deal with the transfer of property to trusts. In general, the transferor must give up nearly all rights to the property (a de minimis reversionary interest is allowed) in order to shift the tax burden to the trust or the trust beneficiaries. Under prior rules, if a ten-year income interest was transferred, the transfer was effective for tax purposes. This rule led to significant amounts of income shifting through trusts and was replaced by the present requirement of complete transfer.

In business relations between related parties, in general, arm's length principles must be followed. A special statutory rule recognizes family members as partners in limited partnerships but requires that partners performing services must be reasonably compensated, thus preventing the indirect shifting of income to the (typically minor) limited partners.

In the case of interest-free or low-interest loans, either an arm's length interest is imputed or the income generated by the loan is taxed directly to the lender, depending on the circumstances of the loan.

As might be expected, *Canada*, which has the most extensive system of individual taxation, also has the most restrictive rules on assignment of income. Where the taxpayer transfers property to a spouse or minor child, any income from the property, or any property substituted for it, is attributed to the transferor. A similar rule applies to any capital gain on the disposition of property to a spouse. The attribution rules also apply to the loan of property. Beyond the spouse or child situation, where the taxpayer assigns the right to income to a third party in a non-arm's length transaction, the income remains the income of the transferor. This rule prevents the assignment of salary income as well as income from property where the transferor retains the underlying property. A special statutory rule attributes the income generated on an interest-free or low-interest loan to a person related to the lender.

The rules in the *United Kingdom* are more liberal. An outright gift of property is effective to shift the burden of tax on the income to the transferee. If property is transferred in trust, the settlor remains taxable if he has retained any interest in the property. Special rules apply to trusts for the benefit of spouses, with the income of the trust remaining taxable to the grantor in most cases, even if there are not other retained interests. The term trust is widely defined for these purposes. There are even wider rules treating income of unmarried minor children of the settlor as income of the settlor but these rules do not apply to income which is accumulated and not distributed.

In *Australia*, as well, outright transfers of property between spouses are effective to shift the incidence of the tax. In addition, various income splitting schemes involving a division of professional income through the leasing of assets and the provision of services by a related trust have had varying degrees of success. Splitting of income with children has been prevented by a special statutory rule which taxes the unearned income of children (with limited exceptions including the income from property received by will) at the highest marginal tax rate, regardless of the rates of the parents. There is also a special provision which prevents short term (less than 7 years) transfers of income rights.

Sweden has no special statutory rules on assignment of income. In the case of earned income, case law principles have required that income be taxed to the person that earned the income. The income source is performance of services and from this it follows that it must be the income of the performer. Thus income earned by an employee which, under contractual arrangements, is received directly by a spouse, is taxed to the employee. The rules are more liberal in the case of income from property. Dividend income can be transferred effectively for tax purposes while the transferor retains the underlying shares. In the case of an outright gift of property, the carryover basis results in the tax on the gain being shifted to the donee. No interest is imputed on interest-free loans, allowing the transfer of the income to the borrower.

The *German* rules on assignment of income are case law-based and focus primarily on the requirement that arm's length principles generally be applied in contractual arrangements between related parties. For example, loans usually must bear a market rate of interest (though some flexibility is allowed), services must be performed for salaries paid to related persons, and the like. Children may be recognized as limited or silent partners if actual legal and economic rights are transferred and exercised.

Most of the case law in the assignment of income area involves the treatment of usufruct (*Niessbrauch*), a civil law institution roughly equivalent to an income interest or term of years in the common law tradition. A usufruct can be created in personal or real property but is most commonly a real property right. There is substantial case law dealing with the tax aspects of usufruct, which can be either gratuitous or for consideration. In general terms, in the case of a gratuitous usufruct, the income is taxed to the transferee-usufructuary. However, where the asset is a wasting one, no depreciation is allowed since the usufructuary has no tax cost in the income right. Correspondingly, the transferor-owner is denied any depreciation expenses or deductions since he is not in receipt of any taxable income. The denial of the deductions makes the transaction unattractive from a tax point of view if the purpose is to shift income.

With respect to income from capital, if only the bare right to income, for example, the dividends on stock or interest on a bond, is transferred, the income will remain taxable to the holder of the underlying asset. In more complex situations, the question is whether the rights transferred amount to an opportunity to influence the economic course of events through voting or management rights which may be sufficient to shift the income stream but may also be found to be a transfer of the asset.

Japan has no special rules on assignment of income. Contractual arrangements to shift earned income would be treated as taxable to the earner with a subsequent gift of the income, possibly subject to the gift tax. Attempts to shift property income have not been an issue since, under civil law concepts, it is not possible to effectively divide the right to the income from the underlying property.

In *France*, because of the aggregate household system of taxation, there are no special assignment of income provisions. Mention should be made, however, of the limit placed on the deductibility of the wages paid by one spouse carrying on a commercial or industrial business to the other spouse as an employee, because wages are more favorably taxed than industrial and commercial profits.

Similarly, in The *Netherlands*, the effect of an assignment of income to a spouse or a minor child is limited by the statutory attribution to the taxpayer of various categories of income of the spouse or child as discussed above. A special statutory rule taxes transferred accrued interest, rentals and similar payments to the owner of the underlying property. With regard to dividend payments, the dividends will generally be taxable to the owner of the shares, though the incidence of dividend taxation may be transferred through the use of a long-term usufruct. Interest free or low-interest loans are frequently used to attempt to shift income to another person and there are no special income tax rules dealing with the situation, though the gift tax may apply to the capitalized value of the foregone interest payments.

Part Three:
Taxation of Business Organizations

The taxation of business organizations generally falls into two basic patterns. "Corporate" taxation typically imposes a tax on the income of certain types of commercial organizations, usually formed under special enabling legislation, and also taxes the profits distributed to the holders of ownership interests, sometimes adjusting the taxation in the hands of the owners to reflect the fact that the income has been taxed to the organization. The other model, "partnership" or "flow-thru" taxation taxes the income derived by the organization directly to the owners whether or not distributed and makes appropriate adjustments to reflect this fact when the income is in fact distributed. The following Subpart A deals with corporate taxation while Subpart B treats partnership taxation.

These two models do not of course exhaust the possible patterns of the taxation of business organizations. In Australia, for example, substantial amounts of closely-held commercial activity is carried on in the form of "trading trusts", and foundations or other types of organization are important in other jurisdictions. Nonetheless, most of the issues in the taxation of business organizations revolve around corporate and partnership patterns.

Subpart A: Corporate-Shareholder Taxation

The corporate tax systems in the countries here under consideration range from traditional "classical" systems of full corporate and individual level taxation on distributed profits (United States, The Netherlands, Sweden) to complete integration of corporate and individual tax on distributed profits (Germany, France, Australia). All other countries have some more limited form of integration.

This Subpart begins with a brief overview of the structure of corporate taxation in each of the countries. The material then examines a number of technical problems which are common to all systems. There is no attempt to describe in any detail the particularities of corporation-shareholder taxation in each system, a topic which has been examined on a comparative basis frequently in the past.[1] Rather, the focus is on a number of design questions raised in all the systems. Of course, the function that a particular rule performs is affected by the system in which it is operating which in turn may partially explain the contours of the rule. For example, a distribution of profits may bring with it a shareholder credit in an imputation system but be subject to unrelieved shareholder-level taxation in a classical system. Thus, the role the rule plays within the particular system must be kept in mind when considering matters on a comparative basis.

1. Overview of corporate tax systems

In the *United States*, corporate profits are generally taxed at 34 % though there is a 35 % rate for income in excess of $15,000,000 and lower rates for the first $100,000 of income. These latter rates are phased out at higher income levels as is the 34 % rate, giving an odd pattern of marginal rates. Distributed profits are taxed to individual shareholders at progressive rates ranging from 15 % to 39.6 %. A phaseout of some exemptions and deductions can again give a "bulge" in marginal rates. For individuals, the tax rate on capital gains is limited to 28 %, thus giving a preference for those upper-bracket taxpayers who would otherwise fall in higher marginal brackets. Corporate capital gains are taxed at normal rates. Capital losses can only be used to offset capital gains, though for individuals, $3,000 of capital losses annually can be used against normal income.

Sweden similarly has a classical system at the present time though for a brief period in 1994 dividends were exempt from individual taxation. The basic corporate tax rate is 28 %, down from 52 % prior to 1991. For individuals dividend income is usually taxed as income from capital at a flat 30 %. Capital gains are also subject to 30 % tax as income from capital.

The classical system in *The Netherlands* has a corporate rate of 35 % with a higher rate on the first ca. $60,000 of income. This latter rate was intended to slightly discourage high-bracket taxpayers from

---

1. See, e.g., United States Department of Treasury, Report of the Department of the Treasury on Integration of the Individual and Corporate Tax Systems: Taxing Business Income Once (1992); A. Warren, Reporter's Study of Corporate Tax Integration (American Law Institute, 1993).

shifting income to personal corporations but is being phased out. Individual rates are progressive from 37.5 % to 60 %. Capital gains on stock are not taxed to individuals unless the level of shareholding amounts to a "substantial interest", currently defined as at least a 33 % interest held by the taxpayer, his spouse, or close relatives (and at least 7 % held directly by the taxpayer or his spouse) at any time within five years of the disposition. Gains on the disposition of a substantial interest are taxed at 20 %.

In contrast to these classical systems, the *German* system combines a split rate on distributed profits with an imputation credit to eliminate fully the impact of the corporate tax on profits distributed to domestic individuals. Retained profits are taxed in general at a 45 % rate. When the profits are distributed, the rate is reduced to 30 % and the dividend distribution carries with it a 30 % credit to domestic taxable shareholders. The shareholder "grosses up" the cash dividend by the amount of the credit and reduces his income tax liability accordingly. The credit is refundable to individual shareholders whose liability is less than the credit. No credit is allowed for domestic tax-exempt organizations or foreign shareholders (apart from investments held in a German permanent establishment). Income and other receipts which are received by the corporation are classified into various baskets or pools, depending on the level of tax the items have borne. Distributions are deemed to come first from the baskets which have borne the highest tax (so-called HIFO stacking method). If the high-tax baskets are exhausted and distributions are made from certain baskets which have borne no tax, for example, tax-free subsidies or certain cancellation of indebtedness income, a "compensatory" tax of 30% is imposed on the distribution thus funding the credit at the shareholder level. Since 1994 compensatory tax is no longer imposed on distributions out of exempt foreign income.

Capital gains on portfolio shares are in general not subject to tax. Capital gains on shares where the individual owns more than 25 % of the outstanding stock are generally taxable at one-half of the normally applicable rates.

The *Australian* system also gives full relief from corporate level tax on distributions but the technique is somewhat different. The basic corporate rate is 36 % currently and has varied between 33 % and 49 % over the last ten years. When fully taxed corporate profits are distributed, domestic shareholders receive a (nonrefundable) credit for the full amount of the corporate tax. The corporation distributing the dividend attaches or "franks" the dividend with the appropriate amount of corporate tax based on the tax which it has paid and dividends which it has received on which tax has been paid. When dividends are paid at a time when there is no balance in the franking account, they do not carry with them any credit and are correspondingly not subject to any compensatory tax. The corporation must inform the shareholder of the amount of credit attached to each dividend payment. There are "anti-streaming" rules to prevent dividends being paid from franked accounts to shareholders entitled to the credit and other nonfranked dividends to other shareholders. Capital gains on shares acquired after the effective date of the capital gains legislation are taxed in full at ordinary rates, after an indexation allowance for inflation.

The *United Kingdom* has had an imputation credit system since 1973, with the rates of tax and the degree of integration varying over the years. Under the current structure, the basic rate of corporate tax is 33 %. A lower 24 % rate (the basic individual rate) is applicable to profits below ca. $370,000 and is phased out as profits exceed that amount, reaching the 33 % rate at ca. $2.8 million. Dividend distributions are subject to an "advance corporation tax" (ACT) of 20/80 of the amount distributed which is the amount of the refundable imputation credit carried out to the individual domestic shareholder. The advance corporation tax is credited against the otherwise applicable "mainstream" corporate tax. When profits are fully distributed, a residual tax of approximately 16 % will have been imposed at the corporate level and not relieved at the individual level. A "franked income" system applies to intercorporate dividends paid between domestic corporations.

France was one of the first countries to adopt an imputation system and the degree of integration has varied over time. Under the current system, the corporate rate is 33.33 % and a credit (*avoir fiscal*) of one-half of the dividend distributed is available to resident shareholders, thus providing full relief for distributed profits. Excess credit is refundable to individual shareholders who include the grossed-up dividend in income and are taxed under a progressive rate schedule which ranges up to 56.8 %. Long term capital gains are subject to a preferential rate. Where dividends are paid from income which has not borne full corporate level tax, a compensatory tax (*précompte mobilier*) is imposed. The compensatory tax is also imposed on fully taxed profits which are not distributed within five years.

The *Canadian* imputation system allows full imputation of the corporate tax in the case of Canadian-controlled privately-held corporations and partial imputation for publicly-traded companies and other private corporations with the degree of integration depending on the nature of the corporate activity. The most striking feature of the Canadian system is that it provides the credit regardless of whether the corporation distributing the dividend has actually paid the corporate level tax. Thus it goes beyond simply eliminating the double tax on distributed corporate profits and amounts to an incentive to Canadians to invest in Canadian corporations.

In contrast, the *Japanese* system has only a modest degree of integration of corporate and shareholder tax. For taxpayers with income below a certain amount, there is a credit for 10 % of the amount of the dividend distribution which can reduce the individual tax on the dividend and the tax on income falling in other schedules. Where the income exceeds the threshold, the credit is limited to 5 % of the dividend in excess of that amount and 10 % on the remaining amount of the dividend.

Table III at the end of Subpart A summarizes these and other features of each of the systems.

2. Defining entities subject to tax

A basic structural decision in the design of a corporate tax is the determination of what entities or organizations should be subject to the tax. Depending on the state's commercial or business organization law, there may be a number of forms of business organization which would be possible subjects for the corporate tax. In some systems, the determination is made on the basis of a statutory list or enumeration of organizations which is exclusive. More typically, there is a non-exclusive list and some more general description of characteristics which will cause an organization to fall under the corporate taxing scheme. For organizations that are not subject to the corporate tax, some pattern of single-level "pass-thru" taxation is typically applicable and is discussed in Subpart B.

In the *United States* system, all entities that are formed under the general domestic corporate laws of the States are treated as corporations for federal tax purposes. Thus the tax applies in principle to both a one-person corporation and a publicly-traded corporation with thousands of shareholders.

Other forms of business organization in the United States may be taxable as corporations if they have certain characteristics typical of corporations. These tests are based on judicial and administrative principles and focus on limited liability, free transferability of interests, centralized and representative management, and continuity of life. Thus, for example, an entity organized as a limited partnership for commercial law purposes but possessing these features could be treated as a corporation for federal tax. These factors reflect the fact that a corporation has limited liability in relation to the shareholders, its shares are typically freely traded, the board of directors functions as the centralized representative management of the corporation, and the existence of the corporation is not affected by changes in the status of its shareholders.

Though these rules originally were concerned with the "substance" of the similarity between incorporated and unincorporated entities, in the United States they have evolved into an arcane and technical morass with differences in classification turning on relatively insignificant factors. A recent proposal has been made to greatly liberalize the rules and in effect give the taxpayer the choice of whether an unincorporated business organization should be treated as a corporation. The rule would be expressly elective, that is, the taxpayer would "check the box" on the appropriate form as to whether the unincorporated organization should be treated as a corporation or a "pass-thru" entity for federal tax purposes. The proposal would not apply to organizations which have publicly-traded interests.

Some of the foreign systems here under consideration have taken an approach to classification for tax purposes which follows more closely the commercial law classifications. Thus in *Canada* entities formed under the corporation law are subject to the corporate income tax while those formed under partnership provisions are treated under pass-thru rules. There is no attempt to classify civil law partnerships as corporations. The *United Kingdom* similarly taxes all incorporated bodies and unincorporated associations other than partnerships.

Swedish rules follow the same pattern. There are no tax rules classifying entities for tax purposes and classification is based on private law characterizations. In general, all entities (except partnerships) which have to be registered are treated as corporations for tax purposes.

In the *German* system, the Corporation Tax Law lists specific organizational forms that are subject to the tax. In general, these forms correspond to the forms of organization under the civil or commercial law and other organizations which are treated for civil law purposes as "juridical persons." A special catch-all provision includes associations, institutions, foundations and other "conglomerations of assets" to the extent that the participants are not subject to tax directly. The list is exclusive and only the enumerated forms are subject to corporate tax. General and limited commercial partnerships as well as civil law partnerships are not subject to the corporate tax. This has led to the construction of limited partnerships with a corporate general partner, typically with low capitalization (*GmbH & Co. KG*). Despite their economic resemblance to corporations, these entities are not subject to corporate tax.

The *Dutch* rules are similar. The "entities" that are subject to corporate tax are enumerated in the Corporate Income Tax Act and include corporations and limited liability companies as well as other entities (including limited partnerships) whose capital is divided into shares. As a result, all entities whose interests are freely transferable and whose income does not accrue directly to the participants but requires a decision as to distribution are subject to corporate tax. Certain other entities are also subject to the corporate tax to the extent they carry on a business.

In *France*, in general, the form of civil organization is determinative for tax classification. The tax code enumerates different types of business organizations, specifically those whose equity interests are evidenced by shares, which are in any case subject to the corporate income tax regardless of their activity. All of these organizations provide limited liability to their participants. The code also contains a catch-all provision under which all entities (other than partnerships) that have a juridical personality under civil law are subject to the corporation tax if they carry on profit-seeking activities.

There are some interesting special rules. The share of profits attributable to limited partners is subject to corporate tax. Thus the corporate tax is the price for limited liability. General partnerships are given an election to be treated as corporations for tax purposes.

The situation in *Japan* is somewhat different. All organizations which constitute "juridical entities" under civil law concepts are, with some explicit statutory exceptions, subject to the corporate tax. Both general and limited partnerships formed under the Commercial Code are juridical entities and are thus subject to the corporate tax. In contrast, unincorporated associations which are not juridical entities are not subject to the tax. This includes, for example, "undisclosed associations" which are structurally similar to "silent" or undisclosed partnerships under Continental civil law concepts. In this situation, the business is operated by the disclosed "partner" in his own name and for his own account and there is a contractual arrangement to share the profits (and, if provided in the agreement, the losses) with the silent partner. Though the arrangement is functionally similar in some respects to a limited partnership, the fact that it is not formally a partnership under the Commercial Code and thus not a juridical entity for tax purposes means that it is not subject to the corporate tax.

In *Australia* the statutory definition of "company" for tax purposes is quite broad, including all "bodies or associations corporate or unincorporate" with a specific exclusion for partnerships and a variety of special rules for associations, clubs, and the like which would formally fall under the definition but are not the usual subjects of corporate-shareholder taxation. In addition, under the Australian rules "corporate limited partnerships," that is, partnerships at least one of whose members is subject to limited liability under partnership law, are subject to a tax regime which is similar to that applied to companies in the strict sense of the term. A similar result applies to certain public unit trusts that either are spun off from public companies or engage in trading as opposed to investment activities.

3. Issues in corporate formation

If a corporation is formed by the transfer of cash to the corporation in exchange for the issuance of its shares, the taxpayer will typically have a tax cost or basis in the shares equal to that amount. From a corporate law point of view, the amount received will usually be accounted for as paid-in capital or capital surplus. In some systems, the corporate law treatment of the capital contribution and its possible subsequent repayment will affect the tax rules applicable to the shareholder and to the corporation. In other jurisdictions, the corporate law treatment is irrelevant for tax purposes.

If appreciated or depreciated property is transferred in exchange for shares on formation, the transfer would in principle be an exchange causing gain or loss realization by the shareholder. Several systems take this approach and require current taxation as the general rule in these circumstances. However, a number of systems allow a tax-deferred incorporation if certain conditions are met. The clearest situation is where a sole proprietorship is continued in corporate form, the former owner receiving all the shares on incorporation. Arguably, the transferor has only changed the legal form of the investment which is now represented by shares rather than direct ownership and to require gain recognition in those circumstances would be inappropriate. There are a number of possible variations, however. Suppose the assets transferred do not constitute a business. Or suppose the transfer is to an existing corporation and the transferor receives back only a small share interest or receives shares and other consideration. The systems here under consideration have given quite different answers in these circumstances. In some cases, there are special rules dealing with corporate formations. In others, more general nonrecognition principles which also apply to corporate reorganizations and restructuring give the possibility of tax-deferred corporate formation.

In the *United States* system, in general, neither gain nor loss will be taken into account, regardless of the nature of property transferred, as long as persons transferring property in the formation transaction collectively have an 80 % or greater stock interest in the corporation following the transaction. The theoretical justification for this rule is that the incorporation merely represents a continuing investment by the shareholder in the underlying assets transferred and is not an appropriate time to require taxation of the gain or allow a deduction for the loss. In addition, if the transaction were taxable, it might discourage taxpayers from changing their form of investment through incorporation. However, such treatment allows several taxpayers to in effect engage in partial exchanges of their assets on a basis which does not require a current payment of tax on the gain. This result is accepted in order to prevent tax impediments to a combining of assets which would be desirable for business reasons. To prevent abuse, there are restrictions on the ability of taxpayers to pool passive investment assets on a tax-free basis.

As is generally the case in exchanges where no gain or loss is recognized currently, the transferor takes as his tax cost or basis in the shares which he receives the historical tax cost of the assets transferred. This "substituted" basis thus potentially preserves the taxation of the deferred gain at the shareholder level on the sale of the stock. In addition, in the United States system, the corporate transferee takes as its tax cost for the assets the historical cost of the assets in the hands of the shareholder. Thus after corporate formation, there is the possibility of two gains or losses for tax purposes for what is economically the same gain (or loss) which would have been taxed (or deducted) only once if it had been realized by the shareholder.

If the transferor receives property other than shares of the transferee corporation, e.g., cash or a debt obligation, the appreciation in the transferred assets is taxed to that extent and the transferor is entitled to increase his tax cost in the shares by that amount. Losses, on the other hand, cannot be recognized whatever the consideration received.

The above rules apply not only to the formation of a new corporation but also to transfers of assets by shareholders to an existing corporation where the 80 % stock ownership requirements are met.

In other systems, the treatment of the shareholder on formation varies considerably and in general offers more explicit selectivity than does the United States system. Thus in the *Canadian* system, in principle, the transfer of property in exchange for shares is a taxable disposition. However, the transferor and the corporation can elect the amount treated as received for the property. By electing to treat an amount equal to the tax cost of the property as the value of the shares received, the taxpayer can defer gain. As a consequence, however, both the shareholder and the corporation keep the historical basis of the property for the assets they hold, thus creating the possibility of two gains in the future. There are some limitations on the elective treatment. The amount elected cannot be more than the fair market value of the transferred property, thus preventing the creation of a potential double loss. Similarly, the elected amount cannot, in general terms, be less than the tax cost of the property, thus preventing the creation of a current artificial loss.

The transferor may receive other property, in addition to shares in the transferee corporation, and the elected amount is allocated to that property to the extent of its fair market value The remaining elected amount is allocated to the shares received. In this way, tax on appreciation in the transferred property is deferred through a reduced tax cost in the shares.

Although originally the transferor was required to own 20 % of the shares of the corporation, there is no current requirement that the transferor control the corporation or receive any minimum percentage of shares. However, there are some special anti-avoidance rules. If the transfer is to a corporation controlled by the transferor or related parties, no loss is recognized. A similar rule prevents the shifting of value to related party shareholders. There are also restrictions on the type of property which can be transferred. Real property held as inventory is excluded.

The *Swedish* rules are somewhat more restrictive but have a similar pattern. The basic statutory rule is that a withdrawal of assets from a business is a realization event and treated as if the assets had been sold for fair market value. However, the statute provides for an exception to realization if "special reasons" are present. This has been interpreted by the case law to allow tax-deferred incorporation if the transfer is for a business purpose, no tax advantages are gained, the assets do not change character, i.e., from inventory to capital, the tax cost of the assets remains unchanged in the hands of both the shareholder and the corporation, and certain other conditions are met.

In practice, incorporation of a business in Sweden is done by selling the assets to an existing corporation at their book value. The excess value of the assets over book value is in principle taxable as a withdrawal but the tax can be deferred if the conditions described above are met. This result is functionally similar to the Canadian result, since the appreciation in the assets remains to be taxed to both the shareholder and the corporation and the setting of the (non-arm's length) sales price amounts to an election by the taxpayer of the amount (if any) which will be subject to tax on the transfer.

In *The Netherlands*, the transfer of a business carried on as a sole proprietorship or in partnership would normally be a taxable event. Under a set of administrative conditions, however, the transfer can be effected without current tax if the entire business (or share of the business in the case of a partner) is transferred to a newly formed corporation in exchange for stock. More technically, the tax-free transfer is conditioned on a number of requirements including: (a) at least 95 % of the consideration must be shares of the transferee corporation, and (b) the shares must be held for at least three years by the transferor. If these (and other) conditions are met, the transferor is not taxed and, in contrast to the situation in the United States, takes a fair market value as the tax cost for the shares received. The transferee corporation, on the other hand, retains the historical cost basis of the assets. Thus the preformation appreciation will be subject to only a single level of tax in the hands of the transferee corporation. The tax claim on the assets is in effect "transferred" to the corporation but the potential imposition of a double level of tax is not considered appropriate.

In *Germany*, the transfer of business assets in exchange for shares would in principle be a realization event, with the transferor realizing gain or loss and taking as the tax cost in the shares the fair market value of the transferred assets. The transfer of private assets would not result in income recognition since the disposition of such assets is generally not subject to tax. Despite the general rule of income recognition where business assets are concerned, the special rules dealing with tax-deferred corporate reorganizations may apply to the incorporation of a business. Basically, the tax treatment of the transfer of an existing business or independent division of a business in exchange for the newly issued shares of a corporation depends on the way the transaction is treated by the transferee. The transferee has the right to enter the assets in its books at any figure between the old book value of the assets and their "going concern" value, and this amount is deemed to be the price paid for the assets transferred. Thus, to the extent that the assets are written up in the books of the transferee, the transferor must recognize gain; if the assets are taken over at book value, the transaction is tax-free. The corresponding figure is the acquisition cost of the shares in the hands of the transferor. This treatment is only available for a business or division and the transfer of individual business assets would be a taxable event.

The *Australian* rules on formation distinguish between types of property transferred and are not comprehensive. The capital gains rules require that the transferor hold 100 % of the issued shares of the transferee company after the transfer. In addition, the provisions do not apply to transfers by several persons unless they first form a partnership which is the formal transferor. However, the formation of a partnership will have capital gains consequences which means that this does not offer a route to overcome the narrowness of the rule. When the rules apply, they provide for a carryover of the tax cost of the transferred assets and a corresponding tax cost for the shares received. Liabilities may be assumed in the transfer. The rollover in theory is done on an asset-by-asset basis and so permits the transfer of a single asset or of a business consisting of many assets. Anti-avoidance rules seek to prevent value shifting in the rollover transactions.

In the *United Kingdom*, a deferral of the otherwise applicable capital gains tax is available if there is a transfer of an entire business by an individual in exchange for shares. The business must be transferred as a going concern and all noncash assets transferred. Consideration other than shares may be received but the rollover relief applies only to the extent of the transfer for shares. If the transferor has unrelieved losses incurred in the business, these may be used against income in the form of dividends, interest, or employment income subsequently received from the corporation. A somewhat different set of rules applies to the transfer of a business from one corporation to another.

In *Japan*, in general the transfer of an asset to a corporation as part of the incorporation process is a taxable event. There is a limited exception in the case of the formation of a subsidiary by a parent corporation. If the parent obtains at least 95 % of the subsidiary's stock, gain recognition will be deferred and the parent will take a tax cost in the subsidiary's stock equal to the tax cost of the assets transferred. More restrictive rules apply if the transfer includes real property. There, 20 % of the gain has to be recognized currently, and to qualify for the 80 % deferral the assets must be used in the same business as the parent and the stock must be held for at least five years. The restrictive rules reflect the substantial appreciation in real estate in Japan and the judgment that nonrecognition rules should be tightened when such assets are transferred.

In *France*, as well, the transfer of assets to a corporation on formation is generally a taxable event. There are two exceptions, however. First, in the case of the transfer of a sole proprietorship for the stock of the transferee corporation, the transferor can elect to defer taxation of the gain on nondepreciable fixed assets until the stock received is disposed of or the assets are disposed of by the corporation. With respect to appreciated depreciable assets, the transferor may be taxed currently or the appreciation may be taxed over a five-year period (fifteen years for buildings) to the transferee (thus roughly correlating income recognition and depreciation). If the assets are disposed of during the period, taxation is accelerated. Inventory may be transferred on a tax-deferred basis as long as the book value is continued by the transferee.

Secondly, a corporation can transfer all of the assets constituting a complete branch of activity for the stock of a newly formed corporation on a tax-favored basis if it agrees to hold the stock for five years.

The shares continue the tax cost of the transferred assets. In addition, the transferee corporation must take into income over a five-year period the capital gain realized by the transferor corporation on depreciable assets and receives a fair market value tax cost for those assets.

4. Issues involving capital structure

Commercial and corporate law principles have traditionally recognized a sharp distinction between ownership interests in a corporation in the form of shares and creditor interests in the form of bonds or other debt obligations. For corporate tax purposes, whatever the pattern of corporate taxation, important tax distinctions have also historically turned on the classification of an investment as "equity" or "debt." In "classical" systems, payments of interest on debt obligations are typically deductible by the corporation, unlike dividend distributions which bear full corporate level tax. The importance of the distinction is reduced somewhat in systems which have some degree of corporate-shareholder integration. Even in such systems, however, the distinction between an interest payment on a debt obligation and a dividend payment on equity can be of significance in some circumstances and is always an issue when the shareholder is not entitled to the imputation credit. Thus all systems must deal with this classification for tax purposes. In addition, whatever the domestic rules, a number of countries have special debt-equity restrictions where the shareholders are nonresidents. These aspects of the problem are discussed in Part Four.

In the *United States*, the debt-equity distinction was initially developed in the case law. In general, courts have not felt themselves bound by the civil or commercial law characterization of the investment. Instead, the case law has examined the legal rights created by the instrument, the economic source of the funds for the payments required, the relation between creditor and shareholder interests, the ability of the corporation to obtain similar financing from third parties, the relation between the amount of equity and debt financing, i.e., whether the corporation is "thinly" capitalized, and other factors. The results of the case law are difficult to reconcile in any principled manner and are very fact specific.

Dissatisfaction with the case law approach led to an attempt to provide clearer administrative rules. Those rules focused more directly on the economic characteristics of the instrument in question and the relative importance of "debt" or "equity" features. The rules were ultimately rejected on the ground that they were too complex. As a result, the case law-based system of classification is still generally applicable.

Some special statutory rules have been enacted with respect to certain types of obligations. These rules often "bifurcate" an instrument with both debt and equity characteristics and treat each part of the obligation separately. The "normal" amount of interest is allowed as a deduction and the remainder is disallowed or deferred and sometimes recharacterized as a dividend. Thus, for example, where a bond issued at a discount bears excessive interest, the excess amount is treated as a dividend in the hands of a corporate lender. Special rules on "earnings stripping" are principally important in the international context and are discussed in Part Four.

Most of the systems here under consideration have traditionally given more weight than the United States to the civil or commercial law classification of the instrument in determining its tax classification. Thus in *Canada* there are no general statutory rules and the case law usually makes the distinction based on the legal form of the obligation. Special rules apply in some circumstances with respect to certain preferred stock. In general terms, the rules are intended to prevent corporations which are unable to use interest deductions from, in effect, transferring the advantage of the interest deduction to corporate investors who receive tax-free intercorporate dividends. While not formally debt-equity rules, they do impose limits on the ability to utilize the interest deduction. When the rules limiting "after-tax financing" apply, they impose a tax on the distributing corporation which can then be offset against the corporation's subsequent income tax liability. This ensures that where the distribution will be tax-free in the hands of the recipient, a single level of current tax will have been paid by the distributing corporation.

Like Canada, *Australia* has no specific rules to distinguish debt and equity and the tax classification generally follows the legal form. Special rules apply to convertible notes that allow debt classification only if certain statutory tests can be met. The same issue with respect to redeemable preference shares discussed in connection with Canada arose in Australia and the response was to deny the availability of intercorporate dividend relief. However, in certain limited circumstances, special "infrastructure" bonds can be issued, the interest on which is nondeductible by the payor but exempt to the recipient.

While Australia has relatively limited and selective rules to deal with classification problems, the approach of those that exist is consistent in that the recharacterization is only one-sided and taxpayers generally end up with the worst of both worlds. For example, while the convertible note rules can deny the deductibility of interest to the payor company, the recipient is still taxed on the amount received as interest (and, in particular, not as a dividend qualifying for intercorporate dividend relief).

The *United Kingdom*, too, has followed commercial form in general in distinguishing debt and equity, for example, treating a perpetual debt instrument as debt. However, there are a number of statutory provisions dealing with special situations such as convertible notes (usually treated as equity) and thin capitalization rules (applicable only to nonresident shareholders). Where an instrument is found to constitute debt but the rate of interest is above the normal commercial rate, the excess is treated as a profits distribution.

In *Sweden*, there are no general statutory rules dealing with the debt-equity distinction though there are specific provisions on participating loans for closely held corporations. If the interest rate is determined by dividends paid or the profits realized by the corporation, the interest deduction is denied. The payment remains interest in the hands of the recipient. Apart from this rule, the civil law characterization is in general controlling. The court will examine whether the instrument was in fact a debt under civil law, and if so, it will be treated as such for tax purposes. Thus where an instrument which was in form a debt but had a provision for conditional repayment, the court found the obligation was not a debt for civil law purposes and denied the interest deduction. The tax authorities have on occasion tried to use transfer pricing principles to recharacterize debt as equity but have not been successful.

In *The Netherlands*, the civil law form of the instrument generally controls its treatment for tax purposes. Courts have recharacterized purported debt, however, if the loan was granted under conditions that made the creditor in effect a participant in the business, the parties' real intention was not to make a loan, or, in the case of corporate shareholders, the circumstances indicate that there was no expectation that the loan would be repaid.

There is little developed law in *Japan* on the debt-equity distinction in the domestic context. It is anticipated, however, with the increasing internationalization of capital markets and the emergence of more complex "hybrid" forms of debt financing, that the issue will receive more consideration. There are already some special rules limiting the deductibility of interest in the case of loans by controlling foreign shareholders, which are considered in Part Four.

France, in contrast, has specific rules that, though they do not recharacterize debt to equity, limit the deductibility of interest. In general, interest paid on a loan by a shareholder can only be deducted to the extent it does not exceed the average corporate bond rate. Excess interest remains taxable in the hands of the lender as a constructive dividend (which does not carry an imputation credit). In addition, there is a special limitation on loans made by shareholders who either own more than 50 % of the capital or voting power of the corporation or in fact manage the company. Interest (calculated at the prescribed rate) is only deductible on the aggregate of shareholder loans which do not exceed one-and-one-half times the stated capital of the corporation. This limitation does not apply, however, if the lender is a corporation entitled to the special intercorporate dividend exclusion discussed below.

The situation in *Germany* gives an interesting example of the evolution of debt-equity rules. Historically, court decisions in Germany have followed the civil and commercial law characterization of obligations as debt or equity for tax purposes. This practice led to an administrative attempt in 1987 to provide regulations which limited the interest deduction in cases of excessive debt financing. These rules were challenged by taxpayers and in 1992 were found invalid by the Federal Tax Court. The court stressed the taxpayer's discretion in determining the form of financing as long as the minimum capital required by corporate and commercial law was provided as equity. The court refused to find any form of debt financing an "abusive legal arrangement" under Germany's general anti-avoidance provision. The German Parliament responded with a statutory provision setting out more detailed tax rules dealing with "excessive" debt capitalization. The rules apply only to shareholders who are not entitled to the imputation credit under Germany's imputation system, that is, foreign shareholders and domestic tax-exempt organizations. They are discussed here because, unlike similar restrictions in other systems, they have a domestic as well as international impact.

In general terms, the new legislation treats interest payments on "hybrid" obligations as constructive dividends if the debt-equity ratio exceeds .5:1. "Hybrid" obligations are any debt obligations which do not bear an interest rate limited to a percentage of the face of the obligation. For "straight" debt obligations the ratio is 3:1 and for holding companies it is 9:1. Relatively detailed rules, implemented by non-binding regulations, provide fairly complex definitions and operating principles. For example, the regulations deal at some length with back-to-back loans and loans from related parties. The regulations take the position that there is a presumption that a parent shareholder will de facto be responsible for the loan to a subsidiary corporation even if there is no explicit guarantee. Thus if a foreign bank makes a loan to the German subsidiary of a foreign parent, the loan will be presumed to be a shareholder loan and subject to recharacterization if the other conditions are met.

5. Taxation of corporate distributions

5.1 Basic structure of distribution rules

All systems must have rules that characterize for tax purposes payments to shareholders with respect to their stock and determine the consequences of that characterization. The payments can potentially be treated as a distribution of corporate profits, a distribution of the corporation's stated capital or capital surplus, or a return of the capital of the shareholder invested in the stock, all with differing tax results.

In the *United States* system distributions to shareholders are only taxable if they are deemed to be from corporate profits. Technically, the distributions must be made from "earnings and profits", a concept that is different from corporate taxable income. Tax preferences or deductions that have reduced corporate taxable income may nonetheless be included in earnings and profits. The composition of earnings and profits and its attendant complexities are historically rooted and have no particular current policy justification.

To the extent that a distribution exceeds earnings and profits, it is treated as a tax-free return of the shareholder's tax cost in the shares. If the distribution exceeds the stock investment, it is treated as gain on the disposition of the stock.

These rules control the treatment of the distribution for tax purposes. The corporate law characterization of the distribution as a formal dividend, a capital reduction, or even an illegal distribution which impairs capital is not relevant. Similarly, the treatment of the distribution on the books of the corporation has no effect on the tax treatment.

The patterns in other systems are generally quite different, in some ways more restrictive and in others more inclusive. Often corporate law and accounting treatment play more of a role in tax characterization. Timing rules tend to relate the distributions to earnings of a particular year. On the other hand, the limitation of taxable dividends to distributions of corporate earnings is frequently not present. In *Canada*, for example, any distribution made by a corporation that is not in liquidation or pursuant to an authorized reduction of capital is taxed as a dividend regardless of the existence of profits at the corporate level. In the *United Kingdom*, the concept of a "distribution" is central for determining the treatment of both the distributing corporation (nondeductible and subject to advance corporation tax) and the shareholder (carrying an imputation credit). The concept is broader than the corporate law concept of dividend and covers almost all transfers of assets from corporation to shareholder other than an authorized return of capital.

Similarly, in *Sweden*, there is no connection between the earnings or income of the corporation and the taxation of the corporate distribution. (Special rules may recharacterize a favorably taxed dividend as employment income in some situations.) In the *Netherlands*, any economic benefit received by the shareholder as such is taxable without regard to the financial results of the corporation. Thus where a corporation with no earnings makes a lawful distribution from capital surplus in anticipation of profits in the future, the amount is taxed as a dividend despite the lack of corporate earnings.

The *Japanese* rules have much the same pattern. From a commercial point of view, the payment of dividends is subject to restrictions and cannot be paid out of the corporation's legal capital or certain required reserves. Dividends paid improperly can be required by creditors to be repaid to the corporation by the shareholders. Nonetheless, the amount is still taxed as a dividend at the shareholder level. The only distributions not taxed as dividends (but potentially taxable as capital gains) are distributions made pursuant to the formal reduction of the corporation's legal capital.

In contrast, in the *Australian* system, a dividend for tax purposes must be "out of profits" which is in practice determined with reference to company accounts or financial statements. In the case of closely-held corporations which do not maintain adequate records, the tax authorities can reconstruct the accounts to establish the requisite profits. The distribution of share premium (amounts paid in excess of stated par value) is possible though court approval is required. Distributions which are treated for corporate law purposes as repayment of share premium are generally tax-free and reduce the tax cost of the stock, with any excess being taxable as a capital gain. If the distribution of share premium is part of a scheme involving the contribution of share premium by one shareholder and its distribution to another, an anti-avoidance rule may treat the distribution as a dividend. Essentially the same rules apply to reductions of stated capital.

In the *German* system, as discussed in more detail below, distributions are related to "baskets" of income at the corporate level, based on the amount of corporate-level tax attributed to the particular basket. Capital reserves are in the "zero" basket and are stacked last with the result that they can only be distributed for tax purposes after all other baskets have been distributed. When capital distributions are made to corporations, they first reduce tax cost in the shares and result in taxable gain to the extent they exceed that amount. The same result should apply to distributions to individual shareholders who are taxable on capital gains, though the question is not completely settled. For individual shareholders who are not taxable on capital gains, the distributions have no tax effect.

The situation in *France* is rather complex. The definition of taxable corporate distributions encompasses much more than dividends in cash or property properly distributed to the shareholders in proportion to their capital interests. A taxable distribution is deemed to occur whenever a corporate decision results in a "disinvestment," i.e., a decrease in the value of the corporation's net assets to the benefit of a shareholder even if the corporation does not have available earnings. Where non-shareholders are benefited, that too can be treated as a taxable distribution if corporate profits are available. Capital distributions as such are prohibited by corporate law. Special rules apply to capital distributed in redemptions or liquidation and are discussed in those sections.

5.2 Relating distributions to corporate earnings

Where a distinction exists for tax purposes between types of distributions, ordering rules are necessary to determine the characterization of the distribution. Thus in the *United States* system, because of the earnings and profits requirement, complex rules are provided which connect distributions and profits. In general terms, profits are deemed to be distributed first, regardless of the formal corporate characterization of the distribution. If the corporation has earnings for the year and an accumulated deficit, a distribution during the year is nonetheless taxable. Distributions are taxable to the shareholder receiving them even if they relate to earnings which were accumulated in years prior to the investment by the shareholder and thus, in an economic sense, represent a return of his original investment in the shares.

For countries which generally tax distributions without regard to the existence of earnings at the corporate level, this type of rule is not necessary. However, in the context of an imputation system which provides a shareholder credit only when distributions have been made from earnings taxed at the corporate level, similar types of rules may be necessary. For example, in *Germany*, corporate profits and other sources of funds for distributions are segregated into baskets according to the amount of domestic corporate tax the amounts have borne. Distributions are deemed to have been made out of the highest-taxed baskets first. Distributions from baskets which have borne no tax may be subject to a compensating tax and carry the imputation credit or may be tax-free to the shareholder if, for example, the distribution is from paid-in capital reserve. *France* as well has complex rules for determining when a distribution is deemed to be from preferentially taxed earnings and is thus subject to the compensatory tax (*précompte mobilier*).

Similarly, for countries that allow the tax-free distribution of share premium or stated capital, rules are necessary to identify such distributions. Often the characterization for corporate law purposes is controlling. Thus in *Australia*, amounts that are paid under a court-approved reduction of capital are tax-free and reduce the tax cost of the shares. Any distribution in excess of the approved amount is taxed as a dividend. Similarly, in the *Canadian* system, distributions of paid-up capital, which may be made under corporate law provisions, are deemed to be made before profits distributions with only the excess over the paid-up capital reduction taxable as a dividend.

5.3 Constructive dividends

All systems have either statutory or case law principles that tax as distributions benefits received by shareholders without the formal declaration of a dividend or profit distribution. In some situations the payment is treated as a dividend for all purposes, though often, to discourage such payments, they will not carry the imputation credit or qualify for intercorporate dividend relief.

The *United States* system has case law-developed rules which treat shareholder benefits as dividends. Under a special provision, unreasonable compensation may be disallowed as a deduction at the corporate level even when the payment is not formally recharacterized as a dividend to the shareholder, though the rule is normally applied only in the case of payments to shareholders. Loans to shareholders may be treated as dividends. Even when a loan is not recharacterized, if the loan does not bear a stipulated interest rate, under a special statutory rule a dividend in the amount of the forgone interest is imputed to the shareholder, followed by a deemed transfer of that amount of interest to the corporation. The deemed interest payment may be deductible by the shareholder subject to the normal limitations and is included in the income of the corporation.

In *France*, there are specific statutory provisions dealing with loans to shareholders, excessive remuneration, excessive interest on loans by shareholders and expenditures deemed extravagant. In addition, case law has developed a principle which treats as constructive dividends any distributions which have been made in situations in which the corporation did not receive an appropriate benefit for the payment. Such an "abnormal management decision" will result in a taxable distribution. Typical situations involve bargain sales or rentals of corporate assets, payment of personal expenses, and the like. In certain circumstances, payments to third parties who are not shareholders may be treated as constructive dividends. Constructive dividends do not carry with them the imputation credit but some may qualify for the intercorporate dividends received deduction.

In *Canada*, any benefit conferred on the shareholder must be included in taxable income. Typical situations are bargain purchases and sales, rent-free use of property, and payment of personal expenses. A special rule, with some exceptions, treats as income loans by a corporation to an individual shareholder or related person if the loan is not repaid within one year. These various shareholder benefits must be included in the shareholders' income but are not treated as dividends. As a result they do not qualify for either the imputation credit or the intercorporate dividend deduction.

In *Australia*, specific legislation treats certain benefits provided to shareholders in closely-held companies as nondeductible dividends, in particular bargain sales of property, interest free loans and excessive compensation or retirement benefits to shareholder-employees or associates. Rent-free use of property probably would not be covered. Payment of personal expenses would typically be covered by the fringe benefits tax. As in Canada, the constructive dividend does not bring with it the imputation credit.

The *United Kingdom* also has special rules dealing with shareholder loans in the closely held context and broadens the concept of "distribution" to cover benefits in kind provided by a closely-held corporation to its shareholders. In addition, a rule applicable to all companies but which is most frequently applied here treats any transfer of assets to shareholders not in exchange for equal value as a distribution.

Dutch case law also deals with constructive dividends. Benefits to the shareholder in his capacity as a shareholder are generally taxable as dividends where both the corporation and the shareholder were aware (or should have been aware) of the advantage to the shareholder. In *Sweden*, there are special statutory provisions dealing with constructive dividends in the case of closely-held corporations. They cover bargain purchases and sales, use of corporate property by shareholders, and loans at less than arm's length. In the case of a bargain sale by a shareholder to the corporation, the taxable amount is the full value received without offset for the tax cost of the asset, a rule intended to discourage such transactions. Any loans made to shareholders which are improper under company law are taxed in full as dividend distributions even if the loans are at arm's length. These rules also apply in the case of benefits made available to related parties, with the party receiving the benefit being the taxable person. In the case of publicly held corporations, constructive dividends have been found in some cases but minor benefits such as rebates to shareholders for purchases in the corporation's stores have not been taxed.

Germany has a highly developed case law on constructive dividends. Any transaction between shareholder and corporation which is not undertaken at arm's length is a potential constructive dividend. To avoid constructive dividend treatment agreements between shareholder and corporation must meet the "prudent manager" test and must be shown to be in the interests of the corporation and not simply undertaken to benefit the shareholder. Agreements between the corporation and its controlling shareholder must be legally binding, in clear terms and concluded in advance. In practice, some rules of thumb have been developed. If a managing shareholder receives a bonus based on profits in addition to a fixed salary, no constructive dividend will be found as long as the bonus does not exceed 25 % of the fixed salary and the total remuneration is not excessive.

5.4 Intercorporate dividends

All of the systems have special rules dealing with distributions by domestic corporations to domestic corporate shareholders. (Special considerations apply if the corporations are foreign, and are discussed in Part Four.) Though the basic purpose of the various provisions is to prevent the "cascading" of levels of corporate tax on distributions which move up a corporate chain to the ultimate individual shareholder, the structure of the provisions have significant differences both in terms of the degree of relief granted and the techniques used. In the *United States*, the mechanism for relief is a deduction for a certain percentage of the dividend received. The amount of the deduction varies with the degree of share ownership. In the case of 100 % share ownership, the full amount of the dividend is deductible while for portfolio investment (below 20 %) the amount is 70 % of the dividend.

A series of special provisions restrict the ability of the corporate shareholder to combine the dividends received deduction with other deductions. Where a portfolio investment is financed with debt, the dividends received deduction is reduced to that extent, thus preventing a tax arbitrage between the fully deductible interest and the partially taxable intercorporate dividend. Similar rules restrict the ability to deduct tax losses which are related to the decline in value of a stock investment due to the payment of a dividend which has only been partially taxed (sometimes referred to as "dividend stripping"). The rules generally require that the stock on which the dividend was received be held for a period of time before the loss on sale will be allowed. In some situations, the amount paid for the stock must be allocated between the dividend to be received and the stock itself, thus limiting the amount deductible as a loss when the stock is sold.

Since intercorporate dividends are taxed at a reduced rate while capital gain on the sale of stock is fully taxable, a corporate shareholder may attempt to withdraw dividends from the corporation prior to the sale in order to reduce the taxable capital gain. Case law principles have limited the use of this technique for "capital gain stripping," especially if the funds used to pay the dividend come indirectly from the buyer. The purported dividend payment is treated as additional sale proceeds.

Canada also allows a deduction for intercorporate dividends but, unlike the situation in the United States, the relief is complete. One hundred percent of the dividends are deducted without regard to the degree of share ownership. To prevent closely-held corporations from being used as "incorporated pocketbooks" to hold portfolio investments of individuals, dividends are subject to a special refundable tax intended to replicate the tax that would have been due if the dividend had been received by an individual shareholder. Other limitations apply to prevent the conversion of taxable capital gain into tax-free dividends. Under these rules, dividends received in some circumstances are deemed to be proceeds of sales of the shares and as such taxable. The rule is in effect limited to gain which is not attributable to previously taxed corporate earnings. In addition, no loss is allowed on the sale of stock preceded by a dividend distribution which is entitled to intercorporate dividend relief.

The situation is similar in *Australia*. Intercorporate dividend relief is given by means of a credit ("rebate") equal to the amount of the dividend multiplied by the recipient corporation's average tax rate. The credit is available whatever the level of interest held in the paying company. In calculating the amount of the dividend subject to the credit, deductions are stacked last against dividends received, so that the benefit of the credit is lost only when a company is in a loss situation apart from the dividends received. The intercorporate rebate system operates independently of the imputation system and the dividend entitled to the rebate still can affect the franked income account. In the case of privately held companies, the intercorporate dividend rebate is denied to the extent that the dividends received are unfranked. This prevents companies being used to avoid the shareholder tax on unfranked dividends payments which would be fully taxable if received directly.

The intercorporate dividend credit in Australia was used in various transactions involving "dividend stripping" schemes. The transactions typically involved the sale of stock by individuals of closely-held corporations which had substantial accumulated earnings. The sale transaction converted the potential dividend income into preferentially taxed (or tax-free) capital gain. The purchasing corporation (the "stripper") could extract the earnings from the purchased corporation on a tax-free basis and then dispose of the stock at a (deductible) loss. Several statutory provisions have dealt with the widespread use of this technique. First, in some cases, under general anti-avoidance principles, the seller of the shares may be deemed to have received a taxable dividend rather than tax-preferred proceeds of sale. In addition, more specific statutory rules either deny the credit to the purchaser or else restrict the deductibility of the loss, depending on the circumstances. In any of these situations, the imputation credits attached to the dividend are lost. The existence of the credit has also given rise to "capital gain stripping" transactions, though there has been some legislative response to the issue. The most recent was in 1995 when the intercorporate dividend credit was denied for any dividends paid out of share premium or revaluation reserves.

In the *United Kingdom*, intercorporate distributions, like all distributions, are in general subject to the advance corporation tax which is paid by the distributing corporation. However, the dividend is not taxed to the recipient corporation and in its hands is referred to as "franked investment income." Such income can be distributed to the recipient corporation's (individual) shareholders without an additional payment of ACT, thus ensuring a single payment of corporation tax and ACT on the distribution of profits through a corporate chain. Special elective group treatment exempts the distribution from the ACT.

The situation in *Japan* is similar to the United States. Intercorporate dividends may be excluded entirely if the share ownership is 25 % or more and 80 % excludable in case of ownership below 25 %. There are special limitations on the deductibility of interest expense incurred with respect to stock paying tax-exempt dividends.

France allows 100 % exclusion if the stock interest is over 10 % or has a value of over ca. $30 million. The exclusion is elective since excluding the income, as opposed to including it but taking an imputation credit, may have implications for the imputation system. In the *German* system, there are no special rules for domestic intercorporate dividends. The split rate/imputation credit mechanism eliminates all tax at the level of the distributing corporation for all distributions and thus there is no problem of cascading corporate level taxes. Special rules prevent the deduction of the decrease in value of the shares of a corporation that result from a distribution, if the shares were purchased from a prior shareholder who was not entitled to the imputation credit.

This prevents an indirect transfer of the benefit of the credit.

In *The Netherlands* there is an exclusion for dividends received on "participations," defined generally as a 5 % or greater stock interest in the distributing company. Unlike the situation in the other jurisdictions, the exemption for participations extends to the gain on the sale of the stock.

Sweden likewise has an exclusion for intercorporate dividends if the recipient corporation has a 25 % or greater voting interest in the distributing corporation or there is a business relation between the two corporations. For other "portfolio" investments, the dividend is taxable in full. Where shares are sold at a loss as the result of a tax-free dividend distribution, the deduction for the loss is disallowed.

5.5 Distributions of appreciated or depreciated property

When appreciated or depreciated property is distributed, if the gain or loss is not recognized at the corporate level at the time of distribution it will no longer be subject to the corporate taxing regime in the hands of the individual shareholder. While the logic of treating the distribution as a taxable event seems clear, the *United States* historically did not take this approach; neither gain nor loss was recognized on distribution. The rule was ultimately changed, however, in 1986 and now, in principle, the distribution is a recognition event, with some exceptions. The rules apply whether the shareholder is an individual or a corporation.

In the case of ongoing dividend distributions, gain is recognized on the distribution of appreciated property but loss is not recognized. The limitation with respect to loss property reflects the fact that the timing of the distribution is in the control of the taxpayer. As a result of the rule, however, the possibility of deducting the loss on the property is totally eliminated since the shareholder takes the fair market value as his tax cost. Where property is distributed in complete liquidation of the corporation, both gains and losses are recognized since the possibility of shareholder manipulation is not present. However, there are restrictions on the deductibility of losses on property that has been recently contributed to the corporation. Distributions in the liquidation of an 80 %-owned corporate subsidiary are not taxed; the parent corporation takes the historical cost of the assets as its tax cost.

The other systems here under consideration typically require the recognition of gain or loss on property distributions. In *Canada*, the corporation is considered to have disposed of the property at its fair market value while the shareholder includes the fair market value in income as a dividend. These rules are intended to ensure that the consequences of a dividend in kind are the same as a sale of the corporate assets followed by the distribution of the proceeds. The *United Kingdom* rules reach the same result. In *Germany*, any distribution of an appreciated asset is a realization event, regardless of whether the distribution is treated as a dividend to the shareholder or is a return of capital. Similarly, in *The Netherlands* the distribution is a taxable event, though there is the possibility of deferring the tax on gains by the use of a replacement reserve if the property is going to be replaced. In *Sweden*, the distribution is treated as removal of the assets from the business which is in principle a recognition event. *Australia*, as well, treats the distribution of an asset as subject to the capital gains tax at the corporate level. Where the transferor is a 100 % subsidiary of the transferee, a rollover is available on the transfer. Special rules restrict the ability to use such property distributions to shift value among shares.

The situation in *Japan* is somewhat more complex. Distributions of dividends in kind are prohibited. If a corporation distributes appreciated or depreciated property in the process of reducing its legal capital, gain or loss will be recognized based on the value of the property and its tax cost. However, if the distribution is in liquidation (or in a merger transaction treated as a liquidation) the gain or loss is calculated as the difference between the fair market value of the property distributed and the amount of the legal capital and statutory profit reserves. A special "liquidation" tax is applicable to this amount. In the case of a merger, the liquidation tax is based on the difference between the par value of the stock (together with the fair market value of any nonstock property) received by the shareholders of the merged corporation, and the amount of the legal capital and the statutory profit reserves.

In *France*, there is no developed law on the distribution of appreciated or depreciated property as a normal dividend, though for accounting purposes it would be treated as a recognition of gain and this treatment may be applicable for corporate tax purposes as well. In the case of liquidations, the rules are quite fully developed. The distributing corporation must realize all gains and losses on distributed assets, which are taxed as capital gain or ordinary income as the case may be. In addition, any income items that have previously escaped tax as deferred income or tax-free provisions must also be included in the tax base.

5.6 Distributions involving changes in corporate capital structure

5.6.1 General

Apart from formal or constructive dividends, many changes in corporate capital structure may involve distributions to shareholders. Typical examples would be distributions in connection with a reduction in capital or a redemption of outstanding shares or the capitalization of earnings through an increase in stated capital followed by a stock dividend. In all these situations, the distribution must be characterized for tax purposes and a recurring issue is the extent that the corporate or commercial law characterization of the transaction will be controlling for tax purposes. Here the systems show wide variation.

In the *United States*, as a general matter, the corporate law aspects of a change in the capitalization of a corporation are not relevant for tax purposes. Thus if a corporation formally reduces its capital and repays that amount to the shareholders, the distribution will be taxed as a dividend as long as the corporation has earnings for tax purposes; the fact that from a corporate law point of view the payment is a return of invested capital is of no significance. Similarly, if a corporation increases its stated capital by transferring undistributed earnings to the capital account, the corporate transfer has no effect on the "pool" of earnings for tax purposes which determines the taxability of later distributions.

In the systems of most other countries, corporate law concepts play a more important role in determining the treatment of such distributions. In *Canada* and *Australia*, for example, amounts received by the shareholder from a reduction in paid-in capital can be received tax-free. However, if the amount received exceeds the portion of stated capital allocated to the shares, the excess is taxed as a dividend, regardless of the absence of accumulated profits. Similarly, if a reserve against earnings is transferred to capital, the transfer will, subject to some exceptions, constitute a dividend since, after the earnings have been transferred to the capital account, they could be repaid free of tax. In some circumstances, distributions of capital by publicly-traded companies are fully taxable as dividends.

In the *United Kingdom*, payments effecting a reduction in capital are not treated as distributions. This rule extends to repayments of loan capital even where the interest payment itself is treated as a distribution. However, repayment of stock dividend shares is treated as a distribution.

France also allows the tax-free distribution of amounts resulting from a capital reduction but only after all profits reserves and undistributed profits have been accounted for as taxable dividends. However, according to case law, the scope of this provision is limited to those repayments of capital that result in the proportionate reduction of the nominal value of all shares.

Germany also allows the repayment of stated capital or capital reserves on a tax-free basis. In the case of capital reserves, they may be distributed only after all profits and profit reserves have been distributed. Distributions of stated capital can be made without distributing retained profits, but a number of special corporate law conditions must be met. The distribution reduces the acquisition costs of the stock and can result in a taxable gain if it exceeds that amount, depending on the status of the stock in the hands of the shareholder. *Sweden*, in contrast, treats distributions of the amount of the reduction in nominal value of stock as dividends without regard to the existence of corporate profits.

5.6.2 Stock dividends

The distribution of dividends in the form of stock or "bonus" shares to existing shareholders typically involves a transfer for corporate law purposes of retained earnings into stated capital. It can been viewed as a deemed distribution of a cash dividend to the shareholders followed by a corresponding contribution to capital or as solely an event at the corporate level which has no effect on the shareholders whose economic interest in the corporation is unchanged by the receipt of additional shares. The systems have taken varied approaches to the stock dividend problem. The treatment is in part a function of the rules dealing with distributions of stated capital.

The *United States* rules on the taxation of stock dividends are quite detailed. The basic rule is fairly straightforward; pro rata distributions of common stock of the same class as the stock on which the distribution is being made are not taxable. The principal justification behind the rule is that the shareholder has not had a significant change of position as a result of the distribution. He simply has more pieces of paper representing an unchanged underlying investment and thus the receipt of the stock dividend is not an appropriate time to treat the underlying corporate profits as having been distributed. This rule is possible in part because the United States system ignores the effects of the capitalization of earnings for corporate purposes which typically accompanies a stock dividend. As soon as one moves beyond the simple pro rata stock distribution, however, the situation becomes more complex. First, if the shareholder has the right to choose between a cash dividend and a stock dividend, the stock dividend will be taxable even if all shareholders elect to receive stock and the distribution is thus pro rata. The shareholder is in effect deemed to have received the equivalent of the cash dividend he could have received.

Where the distribution is not pro rata, and thus results in an increase in the proportionate interest of the shareholders receiving the stock dividend, the distribution is generally taxable. Technically, the distribution will be taxable if it results in the increase in the proportionate interest of some shareholders and the receipt of a property distribution by others. Thus, for example, if a corporation has two classes of stock, one of which pays stock dividends and the other of which pays cash dividends, the stock dividends would be taxable. The increase in proportionate interest of shareholders who do not have their stock redeemed when others are redeemed can also result in a "constructive" taxable stock dividend.

The rules in other jurisdictions are simpler, and the results are varied. In *Sweden*, stock dividends are in principle not subject to tax, being viewed as the equivalent of a split in the old stock. Tax cost of the old shares is allocated between the old shares and the new shares of the same type. If the stock is of a different class or type, it retains a basis of zero. In *Japan*, the commercial law prior to 1990 allowed stock dividends and they were treated for tax purposes as if the corporation had distributed a taxable cash dividend which had been reinvested. After 1990, stock dividends are no longer possible as a matter of corporate law. However, stock splits are still possible. The stock split itself is not a taxable event but if it is (as is usually the case) accompanied by a transfer of amounts from a profits reserve to stated capital, the shareholder will have dividend income in that amount.

In *The Netherlands*, stock dividends received by individuals are taxable in general to the extent that they represent the nominal capital of the distributed shares, which amounts could subsequently be distributed on a tax-free basis. On the other hand, stock dividends based on the transfer of informal capital contributions (share premium) to stated capital are not taxed. A special provision allows tax-preferred stock dividends resulting from the capitalization of retained profits if the capital increase is at least 25 % of the stated capital and the corporation has been paying significant dividends in the past ten years. The provision is intended to encourage the strengthening of paid-in capital. If these and other conditions are met, a special tax rate of 10 % is applicable to the distribution. In addition, a cash distribution in the amount of the tax due is also subject to the 10 % rate. Stock dividends paid to corporate shareholders are not taxable in any event, even if the holding (less than 5 %) does not qualify for the participation exemption.

Canada follows a similar pattern. To the extent that the stated capital attributable to the stock dividend is out of retained earnings, the stock dividend is taxable since the capitalized earnings could be distributed subsequently on a tax-free basis.

Australia also taxes stock dividends (other than dividends paid out of share premium) and the dividends carry with them the imputation credit, with the tax cost of the total shareholding increased by the amount of the dividend. This allows corporations that wish to retain after-tax income for corporate purposes to capitalize the income through the stock dividend, resulting in effect in full integration of corporate and individual tax on undistributed earnings. Australia also permits stock splits and consolidation that do not result in any transfer of profit reserves to stated capital on a tax-free basis.

The *United Kingdom* has a special rule for stock dividends that is related to its imputation system. Stock dividends are not treated as distributions and the distributing company does not have to pay advanced corporation tax on the issuance of the stock. The recipient is taxed only if the tax on the grossed-up value of the dividend would exceed the basic rate of tax and then only on the 16 % difference between the basic rate and the top rate. In effect, the basic rate of tax is deemed offset by tax paid at the corporate level (though no ACT is due and no refund is available) and only the incremental tax is due.

French law distinguishes between stock dividends as such and bonus shares resulting in the capitalization of reserves or earnings. In the former case, the shareholder, as a matter of corporate law, has a choice between the receipt of cash or of a stock dividend. If a stock dividend is chosen, it is taxable in the same way as a cash dividend. In the case of bonus stock, the stock is not taxable currently as it is not viewed as increasing the assets of the shareholder. However, the capitalized earnings, unlike capital attributable to original contributions, cannot be distributed on a tax-free basis on redemption.

Germany represents another variation. If a stock dividend is based on the capitalization of earnings accumulated after the effective date of the imputation system, the stock dividend itself is not taxable. Subsequent repayment of capital increases resulting from stock dividends, however, are taxable dividends but carry with them the imputation credit. For stock dividends created from earnings surpluses arising prior to the introduction of the imputation system, the stock distribution is likewise not taxable. However, if the share capital is repaid within five years of the increase, the dividend is taxed at a flat 30 % rate with no credit.

5.6.3 Redemptions

Redemptions, that is, the purchase by the corporation of its own stock from its existing shareholders, are in form the purchase of shares. If that characterization is followed, the shareholder would have a gain or loss on the shares determined by the difference between the tax cost of the shares and the amount received. This gain or loss would be treated under the normal rules dealing with property dispositions. Thus the gain might be fully taxable, taxed at a preferential rate, or exempt from tax depending on the structure of the capital gains regime. On the other hand, a redemption differs from a sale to a third party in that property is leaving the corporation and remaining in the hands of the shareholder, which is similar in some respects to a dividend distribution and also to a repayment of stated capital. There is a wide variation in the manner in which the systems here under consideration treat redemption transactions.

In the *United States*, specific statutory rules deal with redemptions. A redemption will not be treated as a profits distribution if it is "not essentially equivalent to a dividend." There is substantial case law dealing with this standard which focuses on whether the taxpayer has had a "meaningful reduction" in his ownership interest in the distributing corporation. In addition to this general standard, there are several "safe haven" rules. If the distribution is "substantially disproportionate," exchange treatment is applicable. To meet this test, the shareholder must have a more than 20 % reduction in his ownership interest in the corporation and must own less than 50 % of the corporation after the redemption. Thus a redemption that reduced a shareholder's interest from 50 % to 39 % would qualify for sale treatment. A redemption that terminates a shareholder's interest is also treated as an exchange.

In applying these tests, stock owned by related persons and entities is attributed to the shareholder whose stock is being redeemed. Thus in the above example, if the remaining stock in the corporation was owned by the taxpayer's wife or son, the redemption would not qualify. The ownership rules based on family relationship are waived in some cases where the shareholder being redeemed sells all of the shares he actually owns.

Any redemption that does not qualify as an exchange under the general test or the various safe havens is treated in its entirety as a dividend distribution and is fully taxable to an individual shareholder to the extent it represents a distribution of earnings. For a corporate shareholder, a redemption not treated as an exchange would qualify for intercompany dividend relief. The tax cost of the redeemed shares is attributed to the remaining shares.

In the other systems, redemptions tend to take place less frequently, often because the reduction in stated capital with which a redemption is often accompanied is a complex procedure as a matter of corporate law. In addition, the corporate law accounting for the redemption has an important influence on the tax treatment.

In *Japan*, the treatment of redemptions is tied to the treatment of reductions in stated capital. In general, amounts distributed in connection with a reduction in capital are deemed first to be from legally required profits reserves and, as such, fully taxable. The remainder of the distribution is treated as being in exchange for the shareholder's stock and any excess over the acquisition cost is taxable as a capital gain.

The situation is somewhat different if the corporation repurchases shares out of its retained profits and not in connection with a capital reduction. Those shareholders whose shares are repurchased will receive a dividend equal to their share of retained earnings. The excess is treated as an amount received for the sale of the stock and taxed as a capital gain. Since the redemption has been made out of profits from the corporation's point of view, there is no reduction in stated capital. Since paid-in capital has not been reduced, the amount of paid-in capital allocated to the remaining shares has increased and this increase is taxed as a dividend. In effect, a portion of the profits are allocated to the remaining shareholders to reflect the fact that, in the future, they would be able to receive the paid-in capital on a tax-free basis.

Canada operates with similar concepts but the system is somewhat differently structured. In case of a redemption, the shareholder is deemed to receive his share of paid-up capital first in the redemption transaction. This amount can be received on a tax-free basis regardless of whether or not the redemption changes the shareholder's proportionate interest. If the amount received on the redemption exceeds the paid-up capital of the shares redeemed, the excess is taxed as a dividend. The transaction is also treated as a disposition for capital gains purposes. However, for this purpose the proceeds of disposition are reduced by any amount deemed to be a dividend. Accordingly, if the acquisition cost of the shares is more than their paid-up capital, a capital loss will result; on the other hand, if the acquisition cost is less than the paid-up capital, a capital gain will result. In contrast to these rules that are applicable in the closely-held context, redemptions by publicly-traded corporations in open-market transactions are taxed entirely as capital gains.

Australia also treats redemptions involving traded stock as capital gains transactions (taxability being determined by whether the stock is an asset subject to the capital gains regime). In other situations, the purchase price is treated as a dividend to the extent it exceeds the attributable stated capital and share premium. The dividend portion carries the imputation credit. Where the redemption involves traded stock and receives capital gains treatment in the hands of the shareholder, the transaction is still treated as a dividend for imputation purposes from the company point of view and to that extent, imputation credits are lost to the company and the shareholder.

The *French* corporate law only allows redemptions in limited circumstances. Where redemptions are permitted, the pattern developed by administrative practice is rather complex. For shareholders who hold the stock as a business asset, the difference between the redemption price and the higher of the book value or the nominal value of the stock is a dividend and to the extent the latter exceeds the former, the difference is treated as ordinary income or capital gain, as the case may be. For an individual shareholder, the redemption price is considered as a dividend to the extent it does not exceed the corporation's existing reserves and undistributed earnings, any amount in excess being exempt as a repayment of capital. However, if the acquisition price of the stock is higher than its nominal value, the taxable dividend is limited to the gain actually realized by the shareholder. Any taxable dividend brings with it the imputation credit if all the shareholders are redeemed. The above is the traditional administrative analysis of the redemption situation. Some recent case law suggests that any non pro rata distribution may be treated as an exchange, with pro rata exchanges being treated as dividends, thus reaching roughly the result of the United States system.

In *Germany*, redemptions are quite unusual in the case of public companies because of the corporate law restrictions. While the corporate law limitations are less strict for limited liability companies, even there the transactions are not common. There is little developed tax law dealing with redemptions and the transactions are generally treated as exchanges, taxable to the shareholder if the investment amounts to a substantial participation or is held as a business asset.

In *The Netherlands*, the exchange aspect of the redemption transaction is completely ignored. To the extent that the distribution in redemption exceeds the allocated share of average paid-in capital, the amount is treated as a dividend; the shareholder's tax cost in his shares is not relevant in determining the amount of the dividend (or in determining the amount of capital gain or loss, as private gains or losses are not taxed). In some circumstances, a reduced rate of tax may apply to the redemption.

Share redemptions in the *Swedish* system are generally treated as dividends. In the *United Kingdom*, prior to 1982, share repurchase was not permitted by company law rules. When the company law was changed, a corresponding tax regime was provided. If the redeeming corporation is engaged in a trade and its shares are not quoted on an exchange, the redemption is treated as a capital transaction with capital gains consequences. Capital gain treatment is only available, however, if the company can establish a business purpose for the redemption and meet other anti-avoidance tests. If the conditions for capital gain treatment are not met, the excess of the amount distributed over the amount originally paid for the stock is treated as a qualifying distribution and subject to the advance corporation tax. There are some unresolved technical issues in the treatment of redemptions of corporate shareholders.

6. Liquidations

The liquidation of the corporation is the last opportunity to tax at the shareholder level any undistributed corporate profits that have not yet borne shareholder tax. It is also an occasion to tax the share-holder on the appreciation in value of his stock investment. The systems vary considerably in the extent to which they emphasize one or the other of these two aspects of liquidation. In the *United States*, a liquidating distribution is treated entirely as an exchange transaction. The corporation has a gain or loss to the extent appreciated or depreciated assets are involved and the individual shareholder has a capital gain or loss determined by the difference between the tax cost of the share and the fair market value of the distribution. The property received on liquidation takes the fair market value as its tax cost. No attempt is made to tax the undistributed corporate profits as a dividend; the assets which they represent are simply included in the calculation of capital gain or loss.

Where the liquidating corporation is a subsidiary (at least 80% owned) of a corporate shareholder, a special rule applies. The liquidation is tax-free both to the distributing corporation and the corporate shareholder. The assets transferred to the corporate parent retain their tax cost in the hands of the subsidiary; the parent's tax cost in the stock simply disappears.

This pattern of rules makes the form and timing of the liquidation important. If, for example, the corporation first makes a dividend distribution and then a liquidating distribution to an individual shareholder, the dividend will be taxed in full as ordinary income and the (reduced) amount received on liquidation may be a preferentially treated capital gain. If the entire amount had been distributed in liquidation, only capital gain or loss treatment would have applied. On the other hand, a dividend paid to a corporate shareholder would qualify for the dividends received deduction while a capital gain on liquidation would be taxed in full.

Many of the other systems use the occasion of the liquidation to tax the accumulated corporate profits as a dividend and also to allow the repayment of the paid-in capital on a tax-free basis. In *Canada*, where a corporation makes a liquidating distribution, the rules are essentially the same as for a redemption. The taxpayer's share of paid-in capital can in general be received on a tax-free basis. If the acquisition cost is less than that amount, the difference is a capital gain. Any additional amount is taxed as a dividend. Special rules allow the tax-free liquidation of 90 %-owned domestic corporate subsidiaries.

The pattern in *Japan* is very similar. If the acquisition cost of the shares is equal to or greater than the attributable paid-in capital, the excess of the amount received over the cost is taxed as a dividend. If the acquisition cost is less than the attributable paid-in capital, the difference will be a taxable capital gain; any excess received will be taxed as a dividend. The special "liquidation" tax discussed in Section 5.5 would be applicable at the corporate level.

France also makes a distinction between paid-in capital, acquisition cost, and taxable dividends. For an individual shareholder not holding the shares in a business, any amounts received in excess of the greater of the acquisition cost of the shares or the allocated portion of the paid-in capital is taxed as a dividend and carries the imputation credit; no loss is allowed. When the distribution is received by a business entity and the amount received is less than the acquisition cost of the shares, a loss (ordinary or capital as the case may be) is recognized. If the acquisition cost is in excess of the paid-in capital but lower than the amount received, the difference between the latter and the acquisition cost is taxed as a dividend. If the acquisition cost is below the share of the paid-in capital, then the difference will be a taxable gain (ordinary or capital) with any additional amount taxed as a dividend.

The Australian system treats liquidating distributions to the extent of after-tax taxable income (as opposed to after-tax profits, which is usually larger) as dividends which carry with them the imputation credit. As in Canada, for capital gains tax purposes, the total amount of the liquidating distribution is treated as consideration for the disposal of the stock but the amount of the gain is reduced by the amount taxed as a dividend. No loss is allowed unless the total amount received (whether characterized as a dividend or not) is less than the cost base of the shares. In the liquidation of a 100 % subsidiary, there is a rollover of the tax cost of the subsidiary's assets, though the transaction is still treated as a disposition of the parent company's shares with the tax consequences outlined above. Liquidating dividends carry the intercorporate dividend credit, subject to restrictions. There are no fixed ordering rules distinguishing between distributions of stated capital, share premium, and retained earnings and in practice, the liquidator has considerable flexibility in obtaining the most favorable tax results on the liquidating distribution.

In the German system, where a corporation is wound up and liquidated, the liquidating corporation is generally taxed on the difference between the book value of the assets at the beginning of the winding-up period and the assets which are distributed to the shareholder at the end of the period. If appreciated assets are distributed in kind, the appreciation is subject to tax. In the hands of the shareholder, the amounts in the various income baskets will be treated as distributions with the usual tax results. The difference between the tax basis in the shares and the remaining amount of the liquidating distribution will result in a gain or loss, whose tax treatment depends on the status of the shareholder. If the shares are held as a business asset or amount to a substantial participation, a gain would be taxable and a loss deductible. If the shares are private assets, no gain or loss would be recognized.

Special rules apply if the business is not wound up but is transferred to a partnership composed of the shareholders or is continued as a sole proprietorship. If the taxpayer wants the transaction to be tax free, the book values of the transferred assets are continued. If the tax cost of the shares is lower than the book value of the assets, gain is recognized to that extent by the transferee.

In *The Netherlands*, for individual shareholders not holding their shares in a business, a liquidation distribution up to the amount of the average paid-in capital can be received on a tax-free basis. Any excess is taxed as a dividend. The shareholder's acquisition cost in the shares is not relevant (it should be remembered that private capital gains are not taxed). A special rule treats a sale in certain circumstances as a liquidation if the corporation is liquidated shortly after the sale and the purchaser (e.g., a nonresident) would not be subject to income tax on the amount in excess of paid-in capital. If the shareholder is a corporation whose holding does not amount to a participation or an individual holding the shares in his business, the difference between the tax cost of the shares and the liquidation payment will be subject to tax as a gain on sale. If the corporate shareholder qualifies for the participation exemption, the gain is not taxed. However, losses are then not deductible.

Sweden treats a liquidation entirely as a capital transaction. This means that if a loss results, it is subject to the 70 % deduction limitation discussed above. This result obtains despite the fact that the realization of the loss is typically not a voluntary act by the shareholder and the 70 % rule is generally aimed at intentionally realizing losses while deferring gains. If a subsidiary is in effect liquidated into its parent corporation in a merger, the transaction is tax-free to both parties with a carryover basis in the subsidiary's assets. As in the United States situation, the tax cost in the shares of the subsidiary disappears in the transaction.

The *United Kingdom* also treats liquidating payments as capital distributions, resulting in capital gains treatment to both the corporation and the shareholder. There is no attempt to treat a portion of the payment as a dividend distribution, subject to ACT and bringing with it an imputation credit.

7. Corporate reorganizations and restructuring

7.1 General

Most of the systems here under consideration have special rules dealing with the tax treatment of corporate reorganizations.[2] Transactions covered include corporate mergers and acquisitions, divisions, changes in capital structure, and other similar rearrangements of corporate affairs. There are typically a number of structural issues of corporate taxation involved in such transactions. First, the exchanges and rearrangements of interests that take place in reorganization transactions are usually events that would cause a recognition of gain or loss under normal tax principles. Each system must determine the conditions and circumstances under which those rules will be supplanted by special provisions which permit tax-preferred treatment. The factors taken into account might include the business or commercial reasons for the transaction; the corporate and commercial law aspects of the transaction; and the character of the assets involved and their role in the existing and emerging enterprises. In addition, the change in the extent and character of the ownership interests in the corporation is often an important factor in deciding if the normal recognition rules should be displaced. While the form of the investment may change, that change may not be deemed a sufficient modification of the "continuity of ownership interest" to require a recognition of gain or allow a recognition of loss.

---

2. For France, Germany, The Netherlands, Sweden, and the United Kingdom, the European Union Merger Directive requires domestic legislation to allow mergers, share exchanges, and certain transfers of assets to take place on a tax-deferred basis when the participating companies and shareholders are organized or reside in different EU states. In modifying their legislation to the requirements of the Directive, several of the countries also modified the rules applicable to purely domestic transactions.

Where the judgment is made that the transaction should only be partially tax-free and some income must be recognized, rules must be provided to characterize that gain. To the extent that an exchange is involved, capital gain or loss treatment may be appropriate. On the other hand, if property is coming out of the corporation, it may be similar to a dividend distribution in connection with the otherwise tax-free reorganization. The effect of exchange treatment or dividend treatment will differ in some situations depending on the nature of the shareholder and the extent to which integration relief is available. Finally, rules must be provided for the continuance or carryover of various corporate tax attributes (tax cost, carryovers, etc.) of the corporations involved.

Sometimes these issues are dealt with in detailed statutory rules, sometimes under broad general principles like continuity of business or ownership interest, and sometimes with a combination of both approaches. The basic pattern of reorganization transactions and their effects is considered here. The next section deals with the carryover of corporate tax attributes in these situations and the limitations to which carryovers may be subject.

7.2 Merger transactions

In a typical merger transaction, an existing corporation disappears and its assets and liabilities are taken over by another corporation which continues the business activities of the disappearing corporation. The shareholders of the disappearing corporation may continue as shareholders of the continuing corporation or may receive cash, property, or creditor interests in the continuing corporation for all or a part of their shares. As a formal matter, the merger may take place under special corporate law provisions or may be a "practical" merger where there is an actual transfer of assets in exchange for stock or other property by the corporation ceasing business.

In the *United States*, the rules dealing with mergers have been developed both in the case law and in detailed statutory provisions that apply to all qualifying reorganizations including mergers. Under the statutory structure, a series of corporate rearrangements, including mergers, are defined as "reorganizations"; other rules then determine the consequences of the various transfers and exchanges involved in the reorganization.

Beyond the statutory definition of reorganization, however, there are a number of judicially-developed doctrines which limit the scope of reorganization treatment even when the formal statutory requirements are met. First of all, the reorganization must have a business or commercial purpose. While this requirement is usually easily satisfied, it stands as a barrier to reorganization transactions that are focused exclusively on the tax benefits of reorganization treatment. In addition, the business of the acquired corporation must to some extent be continued, though substantial variation and changes are allowed. Most importantly, the shareholders in the disappearing corporation must have a significant continuing ownership interest in the acquiring corporation. This requirement of "continuity of ownership interest" is based on the idea that tax deferral is only appropriate when the shareholder has not changed the basic nature of his investment. However, as the doctrine has developed, it in fact allows substantial variation in the economic characteristics of the investment as long is it continues in the form of an ownership interest. Thus, for example, a merger transaction in which a target corporation wholly owned by a single shareholder is merged into a publicly-traded corporation in which the former shareholder receives only a small percentage of the stock of the acquiring corporation would still qualify under the continuity of interest test. This would be true even if the stock interest has substantially different characteristics, e.g., limited voting rights.

While the exact degree of required continuing ownership is not clearly defined in the case law, something less than 50 % would be acceptable. That is, if the shareholders of the disappearing corporation, taken together, received at least, say, 45 % of the consideration for their shares in the form of stock in the acquiring corporation, the requirement would be met. Exactly where the lower limit is is not clear. On the other hand, the continuity requirement must be met by, broadly speaking, the corporation's "historical" shareholders. Thus if the shareholders who receive shares in the reorganization have recently purchased their shares, perhaps with an eye to the possibility of the merger, they might not be counted in the "historical" group. Similarly, the cases have required that the shareholders participating in the reorganization transaction intend to continue to be shareholders in the acquiring corporation after the merger. Thus a sale immediately after the reorganization might defeat the required "post-reorganization" continuity.

Assuming that the merger transaction meets the various judicial requirements, the statute provides special rules to determine the tax treatment of the participants. If only stock in the acquiring corporation is used in the merger, neither the acquired corporation which transfers its assets in the merger nor the shareholder who exchanges his shares for shares in the acquired corporation will recognize gain or loss. The tax cost of the assets carries over to the acquiring corporation and the shareholder takes as his tax cost in the new shares his historical cost in his old shares. If other property, e.g., cash or a creditor interest in the acquiring corporation is received, then gain, but not loss, will be recognized. If this receipt of the nonstock property is functionally equivalent to a dividend distribution made in connection with the merger, dividend treatment will result. Otherwise, gain will be recognized on the disposition of the shares, which would ordinarily be capital gain. The shareholder is allowed to increase his tax cost in the new shares by the amount of the recognized gain (or dividend) and the acquiring corporation is given a similar increase in the tax basis of the assets.

Some special provisions allow reorganization treatment when the stock consideration used is the stock of the parent corporation controlling the actual acquiring corporation. The extremely technical rules for these "triangular" forms of merger reorganizations have developed in a haphazard fashion and represent no consistent policies beyond the general notions of continuity of ownership interest and continuation of the business enterprise.

The *Canadian* treatment of the functional equivalent of a merger transaction is determined in part by the nature of the transaction for corporate law purposes. Federal and provincial law allow two or more corporations to "amalgamate" and continue as a single corporation. The amalgamating corporations do not cease to exist for corporate law purposes; rather, they continue in the form of the amalgamated corporation. As a result of this approach, there has formally been no transfer of assets or discontinuation of business; in an analogy often used in the case law (and appropriate for Canada) it is as if two streams flowed together to form a river.

The tax law accepts this characterization to some extent and thus the transfers involved in the amalgamation transaction are not treated as dispositions for purposes of gain or loss recognition. On the other hand, there are some special tax rules that do not follow the corporate concept. Thus for many purposes, the resulting entity is treated as a new corporation and the statute provides detailed rules for the carryover of various corporate tax attributes in the amalgamation transaction.

At the shareholder level, where the shareholders of the "old" corporation receive only shares of the new corporation, the exchange is tax-free and the shareholders continue the tax cost of their old shares. There is no requirement that the shares received be held for any particular period of time. If there is a difference in the values of the shares given up and the shares received and that benefit in effect accrues to a person related to the shareholder, gain is recognized to this extent. As a prophylactic measure, no increase in basis of the shares is allowed for the gain recognized. If the shareholders receive non-share consideration in the amalgamation, the rollover does not apply and the shareholders would be considered to have disposed of their shares in the amalgamating corporations for proceeds equal to the fair market value of the shares in the amalgamated corporations.

Apart from amalgamations under corporate law, the rules discussed in connection with corporate formation may apply to a transfer of property for shares which is, at the corporate level, similar to a merger. However, the distribution of the shares to the shareholders would be a taxable event under normal principles.

Dutch rules on legal mergers are contained in standard provisions issued by the Ministry. They set out the basic framework in which mergers can take place on a tax-deferred basis. When complied with, the tax attributes of the disappearing company are transferred to the surviving company and the shareholders of the resultant company transfer their tax cost of the old shares to the new shares. Any consideration the taxpayer receives in cash is taxable up to the amount of the gain. The standard conditions require, inter alia, that the merging companies be subject to the same tax regime.

Germany has a special statute that deals with reorganizations of all forms, with differing requirements for various types of reorganizations. In the case of mergers, the transaction may take the form of several existing corporations merging or two or more existing corporations merging into a newly-formed corporation. The shareholders of the disappearing corporation are issued shares in the surviving corporation. If the transfer is solely for stock of the surviving corporation and the assets are taken over by the surviving corporation at book value in circumstances in which the potential gain will remain subject to tax, no gain or loss is recognized by the transferring corporation. However, the receiving corporation has to enter the assets on its books at any value chosen by the transferring corporation between the book value and the going concern value, assuming that value is higher. To the extent an amount greater than the book value is used, the transferring corporation must realize gain.

As for the shareholders, the tax cost of the new shares received will in general be the tax cost of the old shares. However, if as a result of the merger, a former portfolio interest becomes a substantial participation which would be subject to tax, the shares take a fair market value tax cost. Similarly, if a substantial participation is changed into a portfolio interest, the tax cost of the shares is carried over and a subsequent disposition of the shares would remain taxable. Cash payments may be received in some circumstances though to that extent gains have to be shown and taxed.

In *France*, as well, reorganizations can take place on a tax-deferred basis under conditions and circumstances precisely stated in the statutory provisions. For corporate and tax law purposes, the merger may take the same forms as in Germany. Gain is normally deferred on the transferred assets provided that they keep their tax cost in the hands of the transferee corporation. However, the transferee corporation can elect to take income into account currently on the transfer of current assets with a corresponding step-up in basis. Special rules apply with respect to depreciable fixed assets. In the hands of the transferee, these assets receive a stepped-up tax cost and correspondingly, the gains (other than those long term gains for which the transferring company elected a current preferential 19 % taxation) are subject to normal corporate tax with the gain taken into account ratably over a five-year period (fifteen years in the case of real estate). At the shareholder level, gain is deferred until the disposition of the shares received on the exchange. Cash up to 10 % of the nominal value of the shares can be received and is currently taxable.

Mergers in the *United Kingdom* are covered by the general rules on reorganizations. Normally, when a corporation makes a distribution which is not treated as income under the usually applicable rules, the distribution is considered a capital distribution and results in a potentially taxable disposal by the shareholder. However, if the transactions qualify as a reorganization, no disposition is deemed to take place and the new holding is treated as a continuation of the old. One of the statutorily defined forms of reorganization is a reconstruction of a company or the amalgamation of two or more companies. To qualify, the reorganization must have a bona fide commercial purpose and the exchange must not be part of a scheme for tax avoidance.

The *Japanese* rules on reorganizations are quite restrictive. In general, the corporation that disappears in the merger is subject to the "liquidation" tax discussed in connection with property distributions. Thus it must recognize gain on its appreciated property and return to income any deferred profits or reserves. The gain is calculated as the difference between the paid-in capital, surplus and legal reserves of the disappearing corporation, and the par value of the stock received, together with the fair market value of any non-stock property received in the merger. This approach allows the fair market value of the stock received in excess of its par value to escape tax; the only concern is the increase in stated capital for the acquiring corporation. However, if the acquiring corporation enters the assets on its books for more than the par value of the stock given and the non-stock consideration, it must realize income to the extent that this value exceeds the book value of the asset in the hands of the merged corporation. Thus, in effect, any increases in paid-in capital resulting from the merger are taxed to the merged corporation and any write-up in asset value beyond the par value of the shares transferred is taxed to the surviving corporation. Shareholders who received shares in the acquiring corporation are taxed to the extent that the par value of the shares received exceeds the par value of the old shares. If the market value of the shares is higher than the par value, that potential gain will be deferred until the shares are disposed of in a taxable transaction.

Sweden has no special rules dealing with merger transactions apart from the merger of a subsidiary into a parent corporation discussed in connection with liquidations. However, other provisions taken together can be used to obtain tax-free treatment for what is in effect a merger transaction. For example, if a shareholder transfers shares to a corporation for newly-issued shares, the exchange is tax-free. Consideration in the form of cash or other property up to 10 % of the nominal value of the stock can be given without affecting the tax-free nature of the stock exchange. The cash will be taxed as gain on the exchange. Thereafter, the acquired corporation can be merged into the acquiring corporation under the general merger provision, thus providing the functional equivalent of a merger of the two companies with the shareholders of the old company becoming shareholders of the acquiring company.

Australia has no specific provisions allowing the tax-free merger of economically independent corporations. Rollovers are permitted in assets transfers, including shares of stock, but only if there is 100 % continuity of economic ownership. These rules permit what are, in effect, reorganization transactions within groups or between a company and its existing shareholders, but not otherwise. The strictness of the Australian rule has to do with the transitional rule used in connection with the introduction of capital gains taxation that restricts taxation to assets acquired after the effective date of the legislation but allows a continuation on nontaxable status in the case of rollovers. If assets could retain their tax-free status through successive corporate reorganizations, the potential scope of the tax would have been substantially limited.

7.3 Share exchanges

A second typical form of reorganization involves an exchange of shares entirely at the shareholder level. Unlike the merger transaction, no transfers of assets are involved and the acquired corporation is unaffected at the corporate level. Normally, a share exchange would be a taxable event in the systems here under consideration but special provisions allow such an exchange to be treated on a rollover basis if certain conditions are met.

In the *United States*, one form of statutorily recognized reorganization is the acquisition by one corporation of 80 % ("control") of the stock of another corporation *solely* in exchange for the voting stock of the acquiring corporation. The voting stock requirement has been very strictly interpreted by the courts and even a de minimis amount of nonqualifying consideration can prevent nonrecognition.

The 80 % control need not be acquired in one transaction as long as the final acquisition results in the 80 % test being met. However, if some of the prior acquisitions have been made for consideration other than voting stock and are considered as part of an integrated acquisition transaction, the entire exchange would be taxable. If the prior acquisitions were for voting stock, subsequent acquisition of control could be done on a tax-free basis. Where the transaction qualifies as a reorganization, the shareholder retains the tax cost of his old shares for the new shares.

The *Canadian* rules are quite different. Shares can be exchanged for shares in the acquiring corporation on a tax-free basis in any amount as long as the acquired shareholders do not have, after the exchange, an interest in the acquiring corporation of more than 50 % in value or have control of the acquiring corporation. In addition, the acquiring corporation and the acquired corporation's shareholders must deal with each other at arm's length. Shares can also be acquired for other consideration in the same transaction as long as the vendor can clearly identify which shares were exchanged for cash and which were exchanged for shares. Similarly, the rollover will apply to a fraction of the shares exchanged for other shares as long as the purchaser's offer indicates that the shares are exchanged for a specified fraction of the acquired shareholder's shares and cash or other consideration for the remaining fraction. The tax-free rollover treatment applies only to the shares or fraction of shares that are disposed of for shares. The shareholder keeps his tax cost in the old shares as his tax cost for the new shares and the acquiring corporation takes as its cost the lesser of fair market value or the paid-up capital allocated to the shares.

The *Dutch* rules allow a tax-deferred exchange of shares if the acquiring corporation obtains over 50 % of the voting stock (reduced from 90 % in compliance with the EU merger directive and made applicable to domestic as well as EU-related transactions) of the acquired corporation. Preexisting ownership of shares may be counted for purposes of the 50 % test. Cash payments of up to 10 % of the nominal amount of the stock are allowed, though it is not clear if these payments must be pro rata or could be made on a disproportionate basis in order to buy out a shareholder. There are special rules to ensure that the later disposition of the shares remains taxable if the status of the shareholder changes from taxable to nontaxable, e.g., if the prior ownership interest amounted to a (taxable) substantial participation and the acquired interest did not.

The *German* rules are similar and also have been changed recently to comply with the EU directive and made applicable to domestic as well as international transactions involving other EU states. An exchange of shares in which the acquiring corporation obtains a majority of the voting rights in the acquired corporation is tax deferred. Previous ownership of the shares of the acquired company is counted in determining if voting control is present. As in the case of mergers, the acquiring corporation has the option of entering the shares acquired at their book value, the "going concern" value or any value in between those amounts. If an amount in excess of book value is chosen, the exchanging shareholder will recognize gain to that extent, the tax treatment of which depends on the status of the shareholder. In addition to the tax-deferred exchange permitted by the reorganizations provisions, prior case law, which is still followed, allows a tax-deferred exchange of shares if the shares received are identical in value, type and function as the transferred shares. In such a situation, the courts have held there is no realization event.

In general, in *France* an exchange of shares is a taxable event. However, rollover treatment is available if 50 % (30 % in the case of traded shares) of the capital of a company is exchanged for newly-issued shares of the acquiring company under certain conditions. The exchanging shareholders must agree to keep the shares received for at least five years and cash consideration cannot exceed 10 % of the nominal value of the shares.

In the *United Kingdom*, certain share exchanges are treated as reorganizations not resulting in a disposition for capital gains purposes. There are several qualifying transactions. First, if the acquiring company already owns 25 % of the stock of the acquired corporation or, as a result of the exchange, obtains voting control the exchange may be made on a tax-deferred basis. Tax-deferred treatment is also available if the exchange is part of a general offer to obtain control. Finally, the exchange is tax deferred if it in fact results in the acquisition of control of the acquired company.

As mentioned above in connection with merger transactions, in *Sweden* shares may be transferred on a tax-free basis for newly issued shares of the transferee corporation. *Australia* and *Japan* have no rules allowing domestic tax-free share acquisitions.

7.4 Nonmerger asset reorganizations

Some systems have special reorganization provisions dealing with asset transfers or "enterprise" mergers that involve the transfer of assets in a transaction that does not formally constitute a merger for corporate law purposes. In the *United States*, this type of "practical" merger is possible if certain statutory requirements are met. The corporation whose assets are being acquired must transfer "substantially all" of its assets to the acquiring corporation. At least 80 % of the consideration received for the assets must be voting stock of the acquiring corporation (or a parent corporation in control of the acquiring corporation). In addition, liabilities of the acquired corporation can be assumed subject to some special limitations. The corporation whose assets were acquired must be liquidated and distribute the consideration received to its shareholders. If these requirements are met, no gain or loss is recognized by the acquired corporation with respect to the transferred assets and the acquiring corporation takes over the tax cost of the assets. At the shareholder level, the shares of the acquiring corporation can be received on a tax-free basis, with the tax cost of the old shares attaching to the new shares. If nonstock consideration within the permissible limits is involved, that amount is taxable, either as gain on the share disposition or as a dividend, depending on the circumstances. The income inclusion increases the tax cost for the new shares. In addition, the acquiring corporation is allowed to increase its tax cost in the assets received by the amount of the income recognized at the shareholder level.

In the other systems, while there are frequently provisions which allow a tax-deferred transfer of assets to an existing corporation in exchange for shares, there is typically no mechanism which allows the shares received in exchange for the assets to be distributed tax-free to the shareholders unless the transaction meets the requirements of a tax-deferred division, discussed in the next section.

Thus in the *Canadian* system, there is no equivalent of the United States "practical" merger described above. The special rollover rules described above in connection with corporate formation allow the transfer of assets in exchange for stock to take place on a tax-deferred basis. However, there is no provision allowing the tax-deferred distribution of the stock of the acquiring corporation to the shareholders of the acquired corporation. The rules in the *United Kingdom* are even more restrictive in that the only permissible consideration is the assumption of liabilities by the transferee corporation.

The *Swedish* system allows a tax-free result by combining the rules that allow tax-free exchanges of shares for newly-issued stock and tax-free parent-subsidiary mergers. Thus all of the shares of the acquired corporation are transferred to the acquiring corporation for newly-issued shares and the now subsidiary corporation can then be liquidated, with both steps being tax-free.

Both *Germany* and *The Netherlands* similarly allow the transfer of, broadly speaking, an independent business unit in exchange for shares on a tax-deferred basis. However, in neither system do the provisions foresee the tax-free distribution of the shares of the acquired corporation.

In the Dutch system, the transferor must be a corporation and there must be an economic consolidation or integration of the transferred business with the business of the transferee. Germany only requires that the transferred business be a potentially independent operation. In addition, in the Dutch system, the transferor corporation takes as its tax cost in the shares received the fair market value of the shares, thus eliminating the potential second corporate level tax on the appreciation in the transferred assets. The transferee corporation takes the assets with their historical tax cost and thus will bear the burden of the tax on disposition. There is a requirement, however, that the stock be held for at least three years to prevent what is essentially a cash sale from being converted into a tax-deferred exchange. In Germany, the treatment of the transaction, as in the merger and share exchange situations described above, depends on the extent to which the transferee corporation elects to write up the assets in excess of their book value. To that extent, the transferor will recognize gain and have a corresponding increase in the tax cost of the shares.

In *France*, it is possible to transfer an independent business activity for shares on a tax-deferred basis. In certain circumstances, the transferring corporation can distribute the shares to its shareholders if prior approval is obtained to waive the normally applicable five-year holding period.

7.5 Corporate divisions: "Demergers"

The division of the assets of an existing corporation can take a variety of forms, but all have in common the splitting of ownership at the shareholder level. In a typical "demerger" situation, shareholders of the original corporation emerge from the transaction with stock interests in two (or more) corporations.[3] The splitting of ownership at the shareholder level raises a number of tax issues. In the first place, since property has left the original corporation, gain might be recognized by the distributing corporation under normally applicable rules. In addition, since the shareholder has received a property distribution, the usual rules for dividends, or redemptions (if shares in the original corporation are exchanged for the distributed shares), are implicated at the shareholder level. Finally, since the shareholder now has two interests in place of his original single interest, it is possible to sell a part of

---

3. In the terminology often used in connection with corporate divisions, the pro rata distribution of the stock of a subsidiary to the existing shareholders is referred to as a "spin-off." If the distribution is in exchange for the stock of the distributing corporation, the transaction is termed a "split-off." A split-off is often done on a non-pro rata basis and results in a change in the ownership of the distributing corporation. Finally, in a "split-up," the distributing corporation transfers assets to new or existing subsidiaries and then liquidates.

his investment while retaining the remainder, thus involving the usual rules, including preferential or tax-free treatment, on the sale of shares. From a policy point of view, the issue is whether and to what extent the results of the normally applicable rules should be modified when the transaction constitutes a corporate division.

The systems here under consideration have reacted quite differently to the tax issues that arise in corporate divisions. In some countries, special rules are provided to allow tax-free treatment and are crafted to limit the perceived tax avoidance possibilities in the transaction. In others, no attempt has been made to change the normally applicable rules to allow tax-free treatment. At one extreme, in Japan, while assets may be contributed on a tax-deferred basis to a newly-formed subsidiary, there are no special rules allowing the tax-deferred distribution of the shares of a corporation; the distribution is treated as a taxable dividend or redemption. In contrast, in the United States, detailed rules allow for a tax-deferred division of, broadly speaking, active businesses but have substantial restrictions intended to prevent the "bailing out" of corporate profits in a divisive transaction. In Canada, there are no special rules on demergers but normally applicable principles may allow divisive transactions in some circumstances, though typically not without administrative approval.

Even among those jurisdictions that allow some form of tax-deferred division, there are substantial differences in the requirements which must be met. Almost all jurisdictions, however, recognize that some sort of "business" or commercial purpose must be established for the division and have rules preventing the division of business and investment assets.

The rules on corporate division are most developed in the *United States* and involve both case law principles and statutory provisions. The rules apply both to the distribution of an existing subsidiary and the transfer of assets to a newly-formed subsidiary followed by the distribution of the stock to the shareholders. As a basic requirement, the division must have a demonstrable business purpose to justify the transaction from a commercial point of view. The purpose must be, in general, a "corporate" purpose, as opposed to a "shareholder" purpose, and must justify the division of ownership at the shareholder level. Thus, for example, a desire to insulate risky activities in a separate corporation is not a sufficient business purpose for the distribution of the stock of the corporation to shareholders. On the other hand, where shareholder disagreement is affecting operations at the corporate level, a corporate division may be commercially justified.

Assuming the division has a business purpose, there are several statutory requirements intended to prevent the division from being used to distribute corporate profits to shareholders. First, both the corporation making the distribution and the distributed corporation must be engaged in the active conduct of a trade or business and have been engaged in such business for at least five years prior to the division. This requirement prevents the concentrating of passive or investment-type assets in one corporation which could then be disposed of at preferential capital gain rates after the division. In addition, the statute requires that the division is not "used principally as a device for the distribution of [earnings]." Although the "device" and "active business" requirements to some extent overlap, the former focuses particularly on the possibility of a post-division sale of one of the businesses and takes this as an important sign of a distribution "device."

If the above requirements are met, then at the corporate level, both the transfer of the assets to a subsidiary corporation (if an existing subsidiary is not involved) and the distribution of the stock do not result in the recognition of gain or loss. The receipt of the stock by the shareholders is similarly tax-free and the tax cost of the shares with respect to which the distribution is made is allocated between the shares of the distributed and distributing companies.

In contrast, *Canada* has no special provisions dealing with divisive transactions but a complex transactional form — the "butterfly" reorganization — allows what is in effect a demerger transaction. The most important structural requirement is that each transferee corporation must receive the same proportionate share of property of the corporation which is being divided, viz. business property, investment property, and cash. Thus the transaction cannot be used to "bail out" cash or liquid investment assets.

The situation in *Australia* is similar. While there are no special rules dealing with demergers, a transactional form of demerger is possible in the context of a corporate group. The subsidiary to be distributed can issue stock rights to the shareholders of the parent company without the distribution being treated as a dividend. The exercise of the right is not taxable and the shareholders now hold stock directly in the subsidiary. The tax cost of the stock is the exercise price of the option and thus any transfer of value will be taxed to the shareholders when the stock is sold. There are no restrictions in general on this form of transaction based on the business or commercial purpose of the transaction, though a special statutory provision is applicable to certain spin-offs taking this form where the distributed entity is a unit trust subject to single-level taxation.

Since 1980, the *United Kingdom* has had extensive statutory rules dealing with demergers. Basically, three situations are covered: (1) the distribution of the shares of an existing subsidiary; (2) the transfer of a subsidiary to another company and a distribution of the shares of that company; and (3) the transfer of a business to a subsidiary and the distribution of the shares of the subsidiary. There are a number of conditions, the most important of which is that the company is a trading company or a member of a trading group and that the demerger is of some benefit to the trading activities. This latter test requires more than merely showing that there is some commercial purpose to the transaction. An advanced ruling or clearance for the transaction can be obtained from the fiscal authorities. If the various requirements are met, the distribution of the shares will not be treated as a distribution for tax purposes and will be tax-free in the hands of the recipient. In general, there will be no capital gains consequences for the company transferring the shares.

In *Sweden*, under a special law for publicly traded corporations (occasioned by the restructuring of ASEA and ABB in 1991) a pro rata distribution of all of the shares of a previously-owned subsidiary corporation is possible on a tax-free basis if, generally speaking, the activities of the distributing and distributed company are of significant size in relation to the size of the activities before the distributions. This requirement indirectly prevents investment asset bailouts. The tax cost of the shares of the distributing corporation are allocated between the distributing and distributed corporation based on fair market values. There is generally no tax at the level of the distributing corporation as long as the shares are investment assets and not current assets.

For nonpublicly-traded companies, there are no special statutory provisions on demergers. Some case law principles have been used to attempt demerger transactions which avoid tax at both the level of the distributing corporation and the recipient shareholder. These results can be obtained if there are good organizational reasons for the transaction. The transaction typically involves the sale of a division at book value to a newly formed corporation owned by the shareholders of the selling corporation.

Germany has modified its domestic laws dealing with demergers to comply with the EU Merger Directive. In the German system, two forms of demerger are recognized; a division and a split-off. In a division, two or more potentially independent businesses are transferred to new or existing subsidiary corporations and distributed to the shareholders of the distributing corporation which is dissolved. In a split-off, one or more businesses are transferred to subsidiary corporation(s) and distributed with the distributing corporation continuing to operate at least one business. The transfer can be done without recognition of gain to the distributing corporation or the shareholders if the parties elect to retain the book values of the assets and shares involved and certain holding period requirements are met. In general, the shares of the distributed corporations must be held for five years and the shareholders receiving the distributed stock must have been shareholders for five years prior to the distribution. In the division, any existing loss carryforward and the pools of net equity are allocated between the surviving corporations on the basis of fair market values.

In *France*, both the transfer of assets to a subsidiary preliminary to a demerger and the distribution of the stock would in principle be taxable events. However, a division can be done on a tax-deferred basis if prior governmental approval is obtained. In addition, under legislation passed in 1995, prior approval is no longer necessary for tax-deferred treatment when a corporation operating at least two independent businesses transfers those businesses to two (or more) corporations whose shares are distributed to shareholders on a pro rata basis and the shareholders hold the stock for at least five years.

In the *Japanese* system, while the transfer of assets to a newly formed subsidiary corporation can be done on a tax-deferred basis, the distribution of the shares of the subsidiary to the shareholders of the distributing company would be fully taxable.

In *The Netherlands*, divisions are presently not possible under Dutch company law, though a statutory amendment is being considered. In general, it is difficult as a practical matter to achieve a demerger on a tax-free basis using generally applicable tax principles.

8. Transfer and limitations on transfer of corporate tax attributes

In many systems, when a corporation goes out of existence in connection with a merger or similar transaction, its tax attributes are transferred to the successor corporation. The tax attributes transferred typically include the tax cost of assets, accumulated profits, various reserves and provisions, and most importantly, loss carryforwards. In connection with loss carryforwards, there are often restrictions on the ability of the successor corporation to use the losses against subsequently arising income. These limitations are intended to prevent the "selling" of loss carryforwards by those who have incurred the losses to third parties. They are typically triggered by changes in the ownership of the loss corporation and/or changes in its business activities.

The *United States* has highly developed rules concerning both the carryover of attributes and limitations on those carryovers. Basically, in situations which qualify as reorganizations under the various statutory definitions, the corporate attributes of the disappearing corporation are inherited by the surviving corporation. In situations involving divisions where there is more than one surviving corporation, some of the existing corporate tax attributes are divided among the surviving corporations. In addition, in the liquidation of a corporate subsidiary, the subsidiary's attributes are inherited by the parent.

There are substantial limits on the carryover of losses, credits and other tax benefits in those situations in which attributes are inherited. The limitations apply generally whenever there is a significant change in the share ownership of the corporation, even if the situation does not involve the transfer of tax attributes. In general, if there is a more than 50 % change in share ownership, the losses of the corporation experiencing the change in ownership will be limited. Thus if there is a sale of over 50 % of the stock of corporation which has loss carryovers, the carryovers will be subject to the limitations. Similarly, if there is a change of over 50 % of the ownership of the loss corporation due to its merger into a profit corporation, the limitations will apply. The "50 % ownership change" is tested by looking back at changes in the prior three-year period. These rules apply only to ownership changes by shareholders who have at least 5 % interests in the corporation but there are complex rules aggregating less than 5 % shareholders for some purposes.

Where the limitations are applicable, the loss carryover can only be used to offset income of the business which generated the losses.

Rather than actually attempting to determine that amount of income, an assumed rate of return is applied to the value of the corporation at the time the change in ownership takes place and the loss is allowed to that extent. The basic theory behind the limitation is that the purchasers of the corporation should be able to make no greater use of the losses economically incurred by the selling shareholders than those shareholders would have enjoyed if there had been no change of ownership. Even this limited carryover is not allowed unless the corporation's business is continued or its assets are used in another business.

The loss limitations also apply to certain credit carryforwards.

Similar limitations apply to losses which have accrued but are not yet realized for tax purposes at the time of the change in ownership. The deduction of such "built-in" losses is limited if the losses are realized within five years after the ownership change.

In addition, there are some broad "purpose-based" anti-avoidance principles applicable to loss situations, but they have largely been supplanted by the more specific statutory provisions dealing with losses.

The *Canadian* rules are somewhat similar though not as extensive. Corporate tax attributes are transferred in the liquidation of a domestic 90 %-owned subsidiary by its domestic parent corporation. In addition, in the amalgamation of two corporations, the existing tax attributes are preserved. Where control of a corporation changes, any existing capital loss carryforwards are eliminated. Similarly, nonbusiness losses may not be carried forward after an ownership change. With respect to operating loss carryforwards, the business of the loss corporation must be continued and the losses may be used only against the income from that business. In addition, any accrued but unrealized losses are deemed to be realized at the time of the change of ownership, thus subjecting them to the above limitations.

In *The Netherlands*, a reorganization in the form of a merger under corporate law can result in the carryover of tax attributes of the disappearing company at the taxpayer's request if certain conditions set out by the Ministry of Finance are fulfilled. A general limitation on the use of losses applies in that situation as well as certain others where changes of business activities or ownership take place; the losses may only be used against income from the same business activity which generated the losses. In addition, if a corporation has "completely or almost completely" ceased activities and there is a 30 % change in share ownership involving those who were shareholders when the business activities ceased, then no carryforward or carryback of losses is allowed. There is substantial jurisprudence around the issue of business cessation but in general the legislation has limited the trading in loss corporations which was previously the practice.

As a general rule, in the *Japanese* system the tax losses may not be transferred from one corporation to another. This has led to a practice of the loss corporation being the surviving corporation in a merger transaction and thus formally retaining its old losses. Often the "acquiring" corporation will pay an amount for the tax loss and write this amount off as goodwill. The tax authorities have challenged such transactions in the past.

In *Sweden*, corporate tax attributes are transferred in a merger transaction, including loss carryforwards. However, where a change of ownership of the loss corporation occurs, as would typically be the case in an acquisition of shares followed by a liquidation, special limits apply on existing loss carryforwards. First, the existing loss can only be used in an amount equal to twice the purchase price of the shares. In addition, the losses cannot be used against taxable "group contributions" from other members of the group, the technique by which Sweden allows a consolidation of profits and losses within a group. However, the loss can be used against the income of the corporation to which the assets were transferred in the merger.

While tax attributes in *France*, in general, are transferred in the case of a merger, there is no transfer of the loss carryforward except in unusual cases with a special agreement by the fiscal authorities. In addition, if a corporation undergoes a radical change of its business activities, particularly if in connection with a change in control, the corporation's existing loss carryforwards will no longer be available.

The *Australian* rules limit the tax attributes of a corporation whose stock ownership undergoes a 50 % or greater change unless the corporation continues the "same business." The test is interpreted strictly and the commencement of a new business will result in the loss of carryforwards of operating losses, bad debts not yet written off for tax purposes, or realized capital losses. There is no limitation on built-in capital losses and the general limitations do not apply to imputation credits or foreign tax credits. The rules are drafted and applied in such a way that they do not apply to normal dealings in a company's shares on the stock exchange. As Australia does not generally recognize the concept of mergers in its corporate law, there are no special provisions dealing with the transfer of tax attributes.

The pattern in the *United Kingdom* is basically the same. If within a three-year period after an ownership change (an elaborately defined statutory concept) there is a major change in the nature and conduct of the business, the utilization of prechange losses is restricted.

Prior to 1990, *German* case law had refused to disallow losses where there was a change in share ownership or business as long as there was no formal change in the legal existence of the corporation. A statutory provision now requires that the corporation that is utilizing the losses must be "economically" identical with the corporation that suffered the losses. It expressly provides that such identity is not present if there has been a transfer of more than three-quarters of the shares of the corporation, it has recommenced business (in the same field or a different field) and the fair market value of newly acquired assets exceeds the value of existing assets.

9. Consolidated corporate taxation

While corporations are generally treated as separate taxpayers, most systems have special provisions under which affiliated corporations can be combined for tax purposes. These rules allow the overall economic results of the group operation to be taken into account despite the existence of formally separate corporate entities. The requirements for consolidation differ substantially, as do the techniques for treating the consolidated entity. In some cases, the separate corporate existence of the members for the group is ignored for most purposes, and in effect each corporation is treated as a division of a single company. In contrast, some systems generally treat the corporations as separate taxpayers but have special rules which allow the separate profit or loss so computed to be transferred among members of the group. The differences in technique can have important consequences in the timing and character of the income in the group. In still other situations, there is no formal mechanism for consolidation but the normal rules of income determination are relaxed in the context of related corporations.

The *United States* has a highly developed system of consolidated taxation. The rules are contained in a complex set of administrative regulations based on a broad statutory authorization. To qualify for consolidated treatment, an "affiliated group" of corporations must have a domestic parent corporation which owns at least 80 % of the stock of another domestic corporation. Lower-tier corporations may be included in the group if their higher-tier shareholder(s) in the group meet the 80 % ownership test with respect to those corporations. Corporations subject to special taxing regimes, for example, life insurance companies, may not be included in the group. Under this definition, two brother-sister corporations owned by an individual or a foreign corporation are not entitled to consolidated treatment. If the definitional requirements are met, the group can elect to file a consolidated tax return.

When consolidated filing is elected, "consolidated" income is calculated by combining the separate incomes of each of the members of the group. The income of each member of the group is determined under normal principles with important modifications to reflect the consolidation. Intercompany transactions are accounted for on a "deferred" basis. In general, no gain or loss is recognized on intercompany sales transactions until the property is sold outside the group. At that time, the gain or loss that would have been involved in the intercompany sale is accounted for by the member who would have realized that amount in the original sale. If the property is depreciable and is used in the business of the buying member, an increased basis for depreciation purposes is allowed, but the selling member has to include a corresponding amount in income as the depreciation deductions are taken. Deferred intercompany transactions also have to be taken into account if the group for some reason stops filing a consolidated return. Intercorporate dividends are eliminated in the calculations of consolidated income.

Consolidation allows losses in one member of the group to offset income of other members.

The overall effects of the consolidation are reflected in the "investment account" with respect to the parent's stock in the subsidiaries in the group. In general terms, earnings in the subsidiary which are included in the consolidated income increase the parent's basis in the subsidiary stock, thus preventing a double taxation of the same economic income if the stock of the subsidiary is sold. Correspondingly, actual dividend distributions reduce the basis in the stock as do losses of the subsidiary that are being used by other members of the group. If the losses exceed the basis of the stock, a so-called "excess loss account" is established, a kind of "negative" basis that will cause the loss in effect to be recaptured if the stock is sold or the member leaves the group.

The *Canadian* system takes a very different approach to the taxation of affiliated corporations. There are no formal provisions which allow the consolidation of profits and losses. While proposals for consolidation have been made, they have been opposed by the provinces, whose tax is usually a percentage of the federal tax. There was concern that the provisions would allow an avoidance of provincial taxes through the shifting of profits and losses in the group. Nonetheless, informal consolidation has been recognized both administratively and legislatively. Most of the anti-avoidance and anti-loss-trading rules do not apply to transactions between related corporations; transactions which are structured to transfer profits and losses among the members of a group are generally effective.

Sweden also does not formally recognize consolidation among group members. However, a special tax rule provides a mechanism which allows for the consolidation of profits and losses. It is possible for corporations connected with at least 90 % ownership to a common parent corporation to make "group contributions" to other members of the group. The group contribution is deductible by the paying corporation and taxable to the recipient corporation. Thus, for example, a profitable parent corporation with a loss subsidiary could make a group contribution to the subsidiary which would reduce the parent's profit and allow the subsidiary to utilize its losses. Group contributions can also be made between subsidiaries of the same parent corporation. Where the stock of a subsidiary corporation that has paid group contributions to its parent is sold at a loss, the loss must be reduced by the amount of the payments. The rules are not, in general, applicable to corporations subject to special tax rules.

The *United Kingdom* similarly does not recognize group reporting of income. However, a number of special rules apply to the taxation of company groups. The most important deals with "group relief." If a parent company owns at least 75 % of the stock of a domestic subsidiary company, then trading losses, capital allowances, and certain other tax attributes can be "surrendered" from one company to the other. In addition, if a "consortium" of 5 % or more corporate shareholders own together 75 % of the stock of a company, group relief is available. Group relief allows, for example, losses in one company to be "surrendered" and offset against income of the other company. Besides group relief, other rules permit the payment of dividends and interest without withholding of advance corporation tax or otherwise applicable withholding taxes if certain levels of share ownership are present.

Special rules apply for capital gains purposes. They allow a tax-free transfer of assets within the group. However, if the corporation receiving the asset on a tax-free basis leaves the group within six years, the transaction is retroactively taxable. In contrast to trading losses, capital losses cannot be transferred among group members.

The Netherlands, in contrast, has a complex system of consolidation based on both statutory and case law principles. Under the statute, a parent corporation and some or all of its 100%-owned subsidiaries can make an application to the fiscal authorities to be treated as a so-called "fiscal unity." While the corporations remain separate for corporate law purposes, for tax purposes, the assets and liabilities and income and losses are deemed to be those of the parent corporation. Generally, both corporations must be formed in the Netherlands (except where treaty nondiscrimination rules require otherwise) and be subject to the same tax rules, i.e., an insurance corporation and a business corporation cannot form a fiscal unity. There are standard requirements for permission to treat the corporations as one entity and special conditions can be applied in individual circumstances. Special rules prevent, inter alia, the shifting of value to a subsidiary whose stock could be sold on a tax-free basis and also limit the use of pre- and post-unity loss offset.

Australia has no provisions dealing explicitly with consolidated taxation of corporate groups. However, operating losses and capital losses can be utilized by members of a 100 %-related group. Basis adjustments in shareholdings where capital losses are transferred are required to prevent the "double counting" of the same economic loss, though the rules are not completely effective. In addition, as discussed above, assets rollovers among 100 %-owned companies are permitted.

There are comprehensive value-shifting provisions to deal with the related problem of transactions within a corporate group which generate a capital loss now in exchange for a capital gain in the future. The rules require appropriate adjustments in the tax cost of the shares or loans involved to reflect the value-shifting transaction. The problems arise mainly in connection with the rollover rules. For example, an asset may be transferred between sister companies for no consideration and a rollover elected. As a result, the value of the transferee company increases with a corresponding reduction in the value of the transferor company which, in the absence of special provisions, would result in a possible loss on the sale of that company's shares.

France allows a consolidation of a domestic parent (or French branch of a foreign corporation) and any 95 % or more domestic subsidiaries (*intégration fiscale*). The holding can be direct or indirect and must be maintained for the entire fiscal period. The election to consolidate is binding for five years but the parent can decide each year which of the qualifying subsidiaries it wants to include.

The income of each member is calculated separately. Losses (capital losses and operating losses) realized by members may be used to offset against income of other members. To the extent so used, they are not available to the subsidiary later should it leave the group. Loss carryforwards arising in years before the consolidation can only be used against income generated by that member. Intragroup financial transactions such as loans, loan forgiveness, bad debt reserves, etc. are eliminated in calculating each member's income. Intercompany sales result in deferred gains or losses that are taken into account when the property is sold outside the group, the member leaves the group, or the group is discontinued. The same is true for deferred intragroup financial transactions. Intercorporate dividends are also eliminated.

Germany has statutory provisions dealing with group taxation which are based on a complex and highly developed case law-based system of de facto consolidation (*Organschaft*). The consolidation is only available between domestic businesses (including the German branch of a foreign corporation and an individual proprietorship) and is possible only where a "dominant" entity has such "financial, economic and organizational domination" over a "dependent" entity that the latter entity is effectively a division of the former. The doctrinal basis for the *Organschaft* relation has a long history and the various requirements have been developed in great detail. Financial integration is present if the dominant entity has a majority of the voting shares in the dependent entity. Economic integration has been interpreted by case law fairly liberally to require simply that the dependent entity serves some business purposes of the dominant entity. A typical example would be a sales subsidiary of a manufacturing company. A holding company can be a dominant entity if it participates in the active management of the dependent entity's business. Organizational integration is present if the dependent entity cannot independently make business decisions. This is often ensured by a special contractual arrangement.

Assuming the above requirements are met, the dominant and dependent entities may, in effect, elect for group taxation by entering into a profit-and-loss pooling agreement (prescribed in the corporation law). Under the pooling agreement, which must last for at least five years, the profit or loss of the dependent entities calculated on a separate basis are transferred to the dominant entity and it includes that amount in its income calculations. The dominant entity is responsible to make up any loss suffered by the dependent entity and takes over its profits. This transfer of profit is not treated as a distribution. As a result of the transfer, the dependent entity shows no income or loss (the loss being offset by the claim against the dominant entity for reimbursement under the agreement). Losses arising prior to the *Organschaft* may not be used while the *Organschaft* arrangement is in effect.

Despite the *Organschaft* arrangement, the participating companies are treated as independent for tax purposes. Thus intercompany transactions generate income or loss that is taken into account currently. If transactions are not undertaken on an arm's length basis, a constructive dividend (treated as an advance transfer of profit and not carrying an imputation credit) or constructive contribution to capital may be found.

Unlike the other systems, *Japan* does not allow any form of formal or informal consolidation. Each corporation is treated as a separate taxpayer and transactions between related corporations have to be undertaken at arm's length.

10. Special tax regimes for closely held corporations

Whatever the basic structure of the corporate tax system, some countries have special rules for the taxation of closely-held corporations. They sometimes reflect the judgment that whatever the appropriate taxing pattern for widely-held corporations, modification should be made for closely held corporations that more nearly resemble partnerships. Nonetheless, the technical details of the rules vary substantially. In some cases, those rules allow a single level of pass-thru taxation on the partnership model. In other situations, the rules are intended to reinforce the normal pattern of taxation by dealing specifically with issues which typically arise in the closely-held context or to prevent income from being shifted from one category to another through the closely-held corporation.

In the *United States*, special rules provide for pass-thru treatment for corporations that meet certain definitional requirements and elect to be treated on a pass-thru basis. In general, the number of shareholders is limited to thirty-five resident individuals. The number of allowed shareholders has varied over the years and there are proposals to increase the limit. Special rules apply to trusts which allow them to be shareholders in certain situations. The corporation can only have a single class of stock that participates in dividends, though voting and nonvoting common stock is allowed. The corporation is not allowed to have any subsidiary corporations though again there is a proposed change to this rule. The technical requirements for qualification have been strictly interpreted and the rules are often criticized as being too complex for the often relatively unsophisticated taxpayers to whom they are intended to apply.

If the corporation elects pass-thru status, each shareholder includes in his income his share of the items of income and deduction which arise at the corporate level. Thus the character of the items passes through and retains its character, e.g., as a capital gain, at the shareholder level. The income is included in the shareholder's taxable year in which the corporation's year ends, whether or not it is distributed. If the share ownership changes during the year, income is generally prorated over the entire year and attributed to the shareholders accordingly. Income which is included increases the shareholder's tax cost in his shares as if the income had been distributed and then reinvested in the corporation. When an actual distribution is made, the tax cost of the shares is reduced accordingly; any excess over the tax cost is treated as a capital gain.

If the corporation operates at a loss, the loss similarly passes through to the shareholder and reduces the tax cost of the stock accordingly. The shareholder is allowed to take a current deduction for the corporate level loss only to the extent of his actual investment in the corporation, whether in the form of stock or debt. If the taxpayer has insufficient investment to use the loss currently, the loss is suspended until the investment is increased, for example, by additional capital contributions or by the recognition of corporate-level income which in effect increases the investment.

Special rules apply if the corporation which has elected pass-thru treatment had previously done business as a "normal" corporation subject to the two-level tax system. The rules are intended to ensure that any previously earned but undistributed corporate income is subject to a second shareholder level tax when distributed. Thus complex "stacking" rules are provided that determine whether distributions are deemed to be from current or prior earnings. Similarly, appreciation which was accrued but unrecognized at the time the corporation became subject to the pass-thru regime may be subject to a double-level tax to approximate the pattern of taxation which would have applied if the appreciation had been realized and distributed while the corporation was subject to the two-level tax system.

While the corporate level income and deduction items are subject to the special pass-thru rules, the other normally applicable tax rules continue to apply to the corporation. Thus, for example, a reorganization is possible between a "normal" corporation and a pass-thru corporation.

None of the other countries here under consideration have special pass-thru treatment for formally organized corporations. However, in *Canada*, full imputation relief is only extended to Canadian-owned "private" corporations, those whose stock is not publicly traded on an exchange. In *Australia*, government-sponsored committees twice recommended a pass-thru regime like the American approach, but no action was taken.

Many countries have more restrictive rules dealing with closely-held companies. In *Sweden*, rules are provided to prevent income from services from being converted to (more lightly taxed) income from capital. The special situation dealt with is dividends from closely-held corporations where the shareholder works on behalf of the corporation. A yield on the shareholder capital invested in the corporation is calculated based on the government borrowing rate plus 5 %. Dividends up to this amount are taxed as income from capital. Dividends above this amount are treated as income from employment in the hands of the shareholder. The dividends are not deductible at the corporate level but also are not subject to social security tax at the corporate level. Given the levels of corporate and social security tax, the result is that the total tax burden on actual salary distributions and "deemed" salary in the form of excess dividends is roughly the same.

Other countries have similar rules to prevent closely-held corporations from taking advantage of possible rate differentials between individual and corporate level taxation. In the *United States*, the reduced rates of tax available to corporations with low amounts of income are not available to personal service corporations owned by employees. In addition, undistributed investment income realized by closely-held investment companies can be subject to a special penalty tax.

As previously mentioned, in *Germany* additional restrictions apply to arrangements between a controlling shareholder (as defined) and the corporation. In addition to the normal arm's length rule, the agreement must be legally valid, clearly expressed and concluded in advance of the transaction in question.

In *Australia*, in the context of private companies, loans to shareholders can be treated as dividends which are not entitled to the imputation credit and cause a loss of potential credit at the company level. A similar restriction applies to excess employee benefits.

The *United Kingdom* also has restrictive rules which apply to closely-held companies, defined as companies where five or fewer "participators" have control of the company. Special rules apply to directors and creditors who can qualify as participators. If the company meets the definition of "close," a loan to a participator is subject to advance corporate tax as if it had been a distribution, though it remains nontaxable in the hands of the recipient. The tax is refunded if and when the loan is repaid. The usual rules applicable to employee fringe benefits are applicable to benefits extended to participators.

The following **Table III** summarizes some of the features of the corporate tax systems discussed in Part III. The notations "Partial imputation" or "Full imputation" refer to the degree to which the tax imposed at the corporate level is relieved in the hands of the shareholder when profits are distributed. The amount of unrelieved corporate tax on distributed profits is shown in the column headed "Residual corporate tax."

Some basic aspects of corporate taxation

	Basic approach	Corporate rate on retentions	Residual corporate tax on distributed profits	Total tax burden (corp tax + max. shareholder tax) on div. distr.	Profits require-ment for taxable distr.	Intercorp. dividend relief	Corp. level tax on distr. of apprec. property	Consol. taxation possible
Australia	full imputation	36%	0%	47%	yes	yes via rebate 100%	yes	no (some equiv. techniques)
Canada	partial imputation	30-46% (depending on province and type of income); lower for Can. small corps.	ca. 24% (depending on province and type of income); 0% in some cases for Can. small corps	51-67% depending on province; lower for Can. small corp.	no	yes (100% relief)	yes	no (some equiv. techniques)
France	full imputation	33%	0%	56.8% (60.7% with surcharge + additional levies)	yes	yes (100% relief)	yes	yes

Some basic aspects of corporate taxation

	Basic approach	Corporate rate on retentions	Residual corporate tax on distributed profits	Total tax burden (corp tax + max. shareholder tax) on div. distr.	Profits require-ment for taxable distr.	Intercorp. dividend relief	Corp. level tax on distr. of apprec. property	Consol. taxation possible
Germany	imputation/ split rate (full relief)	45%	0%	53% (plus surcharge; higher if local trade tax included)	no	yes (through general rules)	yes	yes
Japan	very limited imputation (10% credit)	37.5%	31.25%	62.25%	no	limited (80-100%)	yes	no
The Netherlands	Classical	35%	35%	74%	no	yes (5%+ share holding)	yes	yes
Sweden	classical	28%	28%	49%	no	yes (25%+ share holding)	yes	no (some equivalent techniques)
United Kingdom	partial imputation	33% (or lower)	16.25%	49.75%	no	yes	yes	no (some equivalent techniques)
United States	classical	34/35%	34/35%	60.74%	yes	limited (70-80-100%)	yes	yes

Subpart B: Partnership Taxation

All of the systems here under consideration have rules that allow the income and losses of certain types of commercial organizations to be passed directly through to the participants. These organizations are typically formed as partnerships for commercial law purposes and often the commercial law classification is determinative of the tax regime. In this Subpart, the reference to "partnership" is to an organization, typically but not necessarily organized as a commercial law partnership, to which pass-thru principles of taxation generally apply. Similarly, the reference to "partner" is to the participant to whom the income and losses are attributed.

The taxing patterns here under consideration are all based on the principle that the income of the partnership should be taxed directly to the individual partners in much the same way as if they had earned it directly. Within that framework, however, the techniques and mechanisms used to achieve pass-thru treatment and the actual results vary considerably as does the sophistication of the systems.

In some cases, in *Japan*, for example, there are no specific rules dealing with the taxation of partnerships and little administrative guidance. The same is true, to some extent, in *France* where case-developed principles are important but still leave a number of questions open. In the *United Kingdom*, there are limited statutory provisions dealing with partnerships. In other systems, partnerships have been used frequently, often in connection with tax shelter investments, and the principles are correspondingly highly developed. As usual, the *United States* seems to have the most highly articulated set of rules.

All of the systems, although generally using a pass-thru model, recognize the partnership and the partner as separate tax subjects for some purposes. Thus a consistent theme in all of the systems is the tension between "aggregate," pass-thru treatment in some situations and "entity" treatment in other situations. For example, in some systems, loans made by a partner to the partnership are treated in the same fashion as loans by third parties; interest payments are taxed to the partner making the loan and the interest deduction which arises at the partnership level is deducted by the appropriate partners. To the extent that interest income is treated differently from business profits, the characterization of the income as interest controls. In other systems, the partnership-partner loan is disregarded and the "interest" payments are treated as a distribution of partnership income, with corresponding tax results. The following materials first examine the basic methods of implementing a pass-thru taxation system and then look at several situations in which the aggregate-entity issues arise.

1. Qualification for pass-thru taxation

In most of the systems, entities are treated as partnerships for tax purposes and taxed on a pass-thru basis if they are formally organized under commercial partnership statutes. In addition, more informal arrangements for pooling assets and labor in a business activity may be found to be partnerships for tax purposes. Thus, in the *United States*, any cooperative activity aimed at a profit that goes beyond simple co-ownership of property will be treated as a partnership for tax purposes (assuming that it is not classified as a corporation). The *Canadian* rules are similar. There is no definition of partnership for tax purposes but the typically very broad (provincial) commercial law definition of a partnership as a business carried on jointly with a view to a profit covers most arrangements which extend beyond co-ownership. This characterization is controlling for tax purposes.

The statutory definition in *Sweden* initially included formal partnerships as well as any other "joint" activities which were not specifically dealt with in other tax provisions. Recent changes, however, have limited the definition to organizations which are formally registered as partnerships.

In *France*, there is no general definition of a partnership for tax purposes. Tax status as a partnership is based on a specific enumeration of types of entities, the income of which is taxed directly to the participants.

The definitional rules in *Australia* are quite extensive (going so far as to treat jointly owned property that generates income as a partnership), though the possibility of joint ventures that are not classified as partnerships allows certain operations, typically in the natural resource field, to be treated as in effect separate enterprises of each participant. In the *United Kingdom*, there is no formal definition of partnership as such. The partnership rules apply to joint undertakings which, unlike clubs or associations, are organized to do business. However, income from jointly owned property will not of itself be treated as partnership income.

In *The Netherlands* there are no specific provisions defining the forms of organization which will be subject to pass-thru taxation. Instead, all associations that are not covered by the generic definitions of taxable entities in the corporate tax law are transparent for tax purposes and the income is taxed directly to the participants. A special rule applies to a limited partnership with transferable shares. For these purposes, the partnership is split into two parts. The income allocable to the limited interests is subject to the corporate tax structure; income at the partnership level is subject to corporate tax and distributions are again taxed to the limited partners when distributed. The income allocated to the general partners is directly taxable to them.

In the *German* system, characterization of the organization as a partnership for civil law purposes is a necessary precondition for partnership tax treatment. In addition, there are some special tax rules. In particular, the partner must participate in any appreciation in the value of the assets, at least on the liquidation of the partnership.

Partnerships organized under the Commercial Code in *Japan* are taxed as corporations. While it is possible to organize partnerships under the Civil Code, this form is unusual and there are no statutory rules for their taxation. Some administrative guidance indicates that the partnership would be treated as a pass-thru entity and its partners taxed as if they had received the income directly. Similarly, the contractual relation set up in an "undisclosed association" results in the direct taxation of the undisclosed participants' share of the net income or loss in accordance with the contractual arrangement.

2. Basic structure of pass-thru taxation

In the *United States*, income and deductions arising at the partnership level are either aggregated at the partnership level or are passed through directly to the individual partners to the extent that special computations may be necessary at the partner level. For example, capital gains and losses are separately stated so that they may be aggregated with the individual partner's gains and losses. Most elections, e.g., method of depreciation, are made at the partnership level and are binding on the partners. The partnership income is included in the tax year of the partner in which the partnership's tax year ends, independently of whether it is distributed. There are restrictions to prevent manipulation of the tax years to achieve tax deferral.

The partner's tax cost in his partnership interest is increased by the amount of income attributed to him and decreased by distributions and losses. Distributions are only taxable to the extent they exceed the partner's tax cost in his interest in the partnership. Tax-exempt income increases the tax cost of the interest to avoid an indirect tax on the income on a sale of the interest. Losses incurred at the partnership level can be deducted currently only to the extent of the partner's tax cost in his partnership interest.

Complex rules deal with the allocation of income and deductions among the partners. In very general terms, special allocations of items of income and deductions, i.e., allocations which differ from the normal profit and loss sharing arrangement, will be respected for tax purposes only if they have "substantial economic effect." In other words, the allocation for tax purposes must actually affect the economic situation of the partners apart from the tax consequences of the allocation. The economic effect of the allocation is generally determined by the partners' "capital accounts", which reflect the actual economic relations among the partners. Normally, allocation for tax purposes must be reflected in the capital accounts and those accounts must control the amounts which the partners would receive on the liquidation of the partnership. If a partner had a negative capital account, for example, as a result of receiving a larger share of partnership losses, that amount would typically have to be required to be made up on the liquidation of the partnership for the special allocation of the losses to be recognized. Since nonrecourse debt by definition will not have to be repaid by the partners, additional restrictions apply to deductions based on nonrecourse debt. The special allocation rules are enormously complex and have been criticized as unworkable for unsophisticated partnerships.

The *Canadian* system is in general quite similar though substantially simpler. Partnerships are not taxable entities and the partner's share of the partnership's income is taxed to him in the taxable year in which the partnership's taxable year ends. If a partnership interest is disposed of, the new partner is taxed on his share of the income as if he had been a partner for the entire year and the former partner is not taxable on his share of the partnership's income for the year. The source and character of the income earned by the partnership flows through to the partners. Distributions are not taxable, regardless of whether they are characterized as income or capital distributions. The partnership agreement in general controls the allocation of income and deductions among the partners. Rather than limiting special allocations by detailed regulatory rules, the allocation is subject to a general anti-avoidance rule which allows the allocation to be ignored if the "principal reason" for the disproportionate allocation is reduction or postponement of tax. A similar rule applies if the partners do not deal at arm's length.

The partner's cost basis in his interest is increased by his share of undistributed income and decreased by distributions and losses. Adjustments are made to ensure that income or losses that are subject to special treatment are appropriately reflected in the partnership basis. Thus, for example, where only three-quarters of capital gains are included in income, the full amount of the gain increases the partner's basis to ensure that the gain is not in effect taxed when the interest is disposed of. Unlike the situation in the United States, the cost in the partnership interest can become "negative" if losses in excess of the investment are passed through to the partner. The "negative" basis will increase the gain on the disposition of the partnership interest.

The partnership rules in *Sweden* follow the same general pattern. Income is computed at the partnership level and then attributed through to the individual partners. The income is taxed as business income. The use of losses has been substantially restricted after an explosion of tax-shelter activities in the 1980s. For individual partners, losses from a partnership can only be used against income from the same partnership. Perhaps as a result of this limitation, the rules on special allocations are not well developed. The partner's basis in the partnership interest is increased by capital contributions and retained taxable earnings and reduced by withdrawals and tax deductible losses.

In the *United Kingdom*, the income is calculated at the partnership level according to the schedular system and then each partner pays tax with reference to his share. For capital gains tax purposes, however, the partnership assets are deemed to be owned and disposed of by the individual partners.

In *The Netherlands*, the system is somewhat different. The character of income is basically determined at the individual level. Thus, for example, income of a limited partner is income from capital, in general, since the activities as a limited partner do not constitute a business. On the other hand, if the limited partnership interest is held in a (separate) business, the income would be business income. Each general partner is treated in respect of his share in the partnership's business as being involved in his own business undertaking. Consequently, where options such as rate of depreciation, formation of reserves, etc. are available, each partner may make his own individual choice. Contractual allocations are, in general, respected but limited partners may only offset losses to the extent of their actual contributions.

The *Australian* rules on income computation are a mix of partnership and partner level calculations. In general, gains or losses from the disposition of inventory and business activities are determined at the partnership level and passed through to the individual partners. Partnership agreement allocations are generally respected and based on the accounts at the end of the taxable year. While there is some potential for tax planning through manipulation of the timing of partnership accounts, this has not proved to be a problem. (There is a provision intended to prevent income splitting through family partnerships, which is no longer needed in light of the income attribution rules discussed in Part Two.) Various tax attributes (foreign tax credit, imputation credit, etc.) also flow through. However, capital gains are taxed at the partner level as if each partner had disposed of his share of the partnership capital assets. This treatment applies whether there is a sale of a partnership asset or of the partnership interest, the admission of a new partner, or a change in the relations of existing partners.

Under the *German* system, the character of the income for purposes of schedular classification takes place at the partnership level. However, if the general partner in a limited partnership is a corporation, all of the income in the partnership is usually treated as business income. Elections must be made at the partnership level and income and deductions are determined at that level. In general, no special allocation of income or losses is allowed and the general ratio of sharing profits and losses controls. Thus, for example, it is not possible to allocate foreign income to foreign partners. Special, and controversial, rules apply where the partner has provided assets that the partnership uses without a formal contribution to the capital of the partnership. Complex rules also restrict the ability of limited partners to deduct losses in excess of their capital contributions. Basically, the losses attributable to the partner cannot exceed his share of the assets of the partnership less the partnership-level liabilities, i.e., the net equity in the partnership.

In *France*, income is initially determined at the partnership level, with options or elections, e.g., method of depreciation, determined by the partnership. For purposes of applying the schedular system, in general the nature of the activities at the partnership level are determinative. However, in some situations, the partner's status, e.g., as a corporation, will affect the income classification and computation. The partnership agreement in general controls the allocation of income and loss and applies to the net result at the partnership level; no allocation of specific items of income or deduction is allowed. Each partner is taxed on his allocable share of the partnership's results regardless of whether or not it is distributed. In the French system, there is no ongoing adjustment to the partner's basis in his partnership interest for undistributed income or for distributions. Instead, adjustments are made in the selling price at the time the interest is disposed of for the partner's share of retained earnings.

3. Liabilities, basis and losses

Two basic patterns emerge in the treatment of liabilities at the entity level and their effect on the basis of the partner's interest in the partnership and the ability to take current loss deductions. Under the *United States* system, liabilities incurred at the partnership level are reflected in the partner's tax cost in his partnership interest. The liability is allocated to those partners who ultimately would have to pay the debt if the partnership assets were insufficient to pay the debt in the case of liquidation. This means that usually in a limited partnership, partnership level debt is allocated to the general partners and increases their tax cost; limited partners, who are not liable beyond their capital contributions, are not allocated any portion of the debt and accordingly cannot share in losses financed out of the liabilities. A special rule applies to "nonrecourse" debt, that is, debt which is secured only by the property in question and for which no partner is personally liable. In general, such debt is allocated in accordance with the partners' share of partnership profits. Since no partner is responsible for the debt personally, it will be repaid, if at all, out of partnership profits and is so allocated for tax cost purposes.

The *Dutch* system follows essentially the general principle that liabilities incurred at the partnership level are treated at the level of the partners as if incurred directly. However, it does not have the complex set of allocation rules present in the United States.

In contrast, in *Sweden* and *Canada*, liabilities incurred at the partnership level do not affect the cost basis of the partner in his partnership interest. However, there is no restriction on the ability of a general partner to deduct his share of losses at the partnership level in excess of his actual investment (capital plus retained earnings) in the partnership. Excess losses are accounted for by allowing a "negative" basis in the partner interest which increases the potential gain on the disposition of the interest. In both systems, losses allocated to a limited partner are restricted to the amount of his capital investment.

The *German* system is similar. Liabilities incurred at the partnership level do not affect the partner's basis in his partnership interest. Where limited partners are involved, existence of the liability is taken into account in calculating the partner's equity in the partnership and deductions are correspondingly limited.

In *France*, there is no limitation on the pass-thru of losses to the investment in the partnership, though other quarantining rules may be applicable. For example, if the partnership's activity consists of holding rental real estate, the deductibility of the loss would be restricted. Similarly, liabilities at the partnership level have no effect on the tax treatment of partnership operations but are relevant when the partnership interest is sold.

In the *United Kingdom*, losses sustained by the partnership are claimed by the partners separately. If the allocation of losses results in losses for some partners and profits for others, the losses are reduced to the net amount of partnership loss. Limited partners can, generally speaking, only deduct losses to the extent of their contribution to the partnership.

4. Transactions between partner and partnership

The systems vary considerably in the extent to which transactions between the partner and the partnership will be given independent significance for tax purposes. Under *United States* rules, if a partner engages in a transaction with the partnership "other than in his capacity as a partner," the form of the transaction is generally respected. Thus a partner can receive compensation for services rendered to the partnership or for money loaned to the partnership with a corresponding deduction or capital expense at the partnership level. In addition, the statute recognizes a special form of partner-partnership relation where the partner is guaranteed a payment regardless of partnership profits. Such payments are treated in some respects as payments to third parties for purposes of determining taxation of the recipient partner and the deductibility of the payment at the partnership level.

The rules in *Canada* are generally similar. The partnership is usually treated as a separate entity for tax purposes. A partner can lend funds to the partnership or perform services for it. The latter principle is also followed in *The Netherlands*, though its application in the international context is not clear. _

In the *United Kingdom*, for income tax purposes the partner can have dealings with the partnership as a third party, for example, a lease of property to the partnership will result in rental income to the partner and a corresponding deduction to the partnership. The rules are more complex for capital gains tax purposes as each partner is deemed to own directly his share of the capital assets. Thus a disposal of an asset by a partner to the partnership will be treated as only a partial disposal since the partner retains an interest in the asset.

In *Sweden*, transactions between partner and partnership are ignored. This can be important because the treatment of income as income from services, from capital, or from business may result in different tax treatment at the partner level. Payments by the partnership for partner services or capital are not deductible by the partnership or includable by the partner. The increased partnership income is simply allocated to the partners under normal principles and keeps the character it had in the hands of the partnership.

The *Australian* rules are somewhat similar to the Swedish system though they rest on a different principle. Under private law principles, a partner cannot be an employee of the partnership and any purported "wages" paid to the partner are treated as partnership distributions. This characterization is followed for tax purposes. Similarly, loans by partners which bear interest but are accounted for as interest-bearing capital or retained profits will not generate interest income or corresponding deductions. Other partner loans, however, may be respected.

Similarly, in *France*, since all the participants are considered as co-owners of the operation, in general, no employment relation can exist between the partnership and a partner and everything which a partner receives is deemed to be part of the profit allocation the parties have agreed on. There are some exceptions, however. Rentals of property between partner and partnership are respected; the rental payments are deductible by the partnership and treated as rental income or commercial profits in the hands of the partner, depending on the circumstances. In addition, interest on partner current account loans is deductible, subject to the limitation that the rate does not exceed the average bond rate. To the extent deductible, the interest is treated as securities income by the partner; any excess is treated as partnership income allocated to the partner.

Germany reaches somewhat similar results with different techniques. Payments for services, interest on loans or rental payments on leased property received by a partner from a partnership are accounted for in a separate "special" balance sheet and are in effect included in the partnership income which is then allocated to the partners under the usual rules.

5. Disposition of partnership interest.

While most of the systems in general treat the disposition of a partnership interest as the disposition of a separate asset, thus following an entity approach, some require fragmentation. In the *United States*, a partnership interest is treated as a capital asset and gain or loss is treated accordingly. However, where the partnership holds certain assets the sale of which would generate ordinary income, in particular appreciated inventory and property subject to depreciation recapture, then the sale of the partnership interest generates ordinary income to that extent. *Sweden* also treats the partnership interest as a separate asset and the gain or loss on the disposition is treated as income from capital. *Canada* as well treats the gain or loss on the disposition of a partnership interest as capital gain.

In contrast, in *The Netherlands*, the tax treatment of the gain on disposition depends on the character of the partnership's operating income. If that income is treated as business income in the hands of the individual partner, then the gain or loss will similarly be business income. However, if the income is treated as income from capital, then the gain on the disposition is not subject to tax, since private capital gains of individuals are not generally taxed. If the partner is a corporation, the gain is subject to full corporate tax. The underlying theory is that the partnership, viewed from an aggregate point of view, is simply the sum of the activities of the individual partners. As indicated, the principle extends to allowing, for example, different depreciation methods for different partners for the same asset.

Germany follows the same pattern. The nature of the partnership activities (trade or business, agriculture, etc.) will determine the treat-ment of the gain or loss on the partnership interest.

The *Australian* approach operates on the theory that there is no partnership interest separate from the assets of the partnership. A num-ber of questions have been raised concerning the operation of the capi-tal gains rules in the partnership context which have been resolved as a practical matter by the tax office's flexible interpretation of the new statute. However, the elaboration of the treatment of partnerships in the capital gains setting is in its early stages.

The *United Kingdom* treats any change in ownership interests in a partnership as a disposal of partnership assets.

Several of the systems allow the "inside" basis of partnership assets to be adjusted when there is a sale of a partnership interest. In *Germany*, such an adjustment is mandatory. As a result, the "inside" and "outside" bases of partnership assets and partnership interests are always the same. The increased tax cost at the partnership level is related only to the purchasing partner's tax calculation and is account-ed for in a special "complementary" balance sheet. For purposes of determining the deductibility of losses by a limited partner, the assets shown on the "complementary" balance sheet are considered as part of his equity in the partnership.

The *United States* has similar rules in the case of the sale of a partnership interest, but the system is elective.

The *French* system is different from the others in several respects. During partnership operations, no adjustment to basis in the partner-ship interest is made for distributions, retained earnings taxed to the partner, or losses which have been passed through and deducted. Instead, adjustments are in effect postponed until the interest is sold. Thus, under case law principles, the selling price is decreased by the partner's share of retained earnings and increased by losses which have been passed through to the partner. However, these points have only been established in limited circumstances and many aspects of adjust-ments on sales are uncertain.

As for the gain or loss on the disposition, its treatment depends on a complex set of rules involving in part the status of the partner and in part the nature and extent of activities of the partnership. For instance, regardless of partnership activities, for corporate partners and individual proprietorships holding a partnership interest, a gain or loss is treated as a business capital gain or loss subject to a preferential rate or to the usual loss limitations if long term. The same result applies where the partnership is involved in a trade or business or professional activity and the interest is disposed of by an individual partner who is involved in the business. If the partnership is engaged in real estate or securities investment, the gain, unless realized by a corporate or sole proprietorship partner, is treated as falling within the category of private capital gains.

6. Liquidation of the partnership

When the partnership is liquidated, potential gain or loss may be present both at the partnership level and the partner level, depending on the relation between the fair market value of the partnership assets, their tax cost in the hands of the partnership, and the tax cost of the partnership interest in the hands of the partners. The systems differ substantially on the treatment of the potential gain or loss involved.

The *United States* system provides the most extensive deferral of gain or loss recognition. As a general rule, if property other than cash is distributed, there is no recognition of gain or loss at either the partnership or partner level and the partner's tax cost in his partnership interest becomes the tax cost for the property received. If cash is received, it first reduces the tax cost of the partner's interest and may result in gain to the extent it exceeds that amount. Any additional property received would correspondingly take a zero tax cost. A loss may be recognized if only cash or certain ordinary income assets are distributed.

The situation is more complex if the assets are not distributed pro rata and the partnership holds certain assets the sale of which would have generated ordinary income. In effect, the partners are treated as having made a taxable exchange of the assets to the extent that they receive non-pro rata amounts.

Other systems have more extensive recognition on liquidation. In *Sweden*, the distribution of the property is viewed as a removal of the property from business use unless the property continues to be used in the business of the partner. The withdrawal would result in gain recognition under normal principles. In addition, if the value of the property exceeds the partner's basis in his partnership interest (increased for the gain recognized on the withdrawal), the partner may recognize additional gain since the liquidation is treated as a taxable disposition of the partnership interest.

The *Canadian* rules have the same basic structure. However, there are other possibilities of rollover relief. If the partners receive undivided interests in the property there is no current recognition. In addition, if a single partner continues the business, no gain or loss is recognized as to that partner. Similarly, in the *United Kingdom*, if each partner receives his fractional share of partnership assets, there will be no current recognition of gain which will be deferred through an adjustment to the tax cost of the assets received. If the distributions are non-pro rata, gains will be recognized currently to that extent.

In *Germany*, the distribution of the partnership's property is viewed as a removal of the property from the business which results in the recognition of gain, though the gain would qualify for preferential rate treatment. In addition, if the property is transferred to a business of a partner, the distribution is treated on a tax-deferred basis.

France also treats the liquidation of the partnership as a recognition event for capital gains arising on the cessation of the business. Retained earnings which have previously been taxed may be received on a tax-free basis.

In *The Netherlands*, the same approach is taken as on the disposition of a partnership interest. The transaction is a taxable event and the character of the gain or loss depends on the character of the partnership interest in the hands of the partner as business or investment.

Part Four: International Taxation

The patterns of international taxation examined here show a high degree of similarity, despite significant differences in technical detail. This broad consensus stems in large part from early efforts in international cooperation, particularly in the context of the League of Nations. Those efforts both produced and reflected the conceptual framework for allocating taxing rights in an international context which became the basis of most of the present systems here considered. Generally speaking, a right to tax is asserted on the basis of the personal connection of the taxpayer to the taxing jurisdiction. Most typically that claim extends to all income, though one country does not assert personal taxing jurisdiction over foreign business income of resident corporate taxpayers. Similarly, all jurisdictions claim the right to tax income which can be said to have its "source" within the country, regardless of the personal status of the recipient.

The problem of overlapping tax claims that arise from the parallel assertion of personal and source jurisdiction by different states to the same item of income is resolved by the state of personal jurisdiction ceding either the primary or exclusive jurisdiction to tax to the state in which the income arises. In the former situation, the primacy of source country jurisdiction is recognized through the mechanism of a credit for foreign taxes. In the latter, the income arising outside the jurisdiction is exempted from tax in the jurisdiction of personal connection and taxed exclusively in the source jurisdiction. These broad principles are implemented in both domestic legislation and in bilateral treaty relationships.

The following Subpart A examines the issues which arise in the assertion of personal taxing jurisdiction and the mechanisms for the relief of double taxation. Subpart B considers the structure of source-based taxation and Subpart C examines some selected additional international issues.

Subpart A: Residence Taxation

1. Bases for the assertion of personal taxing jurisdiction

1.1 Individuals

Personal taxing jurisdiction over individuals is typically asserted on the basis of "residence" and is often referred to as residence jurisdiction. The determination of residence often rests on a facts-and-circumstances test which looks at the various social and economic connections the taxpayer has to the taxing jurisdiction as well as the taxpayer's intent with regard to his stay and his connections to other jurisdictions. This general test is frequently supplemented with a mechanical test based on the number of days present in the jurisdiction. Residence for tax purposes may or may not be connected with residence in terms of immigration status.

The *United States* approach combines objective and facts-and-circumstances tests. A person is resident for tax purposes if he possesses the right to permanent entry to the United States under the immigration laws (a so-called "green card") or if he is physically present in the jurisdiction for 183 days or more during the taxable year. In addition, he may be treated as a resident if he is present in the jurisdiction thirty-one days or more and meets a cumulative presence test which looks to the days present in the current year and in the past two years. If the total days in the present year and the weighted days for the past two years is 183 or more, the individual will be a resident for tax purposes unless he can establish that his "tax home," usually his principal place of business, is in another country, and he has a "closer connection" to that country than to the United States. The factors in establishing the "closer connection" are those which are typically used in a residence determination. Special rules apply for students and diplomats which allow them to be present in the country without triggering the mechanical physical presence tests.

Unlike other jurisdictions, the United States also asserts personal jurisdiction based on citizenship. United States citizens are, in principle, taxable on their worldwide income regardless of where they are resident. This basis for personal jurisdiction increases the possibility of overlapping claims for worldwide taxation, an issue that is frequently dealt with in U.S. tax treaties.

In *Canada*, residence is, in general, determined on a case-by-case basis, applying a case law-developed set of factors including the availability of a dwelling in Canada, the residence of family members, physical presence, and social and economic ties. Once residence is established, the intention to return to Canada is relevant in cases where the taxpayer has left the jurisdiction. In addition, a specific statutory provision deems a person resident of Canada if he "sojourns" there for 183 days during the taxable period. The meaning of the term "sojourn" is not entirely clear but it is not synonymous with physical presence; for example, if a person is resident in Canada for part of the year, he is not "sojourning" in Canada.

Australia also applies a facts-and-circumstances test which turns on being "domiciled" in Australia and having no "permanent place of abode" outside the country. Physical presence for more than one-half of the tax year also constitutes residence unless the taxpayer can establish that his usual place of abode is abroad and he does not have the intent of taking up residence in Australia. A special rule treats as residents certain governmental employees who would not normally be taxed under the usual residence rules but typically would be exempt from tax in the foreign jurisdiction to which they were posted.

The *United Kingdom* similarly has no comprehensive definition of residence for individuals and the issue is decided on a facts-and-circumstances approach. This general test is supplemented by a special provision that treats an individual as resident if he is physically present in the United Kingdom for six months or more in the tax year (April 6th to April 5th). As an administrative matter, an individual will be treated as resident if he makes "substantial and habitual" visits. Visits are habitual if they extend over a four-year period and are substantial if they exceed three months.

In *The Netherlands*, the statute requires residence to be determined "according to the circumstances" and case law has focused on "durable ties of a personal nature" to Holland. The principal focus is on the existence of a home in Holland and the abode of the family. Civil servants who are Dutch citizens are deemed to be resident in Holland.

In *Sweden*, an individual is regarded as resident if he has a "real dwelling and home" in Sweden or Sweden is his "habitual abode." This latter test has been interpreted as being met if the taxpayer is continuously present in Sweden for six months. As discussed below,

Sweden also has a complex set of rules which continue to tax residents who have left the jurisdiction but retain substantial connections to Sweden.

Germany treats an individual as resident for tax purposes if he has either his residence or habitual place of abode in the jurisdiction. An individual is only a tax resident if these tests are met; there is generally no option to be treated as a resident even when that could be beneficial for tax purposes (though E.U. case law may require the option in certain situations). Residence is based on the availability to the taxpayer of a home (house, apartment, etc.) which he intends to retain and use. There is a highly developed case law applying this facts-and-circumstances test. Some of the factors considered are the period of time during which the home is used and the regularity and frequency of the use. "Habitual abode" is established by presence in Germany indicating an intention to stay more than temporarily. In practice, a continuous stay of six months (even if spanning two calendar years) will constitute a habitual abode, though there are nuances in the rules.

The *French* system has an extensive statutory definition of residence. Individuals are resident for tax purposes if they have their permanent home in France, or, if their permanent home cannot be determined, if they are physically present in the jurisdiction for over 183 days. In addition, professional or employment activity in France will lead to resident treatment unless the taxpayer can establish that the activity is secondary to activities performed elsewhere. Finally, if the taxpayer has his "center of economic interest" in France, he will be treated as resident regardless of the nature of the activity.

The focus in the *Japanese* statute is on both domicile, defined as the base of personal operations, and more than a year of residence, defined as the place of day-to-day living. An administrative regulation provides that if a person is engaged in a business that ordinarily requires living in the country for one year, he will be treated, unless otherwise provided, as domiciled in Japan for tax purposes when he arrives in the country. However, if personal connections to Japan are significant, domicile will be present even if business activities are conducted outside Japan for significant periods of time. Here the tax law provisions are interpreted in light of the civil law concepts of domicile and the administrative rule is not the exclusive test for domicile.

Japan also distinguishes between ordinary residents and "short-term" residents. A short-term resident is one who meets the normal residence test but does not intend to remain permanently in Japan and has not maintained a residence for five years. Short-term residents are only taxed on domestic source income and foreign source income which is remitted to Japan.

1.2 Corporations

Two basic approaches are used in establishing a personal jurisdictional connection for corporations. One is to focus on some formal legal connection to the jurisdiction such as incorporation or registry in the commercial register. The other is to select some economic or commercial connection such as the place of management, principal business location, or less frequently, residence of shareholders. Many jurisdictions combine these approaches, treating a corporation as resident if either test is satisfied. In some cases, the test of place of management becomes in effect a formal test by focusing on easily controlled events like the place at which the board of directors meets, rather than the situs of day-to-day management decisions.

The *United States* is an example of a jurisdiction which relies on a purely formal test. All corporations organized under the laws of the United States or one of the Federal States are treated as "domestic," i.e., resident, corporations, regardless of any other connection to the jurisdiction. Conversely, all other corporations are "foreign," i.e., non-resident, corporations, even if all of their commercial and economic activities are linked to the U.S. *Japan* also has a formal test, though the technical structure of the rule is somewhat different. Under the statutory definition of resident corporation, a corporation is resident if its "headquarters" or "principal office" is located in Japan. However, these concepts are derived from civil law and commercial law and under those provisions, all corporations incorporated in Japan must have either a registered headquarters (Commercial Code) or a registered principal office (Civil Code) in Japan, thus in effect turning the test into one of incorporation in the case of domestically-organized corporations. On the other hand, a corporation organized in a foreign country can have a registered principal office or headquarters in Japan (if that is possible under the laws of the incorporating jurisdiction) and will also be treated by Japan as a resident corporation.

Sweden also has a formal test which turns on formation and registration under Swedish corporate law.

The *Commonwealth* countries, which traditionally focused on the place of central management and control to determine corporate residence, now combine that test with a test based on formal incorporation. Thus, in the *United Kingdom* prior to 1988, the only test was the factual one of central management and control of the company's business, which was generally, though not conclusively, where the board of directors met. In 1988, this test was supplemented by an incorporation rule which made companies incorporated in the U.K. resident there but left companies incorporated elsewhere to be liable to U.K. resident status under the old rule.

The *Canadian* rules follow the United Kingdom pattern. Either incorporation or place of management in Canada will result in resident treatment. The case law has focused primarily on the place of the meeting of the board of directors, thus giving the test a formal character, though in some situations the courts have examined the question of actual day-to-day control.

Australia has a similar approach. Formal incorporation under Australian law will cause the corporation to be treated as resident. In addition, if the corporation is doing business in Australia and has its place of central management in Australia, it is likewise resident. Since having management in Australia is deemed to constitute doing business there, the test is effectively based on the second factor. The Australian rules also take into consideration the residence of the shareholders. If a corporation is doing business in Australia and a majority of voting power is held by Australian residents, the corporation will be viewed as resident. However, the shareholder test is applied without attributing share ownership through interposed companies and can be avoided by interposing a nonresident entity between the corporation and the ultimate Australian shareholders.

Both *Germany* and *The Netherlands* combine incorporation and management tests. In Germany, a corporation is resident if it has its "statutory seat" in Germany. Since all corporations formed under German corporate law are required to designate a statutory seat in the jurisdiction, they are automatically treated as resident. In addition, if a corporation organized under foreign law has its place of management in Germany, it is treated as a resident taxpayer. The focus is on the activities of day-to-day management and not on the supervisory activities of the legal organ roughly equivalent to the (outside) board of directors.

The Netherlands similarly uses both formal incorporation and, as with individuals, a determination "according to the circumstances."

Case law gives great weight to the place of effective management, i.e. where the day-to-day management takes place. In this regard factors such as residence of directors, and location of board meetings, business and head office may be considered relevant circumstances. In *France*, a corporation formed under French law and having its registered office in France is treated as a resident. However, since France applies the territorial system to corporations, the law on corporate residence is not highly developed as to, for example, the extent to which a corporation must have its place of actual management in France in connection with its registered office.

2. Change of status

2.1 Change of status of individuals

Changing factual circumstances may cause an individual to establish or terminate resident status in a particular jurisdiction. A number of technical issues arise in connection with a change in personal taxing jurisdiction. From the perspective of the receiving country, the principal question is how to establish the "tax history" of the new tax subject. Here, there are basically two approaches. One is, in effect, to reconstruct past events as if they had taken place while the taxpayer was subject to the taxing system of the receiving jurisdiction and then use these historical factors in determining current tax liability. Thus, for example, the historical cost of an asset, adjusted for notional depreciation, could be used to determine the gain on the disposition of the asset in the new jurisdiction. Alternatively, a "fresh start" approach could be taken which focused on market values at the time residence was established.

From the perspective of the departing jurisdiction, the issue is what, if any, attempts should be made to enforce taxing claims on income which arose while the taxpayer was a resident. One approach would be to treat the departure as a realization event for any income which would not later be subject to tax in the hands of the departing taxpayer. Alternatively, modifications may be made to the normal taxing pattern for nonresidents to allow the continued taxation of former residents on certain types of income.

The *United States* uses historical cost of assets in principle, though the rules are not well developed. Termination of residence is not a realization event and there are no general rules extending the tax jurisdiction to former residents. However, in the case of citizens who expatriate for tax-avoidance purposes, an extended tax jurisdiction is applied. Rather than being subject to the usual tax rates and taxing pattern applicable to nonresidents, the former citizen who expatriates and becomes a nonresident is taxed on his U.S source income as if he had remained a citizen. In addition, certain items of income which under normal source rules would be foreign source are treated as U.S. source and hence, subject to tax. The most important source change involves stock or securities in U.S. corporations which are treated as generating U.S source income and subject to net basis taxation. This special taxing pattern extends for ten years after expatriation. Similar rules apply to residents who give up residency, are nonresidents for a period, and then reestablish residence. Thus, it is not possible to avoid U.S. tax on gain on U.S. securities by temporarily breaking the residence period.

Some highly publicized cases of tax-motivated expatriation where expatriates were able to avoid the previously described provisions have led to legislative proposals to treat expatriation as a realization event. The assets held at the time of expatriation would be treated as if sold at fair market value on the expatriation date. Similar treatment would be applied to long-term residents who subsequently lost resident status. An alternative proposal to strengthen the existing expatriation rules and extend them to residents who become nonresidents is also under legislative consideration.

Canada deals with these issues by giving new residents a tax cost for property equal to its fair market value at the time the individual becomes a resident. Thus, only appreciation or depreciation which takes place during the period of residence is taken into account for Canadian tax purposes. Similarly, when an individual ceases to be a resident, he is deemed to have disposed of the property for its fair market value, generating a current gain or loss. An exception is made for property over which Canada still asserts taxing jurisdiction ("taxable Canadian property") such as real estate located in Canada. In some circumstances, Canada extends its taxing right to former residents. If a former resident receives employment income from a Canadian resident, the income remains taxable in Canada unless the taxpayer can establish that the services were rendered abroad and the income is subject to foreign tax.

The *Australian* system is similar. When a nonresident becomes a resident, he is deemed to have acquired assets at their then market value.

When residence is terminated, gain is deemed to be realized on all assets over which Australia does not retain source-based taxation rights, thus ensuring that all (and only) appreciation which took place during the period of Australian residence is subject to tax. It is also possible to elect to defer the tax until the asset is actually disposed of, though in this case all appreciation is subject to tax. If the person terminating residence has not been a resident for five of the last ten years, there is no deemed realization on termination.

In contrast, the *United Kingdom* does not treat change of status as a taxable event and has no special rules for deemed acquisitions when resident status is established.

Sweden uses the historical cost as the basis for taxing gain of incoming residents. With respect to departing residents, there is a special rule which in effect extends the residence concept. If a taxpayer has been resident under the basic statutory definition but no longer is covered by that test, he will continue to be taxed as a resident if he maintains an "essential connection" to Sweden. There is a statutory catalogue of factors which are considered in determining if an essential connection is present. They include the factors of Swedish citizenship, period of former residence in Sweden, existence of permanent residence abroad, reason for being abroad, access to dwelling in Sweden, family business connections in Sweden, and other comparable circumstances. A special evidentiary rule applies if the taxpayer is a Swedish citizen or was a resident of Sweden under the normal rules for at least ten years. There, for the first five years after departure, the taxpayer is deemed to have an essential connection and has the burden of proof of negating sufficient of the factors to establish that no essential connection is present. Thereafter, the tax authorities have the burden of establishing the essential connection with respect to the same factors.

Sweden also retains the right to tax gain on the disposition of shares and other financial assets in Swedish corporations for ten years after departure. A related provision treats departure as a realization event with respect to shares of a foreign corporation (which would not be caught by the ten-year rule) if those shares had been received previously in a tax-deferred exchange.

Germany likewise uses historical cost in determining the tax consequences of transactions undertaken after an individual establishes residence. The termination of residence is generally not considered a realization event. However, in the case of "substantial participations" in companies which would have been taxable on disposition, termination of residence will be a realization event for gain (but not loss) purposes, if the individual has been a tax resident for at least ten years previously. In addition, special rules apply to German citizens who have been resident in Germany for an extended period and then transfer residence to a low-tax jurisdiction (or to no jurisdiction) if they maintain "substantial connections" to Germany. If the provisions apply, the former resident is taxed at the usually applicable domestic rates on income from German sources. The extended tax liability lasts for ten years after the termination of German residence.

The Netherlands has a highly developed system for dealing with the taxation of newly-arrived residents. Business assets which were not previously subject to Dutch tax take a fair market value basis. Existing Dutch business assets keep their historical cost. Where residence is terminated, there is generally a deemed disposition of business assets if none of the assets will any longer generate business income taxable in The Netherlands, though the fiscal authorities recently interpreted this rule as requiring recognition on an asset-by-asset basis. As for nonbusiness assets, the issue generally does not arise on immigration since gains on nonbusiness assets are not taxed. Taxable substantial participations take a fair market value basis. As to emigration, in general, termination of residence does not result in taxation, though The Netherlands retains taxing rights over substantial participations in resident companies and certain annuities and insurance policies if premiums have been deducted in Holland.

No special rules have been developed in *France* on the topic. The departing taxpayer is taxed on his worldwide income (subject to tax treaties) received or accrued before departure and not yet taxed. No gain is deemed realized on the taxpayer's assets and no special rule extends taxing jurisdiction as far as income tax is concerned.

Japan uses historical cost and has no special rules that extend taxing jurisdiction.

2.2 Change of status of corporations

The personal taxing jurisdiction over a corporation can change if the corporation is formally reincorporated or "continued" into another jurisdiction. In addition, for those countries using a management-and-control test of corporate residency, residency can change if modifications are made to the management structure or organization of the corporation. There are several models as to how change of corporate residence might be treated. One approach would be to treat the original domestic corporation as if it had been liquidated with the attendant consequences to the corporation and shareholders. The assets received by the shareholder would then be treated as if contributed to the nonresident corporation with the usual tax results for an outbound transaction in those circumstances. Alternatively, the domestic corporation could be viewed as transferring its assets to the nonresident corporation for its shares, followed by a liquidating distribution of those shares to the shareholders, again with the tax consequences which those transactions would have under normally applicable rules. Only a few of the jurisdictions here under consideration have fully developed rules dealing with this situation.

In the *United States*, the transaction in which a domestic corporation is reincorporated as a foreign corporation would be treated as a reorganization involving an outbound transfer. As a result, the normal nonrecognition treatment given reorganization exchanges would not be available automatically and both the deemed transfer of the assets by the domestic corporation and the deemed share exchange by the shareholders would, potentially, be taxable events. On the other hand, the "continuation" of a foreign corporation as a domestic corporation would in general be treated as a qualifying reorganization. As a result, the new resident corporation would continue the tax cost of the assets received and the shareholders would similarly transfer the tax cost of their old shares to the shares of the continued corporation.

In *Canada*, the same principles are applied to corporations as are applied to individuals. For a corporation which becomes resident in Canada, there is a "fresh start" fair market value for its assets other than taxable Canadian property and property of a business carried on in Canada. A new taxation year is deemed to commence at the time that the corporation becomes a resident of Canada. Loss carryovers are permitted only to the extent that they relate to businesses carried on in Canada.

In the case of a Canadian corporation that becomes nonresident by reincorporation or continuation into another jurisdiction and that is no longer managed or controlled in Canada, the "expatriation" is a realization event with respect to any property over which Canada does not retain taxing jurisdiction. The corporation's taxation year is deemed to have ended immediately before the emigration, and the corporation is deemed to have disposed of all of its assets for their fair market value immediately before that time. This deemed realization gives rise to capital gains and other tax consequences. In addition, a special departure tax of 25 % is imposed on the excess of the fair market value of its property over the aggregate of its paid-up capital and its liabilities. This special tax is intended to prevent corporations from avoiding the withholding tax on dividends by shifting their residence to another country. The 25 % rate is reduced if there is a reduced rate of withholding on dividends pursuant to a tax treaty.

The *United Kingdom* also has explicit rules dealing with the corporate change of residence. At one time, it was a criminal offense for a company to cease to be resident of the United Kingdom without the permission of the Treasury but this rule was repealed in 1990. In the case of a residence change, there is a deemed disposal of, in general, all assets over which the U.K. no longer has a source-based taxing claim. The tax can be postponed if the migrating company is a subsidiary of a parent company that remains resident.

Australia does not allow as a matter of company law the continuation of a Australian corporation into a foreign jurisdiction and outbound changes in place of incorporation are probably treated as liquidations. Foreign corporations can be continued into Australia under special procedures but the tax consequences are generally unclear. When a company is treated as a continuation, then any change of residence which follows the reincorporation in another country will give rise to a deemed acquisition or disposal under the capital gains rules dealing with changes of residence. The qualifications on these rules noted above in the case of individuals are limited to individuals and so the application of the rules is automatic for companies. Reincorporation in Australia will mean that the company becomes an Australian resident under the place of incorporation rule if it is not already.

In *Sweden*, a Swedish corporation cannot under corporate law change its status to become incorporated in a foreign state. If the corporation liquidates in order to reincorporate as a foreign corporation, the transaction will be taxable under normal rules. Where a Swedish corporation has its management abroad and, under the applicable tax treaty, the corporation is deemed to be a resident only of the other country, with the result that Sweden cannot tax non-Swedish source income, the transfer of management is treated as a deemed realization.

In *Germany*, several different situations must be distinguished. If a corporation transfers both its seat and place of effective management abroad for corporate law purposes, there is a liquidation of the corporation and in principle the normal rules on liquidation which require gain recognition on transferred assets would seem to be applicable. However, if the assets remain in a branch in Germany and continue to be subject to German taxing jurisdiction, some take the view that no recognition is required. If the seat of the corporation for corporate law purposes is transferred, but the place of effective management remained in Germany, while there is a technical liquidation, no gain should be recognized since the corporation remains a resident for tax purposes. If the place of effective management is transferred abroad while the seat remains in Germany in circumstances in which a treaty tie-breaker rule gives the taxing right to the other country, it is unclear to what extent recognition is required.

The transfer of the head office of a corporation from *France* to another country yields the immediate taxation of all income not yet subject to tax and is a realization event as far as capital gains are concerned, unless there exists between France and the host country a treaty providing for the continuation of the legal personality of the moving corporation. No such treaty has been concluded yet.

In *The Netherlands*, the transfer by a Dutch-incorporated corporation of management abroad will not affect Dutch taxing rights as corporate residence is still deemed to be in Holland by virtue of domestic incorporation. However, if under a treaty rule the other country has the exclusive right to treat the corporation as a resident, realization is required with respect to all assets over which Holland no longer has taxing rights.

Japan does not have a rule on Japanese corporations moving into a foreign jurisdiction.

2.3 Dual residence

Problems of dual residence are often dealt with in treaties that contain rules to establish a single residence jurisdiction for treaty purposes which in turn limits the taxing rights of the other country. Apart from treaty rules, some jurisdictions have special domestic legislation which prevents taxpayers from utilizing corporations which are treated as residents of two (or more) jurisdictions (so-called "dual resident" corporations) to deduct losses in both jurisdictions. For example, in the *United States*, special rules restrict the use of losses in the United

States by a dual resident company where the losses, generally speaking, can also be used in a foreign consolidated group. On the other hand, the rules do not in general prevent the corporation from using the losses to reduce its own income in both jurisdictions, e.g., through the mechanism of a loss carryover. Since the income is potentially taxable in both jurisdictions, allowance of the loss in these circumstances is not viewed as inappropriate. The perceived problem generally arises when the income which is being offset against the loss in the foreign consolidated group is not subject to the taxing claim of the United States.

In *Canada*, a dual resident corporation that is considered to be resident in another country pursuant to the provisions of a tax treaty is deemed not to be a resident of Canada. This provision has been reasonably effective in preventing most of the tax planning advantages of dual resident companies. Dual resident companies can still be utilized with respect to nontreaty countries.

Australia has also experienced problems with deductions, principally interest, being claimed by dual resident companies. The problem arose first in 1984 when the right to transfer losses among 100 % related companies was introduced. The response was to deny the right to transfer losses by dual resident investment companies. The definition of investment company effectively eliminated many of the dual resident financing structures. Like the Canadian system, the controlled foreign corporation provisions also have a rule which treats an otherwise dual resident corporation whose residence the treaty allocates to the other country as no longer a resident of Australia. It has been proposed to extend this approach to certain tax benefits available to residents such as the intercorporate dividend rebate.

The *United Kingdom* similarly has rules which restrict the use of losses and other reliefs by dual resident investment companies.

France, *Germany* and *The Netherlands* do not have any special statutory rules dealing with dual residence.

3. Mechanisms for relief of double taxation

All of the countries here under consideration have some domestic law mechanism for the relief of the double taxation which results when residence-based and source-based taxing claims are asserted on the same item of income The residence country generally eliminates double taxation by either exempting the item of income from its tax base or by giving a credit against the domestic tax liability for the foreign tax.

Under the foreign tax credit mechanism, foreign income is included in the tax base, and the prior right of the source country to tax is recognized by giving a credit for the foreign tax liability which displaces the normally applicable domestic liability. To the extent that the residence country rate is higher than the foreign rate, a residual domestic tax is collected but international double taxation has been eliminated. If the foreign rate is higher than the domestic rate, all domestic tax is eliminated, and again, double taxation has been avoided.

Beyond resolving the perceived inequity of subjecting the same taxpayer to conflicting taxing claims on the same income, from an economic point of view, the foreign tax credit system is generally viewed as consistent with an overall policy of capital export neutrality. That is, from the perspective of the residence country investor, the credit system tends to ensure that the choice between domestic or foreign investment will not be influenced by tax considerations. In practical operation, the credit systems here considered fall far short of this result, in particular where the tax rate in the foreign jurisdiction is higher than the domestic rate. In addition, in practice, the interaction of the various provisions dealing with international income often makes it difficult to determine if a particular rule does or does not further capital export neutrality. Nonetheless, especially in the context of portfolio investment, capital export neutrality has historically been an important factor in the decision to adopt or maintain a credit system.

International double taxation can also be avoided by exempting from domestic tax certain classes of foreign source income, thus ceding exclusive taxing jurisdiction to the country of source. If the foreign income is simply exempt, and does not affect the taxation of other foreign or domestic source income which is subject to tax, the result is essentially the same as not asserting jurisdiction to tax the income at all. More typically, the exempt income is taken into account in determining the tax treatment of other income, for example, in determining the applicable rate of tax in a progressive rate structure ("exemption with progression").

While the exemption technique is often contrasted with the credit approach, in actual operation the two methods of relieving double taxation often yield quite similar results. In the systems here considered, exemption is usually limited to specific categories of income, most typically active business or employment income, that are likely to be subject to a level of tax comparable to that which would have been applicable in the residence country. Where rates are roughly comparable, in a credit system the residence country will not collect any additional tax on the foreign source income, a result functionally equivalent to exempting the income. Ancillary differences are reduced still further if an "exemption with progression" technique is used.

Nonetheless, there may be some important differences in the effects of the two techniques in particular situations. While rates may be roughly similar in general terms, there may be important variations across industries and with respect to different companies and the choice of exemption means that residual domestic tax may not be collected in some significant cases. In addition, great pressure is put on the source rules, as the decision that a particular item of income is foreign source may mean that it is not taxed anywhere if the source rules of the two jurisdictions are not completely congruent. Similarly, transfer pricing differences have different implications in an exemption system.

Beyond its role as a mechanism for relieving potential double taxation, from a policy point of view, an exemption method is consistent with a policy of capital import or competitive neutrality. It ensures that the income from foreign activities will not be subjected to a higher rate of tax in the foreign jurisdiction than the rate faced by local competitors. It also ensures that foreign tax holidays or preferences are not "washed out" by additional residence country tax. These effects have been a factor in the decision of some countries to utilize the exemption technique.

Another aspect of the exemption technique which is often stressed is its relative administrative simplicity. Since the foreign income is simply exempt, there is no need to establish in detail the foreign tax burden on particular items of income. However, this asserted advantage over the credit system can be overstated, especially in the context of business taxation. As discussed below, while the exemption system eliminates some technical issues, it raises others. The level of simplicity or complexity seems less a question of the basic approach than the degree to which rough and simple solutions are accepted for administrative reasons.

Whatever their relative advantages and disadvantages, in practice, no country uses a "pure" exemption or "pure" credit approach. All of the countries here considered combine these two methods, exempting certain classes of income and giving credit for foreign taxes imposed on others. The relative "mix" between exemption and credit varies substantially, however. The *United States*, the *United Kingdom*, and *Japan* make most use of the credit approach while the *Continental* systems have more exemption features. *Canada* and *Australia* fall somewhere in the middle.

As to the specific systems, the *United States* employs a foreign tax credit for most foreign income, though there is a limited exemption for foreign earned income. The taxpayer has the choice between crediting or deducting foreign taxes. The credit is restricted to foreign income taxes which are comparable to U.S. income tax and are imposed on the item of income from foreign sources. The credit cannot exceed the U.S. tax on the foreign income. However, rather than tracing particular taxes to particular items or segments of income, the limitation is expressed in terms of a formula that allows high and low foreign taxes on various classes or "baskets" of foreign income to be averaged. The credit extends to taxes paid by foreign corporations in which a U.S. corporation owns at least 10 % of the voting stock (the "indirect" credit).

In *Japan*, the foreign tax credit system is also used and the taxpayer has the choice between crediting or deducting foreign taxes. Credit is given for all foreign income taxes as well as excess profits taxes and taxes on distributed earnings. The credit cannot exceed the Japanese tax on the foreign-source income. In general, an overall limitation is used that allows averaging of high and low taxed foreign income. However, there are certain limitations on averaging. For example, two-thirds of untaxed foreign-source income must be eliminated in calculating the credit. An indirect credit is available for 25 % or greater corporate shareholders.

The *United Kingdom* uses a mix of credit and exemption. The credit is limited to the foreign tax on each particular source of income, thus preventing averaging of foreign rates on directly received income. An indirect credit is allowed with respect to dividends received by resident corporate shareholders who own at least 10 % of the voting power of the payor foreign corporation. What is, in effect, an exemption may be allowed for foreign income earned as an employee working outside the UK if certain conditions are met. Similarly, an individual resident in the United Kingdom but not domiciled there may obtain what amounts to exemption by using the "remittance" basis of taxation and restricting the foreign income which is brought into the United Kingdom.

Canada uses both the foreign tax credit method and an exemption system for certain income. Credit is given for "income or profits" taxes paid by a resident taxpayer and is limited to the Canadian tax on the foreign-source income from sources in the particular country, a so-called "per country" limitation. A form of indirect credit is also available for taxes paid by foreign corporations in which there is a direct or indirect 10 % share ownership by a Canadian corporation. The credit takes the form of a grossed-up deduction which in effect limits the credit to the Canadian tax that would have been payable on the foreign income. In addition to the indirect credit, there is an exemption for dividends paid out of active business income from countries with which Canada has a tax treaty.

A similar combination of credit and exemption is used in *Germany*. The basic statutory system provides for worldwide taxation with a foreign tax credit for foreign income taxes on income determined to be foreign source under German source rules. The credit is limited to the amount of the German tax paid and the limitation is applied on a per country basis. An indirect credit is available for taxes paid by foreign corporations in which a domestic corporate shareholder has a direct or indirect 10 % interest. An indirect "tax sparing" credit is also allowed in cases involving developing countries. The taxpayer can also elect to deduct foreign taxes. A special rule allows taxation of foreign-source income at a flat reduced rate in certain circumstances with the approval of the tax authorities. In addition, foreign losses arising from, broadly speaking, foreign activities, that do not amount to an active trade or business, cannot be deducted against other categories of income.

In almost all of its treaties, Germany exempts business income (and dividends from subsidiaries) under varying conditions, sometimes requiring an active business in the foreign country or that the income be subject to tax there. In light of Germany's extensive treaty network, it is effectively an exemption country as far as business income is concerned.

Sweden allows either a deduction or a credit for foreign income taxes. In the case of a credit, the amount is limited to the Swedish taxes due on all foreign income, an overall or general limitation. There is no indirect credit, but dividends from 25 %-owned foreign subsidiaries are exempt from tax. The subsidiary must, in general, be subject to a foreign tax which is "comparable to" the tax the corporation would have borne if it had been Swedish. There is also an exemption for foreign employment income when the resident is present outside Sweden for six months.

The Netherlands provides for double tax relief in domestic law primarily by the exemption method. In addition, a foreign tax credit is applied with respect to passive income received from certain develop-ing countries. Dividends received from foreign corporations qualify for the "participation" exemption on essentially the same terms as divi-dends from domestic companies, with the additional requirement that the corporation be "subject to tax" in the foreign jurisdiction. Profits arising in a foreign permanent establishment, and income from foreign employment and from foreign real estate are formally included in income but then the total tax liability is reduced by the percentage that the foreign income is of the total income, which has the effect of exempting any positive foreign income. The taxpayer may also elect to deduct the foreign tax.

The form of double tax relief in *Australia* depends on the type of income and the level of the foreign tax. Passive investment-type income is dealt with in a credit system that gives a credit for the foreign withholding tax. The treatment of other income depends on whether it is "comparably taxed" in a foreign jurisdiction. If so, then profits arising from direct activities abroad and dividends paid by foreign cor-porations to 10 % or more corporate shareholders ("nonportfolio divi-dends") are exempt from Australian tax. Foreign employment income is exempt if the taxpayer is abroad for at least ninety-one days and is subject to tax in the foreign jurisdiction. In other circumstances, a for-eign tax credit is allowed for foreign taxes on foreign income, including an indirect credit in connection with nonportfolio dividends received by a corporate shareholder from foreign corporations where the divi-dend does not qualify for the exemption.

The *French* system is unique in that it does not normally, apart from treaties, grant relief for double taxation and foreign taxes are sim-ply deductible from the tax base. There are some important excep-tions, however. The principle of territoriality exempts from corporate tax profits arising from a trade or business carried on abroad and divi-dends from qualifying foreign subsidiaries are likewise exempt. In addi-tion, it is possible to obtain special permission to file a consolidated tax return including both domestic and foreign operations, in which case foreign taxes are creditable and foreign losses deductible. Around a dozen companies have taken advantage of the election.

3.1 Issues in the structure of a foreign tax credit system

3.1.1 Creditable taxes

All systems that give a credit for foreign taxes paid against the domestic income tax liability must determine which foreign levies will be entitled to credit. Several approaches are possible. One is to list specific foreign taxes that qualify for the credit. Another is to credit foreign taxes that have a general resemblance to the domestic income tax without too much concern for the technical details of the foreign tax law. Finally, it is possible to define the specific characteristics that a foreign tax must have to be creditable as an income tax. In addition, it is usual in treaties to specify which taxes will qualify for the credit.

Most countries focus on general resemblance. Only the *United States* has detailed regulatory rules setting out the criteria that a foreign income tax must meet. The regulatory structure is based in part on some case law principles developing the concept of an income tax for tax credit purposes. Under the regulatory scheme, the foreign "levy" must be a tax and not a payment for some kind of economic benefit and must be likely to reach net gain in normal circumstances. Taxes imposed by national and sub-national political subdivisions both can qualify for credit.

In determining if the tax is an income tax, the tax must be based on a realization of income, though the regulations permit some departures from the realization requirement. The tax also must use gross receipts in the computation of taxable income. Thus, taxes imposed on the basis of artificially "posted" prices would not qualify. However, a tax based on a likely estimate of gross receipts, for example, costs plus a reasonable profit mark up, would qualify. Finally, the tax base must be reduced by reasonable allowances for expenses in order to fall primarily on net income. Here again, substantial latitude is allowed. A gross-based tax would qualify in circumstances in which it is unlikely that there will be significant expenses and a tax on a gross basis would still leave the taxpayer with a net gain after the payment of the tax. At the other extreme, a subtraction-based consumption tax which allowed a full deduction for what, in an income tax, would be treated as capital expenditures, was reportedly determined not to qualify as a creditable tax.

Social security-type taxes used to fund retirement benefits are generally creditable as long as the payment is not based on age, life expectancy or other similar characteristics. The payments are not viewed as a charge for a specific economic benefit.

Taxes "in lieu of" an income tax are also creditable. A gross-base tax such as the withholding tax typically imposed on investment income of nonresidents is treated as such a tax as long as it is clear the tax is substituting for an otherwise generally applicable income tax. No credit is allowed, however, for so-called "soak up" taxes, taxes which are only imposed in situations in which they would qualify for the credit in the residence country.

Treaties may expand the category of creditable taxes to cover taxes which would not meet the regulatory definition.

Canada restricts the credit to "income or profits" taxes but there is no statutory or regulatory definition and little case law on the question. United States social security taxes have been held to be creditable despite the limited tax base and the fact that the payments are loosely tied to specific benefits. Income taxes paid to political subdivisions are also creditable

Sweden similarly limits the credit to "income taxes" paid to all governmental levels. In addition, credit is allowed for real estate taxes that are similar to the tax which Sweden levies on personal dwellings in lieu of taxing the imputed rental income.

The *Australian* rules are somewhat more complex. The statutory definition covers any tax on income, profits, or gains. (Taxes covered by tax treaties are listed specifically rather than by general description.) Under administrative rulings, creditable taxes must be imposed on a basis "substantially equivalent" to the Australian legislation, which includes a net basis tax on income or gains and a final gross basis withholding tax on passive income. The rulings contain lists of taxes which do or do not meet these criteria. Social security taxes generally are not creditable but credit is given for sub-national income taxes. Special rules exclude credit for unitary taxes, aimed at the taxes of some American states, to the extent they are not applied on a "water's edge" basis. In addition, no credit is allowed for a "soak up" tax, defined as a tax which would not have been imposed if the taxpayer would not have been entitled to credit in Australia.

The *United Kingdom* allows a credit for any tax on income or a tax which has a "similar character." This limitation has been liberally interpreted and a tax on 90 % of gross receipts has been held by the courts to be creditable. The administrative position is to allow credit for taxes which serve the same function in relation to business profits as an income tax, thus excluding turnover taxes but not necessarily taxes on gross receipts. Taxes paid to sub-national governments are creditable. Social security payments do not qualify.

Germany similarly limits the credit to taxes which are comparable to the German income or corporate tax. The tax authorities have
published a detailed list of creditable taxes.

The *Japanese* system has a broad regulatory definition which covers individual and corporate income taxes as well as excess profits taxes,
revenue taxes, and distributed earnings taxes. However, social security
taxes are not creditable and local income taxes are only entitled to a
deduction.

Since the *Dutch* system operates primarily under the exemption
method, the issue of creditable taxes is not as significant. Under Dutch
domestic law, only certain withholding taxes on dividends, interest and
royalties from listed countries are entitled to credit. The credit is
sometimes extended to taxes on other categories of income in treaties.
The situation is the same in *France* where the territorial principle controls the taxation of foreign corporate income. Most credits are granted
by treaty, which identify the tax in question. In the context of elective
worldwide consolidation, there is a general definition of creditable tax.

3.1.2 Limitations on the credit

All systems have limitations on the extent to which foreign tax
paid can displace domestic tax liability. While from a theoretical point
of view, an unlimited foreign tax credit is sometimes urged as the structure most consistent with complete capital export neutrality, practical
revenue constraints make such a policy impossible. In addition, to the
extent that the principal function of the credit is to relieve double taxation on international income, there is no reason to allow the credit to
reduce domestic taxes on domestic-source income. Within these broad
constraints, however, there is a wide variety in the actual form that a
limitation might take. At one extreme, the foreign tax could be traced
to a particular item of foreign income and the credit limited to the
domestic tax on that item. As an alternative, all foreign income and
foreign taxes could be considered together and the credit limited to the
corresponding domestic tax. This approach would allow an "averaging"
between high-taxed and low-taxed foreign income and allow the credit
in full to the extent the domestic tax was not exceeded. Any number
of intermediate structures are also possible. The credit could be limited
to the foreign tax on particular categories of income such as income
from a particular country (a "per country" limitation) or a particular

class or type of income (a "basket" limitation).

The systems here under review all fall somewhere between a per item and an unlimited overall limitation. In most cases, there are restrictions on the ability to average foreign taxes on active business income and passive income, in particular interest income. For those systems that exempt certain forms of income, averaging possibilities are also limited since the exempt income and the corresponding foreign tax do not enter into the limitation calculations. To some extent, the scope of the limitation is related to the breadth of the definition of creditable taxes.

The *United States*, in part because of its historical role as a capital exporting country, has the most complex and developed set of rules limiting the credit. However, since the system does not exempt any foreign-source business income and, in general terms, allows averaging with respect to such income regardless of the tax rate or source, it may in fact be less restrictive than some of the other systems. Under the United States approach, a worldwide limitation is applied to a number of different baskets of income. Most active business income falls into the residual or "general limitation" basket and averaging is allowed across businesses and geographical sources. Passive income is placed in a separate basket, with some exceptions. If the passive income is itself subject to a tax rate comparable to the United States rate, then it is moved to the general basket, thus ensuring that low-taxed passive income will bear some residual U.S. tax. Interest which bears a 5 % or greater gross-based withholding tax is also placed in a separate basket. This isolates interest income which may bear a high effective rate of tax on a net basis. Financial services income is also placed in a separate basket as is income from shipping, oil and gas, and other types of income which are typically taxed on a special basis. Finally, dividends received by corporate shareholders which qualify for the indirect credit are placed in separate baskets if the foreign corporation is not controlled by United States persons. If the foreign corporation is controlled by U.S. persons, dividends, royalties, and interest payments received from it are deemed to be out of the relevant baskets of income determined at the level of the foreign corporation. Thus the character of the income "passes thru" to the U.S shareholder rather than simply falling in the passive basket.

While each of the baskets has its own justification, the interaction of the various baskets, especially in the context of "pass thru" taxation of dividends and other payments, has been subject to substantial criticism for excessive complexity.

In *Japan*, the limitation is calculated by multiplying the domestic tax liability by a fraction in which the numerator is the total amount of foreign-source income subject to tax and the denominator is total global taxable income. There are two special restrictions, however, that were enacted to counteract what was perceived as excess averaging of foreign taxes. First, only one-third of foreign income that was not subject to foreign tax is included in the numerator. Second, the foreign-source numerator of the fraction cannot exceed 90 % of the total income. Income on export sales of inventory is treated as foreign source only if effected through a foreign fixed place of business or in other circumstances which make the income subject to tax in the foreign jurisdiction. Other source rules are the same in general as those applied in the taxation of foreign taxpayers

In *Canada*, a per-country limit is used as the basic limitation on business income that is not exempt. In addition, there is a "basket" limitation for nonbusiness income which is also applied on a per-country basis. For individuals, the credit is subject to an absolute per-country limitation of 15 % of the amount of income sourced in the country. The excess tax can be deducted. The 15 % limitation does not apply to real property rental income. The nonbusiness basket is primarily important for reasons of provincial taxation but does have the effect of limiting averaging for Federal purposes. While source rules are important to the operation of the Canadian system, they are relatively undeveloped. Foreign taxes are generally attributed to foreign income on a tracing basis.

Germany similarly has a per-country limitation. Where the foreign country taxes certain items of income but exempts others, current case law allows the untaxed income to be considered in the credit limitation calculation. *The Netherlands* also uses a per country limitation when applying its somewhat restricted foreign tax credit.

The limitation in *Sweden* is a function of the schedular system of taxation. Business income and employment income are treated together and capital income is in a separate category in the initial limitation computation. Under that limitation, the tax on each category of income is limited to the Swedish tax on the same category. However, if there is an excess limitation in one category, because the Swedish tax is lower than the foreign tax, excess taxes in the other category can be used to absorb the additional limitation currently. The foreign source character of the income is determined by its treatment under foreign law.

Australia has a worldwide limitation based on four baskets: interest income, offshore banking income, certain foreign pension income, and all other income. In practice, the major demarcation is between interest income and all other income. A special additional limitation applies to capital gains. Under administrative practice, where foreign-source capital gain is not subject to tax in the foreign country, it is not included in the credit calculation. It should be noted that "comparably taxed" income from either branch or non-portfolio investment is exempt when earned or repatriated so that such income also does not enter into the credit computation. Thus, the ability to average with respect to business income is substantially limited.

Australia has few explicit legislative source rules dealing with resident taxpayers. The courts have developed some jurisprudence based on a facts-and-circumstances approach. Some rules are fairly clear. For example, interest is sourced where the credit is made available, which may be the place of the contract of loan or of advancing the funds.

The *United Kingdom* limitation is, in principle, quite restrictive. Credit relief is given on a source-by-source basis and unused credits cannot be used against the U.K. tax on other income or carried forward, though excess credits can be deducted in some cases. The strictness of this limitation, however, can be avoided by using a nonresident holding company through which foreign income can be routed. There are no "pass-thru" rules and the income from the intermediate foreign "mixer" company is considered to be from one source, allowing a credit for all associated taxes. The use of a "mixer" company to achieve an averaging of high and low foreign tax rates is a common practice.

3.1.3 Allocation of expenses to foreign-source income

A crucial element in the determination of the credit limitation is the foreign-source *taxable* income of the taxpayer in the various categories to which the limitations apply. To determine this amount, rules must be established which allocate deductions to the appropriate types of positive income (or establish a negative amount in a particular category). Despite the centrality of this issue in applying foreign tax credit limitations, only the United States has any fully developed rules in this area. In other countries, the rules are quite general and leave much to taxpayer choice. To some extent, the rules are influenced by financial accounting practice and generally accepted accounting principles.

Since 1977, the *United States* has had detailed administrative rules dealing with the allocation of expenses between foreign-source and domestic-source income. Under the regulations, deductions are first allocated to general classes of income based on the "factual relationship" between the income and the expense. Deductions allocated to a particular class may exceed the positive income in the class in a given year. Deductions which are not definitely related to a class of income are ratably allocated to all gross income but the specificity of the rules leaves little scope for gross-to-gross allocation. Once allocated to a class of gross income, deductions are then apportioned to the relevant categories of income, in this case foreign source and domestic source. The regulations deal with the factors to be considered in the apportionment and include units sold, gross receipts, cost of goods sold, and the like. Special rules are applied to interest and research and development costs.

In the case of interest, the interest cost is apportioned on an asset method based on the tax cost of assets generating foreign-source and domestic-source income. The tax basis of stock in foreign corporations is adjusted to reflect retained earnings or deficits in earnings, thus in effect accounting for the current operations of the foreign corporations. The taxpayer can elect to use market values if those values can be adequately established.

This method is based on a "fungibility" approach and assumes that borrowing costs relate to all productive assets. However, a special rule requires the allocation of interest expense directly to foreign-source income if there is "excess" borrowing in the United States which has been loaned to foreign subsidiaries. A portion of the domestic interest expense is in effect treated as if it had been incurred abroad in a related subsidiary and was thus directly allocable to foreign-source income.

In the case of a domestic consolidated group of companies, interest expense and associated income must be computed on a consolidated basis. Prior to a statutory change, it was common practice to isolate interest expense in members of a consolidated group that did not have significant foreign-source income.

The approach to research and development costs has been constantly changed since the introduction of the 1977 regulations. Under the original regulations, the research costs were first allocated to the appropriate product categories in broad classifications and then were allocated, in part, on where the research was performed and in part on the basis of sales or gross income, with appropriate adjustments in royalties and other similar payments to arrive at amounts comparable to sales figures Legislative changes suspended the application of the rules for several years and replaced them with a provision which allocated all research expenses incurred in the United States to U.S. source income. Other stopgap legislative measures followed with a 64 % geographical allocation in effect for a time.

Additional regulations were proposed in 1995 that would be effective for periods after 1995 if they are not in turn replaced by additional legislation. Under the proposed regulations, research expenses would be allocated to somewhat narrower product classes than the 1977 regulations. In addition, following one of the various temporary statutory modifications, 50 % of the expenses would be allocated to the place of performance and the sales allocation method would be modified. It is estimated that the new regulations would reduce by about 25 % the amount of research expenses allocated to foreign-source income under the prior regulations.

In *Canada*, interest and other expenses are ordinarily allocated to foreign-source income on a factual tracing basis. This approach allows taxpayers to plan their affairs to "stream" their borrowings to Canadian assets or Canadian income in order to maximize foreign tax credits. If tracing is impossible, Revenue Canada permits expenses to be allocated in accordance with a reasonable formula based on asset values or gross income. There are no specific statutory rules or case law dealing with the allocation of expenses to foreign source income. In addition, Revenue Canada's administrative positions are very general.

Australia distinguishes, in principle, between expenses allocable exclusively to foreign income, expenses allocable to both foreign and domestic income, and expenses that do not relate to particular income ("apportionable deductions"). Expenses falling in the latter category are allocated on the basis of net income. Expenses allocable to both foreign and domestic income may be allocated in any manner deemed appropriate by the fiscal authorities, though there is little guidance in the published material. Interest expense is allocated on a tracing basis.

The *Japanese* system provides in its regulations that expenses are to be allocated on a "rational" basis, with substantial taxpayer choice. The regulations give as examples, allocation based on income, capital investment, or work force size.

In *Sweden*, there are no statutory rules dealing with expense allocation though it is clear that the limitations have to be applied on a net basis. Some principles developed in the context of allocation between domestic and foreign branches may have some application but in general, the area is undeveloped.

The *United Kingdom* likewise has no rules in the area, reflecting perhaps the very restrictive nature of the credit limitations themselves and the basic rule on deductions which prohibits deductions which are not "wholly and exclusively" for the purposes of the trade. There are restrictions on interest deductions for banks and insurance companies.

In *Germany*, case law principles developed to this point require that "directly connected" expenses be attributed to foreign source income. There is no allocation of general expenses. It is anticipated that the general issue of the allocation of deductions in both the credit and exemption context will be reexamined legislatively.

3.1.4 Treatment of losses in the credit computation

Where the expenses in a particular credit category exceed the income, the resulting loss may have an impact on the remaining credit calculations. Several situations must be distinguished. First, if expenses allocated to a given foreign income category exceed the income, the excess could be (a) allocated to domestic income, thus not affecting the other credit calculations; (b) allocated on some basis to the other foreign income baskets only, potentially reducing the amount of credit available in those baskets; or (c) allocated pro rata to foreign as well as domestic income, having a more limited effect on the credit calculation. Assuming that some allocation rule has been established, an ancillary principle must determine what, if any, effect a later positive amount in a basket whose loss had been allocated to other baskets (or to domestic source income) will have. Finally, if the overall results are negative so there is an overall net operating loss that may be carried forward, rules must be provided to deal with the effect of the carryover on the credit computation in later years. The systems here under consideration have taken a variety of approaches. Where active business income is exempt when subject to significant foreign taxation, the issues are generally not of great significance since the credit will be applied in categories of foreign income in which losses are unlikely.

Again the *United States* has the most complex rules for dealing with losses. The complexity is traceable to the extensive use of the basket system and the policy decision that foreign losses in a particular basket should not be allowed to reduce domestic source income in any situation in which there is positive foreign source income in any of the other income categories. Thus, foreign losses in one basket must first reduce proportionally foreign income in other baskets, with any excess reducing United States-source income. When foreign income is subsequently generated in the basket which initially incurred the loss, that income is recharacterized for basket purposes in the same fashion that the loss was used. However, any foreign taxes imposed on the income are not reattributed to the other basket. If the foreign loss exceeds foreign-source income and reduces U.S. income, so that the taxpayer experiences an "overall" foreign loss, subsequently arising foreign-source income is recharacterized as U.S. source for credit limitation purposes. However, in the reverse situation, where domestic losses reduce foreign income, there is no recharacterization rule applicable to subsequently arising domestic-source income, though a provision to this effect has been proposed.

The *Australian* rule is the strictest, affecting not only the credit computation but the underlying domestic tax liability. If the deductions allocated to foreign-source income exceed the income, the loss cannot be used against domestic-source income in the current year but is carried forward indefinitely for use against future foreign income. Special rules are provided that prevent the taxpayer from generating passive income to offset active business losses. The passive income is placed in a separate basket for these purposes. In the opposite situation, current domestic losses do reduce the foreign income for credit purposes. In the case of domestic losses from previous years, the taxpayer can elect to use the losses to reduce the foreign income to the extent necessary to obtain the maximum usable credit.

In *Canada*, the limitation is calculated on a country-by-country basis and, in general, losses in one foreign jurisdiction do not affect the credit calculation for other jurisdictions but reduce domestic-source income. There is no recharacterization of later arising domestic income as foreign for credit purposes. Where domestic losses exceed domestic income and reduce foreign-source income, the credit will be limited to the amount of Canadian tax payable. An overall net operating loss for a year does not have any impact on the foreign tax credit calculations for subsequent years except to the extent that the amount of foreign or Canadian tax payable in those subsequent years is reduced as a result of the loss carryforward.

The *United Kingdom* source approach similarly does not take losses from other sources into account.

Germany, in applying its per-country limitation, does not reduce the positive income from one country with losses incurred in another country. On the other hand, when several different types of income are earned in one country, gains and losses are combined. In addition, certain foreign losses (arising principally in passive activities likely to create tax shelters) are restricted in their deductibility to income from the same source in the same country. Those losses do not affect the credit calculation with respect to other income arising in the same country. An overall foreign loss which reduces domestic-source income has no effect on the calculation of the credit in subsequent years.

In *Sweden*, the rules on the treatment of losses are relatively undeveloped. It is unclear whether foreign losses must be used first against foreign income before reducing income from domestic sources. A leading treatise takes the position that from a theoretical point of view no reduction should be required.

The question of losses in the *Japanese* system is of relatively minor significance since the overall method is used and there is no problem of the allocation of losses among income baskets. Where foreign losses reduce domestic income, there is no provision for later recharacterization of foreign income as domestic.

3.1.5 Carryover of excess credits or limitation

Where limitations on the credit are applicable and excess foreign tax credits are generated, all systems must deal with the structural question of how such excess credits should be treated. Strict adherence to annual accounting principles would require each computation to be made on an annual basis and if credits could not be used in the years in which the foreign taxes were incurred, they would be lost. The most appealing case for some kind of relief from strict annual accounting is where the inclusion of the foreign income in the domestic system differs from the inclusion in the foreign system because of differences in accounting rules. Here, the timing rules can cause the foreign tax and the corresponding domestic tax on the same income to fall in different accounting periods. Other timing differences can arise because of differences in the principles governing the allowance of deductions and the recognition of income. Beyond timing issues, a broader policy question is the extent to which temporal averaging between high- and low-taxed foreign-source income should be allowed as a general matter.

Assuming that some type of temporal averaging is desirable, the question of technical structure is whether the excess taxes themselves should be carried to other periods in which there was "excess limitation" or whether the excess limitations should be allowed in the years the taxes were incurred. Most of the systems use the tax carryover method and allow varying degrees of temporal averaging. The structure of the rules is generally the same though the (essentially arbitrary) periods of carryover differ. The carryover periods may sometimes relate to statute of limitations periods.

In the *United States*, excess credits can be carried back two years and forward five years, subject to the availability of excess limitation in the appropriate basket.

In *Canada*, excess foreign business taxes can be carried back for three years and forward for seven years. No carryforward is allowed for excess taxes arising in connection with nonbusiness income but the excess can be deducted in the year incurred.

In the context of the overall limitation system in *Japan*, excess credits can be carried forward three years. In addition, any excess limitation from the preceding three years can be carried forward and excess credits can be absorbed in the current year to that extent. Any remaining excess credit is then carried forward.

Sweden similarly allows a three-year carryforward but no carryback.

Australia allows a five-year carryforward within each income basket. In addition, credits can be transferred among 100 %-related companies. (There are no general provisions for consolidation of corporate groups.)

The Netherlands has recently adopted an unlimited carryover.

In contrast, no carryover at all is allowed in the *United Kingdom*. *Germany* also has a restrictive system, not allowing any carryforward or carryback for excess credits. As a partial response to the problem, the taxpayer can elect (on a country-by-country basis) to deduct rather than credit the foreign taxes.

3.1.6 Indirect credit for foreign taxes paid by foreign subsidiaries

In all of the systems, there is some mechanism for eliminating or reducing multiple burdens of corporate-level tax when corporate profits are distributed by domestic corporations to domestic corporate shareholders. Similarly, all of the systems have some form of relief when the distributing corporation is a foreign corporation. This relief can be seen as performing two functions. First, as in the domestic context, it avoids a cascading of corporate-level taxes. At the same time, it relieves the potential international double taxation which would result from the taxation of the profits in the state where earned as well as in the state of the residence of the shareholder. This latter effect also makes more comparable the treatment of foreign operations carried out through foreign branches and through foreign subsidiaries.

Several of the countries here considered deal with this problem generally by exempting most intercorporate dividends from the tax base. *Canada, Australia, Germany,* and *France* use an indirect credit system in some situations but the exemption of foreign corporate dividends is much more common in practice. *The Netherlands* uses an exemption method exclusively. The issues which the exemption system raises will be considered below.

3.1.6.1 Share ownership requirements

As is usually the case in the relief from domestic multiple taxation, all of the systems require some minimum level of shareholding before an "indirect" foreign tax credit will be given for foreign taxes paid by the distributing corporation. The requirements are based in part on considerations of administrative simplicity and in part on the more basic notion that the function of the credit is to relieve international double taxation on "direct" foreign investment rather than portfolio investment.

The basic requirement in the *United States* is that the U.S. corporate shareholder own directly a 10 % or greater interest in the voting stock of the distributing foreign corporation. The *United Kingdom* and *Australia* also have a 10 % voting stock threshold. The *Canadian* test is more liberal, allowing the credit where a 10 % or greater share interest in any class of shares is present and is held directly or indirectly. Moreover, the ownership threshold is determined merely by reference to the number of shares of the class owned by the Canadian corporation, not by reference to votes or value. *Japan* requires 25 % ownership of the equity interest in the foreign corporation.

The *German* system for the indirect credit requires a 10 % interest, a minimum holding period of twelve months and, in the case of a subsidiary located outside the European Union, the subsidiary usually must be engaged in an active business. As discussed below, in treaties intergroup dividends from subsidiaries engaged in an active business are usually exempt from tax.

3.1.6.2 Tier limitations

The problem of multiple layers of corporate tax also exists if the first-tier foreign corporation itself receives distributions from lower-tier corporations. Both the *United Kingdom* and *Canada* allow the credit without restriction as to the corporate tier at which the tax was paid as long as the ultimate domestic shareholder owns, directly or indirectly, the requisite 10 % stock interest.

The *United States* rules are more restrictive. The credit only extends for three tiers. At each level there must be at least a 10 % voting stock interest held by the higher-tier corporation and an indirect 5 % interest by the ultimate domestic parent. The tier limits are viewed as a matter of administrative convenience. The *Australian* shareholding requirement is the same, with no limitation as to tiers.

In *Japan*, the credit extends to two tiers and at each level at least a 25 % shareholding is required.

The *German* indirect credit system similarly extends to two tiers, with a required 10 % indirect interest. Direct and indirect interests cannot be combined in meeting the test.

3.1.6.3 Computation of the indirect credit

The computation of the indirect credit involves several structural issues. The profits distributions must be related to particular profits of the foreign corporation and foreign taxes must be attributed to the profits distributions. In addition, since the income inclusion of the actual dividend distribution brings with it the indirect credit, the amount of the credit should in principle be "grossed up" so that the foreign tax itself is included in the domestic tax basis.

In the *United States*, profits and associated taxes were initially computed on an annual, last-in, first-out basis. That approach encouraged tax planning to artificially increase taxes from which distributions were made and also created technical difficulties where years with deficits in earnings occurred. In 1986, the system was replaced with a "cumulative pooling" approach which pools all earnings and foreign taxes (on a prospective basis) and treats all distributions as bringing back the appropriate portion of the total pool. Indirect credits are "grossed up" in the computation of the domestic parent's income.

The *Japanese* system is structured much like the United States system prior to the changes adopted in 1986.

In the *United Kingdom*, the taxes are related to the profits represented by the dividend. Thus, if a dividend is paid for a period, the relevant profits and taxes are for that period. In other situations, the profits of the last complete internal audit are used. In all cases, the relevant profits are those showing in the company's accounts and not the base on which the foreign tax is assessed.

The *Canadian* system is complicated by the fact that profits distributions from "taxable surplus" bring with them the functional equivalent of a credit, and distributions from "exempt surplus" are exempt. In general, foreign taxes are allocated between the two categories. Distributions are deemed to be first out of the "pool" of exempt surplus and thereafter out of taxable surplus, where the calculation of the credit equivalent deduction is made.

In *Australia*, pooling is used for years after the commencement of the foreign tax credit in 1987, and when that pool is exhausted, a last-in, first-out rule is used for years prior to the introduction of the credit. The calculations are based on foreign profits as revealed in financial statements with some adjustments, and not taxable income. While there is no clear guidance on the parallel treatment of the foreign company taxes, the general view is that taxes are treated as having been averaged over the pool (or profits of the years before 1987) and attach proportionately to dividends paid.

The *German* system relates the foreign taxes to the fiscal period from which the dividend is deemed to be distributed. Where a second-tier foreign subsidiary is involved, the credit is only allowed if the second-tier corporation pays a dividend in the same year as the first-tier corporation. In addition, in the case of dividends from "active" subsidiaries in developing countries, a "tax sparing" credit is given to the extent the local tax rate is lower than the German rate.

3.1.7 Interaction between indirect credit and limitation system

Where the ability to average is limited by some kind of basket system, that limitation must be coordinated with the indirect credit. "Passing thru" the various basket limitations is necessarily complex and is a function of the underlying complexity of the basket system itself. It involves both the treatment of profits distributions in the form of dividends and also deductible payments such as interest and royalties which can be viewed as being paid "out of" the various basket categories.

The problem is most acute in the *United States* since it uses the credit system extensively and has a complex basket structure in its limitation rules. In general terms, dividends from a foreign corporation controlled by United States persons are deemed for foreign tax credit purposes to be out of the appropriate baskets of earnings of the foreign corporation on a pro rata basis. Pass-thru also applies to rental and royalty income that reduce the foreign tax base. They are allocated to the category of income they helped to generate under the usual deduction allocation rules. Interest payments are allocated first to any passive income of the foreign corporation and then allocated to the remaining baskets. Complex ordering rules determine which payments are deemed to be made first.

In *Canada*, while a distinction is made between distributions out of exempt surplus and taxable surplus, no attempt is made to pass through the normally used per-country limitation in the case of taxable dividends which qualify for the indirect credit. Thus, it is possible for high and low foreign taxes to be averaged. However, the effective credit is limited on an overall basis with respect to the foreign affiliate paying the dividend to the amount of Canadian tax on the dividend. Generally, in *Australia*, dividends are not recharacterized for the indirect credit based on the nature of the income that is being distributed, but in certain cases they are treated as interest income or offshore banking income with the result that the baskets for these types of income apply and the underlying foreign credit is no longer available on the recharacterized amounts (as the underlying credit only applies to dividends). The precise details of the interactions among these rules are still unclear but with the introduction of an exemption system for most non-portfolio dividends from 1990 where the underlying profits have been comparably taxed, the issue is of little relevance. Most dividends now subject to the indirect foreign tax credit have borne little or no underlying tax and averaging and other tax planning issues no longer are prominent.

In *Germany*, dividend payments made by the second tier corporation are deemed to be received directly by the parent corporation rather than "passing thru" the first tier corporation. It is unclear what effect this has on the application of the per-country limitation.

As discussed previously, in the *United Kingdom*, while the limitation is quite restrictive, no attempt is made to "pass thru" limitations in the case of dividends qualifying for the indirect credit, and the use of "mixer" companies allows averaging. In *Japan*, the issues do not come up because of the use of the overall limitation.

3.2 Issues in the structure of an exemption for foreign income

3.2.1 Structure of the exemption

Where foreign income of a resident taxpayer is exempted from tax, the structure of the exemption can take several forms. The most extensive is to exclude the income for the coverage of the tax system altogether by simply not asserting jurisdiction to tax the income. Thus, for example, in *France*, the tax base for resident corporations in the case of business income is limited to income arising in France; foreign business income is not in principle subject to tax. Alternatively, the foreign income can be included for certain purposes though ultimately relieved from tax liability. One approach ("exemption with progression") is to calculate the tax liability which would have resulted if the income had been included and then apply the resulting rate of tax only to the included income. This is the approach taken, for example, in *Germany*, when foreign income of a resident individual is exempt under a tax treaty. Another approach is to "stack" the excluded income in the lower progressive rates in calculating the rates applicable to the taxable income. This approach has been used in the past in the *United States* and *Australia* in connection with the exemption for foreign-earned income.

3.2.2 Classes of exempt income

As indicated above, none of the systems exempt all foreign-source income of resident taxpayers. Thus rules must be provided to classify exempt foreign income and includable income, with a credit for foreign taxes typically given in the latter case. The distinction is usually between active income such as business income, either earned directly in a foreign branch or as a dividend from a qualifying foreign subsidiary, and portfolio income in the form of interest, royalties, and other passive income. Sometimes, there is a requirement that the exempt income be either actually, or in principle, subject to tax in the foreign jurisdiction. In other cases, the exemption is restricted to income from certain countries, for example, those with which the domestic country has a tax treaty.

Thus in *Canada*, which generally uses a foreign tax credit system, exemption is provided for dividends received out of the "exempt surplus" of foreign subsidiaries ("foreign affiliates") in which the Canadian corporate shareholder holds a 10 % or greater stock interest. Exempt surplus is defined as active business income earned in countries with which Canada has a tax treaty and certain capital gains. The definition of active business income is quite complex and excludes certain real estate rental, licensing, financing, and investment businesses. Pass thru rules apply that treat certain interest, royalties, and other deductible payments made out of the active business of one foreign affiliate to another as active business income to the recipient. In addition, dividends received by one foreign affiliate from another are added to either exempt surplus or taxable surplus, depending on which surplus account of the payor the dividend is paid from. An exemption is also provided for a limited amount of foreign employment income earned in qualifying activities and for certain income from offshore banking centers.

The *French* system exempts all income derived by French corporations from a trade or business carried on abroad, including passive income effectively connected to the trade or business. The level of activities qualifying as a trade or business is roughly equivalent to the treaty concept of permanent establishment. In addition, an exclusion is granted for intercorporate dividends received from foreign subsidiary corporations on the same conditions as for investments in the domestic context, that is, in general if there is a 10 % or greater stock interest. In both cases, the exemption is available whether or not any foreign tax is paid abroad.

As for individuals, bonuses and special payments for working abroad are exempt. Wages in general for working abroad are exempt if they bear a foreign income tax equal to two-thirds of the French tax otherwise due. Special rules apply for workers involved in foreign construction or extraction activities.

In contrast, *Sweden* limits its exemption to dividends received from foreign corporations in circumstances where the dividend would have been exempt under the domestic intercorporate dividends regime and has been subject to foreign taxation that is "comparable" with the corresponding Swedish income tax. If the distribution does not meet the "comparable" test, a special limited credit of 13 % of the dividend is given nonetheless. The justification for the limited credit is that there presumably is some foreign taxation, even if not comparable, and a standardized method of relief is thus appropriate. An exemption is also given to foreign-source employment income if the Swedish resident is abroad for six months and the income is subject to tax in the foreign country.

Australia also exempts foreign business income of corporations if the income is subject to tax in a "comparable tax" country. The exemption extends to profits (and certain capital gains) earned directly in branch form or dividends received by Australian corporate shareholders from nonportfolio (10 % or greater) foreign investments. Countries whose tax systems qualify as comparable are listed in Regulations. Even though a country is "listed," however, some concessionary aspects of its tax system may be "designated" in which event the exemption no longer applies to passive and related party income falling into that class (and in the case of foreign companies, as opposed to branches, the controlled foreign corporation regime can apply if its threshold tests are satisfied, thus subjecting the income to current taxation). Designated concessions can be general, such as the lack of a capital gains tax, or country specific (the offshore and holding company regimes of a number of countries are listed by name). The designation system also serves as the means whereby tax sparing is effectively achieved on a unilateral basis. Where a foreign country operates a tax holiday or concession of the type that Australia considers appropriate for a developing country, it is not listed and the exemption continues to apply. Thus, in the case of Singapore, the offshore regimes are designated but certain tax holidays are not, so that the exemption treatment is still available for the latter. A "subject to tax" test is also applied in the case of branches and where income from an unlisted country is received by a company in a listed country, the test can be satisfied.

Foreign employment income also qualifies for exemption if the Australian resident is abroad for three months and the income is subject to tax (with some exceptions) in the foreign jurisdiction. An "exemption with progression" feature affects the taxation of other income based on average rates.

The *Dutch* system is structured somewhat differently and is not formally an exemption system, though in operation it has that result. Rather than technically exempting foreign income, initially, all income, both taxable and exempt, is included in the tax base and the tax calculated. The tax is then reduced by the percentage which the income qualifying for exemption is of the total income.

The exemption under domestic law applies to foreign income that is derived directly as business income from a foreign permanent establishment, income from real property, and income from employment abroad if the income is "subject to tax" under an income tax in a foreign jurisdiction. The latter requirement has been interpreted as requiring only that the income be "objectively" subject to tax; the fact that the particular taxpayer does not pay tax on the income is not relevant. In the case of employment income, the requirement is deemed to be met if the taxpayer is employed by a Dutch company and is employed abroad for a period of three months. Under tax treaties, no "subject to tax" requirement applies.

The most important part of the Dutch exemption system is the extension of the domestic participation exemption to investments in foreign corporations. Dividends received by a 5 % or greater domestic corporate shareholder from a foreign corporation will be exempt from tax (completely and not proportionately) if the shares are not held as a "portfolio" investment, which requires some connection with the business of the domestic company but includes acting as a holding or coordinating company. (The "no portfolio investment" requirement is dropped with respect to EU subsidiaries.) In addition, the foreign corporation must be subject to a national foreign profits tax.

Because foreign participation dividends are exempt, no credit as such is given for foreign withholding taxes imposed on foreign dividends. However, under a recent change intended to improve The Netherlands' position as a location for holding companies, a portion of the withholding tax on the "inbound" dividend is allowed to reduce the tax which the Dutch company has to remit on the payment of "outbound" dividends if certain conditions are met.

While the *German* domestic system utilizes a foreign tax credit mechanism, its treaties make extensive use of the exemption system for income that arises in a foreign permanent establishment and for dividends from foreign subsidiaries. Even in treaties, however, exemption is generally not provided for investment or portfolio income, employment income or real estate income.

The circumstances in which exemption is available vary substantially, with earlier treaties being less restrictive and newer ones typically restricting exemption to income from an active business or income that is subject to tax in the foreign jurisdiction. The exemption usually extends to dividends paid to German corporate shareholders who own at least 10 % of the stock of the foreign corporation. (The threshold is unilaterally reduced to 10 % in domestic legislation if the actual treaty test is higher.) The exemption is sometimes limited to situations in which the foreign subsidiary is engaged in an active business. In addition, as discussed below, treaty exemption is denied under a recent statutory provision (which is in effect a treaty override) where the foreign corporation or foreign permanent establishment earns certain types of passive investment income in a low tax country.

The *United States* provides a limited exemption for foreign earned income when the recipient is a foreign resident or is abroad for a substantial portion of the tax year. The exemption is limited to $70,000 and does not involve "exemption with progression"; the exempt income reduces the applicable tax rate on the other items of taxable income.

3.2.3 Allocation of deductions to tax-exempt income

Where an exemption system is used to relieve international double taxation, in principle the exemption should only extend to net foreign income. Accordingly, deductions related to the exempt foreign-source income should not be deductible against taxable domestic or foreign-source income. The issue of allocation of deductions to exempt income is functionally the same as the allocation of deductions to foreign-source income for limitation purposes in a credit system. While all of the systems recognize the issue in principle, the rules are not highly developed. In particular, interest is typically allocated on a tracing basis, making it relatively easy to avoid the allocation of interest expense to exempt income.

Thus, *Canada* has no specific rules for allocation of deductions to exempt income and, in general, a tracing approach is used. The deduction of interest expense by Canadian companies in relation to exempt foreign income is recognized as a problem by critics of the present system but is justified as important with respect to international competitiveness of Canadian companies.

While *Sweden* has a relatively sophisticated mechanism for allocating expenses, in particular interest between business and capital income, the rules in the international area are quite rudimentary. *The Netherlands*, too, has no specific rules on the general allocation of deductions to exempt branch or participation income, though under the case law some sort of tracing approach is taken. For participation income, however, there is a specific rule with respect to interest expense. Interest expense attributable to a loan taken up within six months of the acquisition of a foreign participation is presumed to be connected with the investment in the participation and not deductible, unless the taxpayer can establish that the loan was obtained for another purpose.

Australia uses the same allocation rules for exempt income as those used in the context of the foreign tax credit limitation discussed above. Expenses allocable exclusively to foreign income are nondeductible in their entirety. Expenses allocable to both foreign and domestic income may be allocated in any manner deemed appropriate by the fiscal authorities, though there is little guidance in the published material. Deductions allocable to no particular class of income are prorated. Interest expense is allocated on a tracing basis.

In *Germany*, deductions related to foreign-source income that qualify for an exemption are disallowed under the basic statutory provision that treats the issue of expenses and tax-exempt income generally. The statute requires that the expenses be incurred in "direct economic connection" with the income, and the provision has been quite restrictively interpreted. In the case of expenses in connection with participation dividends that are exempt under treaties, the provision has generally been interpreted to apply only to the extent that dividends are received in the year the expense is incurred. Thus, where a foreign stock investment is debt-financed, the interest expense incurred in connection with the investment has been held to be deductible in full if no dividends are paid in the current year. In part, the justification of this rule was that the gain on the sale of the stock of the foreign subsidiary would be subject to tax on disposal. However, this result has recently been changed by statute in order to encourage the use of German holding companies for foreign operations, and capital gains in this situation are no longer taxable. Nonetheless, the Federal Tax Court recently reaffirmed its prior line of cases despite the statutory modification and there may be a legislative change in the allocation rules.

France has no statutory rules on allocation of expenses but under general principles treats expenses directly related to exempt foreign income as nondeductible while allocating expenses that relate to both taxable and tax-exempt income. However, interest related to exempt intercorporate dividends from foreign corporations remains deductible. The allocation of expense to exempt branch income follows in general the approach taken in the OECD Model Treaty article dealing with business profits.

3.2.4 Treatment of foreign losses

The treatment of foreign losses, that is, the excess of deductions allocated to foreign income over gross foreign income, also raises some special problems. In principle, the overall foreign loss arising in a situation which would be entitled to exemption should not reduce otherwise taxable domestic or foreign-source income. The exemption is for the net foreign income, and the existence of a foreign loss simply indicates that there is no net income to exempt. In systems which use an "exemption with progression" approach, however, a foreign loss may affect the rate of tax on domestic income ("negative" progression). Nonetheless, several of the jurisdictions have special rules for foreign losses that allow current deductions.

In *The Netherlands*, foreign losses are deductible against domestic income on a per-country basis, even if other foreign income is positive. There is a recapture of the deducted loss in later years when the operations in the country which generated the loss are positive. The recapture operates by treating the income as taxable in the application of the proportional exemption. The per-country limitation was introduced in 1995. Prior to that time, foreign income and losses from nontreaty countries and under older treaties were combined, and the resulting loss reduced domestic-source income with subsequent recharacterization as taxable income when any foreign-source income was realized. In addition, if foreign losses in a branch have reduced taxable income in the last eight years and the branch is incorporated, the participation exemption is not available until the losses have been compensated for by additional taxable income.

Where *Germany* exempts income under a treaty, in principle, foreign losses have no impact on German income except for the possible effect of "exemption with progression," that is, the foreign loss is taken into account in determining the rate of personal income tax on positive income. However, under a special provision, losses incurred in most active businesses (excluding tourism, arms, and leasing) carried on in a foreign permanent establishment can be deducted currently to the extent they exceed other foreign income from the same country which is entitled to exemption. The overall loss will reduce otherwise taxable domestic or foreign-source income and can be carried forward.

If the operations are profitable in later years, the usually applicable treaty exemption is not available and the income is taxable in Germany, but only in those cases where the losses are usable as a carry-forward under the law of the other country.

In the *French* exemption system, foreign losses are in general not deductible against domestic income. However, as an incentive for the foreign investment, losses from the first five years of branch or subsidiary operation may be deducted currently against domestic income and then are recaptured over a five- or ten-year period, thus providing in effect an interest-free loan in support of foreign investment.

4. Limitations on exemption or deferral of income of foreign corporations

Under the basic jurisdictional principles discussed previously, the income of a foreign corporation is not taxed to the domestic shareholder when earned by the foreign corporation. Taxation occurs, if at all, when the income is distributed. And in the case of countries that use the exemption system to relieve international double taxation, even distributed income may not be subject to tax. In the systems here under consideration, the deferral of or exemption from tax for distributed income usually arose without much consideration of the tax policy implications of that result. Deferral seemed the natural consequence of the recognition of the separate existence of the foreign corporation, and the exemption of the distributed income when received by domestic shareholders was often consistent with the treatment of dividends received from domestic corporations.

All of the systems, however, have recognized that the mechanical application of these basic rules can lead to tax results which are inappropriate in light of other aspects of the country's taxing system. Thus, for example, if as a general rule, dividends from a substantial participation in a foreign subsidiary are exempt from domestic tax but passive portfolio income earned directly is taxed currently, it is questionable whether passive income earned by a foreign corporation and distributed to a domestic shareholder as a dividend should fall under the basic rule that foreign dividend income is exempt. Similarly, even if deferred taxation is taken as a basic principle, the avoidance of current domestic taxation on portfolio investment income by lodging investment assets in a foreign corporation formed in a tax haven jurisdiction would cause concern.

More generally, all of the countries here under consideration have been forced, in varying degrees and at varying times, to reexamine the economic and commercial consequences which flow from the application of the historically accepted principles of taxing jurisdiction and methods of double tax relief. This process has produced a more explicit consideration of when and whether deferral or exemption is appropriate and has led to the introduction of special tax regimes that limit the tax advantages which flow from the normally applicable rules. Though the results of these changes differ in many respects, some basic themes recur and there has been much "borrowing" between systems in terms both of concepts and technical rules.

All systems here considered make some distinction between types or classes of income earned by foreign corporations with domestic shareholders. Active foreign business income is more likely to be entitled to deferral or exemption than passive portfolio or investment income. This distinction is sometimes based on considerations of capital import (or competitive) neutrality. Foreign business activities carried on in a foreign subsidiary must compete with local businesses which face only the local tax rate. Competitive considerations, it is argued, require exemption from, or at least deferral of, the potentially higher domestic tax. These considerations are not present in the case of passive income. The distinction can also be seen as necessary to protect the domestic tax base in the case of "mobile" types of passive income.

Most of the systems are also concerned with the level of foreign tax that the income arising in the foreign corporation bears. This may be tested either by an explicit comparison of foreign and domestic rates on income earned, by some sort of minimum rate benchmark, or by the mere fact that the corporation is organized in a particular jurisdiction with a high or low tax rate.

Finally, many systems apply the limitations on deferral or exemption only in the case of a significant level of shareholder ownership by domestic shareholders. In some cases, the foreign corporation must be controlled by domestic shareholders, while in others a significant but noncontrolling interest is sufficient. Where a significant level of domestic ownership is not present, others mechanisms are often employed to prevent domestic portfolio investors from transferring funds offshore to foreign-owned investment companies.

In the elaboration of these basic concepts, there is a wide variation in the lines drawn and the structure of the tax rules in each country. These differences result in part from different policy judgments and in part because of the choice of different techniques to implement similar policy decisions. In some countries, the issues only arose when exchange controls were eliminated which made foreign investment possible, while in others they have been present in the system for a considerable period of time. Thus some rules have grown "organically" while others have been enacted in a relatively short period of time. The following material will first examine limitations used by exemption countries and deferral countries where there is a significant level of domestic share ownership.[1] The subsequent section will consider the response to domestic portfolio investment in foreign investment companies.

4.1 Limitations on exemption for shareholders in foreign corporations with significant domestic share ownership

From a structural point of view, limitations on the exemption of foreign-source income have arisen in several ways. In the first place, as discussed above, the definition of the situations in which exemption is permitted itself typically restricts exemption to certain classes or categories of income. In addition, the general exemption rules are often limited by special provisions, typically enacted after the more general rules, that eliminate exemption in certain circumstances, for example, where operations in tax havens are involved or where the foreign income is of a certain type. The two approaches can obviously reach the same functional results and it is in part a matter of historical accident as to which features appear as part of the "general" exemption definition and which take the form of special limitations. Thus, for example, both *Canada* and *Australia*, in effect, limit exemption for dividends from foreign corporations to distributions out of active business income earned in countries where it is likely that the income will have borne significant foreign tax. In structural terms, this result is reached by the definition of income that qualifies for exemption rather than as a limitation on a broader class of exempt income. In the case of *Australia*, the limitations on the exemption are closely related to the limitations

---

1. An extensive examination of the policy basis and technical aspects of the provisions in Canada, the United States, Japan, Germany, France, and the United Kingdom is found in Arnold, *The Taxation of Controlled Foreign Corporations: An International Comparison* (Canadian Tax Foundation, 1986).

on deferral considered under the next heading, though there are a number of cases where the exemption is not available for nonportfolio dividends but the limitations on deferral do not apply; e.g., active income from unlisted countries and active income from designated concessionary regimes from listed countries.

In contrast, in *France*, intercorporate dividends distributed by foreign subsidiaries qualify for the intercorporate dividends exemption in the same way as domestic dividends and, under the territoriality principle, profits and losses arising in a foreign trade or business are not taken into account in determining the base of the French corporate income tax as a general matter. However, this treatment is limited if the corporate taxpayer is subject to Section 209B of the tax code, an anti-avoidance provision enacted in 1980 and expanded in 1990 and 1992.

In general terms, the provision is applicable to investments in tax haven jurisdictions where the taxpayer is not actively involved in the local market. More technically, a French corporation is subject to tax currently on foreign income that arises in a foreign branch operation or with respect to a 10 % or more investment of the share capital in a foreign corporation (or for any investment over ca. $30 million) if the foreign branch or foreign corporation is not subject locally to an income tax or is subject to an effective rate significantly less than that which would have been levied in France.

For purposes of such taxation, the tax results of the foreign branch or entity are recalculated under French tax rules. The profits are deemed to pass thru to the French corporate taxpayer on the first day of the month following the end of the foreign branch's or entity's tax year. They are taxed separately and cannot be offset by losses from domestic operations. Conversely, the losses of the foreign branch or entity are not taken into account in determining the tax on domestic income.

Tax paid locally is creditable against the corresponding French separate corporate income tax provided that the foreign tax is of a comparable nature. Withholding taxes on actual distributed dividends also entitle the taxpayer to a credit against such separate tax if the subsidiary is based in a tax treaty country.

Current taxation can be avoided if the French corporate taxpayer can establish that the activities of the foreign branch or entity do not have the effect of the "localization" of profit in the low-tax jurisdiction. This condition is deemed to be fulfilled if the foreign business is engaged in actual industrial or commercial activities performed predominantly in the local market. Thus the provision is aimed principally at the isolation of passive investment-type income in a foreign corporation. It also covers some base company transactions where the activities are not principally undertaken in the local market. In the case of litigation, the burden of proof of the low-tax status of the foreign branch or entity lies on the government. Questions not yet resolved are whether section 209B is compatible with double tax treaties and especially with the business profits article (in the absence of a specific treaty provision permitting the application of the section) and with the principle of freedom of establishment within European Union Member States or with the authorization given by the EU Commission to local low-tax regimes.

In 1992, *Germany* enacted a special provision that limits exemption for foreign dividends which would normally be applicable under the participation exemption found in most German treaties. The exemption is not available to the extent that the foreign corporation realizes "passive income with an investment character." Technically, this rule supplements the German controlled foreign corporation legislation by attributing directly to a 10 % or greater German shareholder (even when German control of the foreign corporation does not exist) the undistributed investment income of the foreign corporation. For the provision to apply, the foreign corporation must be subject to "low tax," defined as 30 % or less, and the investment income must exceed certain thresholds. There are complex exceptions intended to exempt active business income, holding companies, and group finance operations. The provision is technically an override of the exemption typically provided in older treaties that do not restrict the participation exemption to dividends from active businesses. It should be noticed that income which does not meet the "investment character" test may still be passive for purposes of the controlled foreign corporation provisions discussed below; however, the treaty exemption would still apply to such income.

4.2 Limitations on deferral for shareholders of foreign corporations with significant domestic share ownership.

The *United States* has very extensive (and complex) rules limiting deferral. Historically, limits on deferral for portfolio income of individuals were in imposed in 1937 in the foreign personal holding company provisions. Those rules restrict deferral for closely-held individually-owned foreign corporations which have predominantly investment-type income. While the thrust of the rules was at "incorporated pocketbooks," the provisions also apply to personal services income where the corporation is providing the services of its shareholder to third parties. Where the shareholding and income tests are met, all of the undistributed income of the foreign corporation is treated as a dividend to the shareholder and subject to current tax. The tax cost of the shares is correspondingly increased.

In 1962, a comprehensive set of rules restricting deferral was enacted and became the predecessor of similar legislation in several of the other countries here under consideration. The "Subpart F" rules, as they came to be known internationally, were the outcome of a complex legislative compromise between those favoring the complete elimination of deferral for the income of controlled foreign corporations in all circumstances and those who argued for a more limited approach.

Broadly speaking, those supporting elimination of deferral were arguing in terms of capital export neutrality and the need to eliminate the incentive that deferral gave for foreign investment. The justifications for continuing deferral were based on the asserted need to preserve the competitive position of United States enterprises in foreign markets. The resulting compromise eliminated deferral for passive income, about which there could be no argument based on competitive considerations, and so-called "base company" income resulting from transactions between related parties where income can be said to have been diverted through a related company. In those situations, the undistributed income of the foreign corporation must be included currently by the U.S. shareholder.

More technically, deferral is eliminated for the "Subpart F income" earned by a "controlled foreign corporation." While the definition of Subpart F income is extremely complex, there are two basic strands which run through the provisions. One is the attempt to distinguish between passive investment-type income and business income. Thus, for example, rents and royalties are normally included in Subpart F income but are excluded if they are derived in the active conduct of a trade or business. Similarly, income from dealings in commodity transactions is generally covered but is excluded if it arises from a hedging transaction carried out in the normal course of the business of a producer or processor. Second, the provisions attempt to define those situations where the foreign corporation is being used as a "base company." This branch of the provision is aimed at transactions with related parties which have no significant economic connection with the "base" country jurisdiction. A typical situation covered by the provisions is the purchase of goods manufactured by a related party and the sale of the goods outside of the country of incorporation of the selling "base" company. On the other hand, if the goods had been sold in the country of incorporation or had been manufactured there and sold to related parties in other jurisdictions, no Subpart F income would have been involved.

These basic rules are hedged with a number of exceedingly complex refinements. Thus, for example, passive income does not include interest and dividends received from a related party organized in the same country. This permits the use of a holding company structure without creating Subpart F income. The exception for interest, however, does not apply if the interest expense reduced the Subpart F income of the paying corporation. In another refinement, transactions carried out through branches rather than separately incorporated corporations can generate base company income if the overall result had the same economic effect as a related company transaction. An overall relief provision excludes from the base company income definition any item of income which bears a rate of tax equal to 90 % of the maximum U.S. corporate rate and a de minimis rule excepts the lesser of 5 % of the foreign corporation's income or $1,000,000.

In addition to covering passive and base company income, the provisions deal with a number of other situations where, for various reasons, the legislative decision was made that deferral was inappropriate. Thus, deferral is denied for income arising in connection with an international boycott, for certain bribes or illegal payments, and for income attributable to countries which the United States does not recognize diplomatically. Most recently, deferral was eliminated for earnings invested in "excess" passive assets, defined as over 25 % of the foreign corporation's total assets. The basic thrust of the provision is to limit deferral where the earnings on which deferral has been permitted are not themselves reinvested in foreign business assets.

Current taxation of undistributed income only occurs if the income is earned by a "controlled foreign corporation" (CFC). CFC status, in turn, requires that over 50 % of the stock (either in terms of voting power or value) is owned by "United States shareholders," that is, United States persons who own, either directly or by attribution through foreign entities, at least 10 % of the voting stock of the foreign corporation. The focus is thus on control lodged in concentrated

United States ownership. CFC status is avoided, for example, if eleven unrelated persons own ratably 100 % of the voting stock of a foreign corporation or if exactly 50 % voting stock is owned by one United States person with the remainder held by foreign persons.

In general, the rules limiting deferral in other jurisdictions are more restricted in scope. Their focus is primarily on passive income and income that could be said to have been diverted from domestic taxation without any "real" activity by the foreign corporation in a "real" foreign jurisdiction.

Thus in *Canadian* legislation, deferral is eliminated only for passive income (foreign accrual property income or "FAPI") which is directly taxable regardless of the level of foreign tax imposed on the income. There is no concept of base company income and the use of tax haven subsidiaries for sales and services transactions is accepted as necessary to support the international competitiveness of Canadian corporations. Thus the scope of the Canadian rules is more like that of the United States foreign personal holding company rules than the Subpart F provisions. The basic pattern of taxation, however, is quite similar to Subpart F.

Elimination of deferral is restricted to the FAPI of a "controlled foreign affiliate," defined as a foreign corporation which is controlled directly or indirectly by five or fewer Canadian residents. FAPI over a de minimis amount is included directly in the income of 10 % or greater shareholders. Income of lower-tier corporations is attributed directly to the Canadian shareholder. A credit is allowed for foreign taxes imposed on the underlying income. The basis of the shares is increased by the amount of the inclusion. Subsequent distribution of the income as a dividend is tax free and a credit is allowed for withholding tax on the dividend if the distribution is made within five years of the inclusion.

The *Japanese* approach to limits on deferral is quite different. Rather than focusing on transactions, the Japanese legislation looks to the location of the principal office or headquarters of the controlled foreign subsidiary. If the operations are located in a jurisdiction which has no corporate tax or an effective tax rate of 25 % or less, then all of the undistributed income, passive or active, is taxed currently to the Japanese shareholders. The legislation is directed at the use of tax havens for activities that have no connection with the jurisdiction. To carry out this policy, there are several exceptions that allow continued deferral. Deferral is permitted for an active business which has fixed assets in the jurisdiction, carries out local managerial activities there, and operates its principal business in that location. This exception would cover, for example, the operation of a resort hotel in a tax haven. Another exception allows deferral for financial or transportation activities which do not meet the location-of-business-test but generate more than 50 % of gross income from dealings with unrelated parties.

The restrictions on deferral apply to "affiliated foreign corporations." These are foreign corporations where more than 50 % of the stock is owned by Japanese residents or corporations. There is no minimum shareholding requirement for testing control. However, only those shareholders who own 5 % of the shares or are part of an affiliated corporate group which own 5 % are subject to direct taxation on the undistributed tax haven earnings. A foreign tax credit is allowed for the corporate taxes paid on the directly included income.

Sweden takes yet another approach. Prior to 1990 there were no restrictions on the deferral of foreign income earned in foreign corporations. The matter was not regarded as a problem, as exchange controls effectively prevented the use of foreign corporations for portfolio investments and deferral was deemed appropriate for usual corporate activities. When exchange controls were eliminated, restrictions were imposed on deferral through the definition of "foreign corporation." Under the new legislation, a foreign corporation is recognized as a separate taxpayer only if it is subject to tax in its resident state in a manner comparable to Swedish taxation or is organized in a treaty country and entitled to double tax relief under the treaty. All other foreign entities are taxed on a pass-thru basis as partnerships if Swedish persons owning at least 10 % of the shares together hold more than 50 % of the votes or value of the interests in the entity. The usually applicable rules of partnership taxation attribute the income to the "shareholders" who are taxed directly. Thus, in effect, deferral is eliminated for all income arising in low-tax countries. This is a kind of "white list" approach in which only corporations from specified jurisdictions are entitled to deferral. Where income is subject to current tax there is intentionally no basis adjustment in the shares, so the same income could be taxed again on the sale of the shares. Dividends, however, are exempt from tax and the capital gain can be avoided by timely distributions.

The *United Kingdom* legislation is focused on corporations resident outside the U.K. and controlled by U.K. residents where the corporation is subject to a "lower level of taxation" in the residence country, defined as less than three-quarters of the taxes the foreign corporation would have paid if it had been resident in the U.K. Control is defined as a more than 50 % interest in the shares, the voting power, the profits, or the assets of the company; there is no minimum shareholding level in making this determination. However, only U.K. resident companies with at least a 10 % interest in the foreign company will be attributed the undistributed profits.

There are a number of exceptions to income attribution which substantially restrict the reach of the rules. If the company follows an "acceptable distribution policy" and distributes at least 90 % of its profits there will be no attribution of the undistributed amounts. In addition, if the foreign company has a business locus in the country in which it is resident and engages in activities other than investment or the dealing in goods involving the United Kingdom or related parties ("exempt activities"), the provisions will not apply. There is also an exception for publicly-traded companies. In addition, there is a "motive" exception that is applicable if the transactions generating the profits were carried out for reasons other than reducing U.K. taxation. As an aid in the administration of the provisions, the fiscal authorities have published a "white list" of countries. For companies resident in such countries and deriving at least 90 % of their income locally, the attribution provision will not apply.

In addition to the above regime, there are provisions attributing the capital gains of a nonresident company to its "members" if the company would have been classified as "closely held" had it been a United Kingdom resident. Further, preferential capital gain treatment is denied for gains on the disposition of interests in offshore investment funds that do not distribute a substantial portion of their income.

The *German* provisions are focused on "tainted" income realized by a German-controlled foreign corporation in a low-tax jurisdiction. Where the income is attributed to the German shareholder, it is characterized as a dividend and is expressly treated as an actual dividend for purposes of applying the participation exemption in the relevant treaty. Thus, as a practical matter, in the case of a corporate shareholder holding an interest of at least 10 %, the provisions are effective only in situations involving non-treaty countries or treaty countries where the treaty does not extend the participation exemption to passive income. In addition, in the case of income of an "investment character", the treaty exemption may be overridden by the special legislation discussed above.

As to the definitional elements, "tainted" income is defined indirectly by excluding from the definition most active business income, including manufacturing, agriculture, processing, banking and insurance, local distribution and processing. Income from trading and services will generally be active if the foreign corporation conducts its business operations without assistance from the German shareholder and deals with the public even if the goods are purchased from related parties. Thus many situations which would be treated as base company sales or services income under the United States Subpart F rules would not be covered by the German provisions.

The foreign corporation will be subject to low tax if it pays tax on a residence basis at a rate of less than 30 %. In this calculation, operating losses that might reduce tax and foreign tax credits are ignored. Control is defined in terms of more than 50 % of the votes or number of shares held by German residents with the attribution of ownership through other corporations or partnerships. The rules also include former German residents who have moved to low-tax jurisdictions. In contrast to the U.S. Subpart F rules, there is no minimum ownership test.

As indicated in the previous section, if the foreign corporation has significant amounts of portfolio investment income, that income will be taxed directly to 10 % German shareholders even if the foreign corporation is not German-controlled and even if a direct dividend would have been entitled to the participation exemption under a treaty.

Where income is attributed, foreign taxes can be credited or deducted and subsequent distributions of the previously taxed income can be made on a tax-free basis for a four year period.

The *Australian* approach to restrictions on deferral and exemption is interesting and is examined in some detail as it is the most recent attempt by one of the countries considered here to deal with the problem. Unlike many other countries, the controlled foreign corporation legislation in Australia was introduced as part of a general rethinking of the international taxation regime. Australia until 1987 operated an exemption system for the relief of double taxation internationally. With the abolition of exchange control in 1983, the way was opened for passive income in particular to be moved offshore for shelter under the exemption system. In response, the Labor Government announced as part of its 1985 tax reform package that Australia would move to a foreign tax credit for all income apart from employment income. The system was hardly underway when a number of abuses came to light and complaints about complexity and competitiveness were heard from the business community. Accordingly as part of the 1988 Business Tax Reform announcement, the Government proposed a mixed exemption and credit system together with the ending of deferral.

As the result of a complex and continuing political process, a compromise was reached that was modeled on the U.S. Subpart F rules with a "white list" of about sixty comparable countries to which an exemption system would largely apply. The white list would cover a substantial portion of the foreign income of Australian multinational companies and relieve them of the compliance costs of a foreign tax credit system in cases where Australia would collect little or no tax in any event. The original legislation did not cover widely-held corporations with passive investment income. Subsequently, a comprehensive set of foreign investment fund rules was introduced which taxed on a current basis all investments in foreign entities that generated passive income.

Although the public debate centered around deferral and the competitiveness of Australian business overseas, the overall regime is probably best regarded as protecting Australia's domestic tax base because it focuses on income of residents which is easily shifted from Australia to a foreign entity.

As to the technical aspects of the rules, a controlled foreign company (CFC) is a nonresident company (including a dual resident company allocated to another country under a tax treaty) in which five or fewer Australian residents directly or indirectly control 50 % or more of the shares. Only residents with a 1 % or more interest are included. There are several anti-avoidance rules intended to prevent circumvention of the control rules.

Income derived by a CFC measured in Australian terms is directly included in assessable income (that is, not as a constructive dividend) and taxed on a current basis to Australian residents with a 10 % or more interest if it is passive income or related party income (closely modeled on U.S. rules and referred to as "tainted" income) and is derived from a non-listed country or is within certain categories of income derived from a listed country. The regulations list disqualifying features of listed countries tax systems, e.g., offshore regimes where income is exempt or subject to preferential rates. Tax holidays of developing countries have not been included which means that income of listed developing countries protected from local tax by tax holidays or preferences is not taxed on an accrual basis by the CFC regime.

The amount of income attributed is calculated through a multiplication of interests. Tainted income of a CFC will not be attributed if it falls below a threshold (a de minimis test) of 5 % of the gross turnover of the CFC. Similarly if the attributable income from a listed country CFC does not exceed the lesser of $50,000 or 5 % of the CFC's gross turnover, no attribution is made. Dividends paid by a non-listed country CFC to a listed country CFC are also attributed if they are not taxed at ordinary rates in the listed country, but dividends paid between unlisted country CFCs are not, thus permitting group structures extending beyond the borders of one country. Extensive deemed dividend rules apply to catch disguised distributions.

Relief of double taxation at the attribution point takes one of two forms. If the taxpayer concerned has less than a 10 % interest, then foreign taxes are allowed as a deduction against attributable income. (Despite the 10 % threshold for attribution, it is possible to be in this position as the tests used are different, being based here on the rules for the indirect foreign tax credit.) If the taxpayer has a 10 % or greater interest, then the foreign tax is credited rather than deducted. In each case the result parallels what happens for distributions of profits from unlisted countries out of active income referred to below.

Where previously attributed income is distributed, an accounting mechanism ensures that it is not taxed again, but a foreign tax credit is nonetheless available for withholding taxes on such dividends (which goes against other income under the Australian worldwide credit limit). Similarly capital gains tax on disposal of a direct or indirect interest in the CFC in respect of attributed but undistributed income of a CFC is prevented by reducing the consideration received by the appropriate amount. Where income of foreign companies that has not been attributed under the CFC regime is distributed, it will be exempt if the shareholder has a 10 % interest or more in the paying company and the income is from a listed country (including income that is made subject to the CFC regime by the regulations but not CFC-taxed because it is active income).

To make direct investment by branch and subsidiary comparable, an exemption also applies to income derived by a branch of a resident in a listed country.

Where the shareholder does not have the necessary interest, or

the income comes from an unlisted country (not having been attributed because it is active or subject to the de minimis rule), the income
is assessable when distributed with a foreign tax credit. If the
Australian resident has a 10 % interest under the foreign tax credit
rules, then the credit extends to foreign underlying corporate-level
taxes where the listed country exemption does not apply.

4.3 Special provisions dealing with domestic portfolio investment in foreign investment companies

Limitations on exemption or deferral were typically focused initially on situations in which there was a significant level of domestic
investment in the foreign corporation and were often restricted to cases
in which there was actual control of the foreign corporation by domestic shareholders. However, as intermediated investment in foreign corporations became more common, the failure to impose current tax on
undistributed earnings of portfolio investment in foreign investment
funds began to be recognized as a significant problem. Where the level
of domestic investment was not substantial, there was some reluctance
to require direct inclusion of foreign earnings as the domestic shareholder was unlikely to have access to information or an influence on
the distribution policies of the foreign corporation. As a result, a number of surrogate taxing techniques were employed, ranging from taxation on a mark-to-market basis to the taxation of an assumed notional
return on the investment.

In the *United States*, when the Subpart F provisions were introduced in 1962, a provision was included which denied preferential capital gains treatment to gains realized by domestic investors on portfolio
investment in the stock of foreign investment companies. The provision was intended to reduce the incentive for United States investors
to invest in foreign mutual funds where the undistributed earnings
would not be subject to current U.S. taxation and would not be
reached by the foreign personal holding company rules or the Subpart F
rules because of the absence of concentrated United States ownership.
However, the elimination of the capital gains preference in 1986 made
this provision ineffective to discourage United States investment in
foreign investment companies. The legislative response was a rule
aimed more directly at the deferral of United States tax on passive
income earned abroad.

Under the passive foreign investment company ("PFIC") rules

enacted in 1986, an interest charge is imposed on foreign earnings which are accumulated and then subsequently distributed to United States shareholders. The distribution is treated as having been received ratably over the period that the United States shareholder has held the stock, and an interest charge is imposed on the taxes (calculated at the highest marginal rate for the year in question) which would have been due on the hypothetical distributions. Similarly, if the stock is disposed of at a gain, the gain is attributed ratably to the period that the stock has been held and an interest charge calculated accordingly. The interest charge mechanism was chosen because of perceived disadvantages of requiring current taxation where United States interests were not substantial. It is possible for United States shareholders to avoid the interest charge regime by electing to include in income currently the undistributed income of the foreign corporation in some circumstances.

While the provision was aimed primarily at investment in foreign investment companies, the definitional scope is substantially broader. A foreign corporation is classified as a passive foreign investment company if (1) 75 % or more of its income is passive or (2) 50 % or more of the value of its assets generates passive income. Unlike Subpart F, there is no minimum shareholding requirement and no required overall level of United States investment.

Similarly, in *Canada*, in addition to the FAPI rules applicable to controlled foreign corporations, there is a special provision aimed at foreign investment vehicles. If a resident taxpayer invests in "offshore investment fund property," defined broadly as an interest which will derive its value primarily from investments in portfolio investments, the investment will be deemed to generate a notional return which will be currently taxable. The rule only applies, however, if one of the main reasons for the investment was a tax advantage in comparison with a direct holding of the investment.

Likewise, though *The Netherlands* has no general provisions limiting deferral, there are special rules dealing with foreign investment companies. Individual shareholders who invest in foreign investment companies are taxed on a deemed return from such investments. The rate varies based on the nature of the investment. The tax paid by the foreign corporation is not relevant and the treatment is not restricted to tax haven operations. For corporate shareholders who hold 25 % or more of the shares of a foreign investment company, the investment is taxed on a mark-to-market basis.

In *Australia*, a separate foreign investment fund ("FIF") regime applies to noncontrolled foreign corporations with primarily passive income. The foreign investment fund rules apply to interests held by Australian residents in foreign companies and foreign life insurance policies. If the business of the foreign company is not regarded as principally active, the regime applies without distinction as between listed and unlisted countries. The following businesses are in this nonactive category: financial intermediation, investment in passive assets (shares, financial instruments, etc.), insurance, funds management and activities involving real property apart from construction. The principal business can be determined by stock exchange category in the case of listed companies or by the portion of assets used in an active business. For stock exchange listed companies, banks, general insurers, life insurers, real estate companies and conglomerates are also excluded from attribution. Interests in pension plans are excluded as are de minimis holdings.

Three methods of calculation are available for determining the amount of income attributed to interests in FIFs: market value, deemed rate of return and simplified calculation method. The first simply marks the interests to market each year and is to be used unless it is impracticable. In that case, the second applies using a deemed interest rate based on a mark-up on the yield on short-term Treasury Notes (compounded each year less distributions). A taxpayer may elect to use the third method based on actual income where there is sufficient information to do so. Some simplifying assumptions are used in the calculations. The amount of attributable income is reduced by assessable distributions.

No explicit relief for double taxation is generally provided with respect to foreign tax paid by the FIF but in the market value method there is implicitly a deduction for foreign taxes as presumably the market value will be reduced in most cases by foreign tax paid. Where the calculation method is used, a foreign tax credit is available for attributable income on the same terms as for dividends if the resident taxpayer has the necessary interest in the FIF. Similar adjustments for capital gains purposes are made as for CFCs. The FIF rules apply in some cases to foreign trusts and there are also specific trust rules dealing with interests of resident beneficiaries in foreign trusts and foreign grantor trusts. Generally the reconciliation of the CFC and FIF regimes with each other is successful (with the former taking precedence over the latter).

The recently enacted *German* provisions dealing with foreign corporations realizing "passive income with an investment character" are also responsive to the problem of foreign investment companies, though they are only applicable when 10 % or greater domestic share holding is present.

5. Outbound transfers to foreign branches or subsidiaries

Transfers of assets outside the taxing jurisdiction raise issues in both a credit system and an exemption system. From the point of view of an exemption system, any appreciation in the value of an asset which is transferred to a foreign business operation whose income qualifies for exemption will not be taxed by the residence country. Similarly, assets transferred to a foreign corporation will not generate tax if the dividends from the direct investment are exempt. Several of the systems have provisions which ensure that tax will be collected in these situations, either by accelerating the income recognition to the time of transfer or by retaining a tax claim on the income when it is later realized.

From the perspective of a credit system, the transfer of the asset to a foreign branch does not terminate the claim to the taxing jurisdiction. However, the existence of the credit gives the primary tax claim to the country of source and if the rates are similar has the same effect as in an exemption system from the government's point of view. Transfers to foreign corporations raise the same issues where the indirect credit is available, and will involve the problem of deferral since whatever domestic tax may be due will be deferred until repatriation. A number of special rules respond to these problems.

Several countries treat the transfer of an appreciated asset to a foreign branch as a realization event. Thus, in *Sweden*, where the exemption method is often used in treaties for branch operations, the transfer of assets is deemed to be a withdrawal of the assets from domestic business operations and is a realization event. In the case of a transfer to a foreign subsidiary, where the dividends would be exempt, the transfer will be treated as a realization event to the extent that it does not take the form of a sale at an arm's length price.

Germany, on the other hand, while it treats the transfer as a realization event in principle, allows a deferral of the gain (through the use of a reserve) until the asset is sold in the branch. At that time, the deferred gain is taken into account. Where depreciable assets (which are not likely to be sold) are involved, the deferred income must be taken into account over the remaining useful life of the asset. The taxpayer can, at his option, treat the original transfer as a realization event. It should be noted that these rules only apply in the case of the transfer to a branch in a treaty country, since only in those circumstances would the accrued gain escape German taxing jurisdiction. The transfer of an asset to a foreign subsidiary company for less than fair market value is treated as a "hidden contribution" and results in the realization of income.

The *Dutch* rules are somewhat more complex. In principle, the transfer of an asset to a foreign branch is not a realization event. However, case law and administrative regulations require that the fair market value of the asset be considered as its basis for computing depreciation of the asset in the foreign branch in calculating foreign-exempt income. Historical cost, however, is used in computing worldwide income. Thus, over the life of the asset, the appreciation will have been included in the tax base by, in effect, reducing the amount of foreign-source income which will qualify for exemption. Similar principles apply to inventory.

France treats the transfer to a foreign branch as a realization event. A tax-free transfer of assets to a foreign subsidiary, however, can be done in exchange for shares, provided the usual statutory requirements are met.

In *Canada*, the transfer of assets to a branch operation is not a taxable transaction since the income of the branch remains subject to Canadian tax. The fact that the foreign tax credit may allow the transfer of the tax on the appreciation to the foreign jurisdiction is not considered sufficient justification to tax the outbound transfer. On the other hand, transfers to foreign subsidiary corporations are fully taxable since the income may never be taxed in Canada when repatriated as exempt surplus and, in any event, the tax will be deferred. The treatment is thus parallel to the departure tax applied in the case of individuals.

The approach in the *United States* is similar. Transfers to a foreign branch are, in general, not taxable. The only exception is the transfer to a foreign partnership that operates the branch. In that case, a special tax is applicable to appreciated assets. The concern is that the income may not be subject to later United States tax if it could be allocated to a foreign partner, though in fact, that would be unlikely given the restrictions on partnership allocations.

In the case of transfers to a foreign corporation, the transfer may be taxable or tax free, depending on the nature of the assets. In general, the transfer of property that is to be used in an active business and that is not likely to be sold can be transferred to a foreign corporation on a tax-deferred basis under the same conditions as the transfer to a domestic corporation. Thus, for example, machinery and buildings can be transferred without immediate recognition of gain but inventory does not qualify. There are extensive restrictions on transfers of stock or securities, in light of the ease of resale, though tax-deferred transfer is available in some circumstances if the taxpayer enters into an agreement to pay tax if the stock is in fact later sold or disposed of by the transferee corporation. A special rule applies to the transfer of intangibles in the form of patents, know-how, and the like. The United States taxpayer is required to take into income a deemed royalty payment (treated as U.S.-source income) from the transferee foreign corporation over the life of the intangible which reflects the amounts commensurate with the income of the intangible. The deemed royalty rule is aimed at the prevention of the deduction of research costs in the United States and then a transfer of the resulting income stream from the intangible abroad, but it has a much broader scope. In addition, if the branch operations have been operating at a loss and are then transferred to a foreign corporation, gain must be recognized to that extent up to the amount of appreciation in the assets transferred.

Japan, on the other hand, allows both the transfer to a branch operation and to a newly-formed subsidiary to proceed without recognition of income.

Australia takes a strict view (outside the finance industry) that there can be no income realization or deductions in transactions between the head office and branch, whether outbound or inbound. The realization event is the disposal of the asset by the taxpayer to a third party. For inventory, income and deductions are then allocated among the countries and taxed or exempted on the basis of source of income and apportionment of deductions rules (with arm's length transfer pricing principles being used to allocate income and deductions where the books are not in conformity with this principle). Thus in the case of inventory manufactured in Australia and shipped to an overseas branch which sells it, the sale price will be allocated partly to Australia and partly to the country of the branch, and the latter part will be exempted if the country is a listed country and the income is subject to tax there and is not designated concession income. The expenses allocated to the Australian income will be deductible and those allocated to the branch will not be deductible.

In the capital gains area, the principles are more complex. If the asset is depreciable equipment, e.g., a building or land, the branch exemption is available for any capital gain so long as the asset has been used wholly or principally for producing exempt branch income during the year of disposal and the preceding year. If, for example, a piece of equipment is used in Australia for producing assessable income and then is shipped to a branch where it is used to produce exempt income, it will give rise to depreciation deductions while used in Australia but not when used in the branch. If it is then sold for more than depreciated value (which includes notional depreciations for the period of use by the branch), any recapture would probably be apportioned between the head office (taxable) and the branch (exempt). If the sale price exceeds the indexed cost base (which disregards depreciation), then the capital gain would be fully exempt if the asset satisfied the time limitation in the preceding sentence and the other exemption conditions as for inventory. If the asset is not inventory, equipment, building, or land, then the branch exemption is not available and the gain will be taxable with a foreign tax credit for any foreign tax levied on the gain.

In the case of the transfer of assets to foreign subsidiaries, the transfer is a realization event and gives rise to income or capital gain. For assets other than inventory, a rollover will be available if the subsidiary is 100 % owned and the asset transferred is a taxable Australian asset of the transferee. This rule permits the rollover in the case of some assets such as land and buildings in Australia or shares in an Australian resident private company, but not in the case of equipment. As the rollover is limited in this case to taxable Australian assets, there is no escape from the capital gains net as the subsidiary will be subject to capital gains tax on disposal (unless treaty rules prevent taxation).

In the *United Kingdom*, transfers to a foreign branch have no tax consequences as the income remains subject to U.K. tax. As a general matter, the transfer of assets outside of a U.K. group to a foreign corporation would be a disposition triggering capital gains taxation and the recapture of previously deducted capital allowances. However, current taxation can be avoided if the business is transferred solely for shares and the resulting interest amounts to at least 25 %.

The following **Table IV-1** summarized the rules dealing with residence-based taxation of foreign source income. The column "CFC legislation" refers to provisions aimed at foreign corporations with concentrated domestic ownership while the column "Foreign investment company legislation" is focused on portfolio investment in foreign entities with predominately passive income.

Taxation of foreign source income of resident taxpayers

	Double tax relief: business income	Double tax relief: subsidiary dividends	Double tax relief: portfolio income	Controlled foreign corporation (CFC) legislation	CFC basic approach	Foreign investment company (FIC) legislation	FIC basic approach
Australia	mainly exemption; otherwise credit	mainly exemption; otherwise credit	foreign tax credit	yes	jurisdictional and transactional	yes	simplified actual calculation; mark-to-market; deemed return
Canada	foreign tax credit	exemption and deemed foreign tax credit	foreign tax credit and deduction	yes	transactional	yes	deemed return
France	exemption (territorial system)	exemption	no domestic relief (only in treaty)	yes	jurisdictional and transactional	no	n.a.
Germany	exemption on active PE income (treaty)	usually exempt on distribution of active income (treaty)	foreign tax credit	yes	jurisdictional and transactional	yes	direct taxation of investment income

Taxation of foreign source income of resident taxpayers

	Double tax relief: business income	Double tax relief: subsidiary dividends	Double tax relief: portfolio income	Controlled foreign corporation (CFC) legislation	CFC basic approach	Foreign investment company (FIC) legislation	FIC basic approach
Japan	foreign tax credit	deemed foreign tax credit	foreign tax credit	yes	jurisdictional	yes	n.a.
The Netherlands	exemption	exemption	foreign tax credit	no	n.a	yes (indiv. shareholders)	deemed return
Sweden	foreign tax credit	exemption	foreign tax credit	yes	jurisdictional	no	n.a.
United Kingdom	foreign tax credit	deemed foreign tax credit	foreign tax credit	yes	jurisdictional and transactional	yes	ordinary income on disposal
United States	foreign tax credit	deemed foreign tax credit	foreign tax credit	yes	principally transactional	yes	interest charge on deferred distribution or gain on sale

Subpart B: Source Taxation

Regardless of their approach to residence-based taxation, all the jurisdictions here under consideration assert the right to tax income which, broadly speaking, can be said to "arise" in the country. This source-based, or in rem, jurisdiction focuses on the economic connection that the particular item of income has to the taxing jurisdiction. The pattern of taxation applied to such income is similar in all of the jurisdictions. A distinction is generally made between "business"-type income that is taxed on a net basis with the allowance of deductions, and "investment"-type income that is taxed on a gross basis, often collected through the mechanism of a withholding tax. The withholding tax often applies regardless of the status of the recipient of the income, but in the case of taxpayers without a residence connection, it represents a final tax. The following materials will analyze first the issues arising in the structure of net basis taxation of business and employment income and then consider the treatment of investment income. In this area in particular, the normally-applicable domestic rules are often modified by treaties limiting the scope of source-based taxation and the domestic rules should be viewed with these qualifications in mind.

1. Issues in the structure of net basis taxation of business income

1.1 Threshold of activity

Income from business operations is typically taxed only if the activities that take place in the country reach a certain level. This approach is based in part on practical and administrative considerations. If the activities are not significant, it will be difficult to collect the tax, since it would usually not be possible to use withholding techniques and the tax must be directly assessed. In addition, if the local activities are not substantial, the income does not have a real economic "source" in the jurisdiction.

The degree of penetration required varies, as does the formulation of the applicable test. Some jurisdictions impose net basis taxation if the taxpayer carries on any business activities within the jurisdiction, though the contours of what constitutes a "business" can be different. Other jurisdictions only tax if the foreign taxpayer has a

"permanent establishment," which represents a more extensive penetration than simply carrying on business activities. The permanent
establishment concept is often similar to, but not identical with, the
concept used in tax treaties. It involves either the presence of some
sort of fixed location within the country or the presence of agents in
the country with certain types of legal authority.

In the *United States*, the basic threshold for net basis taxation is
engaging in a United States trade or business. The concept has been
developed by case law which in general focuses on the continuous and
regular nature of the activities, though results of the cases and rulings are
hard to rationalize. In addition, there are some specific statutory rules.
The performance of personal services in the United States in most circumstances constitutes a trade or business. There are some specific statutory exclusions for certain financial activities such as trading in stock or
securities with a resident broker for the foreign taxpayer's own account.
An election is permitted with respect to real estate activities that allows
the taxpayer to be taxed on a net basis even where the level of actual
activities does not constitute a trade or business.

Canada also uses a business activities test. There is no statutory
definition of what constitutes carrying on a business in Canada. The
case law focuses on where contracts are entered into and where activities "essential" to the business are performed. Under a special statutory
rule, soliciting orders or offering goods for sale in Canada constitutes
carrying on a business as does any processing, construction, or manufacturing activity. In addition, the disposition of "taxable Canadian property" such as real property or natural resource property is deemed to be
carrying on a business. Special rules impose net basis taxation on
employment income.

In the *United Kingdom*, income received by nonresidents is categorized into the same schedules or cases applicable to domestic taxpayers. With respect to business income, the jurisdictional question is
whether the business is being carried on *in* (as opposed to *with*) the
United Kingdom and the question is determined on a facts-and-circumstances basis. In this connection, the place where contracts are
entered into is an important factor. For corporations, the test is principally in terms of the existence of a branch or agency.

In contrast, *Japan*, in general, uses a permanent establishment
test as the threshold for net basis taxation. The domestic law concept
tracks the scope under treaties, though of course, there are differences

in detail since each treaty definition may be different. Though most business income is taxed only if a permanent establishment is present, some categories of income are taxed on a net basis even in the absence of a permanent establishment. These include income from sale of domestic real estate, income from the "use or holding" of certain assets in Japan, and gain on certain stock sales.

The Netherlands also, in general, uses a permanent establishment approach. Though the term is not defined in the statute, the case law has in general followed the definition in the OECD Model Convention. In addition, there is a statutory rule that treats real property which is held as a business asset as a permanent establishment.

Sweden likewise bases business taxation on the presence of a permanent establishment. The domestic law concept of permanent establishment is interpreted in the light of Swedish treaty practice.

Under German domestic law, business income is subject to tax only if it arises in a permanent establishment or from the presence of a permanent representative in Germany. Both terms are defined in some detail in the legislation and are broader than the corresponding treaty concepts. Thus a permanent establishment is present if a stock of goods is available and a permanent representative does not have to have authority to conclude contracts on behalf of his principal. Income from cultural, sporting, etc. events can be taxed without a permanent establishment. Gain on the disposition of a greater than 25 % interest in a German company is also subject to tax without further connection to the jurisdiction.

The Australian regime revolves around source rules rather than an explicit threshold test. Basically all assessable income with an Australian source is potentially taxable and the derivation of taxable income (assessable income less deductions) gives rise to an obligation to file a tax return. Assessable income does not include exempt income and there is a special withholding tax regime for certain dividends, interest, and royalties payable to nonresidents under which the income subject to this regime is deemed to be exempt income so that it is removed from assessable income and the obligation to file, thus being a final tax. In addition, there are various regimes of greater or lesser specificity mixing assessment and withholding elements for certain types of income and a very broad discretionary power to require withholding on nonresidents' income on a case-by-case basis.

Foreign corporations are taxed in France on the business income they realize through what the tax code calls "a trade or business carried on in France" ("*entreprise exploitée en France*"). As construed in case law, this concept is very close to the permanent establishment concept in the OECD model treaty. It is, however, somewhat broader since, beside fixed places of business and dependent agents, it encompasses the performing in France of "complete commercial cycle" ("*cycle commercial complet*" or "*cycle complet d'opérations*") on a customary basis, e.g., several purchases followed by sales, or even a one-shot but large purchase and sale transaction.

1.2 Attribution of business income for net basis taxation

Whatever the threshold for net basis taxation, rules are necessary to determine what items of income are sufficiently associated with the domestic branch[2] to subject them to tax. Here the approaches used differ substantially. One method is to focus on the actual economic connection between a particular item of income and the branch. All income with such a connection is subject to net basis taxation and all other income is either not subject to tax or subject to the withholding regime. Such an approach typically does not use independent source rules with respect to business income.

A different approach is to treat all income with a domestic source as "attracted" to the branch and thus subject to net basis taxation even when there is no actual economic connection between the item of income and the branch. This "force of attraction" approach usually involves an independent set of source rules since whether an item of income will be subject to net basis taxation depends on whether it has a domestic source. Between these extremes, a number of variations are possible. Under a "limited" force of attraction approach, only certain types of income are subject to net basis taxation without regard to actual economic connection. In some cases, income which technically has a foreign source may be subject to net basis tax if it has an economic connection with the domestic activities.

These "direct" methods attempt to allocate a particular item of *gross* income to the branch operations. A conceptually distinct "indirect" approach is to determine the *net* income of the entire enterprise

---

2 In the subsequent material, the term "branch" will be used to refer to the applicable domestic threshold for taxation, i.e., business activity, "trade or business," permanent establishment, etc.

and then allocate that profit to the various geographic locations. The allocation may be made on the basis of turnover, assets, payroll or other similar factors. This approach is often used in special industries such as banking, insurance, and transportation while the direct approach is used for sales and manufacturing operations. The results of the two approaches can be quite different. A branch operation can show a profit on the direct method but would have no allocable net income on the indirect method if the overall operations resulted in a loss.

While the general outlines of the various approaches are fairly clear, in practice, the details tend to be relatively undeveloped. This is a result in part of the fact that cross-border operations, in general, tend to be done in subsidiary form, except in the case of special industries like banking, real estate, and natural resources.

In addition, special problems arise in determining the income attributable to transactions that involve dealings between the domestic branch and the head office or other foreign branches. Those issues arise both in connection with income attribution and with the determination of appropriate deductions for the branch and will be discussed in the following section.

The *United States* combines a "limited" force of attraction approach with a focus on the economic connection of the income and the domestic activities. The rules for establishing the tax base are related to the complex set of rules for establishing the source of income which apply to both resident and nonresident taxpayers. With respect to investment-type income like dividends, interest, etc. from United States sources, the income is subject to net basis taxation if it is "effectively connected" with the United States business activities. The focus is on the function the asset generating the income plays in the business and the business activities with respect to the asset. The same rules apply to determine if capital gains from the disposition of assets are effectively connected and thus subject to net basis taxation. (Income in these categories which is not effectively connected is either taxed on a gross basis or not taxed at all.)

With respect to other items of income from United States sources, the income is treated as effectively connected even if there is no factual connection between the item of income and the U.S. business activities. Thus, for example, sales of inventory property in the United States that were done directly from the foreign head office with no involvement of the U.S. business would nonetheless be treated as effectively connected income.

A special set of rules applies to income which is foreign source under the normally applicable source rules but nonetheless has a connection with United States business activities. Rather than simply recharacterizing such income as United States source income, the statutory pattern subjects such income attributable to the United States business to net basis taxation despite the formally foreign source of the income. The rules only apply to a very limited class of income, principally income resulting from financial services and the licensing of intangibles. Where foreign-source income is subject to net basis taxation, a credit is allowed for foreign taxes imposed on the income, thus restricting the United States to a "residual" taxing jurisdiction. Under prior law, foreign-source sales income could in some circumstances be subject to U.S. tax under the above approach, but subsequent changes in the source rules redefined such income in most cases as United States source, thus subjecting it to tax under the normal pattern of rules.

As for the *Australian* situation, as noted above the regime for taxing nonresidents starts with the basic assumption that all Australian source income is assessable and taxed on a net basis. This applies generally to business income. The source rules for business income come mainly from judge-made law and operate on a facts-and-circumstances approach, though in the case of income derived from the sale of goods there have been suggestions that the sales profit is sourced where the contract is made. The tax administration is given power to determine the source and amount of business income under some old provisions in the tax legislation but the power seems to have fallen into disuse.

There are a few special regimes for certain types of business income that mix assessment and withholding elements and may be regarded as cases of the indirect approach. For example, in the case of insurance with nonresidents and overseas ships, a certain percentage of receipts are deemed to be Australian-sourced taxable income and an assessment, which effectively operates as a kind of withholding mechanism, is raised against a convenient local deemed agent (master of a ship, insurer's agent). In practice, tax treaties govern most of the business income derived in Australia by nonresidents (though the domestic insurance rules are sometimes preserved in whole or part) and the source rules for business income (profits attributable to a permanent establishment) effectively govern since Australia's tax treaties, as already noted, provide that the source rule in the treaty becomes the rule for all purposes of Australian tax law.

Canada does not use the force of attraction principle in general, though certain items of Canadian source income become subject to tax if the taxpayer is otherwise subject to net basis taxation. There are no detailed source rules specifying the geographic source of income. In the case of branch operations, income which may be allocated in a "reasonable manner" to the Canadian branch is treated as domestic-source income and is taxed on a net basis to the foreign taxpayer. A nonresident's Canadian branch income must be computed on the assumption that the nonresident's only income is from carrying on business in Canada. Moreover, the nonresident is entitled only to those deductions that are reasonably attributable to the Canadian business. No other statutory or administrative guidance as to the allocation of profits to a Canadian branch is provided.

The *Dutch* rules likewise do not apply a force of attraction approach and are similarly open-ended. Income which is "realized" by a Dutch branch is treated as domestic source and is subject to net basis taxation. Income and expenses as well as assets and liabilities are attributed to a branch if they are functionally related to the branch activities. Thus, for example, a payment attributable to branch activities but received after the branch activities had ceased was still considered attributable to the branch. Investment-type income such as dividends and interest are taxed to the branch only if the assets which generate the income are part of the business assets of the branch. Here, the manner in which the assets are carried on the books of the branch is an important factor in determining the business character of the assets but is not controlling.

In *Germany*, income is generally attributed to the permanent establishment on a "direct" method, focusing on the activities in Germany; the force of attraction principle is not used.

Sweden attributes income based on a "true and fair" calculation of the economic results of the operations in Sweden, based to some extent on the accounting principles used to allocate income between the divisions of a single company.

In the *United Kingdom*, income is attributed to the United Kingdom business activity on a factual connection basis. If the income can be said to "arise" in the business, it will be subject to net basis taxation. In addition, income from rights or property used or held in the business is subject to tax, as is gain on the disposition of business assets.

A special rule in connection with goods manufactured outside the United Kingdom and sold within allows the taxpayer to elect to be taxed only on the sales portion of the profit, determined by looking at the profit an unrelated sales agent would have obtained.

Since a branch is in principle assimilated to an independent enterprise, *France* does not follow the force of attraction approach, and the indirect or unitary method is used very exceptionally. Emphasis is generally placed on the branch's books, and the branch is taxed only on the active income attributable to it and to passive income effectively connected with it. There are no special source rules with respect to business income in that the existence of a "trade or business carried on in France" is the criterion of both taxability and source.

Japan has developed a system which relies to a large extent on source rules, income classes, and types of activity in determining the income taxable to Japanese branch activities. Foreign corporations are divided into categories depending on the type of branch activity they conduct. There are eleven types of domestic source income and four types of corporate activities. Two basic patterns emerge from these rules. For some categories of operations, most importantly those with offices, warehouses, or other fixed operations which would constitute a permanent establishment under general international rules, an extensive force of attraction principle is followed. For such operations all (and only) income which is deemed to be from Japanese sources under the source rules is taxed to the branch on a net basis. If some of the "attracted" items are subject to a withholding tax, that tax is credited against the final tax liability. Thus, if the sales branch of a foreign company also had interest income from Japanese sources which was unconnected in fact with the branch activities, that income would nonetheless be attributed to the branch and subject to net basis taxation. On the other hand, if the sales branch had sales income which, under the source rules, did not have a Japanese source, it would not be subject to tax, even if the branch activities were important in the generation of the income and the income could be said to be "attributable" to the Japanese branch operations. The overall pattern of the rules resembles that of the United States prior to the changes in 1966.

A different approach is taken where the Japanese permanent establishment is not a fixed location but is a construction site or a trading agent. There again all (and only) domestic-source business income is taxable. Other types of income are subject to tax in the permanent establishment only if they are in fact "attributable" to the activities of the permanent establishment; the force of attraction principle does not apply.

There are two important modifications to the above described pattern. In some treaties, the source rules are modified to provide that income attributable to the activities of a domestic branch are domestic source income, thus allowing the taxation of income which would otherwise be technically exempt under the domestic-source rules. In addition, administrative regulations have attempted to extend the definition of domestic-source income to investment-type income, normally foreign source, which is generated by investments made by the Japanese branch.

1.3 Determination of deductions in the net basis taxation of business income

The rules for determining the deductions attributable to business income arising in a branch generally focus on the factual or "causal" connection between the expenditure and the income. Following treaty practices, some of the domestic rules give considerable weight to the manner in which the expense is accounted for on the books of the branch or head office. Some expenses are allocated on a formulary basis that takes into account factors such as the relation of the branch assets to total assets or relative sales volume.

Also following treaty practices, in general none of the jurisdictions in their domestic rules recognize "self-charged" expenses for payments or transfers made between the branch and the head office. Thus, internally computed "interest" or "royalty" charges do not affect the income of the branch or head office. Only expenses which are actually paid or accrued to third parties will support deductions, determined either on a "direct" or formulary basis.

In the case of individuals, deductions for personal allowances and other personal costs are generally quite limited or not allowed at all.

Under the *United States* approach, the same allocation-of-deduction rules applicable to domestic taxpayers for purposes of the foreign tax credit limitation are used to determine the net income of foreign business operations. No deduction is allowed for self-charged expenses and no income results from transactions between the head office and the branch operations. The focus is on expenses which are "definitely related" to the income generated by the U.S. business activities. In addition, a formulary approach is allowed for certain expenses. Thus general and administrative expenses can be allocated on a sales or gross income basis between U.S. and foreign-source income.

A special rule applies to the allocation of interest expense to U.S. business operations. The basic approach is to look to the overall capital structure of the foreign taxpayer and the relation of that structure to the assets used in the United States. It combines what is in effect a tracing rule with a residual allocation rule. In determining the relation between U.S. assets and related liabilities, the taxpayer may either use the actual ratio of assets to liabilities or a fixed arbitrary percentage. Actual and "allocated" interest expenses deducted by the branch may be subject to gross basis taxation. The special allocation rules are of principal importance to foreign banks who typically operate in the United States in branch form for regulatory reasons.

In *Canada*, expenses are generally allocated on a factual tracing basis, though a formulary apportionment of interest and depreciation expense is allowed. If all or substantially all of a nonresident's income is earned in Canada, the nonresident is, in effect, assimilated to resident status and other deductions are available to the extent they can be considered applicable to the income earned in Canada.

The *Japanese* approach also combines elements of direct and indirect allocation of costs. Costs must be allocated on a "rational" basis. For assets located in Japan, this generally means a direct determination of the relevant deductions, for example, for depreciation. For other expenses, they may be deducted if they have a factual connection to the domestic-source income regardless of where they are incurred. However, there are strict rules of documentation for claimed deductions for expenses incurred abroad. For expenses related to both domestic-source and foreign-source income, a formulary approach is used which allocates the expenses on the basis of revenues, assets, etc. depending on the nature of the expense. Interest expense may be deducted directly if it can be traced to domestic activities; otherwise, it is allocated on a formulary basis.

The *Swedish* rules on allocation of deductions are quite undeveloped. For clearly identifiable costs incurred in the branch, for example, salaries of local employees, the expenses are directly deductible. In other situations, a formulary approach based on gross sales, a standardized head office charge, etc. may be used. The *United Kingdom* leaves the question to a factual determination.

Germany in general focuses on the economic connection

between the expense and the German activities, though there is no requirement that the expense be undertaken in Germany. In the case of management and general expenses, an allocation of the headquarters costs of the enterprise has been permitted as long the connection between the cost and the German activity can be established. While interest attributable to debt directly allocated to the branch would be deductible, it is unclear how the overall interest expense of the enterprise would be attributable to the branch. As the branch is a dependent part of the business, contractual arrangements between the branch and the head office generally are not accepted (with some exceptions in the banking and insurance industries). Thus, usually only an allocated portion of costs paid to third parties can be deducted. A "cost-plus" charge for control and coordination centers has been accepted in practice.

In *The Netherlands*, the same "functional" approach as is taken with income attribution is applied to deductions. Unlike other jurisdictions, there is some tendency in the Dutch case law to allow self-charged expenses in some situations. For example, it might be possible for the branch to deduct an arm's length rental for the use of assets of the overall enterprise for a short period of time.

All expenses effectively connected with and borne by the *French* branch of a foreign corporation, whether incurred by it or on behalf of it and wherever incurred, are deductible from taxable income. An expense incurred for the purposes of several branches must be allocated between them according to appropriate criteria. The general administrative expenses of the head office are usually allocable on the ratio the branch's turnover bears to that of the corporation as a whole. No allowance is normally to be made for payments by the branch to the head office in return for money loaned or patent rights conceded by the latter to the former, when they do not constitute the reimbursement of expenses paid or accrued to third parties. Nonresident individuals, unless provided to the contrary by statute, are denied the deductions from global net income and tax credits which residents are entitled to for personal expenses.

In *Australia*, the normal allocation rules for deductions apply in this area as in others. The foreign-source income of nonresidents is exempt income as are dividends, interest, and royalties subject to the nonresident withholding regime. Accordingly deductions that relate to these classes of income are not deductible whereas deductions that relate to the Australian source assessable income of the branch are. Australia is very strict in not allowing notional deductions for head office charges both for inbound and outbound cases. The special regimes that apply to overseas ships and insurance with nonresidents deem a certain percentage of freight charges (5 %) or premiums (10 %) to be taxable income to which the normal tax rates are applied and thus amount to formulary measures allowing deductions for expenses of 95 % and 90 % of income respectively. In some cases, the local agent of the taxpayer can elect out of the special regime into net basis taxation.

When the operation of branches of foreign banks became possible in Australia in 1994, a special regime was enacted for the calculation of their income. In this case, internal interest charges are allowed; 4 % of the branch's liabilities are treated as equity and the rest attracts a tax deduction based on the LIBOR interest rate; 50 % of this deemed interest payment is subject to interest withholding tax (in effect a one-half reduction in the 10 % interest withholding tax rate, recognizing the problem of applying full interest withholding tax rates to banks) and the general thin capitalization rules do not apply. A branch of a foreign bank may elect to be taxed under tax treaty rules where one is applicable which ensures that the regime is not in breach of treaty obligations.

1.4 Taxation of employment income

Most jurisdictions tax employment income earned by nonresidents on a net basis, typically with an exemption where the contacts with the jurisdiction are not extensive. Two basic approaches are used in determining the source of employment income. One focuses on the place where the services are performed, taking into account the days of physical presence. The other considers where the services are "utilized," that is, the locus of the benefit from the services. Deduction for attributable expenses of earning domestic-source employment income are allowed but personal allowances or preferential rate schedules are generally not available or are limited.

The *United States* considers services income to have its source where the services are performed. The provision of personal services is treated as a trade or business, thus satisfying the threshold for net basis taxation. A de minimis rule exempts the income where both the presence in the jurisdiction and the amount of income are minimal and the payor is a foreign person.

In *Japan*, income from personal services likewise has a domestic source if the services are performed in Japan and there is no further requirement for the income to be subject to net basis taxation. The income is subject to tax on a net basis but in the case of employees, domestic law allows only very limited deductions. A special rule treats director's fees paid by a domestic corporation as Japanese source income regardless of where the services are performed, thus assimilating such payments to corporate distributions.

The *Canadian* rules also focus on employment performed in Canada. Income from such employment is taxed on a net basis. Under a special provision, if a nonresident was formerly a resident of Canada, his entire employment income received from a Canadian payor is subject to Canadian tax except to the extent that the amount received for employment outside of Canada is subject to tax in a foreign jurisdiction.

The Netherlands taxes income from employment in the country on a net basis. Director's fees paid by domestic corporations are taxed even if the services are performed abroad.

In *Australia*, the source rule for employment income apart from treaties is a mixture of place of performance, place of contract and place of payment. The original cases establishing these rules concerned seamen based in Australia in the days when tax was only levied on a source basis. In those cases, no jurisdiction would have taxed the sailors on their income earned on the high seas if Australia did not, which partly explains the emphasis on place of contract and payment. Nonetheless, the mix of factors continues to apply. It was held that the income derived by Robert Mitchum for acting in "The Sundowners" filmed on location in Australia, was not necessarily domestic sourced and conversely that the salary paid by an Australian university to a resident academic on sabbatical leave overseas was sourced in Australia.

The normal deduction, assessment, and withholding collection rules apply to nonresident employees, though a different rate scale is in operation for the first $20,700 of taxable income and the personal tax rebates (credits) are not available. Treaties are the only means of providing a liability threshold if the income is Australian source, though in practice nonresidents with limited contacts may avoid the net basis tax. The international jurisdiction rules for the fringe benefits tax effectively track those used for employment income. Thus, liability arises in respect of benefits provided to a nonresident employee whose salary is sourced in Australia. However, nonresident employers will often not be aware of this liability which usually cannot be enforced apart from voluntary compliance in this case.

The *United Kingdom* taxes all compensation for services rendered within the jurisdiction. Where duties are performed partly within and partly without the U.K., the income is generally apportioned on a time basis. Taxation is on a net basis though certain personal deductions are not available.

Germany taxes employment income if the services are carried out in Germany or "utilized" by a German resident employer. The same rule applies to income from self-employment. Taxation is on a net basis, though in the case of employment income some deductions are limited. Special rules apply to cross-border workers.

France levies a progressive (15 % and 25 %) withholding tax (which does not exist for French residents) on employment income of nonresident individuals performing their activity on its territory. It is assessed on a net basis in that the salary is reduced by the standard 10 % professional expense deduction, but the election to deduct actual expenses open to residents is not available. The base is then reduced by the general 20 % allowance accorded to all salary income. The 15 % tax is final. But the income taxed in the upper bracket (over ca. $700 a week, $3,000 a month, $35,000 a year) is included in the global annual income and so subject to progressive individual income tax according to the same rules that apply to wages earned by French residents. The 25 % withholding tax is then creditable against such income tax and the excess may be refunded.

1.5 Other situations involving net basis taxation

A number of other types of income are often taxed on a net basis, though there is considerable variation in approach. Most often, the income has substantial associated deductions or deduction levels that vary from situation to situation so that gross taxation, even at a low level, would yield inappropriate results. Often, net basis treatment is available for real estate income where depreciation and interest deductions can be important. Gain from the disposition of substantial investments in domestic corporations are also often taxed on a net basis, with the underlying domestic business activity of the corporation, in effect, attributed to the nonresident shareholder for purposes of taxing the gain.

The *United States* allows election for net basis taxation in the case of real estate. If the real estate activities constitute a trade or business, the income would be subject to net basis taxation even without a special rule. However, in other cases, the rental income would be subject to gross withholding tax. A special election allows the taxpayer to elect to have all real estate income taxed on a net basis. In addition, gain on the sale of domestic real estate is also taxed on a net basis and that treatment is extended to gain on the shares of domestic corporations which have substantial domestic real estate holdings.

Canada similarly has an election to have real estate rental income taxed on a net basis. In the absence of an election, the rentals are subject to gross basis withholding tax at 25 %.

Most other jurisdictions tax real estate income on a net basis regardless of the level of activity or whether the real estate activities would otherwise qualify as a business. In Germany, special legislation makes it clear that real estate activities of foreign corporations can be taxed even in the absence of a permanent establishment; individuals, however, are only taxed if the activities amount to a business.

Results are more varied on substantial domestic corporate investments. The United States, Japan, Sweden, and the United Kingdom in general do not impose tax on this category of income. In contrast, Germany, The Netherlands, Canada, and Australia, under varying conditions, include such gain in domestic-source income and impose a net basis tax. Thus in Germany, for example, nonresidents are subject to tax on gains from the disposition of a greater than 25 % interest in a German corporation. Australia also taxes any interest in a resident closely-held corporation or trust.

Other miscellaneous types of income are often subject to tax on a net basis independent of the general classification of the activity generating the income as a business or permanent establishment. For example, Australia levies a withholding tax on natural resource payments to nonresidents but the rate is negotiated with the tax administration and is meant to reflect expenses; the taxpayer can file returns for refunds or be assessed on a net basis if it turns out that the estimated expenses are incorrect.

2. Issues in the structure of gross basis taxation

All of the systems here under consideration impose a gross-based withholding tax on certain categories of income. Sometimes the withholding tax is part of the domestic system and is applied to residents and nonresidents alike, though for nonresidents it represents a final tax. In other cases, the withholding tax is aimed only at foreign persons. The income subject to withholding is typically investment-type income that is not connected with a business activity and that is deemed to have a domestic source. Thus, the structural rules involve issues as to classification of the income by type as well as by source. In some cases, the source rules are the same as those used for domestic persons in determining the income entitled to double tax relief and in some cases, there are special source rules for income accruing to foreign persons.

The *United States* rules imposing gross basis taxation on foreign persons apply to "fixed or determinable annual or periodic" income from domestic sources. The taxable category has been broadly interpreted and applies essentially to all income that does not involve the sale of property. Thus, for example, isolated gambling winnings have been held to be subject to tax, despite difficulty of fitting such income into the statutory definition. The rate of tax is 30 % regardless of the type of income. However, there are statutory exceptions which exempt interest on domestic bank deposits and most interest paid by United States corporations or the United States government on publicly-traded debt.

Detailed statutory source rules deal with the commonly recurring types of income such as dividends, interest, royalties, etc. In general, the same source rules apply to domestic persons as to foreign persons. The source rules focus in part on the economic connections and in part on formal legal relations. For example, royalties are sourced where the property is used while interest, in general, is sourced based on the residence of the payor. Special rules apply to interest paid by a U.S. trade or business. The interest is treated as if paid by a U.S. corporation and as such is subject to tax in the hands of a foreign recipient. In addition, if, under the rules allocating interest expense to the U.S. branch, more interest has been deducted then paid directly, that excess is subject to the usually applicable gross basis tax in the hands of the branch.

Domestic-source income is subject to withholding by the payor and the withheld amount functions as a final tax. No withholding is required if the income is part of the business income of the foreign taxpayer. If for some reason the appropriate tax is not withheld, the foreign person as well as the domestic withholding agent are both liable for the tax. Special withholding rules also apply to partnerships with nonresident partners and to dispositions of United States real estate.

Japan takes a somewhat similar approach. Source rules deal with rentals, interest, dividends, royalties, prizes, annuities, income from certain financial instruments, and "silent partnership" income. All such income is subject to withholding even if it arises in connection with a business which is taxed on a net basis. (The corporation can ask for non-withholding treatment in certain circumstances.) The withheld tax is credited against the net basis tax liability. The source rules are generally the same for both inbound and outbound transactions.

The *Swedish* system does not have extensive source rules and simply defines certain categories of income which are subject to withholding as a final tax. Unlike other systems, Sweden taxes employment income from services performed in Sweden on a gross basis. Withholding is imposed on the following types of income at the given rates; employment income, director's fees, pensions (25 %); dividends (30 %); artists and entertainers (15 %). The rates of withholding were set at a level which tries in a rough way to take into account the costs associated with the income.

Canada imposes a 25 % withholding tax on a statutory catalogue of income categories when paid by Canadian residents to a nonresident. The statute is not structured in terms of source rules but the operative taxing provisions function in that manner. Thus, in general, all interest payable by a Canadian resident is subject to the withholding tax. This is functionally the same result as in the United States, which relies on explicit source rules.

Withholding is required on many types of interest, but exceptions are made for interest on governmental obligations, medium and long-term portfolio interest, and certain bank interest. Estate and trust income is generally subject to withholding when paid to a nonresident. Amounts paid by a resident for the use of property in Canada, including intangibles, is subject to tax, with the charging provision in effect functioning as a source rule. Dividends paid by Canadian corporations, including constructive dividends, are subject to tax as are alimony, pensions and other deferred compensation, and the interest element in annuities.

The scope of the withholding regime is extended substantially by rules deeming certain payors to be Canadian residents and thus subject to withholding obligations and by parallel rules deeming recipients to be nonresidents, again triggering a withholding tax liability. Thus, payments by a nonresident which are deductible in computing Canadian business or real estate profits are deemed to be made by a Canadian resident and thus, subject to withholding when paid to a nonresident. A specific rule applies to partnerships that treats them as resident as regards amounts paid to nonresidents which are deductible in Canada.

The *United Kingdom* requires withholding at the basic rate of 24 % on a wide range of investment income. Sometimes, for example in the case of rent, the withholding only applies to payments to nonresidents. The rules with regard to interest are being reconsidered.

In *Germany*, withholding taxes are imposed on some categories of income regardless of the status of the recipient and also are imposed specifically on certain income paid to nonresidents. With respect to capital income (dividends, certain types of interest, income of silent partners), the normally applicable withholding tax represents a final tax for nonresidents. The tax is at a 25 % rate unless the agreement requires a payment net of tax, in which case the rate is 33 %. In addition, a final 25 % withholding tax is imposed on income from artistic, sporting or cultural activities, royalties on intangibles, and rentals on personal property. A final 30 % withholding tax is imposed on director's fees. Under a court-developed principle which was later incorporated into the statute, the usual rule that all the income of a corporation is treated as business income is not applied in the case of nonresident corporations. Thus they can be taxed on, for example, royalty or dividend income from German sources even in the absence of a permanent establishment.

The interaction of net basis and gross basis rules in *Australia* is quite complex. The Australian nonresident final withholding tax on dividends, interest, and royalties is levied at rates of 30 %, 10 % and 30 %, respectively. The interest withholding tax has an important exemption for widely-held offshore fund-raisings which the government has recently announced will be extended to all cases where the loan is open to public bidding even if one lender takes the whole loan. The implicit source rule in each case is payment by a resident to a nonresident, which will differ in many cases from the judge-made source rules in these areas. Thus, the theoretical possibility is opened up of a payment derived by a nonresident which is not subject to the withholding regime but is sourced in Australia and so assessable on an assessment basis; such cases seem to be ignored in practice.

The interest withholding rule also reflects the permanent establishment thinking of tax treaties in the sense that the tax applies to payments of interest *by* on-shore permanent establishments of nonresidents and payments *to* offshore permanent establishments of residents. The basic criterion is use of the borrowed funds in an Australian business. In the case of payment to an offshore permanent establishment of a resident, the interest income is still included in assessable income (unlike all other payments subject to the nonresident withholding tax) but no credit is given for the tax withheld which in this case is operating as a surrogate tax on interest payments made by the offshore permanent establishment to third parties. In contrast, the royalty rule is only extended to the case of payment by an onshore permanent establishment of a nonresident.

Dividends are in a special position because of the imputation system. The franked part of dividends is not subject to withholding tax when paid to nonresidents but remains exempt income outside the net basis regime whether or not there is an onshore permanent establishment to which the dividend is attributable. This reflects the fact that the underlying corporate profits will have borne corporate-level tax, though the imputation credit is not extended to nonresidents. The unfranked part of dividends is subject to the treaty-reduced withholding tax of 15% normally.

Where an Australian resident company receives foreign dividends (which will usually be exempt from Australian tax in the case of a headquarters company under the non-portfolio dividend exemption discussed above) and then pays out unfranked dividends to nonresident shareholders, it may keep a foreign dividend account to match dividends received and dividends paid that will not be subject to nonresident dividend withholding tax to that extent. Although this benefit is in theory available to Australian multinational companies with nonresident subsidiaries and nonresident shareholders, strict rules to prevent streaming of dividends under the imputation system and the foreign dividend account mean that the benefit will generally have greatest relevance to headquarters companies. The anti-avoidance rules hedging around these regimes mean that they are less generous in many cases than comparable regimes in other countries in the region and a common perception is that they were introduced by the government without much enthusiasm in response to pressure from the private sector.

The *French* tax code contains a list of French-source income, foreign source income being defined a contrario. Source is determined, according to the categories, on the basis of economic connections or formal legal relations or a combination of both. Some categories of income are subject to withholding taxes. These are assessed to some extent on a net basis (salaries, gains on the sale of real property) and are final or creditable against income tax. In other cases (income from independent personal services, copyrights, industrial property rights, remunerations for services of any kind supplied or used in France, remunerations of artists and sportsmen), the withholding tax is assessed on a gross basis but creditable against income tax levied on a net basis. The only withholding taxes that are both final and levied on gross income are the 25 % tax on distributed income, 15 % on interest (but there are many exemptions), and 16 % on gains from the disposition of substantial interests in French corporations.

Of all the jurisdictions here considered, *The Netherlands* has the least extensive gross basis source taxation. Historically, this appears to reflect a conscious policy to encourage the use of The Netherlands as the location for holding and intermediate companies, often engaged in treaty shopping activities. Only dividends paid by Dutch companies are subject to withholding tax at the rate of 25 %. For nonresidents, this tax is a final tax unless the dividends are attributed to a permanent establishment in which case the tax is credited against the net basis tax liability. Interest which is based on profits is treated as a dividend for these purposes. Other interest, royalties, and like payments are in general not subject to gross basis taxation when paid to nonresidents.

3. Branch profits tax

Absent special rules, the remittance of profits from a branch activity would not be subject to any further source-based taxation. In contrast, dividends paid by a domestic corporation would typically be subject to a withholding tax. This difference in treatment of alternative investment structures has led some countries to impose a second "level" of tax on branch income of foreign corporations. Though the technical rules differ in many respects, the basic impact of the tax is to subject the net after-tax profits of the branch to a tax roughly equivalent to the tax that would have been applicable to a profits distribution by a domestic subsidiary.

Until 1986, the *United States* attempted to impose a second "level" of tax when the foreign corporation with United States branch activities made a dividend distribution to its shareholders. The tax was very difficult to enforce and was resented by other countries as an attempt at "extraterritorial" taxation, involving as it did the taxation of a distribution of a foreign corporation to a foreign shareholder. In 1986, this second-level withholding tax was replaced in most situations by a branch profits tax imposed on the net after-tax income of the branch. After-tax profits which are not reinvested in the United States business are subject to the same 30 % tax that a dividend distribution would have attracted. If the tax is avoided currently by reinvesting profits, subsequent decreases in investment will trigger a "recapture" of the tax. If branch activities are terminated, there is no recapture of the tax previously avoided through reinvestment. If the assets are transferred to a U.S. corporation, the taxpayer can avoid current tax by agreeing that a subsequent sale of the stock will result in recognition of the deferred branch tax. The treatment is based on the model of a liquidating distribution by a domestic subsidiary that similarly would not have attracted a dividend withholding tax. As discussed above, a somewhat similar "branch interest" tax is imposed on interest expense which has been allocated to U.S. branch activities.

Canada has a similar branch profits tax that antedated the United States tax. It is imposed at a 25 % rate, the normal withholding rate on dividends, on the after-tax profits of a Canadian business operated by a foreign corporation which are not reinvested in the Canadian operations. Any amount claimed by a nonresident corporation as reinvested profits in computing the branch tax payable for a particular year must be included in computing the base for the branch tax for the succeeding year. Accordingly, as in the U.S. system, if a nonresident corporation decreases its branch investment in subsequent years, the prior reduction of the branch tax will be recaptured. A similar result occurs if a branch operation is terminated. However, where a nonresident corporation forms a Canadian corporation and transfers to the corporation the assets of the Canadian branch, the recapture is effectively deferred. In effect, a nonresident corporation may transfer the assets of a branch operation to a wholly-owned Canadian subsidiary on a rollover basis.

France has a related method of imposing a second level of source-country tax on foreign corporate operations. France levies its 25 % withholding tax normally applicable to distributed income on the net after-tax amount of profits of foreign corporations operating in France. In effect, those profits are deemed to be distributed to nonresident shareholders and the tax is equivalent to the withholding tax which would have been imposed on distributions by a resident company. However, this second-level tax can be refunded if the foreign corporation can prove that, in the year following the realization of the income, it has distributed no dividends or that all shareholders are French residents. It is partially refunded when the corporation can demonstrate that it has distributed less money than its earnings in France and/or in proportion to the percentage of French residents among its shareholders.

Australia previously had a branch profits tax but it was eliminated when, in connection with the introduction of the imputation system, the corporate and maximum individual tax rates were aligned which meant, in the Australian view, there was no justification for an extra branch tax to match the shareholder tax on dividends. For the same reason, the nonresident dividend withholding tax on the franked part of dividends was also abolished. Although the corporate rate is now significantly below the maximum individual rate, which would provide some justification for both a nonresident dividend withholding tax and a branch profits tax, neither has been reintroduced (perhaps to forestall efforts by the United States to obtain imputation benefits by treaty).

Sweden, The Netherlands, Japan, the *United Kingdom,* and *Germany* do not have a branch profits tax.

4. Limitations on base-eroding payments to nonresidents

Where, as is usually the case, rates on business income taxed on a net basis are higher than rates on deductible gross basis taxed payments, taxpayers have an incentive to reduce the net basis tax base as much as possible. This is particularly true where treaties reduce or even eliminate the gross basis taxation. In response, a number of countries have imposed restrictions on the deductibility of such base-eroding payments. The focus here is on restrictions which are exclusively or primarily aimed at nonresident-owned domestic operations.[3] The most common problem is debt financing of domestic subsidiary operations with the attendant interest deduction. Here, special debt-equity

---

3 The limitations are sometimes applied to all "tax-exempt" recipients, thus covering domestic tax exempt organizations as well as foreign taxpayers but the main impact of the rules usually is, and is intended to be, on foreigners, with the extension to tax-exempt organizations aimed at avoiding treaty-based complaints of discrimination.

rules are sometimes applied to nonresident-owned domestic corporations. Other provisions limit the extent of the interest deduction if interest payments are deemed excessive in relation to the domestic income. These "earnings stripping" rules are also typically focused on payments to nonresidents.

In the *United States*, there are no special debt-equity rules applicable to nonresidents. However, "earnings stripping" restrictions do limit the deductibility of certain interest payments. The rules are applicable to payments of interest to related parties who are tax-exempt and thus cover loans by domestic tax-exempt organizations, though the thrust of the provisions is clearly at nonresident investors who are often exempt by treaty from withholding tax on outbound interest payments. Originally limited to loans made directly by related tax-exempt persons, the provision was expanded recently to cover loans by third parties which are guaranteed by foreign persons. For the interest deduction to be limited, the corporation's debt-equity ratio must exceed 1.5:1 and the corporation must have "excess" interest expense, defined as interest in excess of 50 % of the corporation's adjusted taxable income for the period. In that case, deduction for any excess interest paid to related tax-exempt persons is not deducted currently but can be carried forward and deducted in a later year, subject to the 50 % limitation in that year. In addition, any "excess" limitation can be carried forward and used to increase the amount of deductible interest in a future year. Where the interest paid to a foreign person is subject to some tax, but the tax is reduced under a treaty, the amount of the disallowed interest expense is determined by treating a proportionate part of the interest as being tax exempt. Thus, if the treaty reduced the normal 30 % rate to 10 %, two-thirds of the interest expense would be treated as payable to a tax-exempt person and potentially subject to disallowance.

In addition, the interest deduction can be disallowed if the interest is paid to a third-party lender who is not subject to a gross basis tax and the obligation is guaranteed (formally or informally) by a related foreign person. In this case, the interest deduction can be disallowed even if it is subject to net basis taxation in the hands of the recipient, i.e., when received by a U.S. bank.

Canada has debt-equity rules that apply to loans by nonresident shareholders. Canadian thin capitalization rules apply to foreign shareholders of a Canadian corporation who own at least 25 percent, by votes or value, of the shares of a Canadian corporation. Constructive ownership rules apply for this purpose. The rules also apply to debt of the Canadian corporation held by a nonresident who does not deal at arm's length with such shareholders. A 3:1 debt-equity ratio is required and is calculated on the basis of the greatest amount of debt outstanding to the specified shareholders and persons not dealing at arm's length with them. The equity of the corporation is defined as the aggregate of its retained earnings, any surplus contributed by the specified nonresident shareholders, and the greater of the opening and closing paid-up capital of the shares owned by such shareholders. Equity is computed on a non-consolidated basis. A special anti-avoidance rule prevents the circumvention of the thin capitalization rules through the use of back-to-back loans. The Canadian thin capitalization rules do not apply to partnerships, trusts, or branches. The rules, first introduced in 1972, are generally thought to be ineffective.

In *Australia*, interest deductions are denied to the extent debt-equity ratios exceed 3:1 in the normal case or 6:1 for financial institutions on loans by 15 %-related nonresidents to Australian branches of nonresidents and to Australian companies (which are grouped for this purpose where there is an onshore holding company with resident 100 % subsidiaries). The ratio is based only on related party debt-to-equity, not total debt-to-equity, and is thus very generous compared to regimes in other countries. Further, despite strict back-to-back rules the regime is relatively limited. Parent guarantees are not currently covered (though there are proposals for change) and the definition of interest for this purpose does not include close interest substitutes such as foreign exchange gains/losses and so can be circumvented by modern financial instruments.

The generosity of the regime is such that rules were introduced at the same time (referred to as "debt creation") designed to prevent 50 %-related parties from substituting debt for existing equity and so increasing their debt up to the permitted limit. These latter rules go beyond related-party debt, however, and cover, for example, sales of assets between related parties where the purchase is financed by a bank loan and used to retire equity of the seller. This aspect is explained by the origin of Australia's rules on base erosion in the foreign investment approval process, which sought to ensure not only that the Australian tax base was not eroded by excessive related party funding but also that once the investment was made, a certain agreed amount of equity funding was committed in Australia and could not be surreptitiously withdrawn after approval was forthcoming.

The *United Kingdom* also has a complex set of thin capitalization rules which apply primarily to nonresidents. The most important is a rule which denies deduction for interest in certain circumstances where the U.K. company is a 75 % or greater subsidiary of a foreign parent.

Japan has thin capitalization rules which restrict the deduction of interest paid by domestic corporations to foreign shareholders under certain conditions. The legislation, enacted in 1992, provides that the interest deduction on loans to Japanese corporations by controlling foreign shareholders is limited if the debt-equity ratio of both related party and overall borrowing exceeds 3:1. If the taxpayer can establish that comparable Japanese companies have higher ratios, those ratios will be used. Where the provision applies, it disallows deduction for interest on that portion of the debt that exceeds the relevant ratio. The rule applies to branch operations as well.

The *German* thin capitalization rules, which apply both to nonresidents and domestic tax-exempt organizations, play a significant role in the domestic context and are described in Part Three.

Sweden and *The Netherlands* have no special provisions dealing with base-eroding payments to nonresidents, though there have been legislative proposals for such rules in The Netherlands.

5. Restrictions on source-based taxation of nonresidents within the European Union

The differential treatment of residents and nonresidents reflected in source based taxation has recently raised some important issues in the European Union. The provisions on freedom of movement of employees, business, services and capital date back to 1957 when the EC Treaty was concluded. It was not until 1986, however, that the EC Court of Justice ruled that these provisions were applicable to differential taxation by one Member State of resident taxpayers of another Member State. To the extent taxes have not been harmonized — individual income tax has not been harmonized in any respect and in the corporate tax field harmonization has remained limited to the Parent-Subsidiary and Merger Directives — the Court has ruled that the application of the domestic tax laws may not interfere with intra-Community movements of individuals and businesses. While these freedom of movement provisions forbid Member States to treat differentially on the basis of nationality, the Court in a liberal construction of these provisions has ruled that since nonresidents typically will have a foreign nationality, discrimination in the treatment of nonresident taxpayers as compared to resident taxpayers is forbidden by these rules.

A substantial jurisprudence has developed significant limitations on source country taxation of nonresidents. As of 1996, the Court has decided more than ten cases dealing with various aspects of the problem. Forms of differential taxation that the Court declared as violating the Treaty include individual income tax rates (the *Asscher* case on the Netherlands 25 % tax rate in first bracket for nonresidents in contrast to the 6.5 % rate for resident taxpayers), the right to file for a refund (the *Biehl* and *Schumacker* decisions), the right to personal deductions (e.g., medical expenses, alimony) and to income splitting (*Schumacker*) (provided the nonresident taxpayer derives virtually all of his income from the source state), and the right to the imputation credit (*avoir fiscal*) (where shares of a French company were held in a French branch of a nonresident taxpayer).

In developing the restrictions on the taxation of nonresidents, the Court does not always seem to be fully aware of the extensive impact of its decisions in the highly technical area of international taxation. Apparently animated by a desire to do away with all potentially discriminatory national restrictions, whatever form they take, the Court has increasingly limited the right of source countries to apply traditionally accepted methods of taxing nonresidents. The governments of the Member States have become more and more aware of the vast number of long standing rules that may not withstand the scrutiny of the Court. One should add to this that the 1992 Maastricht Treaty expanded the scope of the EC Treaty beyond restrictions of an economic nature. As a result, the prospect is that where the Court in the past has denied the applicability of the Treaty in situations which only personal matters were involved, such cases will in the future be found to be within the scope of the EC Treaty as amended by the EU Treaty. This development may trigger further voluntary harmonization of the taxation of nonresidents by the Member States. On the other hand, it may lead the Member States to restrict the power of the Court through amendments to the Treaty.

The following **Table IV-2** summarizes the rules dealing with the taxation of various types of domestic source income received by nonresident taxpayers. The typically applicable treaty rates are indicated, though there can be substantial variations in individual treaties. The column "Sale of stock" deals with source-based tax on gains derived from the sale of stock in a domestic corporation by a foreign shareholder who has no other contact to the source country. Likewise, the column "Financial product income" is focused on source-based taxation of income from derivative financial instruments where there is no other jurisdictional connection.

Taxation of domestic source income of nonresident taxpayers

	Dividends	Interest	Royalties	Business income threshold	Employment income threshold	Sale of stock of domestic corporation	Financial product income (no domestic PE/ business)
Australia	0% if corp. tax paid; 30% gross withholding if not; treaty 15%	10% gross withholding (publicly offered debt exempt); treaty 10%	30% gross; treaty 15%	any Australian source	Australian source (place of performance in general)	any private company shares, 10%+ of public company taxable	generally exempt but Australian source taxed
Canada	25% gross withholding; treaty 5-15%	25% gross withholding (long term debt exempt); treaty 10%	25% gross withholding; treaty 10%, 0% for technology royalties	carrying on business	any employment in Canada	any private company shares, 25%+ of public company or real estate taxable	generally exempt

Taxation of domestic source income of nonresident taxpayers

	Dividends	Interest	Royalties	Business income threshold	Employment income threshold	Sale of stock of domestic corporation	Financial product income (no domestic PE/ business)
France	25% gross withholding; treaty 5-15%	15% gross withholding (many important exceptions); treaty 0-10%	33.33% withholding; (creditable against net basis tax); treaty 0-10%	permanent establishment (some differences from treaty rule)	any services performed in France	25% + interest in domestic company taxable (real estate no minimum shareholding)	generally exempt
Germany	25% gross withholding tax; treaty usually 15%	generally exempt	25% withholding tax; treaty exempt	permanent establishment/ permanent representative	services "utilized" in Germany	25% + interest in domestic company taxable	generally exempt
Japan	20% gross withholding; treaty 10-15%	15% gross withholding; treaty 10%	20% gross withholding: treaty 10%	permanent establishment	any services performed in Japan over de minimis	generally exempt	generally exempt
The Netherlands	25% gross withholding; treaty 5-15%	exempt	exempt	permanent establishment/ permanent representative	any services performed in NL	substantial interest (33%+) taxable	generally exempt
Sweden	30% gross withholding; treaty 5-15%	generally exempt	taxed as business income; treaty exempt	permanent establishment	services performed in Sweeden	exempt	generally exempt
United Kingdom	20% withholding; taxed at 20% or 40%; treaty 5-15%	20% withholding; taxed at 20% or 40%; treaty 10-15%	24% withholding; taxed at 20% or 40%; treaty 10-15%	trade or profession in UK	any services performed in UK	exempt	generally exempt
United States	30% gross withholding; treaty 5-15%	30% gross withholding (portfolio exempt); treaty 0%	30% gross withholding; treaty 0%	trade or business	any services performed in US over de minimis	generally exempt; interest in domestic real estate corp. taxed	generally exempt

Subpart C: Additional International Topics

1. Special international anti-avoidance rules.

The general approach of the jurisdictions here under consideration to tax avoidance schemes is discussed in the material in Part One. Beyond these generally applicable principles and rules, several countries have provisions that are aimed specifically at certain international transactions. In some cases, the same results might have been reached under normally applicable principles and the international rule only clarifies the situation. In others, there are principles which are unique to the international area.

In the *United States*, general substance-over-form and "step-transactions" principles have allowed interrelated financing arrangements to be recharacterized where the particular structure was tax motivated. However, questions about the extent to which the rules would be applied and their limits gave room for substantial aggressive tax planning in the international area. Congress responded by authorizing regulations to recharacterize "multiple-party financing transactions" as occurring directly between participants, ignoring intermediate parties. Regulations recently issued under this provision deal with international "back-to-back" arrangements designed to take advantage of reduced treaty rates available to the intermediate entity. Interest paid to the intermediary is treated as paid directly to the ultimate source of the financing and taxed as such. The recharacterization will only occur if the financing transaction was part of a "tax avoidance plan," one of the principal purposes of which is the avoidance of U.S. tax. The regulations list a number of factors to be taken into account in making this determination.

Special *Canadian* rules are aimed at attempts to convert tax-free capital gains realized by nonresidents on the sale of shares in Canadian resident corporations into paid-up capital of a purchasing Canadian corporation. The sales amount is recharacterized as a dividend (or reduction in the paid-up capital of the transferred corporation) that defeats the double benefit which would otherwise be available.

Similar rules apply in *Germany* in connection with sales of shares in German corporations by nonresidents who would not otherwise be entitled to the imputation credit. In a typical transaction, a nonresident shareholder in a German corporation would sell his shares to a German resident shortly before the declaration of a dividend at a price reflecting the amount of the potential dividend. The gain could escape German tax under a treaty exemption. When the dividend was paid to the German shareholder, the dividend would bring with it the imputation credit and the dividend income could be offset by the write-down of the decline in value of the stock. The shares could subsequently be resold to the nonresident who would have in effect obtained the economic equivalent of the imputation credit in the initial purchase price. To block this dividend-stripping technique, anti-avoidance legislation was passed that denied the German taxpayer the ability to write down the shares purchased from a shareholder not entitled to the imputation credit in many situations. Other more sophisticated schemes were developed involving stock lending and repo agreements, and legislation in 1994 responded by denying the German shareholder the credit in those circumstances.

The *French* anti-avoidance theories of abuse of law (*abus de droit*) and abnormal management decision (*acte anormal de gestion*) apply both to international and domestic tax matters. But some statutory provisions specifically embody these theories in order to combat more easily certain types of international tax avoidance, especially by placing the burden of proof on the taxpayer.

Thus, according to the so-called "rent-a-star company" provision, compensation for services rendered by an individual or a corporation in France, or rendered abroad if such person is resident or has an establishment in France, is taxed to such person if it is received by a person residing or established abroad and who is either based in a low-tax jurisdiction or controlled by the person providing the services or not shown to be predominantly engaged in an industrial or commercial business other than supplying services.

Similarly, deduction from the income tax base is denied to interest, royalties, and remunerations for services paid to individuals or legal entities residing or established in a low-tax jurisdiction, as well as to payments of any kind to an account in a financial institution established in such jurisdiction, unless the French taxpayer can prove the bona fide character of the transaction and that the amount paid is not exaggerated.

Finally, a French corporation is taxed on income arising from assets it has previously directly or indirectly transferred to a foreign person or trust without any immediate consideration in order for the transferee to manage such assets or pay interest and capital on a debt on behalf of the transferor.

Japan, Sweden, and *The Netherlands* do not have any special anti-avoidance rules in the international area.

2. Selected intercompany pricing issues

All of the systems recognize as a general principle that dealings between related parties must be undertaken at arm's length, though the specific formulation takes different forms. The arm's length principle usually is applied on a transactional basis and formulary rules are not used. Some countries have detailed administrative rules while others take a more "facts-and-circumstances" approach.

The general framework for analyzing intercompany pricing issues set out in the 1979 OECD Report on Transfer Pricing and Multinational Enterprises seems to be widely followed. The terminology and methodology of comparable uncontrolled price ("CUP"), resale price, cost-plus, and "other" methods are thus present in most of the systems. The revised 1995 OECD guidelines will undoubtedly also be important in the future, though the extent to which profit-based methodologies will be accepted remains unclear. The following discussion is limited to the general approach taken by the countries and any special or distinguishing features which might be of interest.

The *United States* has historically been a leader in the development of transfer pricing rules and its system is still the most highly developed. The recent revisions in the regulation, effective in 1994, make some important changes in the general approach to transfer pricing. Rather than establishing an order of preference for a particular transfer pricing technique, the new Regulations instruct the taxpayer to use the "best method," that is, the method which will provide the most reliable measure of an arm's length price under the circumstances. Taxpayers may use transactions which involve "inexact" comparables if adjustments can be made to improve the reliability of the comparison between the controlled and uncontrolled transactions. The factors involved in determining comparability include the functions performed by each party, the contractual terms involved, and the allocation of risks. The focus is on arriving at a range of possible arm's length prices, using statistical techniques to establish the limits of the appropriate range.

The new Regulations introduce two new methods which can be used in the absence of reliable data establishing comparability. First, a profit-split method is permitted in which the aggregate profit is allocated between the controlled parties in the light of the functions performed, risks assumed, and resources provided by each party. Under the previous Regulations, profit-splits, though common in practice, were only recognized as an unspecified "other" method.

The most important and controversial aspect of the new Regulations is the introduction of the "comparable profits" method (CPM) of price determination. Under the CPM approach, the determination of an arm's length price is based on comparable profit level indicators that measure the relationship between profits and costs involved and resources employed. The price charged the controlled taxpayer with respect to particular transactions must result in appropriate profit levels from those transactions as determined by the profit level indicators of comparable but unrelated parties. Unlike previous proposed regulations, which stressed the importance of a profit-based methodology as a check on other methods, under the final regulations the CPM is simply another possible method and subject to the "best method" principle. Thus, where better information with respect to some of the traditional methods exists, those approaches are to be used. Only where the information used to establish the appropriate profit margins is more reliable than that needed for one of the other methods will the CPM be the method of choice.

Beyond the substantive rules, there are important procedural requirements that must be followed to avoid significant penalties in case of a subsequent transfer price adjustment. The penalties can be avoided only if the taxpayer has followed one of the prescribed methods of price determination and has contemporaneous documentation establishing how the price was determined. Thus the new regulations offer a substantial degree of flexibility in the choice of the method but the taxpayer must be prepared to demonstrate in detail how prices were in fact arrived at.

In addition, the United States has encouraged the use of Advance Pricing Agreements through which taxpayers can obtain a binding commitment in advance from the fiscal authorities as to the appropriateness of the methodology to be used in establishing the transfer price. In many cases, these agreements involve both the United States and the other countries impacted by the business activities in question.

Germany similarly has detailed "administrative principles" on transfer pricing which have been issued by the fiscal authorities. While not binding on taxpayers, they are followed in practice. They are based in part on the 1979 OECD Report and in part on prior German judicial and administrative practices. The Finance Ministry has recently repeated the position taken in the administrative principles that only "transactional" methods of price determination are acceptable, expressly rejecting profit-based methods such as profit-split or the comparable profits method. Germany in principle is ready to enter into advance pricing agreements but lack of staff has limited the use of such agreements. Given their stress on arbitration in treaty negotiations, it appears that the German tax authorities seem to prefer arbitration to advance pricing agreements in the resolution of intercompany pricing disputes. However, there are some APA's in process.

In 1986, *Japan* adopted legislation dealing with transfer pricing. The provision applies to transactions between affiliated corporations where one party is Japanese (or a foreign corporation subject to corporate tax in Japan) and the other is foreign. It allows the tax authorities to make an assessment based on arm's length prices. The statutory provision is quite extensive and sets out at length the details of comparable price, resale price and cost-plus methods. There is no priority of method. If none of the "basic" methods can be applied, then "alternative" methods can be used; profit-split may be used though tax authorities clearly favor the use of the "basic" methods if possible. Advance pricing agreements have been available since shortly after the legislation was enacted.

In *Canada*, statutory provisions require that transactions between resident and nonresident related parties be at prices which would have been "reasonable" had the parties been unrelated. While there are no detailed regulations interpreting the statute, the tax authorities have issued an information circular setting forth its approach to transfer pricing. The positions taken are clearly based on and consistent with the approach of the 1979 OECD Report. There is little case law, however, and it is unclear how the positions taken in the circular would be dealt with by a court. In practice, the tax administration seems to be willing to allow corporations to set transfer prices within broad ranges of "reasonability," concentrating resources on "abusive" situations. There is a special procedure for advance pricing agreements, both unilateral and bilateral.

Canada has in the past indicated that it will not in principle follow a comparative profit method and will not make corresponding
adjustments based on that approach. On the other hand, the acceptance of a profit-based approach in the 1995 OECD Report as a "last
resort" may change that view, given the respect which Canada has historically given to the OECD positions.

Australia replaced its original defective provisions on transfer
pricing in 1981 with fairly elaborate provisions which, however, focus
on when adjustments may be made and the mechanics of doing so
(including adjustments to other taxpayers' positions) rather than the
pricing methodologies to be used. The "arm's length consideration" is
the only guide provided and where this cannot be determined because
of lack of information, the tax administration has power to determine
the amount it considers appropriate. The provisions apply to supply or
acquisition of property or services under international agreements
defined as the supply or acquisition by a nonresident otherwise than in
connection with a business of an onshore permanent establishment of
the nonresident or by a resident carrying on a business outside
Australia. There is no requirement that the parties to the transaction
be related. Thus the provision deals with situations where unrelated
parties enter into two transactions which together may be arm's length
but the one that affects Australia may not have an arm's length price
because it is compensated for in the pricing of the other agreement
which does not affect Australia. The rules also cover the branch case
where instead of adjustment through an arm's length pricing of the
transaction, the tax administration is given power to adjust the source
of income and related expenses on the basis of criteria that include the
separate entity and arm's length pricing hypothesis found in the business profits article of tax treaties.

The tax administration has recently begun to release a set of rulings on transfer pricing that already amount to many hundreds of pages
with much more to come. Generally these rulings follow the 1995
OECD guidelines and, like the U.S., look favorably on profit-based
"fourth" methods. Advance pricing agreements are available; indeed
Australia was the first country to enter into a bilateral APA with the
U.S. in relation to Apple Computer's operations in Australia. The
APA procedure is similar to that in the U.S. Penalties in the transfer
pricing area distinguish between tax avoidance schemes and other situations resulting in income understatement.

The *United Kingdom* has a fairly general statutory rule which allows the Revenue to substitute market value for whatever price may have been agreed upon between related parties in a particular transaction. There is some disagreement on the scope of the provision, which by its terms does not explicitly cover a number of transactions. There is very little administrative guidance and in practice, the issues are subject to negotiation between the tax authorities and the taxpayer which generally result in settlements. As a result, there is almost no case law on the application of the principles. There is some dispute about the relation between the domestic legislation and the corresponding treaty article authorizing arm's length price adjustments. The fiscal authorities have not yet taken a formal position on APA's.

While *Sweden* has a statutory provision that requires arm's length dealings where an "economic community" exists between the parties, there are no administrative regulations interpreting the provision and the case law is also quite sparse. In an important recent case, the Supreme Administrative Court indicated that the principles set out in the OECD 1979 report would be considered as "guidelines" in establishing an arm's length price. That case also stressed that the commercial situation should be judged at the time the agreements were entered into. The court seemed to indicate that price adjustments required under the "commensurate with income" standard would not be accepted. From a procedural point of view, the burden of proof is initially on the government to show that a deviation from an arm's length price has taken place which has resulted in lower taxable income in Sweden. Thereafter, the taxpayer has the burden to show that the reduced income was compensated for in other ways, by offsetting transactions or by other commercial factors. The offset rules are quite liberal. Thus, in some cases, failure to charge an arm's length price for services provided by a Swedish company can be justified by the benefit which the Swedish company could be expected to have from future sales to the foreign company. While Sweden in general allows advance rulings on tax issues, there is no special procedure for advance pricing agreements.

In *France*, the requirement to deal at arm's length to determine transfer prices results from the abnormal management decision theory (a decision that is not in the interest of the enterprise) which has, since 1933, been embodied in Section 57 of the tax code as far as international matters are concerned. There are few formal administrative guidelines and the approach has always been a facts and circumstances one.

The tax service has to show that a deviation from an arm's length price has taken place and, except when the foreign person is resident in or established in a low-tax jurisdiction, that the parties to the transaction are related to each other. Such transferred income is then added back to the tax base and, since it is treated as a deemed distribution of income to a foreign resident, subject to a 25 % withholding tax, unless the taxpayer can prove that the price was normal or that failure to charge an arm's length price is justified according to the particular economic circumstances or has or could have resulted in an equivalent increase in French-source income, e.g., because of subsequent sales. Case law is quite liberal in these matters.

Appropriate correlative adjustments are now available through a European Union arbitration mechanism, after the mutual agreement procedure has failed to arrive at a satisfactory solution.

The French tax authorities are generally reluctant as regards ruling practices, and no APA procedure exists. The powers of tax auditors to make requests for clarification about relationships of French businesses with foreign persons and for documentation substantiating transfer prices have been increased in 1996. When in the course of an audit, the authorities have gathered information which leads them to believe that there has been an indirect transfer of profits to an associated foreign enterprise, they may require the French enterprise to produce appropriate documents and information specifying the nature of the transactions and the methods used in determining the intercompany pricing of transactions. Failure to comply entails a fine and entitles the tax authorities to assess the income on the base of the data that it has available. In addition, the statute of limitations is extended when French tax authorities request international administrative assistance in connection with transfer pricing issues.

Although *The Netherlands* has no specific statutory provision requiring arm's length pricing between related parties, the principle that profits can be "corrected" in transactions between a corporation and its shareholders is firmly established in the case law. There are no formal administrative rules, but the 1979 OECD Report has been used both by taxpayers and tax authorities in evaluating and justifying pricing practices. The extent to which courts would consider those principles controlling is less clear, though there are a number of cases which use some sort of cost-plus method. An administrative circular also accepts a cost-plus approach to services. Advance rulings on transfer pricing have long been common in Holland and bilateral advance pricing agreements also available.

3. Selected treaty issues

All of the countries have treaties which are broadly based on the OECD Model Convention. Canada and Australia, whose interests as source countries are greater than the other jurisdictions, generally insist on greater recognition of source-base taxation. The following materials consider several topics which have been important in treaty policy discussions.

3.1 Relation between domestic law and treaties; treaty override

Under constitutional principles in the *United States*, statutory law and treaties are of equal status. As a consequence, in the case of conflict between domestic legislation and treaty provisions, the later in time prevails. Thus, in principle, treaty obligations can be overridden by later, inconsistent domestic legislation. Nonetheless, the courts have required that the legislative intent to override a treaty obligation must be "clearly expressed" and historically there have been relatively few examples of treaty overrides, though the introduction of the taxation of foreign-owned real estate in 1980 is an important exception. In addition, Congress enacted several technical provisions in connection with the extensive tax reform in 1986 which did explicitly override treaty obligations. Thus, for example, the treaty obligation to give a foreign tax credit for the treaty partner's taxes was overridden by legislation that in some circumstances requires that the credit be allowed only to the extent of 90 % of the taxpayer's U.S. tax liability. In addition, the Internal Revenue Code was amended to make explicit that treaties have no "preferential status" in relation to domestic law.

In *Canada*, treaties are put into force by an implementing act which typically provides that the treaty will prevail over domestic law in the case of conflict. In principle, treaties can be overridden by subsequent legislation. However, treaty overrides are infrequent, are often simply clarifying in nature, and are intended to bring Canadian treaty practice into conformity with its treaty partners. For example, domestic legislation was intended to overrule the position taken by a domestic court with respect to the static interpretation of a treaty. In addition, a number of terms, such as "annuity," "Canada," "immovable property," "real property," and "period pension payment" have been defined by statute for purposes of Canada's tax treaties despite the absence of any definition in the treaties.

Sweden in general does not allow subsequent legislation to increase the tax liability that would have been established using treaty rules. In a recent situation, legislation was passed that was intended to make it clear that a certain tax holiday regime was not covered by a treaty and could be viewed in a sense as a treaty override. However, the position taken in the legislation is also a plausible reading of the treaty without the legislative gloss.

It is now clear in *French* case law that, according to the Constitution, duly ratified and published treaties take precedence over prior or subsequent conflicting domestic law. The French situation is special in that income can be taxed on the basis of treaty clauses, even where it would not be subject to tax under the provisions of the tax code defining the territorial scope of French taxes.

Japan as well does not allow domestic legislation to override treaty obligations. A Japanese constitutional article states that treaty obligations should be "faithfully observed." This article has been interpreted as establishing the superiority of international rules over domestic rules, even if the latter are later in time. Thus, under this approach, treaty override through domestic legislation is not possible. Treaty rules can only be displaced if the treaty itself contains a "saving" clause which, within the context of the treaty, preserves the application of domestic legislation.

Some Japanese treaties provide specific source rules for certain categories of income, often giving a domestic source to income which would have had a foreign source under domestic law rules. It seems accepted that the change in source rules can result in income being subject to Japanese taxation in the hands of a foreign taxpayer, even though the income would not have been taxed under the normally applicable domestic-source principles.

Australia gives effect to treaties by enacting them through the normal Parliamentary process as Schedules to the International Tax Agreements Act of 1953. This Act states that its provisions have effect notwithstanding anything inconsistent in the basic domestic tax law, with the conspicuous exception of the general anti-avoidance rule. Under normal interpretation rules this Act could be overridden by later inconsistent legislation but generally Australia is at pains to avoid treaty overrides and courts would be reluctant to reach such a conclusion. The closest things to treaty overrides that have occurred are provisions enacted in the Agreements Act itself as interpretative measures (generally after consulting with treaty partners). For example, a provision was enacted in 1985 that unit holders in a unit trust with a permanent establishment in Australia would also be deemed to have a permanent establishment to forestall arguments then being made that such taxation was not permitted under the business profits article of tax treaties. A provision to similar effect has been included in subsequently negotiated treaties. The exclusion of the general anti-avoidance rules from the overriding effect of treaties is presumably justified on the basis that it is a domestic recognition of an abuse of treaties doctrine in international law.

In the *United Kingdom*, treaties come into effect through a special legislative mechanism and it is that version of the treaty relief and not the treaty itself that is controlling. As a result, what is in effect a treaty override would be possible but has happened only very rarely in practice. In one case, a legislative grant of authority to the Inland Revenue to deny tax credits in connection with jurisdictions which use unitary taxation would have amounted to treaty override.

Under the *Dutch* constitution, domestic law can only be applied to the extent that it does not violate directly applicable treaty provisions.

3.2 Approach to treaty interpretation

The *United States* has signed but not ratified the Vienna Convention and there is no consensus as to whether or to what extent the positions taken there are reflective of customary international law. The interpretative methods used by United States courts are often consistent with the Vienna Convention approach, though there is generally more tendency to look beyond the "ordinary meaning" of the treaty language to the purposes and objects of the treaty in general and the treaty article in particular. "Context" is thus given a broader interpretation than the Vienna Convention would seem to allow. On the other hand, recent cases have shown more of a tendency to reject the use of unilateral material such as the Treasury's Technical Explanation of the treaty or the legislative history of the treaty's consideration by the Senate.

Canada has ratified the Vienna Convention and its courts frequently refer to its provisions in the interpretation of tax treaties.

Commentaries to the various articles of the OECD Convention are also often relied on, though the theory of how such material is available under the Vienna Convention's restrictions on the use of extrinsic material is not entirely clear. Canada has a specific statute dealing with tax treaty interpretation. The legislation makes clear that treaties' references to domestic law concepts are to be interpreted in an "ambulatory" fashion, reflecting domestic law changes which occur subsequent to the ratification of the treaty.

Sweden has also ratified the Vienna Convention and tax treaties are interpreted under its principles. Following the Vienna Convention reference in Article 31(3) to the subsequent administrative practices of the parties, an important case held that a treaty term should be interpreted in the light of those practices rather than using the domestic law concept. While the Swedish text is the starting point for interpretation, the English version will also be given special weight when, as is often the case, the treaty was negotiated in English.

Although *Japan* is a signatory of the Vienna Convention, it seems to have had little impact on treaty interpretation practice in Japanese courts. Courts have not referred to the Convention in connection with tax treaties and the topic is not dealt with extensively in academic writing. On the other hand, the actual results of what sparse case law there is can be said to be consistent in results that would have been produced under the Convention.

In *The Netherlands*, the Supreme Court has not referred directly to the Vienna Convention, possibly due to the fact that Holland acceded to the Convention only in 1985 and most of its treaties antedate the coming into effect of the Convention. However, there has been a lively academic discussion of tax treaty interpretation and the role of the Convention. In addition, court references to Article 3(2) of the OECD Model are quite frequent and there is greater indication of the courts' awareness of the need to restrict the reference to unilateral materials.

Australia is a party to the Vienna Convention and in an important recent case, the highest court used it (Article 32, one judge expressing the view that the Article 31 context was available) to interpret a tax treaty on the basis of the OECD commentaries. The approach to the Vienna Convention in this case by the court was more in the spirit of international law which regards these parts of the Convention as a codification of a fairly diffuse tradition, rather than interpreting Articles 31 and 32 like a tax statute, as sometimes occurs in other settings. This approach is in line with the recent relaxation that has occurred in Australia in the use of extrinsic materials in the interpretation of tax law in general.

The *United Kingdom* courts have referred to OECD commentaries for interpretive assistance and have approached treaty interpretation in a different manner than statutory interpretation, with more focus on purpose and intent.

Since the *French* administrative supreme court in 1990 reversed its prior policy of referring to the Ministry of Foreign Affairs for the interpretation to be given to ambiguous treaty wording, the French tax judge is fully competent in the field of treaty interpretation. Courts never refer to the Vienna Convention, to which France is a party, and they do not explicitly specify the construction methods and rules they apply. There is almost no academic writing on the subject. But the practice of the courts seems mainly based on a narrow, literal construction principle, with no reference to the interpretation given in the other contracting state and very few references to OECD commentaries, and a wide recourse to the meaning of corresponding terms in domestic tax law.

In *Germany*, also a signatory to the Vienna Convention, the courts tend to follow an "autonomous" interpretation, focusing on the wording of the treaty and the treaty context. The courts have stressed the need to come to a uniform interpretation by both parties which is facilitated by an "objective" approach. The Vienna Convention has had some impact on German interpretative practice, moving it in an "objective" direction.

3.3 Anti-treaty shopping policy

United States treaty policy for the last fifteen years has been to insist on a limitation of benefits, or anti-treaty shopping, article in its treaties and all treaties approved by the Senate since 1981 have had such an article. While the details of the articles differ, they have in common the focus on the lack of economic connection between the "resident" corporation claiming treaty benefits and the foreign jurisdiction. While the provisions originated in connection with jurisdictions with relatively low effective tax burdens, they are now present even in treaties involving high-tax jurisdictions. Thus, the recently concluded treaty with Germany, a traditionally high-tax country, contains a complex limitation on benefits article. Companies which are otherwise res-ident for treaty purposes are entitled to treaty benefits only if they meet certain share ownership and base erosion tests, are engaged in the active conduct of a trade or business, are publicly traded, or can obtain a competent authority agreement permitting treaty benefits.

Other countries have seemed less concerned with insisting in all cases on detailed treaty shopping rules. The reasons for this difference in attitude are varied. In the case of *Canada*, treaty shopping has not been viewed as a problem since Canada has a fairly uniform policy con-cerning the level to which it will agree to a reduction of source-based taxation. As a result, there is typically no advantage for a third country resident to enter Canada from a particular jurisdiction. Only in the case of residents from countries which have no treaty at all could treaty shopping be a problem and there Canada's extensive treaty network makes these situations fairly uncommon.

This difference in approach is reflected in the recent Third Protocol to the United States-Canada treaty. There, the anti-treaty shopping article applies only when the United States is applying the treaty to investments from Canada. Canada apparently did not feel it needed an anti-treaty shopping provision to deal with third country investment into Canada from the United States. However, the protocol explicitly states that either state can deny benefits under the treaty if the granting of such benefits would result in an "abuse" of the treaty. This makes it clear that Canada could apply its domestic anti-abuse provisions in appropriate cases of inward investment from the United States, which was apparently all the protection Canada thought it needed.

Australia is in a similar position to Canada. Its treaties reflect a very strict adherence to 15 %/10 %/10 % for dividends, interest, and royalties respectively, and so the major scope for treaty shopping relates to the use of treaties by residents of non-treaty countries. The one major example of the opportunity for treaty shopping that has come to light was quickly fixed by a rapid renegotiation of the offending provi-sion. Apart from the U.S. treaty, there are only one or two minor treaty shopping provisions in Australia's treaties. Australia may be able to use its general anti-avoidance rules against treaty shopping, since these rules are not overridden by tax treaties, as noted above, but there have been no examples of this to date and a recent decision involving the application of the rules in the international area suggests that any attempt to do so may fail.

The Netherlands, naturally enough, has not pursued an anti-treaty shopping policy since it has historically been a base for treaty shopping activities. Under pressure from the United States, it has agreed to an extensive anti-treaty shopping article in the new treaty with the United States. The effect of the article is to preserve treaty benefits for the limited number of "real" Dutch companies while substantially tightening the limitations on "letter-box" companies.

Swedish treaty policy has been guided very much by the OECD Model Convention. Since prior to the 1992 and 1994 revisions of the Commentary to the Convention there was only very limited reference to the problems of treaty shopping, Swedish treaties generally have not had anti-treaty shopping articles unless such articles were insisted upon by the treaty partner. Even after the changes in the Commentary in 1992 and 1994 recognizing the problem of treaty shopping and the possibility of requiring shareholders be residents of the contracting states, Sweden's policy has remained unchanged.

Japan has taken no serious measures to deal with treaty shopping problems. To some extent, this may reflect its interests as a residence country concerned with achieving source reductions for its corporations.

French tax treaties rarely contain anti-treaty shopping clauses other than those in the OECD Model Convention, in spite of the fact that France has an extensive treaty network (about 90 treaties, including Eastern Europe, African, and South American countries) which third countries residents would perhaps like to utilize. Besides the limitation on benefits clause in the 1994 French-U.S. convention, some specific exclusions can be found in treaties with countries whose tax law could provide some incentive to tax avoidance (e.g., Switzerland or Luxembourg).

The *United Kingdom* as a general matter has been opposed to broad anti-treaty shopping articles. Concern has been expressed with the uncertainty such articles generate, the administrative problems they entail, and the difficulty in distinguishing among abusive and nonabusive cases.

Germany does not typically include anti-treaty shopping rules in its treaties, though such rules exist in the United States and Swiss treaties. The general domestic anti-avoidance rule can be used in some treaty shopping situations unless it is clear that the case in question has been dealt with in the treaty itself.

In addition, there is a special legislative provision aimed mainly at "letterbox" companies claiming treaty benefits. The provision denies treaty-based claims to tax relief when third country shareholders who would not be entitled to treaty relief on directly-received income interpose a treaty country company which does not itself engage in significant economic activities and there is no economic or other significant reason for the use of the foreign company.

3.4 Nondiscrimination

While most of the countries here considered usually have nondiscrimination articles in their treaties, there are some important exceptions and restrictions. Most striking is the case of *Australia* which has a nondiscrimination article only in its treaty with the United States. That article is itself quite limited. While its formal coverage follows the general outline of the OECD Model Convention article, the range of situations treated is more limited. More significant, the article is framed in terms of the state's duty to ensure nondiscrimination. It does not give any right to the individual taxpayer to complain about possible discrimination in domestic courts. The discriminating state is only required to "consult" in an endeavor to remove the discrimination. Finally, the provision was never included in adopting legislation applicable to the other articles of the treaty.

Reflecting its general policy against nondiscrimination provisions in tax treaties, Australia has entered a reservation to the OECD Model Convention discrimination article. The basic reason for the rejection of the traditional nondiscrimination formulations is a concern that measures deemed appropriate for the taxation of nonresidents might be held to run afoul of these provisions.

Canada's approach to nondiscrimination articles is also in contrast to the other countries here considered. While the scope of nondiscrimination clauses in Canadian treaties varies, they typically do not grant to nonresidents the usual protections against nondiscrimination found in the OECD treaty and others following that model. Thus, Canadian treaties do not contain an article guaranteeing national treatment of domestic corporations owned by nonresident shareholders. Instead, such investments are entitled only to a kind of "most favored nation" treatment according to which they will not be treated in a less favorable fashion than comparable investments held by third country residents. In addition, the provision ensuring nonresident enterprises the right to deduct expenses on the same terms as residents is usually not present. Thus, it would be possible in the absence of such an article to extend the "thin capitalization" rules which apply to nonresident shareholders in Canadian corporations to branch operations of nonresidents. As in the case of Australia, in Canada the desire to implement certain domestic tax policies that might be viewed as contravening traditional concepts of nondiscrimination has led to a much more limited acceptance of treaty limitations on domestic action.

In contrast, *Sweden* has followed the OECD Model nondiscrimination article in its treaty practice and has given it a fairly wide interpretation. Thus, a domestic provision allowing the deduction of an intragroup contribution only where the members of the group were all domestic corporations was found to be discriminatory when applied to two Swedish subsidiaries owned by a treaty country parent company. Similarly, where a foreign company with Swedish branch operations was merged into another foreign company, losses accruing to the branch operations were held to carry over to the merged company in the same way they would have had the merger been between two Swedish companies.

French courts have liberally applied treaty nondiscrimination clauses, under which they have, for instance, granted French permanent establishments of treaty country corporations the exemption from withholding tax on French-source dividends, the imputation credit and the intercorporate dividends exemption.

French treaty practice generally follows the OECD pattern. But France has entered a few reservations to the nondiscrimination article that it tries to incorporate in its bilateral tax conventions. It wishes to apply to French subsidiaries of foreign corporations its domestic provisions limiting the deductibility of interest paid to shareholders even when such limitation does not affect French parents, and to grant only to French nationals its exemption of the gain from the disposal of immovable property that constitutes the French home of nonresidents. Lastly, it is willing to apply the general antidiscrimination provision contained in paragraph 1 of the OECD article only to individuals, in view of the French case law which assimilates the nationality of corporations to their residence.

The other jurisdictions generally follow the pattern in the OECD Model article, with some differences in detail. In *The Netherlands*, there have been a number of nondiscrimination cases in the past decade, generally decided favorably to the taxpayer.

3.5 "Model" treaties

A number of countries have published, formally or informally, "Model" treaties which set forth the basic positions that their treaty negotiators will be taking in the opening round of treaty discussions.

The *United States* Model Convention, first published in draft form in 1977 and modified in 1981, is currently undergoing revision and has been withdrawn pending completion of the review process. Some of the issues to be considered in the new Model are the permanent establishment rules, in particular the rules on the disposition of permanent establish assets; the treatment of partnerships; the appropriate level of withholding taxes including the possibility of special rates on payments to related parties; the treatment of income from new financial instruments; classification issues in connection with royalties, in particular, software; treaty shopping and other anti-abuse rules; nondiscrimination issues and the structure of the competent authority process. In part, the changes in the Model were necessary to reflect changes in domestic legislation that have taken place since the original Models were proposed. The Model is intended to apply only to relations between developed countries. In treaties with developing countries, the United States in the past has been willing to accept substantially more source-based taxation than is foreseen in the Model treaty.

Canada likewise has a model treaty for use in negotiations, though the model has not been published formally. In a recent change in policy, Canada has indicated that it will be willing to agree to reduce withholding rates on direct investment dividends to 5 % while insisting on a 10 % rate on royalties and interest. However, computer software and technology royalties will not be subject to withholding tax. In general, the OECD permanent establishment pattern is followed in the model.

Sweden does not have a public model treaty but some of its negotiating positions are well known. It favors as low withholding taxes as possible on dividends, interest, and royalties in the direct investment context. Sweden also attempts to establish the principle of source-based taxation of pension income with a credit in the resident country for the source tax. The position is a result of the large number of Swedes who retire to warmer climes. The permanent establishment pattern génerally follows the OECD Model.

Japan has not published a model treaty and in general follows the OECD Model, though it typically seeks a 10 % withholding tax on royalties.

In *The Netherlands*, there is a standard treaty (1987) that in general follows the OECD pattern. Since dividends on direct investments are exempt from Dutch tax, Holland aims at reducing dividend withholding tax in such cases to zero, since no credit is allowed for the tax. The model also provides for no source taxation on interest payments. In addition, the right to tax capital gains of nonresident individuals on substantial participations in domestic corporations is part of the model.

The *United Kingdom* has no published model treaty and generally follows the OECD Model. Likewise, *France* has no formal model, and its treaties generally follow the OECD pattern. Its modern treaty practice is, however, characterized, by the following specific features: a wide definition of dividends encompassing all kinds of deemed distributions under French law, a 10 % minimum shareholding as a prerequisite to the benefit of the reduced rate of withholding tax on dividends, exemption of interest from withholding tax, right of the source country to tax income and gains from shares in real property companies and gains from the sale of large shareholdings in local corporations, special clauses in favor of developing countries and clauses extending (in one-third of the French conventions) the benefit of the imputation credit to residents of the other Contracting State.

Although the *Australian* tax administration has been considering the publication of the Australian model on and off for at least a decade, it has not seen the light of day because of the ongoing revision of the model. The contents of the model can be readily deduced as Australia's tax treaties reflect much greater uniformity than most countries. One notable difference is that different language is often used to express what seem to be the same concepts as in the OECD Model. The language used is regarded as more precise than OECD wording and was adopted in an era when Australian courts took a very literal and strict view of interpretation of tax law.

On substantive matters, Australia gives greater emphasis to source taxation than the OECD Model given that it is a substantial net capital importer. Thus, the definition of permanent establishment is wider and a 10 % minimum tax rate on royalties is insisted on. A notable change in policy has just occurred in the dividends area. Instead of the flat 15 % for all dividends that was insisted on in the past, Australia now is prepared to remove withholding tax on dividends out of profits which have borne full company tax (franked dividends in Australian terminology) though in practice the result of negotiations is likely to be a rule for direct investment dividends as in the OECD Model.

Despite the reintroduction of an exemption system for most direct investment overseas by Australian companies in 1990, Australia continues to rely exclusively on a credit provision in its tax treaties on the theory that an exemption is always more generous than a credit and so involves no conflict with treaty obligations. In this way, freedom to reintroduce a credit-only system or extend the existing credit areas is maintained.

3.6 Tax sparing by treaty

Tax sparing, or the crediting of taxes not actually paid, has been an important issue in treaty relations with developing countries. Where the developed country uses the foreign tax credit method to relieve double taxation, any tax reductions or exemptions that developing countries may enact usually benefit the treasury of the developed country rather than the treaty investor. The issue comes up both with respect to net basis taxes on business profits and withholding taxes on investment income.

The *United States* has historically rejected tax sparing as a matter of treaty policy, viewing tax treaties as an inappropriate vehicle to administer what is in effect a program of assistance to foreign investment. Other countries, however, have included tax sparing credits in their treaties with developing countries, both for foregone business taxes and for reduced withholding taxes.

For example, *The Netherlands* uses an exemption method for the foreign business profits but has a credit method for dividends, interest and royalties. It has granted tax sparing credits with respect to such payments in some nineteen treaties. In more recent treaties, the credits are typically limited to payments made within ten or fifteen years from the entry into effect of the treaty.

Canada, in contrast, does not give tax sparing credits for investment income but does accept such credits for business income. Canada gives credits for spared taxes on business income for a limited period, usually ten years. A few older treaties also provide for tax sparing in respect of certain dividends, interest, and royalties. Where a Canadian corporation receives dividends out of the exempt surplus of a foreign corporation, the dividends are not taxable in Canada and tax sparing credits are irrelevant. Therefore, the only dividends that give rise to tax sparing credits are dividends that are taxable in Canada (i.e., dividends received out of the taxable surplus of foreign affiliates and dividends received from foreign corporations that are not foreign affiliates).

Japan gives tax sparing credits for both business income and withholding taxes, as does *Sweden* and *Germany*.

The *United Kingdom* has granted tax sparing credits in a limited number of treaties, typically involving former colonies. The use of the credit has been heavily criticized, primarily on the ground that it is inconsistent with the neutrality of treatment between domestic and foreign investment that underlies the granting of the basic foreign tax credit.

Australia is happy to grant tax sparing for both tax holidays and withholding tax reliefs in developing countries and includes such provisions in many of its treaties, especially with Asian countries. The areas of tax sparing are usually specified in some detail and are limited in time with the possibility of extension by mutual agreement. Extension is routinely agreed upon though the many extensions in the case of the 1969 Singapore treaty will finally expire in the near future.

The original tax sparing provisions had mechanical defects in that there was gross-up for the tax forgone which meant that the tax relief was not total, but this problem has been corrected in more recent treaties. The Australian domestic law foreign tax credit provisions enacted in 1987 provided for the making of regulations to give tax sparing on a unilateral basis but this power has never been used and by and large has become irrelevant since the return to a modified exemption system in 1990.

In *France* traditional tax treaty policy has used the tax sparing credit technique as well as a wide definition of the permanent establishment concept as a way to support the fiscal revenues of developing countries. Many treaties with Asian, South American, and African countries provide for tax sparing credits for passive income (dividends, interest, royalties). A special technique ("*la décote africaine*") grants French investors tax credits inversely proportional to local withholding taxes on dividends distributed by corporations based in French-speaking Africa or deemed distributed from benefits of permanent establishments (extraterritorial taxation) in those countries.

But these tax sparing mechanisms are of less interest because the rate of withholding taxes in developing countries has often greatly increased and many statutory incentives to local investment have been eliminated, thus eliminating the need for tax sparing credits.

Part Five: Selected Bibliography

The following Selected Bibliography is intended to assist the reader in "picking up the thread" of research on particular topics discussed in the materials. It is in no sense exhaustive and merely contains a representative selection of the types of materials that one might use to go further with a particular subject. The references follow the order of the topics in the text with general sources given at the beginning of each section, if appropriate. The references are thereafter organized by country within each topic. The citation style of the particular jurisdiction has usually been followed, though in the interests of uniformity, titles of articles are indicated by quotation marks and titles of books and periodicals are in italics.

Some other potential research sources which are not dealt with directly in the Bibliography should be mentioned. In most countries, there are often useful official and unofficial studies and reports. In the United States, Congressional Hearings and Reports typically provide important information about legislative enactments. Sometimes the Joint Committee on Taxation prepares a "Bluebook" analyzing the legislation after it has passed. The American Law Institute has also undertaken some important research projects, some of which are cited in the materials.

In the United Kingdom, the Institute for Fiscal Studies has prepared many important studies and reports, including the "Meade Report" in 1978. Governmental discussion documents ("Green Papers") are also often useful sources of information. The Canadian Tax Foundation has an extensive list of publications, some done on a comparative basis. In addition, the Royal Commission on Taxation, known as the Carter Commission, considered a range of tax issues in 1966. In Australia as well, "White Papers" on proposed reforms and the Taxation Review Committee reports contain a great deal of material. The Swedish studies which typically precede any major piece of legislation usually contain an English language summary which is quite helpful.

The international law and accounting firms provide practice-oriented descriptions of foreign systems which can be of use in obtaining basic information on particular systems. The publications of the

International Bureau of Fiscal Documentation in Amsterdam also have useful summaries of foreign law, often organized around a particular subject or topic.

For a number of the countries here considered, there are World Tax Series volumes published by the Harvard International Tax Program. While all of these studies are now seriously out of date in their detailed treatment of particular issues, they provide excellent overviews of the general system which are still useful. They also supply good introductions to further research sources, legislative history, judicial decisions and secondary material.

General Descriptive Material by Country

Australia

R. W. Parsons, *Income Taxation in Australia: Principles of Income, Deductibility and Tax Accounting* (Sydney: Law Book Company Ltd, 1985)

R. W. Parsons, "The Fundamentals of Income and Deductibility Revealed and Unrevealed: Myer and John" (1989) Taxation Institute of Australia - State Convention Papers, New South Wales Division 1-11

G. S. Cooper, R. L. Deutsch and R. E. Krever, *Cooper, Krever & Vann's Income Taxation -Commentary and Materials*, 2nd ed. (Sydney: Law Book Company, 1993)

G. Lehmann and C. Coleman, *Taxation Law in Australia*, 4th ed (Sydney: LBC Australian Tax Practice, 1996)

R. Woellner, T. Vella, L. Burns and S. Barkoczy, *Australian Taxation Law*, 6th ed. (Sydney: CCH Australia Ltd, 1996)

Taxation Review Committee, *Full Report* [the "Asprey" Committee] (Canberra: Australian Government Printing Service, 1975)

Draft White Paper, *Reform of the Australian Tax System* (Canberra: Australian Government Printing Service, 1985)

Canada

J. Harvey Perry, *Taxation in Canada*, 5th ed., Tax Paper No. 89 (Toronto: Canadian Tax Foundation, 1990)

Brian J. Arnold et al., eds., *Materials on Canadian Income Tax*, 11th ed. (Scarborough: Carswell, 1996)

Peter W. Hogg and Joanne E. Magee, *Principles of Canadian Income Tax Law* (Scarborough: Carswell, 1995)

Robin W. Boadway and Harry M. Kitchen, *Canadian Tax Policy*, 2nd ed. (Toronto: Canadian Tax Foundation, 1984)

Vern Krishna, *The Fundamentals of Canadian Income Tax*, 5th ed. (Scarborough: Carswell, 1995)

Report of the Royal Commission on Taxation (Carter Commission) (Ottawa: Queen's Printer, 1966)

France

Bienvenu J. J., *Droit fiscal*, (PUF 1987)

Schmidt, J., *Les principes fondamentaux du droit fiscal* (Dalloz, 1992)

Mercier, J-Y and Plagnet, B., *Les impôts en France* (Francis Lefebvre, 1996)

Martinez, J. C., et Di Malta P., *Droit fiscal contemporain* (Litec, 1989)

Mémento fiscal (Ed. Francis Lefebvre, Paris, 1996)

Gouadain D., "Les prélèvements directs sur les revenus des ménages à la croisée des chemins", *Droit Fiscal* 1995, n. 26, 1057-62

Gouadain D., "La fiscalité directe sur les revenus des ménages sur les voies de la singularité. Vers un nouveau modèle de référence", *Droit Fiscal* 1996, n.42, 1292-97

Dubergé J., *Les Français face à l'impôt. Essai de psychologie fiscale* (LGDJ, Paris, 1990)

Conseil des impôts, *L'impôt sur le revenu* (Journaux Officiels, Paris 1990)

David C., *L'impôt sur le revenu des ménages. Assiette imposable* (Economica, Paris, 1988)

Racine P.-F., "Réflexions sur la notion de revenu", *Bulletin Fiscal* 1984, n. 2, 67-77

Cozian M., "Le revenu imposable est un revenu net", *Droit Fiscal* 1996, n. 14, 480-3

Germany

Commerce Clearing House (CCH) Europe, *German Tax & Business Law Guide*, (Bicester: CCH Editions Limited) (loose-leaf)

Leibfritz, Büttner, van Essen, "The Tax System of Germany", 10 *Tax Notes International* 465 - 483 (1995)

Tipke, *Die Steuerrechtsordnung* (Köln: Verlag Dr. Otto Schmidt KG, 1993)

Tipke/Lang, *Steuerrecht*, 14th ed. (Köln: Verlag Dr. Otto Schmidt KG, 1994)

Blümich, *EStG-KStG-GewStG* (München: Verlag Franz Vahlen GmbH)

Herrmann/Heuer/Raupach, *Einkommensteuer- und Körperschaftsteuergesetz mit Nebengesetzen* (Köln: Verlag Dr. Otto Schmidt KG) (loose-leaf commentary)

Kirchhof/Söhn, *Einkommensteuergesetz* (Heidelberg: C.F. Müller Verlag GmbH)

Lademann/Söffing, *Kommentar zum Einkommensteuergesetz* (Stuttgart: Richard Boorberg Verlag GmbH & Co. KG)

Littmann/Bitz/Hellwig, *Das Einkommensteuerrecht* (Stuttgart: Schäffer-Poeschel Verlag GmbH)

Schmidt, *Einkommensteuergesetz*, 14th ed. (München: Verlag C.H. Beck, 1996)

Japan

The Income Tax Law of Japan. (Eibun-Horei-Sha)

National Tax Collection Law of Japan. (Eibun-Horei-Sha)

Griffith, Brookman & Otsuka, Tax Management, Foreign Income

Portfolios, 51-7th, *Business Operations in Japan* (Tax Management, 1991)

Ishi, Hiromitsu, "The Tax System of Japan", 10 *Tax Notes Int'l* 1407 (1995)

Ministry of Finance, Tax Bureau. *Outline of Japanese Taxation* (various years)

Kaneko, Hiroshi. *Sozei ho* [Tax Law]" (5th ed.). 1995

Kaneko, Hiroshi, Tadatsune Mizuno & Minoru Nakazato (eds.). "*Sozei hanrei hyakusen* [100 cases in Tax]" 3d ed..(1991)

Sozei hogakkai (ed.). "*Sozel ho kenkyu* [Studies in Tax Law]" Annual journal

Nihon zeimu kenkyu sentaa (ed.). "*Nichi zei ken ronshu* [Essays in Japanese Tax Studies]." Essay collection; first volume completed

The Netherlands

te Spenk and Lier, *Taxation in The Netherlands* (Kluwer, 1992)

van Raad, Tax Management, Foreign Income Portfolios, 150-5th, *Business Operations in The Netherlands* (Tax Management, 1989)

Sweden

Andersson, Krister and Mutén, Leif, "The Tax System of Sweden", 9 *Tax Notes Int'l* 1147 (1994)

Lindencrona, Gustaf, *Trends in Scandinavian Taxation*, (Kluwer, 1979) (IFA seminar)

Ljungh, Claes: "Sweden" in *World Tax Reform: A Progress Report* (Joe Pechman ed.) (The Brookings Institution, Washington D.C. 1988)

Lodin, Sven-Olof, *The Swedish Tax Reform of 1991 - an Overview*, (Federation of Swedish Industries, Stockholm 1990)

Mutén, Leif and Faxen, Karl, "Sweden" in *Foreign Tax Policies and Economic Growth* (NBER and The Brookings Institution, New York 1966)

Steinmo, Sven, *Taxation and Democracy: Swedish, British, and American Approaches to Financing the Modern State*, (Yale University Press, 1993)

Nordic Council for Tax Research, *Tax Reform in the Nordic Countries*, (Gothenburg 1993)

United Kingdom

J A Kay and M A King, *The British Tax System* 5th ed. (Oxford, Oxford University Press 1990).

Butterworth's UK Tax Guide 1995-96, consultant editor J Tiley (London, Butterworths 1995)

Whiteman on Income Tax 3rd ed., edited by Peter G Whiteman QC and others (London, Sweet and Maxwell Ltd 1988) (plus cumulative supplements)

Royal Commission on the Income Tax (1920) (London HMSO)

Royal Commission on The Taxation of Profits and Income Final Report (1955) London HMSO Cmd 9474

The Structure and Reform of Direct Taxation ("Meade Report) (Institute for Fiscal Studies, London and Boston, Allen and Unwin, 1978)

United States

B. Bittker and L. Lokken, *Federal Taxation of Income, Estates and Gifts* (Warren, Gorham & Lamont, 2nd ed. 1989)

B. Bittker and M. McMahon, *Federal Income Taxation of Individuals* (Warren, Gorham & Lamont, 2nd ed. 1995)

M. Chirelstein, *Federal Income Taxation* (Foundation Press, 1994)

D. Kahn, *Federal Income Taxation* (Foundation Press, 1992)

J. Bankman, T. Griffith and K. Pratt, *Federal Income Taxation* (Little, Brown and Co. 1996)

U.S. Treasury, *Tax Reform for Fairness, Simplicity, and Economic Growth* (1984)

Part Two: Basic Income Taxation
Subpart A: Inclusions in the tax base

1. Employee Fringe Benefits

<u>Australia</u>

R. J. Vann, "General Principles of the Taxation of Fringe Benefits" (1983) 10 *Sydney Law Review* 90

P. Burgess, "Reforming Fringe Benefits Taxation" (1987) 10 *University of New South Wales Law Journal* 241-259

<u>Canada</u>

Douglas J. Sherbaniuk, *Specific Types of Personal Income*, Study for the Royal Commission on Taxation No. 16 (Ottawa: Queen's Printer, 1966)

<u>United States</u>

Note, "Federal Income Taxation of Employee Fringe Benefits", 89 *Harv. L. Rev.* 1141, 1163 (1976)

W. Shaller, "The New Fringe Benefit Legislation: A Codification of Historical Inequities", 34 *Cath. U.L. Rev.* 425 (1985)

T. St. Ville, "Final Regulations of Fringe Benefits Fail to Resolve Many Substantive Issues", 72 *J. Tax'n* 210 (1990)

2. Imputed Income

<u>Canada</u>

A.F. Sheppard, "The Taxation of Imputed Income and the Rule in *Sharkey v. Wernher*," (1973) 51 *Canadian Bar Review* 617-41

United States

T. Chancellor, "Imputed Income and the Ideal Income Tax", 67 *Or. L. Rev.* 561 (1988)

N. Staudt, "Taxing Housework", 84 *Geo.L.J.* 1571 (1996)

D. Marsh, "The Taxation of Imputed Income", 58 *Pol. Sci. Q.* 514 (1943)

R. Goode, "Imputed Rent of Owner-Occupied Dwellings Under the Income Tax", 15 *Journal of Finance* 504 (1960)

3. Gifts

United States

J. Dodge, "Further Thoughts on Realizing Gains and Losses at Death", 47 *Vand. L. Rev.* 1827 (1994)

J. Dodge, "Beyond Estate and Gift Tax Reform: Including Gifts and Bequests in Income", 91 *Harv. L. Rev.* 1177 (1978)

L. Zelenak, "Taxing Gains at Death", 46 *Vand. L. Rev.* 361 (1993)

M. Kornhauser, "The Constitutional Meaning of Income and the Income Taxation of Gifts", 25 *Conn. L. Rev.* 1 (1992)

D. Shaviro, "A Case Study for Tax Reformers: The Taxation of Employee Awards and Other Business Gifts", 4 *Va. Tax Rev.* 241 (1985)

4. Prizes and awards

Germany

Federal Ministry of Finance, 5. September 1996, "Einkommensteuerliche Behandlung von Preisgeldern (§ 2 Abs. 1 EStG)", BStBl. I 1996, 1150

United States

D. Shaviro, "A Case Study for Tax Reformers: The Taxation of Employee Awards and Other Business Gifts", 4 *Va. Tax Rev.* 241 (1985).

B. Kogan, "The Taxation of Prizes and Awards — Tax Policy Winners and Losers", 63 *Wash. L. Rev.* 257.(1988)

5. Scholarships and grants

United States

J. Dodge, "Scholarships Under the Income Tax", 46 *Tax Law.* 697 (1993)

C. Crane, "Scholarships and the Federal Income Tax Base", 28 *Harv. J. on Legis.* 63 (1991)

B. Wolfman, "Federal Tax Policy and the Support of Science", 114 *U. Pa. L. Rev.* 171, 186 (1965)

6. Cancellation of indebtedness

Canada

Brian A. Felesky and Dennis F. Sykera, "The Debt Forgiveness and Foreclosure Rules: Is There a Better Way?" (1995) 43 *Canadian Tax Journal* 1316-42

Germany

Dziadkowski/Treisch, "Zur Steuerfreiheit des Sanierungsgewinns nach § 3 Nr. 66 EStG", 1995 *Finanzrundschau* 330 - 334

Helmar Fichtelmann, "Neuere Entwicklungen zur Steuerfreiheit des Sanierungsgewinns nach § 3 Nr. 66 EStG," 1992 *Deutsches Steuerrecht* 237 - 242 Teil I, 314 - 317 Teil II"

Manfred Groh, "Abschaffung des Sanierungsprivilegs? - Anm. zum BFH-Urteil vom 18.4.1996 IV R 48/95", 1966 *Der Betrieb* 1890 - 1893

United States

F. Witt, Jr. and W. Lyons, "An Examination of the Tax Consequences of Discharge of Indebtedness", 10 *Va. Tax Rev.* 1 (1990)

J. Eustice, "Cancellation of Indebtedness and the Federal Income Tax: A Problem of Creeping Confusion", 14 *Tax L. Rev.* 225 (1959)

L. Del Cotto, "Debt Discharge Income: Kirby Lumber Co. Revisited Under the 'Transactional Equity' Rule of Hillsboro", 50 *Tax Notes* 761 (1991)

D. Shaviro, "The Man Who Lost Too Much: Zarin v. Commissioner and the Measurement of Taxable Consumption", 45 *Tax L. Rev.* 215 (1990)

B. Bittker and B. Thompson, Jr., "Income From the Discharge of Indebtedness: The Progeny of *United States v. Kirby Lumber Co.*", 66 *Calif. L. Rev.* 1159 (1978)

J. Dodge, "Zarin v. Commissioner: Musings About Debt Cancellations and 'Consumption' in an Income Tax Base", 45 *Tax L. Rev.* 677 (1990)

C. Johnson, "Zarin and the Tax Benefit Rule: Tax Models for Gambling Losses and the Forgiveness of Gambling Debts", 45 *Tax L. Rev.* 697 (1990)

7. Gambling

United States

S. Zorn, "The Federal Income Tax Treatment of Gambling: Fairness or Obsolete Moralism?", 49 *Tax Law.* 1 (1995)

8. Illegal income

United States

B. Bittker, "Taxing Income from Unlawful Activities", 25 *Case W. Res. L. Rev.* 130 (1974)

10. <u>Subsidies</u>

<u>Germany</u>

Karlheinz Küting, "Die Erfassung von erhaltenen und gewährten Zuwendungen im handelsrechtlichen Jahresabschluß", 1996 *Deutsches Steuerrecht* 276 -280 Teil I, 313 - 316 Teil II

11. <u>Realization and recognition of gain</u>

<u>Australia</u>

G. S. Cooper, "Profits of Isolated Venture Businesses", (1985) 14 *Australian Tax Review* 32

S. Barckoczy and P. Cussen, "When are Profits Realised from the Sale of Leased Equipment Income in Nature? The Inconsistent Approach of the Full Federal Court", (1994) 23 *Australian Tax Review* 153

<u>Canada</u>

B.J. Arnold, *Timing and Taxation: The Principles of Income Measurement for Tax Purposes*, Canadian Tax Paper No. 71 (Toronto: Canadian Tax Foundation, 1983)

<u>United States</u>

H. Ordower, "Revisiting Realization: Accretion Taxation, The Constitution, Macomber, and Mark to Market", 13 *Va. Tax. Rev.* 1 (1993)

N. Cunningham, & D. Schenk, "Taxation Without Realization: A 'Revolutionary' Approach to Ownership", 47 *Tax L. Rev.* 725, (1992)

D. Shakow "Taxation Without Realization: A Proposal for Accrual Taxation", 134 *U. Pa. L. Rev.* 1111 (1986)

P. White "Realization, Recognition, Reconciliation, Rationality and the Structure of the Federal Income Tax System", 88 *Mich. L. Rev.* 2034 (1990)

12. Capital gains and losses

Australia

C. J. Taylor, *Capital Gains Tax: Business Assets and Entities* (North Ryde: Law Book Company, 1994)

M. W. Inglis, *Inglis on Capital Gains Tax* (Sydney: College of Law, 1990)

K. Burges, "Capital Gains Tax: The Reborn Terrible Twins", (1995) 3 *Taxation in Australia: Red Edition* 187-198

United Kingdom

Whiteman on Capital Gains Tax 3rd ed., P.C. Whiteman et al. eds. (London, Sweet and Maxwell) (cummulative supplements)

United States

J. Hoerner, *The Capital Gains Controversy: A Tax Analysts Reader.* (Tax Analysts, 1992)

S. Surrey, "Definitional Problems in Capital Gain Taxation", 69 *Harv. L. Rev.* 985 (1956)

G. Zodrow, "Economic Analyses of Capital Gains Taxation: Realization, Revenues, Efficiency and Equity", 48 *Tax L. Rev.* 419 (1993)

"Colloquium on Capital Gains", 48 *Tax L. Rev.* 315 (1993)

"Tax Treatment of Capital Gains and Losses", Staff of the Joint Comm. On Taxation, 101st Cong., 1st Sess. (*Jt. Comm. Print* 1989)

C. Blum, "Rollover: An Alternative Treatment of Capital Gains", 41 *Tax L. Rev.* 385 (1986)

W. Blum, "A Handy Summary of the Capital Gains Arguments", 35 *Taxes* 247 (1957)

N. Cunningham & D. Schenk, "The Case for a Capital Gains Preference", 48 *Tax L. Rev.* 319 (1993)

M. Kornhauser, "The Origins of Capital Gains Taxation: What's Law Got to Do With It?", 39 *Sw. L.J.* 869 (1985)

J. Lee, "Critique of Current Congressional Capital Gains Contentions", 15 *Va. Tax Rev.* 1 (1995)

C. Walker & M. Bloomfield, "The Case for Restoration of a Capital Gains Tax Differential", 43 *Tax Notes* 1019 (1989)

A. Warren, "The Deductability by Individuals of Capital Losses Under the Federal Income Tax", 40 *U. Chi. L. Rev.* 291 (1973)

C. Johnson, "Seventeen Culls from Capital Gains", 48 *Tax Notes* 1285 (1990)

International Fiscal Association, Cahiers de droit fiscal international, vol. 61b, *The definition of capital gains in various countries* (Jerusalem 1993)

Subpart B: Deductions

1. Mixed business and personal expenses

Canada

Claire F.L. Young, "Deductibility of Entertainment and Home Office Expenses: New Restrictions to Deal with Old Problems", (1989) 37 *Canadian Tax Journal* 227-66

France

Bayart G., "La déduction des frais de transport des salariés: une évolution réaliste", *Droit Fiscal* 1996, n.12, 411-4

Germany

Walter Drenseck, "Die Abgrenzung der Betriebsausgaben und Werbungskosten von den Lebenshaltungskosten", 1987 *Der Betrieb* 2483 - 2487

United States

D. Halperin, "Business Deduction for Personal Living Expenses: A Uniform Approach to an Unsolved Problem", 122 *U. Pa. L. Rev.* 859 (1974)

M. Heen, "Welfare Reform, Child Care Costs, and Taxes: Delivering Increased Work-Related Child Care Benefits to Low-Income Families", 13 *Yale L. & Pol'y Rev.* 173 (1995)

W. Shaller, "Reforming The Business Meal Deduction: Matching Statutory Limitations With General Tax Policy", 24 *Duq. L. Rev.* 1129 (1986)

W. Klein, "The Deductibility of Transportation Expenses of a Combination Business and Pleasure Trip - A Conceptual Analysis", 18 *Stan. L. Rev.* 1099 (1966)

2. "Hobby losses" and the criteria for determining - business versus personal activities

Canada

Cy Fien, "To Profit or Not to Profit: A Historical Review and Critical Analysis of the 'Reasonable Expectation of Profit' Test", (1995) 43 *Canadian Tax Journal* 1287-1315

Germany

Günter Söffing, "Einkünfteerzielungsabsicht - Liebhaberei", 1992 *Steuerliche Vierteljahresschrift* 235 - 248

Siegbert F. Seeger, "Die Gewinnerzielungsabsicht - ein unmögliches Tatbestandsmerkmal", 1993 *Festschrift Ludwig Schmidt* 37 - 50

Wolfgang Maaßen, *Kunst oder Gewerbe? Die Abgrenzung der künstlerischen von der gewerblichen Tätigkeit im Steuerrecht, Handwerksrecht, Künstlersozialversicherungsrecht*, (C.F. Müller Juristischer Verlag, Heidelbert, 1991)

United States

A. Samansky, "Hobby Loss or Deductible Loss: An Intractable Problem", 34 *U. Fla. L. Rev.* 46, 55-59 (1981)

3. Capital costs and recovery methods

<u>Australia</u>

G. S. Cooper, "The Treatment of Expenditure on Environmental Protection under the Income Tax: A Note on the Operational Distortions of Nothings", (1991) 8 *Australian Tax Forum 135*.

G. S. Cooper, "The treatment of demolition expenses under the Income Tax: the Mount Isa Mines case", (1991) 13 *Sydney Law Review* 605-619.

Alvin C. Warren, Jr., "Accelerated Capital Recovery, Debt, and Tax Arbitrage", 38 *Tax Law.* 549 (1985).

<u>Canada</u>

Israel Mida and Kathleen Stewart, "The Capital Cost Allowance System", (1995) Vol. 43 *Canadian Tax Journal* 1245-64

<u>United States</u>

A. Gunn, "The Requirement that a Capital Expenditure Create or Enhance an Asset", 15 *B.C. Indus. & Com.L.Rev.* 443 (1974)

4. Educational costs

<u>United States</u>

M. Schoenfeld, "The Educational Expense Deduction: The Need for a Rational Approach", 27 *Vill.L.Rev.* 237 (1982)

P. Stephan III, "Federal Income Taxation and Human Capital", 70 *Va. L. Rev.* 1357 (1984)

D. Davenport, "Education and Human Capital: Pursuing An Ideal Income Tax and A Sensible Tax Policy", 42 *Case W. Res. L. Rev.* 793 (1992)

C. Gross, "Comment: Tax Treatment of Education Expenses: Perspectives from Normative Theory", 55 *U.Chi. L.Rev.* 916 (1988)

J. McNulty, "Tax Policy and Tuition Credit Legislation: Federal Income Tax Allowances for Personal Costs of Higher Education", 61 *Cal. L. Rev.* 1, 16-18 (1973)

5. Deduction of personal costs

Australia

R.W. Parsons, "Roberts and Smith: Principles of Interest Deductibility" (1993) *Taxation in Australia - Red Edition* 261-270

R. Krever and G. Kewley, *Charities and Philanthropic Organisations: Reforming the Tax Subsidy and Regulatory Regimes* (Melbourne: Australian Tax Research Foundation and the Comparative Public Policy Research Unit, Monash University, 1991)

Canada

Edward Tamagno, "The Medical Expenses Deduction", (1979) 1 *Canadian Taxation* 2-58

Gwyneth McGregor, *Personal Exemptions and Deductions*, Canadian Tax Paper No. 31 (Toronto: Canadian Tax Foundation, 1962)

Germany

Walter Drenseck, "Ist die Wiedereinführung des allgemeinen Schuldzinsenabzugs aus verfassungsrechtlichen Gründen geboten?", 1993 *Deutsches Steuerrecht* 1429 - 1436

Reinhard Sunder-Plassmann, "Zur Berücksichtigung von Vermögensschäden als außergewöhnliche Belastung", 1995 *Deutsche Steuerzeitung* 193 - 194

Jochen Thiel/Horst Eversberg, "Das Vereinsförderungsgesetz und seine Auswirkungen auf das Gemeinnützigkeits- und Spendenrecht", 1990 *Der Betrieb* 395 - 401

Jochen Thiel/Horst Eversberg, "Kultur- und Stiftungsförderungsgesetz" 1991 *Der Betrieb* 118 - 128

Gottfried Breuninger/Ulrich Prinz, "Neues zum Sozio-Sponsoring aus steuerlicher Sicht" 1994 *Deutsches Steuerrecht* 1401 - 1408

United States

W. Andrews, "Personal Deductions in an Ideal Income Tax", 86 *Harv. L. Rev.* 308 (1972)

T. Griffith, "Theories of Personal Deductions in the Income Tax", 40 *Hastings L.J.* 343 (1989)

M. Kelman, "Personal Deductions Revisited: Why They Fit Poorly in an 'Ideal' Income Tax and Why They Fit Worse in a Far from Ideal World", 31 *Stan. L. Rev.* 831 (1979)

S. Koppelman, "Personal Deductions Under an Ideal Income Tax", 43 *Tax L.Rev.* 679 (1988)

M. McIntyre, "An Inquiry Into the Special Status of Interest Payments", 1981 *Duke L.J.* 765

W. Turnier, "Evaluating Personal Deductions in an Income Tax - The Ideal", 66 *Cornell L. Rev.* 262 (1981)

6. Limitations on deductions and losses

Australia

R. Krever, "The Deductibility of Fines", (1984) 13 *Australian Tax Review* 168

Canada

Neil Brooks, "The Principles Underlying the Deduction of Business Expenses", in *Essays on Canadian Taxation* (Scarborough: Carswell, 1981)

Vern Krishna, "Public Policy Limitations on the Deductibility of Fines and Penalties: Judicial Inertia", (1978) 16 *Osgoode Hall Law Journal* 19

Germany

Friedrich E.F. Hey, "German Court Sympathetic to expense deduction for acquisition of foreign subs", *The Journal of International Taxation* 81 - 84 (1996)

Gottfried Breuninger, "Abschied vom Betriebsausgabenabzug bei DBA-Schachtelbeteiligungen", 1995 *Finanzrundschau* 561 - 568

United States

Shoemaker, "The Smuggler's Blues: Wood v. United States and the Resulting Horizontal Inequity Among Criminals in the Allowance of Federal Income Tax Deductions", 11 *Va. Tax Rev.* 659 (1992)

G. Cooper, "The Taming of the Shrewd: Identifying and Controlling Income Tax Avoidance", 85 *Colum. L. Rev.* 657 (1985)

C. Rock and D. Shaviro, "Passive Losses and the Improvement of Net Income Measurement", 7 *Va. Tax Rev.* 1 (1987)

Subpart C: Accounting

1. General

Australia

G. S. Cooper, "Tax Accounting for Deductions" (1988) 5 *Australian Tax Forum* 23

Canada

B.J. Arnold, *Timing and Taxation: The Principles of Income Measurement for Tax Purposes*, Canadian Tax Paper No. 71 (Toronto: Canadian Tax Foundation, 1983)

Al Meghji, "The Role of GAAP in Computing Taxable Profits", in *Report of Proceedings of the Forty-sixth Tax Conference*, 1995 Conference Report (Toronto: Canadian Tax Foundation, 1996) 33:1 - 33:25

France

Hinard M. and Mitaine-Chenevier A.-C., *Comptabilité et fiscalité*, (Presses Universitaires de France, Paris, 1988)

Cozian M., "La méthode de la comptabilité d'engagement (ou la théorie des créances acquises)", *Bulletin Fiscal* 1995, n. 4, 219-28

Goulard G., "Les charges de sous-activité", *Revue de Jurisprudence Fiscale* 1994 n. 8-9, 510-2

Germany

Georg Döllerer, "Statische oder dynamische Bilanz", 1968 *Betriebs-Berater* 637 - 641

Manfred Groh, "Struktur der betrieblichen Überschußrechnung", 1986 *Finanzrundschau* 393 - 397

Manfred Groh, "Vor der dynamischen Wende im Bilanzsteuerrecht?", 1989 *Betriebs-Berater* 1586 - 1588

Walter Schoor, "Die Gewinnermittlung nach § 4 Abs. 3 EStG", 1982 *Finanz-Rundschau* 505 - 509

Günter Söffing, "Die Überschußrechnung nach § 4 Abs. 3 EStG", 1970 *Deutsche Steuerzeitung* 17 - 23

Lothar Woerner, "Zeitpunkt der Passivierung von Schulden und Verbindlichkeitsrückstellungen - Problematik der wirtschaftlichen Verursachung ", 1994 *Festschrift Adolf Moxter*, 483 - 506

Herbert Biener, "Rezeption der USGAAP über IOSCO und IASC", 1995 *Festschrift Wolfgang Dieter Budde* 87 - 103

United States

C. Blum, "Should Professionals Accept 'Accrual' Fate?", 6 *Va. Tax Rev.* 593 (1987)

N. Cunningham, "A Theoretical Analysis of the Tax Treatment of Future Costs", 40 *Tax L. Rev.* 577 (1985)

H. Dubroff, et al. "Tax Accounting: The Relationship of Clear Reflection of Income to Generally Accepted Accounting Principles", 47 *Alb. L. Rev.* 354 (1983)

A. Gunn, "Matching of Costs and Revenues as a Goal of Tax Accounting", 4 *Va. Tax Rev.* 1 (1984)

D. Halperin, "The Time Value of Money-1984", 23 *Tax Notes* 751 (1984)

D. Halperin, "Interest in Disguise: Taxing the 'Time Value of Money'", 95 *Yale L.J.* 506 (1986)

D. Halperin & W. Klein, "Tax Accounting for Future Obligations: Basic Principles Revised", 38 *Tax Notes* 831 (1988)

E. Jensen, "The Supreme Court and the Timing of Deductions for Accrual-Basis Taxpayers", 22 *Ga. L. Rev.* 229 (1988)

E. Jensen, "The Deduction of Future Liabilities by Accrual-Basis Taxpayers: Premature Accruals, the All Events Test, and Economic Performance", 37 *U. Fla. L. Rev.* 443 (1985)

W. Raby, "Meaning of 'Accrued' - Accounting Concepts Versus Tax Concepts", 57 *Tax Notes* 777 (1992)

E. Sunley, "Observations on the Appropriate Tax Treatment of Future Costs", 23 *Tax Notes* 719 (1984)

2. Advanced/Deferred Payment

Germany

Herrmann Clemm, "Der Einfluß der Verzinslichkeit auf die Bewertung der Aktiva und Passiva", in: Arndt Raupach (ed.), *Werte und Wertermittlung im Steuerrecht*, DStJG 1984 219 - 243

Alfred Christiansen, *Steuerliche Rückstellungsbildung - Darstellung der Systematik aufgrund von Rechtsprechung und Verwaltungsanweisungen*, (Berlin: Erich Schmidt Verlag, 1993)

Adolf Moxter, "Rückstellungskriterien im Streit",1995 *Zeitschrift für betriebswirtschaftliche Forschung* 311 - 326

Wolfgang Schön, "Der Bundesfinanzhof und die Rückstellungen", 1994 *Betriebs-Berater*, Beilage 9 zu Heft 15

Lothar Woerner, "Zeitpunkt der Passivierung von Schulden und Verbindlichkeitsrückstellungen - Problematik der wirtschaftlichen Verursachung -", 1994 *Festschrift Adolf Moxter* 483 - 506

United States

C. Johnson, "The Illegitimate 'Earned' Requirement in Tax and Nontax Accounting", 50 *Tax L. Rev.* 373 (1995)

W. Klein, "Tailor to the Emperor With No Clothes: The Supreme Court's Tax Rules for Deposits and Advance Payments", 41 *UCLA L. Rev.* 1685 (1994)

4. Accounting for original issue discount and complex financial instruments

United States

L. Lokken, "The Time Value of Money Rules", 42 *Tax L. Rev.* 1 (1986)

T. Sims, "Long-Term Debt, The Term Structure of Interest and the Case for Accrual Taxation", 47 *Tax L. Rev.* 313 (1992)

J. Bankman and W. Klein, "Accurate Taxation of Long-Term Debt: Taking into Account the Term Structure of Interest", 44 *Tax L. Rev.* 335 (1989)

D. Hariton, "The Taxation of Complex Financial Instruments", 43 *Tax L. Rev.* 731 (1988)

R. Kau, "Carving Up Assets and Liabilities - Integration or Bifurcation of Financial Products", 63 *Taxes* 1003 (1990)

S. Kolbrenner, "Derivatives Design And Taxation", 15 *Va. Tax Rev.* 211 (1995)

E. Kleinbard, "Equity Derivative Products: Financial Innovation's Newest Challenge to the Tax System", 69 *Tex. L. Rev.* 1319 (1991)

R. Shuldiner, "A General Approach to the Taxation of Financial Instruments", 71 *Tex. L. Rev.* 243 (1992)

R. Shuldiner, "Consistency and the Taxation of Financial Products", 70 *Taxes* 781 (1992)

J. Strnad, "Periodicity and Accretion Taxation: Norms and Implementation", 99 *Yale L.J.* 1817 (1990)

J. Strnad, "Taxing New Financial Products: A Conceptual Framework", 46 *Stan. L. Rev.* 569 (1994)

J. Strnad, "The Taxation of Bonds: The Tax Trading Dimension", 81 *Va. L. Rev.* 47 (1995)

A. Warren, Jr., "Financial Contract Innovation And Income Tax Policy", 107 *Harv. L. Rev.* 460 (1993)

International Fiscal Association, Cahiers de droit fiscal international, vol. 80b, *Tax aspects of derivative financial instruments* (Cannes 1995)

Subpart D: Attribution of Income

1. Definition of taxable unit

Australia

J. G. Head and R. Krever eds, *Tax Units and the Tax Rate Scale* (Burwood: Australian Tax Research Foundation, 1996)

Canada

Jack London, "The Impact of Changing Perceptions of Social Equality on Tax Policy: The Marital Tax Unit", (1988) 26 *Osgoode Hall Law Journal* 287

John W. Durnford and Stephen J. Toope, "Spousal Support in Family Law and Alimony in the Law of Taxation", (1994) 42 *Canadian Tax Journal* 1-107

France

Bienvenu, J. J., "L''impôt sur le revenu et le droit de la famille", 1986 *Revue Francaise de Finances Publiques* 69

Liau P. and Herschtel M.-L., "Quotient familial et situation fiscale des famillies", *Revue Francaise de Finances Publiques* 1986, n. 14, 79-87

United Kingdom

Parker, *Taxes, Benefits and Family Life* (Institute for Economic Affairs 1995)

United States

B. Bittker, "Federal Income Taxation and the Family", 27 *Stan. L. Rev.* 1389 (1975)

P. Gann, "Abandoning Marital Status as a Factor in Allocating Income Tax Burdens", 59 *Tex. L. Rev.* 1 (1980)

P. Gann, "The Earned Income Deduction: Congress's 1981 Response to the 'Marriage Penalty' Tax", 68 *Cornell L. Rev.* 421 (1983)

M. Kornhauser, "Love, Money, and the IRS: Family, Income-Sharing, and the Joint Income Tax Return", 45 *Hastings L.J.* 63 (1993)

M. McMahon, Jr., "Expanding the Taxable Unit: The Aggregation of the Income of Children and Parents", 56 *N.Y.U. L. Rev.* 60 (1981)

M. McIntyre, "Taxation of the Family: Economic Mutuality and the Need for Joint Filing", 1 *Can. Tax.* 14 (1979)

M. McIntyre & O. Oldman, "Taxation of the Family in a Comprehensive and Simplified Income Tax", 90 *Harv. L. Rev.* 1573 (1977)

L. Zelenak, "Marriage And The Income Tax", 67 *S. Cal. L. Rev.* 339 (1994)

E. McCaffery, "Taxation and the Family: A Fresh Look at Behavioral Gender Biases in the Code", 40 *UCLA L. Rev.* 983 (1993)

2. Alimony and child support

United States

L. Hagan, "A Policy Analysis of Alimony", 41 *Tax Notes* 971 (1988)

W. Klein, "Tax Effects of Nonpayment of Child Support", 45 *Tax L. Rev.* 259 (1990)

L. Malman, "Unfinished Reform: The Tax Consequences of Divorce", 61 *N.Y.U. L. Rev.* 363 (1986)

3. Limitations on assignment of income

Canada

Claire F. L. Young, "The Attribution Rules: Their Uncertain Future in the Light of Current Problems", (1987) Vol. 35 *Canadian Tax Journal* 275-313

Germany

Federal Ministry of Finance, 25. May 1993, "Steuerliche Anerkennung von Darlehensverträgen zwischen Angehörigen", BStBl. I 1993, 410

Federal Ministry of Finance, 15. November 1984, "Schreiben betreffend einkommensteuerrechtliche Behandlung des Nießbrauchs und anderer Nutzungsrechte bei Einkünften aus Vermietung und Verpachtung", BStBl. I 1984, 561 - 567

United States

J. Eustice, "Contract Rights, Capital Gain, and Assignment of Income - The *Ferrer* Case", 20 *Tax L. Rev.* 1 (1964)

C. Lyon & J. Eustice, "Assignment Of Income: Fruit and Tree as Irrigated by the *P.G. Lake* Case", 17 *Tax L. Rev.* 293 (1962)

R. Rice, "Judicial Trends in Gratuitous Assignments to Avoid Federal Income Taxes", 64 *Yale L.J.* 991 (1955)

S. Surrey, "Assignments of Income and Related Devices: Choice of the Taxable Person", 33 *Colum. L. Rev.* 791 (1933)

Part Three: Taxation of Business Organizations

Subpart A: Corporate-Shareholder Taxation

1. Overview of corporate tax systems

OECD, *Company Tax Systems* (Paris: OECD 1973)

OECD, *Taxing Profits in a Global Economy: Domestic and International Issues* (Paris: OECD 1991)

McLure, C.E., *Must Corporate Income be Taxed Twice?* (Washington: The Brookings Institution 1979)

Norr, M., *The Taxation of Corporations and Shareholders* (Deventer: Kluwer 1982)

Australia

M. Butler, *Australian Federal Company Taxation* (North Ryde: Butterworths, 1994)

Marks, *Corporate Taxation in Australia: Distributions and Imputation* (North Ryde: CCH, 1990)

W. Scholtz, *Australian Corporate Taxation: Dividends, Imputation, Reorganisations, Liquidations, Losses* (Melbourne: Longman Cheshire, 1995)

R. J Vann, ed., *Company Tax Reform* (North Ryde: Law Book Company, 1988)

R. J. Vann, "The New Zealand Imputation System: A Comparison with Australia" (1989) CCH *Journal of Australian Taxation* 60-78

T. Magney, "Equity Raising Post Imputation" in Krever, Grbich and Gallagher, eds, *Taxation of Corporate Debt Finance* (Melbourne: Longman Professional, 1991)

Canada

Howard J. Kellough and Peter E. McQuillan, *Taxation of Private Corporations and their Shareholders*, 2nd ed., Canadian Tax Paper No. 95 (Toronto: Canadian Tax Foundation, 1992)

Tim Edgar, "Imputation Canadian Style", (October 17, 1994) 9 *Tax Notes International* 1231

France

Castagnede, B., "L'entreprise et la profession en droit fiscal" 1992 *Droit fiscal* 757

Cozian, M., *Précis de fiscalité des entreprises*, (Litec, Paris, 1992)

Conseil des impôts, *Fiscalité et vie des entreprises* (Journaux Officiels, Paris, 1994, 2 vols.)

Cozian M., *Les grands principes de la fiscalité des entreprises* (Litec, Paris, 1996)

Cozian M., *Précis de fiscalité des entreprises* (Litec, Paris, 1996)

Serlooten P., *Droit fiscal des affaires*, in Ripert G., and Roblot R., *Traité de droit commercial* (LGDJ, Paris, 1995)

Germany

Dötsch/Cattelaens/Gottstein/Stegmüller/Zenthöfer, *Körperschaftsteuer, 11th ed.* (Stuttgart: Schäffer-Poeschel-Verlag, 1994)

Dötsch/Eversberg/Jost/Witt, *Die Körperschaftsteuer* (Stuttgart: Schäffer-Poeschel Verlag GmbH)

Herrmann/Heuer/Raupach,*Einkommensteuer- und Körperschaftsteuergesetz mit Nebengesetzen* (Köln: Verlag Dr. Otto Schmidt KG)

Streck, *Körperschaftsteuergesetz, 4th ed.* (München: Verlag C.H. Beck, 1995)

Japan

The Corporation Tax Law of Japan (Eibun-Horei-Sha)

Sweden

Sven-Olof Lodin, *The Nordic Reforms of Company and Shareholder Taxation - A Comparison* (1994)

Leif Mutén",Dual Income Taxation: Swedish Experience" in Mutén, Sorensen, Hagen and Genser, *Towards a Dual Income Tax? Swedish and Austrian Experiences*, (Foundation for European Fiscal Studies, Erasmus University Rotterdam, Kluwer, 1996)

Bertil Wiman, "The Implementation of EC Tax Directives in Swedish Law", 1995 *EC Tax Review* 151

The Netherlands

S.R. Schuit, *Dutch business law: legal, accounting and tax aspects of doing business in the Netherlands*, (Kluwer) (loose-leaf)

United Kingdom

Report from the Select Committee on Corporation Tax HC (1970-71 No. 622)

Corporation Tax 1982 Cmnd. 8456 (Green Papers)

United States

B. Bittker and J. Eustice, *Federal Taxation of Corporations and Shareholders* (Warren, Gorham & Lamont, 6th ed., loose-leaf)

Treasury Dep't, *Report on Integration of the Individual and Corporate Tax Systems: Taxing Business Income Once* (1992)

C. McLure, "Integration of the Personal and Corporate Income Taxes: The Missing Element in Recent Tax Reform Proposals", 88 *Harv. L. Rev.* 532 (1975)

A. Warren, "The Relation and Integration of Individual and Corporate Income Taxes", 94 *Harv. L. Rev.* 717 (1981)

2. Defining entities subject to tax

Canada

Robin J. MacKnight, "What's in a Name? Classifying Partnerships, Associations, and Limited Liability Companies for Income Tax Purposes", in *Tax Planning for Canada-US and International Transactions*, 1993 Corporate Management Tax Conference (Toronto: Canadian Tax Foundation, 1994) 21:1 - 21:22

United States

M. Schler, "Initial Thoughts on the Proposed 'Check-the Box' Regulation" 12 *Tax Notes International* 1679 (1996)

3. Issues in corporate formation

Canada

Andrew W. Dunn and Kimberley A. Neilsen, "Exchanges of Property for Shares: Section 85 — Part I", (1995) Vol. 43 *Canadian Tax Journal* 203-21 and "— Part II", (1995) Vol. 43 *Canadian Tax Journal* 496-515

United States

D. Herwitz, "Allocation of Stock Between Services and Capital in the Organization of a Close Corporation", 75 *Harv. L. Rev.* 1098 (1962)

R. Jensen, "Of Form and Substance: Tax Free Incorporations and Other Transactions Under Section 351", 11 *Va. Tax Rev.* 349 (1991)

4. Issues involving capital structure

Ruud A. Sommerhalder, "International Approaches to Thin Capitalization", 1996 *European Taxation* 83

Australia

Burges, Magney and Vann, "Income Tax—A Driving Force Behind Financing Transactions" in Austin and Vann, eds, *The Law of Public Company Finance*, ch. 2 (Law Book Company, 1986).

Germany

Eugen Bogenschütz/Georg Edelmann, "German Ministry of Finance publishes guidelines on shareholder debt financing rules", 10 *Tax Notes International*, 279 - 282 (1995)

Friedrich E.F. Hey, "Gesellschafterfremdfinanzierung, einige Zweifelsfragen zur Anwendung von § 8a KStG", 1994, *Recht der Internationalen Wirtschaft*, 221 - 230

Reinhard Pöllath, "Final thin capitalization proposals issued", 1993 *International Tax Review* 50

Rosenstock/Gedig, "Sec. 8a Corporate Income Tax Act", 1993 *Intertax* 460

Schauhoff, "Tax Planning under Germanies New 'Thin Capitalization' Rules", 1993 *Intertax* 466

United States

W. Plumb, "The Federal Income Tax Significance of Corporate Debt: A Critical Analysis and a Proposal", 26 *Tax L. Rev.* 369 (1971)

W. Andrews, "Tax Neutrality Between Equity Capital and Debt", 20 *Wayne L. Rev.* 1057 (1984)

5. Taxation of corporate distributions

Australia

Richards and Doherty, *Taxation of Dividends* (North Ryde: Butterworths, 1987)

Graw, "Company Share Buy-Backs: The Taxation Problem" and "Company Share Buy-Backs—The Sequel" (1989) 6 *Australian Tax Forum* 369-409 and 495-507

Hodgson, "Buy-Backs" (1993) 5 CCH *Journal of Australian Taxation* 38-48

Graw, "Division 16K: An Incomplete Solution" (1991) 26 *Taxation in Australia* 9

A. H. Slater, "What is a Dividend for Imputation Purposes" in Vann, ed., *Company Tax Reform*, ch 3 (North Ryde: Law Book Company, 1988)

Canada

H. Heward Stikeman and Robert Couzin, "Surplus Stripping", (1995) Vol. 43 *Canadian Tax Journal* 1844-60

France

Plagnet B., "Une évolution dans la définition des revenus distribués", *Droit Fiscal* 1990, n. 9, 368-70

Turot J., "Rehaussement du bénéfice social et appréhension de revenus distribués", *Revue de jurisprudence fiscale* 1990, n.1, 3-8

"Les distributions irrégulières de bénéfices ou quand un redressement peut en cacher un autre", *Bulletin Fiscal* 1996, n. 8-9, 431-7

Germany

Georg Döllerer, *Verdeckte Gewinnausschüttungen und verdeckte Einlagen bei Kapitalgesellschaften*, 2nd ed. (Heidelberg: Verlag Recht und Wirtschaft, 1990)

Joachim Lange, *Verdeckte Gewinnausschüttung*, (Herne: Verlag Neue Wirtschaftsbriefe, 6th ed. 1993)

Gottfried Breuninger, "Zur Rechtsnatur eigener Anteile und ihre ertragssteuerliche Bedeutung, Festbeitrag zum 70. Geburtstag von Georg Döllerer" 1991, *Deutsche Steuerzeitung* 420 - 425

Franz Wassermeyer, "Der Erwerb eigener Anteile durch eine Kapitalgesellschaft - Überlegungen zur Rechtsprechung des I. Senats des BFH", Festschrift Ludwig Schmidt, 621 - 638

The Netherlands

Theodoor Huiskes, "Netherlands: Capital Gains on a Company's Repurchase of Shares", 1994 *European Taxation* 472

United States

W. Andrews, "Out of Its Earnings and Profits: Some Reflections on the Taxation of Dividends", 69 *Harv. L. Rev.* 1403 (1956)

W. Blum, "The Earnings and Profits Limitation on Dividend Income: A Reappraisal", 53 *Taxes* 68 (1975)

R. Clark, "The Morphogenesis of Subchapter C: An Essay in Statutory Evolution and Reform", 87 *Yale L.J.* 90 (1977)

L. Stone, "Back to Fundamentals: Another Version of the Stock Dividend Saga", 79 *Colum. L. Rev.* 898 (1979)

6. Liquidations

Australia

W. Scholtz, "Tax Aspects of Liquidations Distributions" (1992) 4 CCH *Journal of Australian Taxation* 34-46

Canada

Joel Shafer, "Liquidation", in *Report of Proceedings of the Forty-second Tax Conference*, 1991 Conference Report (Toronto: Canadian Tax Foundation, 1992) 10:1 - 10:48

France

Gouaislin G., "Réductions de capital et dissolutions. L'évolution législative et jurisprudentielle en matière de revenus distribués", *Droit Fiscal* 1993, n. 45. 1788-93

Streichenberger R., "Réductions de capital liées à un désinvestissement dans les sociétés de capitaux", *Revue de jurisprudence fiscale* 1996, n. 3, 147-51

Germany

Herbert Grziwotz, "Sonderfälle der Liquidation von Gesellschaften", 1992 *Deutsches Steuerrecht* 1813

United States

T. Farer, "Corporate Liquidations: Transmuting Ordinary Income Into Capital Gains", 75 *Harv. L. Rev.* 527 (1962)

G. Yin, "Taxing Corporate Liquidations (and Related Matters) After the Tax Reform Act of 1986", 42 *Tax L. Rev.* 573 (1987)

E. Zolt, "The General Utilities Doctrine: Examining the Scope of the Repeal", 65 *Taxes* 819 (1987)

B. Bittker and N. Redlich, "Corporate Liquidations and the Income Tax", 5 *Tax L. Rev.* 437 (1950)

P. Blawie, "Some Tax Aspects of a Corporate Liquidation", 7 *Tax L. Rev.* 481 (1952)

7. Corporate reorganizations and restructuring

Canada

David Tetrault and Robert F. Lindsay, "The Taxation of Corporate Reorganizations: How Are We Doing So Far?" (1995) Vol. 43 *Canadian Tax Journal* 1441

France

Fusions, scissions et apports partiels d'actif (Ed. Francis Lefebvre, Paris, 1995)

Chadefaux, M., *Les fusions de sociétés, régime juridique et fiscal* (Editions La Villeguérin, Paris, 1995)

De Kergos Y., Raffin M.-H. and Martin Ph., *Fiscalité des fusions et apports partiels d'actif* (Editions EFE, Paris, 1994)

Serlooten P., *Fiscalité de la transmission des entreprises* (Economica, Paris, 1994)

Germany

Dieter Enders/Geoffrey Twinem, "Tax Strategies for acquisitions in Germany", 10 *Tax Notes International* 1335 - 1342 (1995)

Manfred Benkert/Annegret Bürkle, *Umwandlungsgesetz/ Umwandlungssteuergesetz, zweisprachige Ausgabe (dt./engl.) mit umfassender Einführung* (Köln: RWS Verlag Kommunikationsforum, 1996) (German-English version of Reorganization Law)

Hans Dehmer, *Umwandlungsgesetz-Umwandlungssteuergesetz*, (2nd ed. München: Verlag C.H. Beck, 1996)

Norbert Herzig (ed.), *Neues Umwandlungssteuerrecht - Praxisfälle und Gestaltungen im Querschnitt* (Köln: Verlag Dr. Otto Schmidt KG, 1996)

Sagasser/Bula, *Umwandlungen*, (München: Verlag C.H. Beck, 1995)

Widmann/Mayer, *Umwandlungsrecht: Umwandlungsgesetz-Umwandlungssteuergesetz* (Bonn: Stollfuß Verlag)

United States

M. Ginsburg and J. Levin, *Mergers, Acquisitions, and Buyouts* (Little Brown, 1996)

W. Hellerstein, "Mergers, Taxes and Realism", 71 *Harv. L. Rev.* 254 (1957)

S. Surrey, "Income Tax Problems of Corporations and Shareholders: American Law Institute Tax Project - American Bar Association Committee Study on Legislation Revision", 14 *Tax L. Rev.* 1 (1958).

W. Hellerstein, "Mergers, Taxes and Realism", 71 *Harv. L. Rev.* 254 (1957)

M. Sandberg, "The Income Tax Subsidy to 'Reorganizations'", 38 *Colum. L. Rev.* 98 (1938)

8. Transfer and limitations on transfer of corporate tax attributes

Canada

Rosemarie Wertschek, "Corporate Reorganizations and Other Transfers of Tax Attributes: A Question of Taxable Benefits", (1994) Vol. 42 *Canadian Tax Journal* 268-87

United States

R. Jacobs, "Tax Treatment of Corporate Net Operating Losses and Other Tax Attribute Carryovers", 5 *Va. Tax Rev.* 701 (1986)

D. LaRue, "A Case for Neutrality in the Design and Implementation of the Merger and Acquisition Statutes: The Post-Acquisition Net Operating Loss Carryback Limitations", 43 *Tax L. Rev.* 85 (1987)

D. Simmons, "Net Operating Losses and Section 382:Searching for a Limitation on Loss Carryovers", 63 *Tul. L. Rev.* 1045 (1989)

9. Consolidated corporate taxation

Canada

Robert C. Strother, "Creative Corporate Tax Planning", in *Report of Proceedings of the Forty-fifth Tax Conference*, 1994 Conference Report (Toronto: Canadian Tax Foundation, 1995) 11:1 - 11:23

France

Morgenstern P., *L'intégration fiscale, principes et pratique* (Editions La Villeguérin, Paris, 1996)

Moine P., *Le régime fiscal des groupes de sociétés* (Editions EFE, Paris, 1996)

Germany

Schmidt/Müller/Stöcker, *Die Organschaft* (4th ed. Herne: Verlag Neue Wirtschaftsbriefe 1993)

United States

H. Lerner, R. Antes, R. Rosen and B. Finklestein, *Federal Income Taxation of Corporations Filing Consolidated Returns* (Matthew Bender, loose-leaf)

10. Special tax regimes for closely held corporations

Canada

Howard J. Kellough and Peter E. McQuillan, *Taxation of Private Corporations and their Shareholders*, 2nd ed., Canadian Tax Paper No. 95 (Toronto: Canadian Tax Foundation, 1992)

Subpart B: Partnership Taxation

Canada

Howard J. Kellough and Peter E. McQuillan, "A Quarter Century in Partnerships", (1995) Vol. 43 Can. *Tax Journal* 1465-85

France

Bourtourault P.-Y., de Givré Y. and Goulard G., *Sociétés de personnes. Fiscalité française et internationale* (Editions EFE, Paris, 1995)

Puyraveau P., *La fiscalité des sociétés de personnes* (Nouvelles Editions Fiduciaires, Paris, 1986)

Cozian M. and Peignellin N.-S., "Un sac d'embrouilles: le régime fiscal des sociétés", *Droit Fiscal* 1994, n. 5

Germany

Günter Söffing, *Die Besteuerung der Mitunternehmerschaften*, (Herne: Verlag Neue Wirtschaftsbriefe, 1994)

Zimmermann/Reyher/Hottmann, *Die Personengesellschaft im Steuerrecht*, 5th ed. (Achim: Erich Fleischer Verlag, 1995)

The Netherlands

Ton H. M. Daniels, *Issues in International Partnership Taxation* (Kluwer Law and Taxation, Deventer, 1991)

United States

W. McKee, W. Nelson & R. Whitmore, *Federal Taxation of Partnerships and Partners* (Warren, Gorham & Lamont, loose-leaf)

A. Willis, J. Pennell & P. Postlewaite, *Partnership Taxation* (Shepards, loose-leaf)

Part Four: International Taxation

General Descriptive Material by Country

Australia

Hamilton and Deutsch, *Guidebook to Australian International Taxation* (Sydney: Legal Books, 1996)

France

Gouthière, B., *Les impôts dans les affaires internationales* (Francis Lefebvre, 1994)

Gest, G. and Tixier, G., *Droit fiscal international* (Presses universitaires de France, Paris, 1990, new edition in 1997)

Tixier, G. and Rohmer, X., *Fiscalité internationale des personnes physiques* (Les Editions du CFCE, Paris, 1995)

Germany

Commerce Clearing House (CCH) Europe, *German Tax & Business Law Guide* (Bicester: CCH Editions Limited)

Karl-Heinz Baranowski, *Besteuerung von Auslandsbeziehungen*, (Herne: Verlag Neue Wirtschaftsbriefe, 2nd ed. 1996)

Otto H. Jacobs, *Internationale Unternehmensbesteuerung - Handbuch zur Besteuerung deutscher Unternehmen mit Auslandsbeziehungen* (München: Verlag C.H. Beck, 3rd ed. 1995)

Jörg-Manfred Mössner, *Steuerrecht international tätiger Unternehmen* (Köln: Verlag Dr. Otto Schmidt KG, 1992)

Harald Schaumburg, *Internationales Steuerrecht* (Köln: Verlag Dr. Otto Schmidt KG, 1993)

Brezing/Krabbe/Kupenau/Mössner/Runge, *Außensteuerrecht* (Herne: Verlag Neue Wirtschaftsbriefe, 1991, aktuelle Änderungen nach Drucklegung 1993)

Flick/Wassermeyer/Becker, *Kommentar zum Außensteuerrecht* (Köln: Verlag Dr. Otto Schmidt KG)

Wöhrle/Schelle/Gross, *Außensteuergesetz* (Stuttgart: Schäffer-Poeschel Verlag)

Federal Ministry of Finance, 2. December 1994, "Schreiben betr. Grundsätze zur Anwendung des Außensteuergesetzes", BStBl. I 1995, extra edition no. 1

Japan

J. Huston, T. Miyatake & G. Way, *Japanese International Taxation* (loose leaf)

Komatsu, Yoshiaki, "*Sozei joyaku no kenkyu* [Studies in Tax Treaties]" (rev. ed.). 1982

Nakazato, Minoru, "*Kokusai torihiki to kazei* [International Transactions and Taxation]" 1994

United States

J. Kuntz and R. Peroni, *U.S. International Taxation* (Warren, Gorham & Lamont, loose-leaf)

J. Isenbergh, *International Taxation* (Little, Brown, loose-leaf)

B. Bittker, & J. Eustice, *Federal Income Taxation of Corporations and Shareholders*, *Chapter 17*. (Warren, Gorham and Lamont, looseleaf)

American Law Institute (H. Ault and D. Tillinghast, Reporters), *Federal Income Tax Project: International Aspects of United States Income Taxation: Proposals on United States Taxation of Foreign Persons and of the Foreign Income of United States Persons*. Philadelphia, PA: American Law Institute (1987)

C. Kingson, "The Coherence of International Taxation", 81 *Colum. L. Rev.* 1151 (1981)

J. Slemrod, "Twenty Books No International Tax Economist Should Be Without", 3 *Tax Notes Int'l* 202 (1991)

B. Rollinson, "Guidelines for Taxing International Capital Flows: An Economic Perspective", 46 *Nat'l Tax J.* 309 (1993)

S. Ross, "National Versus International Approaches to Cross-Border Tax Issues", 54 *Tax Notes* 589 (1992) (also published in 4 *Tax Notes Int'l* 719 (1992))

Subpart A: Residence Taxation

1. <u>Bases for the assertion of personal taxing jurisdiction</u>

K. Vogel, "Worldwide vs. source taxation of income - A review and re-evaluation of arguments", 1988 *Intertax* 216-29, 310-20

International Fiscal Association, Cahiers de droit fiscal international, vol. 72a., *The fiscal residence of companies* (Brussels 1987)

Canada

Donald J.S. Brean, "Here or There? The Source and Residence Principles of International Taxation", in Richard Bird and Jack Mintz, eds., *Taxation to 2000 and Beyond*, Canadian Tax Paper No. 93 (Toronto: Canadian Tax Foundation, 1992) 303-73

Edwin G. Kroft, "Jurisdiction to Tax: An Update", in *Report of Proceedings of the Forty-fourth Tax Conference*, 1993 Conference Report (Toronto: Canadian Tax Foundation, 1994) 1:1 - 1:38

United States

Gary Clyde Hufbauer *U. S. Taxation of International Income - Blueprint for Reform* (Institute for International Economics, Washington DC 1992)

M. Norr, "Jurisdiction to Tax and International Income", 17 *Tax L. Rev.* 431 (1962)

R. Avi-Yonah, "The Structure of International Taxation: A Proposal for Simplification", 74 *Texas L. Rev.* 1301 (1996)

2. **Change of status**

E. Brood, "Dual residence of companies", 1990 *Intertax* 22

Canada

Allan R. Lanthier, "Corporate Immigration, Emigration and Continuance", in *Tax Planning for Canada-US and International Transactions*, 1993 Corporate Management Tax Conference (Toronto: Canadian Tax Foundation, 1994) 4:1 - 4:42

Germany

S. N. Frommel "Germany: The real seat doctrine and dual-resident companies under German law: another view", 1990 *European Taxation* 267

The Netherlands

M. J. Ellis, "The Netherlands refines the dual resident company", 1990 *International Tax Review* 31

United States

S. Shay and R. Watson, "Final Dual Consolidated Loss Regs", 4 *Int'l Taxation* 52 (1993)

3. Mechanisms for relief of double taxation

Australia

R. J. Vann and R. W. Parsons, "The Foreign Tax Credit and Reform of International Taxation" (1986) 3 *Australian Tax Forum* 131

L. Burns, "The Taxation of Branch Profits" (1991) 3 CCH *Journal of Australian Taxation* 28-39

Canada

Richard G. Tremblay, "Foreign Tax Credit Planning", in *Tax Planning for Canada-US and International Transactions*, 1993 Corporate Management Tax Conference (Toronto: Canadian Tax Foundation, 1994) 3:1-3:53

Germany

Gaßner/Lang/Lechner, *Die Methoden zur Vermeidung der Doppelbesteuerung* (Wien: Linde Verlag, 1995)

United Kingdom

Davies, D. R. (1985), *Principles of International Double Taxation Relief* (London: Sweet & Maxwell)

United States

E. Owens, *The Foreign Tax Credit: A Study of the Credit for Foreign Taxes Under United States Income Tax Law*, Cambridge, MA: Harvard Law School International Tax Program (1961)

E. Owens & G. Ball, *The Indirect Credit: A Study of Various Foreign Tax Credits Granted to Domestic Shareholders Under U.S. Income Tax Law.* Cambridge, MA: Harvard Law School International Tax Program (vol. I, 1975; vol. II, 1979)

C. Kingson, "The Foreign Tax Credit and Its Critics", 9 Am. J. Tax Pol. 1 (1991)

4. Limitations on exemption or deferral of income of foreign corporations

Brian J. Arnold, *The Taxation of Controlled Foreign Corporations: An International Comparison* (Toronto: Canadian Tax Foundation, 1986)

Brian J. Arnold, "The taxation of investments in passive foreign investment funds in Australia, Canada, New Zealand and the United States", *Essays on International Taxation - in honor of Sidney I. Roberts* (Kluwer, Deventer 1993)

Australia

Australian Treasury, *Taxation of Foreign Source Income: A Consultative Document* (Canberra: Australian Government Printing Service, 1988)

Australian Treasury, *Taxation of Foreign Source Income: An Information Paper* (Canberra: Australian Government Printing Service, 1989)

Australian Treasury, *Taxation of Interests in Foreign Investment Funds: An Information Paper* (Canberra: Australian Government Printing Service, 1992)

L. Burns, *Controlled Foreign Companies: Taxation of Foreign Source Income* (Melbourne: Longman, 1992)

Canada

Patrice Simard, "Foreign Affiliates: An Overview", in *Report of Proceedings of the Forty-fifth Tax Conference*, 1994 Conference Report (Toronto: Canadian Tax Foundation, 1994) 25:1 - 25:46

Germany

Martina Baumgärtel, Helmut Perlet, *Hinzurechnungsbesteuerung bei Auslandsbeteiligungen* (Neuwied: Luchterhand Verlag, 1996)

Helmut Debatin, "StÄndG 1992 und 'Treaty override'", 1992 *Der Betrieb*, 2159

Eugen Bogenschütz and Gerhard Kraft, "Konzeptionelle Änderungen der erweiterten Hinzurechnungsbesteuerung und Verschärfung im Bereich der Konzernfinanzierungseinkünfte durch das StMbG", 1994 *Internationales Steuerrecht* 153

Thomas Menck, *Rechtsmechanismus und Rechtscharakter der Zugriffsbesteuerung - Zur Systematik der §§ 7 bis 14 AStG*, 1978 *Deutsche Steuerzeitung, Ausgabe A* 106 - 110

Arndt Raupach, "Außensteuerrechtliche Wirkungen der Außensteuerreformgesetze", in *Jahrbuch der Fachanwälte für Steuerrecht* 1977/78 424

5. Outbound transfers to foreign branches or subsidiaries

Germany

Jörg-Dietrich Kramer, "Germany's Treatment of Asset Transfers From a German Branch to a Foreign Headquarters Examined", 1993 *Tax Notes International* 578

International Fiscal Association, Cahiers de droit fiscal international, vol. LXXIa, *Transfer of assets into and out of a taxing jurisdiction* (New York 1986)

United States

C. Kingson, "The New Theory and Practice of Section 367", 69 *Taxes* 1008 (1991)

C. Kingson, "International Acquisitions and Combinations Involving U.S. Companies", 56 *Tax Notes* 1761 (1992)

Subpart B: Source Taxation

1. Issues in the structure of net basis taxation of business income

OECD Committee on Fiscal Affairs, *Attribution of income to permanent establishments* (OECD, Paris 1994)

Sidney I. Roberts, "The Agency Element of Permanent Establishment: The OECD Commentaries from the Civil Law View", 1993 *Intertax* 396-420; 488-508

Australia

Blaikie, "International Aspects of Capital Gains Tax", (1987) 21 *Taxation in Australia* 742

Burns and Hamilton, "Application of Australian Capital Gains Tax to Non-Residents", 12 *Tax Notes International* 199 (1996)

Canada

Constantine A. Kyres, "Carrying on Business in Canada", (1995) Vol. 43 *Canadian Tax Journal* 1629-71

France

Martin Laprade B., "Relations intragroupe et territorialité", *Fiscalité Internationale*, vol. 2., 49-106 (Ed. de fiscalité et de gestion, Paris, 1989)

Douvier P.-J., "L'internationalisation des affaires et la répartition de l'assiette imposable: notion d'établissement stable", *Bulletin Fiscal* 1993 n. 12, 745-58

Germany

Jörg-Dietrich Kramer, "Germany: Place of Activity and Taxation of Executive Directors' Salaries" 10 *Tax Notes International*, 395 - 398 (1945)

Wilhelm Haarmann (ed.), *Die beschränkte Steuerpflicht*, (Köln: Dr. Otto Schmidt Verlag, 1993)

Franz Wassermeyer, "Die beschränkte Steuerpflicht", in: Klaus Vogel (ed.), *Grundfragen des internationalen Steuerrechts* (Köln: Dr. Otto Schmidt Verlag, 1985), 49 et seq.

Helmut Debatin, "Das Betriebsstättenprinzip der deutschen Doppelbesteuerungsabkommen", 1989 *Der Betrieb* 1692 - 1697 Teil I, 1739 - 1744 Teil II

Wolfgang Kumpf, "Ergebnis- und Vermögenszuordnung bei Betriebsstätten", 1988/89, *Steuerberater-Jahrbuch* 399 - 422

United States

R. Dailey, "The Concept of the Source of Income", 15 *Tax L. Rev.* 415 (1960)

H. Dale, "Effectively Connected Income", 42 *Tax L. Rev.* 689 (1987)

S. Ross, "United States Taxation of Aliens and Foreign Corporations: The Foreign Investors Tax Act of 1966 and Related Developments", 22 *Tax L. Rev.* 279 (1967)

S. Surrey, "Reflections on the Allocation of Income and Expenses Among National Tax Jurisdictions", 10 *Law & Pol'y Int'l Bus.* 409 (1978)

International Fiscal Association, Cahiers de droit fiscal international, vol. 81 a. *Principles for the determination of the income and capital of permanent establishments and their applications to banks, insurance companies and other financial institutions* (Geneva 1996)

2. Issues in the structure of gross basis taxation

Canada

David G. Broadhurst, "Issues in Withholding", in *Income Tax Enforcement, Compliance and Administration*, 1988 Corporate Management Tax Conference (Toronto:Canadian Tax Foundation, 1989) 11:1 - 11:18

United States

R. Green, "The Future of Source-Based Taxation of the Income of Multinational Enterprises", 79 *Cornell L. Rev.* 18 (1993)

3. Branch profits tax

Canada

Paul B. Singer, "Branch Tax Planning", in *Report of Proceedings of the Thirty-eighth Tax Conference*, 1987 Conference Report (Toronto: Canadian Tax Foundation, 1988) 21:1 - 21:49

4. Limitations on base-eroding payments to nonresidents

International Fiscal Association, Cahiers de droit fiscal international, vol. 81 b, *International aspects of thin capitalization*, (Geneva 1996)

Australia

Williams, "The Application of Thin Capitalisation Measures in Australia" (1988) *22 Taxation in Australia* 577

Canada

Tim Edgar, "The Thin Capitalization Rules: Role and Reform" (1992) Vol. 40 *Canadian Tax Journal* 1-54

<u>Germany</u>

Brigitte Knobbe-Keuk, "Developments in Thin Capitalization and Some Legal Obstacles to Legislation", 1992 *European Taxation* 405

<u>United States</u>

J. Roin, "Adding Insult to Injury: The 'Enhancement' of § 163(j) and the Tax Treatment of Foreign Investors in the United States", 49 *Tax L. Rev.* 269 (1994)

Subpart C: Additional International Topics

1. Special international avoidance rules

Ward (ed.), *How Domestic Anti-Avoidance Rules Affect Double Taxation Conventions* (IFA Seminar, 1994)

<u>France</u>

Levine P., *La lutte contre l'évasion fiscale de caractère international en l'absence et en présence de conventions internationales* (LGDJ, Paris, 1988)

<u>Germany</u>

Ewald Dötsch, "Standortssicherungsgesetz: Auseinanderfallen von Stammrecht und Dividendenschein - Dividendenstripping", 1993 *Der Betrieb*, 1842 - 1848

Jochen Thiel, "Umwandlung von Kapitalgesellschaften auf Personengesellschaften mit beschränkt steuerpflichtigen Gesellschaftern", 1995 *GmbH-Rundschau*, 708 - 712

2. Selected intercompany pricing issues

International Fiscal Association, Cahiers de droit fiscal international, vol. 77 a, *Transfer pricing in the absence of comparable market prices* (Cancun 1992)

Australia

T. P. W. Boucher, "International Transactions: The Implications of Division 13" (1983) 17 *Taxation in Australia* 883-895

Killaly, "Transfer Pricing Methodologies" in Krever & Grbich, eds, *Australian International Tax*, ch 7 (Sydney, Law Book Company, 1994)

G. Rozvany, *Transfer Pricing* (Sydney: Legal Books 1995, loose-leaf

Canada

Carl F. Steiss and Luc Blanchette, "The International Transfer Pricing Debate", (1995) Vol. 43 *Canadian Tax Journal* 1566-1602

France

LeGall J.-P., "Quelques réflexions sur l'arm's length prinicple", *Droit Fiscal* 1992, n. 50, 1941-4

Turot J., "Avantagés consentis entre sociétés d'un groupe multinational", *Revue de Jurisprudence Fiscale* 1989, n. 5, 263-271

Uettwiller J.-J., "Comment determiner les prix de cession intragroupe", *Revue des Sociétés*, July-Sept. 1995, 459-92

Dibout P., "L'extension des prérogatives de l'administration fiscale dans le controle des opérations internationales", *Droit Fiscal* 1996, n. 18-19, 651-8

Germany

Federal Ministry of Finance, 23. February 1983, "Schreiben betr. Grundsätze für die Prüfung der Einkunftsabgrenzung bei international verbundenen Unternehmen (Verwaltungsgrundsätze)", BStBl. I 1993, 218, (translated by Albert J. Rädler/Friedhelm Jacob, "German Transfer Pricing/Prix de transfert en Allemagne" (Metzner Verlag, Frankfurt am Main, 1984))

Reinhard Pöllath/Albert J. Rädler, "Gewinnberichtigungen zwischen verbundenen Unternehmen ohne Rücksicht auf Abkommensrecht?", 1982 *Der Betrieb*, 561 - 565, 617 - 620

Albert J. Rädler, "Stellungnahme zu dem Entwurf des OECD-Berichts über Verrechnungspreise", 1995 *Der Betrieb*, 110 - 111

Bertil Wiman, "Swedish transfer pricing rules", 1990 *Bulletin for International Fiscal Documentation* 404

United States

E. Aud & J. Fuller, "The Final Section 482 Regulations", 9 *Tax Notes Int'l* 265 (1994)

R. Culbertson, "Speaking Softly and Carrying a Big Shtick: The Interplay Between Substantive and Penalty Rules in the U.S. Transfer Pricing Regulations", 11 *Tax Notes Int'l* 1509 (1995)

J. Guttentag & T. Miyatake, "Transfer Pricing: U.S. and Japanese Views", 8 *Tax Notes Int'l* 375 (1994)

3. Selected treaty issues

International Fiscal Association, Cahiers de droit fiscal international, vol. 78a, *Interpretation of double taxation conventions* (Florence 1993)

International Fiscal Association, Cahiers de droit fiscal internationa, vol. 78b, *Non-discrimination rules in international taxation* (Florence 1993)

Vogel, K. (1991), *Klaus Vogel on Double Taxation Conventions: A Commentary to the OECD-, UN- and US Model Conventions for the Avoidance of Double Taxation of Income and Capital: With Particular Reference to German Treaty Practice*, 2nd ed. (Kluwer, 1990)

Skaar, A. *Permanent Establishment- Erosion of a Tax Principle*, (Kluwer, 1991)

van Raad, K. *Nondiscrimination in International Tax Law* (Kluwer, 1980)

John F. Avery Jones et al., "The interpretation of tax treaties with particular reference to Article 3 (2) of the OECD Model", 1984 *British Tax Review*, 14-54; 90-108

John F. Avery Jones et al., "The Non-discrimination Article in Tax Treaties", 1991 *European Taxation* 310

Brian J. Arnold, *Tax discrimination against aliens, non-residents, and foreign activities: Canada, Australia, New Zealand, the United Kingdom and the United States* (Canadian Tax Foundation, Toronto, 1991)

Ken Messere, "The 1992 OECD Model Treaty: The Precursors and Successors of the New OECD Model Tax Convention on Income and Capital", 1993 *European Taxation* 246

John F. Avery Jones et al., " International: Credit and Exemption under Tax Treaties in Cases of Differing Income Characterization", 1996 *European Taxation* nr. 4, p. 118-146

Australia

R. J. Vann, "A Model Tax Treaty for the Asia-Pacific Region?" (1991) *Bulletin for International Fiscal Documentation* 99 and 151 (in two parts)

T. Magney, *Australia's Double Tax Agreements: A Critical Appraisal of Key Issues* (Sydney: Legal Books, 1994)

T. Magney, "Australia's Double Taxation Agreements: Does the OECD Model Serve Australia's Interest?" in Krever & Grbich, eds., *Australian International Tax*, ch. 3 (Sydney, Law Book Company, 1994)

Canada

David A. Ward, "Canada's Tax Treaties", (1995), Vol. 43 *Canadian Tax Journal* 1719-58

Stephen R. Richardson and James W. Welkopf, "The Interpretation of Tax Conventions in Canada", Vol. 43 *Canadian Tax Journal* 1759-91

France

Jean-Pierre Le Gall, "Treaty shopping: the French policy", 1989 *Intertax* 364

Service de la Législation fiscale, "La France et les conventions internationales", *Droit Fiscal* 1996, n.7, 236-7

Tournié G., "Conventions fiscales et droit interne", *Revue Française de Finances Publiques* 1995, n. 5, 193-204

Gouthière B., "Trois questions relatives au principe de non-discrimination", *Bulletin fiscal*, 1993, n. 6, 399-410

Gest G., "Le nouveau crédit d'impôt étranger: une réforme en trompe-l'oeil?", *Revue Française de Comptabilité*, June 1993, 52-8

Germany

Dieter Blumenwitz, "Die Auslegung völkerrechtlicher Verträge", in: Mössner/ Blumenwitz (eds.): *Doppelbesteuerungsabkommen und nationales Recht* (1995) 5-18

Walter Leisner, "Abkommensbruch durch Außensteuerrecht?", 1993 *Recht der Internationalen Wirtschaft* 1013 - 1020

Jörg-Manfred Mössner, "Rechtsschutz bei treaty overriding", in: Lutz Fischer (ed.): *Besteuerung internationaler Konzerne* (1993) 113 - 136

Jakob Strobl, "Zur Auslegung von Doppelbesteuerungsabkommen", in: *Festschrift Georg Döllerer* (1988), 635 - 659

Klaus Vogel, "Abkommensbindung und Mißbrauchsabwehr", in: *Festschrift Ernst Höhn* (1995) 461 et seq.

Franz Wassermeyer, "Die Auslegung von Doppelbesteuerungsabkommen durch den Bundesfinanzhof", 1990 *Steuer und Wirtschaft* 404 - 412

Franz Wassermeyer, "Die Auslegung völkerrechtlicher Verträge - Haltung des BFH", in: Mössner/Blumenwitz (eds.) *Doppelbesteuerungsabkommen und nationales Recht* (1995) 19 - 27

Rosemarie Portner, "Vereinbarkeit des § 8a KStG mit den Doppelbesteuerungsabkommen", 1996 *Internationales Steuerrecht* 23 - 30 Teil I, 66 - 70 Teil II

United States

J. O'Brien, (1978), "The Nondiscrimination Article in Tax Treaties", *Law and Policy in International Business*, Vol. 10, No. 2, p. 545

R. Green, "The Troubled Rule of Nondiscrimination in Taxing Foreign Direct Investment", 26 *Law and Policy in International Business* 113 (1994)

D. Rosenbloom, "Tax Treaty Abuse: Policies and Issues", 15 *Law and Policy in International Business* 763 (1983)

W. Streng, " 'Treaty Shopping': Tax Treaty 'Limitation of Benefits' Issues", 15 *Hous. J. Int'l L.* 1 (1992)

H. Ault, "Corporate Integration, Tax Treaties and the Division of the International Tax Base: Principles and Practices", 47 *Tax L. Rev.* 565 (1992)

R. Doernberg & K. van Raad, "The Forthcoming U.S. Model Income Tax Treaty and the Saving Clause", 5 *Tax Notes Int'l* 775 (1992)

R. Doernberg, "Overriding Tax Treaties: The U.S. Perspective", 9 *Emory Int'l L. Rev.* 71 (1995)

Index